Lost in a Book

VICTOR NELL

Lost in a Book

THE PSYCHOLOGY OF
READING FOR PLEASURE

YALE UNIVERSITY PRESS

NEW HAVEN AND LONDON

Designed by Nancy Ovedovitz and set in Baskerville type by Huron Valley Graphics. Printed in the United States of America by Vail-Ballou Press, Binghamton, N.Y.

Library of Congress Cataloging-in-Publication Data
Nell, Victor.
    Lost in a book.
    Bibliography: p.
    Includes index.
    1. Books and reading—Psychological aspects. I. Title. [DNLM: 1. Leisure Activities. 2. Psychology. 3. Reading. BF 456.R2 N421L] Z1003.N426 1988
    028'.9'019 87–14283 ISBN 0–300–04115–2 (alk. paper)

The paper in this book meets the guidelines for permanence and durability of the Committee on Production Guidelines for Book Longevity of the Council on Library Resources.

10 9 8 7 6 5 4 3 2 1

*To Myrna, who
gave me clarity*

Contents

Figures

Tables

Preface

This is a book about readers and for them. It describes the delights of reading and the psychological mechanisms that take skilled readers out of the world and lead them, absorbed or entranced, into the world of the book. Students of reading—librarians, critics, cognitive psychologists, and reading specialists—may also find it useful.

Part I explores the social forces that have shaped reading: the growth and consolidation of the reading habit, the social value system, and the pervasive appeal of narrative. Reading for pleasure is often light reading, but not always: one of pleasure reading's paradoxes is that for many sophisticated readers, a wide range of materials, from the trashiest to the most literate and demanding works, may induce reading trance, and such readers are intrigued by the pleasure they derive from material they know to be culturally worthless.

Reading for pleasure ("ludic reading") is an enormously complex cognitive act that draws on an array of skills and processes in many different domains—attention, comprehension, absorption, and entrancement; reading skill and reading-rate variability; readability and reader preferences; and reading physiology. These component processes of ludic reading are the subject matter of Part II.

Ludic reading is a consciousness-changing activity, and Part III relates reading to fantasy processes such as dreaming and hypnotic trance, on the one hand, and to the sovereignty of the reading experience and the uses readers make of it, on the other, in order to show how the components of reading relate to one another in achieving the capture of consciousness.

The research on which this book is based was carried out at the Institute for Behavioural Sciences of the University of South Africa. I owe a great debt of gratitude to the Institute's staff and especially its director, Professor R. D. Griesel, who funded and supported my research with unfailing generosity over a six-year period.

I owe a great deal to two tenaciously critical readers of the manuscript, Kerneels Plug and Gladys Topkis. Their close reading and lucid emendations have helped me tighten and extend the argument in ways that have greatly strengthened it.

Nearly 300 subjects took part in the six empirical studies reported in Part II—friends, colleagues, students, librarians, and the ludic readers who volunteered for the laboratory study. They sacrificed many hours of entrancement in order to tell me, overtly and covertly, about the delights reading gives them, and they are the true authors of large parts of this book.

Lost in a Book

Introduction:
The Insatiable Appetite

I t seems incredible, the ease with which we sink through books quite out of sight, pass clamorous pages into soundless dreams.

—Gass, 1972, p. 27

We are not now in possession of a complete list of components of reading skill, but the information we now have is converging toward such a catalog. . . . Furthermore, it is now possible to state how the components of reading skill interact, and how they form a hierarchy leading to effective total reading performance.

—Carroll, 1981, p. 18

Reading for pleasure is an extraordinary activity. The black squiggles on the white page are still as the grave, colorless as the moonlit desert; but they give the skilled reader a pleasure as acute as the touch of a loved body, as rousing, colorful and transfiguring as anything out there in the real world. And yet, the more stirring the book the quieter the reader; pleasure reading breeds a concentration so effortless that the absorbed reader of fiction (transported by the book to some other place, and shielded by it from distractions), who is so often reviled as an escapist and denounced as the victim of a vice as pernicious as tippling in the morning should instead be the envy of every student and every teacher.

These are the paired wonders of reading: the world-creating power of books, and the reader's effortless absorption that allows the book's fragile world, all air and thought, to maintain itself for a while, a bamboo and paper house among earthquakes; within it readers acquire peace, become more powerful, feel braver and wiser in the ways of the world.

Absorption may sometimes deepen to become entrancement, the signs of which are greater resistance to interruption and the returning reader's momentary bewilderment, as of someone waking from a dream. "Oh," says the reader, half-apologetically, "I was so deep in the book!"— and indeed, a person emerging from reading trance does appear to be surfacing from a depth or returning from another place. Absorption seems to accompany all pleasure reading, but trance is less common and resembles an altered state of consciousness: reverie, or dreaming, or perhaps even hypnosis. Neither absorption nor trance is restricted to fiction: the final entries in Captain Scott's journals can transport a reader to the icy Antarctic wilderness as surely as any novel or short story; and a newspaper account of a tankcar derailment that sends poisonous fumes creeping toward a sleeping community can entrance as fully as any imaginary disaster story. Nor does narrative nonfiction (travel, biography) seem to be in any way distinct from fiction in the effects it produces on the reader. But fiction is the most common vehicle of pleasure reading and will accordingly occupy most of our attention.

Pleasure reading is playful: it is free activity standing outside ordinary life; it absorbs the player completely, is unproductive, and takes place within circumscribed limits of space and time (Huizinga, 1938; Caillois, 1958). "Ludic reading" (from the Latin *ludo*, I play: Stephenson, 1964) is therefore a useful characterization of pleasure reading, reminding us that it is at root a play activity, intrinsically motivated and usually paratelic, that is, engaged in for its own sake (Deci, 1976; Apter, 1979). Ludic readers often describe themselves as reading addicts, and they do indeed spend a great deal of time reading a great many books. Some read ten books a week, others even more. As a convenient rule of thumb, the term *ludic reader* is here reserved for those who read at least one book a week.

READING AS CONSCIOUSNESS CHANGE

Like dreaming, reading performs the prodigious task of carrying us off to other worlds. But reading is not dreaming because books, unlike dreams, are subject to our will: they envelop us in alternative realities only because we give them explicit permission to do so. Books are the dreams we would most like to have, and, like dreams, they have the power to change consciousness, turning sadness to laughter and anxious introspection to the relaxed contemplation of some other time and place. Indeed, consciousness change and the means by which it is achieved in ludic reading and related activities are the central concern of this book. This is unfamiliar territory, because studies of pleasure reading have traditionally dealt with the reader's aesthetic responses to literature; here, these responses are considered only in their relation to the psychological processes by which reading takes over consciousness.

The newspaper reader is absorbed and transported as readily as the fiction reader (though usually for a shorter time and to a disjointed succession of places), and my own curiosity about the nature of the reader's experience goes back to 1974, when I returned to journalism after a long break. I soon began to wonder how it was that even the least experienced of our number in the copy editor's room of a provincial morning newspaper were repeatedly able to demonstrate perfectly correct newsworthiness judgments in distinguishing big stories from small ones, and small stories from non-stories. In 1949, Wilbur Schramm, the doyen of mass media researchers, wrote that no aspect of communication is as impressive as the enormous number of choices and discards that have to be made between communicator and receiver (p. 289). To me, there are two much more impressive phenomena. The first is the extraordinary agreement among journalists about news-value rankings, which seems to have nothing to do with experience or formal knowledge of news criteria (Nell, 1978b); for example, when I first began work as a journalist (I was a news editor on Israel Radio during the heady days of the Eichmann trial), I could rank stories for newsworthiness as accurately as thirty-year veterans. The second phenomenon is the nature of the public appetite for news, "a crying primal want of the mind, like a hunger of the body" (Will Irwin in Boorstin, 1964). To me, this news hunger can best be seen as a variant of story hunger, the appetite that drove our ancestors to listen, rapt, to tribal storytellers, and that drives us today to theaters and television shows, to libraries and newsstands. To me, this insatiable appetite is the most impressive aspect of communication, not only because of its economic importance (it underpins the entertainment industry), but also in purely psychological terms, as the provider of reinforcements sufficiently strong to sustain many consecutive hours of attention (to anecdotal conversation and informal storytelling as well as to books, radio, and television programs) on every day of every normally functioning person's life.

Entertainment is that aspect of play which stands within the economic sector, and the huge and immensely lucrative entertainment industry has consciousness change as its entire stock in trade. We pay handsomely for the spectacles, titillations, and close-ups of catastrophe that take us out of ourselves by taking over consciousness. But books—the most portable and ubiquitous product of the entertainment industry—often come to us free or nearly free, from libraries, used-book exchanges, and friends. Pleasure reading thus straddles two sets of boundaries: it stands between the entertainments we pay for and those adult play activities for which no money changes hands—chatting and visiting, backyard games, willing sexuality, and the like. Next, within the play domain, reading is both a spectator and a participant activity. It is participant because, until the reader's eye lights on the page, the book does not exist (this phenomenological puzzle is explained in chapter 2). Nonetheless, the reader, like other spectators, is acted on by the world rather than primarily acting on it. The permeability of these boundaries is underscored by bearing in mind that the fundamental distinction between activities performed for their own sake (paratelic) and those we labor at because of external rewards (telic) is itself reversible. As mood and intention change, the chore I begin this morning (reading *Pride and Prejudice* to prepare for an examination) becomes a delight by afternoon. Here, Michael Apter's notion of reversals (1979), which suggests that telic acts may quite suddenly become paratelic, is especially helpful (chapter 9).

THE ELITIST FALLACY

Critics and literary historians have traditionally subscribed to the view that readers are either lowbrow or highbrow and, as a corollary, that trained and untrained minds do not share the same tastes. If this division correctly reflects the way in which culture is produced and consumed, can this book accommodate the richness and diversity of the ludic reading experience of those who read intently and deeply, or will it, on the contrary, focus on the lumpenproletariat, the "ignorantly contented lower orders" (Oxford, 1976) who flourish on the fecund dung heap of popular fiction? If my concern is with "the effect of cheap novels on the minds of uneducated people" (Sterba, 1939), this book will have little interest for sophisticated readers because it will offend them by its implied arrogance while failing to reflect their own experience of ludic reading.

My intentions are neither highbrow nor lowbrow, because the two classes of reader as defined by the elitist critics do not exist; the view that they do contains a fundamental error so common that it deserves to be labeled "the elitist fallacy"—the belief that as sophistication grows, coarser tastes wither away. If today I delight in *The Unbearable Lightness of Being* or *Foe* (Kundera, 1985; Coetzee, 1986), I cannot tomorrow return to *Biggles and the Blue Moon* or *Just William* (Johns, 1934; Crompton, 1922), which I enjoyed as a child, or lose myself in the Harlequin romance offered by the airline passenger in the next seat.

On the contrary: though sophisticated readers have the capacity and the desire to enjoy deeply felt and delicately wrought literature, and habitually do so, they continue, on occasion and if their consciences allow them, to delight in the childlike triumphs of His Majesty the Ego (Freud, 1908) and in the stereotyped narratives that recount the endless victories of invincible heroes and heroines.

For example, the thirty-three ludic readers recruited for some of the experiments described later, among whom trained minds were well represented, rated an average of 42.6 percent of their own pleasure reading as "trash"; the highest individual rating, 90 percent, came from a person working on a doctoral dissertation in English literature. Among the nearly three hundred subjects in some of the other experiments were many others of equal depravity. A correspondent of austere tastes, who does not trouble to conceal her contempt for the dolts, oafs, and freaks who trade subtlety for stereotypes—and worse, do so in great quantity—confesses to enjoying "good trash—good enough for airplane or before-sleep reading, not for one's permanent library or for bothering to remember" (on deliberate forgetting, see "Reading Gluttony" in chapter 11).

Of course, the fallacy is unidirectional, because, for untrained or unwilling minds, much reading matter must remain inaccessible. In the sense that there is a class of lowbrow readers who avoid the products of elite culture, the critics are correct; but, as even fleeting examination of culture consumption in the world around us shows, the doors from high culture to low remain open, and earlier tastes do not wither and die as more refined appetites develop. At least metaphorically, evolutionary theory, which teaches that ontogeny recapitulates phyogeny (Haeckel's "fundamental biogenetic law," 1867) and that new systems do not replace older ones but are superimposed on them (see, for example, McLean, 1973), prepares the ground for the suggestion that more primitive cultural levels remain accessible despite later accretions. Psychoanalysis, in Freud's careful archeological metaphor for the structure of consciousness (for example, 1909, p. 57)—and quite specifically in his account of literary creation (chapter 10)—also suggests that earlier and more primitive needs and desires are not rooted out by maturation and education but merely overlaid and that they remain active in disguised or flamboyant ways throughout life.

The arrogant dismissiveness with which elite critics have studied the workings of lower-class minds since the birth of the mass reading habit thus appears to rest on the faulty premise that the critics' own minds have nothing of cultural importance in common with those of the lower classes they study. A humility that derives from the realization that elite and lowbrow minds share a multitude of drives and gratifications, in literature as in life, might be more appropriate, and would certainly be more productive. Moreover, the new trends in literary criticism (chapter 2) make it increasingly difficult to defend the premises on which the elitist fallacy is founded.

Of course, it may be that I have substituted a populist fallacy for the elitist error; time will tell. Nonetheless, ideology has of course molded my method. I have not stratified my subjects by taste culture because I believed from the beginning of these studies ten years ago that within every elite reader lurks a vestigial or fully formed lumpenprole, so that both classes are contained in one.

Some of my readers are mightily eccentric, especially those who took part in the group discussion reported in chapter 11. A perceptive reader of this book manuscript remarked that one of them, an entertainment glutton, seemed to crave a lobotomy more than books or movies: "What can one learn from accounts of people who are this eccentric?" she asks.

About ourselves: the elitist fallacy has a moral variant, which encourages its proponents to believe that people who behave in morally reprehensible ways—police torturers, Eichmann, Conrad's Kurtz (on the last two, see Nell, 1981)—are abnormal and, comfortingly, less than human; escapists and reading addicts, the tipplers at literature's tuppeny dram shops, are tarred by the same brush. There is by now a great body of literature affirming that at least the capacity to behave in brutal and immoral ways is part of the fabric of our humanity: Milgram's *Obedience to Authority* (1974), Arendt, 1963; Jones, 1976; and the Stanford simulated prison study (Haney, Banks, and Zimbardo, 1973). Accordingly, the aberrant readers whose habits are described in chapter 11 may be "abnormal" but are not less human, or less interesting, for it.

Readers startled by this assertion might like to look back at one of psychology's early texts, Henry Murray's *Explorations in Personality* (1938). In the concluding study of this clinical study of "50 men of college age" (all were students at Harvard), Murray remarks:

> Most of our subjects were carrying what seemed to us a heavy load of crippling anxiety, inferiority feelings, guilt feelings or dejection. . . . They doubted that they could live up to their own standards or to the expectations of their parents. Frequently, they suffered from memories of stinging humiliations, and when they went to their books in the evening, overriding apprehensive thoughts of future failure or depressing feelings of separateness and forsakenness prevented concentration. A basic sense of insupport aggravated by dissensions with one or both parents was a frequent finding (pp. 730–31).

And this of a group representative of the most talented and high-achieving of America's youth!

ESCAPISTS, ADDICTS, OR OTHERWISE MALADJUSTED

Over the past ten years I have talked with hundreds of ludic readers on two continents, singly and in groups, and the extent to which they share concerns that derive from the elitist and moral fallacies is quite striking. They wonder whether the way they enjoy books is unique or shared by other readers; if they read inordinate quantities, or at exceptional speed; why they enjoy good literature as well as reading matter they know to be trash, and why they can be equally moved by both; why they reread old favorites with undiminished enjoyment; why reading in bed is so enjoyable, and why reading books seems to give a deeper pleasure than watching television or going to the theater; and, finally, whether they are escapists, or addicts, or otherwise maladjusted.

In Western society, in which ludic reading is so commonplace that it passes largely unnoticed, the opportunities readers have to talk about their personal experience of reading are strangely circumscribed. When a group of ludic readers is brought together to talk about reading, they respond first with amazement and then with delight. They soon discover that they have a great deal in common (whether as a precondition for ludic reading or as a consequence of it, ludic readers are articulate, well informed, and endlessly curious), and there is a great deal of unembarrassed self-disclosure about childhood fears, reading matter that touches raw places, and authors that speak most deeply to them. (Appendix D contains a verbatim transcript of such a conversation, and a good deal of chapter 11 is made up of readers' reports about their reading experience.)

The following pages are devoted to answering some (though not all) of the questions readers ask about their reading and the ways in which it soothes and captivates them.

A MOTIVATIONAL MODEL OF LUDIC READING

The inquiry that follows is complex, as it needs to be in order to describe the complex route readers follow from the printed page to reading enjoyment. The simplest way of introducing these complexities is by means of a model of ludic reading that will accommodate all aspects of the subject in orderly fashion. In this introductory chapter, the model is skeletal; in chapter 12, at the end of our investigation, it appears in an elaborated form (figure 12.1) and serves as the vehicle around which to build a summary of the findings. (Both here and in chapter 12, I use "model" in the sense of a careful analogy that displays the relations of the part to the whole. Models, note English and English [1958], are useful for discovering hypotheses, which admirably suits our purpose in this exploratory study.) Both the preliminary and elaborated models are motivational in the sense that they relate reading to the reward systems that set it in motion and determine whether it will be continued or terminated in favor of another activity.

Figure 1.1 shows that the point of entry to the model is a person—we do not know yet whether he or she is going to be a ludic reader.

Certain preconditions must be met before ludic reading can begin. In the first place, ludic readers seem by and large to be skilled readers who rapidly and effortlessly assimilate information from the printed page. It seems likely that this skill can be expressed as a minimum reading speed

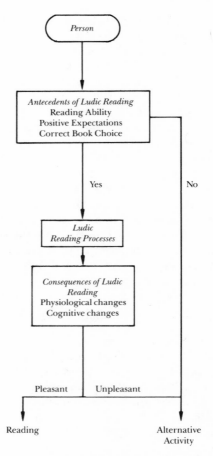

Figure 1.1. A Preliminary Model of
Ludic Reading

below which reading books or other long, continuous texts will be too
slow and tedious to be rewarding. These issues are experimentally investigated in chapter 5.

The second antecedent is the expectation that reading will be a pleasurable experience. First exposure to the delights of storytelling takes
place in early childhood (chapter 3); later, the child reader may find that
books offer similar delights and learn to turn to them for the kind of
consciousness change that narrative produces so readily. The third antecedent is selection of an appropriate book. I shall show that readers
develop great skill in selecting the kind of book that promises "a good
read" (chapters 7 and 8). Of course, this is a very personal preference:

my good read will likely end up in another reader's garbage pail. For this reason, the ludic readers who participated in the laboratory study described in chapter 9 were not all given the same book to read but were asked to bring along with them books of which they had sampled the first fifty pages and which they felt sure they would enjoy.

In the absence of any one of these antecedents, ludic reading is either not attempted or fails. If all three are present, and reading is more attractive than the available alternatives, reading begins and is continued as long as the reinforcements generated are strong enough to withstand the pull of alternative attractions. These reinforcers appear to be of two kinds. One is a series of physiological changes in the reader mediated by the autonomic nervous system, such as alterations in muscle tension, respiration, heart beat, electrical activity of the skin, and the like. These events are by and large unconscious and feed back to consciousness as a general feeling of well-being. Chapter 9 looks at the ways in which excitement and tranquility interact to form the matrix within which reading pleasure is achieved.

The second kind of reinforcer is cognitive changes, which are numerous and profound (chapter 10). Reading changes the focus of attention from self to environment. Because of the heavy demands reading makes on conscious attention, the reader is effectively shielded from other demands, whether internal or external. At the same time, the intense attention brought to bear by the entranced reader may have the effect of transfiguring both book and reader. The absolute control readers exercise over their reading with regard to pace (chapter 6), content, initiation, and duration means that reading can be used to accomplish two very different goals, to dull consciousness or heighten it. I shall argue in chapter 11 that readers' personality dispositions and current concerns determine which of these goals is pursued: for most readers, most of the time, it is likely that one of these two modes will consistently be preferred.

Between the antecedents of ludic reading and its consequences is the reading process itself, in which meaning is extracted from the symbols on the page and formed into inner experience. The quotes from Gass and Carroll at the beginning of this chapter allude to these two processes: one is meaning extraction, addressed by the tough-minded empiricism of Carroll's approach and explored in chapters 4 and 5; the other is the mystery of reading, the "otherness" of the reader's experience, the easy sinking through the pages into soundless dreams. This theme is elaborated in chapter 3, which deliberately deepens the mystery, while in chapters 10–12 I attempt to bring reading's otherness into the domain of established psychological theory and to show how a shift of attention can become a transfiguring experience. However, the skills and the otherness are not disjunctive. The simplest definition of reading, and the one on which most opinion now converges, is the extraction of meaning from a printed or written message. In this sense, both Gass and Carroll are concerned with meaning, one with how the reader extracts it, and other with what he or she does with it once it has been extracted.

Empirical Studies

For those with a professional interest in reading research, the conceptual frame in the previous section may usefully be supplemented by a brief note on the six interlinked studies which form the empirical basis for this book. They are, first, the relations between reading ability and reading habits (chapter 5); second, reading-speed variability during natural reading (chapter 6); third, the sequence in which readers rank reading matter for preference, literary merit, and difficulty (chapter 8); fourth, how these rankings compare with those derived from readability-score rankings (chapters 7 and 8); fifth, the physiology of ludic reading (chapter 9); and sixth, how readers describe and quantify various aspects of the reading experience (chapter 11).

Taxonomy

Of course, reading, like play (Berlyne, 1969, p. 843), means too many things to too many people to be a useful category for psychology. A commuter reads the billboards and road signs that flash by, and a preschool child, paging through a well-loved book, "reads" the story by interpreting the pictures; a student, heavy with effort, reads a statistics text and a moment later, with a sigh of relief, settles down with a Somerset Maugham anthology. Any attempt to devise a model that accommodates all these diverse activities will produce statements of high generality and low heuristic value (Nell, 1978a), and the literature contains some lurid examples of the results that emerge from an inadequately defined approach to reading. Bernard Berelson, for example, produced an essay with a resounding title "Who Reads What Books and Why" (1958). The findings are rather less resounding: "Some Americans read books frequently, some read them occasionally, some seldom and some not at all" (p. 120); or "People read what interests them" (p 124); or "The general moral of this tale . . . is that the state of popular reading is complicated, uneven, shifting, sometimes obscure" (p. 125).

Such generalizations are not helpful, and some arise in faulty taxonomies of reading. Data gathering must be preceded by an act of classification (otherwise data overwhelm us), and interpretation cannot begin until we know what it is that we are interpreting (otherwise meaning eludes us).

Berelson's study and others similar to it exemplify the communications-research tradition, which Lewis (1978, p. 47) characterizes as "productive in the accumulation of data [but] much less successful in the interpretation of this complex material." Some of these problems can be avoided by carefully circumscribing the investigation and restricting it to ludic reading only—that is, the reading of fiction and near-fiction for pleasure by skilled readers.

A Precipitous Landscape

The first chapter of Huey's pioneering 1908 study of reading is entitled "The Mysteries and Problems of Reading": eighty years later, these mysteries are still the subject of diligent investigation. But that "acme of a psychologist's achievements," the complete analysis of what we do when we read, which "would be to describe very many of the most intricate workings of the human mind" (1908, p. 6), seems even more remote today than it must have appeared to Huey, if only because the length of the road and the difficulty of the terrain are clearer now than they were at the beginning of the century. In the rest of this book, we follow a route through this precipitous landscape that leads us through some rather beautiful and mysterious parts of the ludic reader's world and allows us, here and there, between peaks we shall not attempt to scale, to catch a glimpse of distant countries that have not yet been explored.

Reading and
Popular Culture

Ludic reading is shaped by social and cultural values. The meanings a Bostonian and a reader on the Russian steppes assign to Saul Bellow's *Herzog* will be very different, and they are also likely to feel differently about reading it: the culture determines not only what a reader reads but also the effects of this choice on self-esteem and the positive rewards it is able to offer.

The next three chapters deal with these issues, setting the stage for the more specific investigations that follow. Chapter 1 looks at the development of the mass reading habit, at its economic importance, and at the time those who do read for pleasure spend reading. Chapter 2 examines the ways in which elite culture assigns "literary merit" to some works and denies it to others, how value conflicts are created in the ludic reader, and the strategies available for their resolution. Chapter 3 is about storytelling; it asks what narrative is and how it weaves its spell, and, by examining a set of five paradoxes, shows that the ability to cast the spell, even over oneself, is not an arcane gift but one that we all have.

1
Mass Reading: From Penny Papers to The Mammoth Hunters

A BRIEF HISTORY OF MASS READING

Literacy

Literacy rates in a given population might seem to offer a quick guide to the likely extent of ludic reading, but they must be treated with great caution. For example, in North America only 3 to 4 percent of the population over the age of fifteen was illiterate in 1950, and a mere 1 to 2 percent in Western Europe (UNESCO, 1957). However, these figures derive from the comfortable definition that literacy is the ability to read and write one's own name; they are not unexpected since 2.2 of the general population score 69 or below on the Wechsler Adult Intelligence Scale and can thus be classified as mentally defective. When the more stringent criterion of functional literacy is applied—reading and writing abilities equivalent to those of a child who has completed four full years of education—the illiteracy figure for North America soars to 11 percent. Nevertheless this cannot be taken to mean that 89 percent of the population reads books.

For all their shortcomings, contemporary estimates indicate that literacy is a mass phenomenon, the roots of which, in England, go back to the eighteenth and nineteenth centuries (Hoggart, 1959; Leavis, 1932; and especially Altick, 1957). Neuberg (1971) notes that "by the end of the 18th century, the ability to read had become widespread among the English poor" (p. v), partly because of the extensive net of Charity Schools (founded by the Society for Promoting Christian Knowledge, which held that teaching the poor to read would render them more docile and grateful to their betters), and partly because of the ready availability of chapbooks, a cheap popular literature of ballads and adventures. In the 1790s, the political implications of reading came to a sharp focus; Thomas Paine's *Rights of Man,* published in two parts in 1791 and 1792, seemed to the ruling classes to be outright Jacobinism, and the book's huge sales (a million and a half copies, Paine claimed [Altick, 1957, p. 70]) did little to allay these anxieties. "What ploughman who could read . . . would be content to whistle up one furrow and down another, from dawn in the morning, to the setting of the sun?" (George Hadley in 1786, in Neuberg, 1971, p. vi). Hannah More, author of many titles for the prodigiously successful Cheap Repository Tracts, has one of her characters say, "Of all the foolish inventions and new-fangled devices to ruin the country, that of teaching the poor to read is the very worst" (Altick, 1957, p. 69).

But as the nineteenth century drew on, fears of a revolutionary uprising in England abated, and the conviction that literate workers are more productive than illiterates took hold. In 1833, the government began providing limited funding for elementary schooling, although rote-learning, the monitorial system (in which older children taught their juniors), and teacher brutality (recalcitrant students were sometimes suspended in cages from the ceiling) rendered much education so ineffective that in many schools not even half the pupils could read at all. However, the deficiencies of the educational system were to some extent compensated for by forces outside the classroom, among them an increasing demand for literate workers, the introduction in 1840 of the penny post and the impetus it gave to personal communication, and the plentiful availability of cheap books from peddlers and in popular libraries (Altick, 1957). The Forster Act of 1870 finally ended many abuses and greatly extended the scope of elementary education. By the end of the century, literacy rates in Western Europe and North America had reached virtually their present levels (Gray, 1971).

Bestsellers and Penny Papers

Samuel Richardson's *Pamela* (1740) is considered to be the first English novel, but major elements of the genre can be traced back through Defoe and Bunyan to Malory's *Morte D'Arthur* (1485). In the hands of such practitioners as Fielding, Goldsmith, and Austen the novel developed through the eighteenth and early nineteenth centuries until the reign of Queen Victoria (1837–1901), when it "became unquestionably the dominant literary genre. The growth of the reading public and the further consolidation of the middle class enabled the great Victorian novelists [including Dickens, George Eliot, Thackeray, Trollope, and the Brontës] to command a public of unprecedented size" (Watt, 1971, p. 678).

In Victorian times, the main outlet for fiction was serial publication, a system that encouraged very long novels ("three-deckers"). These small quarto publications sold for 1d. (one penny) each in quantities of up to a half-million copies a week. Wilkie Collins, himself distinguished as the author of the first English detective novel (*The Moonstone*, 1868), describes their readers as members of "the unknown public, the mysterious, the unfathomable, the universal public of the penny-novel-journals . . . which reads more for its amusement than for its information." Sold in "oyster shops, cigar shops, lozenge shops," these penny journals had a dreadful sameness; many "might have been produced by the same pen," so that "no-one not a member of the unknown public could be got to read them" (Collins, 1859, p. 13).

One of the first bestselling authors was Lord Byron, whose *Corsair,* a poem in rhyming couplets, sold 10,000 copies on the day of its publication in 1814 (Escarpit, 1966). Stowe's *Uncle Tom's Cabin,* published in 1850, sold one and a half million copies within a year. Leavis (1932, pp. 64–65) rather peevishly designates Marie Corelli, whose great successes were *Barabbas* (1893) and *The Sorrows of Satan* (1895), and Hall Caine (*The Shadow of a Crime,* 1885, and *The Deemster,* 1887) as the two authors who first applied a bestseller "formula" to their work. In the late nineteenth century, an "absolute bestseller" was reckoned to be a book that sold a quarter- to a half-million copies; a "middlebrow" novel regarded as literature sold 20,000 to 30,000; a "highbrow book sold perhaps 3,000 copies (Leavis, 1932). Voltaire's witticism—that a serious book has fifty readers and an entertaining one five hundred (in Escarpit, 1966)—is apposite.

Today's unknown public are the paperback buyers. The oyster, cigar, and lozenge shops that stocked the penny papers in the 1860s are now supermarkets, drugstores, and airport shops, but the principle of increasing sales by utilizing non-traditional book outlets remains the same. It is not the paperback's binding that brings down its price but its huge additional sales, served by 100,000 outlets in the United States and Canada, most of which bypass the traditional bookseller (Petersen, 1975; Smith, 1963). The analogy may be carried further: what the penny papers did for leisure reading in the mid-nineteenth century, paperbacks are doing in the late twentieth. In 1970, half of all U.S. books produced were in paperback (Barker and Escarpit, 1973), and the proportion was probably higher in Europe. In 1974, 380 million paperbacks were sold in the United States, a revolution brought about by web offset (which prints continuous reels of paper rather than separate sheets), by the practice of leasing reprint rights from hardcover publishers, and by sale-or-return newsstand distribution (Petersen, 1975). The consequence of these developments is that the most popular paperback fiction commands first printings of over a million, though a more usual figure is 100,000.

Library Development

Although in late-eighteenth-century England Woolworth's, "the book-shop of the working class," supplied "paper novels" at 2*d*., 3*d*., and 6*d*. apiece (Leavis, 1932, p. 14) and serialized multi-part novels at 1*d*. each, these were not books; full-length quartos cost 12*s*. (shillings) and bound novels 3*s*. (2*s*. 6*d*. in paper wrappers). At the time, the average wage in London was 8*s*. a week and rather less in the country (Altick, 1957, pp. 51–53), so that novels were beyond the reach of the masses. Under these circumstances, the circulating library "was destined shortly to complete the triangle, whose other legs were the expanded middle-class audience and the new fascination of the novel" (p. 61). Novels, indeed, were the staple diet of these circulating libraries, which were often located in drap-ers' or milliners' shops and had a clientele of middle-class women "who had acquired the habit of novel reading" (Irwin, 1971, p. 1,035). Some circulating libraries encouraged an exclusive clientele by charging high subscriptions—for example, William Lane's famous Minerva Library in 1814 charged two guineas a year for an ordinary subscription—but the circulating libraries that catered to the lower classes charged a rental of 1*d*. a volume, so that, as Leavis noted with patent disapproval, "even the poorest class changes books sometimes even daily" (1932, p. 13). In 1850, the Public Libraries Act put in motion the process that led to the provision of library services as we know them today. From the nineteenth century to the present, the debate on whether public funds should be used to supply readers with what they want to read or only what they ought to has been a central issue in formulating public-library policy.

THE LUDIC READING HABIT

The Publishing Industry

Though it is tempting to equate ludic reading with the reading of fiction, it would be incorrect to do so. In 1985, "the year that the hardcover bestseller went mass market" (Simora, 1986, p. 535), a nonfiction work, Lee Iacocca's autobiography, was overall bestseller in the United States with 1.51 million copies (in 1984, it also sold over a million). Next came the third of Jean Auel's prehistoric novels, *The Mammoth Hunters* (1.47 million), another novel (James Michener's *Texas*, 1.37 million), and Garri-son Keillor's *Lake Wobegon Days* (1.10 million). The fifth and sixth places were occupied by nonfiction: Chuck Yeager's autobiography (1.05 mil-lion) and Priscilla Presley's *Elvis and Me* (800,000). This mix of fiction and nonfiction in the hardcover bestseller list is not at all unusual. In 1979, the year in which Robert Ludlum's *Matarese Circle* sold 250,000 copies, Erma Bombeck's *Aunt Erma's Cope Book* sold 692,000 and a new edition of *The Fanny Farmer Cookbook* sold nearly as well as William Styron's *Sophie's Choice*. For pleasure and relaxation, therefore, hardcover buyers are as likely to read nonfiction as fiction.

On the other hand, a great deal of evidence suggests that fiction occupies a uniquely important place in ludic reading. Fiction borrowing, for example, accounts for over three-quarters of public-library loans. Moreover, the 1986 *Bowker Annual of Library and Book Trade Information* (Simora, 1986, p. 421) shows that fiction accounted for 70.0 percent of all mass-market-paperback titles published in 1984 and 1985 (2,663 and an estimated 2,477 fiction titles, respectively). There is no reliable method of converting titles to individual book units, but it seems likely that the proportion of fiction is actually greater because fiction print runs are usually higher than those for the other twenty-two subject categories (agriculture, art, biology, and so on). For fiction titles expected to become smash bestsellers, first printings can be enormous: for example, 2.5 million for Jacqueline Susann's *Valley of the Dolls* (which sold 4 million copies in the first week) and 3.3 million for Puzo's *The Godfather* (Petersen, 1975).

The data suggest that for many readers, relaxing with a book does not necessarily or always mean relaxing with fiction. But for most, it does, and this is certainly true of the thirty-three reading addicts described in chapter 11 and probably of most other heavy readers.

Although arriving at a precise dollar figure is impossible, the leisure reading habit in the United States and in the world is of substantial economic importance. The *Bowker Annual* puts 1984 U.S. publishing-industry sales at $9.1 billion, of which leisure-reading materials are estimated at a mininum of $1.3 billion, or 13.8 percent. This calculation assumes that fiction accounts for 6.2 percent of adult hardbound trade sales and 70 percent of mass-market-paperback sales, and includes total bookclub sales of $660.9 million (all data from Simora, 1986). However, this is a systematic underestimate, since leisure reading comprises an unknown proportion of books classified as juvenile, school and college materials, and other adult sales (which include books in such categories as sport, travel, biography, literature, and so on), totaling some $4.3 billion.

The 1985 UNESCO *Statistical Yearbook* put world book production in 1983 at 772,000 titles, of which some 80 percent were produced in the developed countries. Barker and Escarpit (1973, p. 17) suggest that the average printing worldwide is 15,500 copies; applied to the UNESCO titles total, this yields a world production of 11.9 billion volumes annually. It is quite impossible to arrive at either a dollar value or a leisure reading proportion of this enormous output, but the latter is unlikely to be lower than the 13.8 percent value estimate made for the United States.

Fiction Time Budgets

Although the strength of the fiction-reading habit can be inferred from world fiction-production figures, a more direct indication of its psychological importance is the amount of time fiction reading occupies within an individual's daily round of activities. Two complementary approaches can be used to measure this indicator: one is to look at population means, in which all levels of reading skill and all types of leisure preferences are included; the other is to look only at ludic readers, who occupy the high end of the reading-time continuum.

A major source for statistics of both kinds is Szalai's monumental *The Use of Time* (1972), an eight-year project involving some 27,000 subjects in eleven countries and three continents. The reading of books and related activities are grouped under the following two categories:

Code 5: *Adult education and professional training*
    54: Homework prepared for different courses and lectures
    55: Reading of scientific reviews of books for personal instruction
Code 9: *Passive leisure*
    90 Listening to the radio
    91 Watching television
    92 Listening to records
    93 Reading books
    94 Reading reviews, periodicals, pamphlets, etc.
    95 Reading newspapers

Time budgets are reported for fifteen sites in the eleven countries surveyed, of which four have been arbitrarily selected for examination here: a national sample (N = 2,077) from Belgium and samples from Torun, Poland, with a population of 113,000 (N = 2,759); Maribor, Yugoslavia, with a population of 96,000 (N = 1,995); and Jackson, Michigan, with 72,000 inhabitants (N = 778). Szalai's data for these four sites are presented in table 1.1

A striking feature of this table is the wide discrepancy between the first and the parenthesized figures in each column, indicating that for all the activities, those who participate in the specified activity do so for much longer, on average, than the mean for the whole sample. Students, for example, study for 3 to 5 hours daily, 10 to 20 times longer than the mean for their sample. (It should be noted that since mean participant time is based on different individuals for each activity, the total of these times per locality is some 72 hours per day.) Similarly, book readers read for 70 to 90 minutes a day as against 4 to 15 minutes for the sample as a whole. To observe that participants spend more time on activities than the sample as a whole is not merely to state the obvious: the figures for participant readers provide an approximation of how much ludic readers read. Szalai's figures indicate that since readers read from 6 to 22 times longer than the rest of the sample, book reading does appear to be a habit distributed bimodally in the population: either one is hooked on book reading and reads a lot, or one isn't and reads very little.

Magazine reading is considerably less important than other media inputs. Szalai (1972, table 2.2.1B) indicates that 7 percent of the 27,000 subjects in all samples pooled read magazines as against 14 percent who read books, 36 percent who read newspapers, and 47 percent who viewed television.

Newspaper reading, on the other hand, accounts for a substantial amount of time in the sample as a whole, and in the American city for seven times more than book reading. Across a large sample, approximately half an hour a day is devoted to the total of leisure reading activities (see table 1.1). Across all fifteen survey sites, this total varies from 19 minutes in Peru to 39 in Pskov, U.S.S.R. (mean = 31.8, S.D. = 5.6). However, the three categories of reading are not compensatory, because the sample populations that read books less do not read magazines or newspapers for appreciably longer than those who spend longer time reading books. This finding is entirely to be expected since averaged data do not indicate whether or not a compensatory mechanism exists. For the individual who habitually reads at certain times of the day, it is very likely that there is such a mechanism, reducing the time allotted to one kind of reading as another increases. But for a given population, my increased newspaper time will be canceled out by my neighbor's increased book time. Thus Szalai's figures do not reveal whether individuals habitually have a certain amount of time available for reading, which they fill with what is at hand, or whether total reading time on a particular day is determined by an individual's regnant needs and motives.

Szalai's figures also indicate that reading habits vary according to the occupational level of respondents (1972, tables 3:1.25–3:1.27). For example, Robinson and Converse (in Szalai, 1972, p. 202) report that in the United States, newspapers accounted for 80 percent of the reading time of those who had not completed high school but only 48 percent of the reading time of the college-educated. Similarly, Skorzynski (in Szalai, 1972) shows that the proportion of those who read books increases with rising education: in Poland, books are read by 7 percent of unskilled workers, 14 percent of skilled workers, 26 percent of white-collar workers without higher education, and 30 percent of those with a higher education. For Yugoslavia, the equivalent figures are 5, 4, 13, and 15 percent. When book and newspaper reading are compared in terms of mean minutes per day, the reciprocal nature of the relationship between education and newspaper or book reading appears most markedly for

Table 1.1. Study and Leisure Activity Time Budgets

		Belgium (2,077)		Toruń, Poland (2,759)		Jackson, Michigan (778)		Maribor, Yugoslavia (1,995)	
		Time per activity in minutes per day							
Code	5 *Study*[a]	16.0	(288)[b]	21.0	(196)	9.0	(192)	20.0	(243)
	54 Homework	7.0		8.0		3.9		7.3	
	55 Read to learn	0.3		2.9		0.3		3.1	
Code	9 *Passive Leisure*								
	90 Radio	8.3	(61)	10.1	(56)	2.6	(43)	5.7	(43)
	91 TV	83.2	(249)	70.3	(255)	101.4	(208)	41.0	(206)
	93 Read books	13.7	(87)	16.4	(75)	3.7	(71)	8.4	(74)
	94 Read magazines	5.4	(61)	3.1	(52)	4.9	(55)	0.9	(56)
	95 Read newspaper	16.4	(46)	16.2	(41)	25.4	(44)	18.8	(45)
Total reading		35.5	(194)	35.7	(168)	34.0	(170)	28.1	(175)
Total mass media[c]		131.0	(154)	120	(143)	138	(158)	80	(114)

Source: Szalai, 1972.

[a]This table uses the condensed categories, so that *Study*, for example, subsumes 54 and 55, plus attending classes of various kinds and travel for study.

[b]Figures in parentheses are mean minutes per day for only those respondents who participate in the activity in question (Szalai, 1972, table 2:2.1C).

[c]This includes Items 90 to 95 plus movies, which are listed under Code 7, *Spectacles and Entertainment*.

men on workdays in Poland, again in the sequence of least to most educated: 4 minutes for books and 29 for newspapers; 9 and 22 among skilled workers; 17 and 19 among white-collar workers; and, in the white-collar elite, 19 minutes for books and 18 for newspapers.

That the relation between book and newspaper reading is probably a function of educational level is further reinforced by a 1978 U.S. readership survey (Cole and Gold, 1979), which found that book readers (55 percent of the sample) were better educated than newspaper and magazine readers who did not read books (39 percent of the sample). Unlike book readers, who are prepared to read at odd moments and under time pressure, non-book readers need to feel that they have a long period available before embarking on a book (Cole and Gold, 1979, pp. 60–61)—an attitude not unexpected of those to whom reading a book is an unfamiliar and therefore daunting prospect.

Szalai's time budgets are unique in their cross-cultural scope and the great care taken to gather accurate data, but many other studies of reading time have been conducted, including Sharon in the United States (1974), Mann in the United Kingdom (1971), Fouché (1972) and de Wet (1968) in South Africa. A word of caution is in order here: when reading professionals (teachers, librarians, and the like) study reading, there may be an unspoken bias in favor of reading; and subjects may feel encouraged to inflate self-reports of how much they read—a failing to which this study is not immune.

Sharon's 1974 study of a national sample of 5,067 Americans aged 16 and over found that 6 percent read for less than 5 minutes a day, 71 percent for more than an hour, 45 percent for more than two hours, and 6 percent for more than 8 hours a day, with a national mean of 106 minutes (113 minutes for men and 101 for women)—a figure three times higher than the 34 minutes a day Szalai reports for Jackson, Michigan (table 1.1). This discrepancy can readily be traced to a pro-reading bias, which is indirectly confirmed by Sharon himself (1974, p. 154), who reports that having obtained an hour-by-hour record of the interviewee's activities on the previous day, he then "asked questions designed to bring to mind any reading that had been done in connection with these activities." The probing even elicited reading done in conjunction with shopping, preparing meals, and so forth. This kind of prompting presents two methodological difficulties. One is that respondents, ever willing to please interviewers, are encouraged to inflate reading time and even invent some. Second, Szalai's solution to the parallel-activities problem is to list only the primary activity, so that the daily time budget totaled 24 hours, whereas Sharon's method clearly leads to daily totals considerably in excess of 24 hours.

Sharon confirms that reading time is a function of socioeconomic status: low-income whites read for 77 minutes a day, and both blacks and whites with only elementary education read for 55 minutes. An interesting finding is that reading declines with age, from 123 minutes for the 16 to 20-year-olds to 89 minutes for those over 60 (Sharon, 1974, p. 158).

Sharon finds book reading restricted to 33 percent of the population, for an average of 47 minutes a day, but unfortunately his reporting method cannot determine the proportion of fiction readers and the time spent reading fiction. However, 5 percent of his total sample (about 15 percent of book readers) read general fiction for an average of 46 minutes a day, and another 2 percent of the total sample read mysteries, which, together with adventure novels and historical novels, are excluded from the general-fiction category. Given these omissions, Sharon's mean of 47 minutes a day for book reading by book readers is, not unexpectedly considerably below Szalai's 71 minutes.

Other studies of book-reading habits are not free of interviewer skewing and inadequate definition. De Wet (1968) reports three studies of leisure reading among U.S. college students which give weekly book-reading times of 7.2 hours, 2.7 hours, and 1.1 hours, respectively. This near sevenfold difference points to serious unreported measurement differences. His own study of 2,128 undergraduates at the University of South Africa (a group representative neither of the population at large nor of university students in South Africa) found that they spent 2.8 leisure hours a week (24 minutes a day) reading books and 4.3 hours reading magazines and newspapers.

Cole and Gold (1979) report that no one in their U.S. national sample of 1,450 respondents read books who did not also read magazines and newspapers, but that 39 percent of the respondents read only magazines and newspapers, while 55 percent read magazines, newspapers, and books. They report that the book-reader market is "heavily upscale and female" (58 percent of book readers are women). Of the total U.S. population, Cole and Gold (1979) found that only 55 percent are book readers. Among those who do read books, 55 percent are light readers (1–9 books in six months) and 45 percent are moderate or heavy readers (10 or more books in six months).

It thus appears accurate to say that "a fairly large proportion of those who are able to read, never read books" (Barker and Escarpit, 1973, p. 107). The proportion of what they term "literate non-readers" (that is, non-readers of books) is lower in the developing countries (where, because of lower literacy rates, literates are more strongly motivated to read by having to read for others) and among younger readers. In France in 1967, 53 percent of 6,865 literate persons did not read books, but among 15 to 19-year-olds, the percentage dropped to 18—probably more as a result of school attendance than of a youthful love of literature; in Hungary in 1964 non-book readers were 36 percent of a sample of 2,227; in Italy and Holland the percentage was 40; but in East Paki- stan in a small sample of 145 it was only 11.

The Fiction Habit in Perspective

A number of general conclusions can be drawn from these data on publishing output and reading habits. First, it seems clear that Escarpit's estimate that literary works comprise 28.2 percent of the books pro- duced is probably far too high. However, in the absence of data on either print runs or fiction sales value as a percentage of total sales, no firm estimate can be made; we can say only that fiction almost certainly ac- counts for less than a quarter of world book production, and that this figure is probably close to 15 percent.

Second, the world adult population as a whole spends only 35 minutes a day reading, and of that as little as 5 minutes is spent reading books. Book readers are variously estimated to comprise between 33 and 55 percent of the total adult population, and they spend between 45 and 70 minutes a day reading books. The light readers (55 percent of the book- reading population) read fewer than ten books a year, or less than one a month.

The economic importance of the leisure reading of fiction, whether in terms of book production or time invested, should therefore not be overestimated. But even 15 percent of a very large industry is, purely quantitatively, worth looking at; and so is an activity that at the most conservative estimate occupies nearly an hour a day of the time of one- third of the adult population. But the psychological issue—the nature of rewards ludic reading offers—has nothing to do with scale or quantity. Broca's 1861 study of a single patient with a brain lesion revolutionized our views of language acquisition and production and founded the sci- ence of aphasiology; even if reading trance were identified in only one reader in a thousand, it would remain a phenomenon of the greatest psychological interest.

2

Plague of the Spirit, Death of the Mind: Pleasure Reading and the Social Value System

Although ludic readers see themselves as reading what they like, the book-selection process is not a free interaction between the skilled reader and the universe of reading matter. Readers are consumers of popular culture and are therefore subject to the factors that determine consumption patterns within this broader context. Lewis (1978) notes that at least until the 1960s popular culture was studied under the shadow of an ideology which judged it negatively on four counts: it is created by profit-minded entrepreneurs and sold to paying audiences; it debases high culture and lures away many of its potential customers; it provides its audience with spurious gratifications and is emotionally harmful; and, finally, it creates a passive audience that is a ready target for the persuasive techniques of totalitarianism.

Mass culture is a brutally contradictory term that plays on the widely held belief that an inverse relationship exists between the quality and quantity of culture. Lewis (1978) suggests that the emotionally neutral "popular culture" be used instead, adding that there is "no empirical evidence whatsoever" (p. 13) that mass culture harms its consumers.

The view of popular culture as a noxious influence can be traced to roots far older than the current criticisms that Lewis has suggested, namely to the sixteenth-century Protestant Reformation, which led to a revolutionary restructuring of the Western conscience with regard to the proper use of time, the importance of work, and the sinfulness of pleasure. The invention of printing a bare seventy years earlier greatly facilitated Luther's revolution and allowed what might have remained a purely local controversy, easily contained by the papacy, to spread rapidly through all of Germany. Moreover, the first appearance of ephemeral literature intended for the lower classes—and literally consumed by them until not a shred remained—occurred in the decades immediately before the Reformation.

Mass reading thus coincided with the Reformation and has for centuries attracted the wrath of the Protestant conscience. And although the Protestant origins of the austerity, social purpose, and elitism of those Johnson (1979) has conveniently labeled "the cultural critics" are now obscured, these have in fact shaped their thinking. In Western society, this critical tradition retains immense force, whether in consciously intellectual guises or in the matter-of-fact, "commonsense" censorship applied by librarians.

The power of this merciless critical asceticism to mold our cultural values and tastes (including, of course, our reading tastes) would collapse were it not continually reinforced, in an entirely circular process, by our own superego's pronouncements on worth and worthlessness. Our conscience and the critics' have been tempered in the same fires, and the force of their judgments is greatly augmented by our fundamental acceptance of the Protestant Ethic values on which they are based.

Recent critical trends toward an interactionist view of the reading process, which assigns considerable weight to the reader's interpretive contribution, are at this stage no more than a tiny cloud on the horizon of the elitist world in which popular culture struggles for respectability. But because it arises from a powerful new relativism in the analysis of social values and adopts the heretical view that authoritative social value judgments are created and not revealed, the tiny cloud, like Elijah's, is likely eventually to blacken the heavens of absolutist criticism.

These issues, which might seem to have more relevance for the sociology of mass culture than for the psychology of reading, do in fact bear directly on the social and personal determinants of the individual ludic reader's choice of reading material, and how he or she feels about that choice. If ludic readers see themselves as depraved, like cigarette smokers or habitual masturbators, they will be compelled to deal with the resulting discomfort by a variety of strategies. And the nature and quality of the resolution readers find for the dissonance they experience will necessarily affect the rewards they derive from their reading, since the reinforcements to be derived from such socially sanctioned activities as painting in oils and attending the opera are likely to have a very different subjective quality than those gained from voyeurism or overeating. In terms of Daniel Berlyne's aesthetics, "our perceptions of what is aesthetic and what is not, of which hedonism is sanctified and which profane, is radically moulded by our values. . . . We admire most that which we believe to be admirable: the arousal boost we derive from a work judged to be art is therefore larger and more rewarding than that from one judged to be kitsch" (Nell, 1980, p. 8).

This chapter explores four social-psychological issues: the role of literary criticism in the development of the social values by which popular culture is judged; the emergence of such socially appointed custodian groups as teachers and librarians, whose function it is to implement these standards; the new interactional relativism in criticism, which is radically subversive of these judgments; and, finally, the cognitive strategies ludic readers develop in order to justify what they are still constrained to regard as their vice.

READING AND VALUES

Since the sixteenth century, Western views of the correct use of time and the sinfulness of worldly pleasure have been powerfully influenced by Protestantism and especially by its radical variant, Puritanism. In his famous examination of the Protetant Ethic, Max Weber (1904) notes that the asceticism central to Puritanism is achieved through the discipline of hard, continuous labor, whether mental or physical. This regime defends one against both waste of time, which in Benjamin Franklin's famous discourse is described as the most terrible of all sins (in Weber, 1904, pp. 48–50), and an unclean life (sexuality is permitted for reproduction only). Work, not pleasure, serves God, and Puritan asceticism "turned with all its force against one thing: the spontaneous enjoyment of life" (p. 166). The use of time or wealth for any purpose "which does not serve the glory of God but only one's own enjoyment" is powerfully condemned; thus fine art, the theater, personal decoration, and idle talk are all censured (pp. 166–70). These values are also reflected in the modern conviction that pleasures must be earned by hard work and that the deepest pleasure is consequent upon suffering—for example, the exhilaration of the climber standing exhausted on the mountain peak, or the satisfaction of the reader who has just finished *Moby Dick.*

Squandering time and money on the purchase of profane works of fiction for pleasure reading is therefore an offense against every aspect of the Protestant Ethic—the basis for the moralizing tone in which reading by "the masses" has been condemned since the late eighteenth century. In 1817 Coleridge, in his *Biographia Literaria,* wrote that nine-tenths of the reading public were "that comprehensive class characterized by the power of reconciling . . . indulgence of sloth and hatred of vacancy." Theirs was not reading but rather a "beggarly day-dreaming, during which the mind of the dreamer furnishes for itself nothing but laziness, and a little mawkish sensibility," akin to swaying on a gate or spitting over a bridge (Altick, 1957, pp. 368–69; Taylor, 1943, has collected thirty pages of excerpts from other contemporary attacks on mass reading). Victorian observers agreed, writes Altick, that as reading became more and more passive, "the eye would remain active, but the nerve that connected it with the brain would simply wither away from disuse" (p. 370). A modern critic echoes the view that slothful reading damages the brain: The most popular works of art feed the senses with illusions and indulge the cheapest emotions, which "wither or become loose and deliquescent . . . and the unaroused brain degenerates" (Davis, 1973, p. 17).

Worse, reading is a drug: "the effect of inordinate addiction to light reading . . . came under the head of 'dissipation', and to read novels, as to drink wine, in the morning, was far into the [nineteenth] century a sign of vice" (Leavis, 1932, p. 50). Moreover, the reading habit has often been branded as a form of the drug habit, and the circulating libraries, in which reading means fiction and a book means a novel, as "tuppenny dram shops" (pp. 7–8). Forty years after Leavis, but no less judgmentally, Davis writes that the reading drug may be quite as pernicious as "overindulgence in alcohol or aspirin" (1973, p. 11).

The Wages of Sin

So dire are the physical and moral consequences of these unearned pleasures, so readily available to the least worthy members of society, that the punishments visited on the depraved are exactly those previously reserved for the masturbator, that other class of person who by his own hand confers on himself unearned pleasures proper to those in another estate. Maddi (1976, pp. 280–81) quotes this chilling extract from an authoritative 1901 treatise on the education of small boys:

> Teach him that when he handles or excites the sexual organs, all parts of the body suffer . . . because they are very closely connected with the spine and the brain by means of the nerves, and . . . this lays the foundation for consumption, paralysis, and heart disease. It weakens the memory and . . . even makes many lose their minds; others, when grown, commit suicide.

To readers in the late twentieth century, a puzzling aspect of Huey's otherwise admirably lucid study of reading (1908) is his emphasis on "reading fatigue," which he specifies in the first lines of his preface (p. xii) as an important aspect of his study, and to which he devotes an entire chapter:

> Reading makes certain severe demands upon the psycho-physical organism. These demands fall most heavily upon the eye, upon the mechanism of inner speech, upon mind and brain in the rapid functioning of attention, apperception, association, imagery, feeling, etc., and upon the general nervous mechanism. The causes of the peculiar fatigue experienced after continued reading

have not all been satisfactorily made out as yet. . . . Provisionally, we may here point out certain functionings more or less peculiar to reading which condition part of the fatigue and degeneration which is thus induced (Huey, 1908, p. 387).

Huey then explores the consequences of this "degeneration"—myopia, strabismus, and stuttering (which is attributed to faulty reading instruction). Fatigue is further ascribed to the rapidly changing direction and content of attention, which result in "nerve exhaustion" (p. 403) and the reduction of "nerve reserve." Reading, "though often a helpfully recreative employment, . . . lacks the freedom and the rejuvenating effect of free play" (p. 404). Now, the fatigue that I experience after sixteen hours of reading and writing is most marked in my *glutei maximi;* Huey's nosology falls strangely on our ears. Does the expectation that reading inevitably results in "peculiar fatigue" perhaps have its origin in the same ascetic mythology that predicted the dire physiological consequences of masturbation?

But, despite this apparently new concern with the likely results of too much reading and the continuous decline in moral and artistic standards to which each new generation of critics feels impelled to bear personal witness (such as Richard Hoggart in 1958: "most of our popular journals have become a good deal worse in the last 15 or 20 years," p. 173), the problem of excessive indulgence in narrative products has been around for a long time. For example, at the Cape of Good Hope, large numbers of novels were available from the 1830s and "were anathema to more than one section of society" (Varley, 1958). The novelist is the linear descendant of the tribal storyteller, and in primitive societies, in which social control is exercised through shame mechanisms rather than guilt (Albee, 1977) a taboo was placed on storytelling before sunset lest unregulated indulgence in this most popular of pastimes cut too far into the working day. Among the Tsonga of North Natal, writes Marivate (1973, p. 212), storytelling while the sun is up is forbidden. Jordan (1966) confirms a similar taboo enforced against the Xhosa "ntsomi," and Berry (1961) notes that the same rule applies in West Africa.

The Stratification of Taste

Leavis (1932, p. 99) suggests that the eighteenth-century peasant who could read, read what the gentry read, while the outstanding characteristic of nineteenth-century literature was its stratification, with different writers addressing themselves more and more to different publics, some literally felt to be "unknown" (as in the title of Collins' 1859 essay on the readers of the "penny-novel-Journals"). The stratification of taste, most marked between educated and working-class readers, was also felt within the more restricted class of book readers themselves: "the kind of book the middlebrow press will admire . . . the highbrow reviewer will diagnose as pernicious" (Leavis, 1932, p. 21). Thus *Everyman* in the 1930s praises a work of fiction as "a brave honest philosophy with no nonsense about it," while the *Nation and Athanaeum* describes the same novel as "a really bad book . . . so much quackery and gush."

But is Leavis correct in tracing this stratification to the nineteenth century? On the contrary: though the social factors that led to the spread of literacy and the availability of cheap reading matter vastly increased the size of the reading public in the 1800s, other evidence suggests that "literate peasants" had their own tastes, which were not those of the gentry, long before 1800. Scholderer (1971) notes that a "considerable percentage" of the 20 million incunabula (produced between 1450 and 1500) consisted of ephemeral literature, including cheap romances and ballads, which have perished entirely because they circulated among lower-class readers who passed them from hand to hand until they literally disintegrated. Altick notes (1957, pp. 28–29) that for the very lowest classes, the apprentices, common laborers, peasants, and rivermen, among whom reading in the eighteenth century was rare, there was a separate class of reading matter, contained in broadside ballads ("never was a celebrated highwayman executed or a catastrophe visited upon a hapless town but the event was described in crude language and cruder woodcuts") and in chapbooks, which contained vulgarized versions of old chivalric tales. Production of chapbooks and ballads continued until the advent of penny periodicals in the late eighteenth century provided alternative reading for the common people.

Value Constancy

The condemnation of mass reading has remarkably ancient roots, and even in tribal societies, social-control mechanisms are brought to bear on storytelling activity. Printed ephemeral literature antedates the Reformation, and the first critical judgments of light reading appear in the sixteenth century. The constancy of these judgments (which explicitly or tacitly warn against the sins of idleness, sloth, and unearned pleasure) across four centuries, which have left nothing else unchanged, is nothing less than amazing. In the sixteenth century, for example, it was thought necessary to forbid children to read fables and fantasies, and it was not until the eighteenth century, through children's chapbooks and the zeal of John Newbery, that a children's literature of fairy tales and adventure was provided, though the opposition between the "should" of stifling moral tales and the "would" of fairy stories persisted into the nineteenth century (Hansen, 1973). The conflict today between what children like to read and what they ought to read can be traced quite explicitly to its sixteenth-century origins, as with Pearce (1974), writing in *New Library World:* "It is possible that the child or adult who is *doing*— . . . building a dam, falling out of a tree—is perhaps rather healthier than the one who is playing parasite on the imaginations and words of others" (p. 214). It is not too difficult to find the Protestant Ethic origins of these ostensibly modern remarks: "playing parasite" is a form of sloth, which the view that climbing trees is "healthier" than reading (shades of Huey's "reading fatigue"!) endorses the very old idea that the most legitimate use of leisure is for recreation—that is, to recreate one's energies for the real business of living, which is work (see de Grazia, 1962, for an illuminating analysis of these themes). In the same issue of *New Library World*, Codlin (1974) writes disapprovingly of the "stupefying goo" old ladies take home by the basketful. Mott (1960) refers to the "new subliterary reading experience" and the "holiday world of commercial culture"; the reading bazaar, he says, "belongs to an unpurposeful fun world," a world opposed to the serious workfulness that this critic, like so many others, feels to be the only one that is right and true. "Holiday" is tainted by another unspoken judgment; namely, that pleasure must be earned, and that the effortlessness of ludic reading makes its pleasures as hollow as the euphoria of the junkie or the orgasm of the masturbator.

Escapism

The most richly pejorative of the descriptors applied to ludic reading is *escapist,* a new coinage that appears in the 1956 *Addenda* to the *Shorter Oxford English Dictionary* (1933b) and has the sense of seeking mental or emotional distraction from the realities of life. In a more specifically psychological sense, it is defined as "a tendency to retreat from the unpleasant, especially when it should be dealt with realistically" (English and English, 1958). Mass communication researchers who have spent a great deal of energy proving that the mass media and their users "have been sinful where they should have been good" (Stephenson, 1967, p. 45), have dutifully shown that escapist readers are sick people (see Klapper, 1960, chap. 7) and that children are especially susceptible to escapist temptations (for example, Schramm, Lyle, and Parker, 1961). Unfortunately, neither the term *escapism* nor the literature on it is helpful to a study of ludic reading. To say "escapist" is to make a judgment, and even a perceptive article that challenges many premises of the escapist view (Katz and Foulkes, 1962) remains within the moralist framework, condemning the "narcotizing dysfunction" of the media that fail to feed back to real-life roles (p. 388).

Escapism is most usefully seen as a pejorative synonym for fantasizing, and the judgment implied by the term is that the fantasizer is woolgathering at a time when the work of the world calls him. Ludic readers, who judge themselves harshly, quite readily admit to this sin. (We shall defer a full consideration of this question until chapter 11. By then, in light of our review of fantasy processes in chapter 9, we shall be in a better position to appreciate the true nature of escapism and in what ways ludic readers' judgments of themselves may be unduly severe.)

Leo Dillon's Sin

In "An Encounter," the second story in James Joyce's *Dubliners* (1914), there is a passage set at the turn of the century that encapsulates the entire panorama we have surveyed—the vehicles of mass reading, guilt at self-indulgence and its obligatory apologia, elite culture's censure (here transferring the vice of tippling from reader to author), and, finally, the reader's confessed addiction to the "wild sensations" of consciousness change:

> It was Joe Dillon who introduced the Wild West to us. He had a little library made up of old numbers of *The Union Jack, Pluck,* and *The Half-penny Marvel.* Every evening after school we met in his back garden and arranged an Indian battle. . . . A spirit of unruliness diffused itself among us and, under its influence, differences of culture and constitution were waived. We banded ourselves together, some boldly, some in jest, and some almost in fear: and of the number of these latter, the reluctant Indians who were afraid to seem studious or lacking in robustness, I was one. The adventures related in the literature of the Old West were remote from my nature, but, at least, they opened doors of escape. I liked better some American detective stories which were traversed from time to time by unkempt fierce and beautiful girls. Though there was nothing wrong in these stories and though their intention was sometimes literary they were circulated secretly at school. One day when Father Butler was hearing the four pages of Roman history, clumsy Leo Dillon was discovered with a copy of *The Halfpenny Marvel.* . . .
>
> Everyone's heart palpitated as Leo Dillon handed up the paper and everyone assumed an innocent face. Father Butler turned over the pages, frowning.
>
> —What is this rubbish? he said. *The Apache Chief!* Is this what you read instead of studying your Roman History? Let me not find any more of this wretched stuff in this college. The man who wrote it, I suppose, was some wretched scribbler that writes these things for a drink. I'm surprised at boys like you, educated, reading such stuff. I could understand it if you were . . . National School boys. Now, Dillon, I advise you strongly, get at your work or . . .
>
> This rebuke during the sober hours of school paled much of the glory of the Wild West for me and the confused puffy face of Leo Dillon awakened one of my consciences. But when the restraining influence of the school was at a distance I began to hunger again for wild sensations, for the escape which those chronicles of disorder alone seemed to offer me (pp. 16–17).

INFORMER OR ENTERTAINER: THE DILEMMA OF THE PUBLIC LIBRARIAN

There is an unlikely but illuminating parallel between newspaper editors and public librarians: both see themselves as informers and educators, whereas they are in fact entertainers. Though in our society entertaining is a less honorable profession than teaching, both editors and librarians might save themselves much anxious introspection if they frankly accepted their role as entertainers and made the most of the not inconsiderable opportunities an entertainer has to broaden and deepen his audience's understanding of the ways of the world—which is the goal of education.

Editors and librarians are of course not the only arbiters of public taste. Schoolteachers probably exert a great deal more influence and more lastingly, and many other professions and groups have a social license to make authoritative pronouncements on cultural products. Among these are ministers of religion, reviewers of books, movies, and television programs, academics, and such functionaries of the entertainment industry as authors, playwrights, actors, and directors.

However, librarians are especially relevant to the present study because they deal almost exclusively with books and reading, whereas reading is only one among many activities that concern teachers, ministers, and other authority figures. For this reason, the position of the public librarian is rather less comfortable than, for example, that of the newspaper editor, who may pretend to ignore the trivia and pseudo-events on which the circulation depends and give undivided attention to political opinion-forming. The public librarian, on the other hand, trained to see the profession as educational, knows that light fiction accounts for around 80 percent of the total books borrowed (Fouché, 1981; Leavis, 1932). Librarians are rather thus at the cutting edge of the ancient anomaly between "would" and "should," between informing and entertaining, and the ways in which they deal with this issue may prove relevant to ludic reading in two respects.

First, librarians determine the buying policy of their institutions. The decision to ban comics but stock Enid Blyton will have a large influence on the direction in which young readers' tastes develop (a lifelong hatred of Little Noddy and a devotion to Captain Marvel is one possible outcome). In a very real sense, the librarian's perceptions of art and kitsch, of good reading and trash, will determine what library users are able to read, especially since public libraries are a major source of fiction reading matter.

Second, the way librarians solve the would/should problem affects ludic readers in other, more subtle ways. If in a given library reading fiction is penalized (by borrowing limits or extra fees), readers may turn to narrative nonfiction; if Harlequin romances are banned but their imitators allowed, readers may feel that the imitators are "better" than the originals and pass this judgment on to their children. Finally, the person behind the circulation desk (who, although probably an un-trained library assistant, will have absorbed at least some of the library's cultural values) is for many readers a more visible and therefore salient authority figure within the world of books than critics, teachers, and ministers. The librarian's half-concealed or overt approval or disdain for the books the child or adult has chosen may direct developing tastes into new channels.

In seeking a further understanding of the cultural and professional pressures that mold public-library policy, let us first examine the status of fiction lending. In 1924, fiction accounted for 78 percent of the books borrowed from urban British libraries, but for only 37 percent of their book stock; in other words 63 percent of the volumes on the shelves were nonfiction (Leavis, 1932). Fifty years later, in 1974, fiction accounted for 77 percent of the books loaned by Port Elizabeth Public Library but for only 49 percent of the total stock—despite numerous devices to encourage borrowers to read more nonfiction. Since available stocks of goods usually reflect demand for them, perhaps a hidden motive explains why book-stock figures are inconsistent with demand figures. Publicly funded librar-ies might need to escape the infamy that attached to the eighteenth- and nineteenth-century circulating libraries ("a circulating library in a town is an evergreen tree of diabolical knowledge," complained Sheridan's Sir Anthony Absolute) and to preserve "the intellectual self-respect of the community" (Shera, 1965, p. 152) by maintaining an adequate stock of socially approved material.

The view that an obligation to elevate public taste rests on the public librarian, among others, is widely held: "to form a literate population into a people that is emotionally and intellectually strengthened by books remains . . . an impressive challenge," writes Altick (1957, p. 375). A former head of the English department at the University of Port Eliza-beth, Tom Smailes (personal communication, August 1976), said: "The librarian is there to serve the public, not to give it what it wants. I teach discrimination. The librarian should do the same. A library is not a second-hand book exchange. It has a social responsibility." The editor of the *South African Journal for Librarianship and Information Science* writes that "librarians wish to do their work for a worthwhile purpose and would want to know why they should spend their lives providing some-thing just because the public wants it" (R. B. Zaaiman, personal communi-cation, September 30, 1981).

Heartbreak House

But educating the public is the librarian's Heartbreak House. Earlier this century, Nicholas Rubakin formulated the idea of "bait": "The librarian must not neglect to acquire a number of what we can call 'bait books,' whose authors are popular with the uneducated reader" (Rubakin and Bethmann, 1937, p. 20). The bait strategy is still current (D. Sanderson, personal communication, August 1976), though the public, with no more morality than the fish they are expected to emulate, makes off joyously with the bait but cannily refuses to be landed on the rocky shores of Good Reading. Predictably, public librarians are heartily contemptuous of this obstinately ineducable public. The richly pejorative English term *trash* is archetypically represented by the romantic library published by Silhouette and Harlequin and banned by many public libraries in South Africa. "No self-respecting person should read that, no one with an ounce of intelligence," says an anonymous librarian; "For the kind of person who reads one book a day, it doesn't much matter if it's the same book every day. They can put a book back on the shelf and turn around and take the same book off the shelf again and never notice. It doesn't matter in the least to them."

An interesting question now arises: what instruments does the librarian have available in order to fulfill this duty of protecting the public against its own depravity by ensuring that it is denied trash and provided with good literature? This is an exercise in normative aesthetics, requiring that distinctions be drawn in terms of widely accepted social standards between artifacts possessing positive aesthetic value and those lacking it. But there is another ambiguity with which librarians must grapple; namely, that despite the cultural stewardship society assigns to them (and which they themselves willingly embrace), they stand in a deliberately external relation to books, in the same sense that the printer judging the ink coverage and color registration on the proof copy of a magazine stands outside the headlines and advertisements. Printers are trained to judge print, not politics, and a librarian functioning *qua* librarian is trained to transmit social judgments but not to make them. How, then, are librarians to judge the daily questions of literary and educational value thrust upon them? How are they to judge whether Richard Brautigan is "better" than Djuna Barnes? Which is the unsung genius, which the producer of malicious artifacts? The most obvious yardstick available in such abstruse matters is the Protestant Ethic axiom that virtue and pain are constant companions: "To perceive more richly . . . and think more vigorously . . . we must have recourse to the products of minds superior to our own . . . which must initially bring more pain than pleasure. . . . This pain is one of the symptoms by which the critic recognizes great writing" (Davis, 1973, p. 21). The best medicine tastes the worst, the best exercise hurts the most. Compelled to choose between the prose of Djuna Barnes (1936):

> The number of our days is not check rein enough to look upon the death of our love. While living we knew her too well, and never understood, for then our next gesture permitted our next misunderstanding. But death is intimacy walking backward. (p. 183).

and that of Richard Brautigan (1976):

> The Logan brothers kicked in the front door and ran into the apartment looking for the bowling trophies and the first one in ran down the hall into the bedroom shouting, "BOWLING TROPHY THIEVES DIE!" and shot the two people, one of whom was sitting on the bed reading from a book while the other one was lying in bed, listening to him as he read with her eyes closed.

the librarian is likely to ascribe greater aesthetic value to the former than to the latter. But, if merit is indeed to be judged by difficulty, there is little to prevent the conclusion that a Chevrolet workshop manual and T. S. Eliot are of equal worth. This coupling of quality with difficulty is explicit in de Wet's readership study (1968), in which one of the questions he puts (in Afrikaans) is as follows: "Do you prefer to read (i) light fiction in which a gripping story is the most important element; (ii) heavier fiction in which character development and realism are important; (iii) really difficult fiction of the highest literary quality?" (p. 162).

Other anomalies arise in libraries as a result of the application of Protestant Ethic values to the complex issues raised by popular culture. The first is the arbitrary nature of the distinction between fiction (which, on the whole, is judged to be escapist and bad for one) and nonfiction (real, educational, and therefore good for one). Some librarians feel so strongly on this point that borrowers are allowed to take out twice as many nonfiction as fiction works (D. Sanderson, personal communication, August 1976; Westra, 1981). Travel and biography, which may not be as well researched and written as a John Le Carré spy story set in Hong Kong, are "better" than their fictional counterparts; *Armies of the Night*, Norman Mailer's record of a 1968 antiwar demonstration, which is news that reads like a novel, is "better" than Patrick White. Absurdities multiply, and nowhere more than in the arbitrary distinction between news and fiction.

The second anomaly is that what librarians call trash, in which bestsellers by Wilbur Smith and Arthur Hailey can probably be included, is dismissed as a worthless killtime. But even that austerely highbrow critic Q. D. Leavis says of Marie Corelli, Hall Caine, and Florence Barclay, the blockbuster writers of the late nineteenth and early twentieth centuries, that the "bad writing, false sentiment, sheer silliness and preposterous narrative are all carried along by the magnificent vitality of the author"; she speaks of the fascinated envy that more intellectual writers have for these lower organisms "that exude vital energy as richly as a manure heep" (1932, pp. 62–63). When Davis (1973) warns of atrophy of the mind or Gass (1972, p. 273) writes that the products of popular culture "have no more aesthetic quality than a brick in the street . . . only art enlarges consciousness like space in a cathedral," this power is overlooked, as well as the incontrovertible ability of the Haileys, the Le Carrés, and the Flemings to people our memories and to enlarge our consciousness as well as any cathedral space.

The third anomaly is that the pejoratives are finally misplaced because they overlook the need met by popular art, which critics and librarians share with John Q. Public: to fasten onto the words of the storyteller, to dream a personal triumph, to participate in other lives. The need satisfied by reading what the stewards of high culture call trash is as old as human history, and condemning it as depraved will not change very much.

Legitimation

The dilemma in which public librarians find themselves is uncomfortable. Trained as disseminators of information, they find that their main stock in trade is light fiction, and that they are authoritatively described as practitioners in the field of entertainment: "An entire entertainment industry utilising the mass media is based on this need for escapism. The public library is in practice also undoubtedly located in this area" (Fouché, 1981, p. 8). In order to resolve their dilemma, public librarians may either withdraw from the entertainment field or embrace it wholeheartedly. A recent issue of the *Drexel Library Quarterly* offers a perspective on public libraries in relation to popular culture: "While some public librarians are still embarrassed about 'light' materials in the library, any public library playing the circulation statistics game is frankly popular because that is what folks footing the bills want to read and see and hear. . . . Public library collections . . . also must have major collections of current best sellers, light fiction, popular political commentaries, mysteries, westerns and science fiction" (Schroeder, 1981, p. 65). Other essays in the same issue plead for the establishment of popular-culture collections that will include comic books, pop records, magazine subscriptions (to *Playboy, Mad, Wrestling*), popular photographs, and posters.

Unfortunately, there is no middle road on this fundamentally political issue: one either ascribes value to popular culture or dismisses it as kitsch (a high-culture term as useful as *trash* and *escapism*). Perhaps if public librarians acknowledged their role as entertainers and vigorously set about filling it, they would be less conflicted and our libraries happier places.

LITERARY CRITICISM AND THE DESTRUCTION OF ABSOLUTES

Just two questions within the domain of literary criticism are of interest to the study of ludic reading. One is an almost purely psychological question, long recognized as important, but little explored; namely, "the secret of popularity in art" (Leavis, 1932). This secret, Janus-like, has one face toward the writer's work as an *encoder* of texts, what Wayne Booth calls "the author's means of controlling his reader" (1961, p. ii), and the other toward the reader's work as the *decoder* of texts. The mixed curiosity and disdain bearers of the high culture feel toward the appeal popular art has for its audience is neatly captured by I. A. Richards, author of *Practical Criticism* (1929) and founder of an important critical school: "Best sellers in all the arts are worthy of very close study. No theory of criticism is satisfactory which is not able to explain their wide appeal and to give clear reasons why those who disdain them are not snobs."

Aspects of the second question, the cultural values by which ludic readers judge their activity and its vehicles, have been considered in earlier sections of this chapter: we now turn our attention to the core of this process: the ways in which cultural and especially literary values are created and destroyed. We examine below the three major emphases that have emerged in literary criticism since the 1920s: a focus on the text, on the writer, and on the reader. These and related issues are reviewed in Ryan (1985).

The Geneva School

The Geneva School has little to offer the student of ludic reading because it focuses primarily on the writer's work. The reader is viewed as re-creating the writer's creative experience, and the coded forms of the text become transparent as they release their energy into the mind of the receptive reader (Ryan, 1982). This is a prescription for an essentially effortful experience, very different from sinking through the page into the book. The ludic reader becomes the fictional hero and sees the book-world through the protagonist's eyes, whereas Ryan's receptive reader must locate the author, who broods invisibly behind the page. "Through the act of reading the reader tries to identify himself with another mind and to re-experience from the inside the feelings of that mind" (George Miller, in Ryan, 1982). The word "tries" points to the effortfulness of this endeavor.

The Geneva School's focus on the author led it to attempt to characterize the inner unity of an author's work by defining the quality that "binds the diverse expressions of a single consciousness" (Ryan, 1982). This is a question of the greatest interest to the ludic reader, who needs to know whether a new book by Georges Simenon or Ian Fleming will deliver what has delighted him or her in the past. However, ludic readers want stable qualities (Cawelti, 1976), whereas the "literary" writer's inner unity may nonetheless sanction wide variations in theme, diction, and tone. The Geneva School reader is delighted by the unity-in-diversity exhibited by Doris Lessing in *A Proper Marriage* and *Shikasta,* or Henry Miller in *Tropic of Capricorn* and *Smile at the Foot of the Ladder;* the ludic reader feels cheated.

The New Criticism

The view that criticism rests on a close study of the text ("practical criticism") without reference either to the author's assumed purpose (the "intentional fallacy") or to the reader's response (the "affective fallacy") was put forward by I. A. Richards, first at Cambridge and later at Harvard, and in Eastern Europe, by Roman Jakobson and the Prague Linguistic Circle. These New Critics held that a literary work is an objective artifact with a determinate and recoverable meaning; literary studies should thus adopt a scientific and rule-governed approach. This formalist view postulates the existence of a unique genus, literature, which may unerringly be identified by a scientifically trained critic. Richard's famous exercise in practical criticism (1929) therefore required students to write appreciations of thirteen printed sheets containing anonymous extracts from Shakespeare, John Donne, and various unknowns. One of these authors was the Rev. G. A. Studdert Kennedy, also known as Woodbine Willie, who, in a letter giving Richards permission to use "any of my poems for any purpose you like," added, "the criticisms could not be more . . . slaughterous than my own would be" (Richards, 1929, p. 367). "I would as a rule hint that the poems were perhaps a mixed lot, but that was the full extent of my interference," notes Richards.

Implicit in this exercise, and in the formalist system as a whole, is the belief that poetic and non-poetic language—that is, literary and non-literary discourse—can be distinguished on scientific grounds, and that this distinction is likely to be founded in determinable linguistic differences (as held by the Prague School: Pratt, 1977, chap. 1; Erlich, 1969), in peculiarly literary modes of diction such as ambiguity (Empson, 1939), or both. The formalist view has several corollaries. One is that "literature is somehow intrinsically superior" to non-literary discourse (Pratt, 1977, p. xvi); a second is that "psychology is unnecessary to art and not in itself of artistic value" (Welleck and Warren, 1955, p. 92). Or, in other words, studying the psychological processes of encoders or decoders of literature (what formalists see as the intentional and affective fallacies) is irrelevant to criticism.

The third corollary is that the ultimate test of critical competence is to be able to distinguish reliably between literary and non-literary works (or between art and fakes) on textual grounds alone. Formalism admits of the possibility of the clever fake, which I prefer to call "the malicious artifact" (chimpanzee art masquerading as abstract expressionism, or a "poem" composed by an IBM 3084). It is malicious because it lies in ambush for the unwary critic, who, if duped, is stripped of his authority and becomes the legitimate object of ridicule. The specter of the malicious artifact collapses if aesthetic quality is located elsewhere (in the audience, for example, which in fact means in social values); but by moving the aesthetic locus from text or artifact to the audience, we radically alter the nature of criticism. The critic ceases to be a judge, delivering pronouncements *ex cathedra*, and becomes instead the channel through which social values are articulated. This is an uncomfortable change, unlikely to be welcomed by the socially appointed guardians of aesthetic standards, simply because it is easier for hack critics to ape authoritative views (even at the risk of embarrassing error) than to arrive at their own views in the absence of authority. For those who have to judge literature, the change will be especially difficult. Though not trained as critics and therefore lacking the prerequisite scientific apparatus, librarians and their assistants are called upon to make only one all-or-nothing distinction: is a given book trash or is it not? This crude distinction is further aided by the availability of copious indicators on the book itself of its likely literary standing: author, publisher, and design of the dust jacket (which may even quote authoritative reviews). The chances of error are small, and those that are made can be condoned because they are committed in the public's best interests.

But in literature, as in the fine arts, critics' and librarians' comfortable certainties that art and trash, originals and fakes, can be reliably distinguished by internal evidence alone are slowly beginning to crumble under the double impact of a relativism about values, examined below, and the twofold relativism introduced by the speech-act school of literary critics.

The New Readers

The new-readers school (Fish, 1980; Pratt, 1977) holds, first, that literature and non-literature are not structurally distinct and, second, that the reader's expectations create the quality of literariness in a text, not the text itself. Proof of the first assertion is that a single linguistic apparatus can be constructed to account adequately for language use both within and outside literature, thus collapsing the Prague School's textoid contention that "there are such things as 'poetic' and 'prosaic' languages, each with their different laws" (Ejxenbaum in Pratt, 1977, p. 4). The second line of proof seeks to establish whether the quality of "literariness" exists outside literature by examining the speech acts of ordinary people with no artistic pretensions. Evidence that this may be true derives largely from the work of the sociolinguist William Labov (1972), who studied Black English vernacular speakers in New York City (a relevant parallel study is Kochman's *Rappin' and Stylin' Out,* 1972). Labov asked his adolescent subjects whether they had ever been in a situation in which they felt their lives to be in danger, and whether they had ever been in a fight with someone bigger than themselves. Two of his findings concern us. First, although these vernacular speakers usually modify their speech when talking to an outsider, "because the experience and emotions involved here form an important part of the speaker's biography, he seems to undergo a partial reliving of that experience, and he is no longer free to monitor his own speech as he normally does in face to face interviews" (p. 355). Labov is telling us something of the greatest psychological importance for our understanding of the spell storytelling casts on its audience: the teller casts a spell not only over his audience but also over himself.

The second important finding is that the extra-literary productions of ordinary people telling stories about their own experiences—what Labov calls natural narratives—follow a fixed six-step structural pattern that closely corresponds to the organization of narrative literature (Pratt, 1977, p. 50). Both literary and natural narratives begin with an *abstract* that briefly encapsulates the point of the story, offer an *orientation,* recount the *complicating action* and its *resolution,* offer an *evaluation* that explains why the story was worth telling (the more skillful the narrator, the more deeply the evaluation is embedded in the story), and conclude with a *coda* that leaves the listener with a feeling of satisfaction and completeness.

Although natural and literary narratives are indistinguishable on linguistic or organizational grounds, enthronement of the text as the source of literariness is subject to a further attack—the relocation of the literary experience to within the reader. Stanley Fish (1980) argues that the reader's response is not *to* the meaning of the text, it *is* the meaning (p. 3). Nevertheless, this radical view is in fact no more than a restatement in stronger terms of the critical cliché that the book is created by the reader. Thus the methodical Tinker: "Reading is creative . . . what any reader derives from the printed page, therefore, is not exactly what some other reader would get or even what the author had in mind, but to a certain degree at least a personal recreation on the part of the reader" (1965, p. 5). Or Percy Lubbock: "The reader of a novel is himself a novelist: he is the maker of a book . . . for which he must take his own share of responsibility" (1957, p. 17). Or Jorge Luis Borges: a book "is the dialogue it establishes with its reader and the intonation it imposes on his voice. . . . A book is not an isolated entity: it is a relationship, an axis of innumerable relationships" (1964, p. 213). Or Robert Escarpit: "when we hold a book in our hands, all we hold is paper. The book is elsewhere" (1966, p. 17).

Fish merely carries these views to their radical conclusion: literature has no formal properties that compel a certain kind of attention; rather, "paying a certain kind of attention results in the emergence into noticeability of the properties we know in advance to be literary" (1980, p. 10). In other words, "the reader makes literature" (p. 11). Fish brilliantly illustrates this point in a chapter entitled "How to Recognize a Poem When You See One," in which he tells a poetry class that a list of six linguists' names written one under the other on the blackboard for an earlier class is a medieval liturgical poem of a kind they had been studying, and the students duly interpret the list as if it were a poem. The received creed, comments Fish, is that a poem is poetic because its language displays appropriate characteristics, whereas in fact "the acts of recognition, rather than being triggered by formal characteristics, are their source; . . .paying a certain kind of attention results in the emergence of poetic qualities" (p. 326). Fish, rightly appalled by the radical indeterminacy into which his position plunges the study of literature, takes refuge in the idea of an interpretive community (p. 14), but once meaning (and quality) are dislodged from the text and placed between it and the reader, no subterfuge can return one to the traditional certainties.

The implications of this view are so subversive of the established aesthetic order that one may confidently expect librarians, schoolteachers, and professional critics to defend against it to their last breath.

The New Relativism

Fish is a product of the times. In the past decade, a fundamental relativism has invaded the social sciences. With the wisdom of hindsight it would now appear that one of its more important points of origin was the demonstration by Rokeach (1971) that deeply held values can be permanently modified by a brief experimental procedure. Since values are identified as "universal determinants in all human decision-making" (Sperry, 1977, p. 237), the repeatedly demonstrated ease with which they can be manipulated (McClelland, 1977; Eron, 1980) introduces a fundamental uncertainty about the ways in which we judge ourselves and the world. This uncertainty has one outcome in labeling theory (Lewis, 1978, pp. 18–21), which holds that elite culture, for example, is a social value judgment rather than an inherent quality, and another in Michael

Thompson's radical variant of labeling theory in *Rubbish Theory: The Creation and Destruction of Value* (1979).

In psychology as in aesthetics, this fundamental relativism will make it increasingly difficult to pronounce authoritative value judgments in any area, though for the foreseeable future this difficulty will be felt more keenly by scholars and researchers than by the custodians of the threatened values. Ever greater moral forces will continue to be ranged against the specter of cultural relativism, so that it will be a long time before the winds of change ruffle the hair of the lady behind the lending desk.

BOOK-SELECTION STRATEGIES

Social value judgments bear directly on the reader's choice of ludic vehicle, requiring, first, a resolution of the dissonance between preference and conscience and, second, the establishment of a personal selection system.

The Resolution of Dissonance

Two cognitions are dissonant if the obverse of one follows from the other (Festinger, 1957). Since bad taste (the enjoyment of the aesthetically worthless or, worse, of the aesthetically repulsive) is a quality I attribute to my neighbor and never to myself, it follows that the books I choose for my ludic reading are in good taste. However, authoritative voices in my society judge them to be trash; the same voices tell me my time would be better employed in work, study, or devotion than in giving myself pleasure I may not have earned, the penalty for which is blindness and decomposition of the brain. There are two ways in which I can resolve the dissonance and recover my self-respect. One is to acknowledge that I do in fact read trash, but that I have a moral license to do so; the other is to argue that while many people read trash, of which bookshops and libraries contain an abundance, my own reading matter is clearly not trash.

Moral license may be claimed through a number of strategies. For example, in researching this book, I read Harlequin and Silhouette romances, Louis L'Amour Westerns, Wilbur Smith and Arthur Hailey blockbusters, all with enormous enjoyment and all in the cause of science, adopting the frame of mind of a participant observer at the rites of the Trobriand Islanders. I could not now bring myself to enjoy another Harlequin or Silhouette: the license has lapsed. Second, one can argue that productivity requires recreation: I work so hard and under such tension that relaxing with a mindless book—of course it's rubbish!—is the only way in which I can guarantee my sanity; insanity, of course, depresses work output. Third—a thinner argument—I can plead "new worlds": although my reading may be trashy, it does teach me about places and situations I would not otherwise encounter, thus serving a broadly educational purpose.

The "Trash?—not me!" defense has equally rich possibilities and includes three basic options. First, I may have implicit recourse to the concept of taste cultures (Gans, 1974), arguing that while "they" read trash, I don't. "They" would usually be groups lower than myself in the culture scale: younger people (my children read comics), the less educated, and so on. My own reading is clearly superior and certainly not trash. The second course is even more attractive: since trash, as we have seen, is universally identified with fiction, and the librarian's eternal plea is that borrowers read more nonfiction, I can easily remove all suspicion from myself by reading nonfiction only. Since most books of travel, biography, and current-events reporting have story lines as strong as anything in Wilbur Smith, I achieve the stature of a person who reads only "good stuff" at no personal hardship whatever. Third, especially for genre reading, I can have recourse to alternative sources of normative judgment located in connoisseurs of the genre in question: sure, I will argue, the university big shots say that Isaac Asimov is a nothing, but people who know their science fiction will tell you that he has no equal; similarly, Louis L'Amour? You'll never fault him on the facts! why, he knows more about the Old West than all your history professors put together! These judgments reassure me that though the world may see my reading as trash, those best qualified to judge find it to be of the highest quality. I may, if my self-esteem is high enough, choose to locate the source of the authoritative judgment in myself: Georgette Heyer? her command of Regency manners is superb—believe me, I've made a study of the period!

Is Taste Universal?

The immense and immensely diverse audiences commanded by a hit movie or novel have two possible interpretations. One is that taste is indeed universal and that certain techniques allow one to touch a universal sensibility. For example, Lord Northcliffe, the British newspaper magnate, reputedly placed a notice in all his company's offices to remind his writers of the mental age of their readers: "Remember, they are all 10." The legendary advice of a nameless American editor to magazine authors was even more brutal: "Write so a blind man can read it!" The critics' scorn for the readers of "trash" in turn infects the writers, who feel contempt both for their ten-year-old audience and for themselves.

If indeed we are all ten, would an "educated" taste truly recoil from popular fiction? If the constraints of the Protestant Ethic were removed by marooning a highbrow reader on a desert island with a vast store of fiction, both Harlequin romances and classics, all carefully stripped of their original covers and served up anonymously in brown paper wrappers, and an unseen eye logged his daily reading in that echoing privacy—would the distinctions of choice disappear? Would the highbrow turn for pleasure, relaxation, and reading trance to exactly the same books as the lowbrow on the adjacent island?

It is possible that taste is more universal than even the most pessimistic critics have imagined, that James Bond, the apotheosis of sophistication, is in fact no more than Tarzan of the Apes with a gunmetal cigarette lighter and Savile Row suit, and that our conviction that good reading demands an effort of will—that Saul Bellow is therefore "better" than Ian Fleming, and *Mathematics for the Millions* better even than Thomas Mann—is entirely a product of our conviction that true pleasure is consequent on suffering (a conviction that may turn out to have very little to do with what we like best). This would explain the almost universal appeal of certain cultural products, such as Disneyland, which rivet the attention of the critics who scoff at them no less than they do John Q. Public's.

The alternative interpretation is that taste is not universal and that the mass audience is divided into separate taste cultures, each of which responds in more or less uniform ways to a given set of cultural stimuli. Lewis (1978, p. 48) reports some evidence pointing to a differentiated mass audience. There are advantages to this view. First, it accounts for the fact that certain cultural products clearly have a limited market—for example, picture stories at one end of the "quality" spectrum and the novels of Patrick White at the other. Second, the blockbuster phenomenon could still be accounted for by arguing that it bridges the gap between the separate taste cultures; this explanation raises the question of what these "universalizing" mechanisms are.

It may be possible to resolve these intricate problems by preparing a range of cultural artifacts of unknown provenance (a set of anonymous extracts from a variety of books, an unsigned set of paintings by different hands) and asking representatives of the culture under investigation to rank them in the sequence of their personal preferences. To the extent that both the artifacts and the subjects are representative of the respective populations, the concordance of the rankings along this "ludic continuum" would determine whether taste is in fact universal or differentiated.

We return to these questions in chapter 8. Here we turn to a broader analysis of the judgments on which reader preferences and the ludic continuum are based.

3
The Witchery
of a Story

As the giant grey shadow rises slowly in the East . . . and night comes on without a shade of gloaming . . . the camp foregathers. The Shaykhs and "white-beards" of the tribe gravely take their places . . . around the camp fire. . . . The women and children stand motionless as silhouettes outside the ring; and all are breathless with attention; they seem to drink in the words with eyes and mouth as well as with ears. The most fantastic flights of fancy, the wildest improbabilities, the most impossible of impossibilities, appear to them utterly natural, mere matters of everyday occurrence.

—Burton, 1897, p. xviii

Like a set of chinese boxes nested inside one another, answers to the questions in the introduction about the origin of our insatiable appetite for narrative are shown to have successive answers, each smaller and more finely wrought than the one before. "Insatiable" is a very large word, but we do spend huge amounts of time every day in narrative activity: dreaming, daydreaming, telling stories and listening to them, reading, and watching television. Moreover, this appetite compels us to "trail the entertainer like a child his mother, restless, bored, and whining: What can I do? What will amuse me? How shall I live?" (Gass, 1972, p. 252). Authors, actors, opera singers, racing drivers, and professional athletes are all entertainers, and Daniel Berlyne has noted that "in our society, those who devote themselves professionally to the provision of such opportunities [for play and laughter] are among the most lavishly remunerated and fulsomely idolised" (1969, p. 806).

In this chapter, we attempt to clarify the nature of the rewards offered by narrative activity, first taking up the examination of reading as a cultural phenomenon, begun in chapters 1 and 2, from a very different point of view. There, our concern was with the conflict between the "would" of ludic reading and the "should" of elite culture, and the resolution of this conflict; here, the concern is satisfactions. First, we look at the origins of printed narratives in folktales and at the parallels between storytellers and authors, which indicate that the needs the storyteller satisfies are very old (throughout this chapter, "storyteller" can be read as "author," and "listener" as "reader"). Then five paradoxes are proposed, which plunge us more and more deeply into the mystery of the storyteller's power, to which increasingly specific solutions are offered.

STORY MAGIC

In 1905, a teacher named Sarah Cone Bryant wrote an extraordinarily vivid account of storytelling in its most basic form. Combing the hair of a cross little girl, she tells her about the tingly-tanglies that had tied knots in her hair as they climbed through it: "Never had the witchery of the story to the ear of the child come more closely home to me. . . . The surrender of the natural child to the storyteller is as absolute and invariable as that of a devotee to the priest of his own cult" (Bryant, 1905, p. 8). She describes a rowdy group of children who have been taken over by a story: "I was suddenly conscious of a sense of ease and relief, a familiar restful feeling in the atmosphere; and then, at last, I knew my audience was with me. . . . Absolutely quiet, entirely unconscious of themselves . . ." (p. 11). Bryant's account has an echo three thousand years old: "Odysseus' tale was finished, and such was the spell he had cast on the whole company that not a sound was heard throughout the shadowy hall" (Homer, *Odyssey*, XIII). Indeed, all of Homer is a study in story magic, very clearly seen, for example, in the story of the Phaecian games, or Alcinous' invitation to Odysseus: "And now I call upon you for a true account of your wanderings" (*Odyssey*, VIII). Implicit in stories about the spell of storytelling is the narrator's own sense of power, the awareness that a recalcitrant audience may be bent to one's will and swayed by one's moods. It is a power relationship that strongly parallels the induction of hypnotic trance. In tribal African societies, as we have seen, storytelling was forbidden during the daylight hours because of its great popularity. Marivate (1973) writes that, despite the significant inroads made by non-traditional radio stories, among the Tsonga people of the Transvaal province in South Africa, storytellers still use voice modulation, gesture, and mimicry to such effect that the best among them, usually middle-aged women, "can keep their audience hypnotised with their performance and dramatic artistry" (p. 26); "by her voice, facial expressions, movements of her body and hands, [one famous narrator] carried her audience away with her" (p. 22). At the end, the tale is ceremonially "killed" so that its characters "will not pursue the people into their dreams" (p. 56).

Tribal storytelling is the contemporary expression of an older tradition of oral literature, and the importance of the needs served by folk-tales can be gauged by the sheer volume of folk literature. Notable collections are Sir James Frazer's twelve-volume *Golden Bough* (1910), Ireland's 779-page index of fairytales (1973), and Stith Thompson's monumental six-volume cross-cultural index of folktale themes (1955), which is in turn based on very large single-culture collections—for example, Louis Ginzberg's seven-volume *Legends of the Jews* (1954–59).

Storytellers today and jokes. Even though the Tsonga now "generally crowd around the radios listening to modern stories" (Marivate, 1973, p. 146), the advent of electronic media does not necessarily herald the death of traditional storytelling. Newall (1980) notes that a famous Hungarian storyteller died as recently as 1964, while in the Soviet Union in Stalin's lifetime, old tales were retold with an emphasis on revolutionary ideology. And in present-day Japan, storytelling continues to flourish (J. Mayumi, personal communication, October 15, 1981). In Tokyo today there are at least three story theaters, each offering shows from early afternoon until late evening, with additional performances on Saturdays and Sundays. Each theater has a complement of five or six storytellers; most are men, and the best are said to be in their fifties. Their repertoire includes both classic and comic tales. As in Africa, the storyteller is a one-man theater, acting the roles of each protagonist and mimicking animal calls.

Curiously, the only surviving form of oral literature in Western society is the joke; its primary carriers are men, and it is largely spread by public telling but sometimes passed privately from one joke-teller to another, as a gift: "I have a joke for you." The power needs served by storytelling are especially well met by jokes because of the powerful and highly visible effect they produce: it is tempting to speculate that habitual jokesters have a higher need for power (Winter, 1973) than the more sober-minded members of their social groups. Jokes and anecdotes have in fact contributed to the survival of professional storytelling within the entertainment industry in the form of cabaret artists and stand-up comics.

Functional equivalence. There is no great distance from storyteller to author, or from listening to reading: "Folktales are the earliest form of romantic and imaginative literature, the unwritten fiction of early men and of primitive people in all parts of the world. They represent fiction in its childhood. . . . They owe their birth in a great part to that universal human desire to listen to a story" (MacCulloch, 1905, p. 1). Can these parallels between storytelling and story-writing be extended to include an equivalence of function? There is some evidence that they can. The storytelling descriptions by Bryant and Marivate make it clear that the storyteller's function is to transport the audience to some other place, to remove them from themselves; and in everyday language, there are indications that ludic books have a similar purpose. The English phrase "to be carried away by a book" has equivalents in many languages. For example, in Dutch the phrase is "om in een boek op te gaan"; in German, "in einem Buch versunken zu sein"; and in French, "être pris par un livre." Some of these expressions have the sense of being taken away or carried off; others of being steeped or sucked in; others of sunk in. But whether the reader remains still while the book impregnates him or is carried off to some other place where the book reigns, the sense of the power of reading to effect a change of state is very strong, whether in Spanish, Hebrew, or Czech. Accordingly, the functions of storyteller and author do have in common at least this transport of their users.

FICTION AND THE TRUTH

The first of the five paradoxes specified earlier is that although fiction is the usual vehicle for ludic reading, it is not its lack of truth—its "fictivity"—that renders it pleasurable. This is in marked contrast to the traditional view, which holds that it is our special relation to fiction that allows us to enjoy it. For example, Richard Ohmann (1971) argues that "a literary work creates a world by providing the reader with impaired and incomplete speech acts which he completes by supplying the appropriate circumstances" (p. 17). Ohmann ascribes this incompleteness to the suspension of "illocutionary force" in the literary work—that is, the describing, urging, commanding, and contracting functions of speech that solicit us to act; it is the unreality of these commanding and contracting functions in fiction that leaves the reader free to attend to its literary qualities.

On the contrary, argues Pratt (1977): lack of illocutionary force is not unique to fiction but is equally characteristic of a war scenario or a scientific hypothesis. Accordingly, "it is not its quasi-ness which gives literature its world-creating capacity. Nonfictional narrative accounts are world-creating in the same sense as are works of literature, and, say, accounts of dreams" (p. 95). Pratt notes two further reasons for rejecting a fictivity criterion for literature: the bestseller lists show that nonfictional narratives are as much part of the public's literary preference as fiction (and the bestseller figures cited in chapter 1 show they are even more to the public's taste). Second, there is no clear line between fiction and nonfiction. *Robinson Crusoe* and *The Agony and the Ecstasy* are clearly fiction despite their pretensions to be chronicles, while Capote's *In Cold Blood*, an account of two drifters who murdered a Kansas farm family, is nonfiction despite its novelistic form.

News Hunger

The most striking evidence that fact grips us at least as strongly as fiction is the self-evident but almost entirely unremarked phenomenon that the way we lose ourselves in a newspaper (especially when a big story runs: the assassination of a president or a great pollution threat) cannot be distinguished from the way we lose ourselves in a novel. The traditional definitions of news (Nell, 1978b) fail to account for its fascination because they deal with news in isolation, as a unique phenomenon, instead of seeing it for what it most truly is, a kind of storytelling.

Two lines of evidence support this contention. First, both newsroom jargon and the classic news criteria acknowledge the identity of news and storytelling. "I'm writing a story," say reporters at their typewriters—about a murder, a fire, or a dog show. And timeliness, proximity, scale, and importance, are also the criteria for successful plays and novels (*The Godfather, Airport, The Crucible,* and Aesop's *Fables*), which mirror the issues of their time with no less accuracy than the daily newspaper.

Second, the history of the word *news* points to its storytelling origins. The *Oxford English Dictionary* (1933a) offers a synopsis-by-quotation of the development of *news,* derived from the Old French *noveles.* In the sense of "tidings, the report or account of recent events or occurrences," the word appears from the fifteenth century. It is a source of delight ("I bring the newis glad, that blisfull ben": 1423); of sorrow ("He was right pensyve and sore troubled with those newes": 1581); or of wonderment ("The amazing news of Charles at once were spread": 1685). There is also an early awareness of the swiftness of news: "These newes were sodainly spread throughout the citie of Cherona" (1581). Moreover, big news was soon perceived to be compulsive reading, pushing aside "better" material: "A daily swarm. . . . Come flying forth, and mortals call them News: For these, unread the noblest volumes lie" (1785). This early perception of the functional equivalence of news and novels has a modern echo: Katz and Foulkes (1962) remark that "the latest news from Luang Prabang may provide as much escape as does [an account of] a frontier town of the Old West" (p. 383).

It is in this sense that newspaper editors are entertainers rather than informers: Le Carré may inform us about Hong Kong in the course of *The Honorable Schoolboy,* but that is not why we read Le Carré; similarly, news is a story and a newspaper in an assemblage of short fiction: the information we glean during breakfast is an incidental by-product of reading ten or twenty short stories.

Cultural isomorphism. Reporters and their editors make a mystique of news. In the late 1940s, *Time* magazine ran a full-page advertisement in its sister publication, *Life* (reproduced in Marshall McLuhan, 1951, p. 10). Above a somber wash drawing of a reporter rushing through the swinging doors of a bar to the tocsin of a distant fire alarm, the headline proclaims, "A nose for news—and a stomach for whiskey" (on the latter, see Hirschowitz and Nell, 1983). The sonorous text assures us that a nose for news is an arcane gift, "as peculiar and authentic a possession as the eye of a painter or the ear of a musician." On the contrary: it is only because readers and journalists share the same sense of news that editors are able to produce newspapers that sell. A fundamental cultural isomorphism underlies news value judgments. We do not need a news editor to tell us that "The King Is Dead" is big news: we can tell him, with a certainty that has its origins in our sense of the personal newsworthiness of intimate events (the birth of a child, the death of a parent). From the personal, we readily extrapolate to the national and international. Critical personal and public events imprint on our mind the exact time, place, and personal circumstances of their occurrence. Just as an alcoholic (but not a moderate drinker) recalls exactly where and how he had his first drink (Ullman, 1952), so all of us know where we were and what we were doing when we heard the king had died, Pearl Harbor had been bombed, or the first Sputnik launched. Moreover, laymen share the journalist's compulsion to tell the news: over 90 percent of Americans knew of Kennedy's assassination within an hour, because each person who heard the news passed it on to five or six others (Schramm, 1965). At some level, we all want to be hypnotic storytellers, see our friends raise their hands in horror and say "My God!"

Labov's sociolinguistic studies demonstrate that this cultural isomorphism has its roots in a much earlier activity than telling the news: it goes back to telling stories, and the reason we can all judge the weight of a story so accurately is that we tell stories all the time and judge other people's continually. We all share the ability to weave formless experience into narratives, we are all authors, we are all newsmen. "Look," we say, "just see what rubbish they've put on the front page!" or, of a book, "I wonder how that ever got into print." The broad claim made by this argument is twofold: first, that this near-universal critical sensibility is restricted to narrative products (newspapers, novels, jokes, and other stories) and does not generalize to music or art. Indeed, many readers who unhesitatingly judge novels blush and squirm if asked for an opinion of a painting or a symphony. Second, the criteria by which narrative products are judged form part of the intellectual equipment of almost every adult (and most children) because the production and consumption of narrative are near-universal human experiences.

News and the Novel

In his essay on the phenomenon he calls New Journalism, Tom Wolfe (1972) deals with two issues that concern us: the nature of the relationship between news reporter and novelist, and the source of the novel's power to absorb and entrance the reader.

There is a clear link between the major novels and news reporting, writes Wolfe, as in Balzac, Tolstoy, and Dickens (who penetrated Yorkshire boarding schools under a false name to gather material for *Nicholas Nickleby*). However, though novelists may use reporters' techniques, no reporter until recently had dared model his journalism on the novel. In 1962, however, an essay by a young reporter named Gay Talese appeared in *Esquire*—"Joe Louis: The King as a Middle-Aged Man." Though ostensibly straight reporting, it had the tone and mood of a short story or part of a novel. Talese had demonstrated that a reporter could write like a novelist, and soon there were others: Capote, Mailer, John Sack, who joined an infantry brigade as a reporter and wrote a book on Vietnam; Hunter S. Thompson, who ran with the Hell's Angels for eighteen months and wrote the "strange and terrible saga" of the outlaw motorcycle gang.

These developments (which support the contention that news and novels are species of the same class) caused what Wolfe calls a status panic in the American literary community, threatening what had appeared to be an eternal class structure. Novelists, the incumbents of a sacred literary office, were the upper class; they had "exclusive entry to the soul of man" (p. 39). Second in line were the critics, essayists, and other men of letters, the middle class. The day laborers, the lumpenproles, were the journalists. Moreover, to Write a Novel had for decades been part of the American Dream. Small wonder that Capote's "nonfiction novel" (his own term), Talese's study of the Mafia, and Wolfe's own work (*The Electric Kool-Aid Acid Test*) caused a panic: one no longer had to be a novelist to write a novel, and the class structure was shattered.

Seizing the power. Wolfe's analysis of the sources of the modern novel's narrative power is especially useful to us. He specifies four devices "that give the realistic novel its unique power, variously known as its 'immediacy,' . . . its 'emotional involvement,' its 'gripping' or 'absorbing' quality" (p. 46). The first is scene-by-scene construction, which eliminates bridging narrative. The second is dialogue recorded in full, because "realistic dialogue involves the reader more completely than any other single device" (p. 46); Dickens, for example, uses dialogue rather than description to establish character vividly. The third device is the third-person point of view, which presents each scene to the reader through the eyes of a participant character. And the fourth, the least understood and the most important, claims Wolfe, "lies as close to the center of the power of realism as any other device in literature. It is the very essence of the absorbing power of Balzac, for example"; it is the recording of all symbolic details of the protagonists' status life—their gestures, habits, furniture, clothing, housekeeping, behavior toward children and servants: "The introduction of realism into literature by people like Richardson, Fielding and Smollet was like the introduction of electricity into machine technology. . . . It raised the state of the art to a new magnitude. The effect of realism on the emotions was something that had never been conceived of before" (p. 49). Realism, continues Wolfe, renders the novel's power to absorb the reader superior to that of fable and myth, in which the protagonists have no personal background and move in a timeless and elemental terrain. It is because of its deliberate anti-realism, Wolfe implies, that "the fable was never able to compete with the power of the realistic printed story and can't now" (p. 56).

The Reader's Relation to Truth

Though the devices listed by Wolfe are important elements of the novel's power, they do not deal with the ultimate source of that power, which is inside the reader's head. The psychologist's question here is what cognitive mechanisms allow the reader or listener or audience to attribute reality to something that the author claims to be true (because, as I argue below, his role constrains him to make this claim) but which the reader knows perfectly well to be false. How the author constructs a fictive reality, and why the reader accepts it, are among the most fundamental questions in literary criticism (see, for example, Auerbach's *Mimesis*, 1946). The epigraph to this chapter reflects a storyteller's own wonder that his wild improbabilities are so readily and naturally accepted by his audience. This is a matter to which we shall return in a variety of contexts; here, we are concerned with the mechanisms by which manifest fictions so readily attain a form of internal reality.

In developmental terms, the relations between fantasy and reality are important. One of the earliest and most fundamental distinctions a child learns is between fantasy and reality, falsity and truth—for example, that illness and death in a television play are sad but not real, that what happens in movies is never personally threatening, and that the protagonists themselves are unhurt even if, like the Pink Panther, they are flattened under a steamroller. So, when the child listening to a tale of magic and enchantment asks, "Daddy, did that really happen, that the puppy dog flew up to the top of the tree?" the question is acutely important, setting limits for the possible in a world in which nothing is yet wholly impossible. Ernest Hilgard (1965) has suggested that the parent who tells a child tales of ghosts and castles, and at the end of each adventure brings the child safely back from the animistic to the objective world, is creating a lifelong openness to fantasy: the path to the other world is well worn, the entrance and exit swift and safe. The consequence, argues Hilgard, is greater hypnotic susceptibility. We may extrapolate and say that if on the other hand the child is confused about the status of fantasy ("Of course fairies are real! Well, if you didn't see the witch at midnight, you just weren't trying hard enough . . ."), it seems likely that the door to other worlds will be kept firmly closed.

With passing years and growing sophistication (which, we should remember, has the literal meaning of corruption by worldly wisdom), individuals learn to apply their acquired fact-fiction discriminations to every cultural input: he says he loves me, does he really? the news bulletin said all our aircraft returned safely to base, I wonder if that's true? that the Afghanistan rebels have laid down their arms, that the economic recession is over . . . true? false? It is a dreadful blow to discover that there is a higher criticism of Scripture, or that historiography reflects the perceptions of historians and not the objective truth, which, in history as in other human affairs, is irrecoverable. This bottomless skepticism means that for the adult, the only narrative products that falsely but imperatively claim reality are dreams, and sometimes daydreams, but only for a moment; while the adult listener is awake, the storyteller's product, no matter how compelling, is known to be a fiction. Let us examine the implications of this state of affairs.

In the first place, the storyteller (who we shall assume to be female) knows where she stands in relation to truth and falsity. She may have witnessed the events personally or have them on excellent authority; she may be unsure, as with legends and hearsay experiences, whether they really took place or not; or she knows they never could have happened, because she is making them up as she tells. If she claims veracity, she is committed to a multitude of incidental details, checkability criteria, time intervals, and the actions of characters, among whom some may be personally known to the audience (or reader). Against these disadvantages, the veracious narrator balances the greatly added force her story gains by locating itself in the real world (these options are displayed in figure 3.1).

More usually, however, the narrator is telling a fictional story, and this case is most interest to us both in the context of truth testing and in relation to ludic reading. Whichever of the untruth alternatives is selected (the "maybe" or the fiction), the narrator is obliged to answer "yes" to the implied audience question, "Did that really happen?" The convention that causes the question to be asked (even though the audience knows perfectly well that the truth claim is specious) is as powerful as the parallel convention that dictates the answer. In literature, those genres which are the least constrained by reality, such as science fiction and stories of the supernatural, are at special pains to establish conventions acceptable to the reader. For example, science fiction writers eschew technical devices inconsistent with the technology of the world in which they have set their story. Or, as in *Lord of the Rings* (Tolkien, 1954), magical powers are vested in a very limited number of protagonists, and the powers themselves are carefully circumscribed. Clearly, a consistent world is an articulated world: the workings are visible, the way its illogicalities are put together is logical. Other truth constraints may be determined by the genre (Westerns allow less latitude than science fiction); by the author's preferences (Le Carré's Smiley has a creased, puffy-eyed reality while Fleming's Bond is a dream-figure in a make-believe world); or by a multitude of other criteria. The narrator or author who flouts these conventions loses her audience, since absorption cannot be commanded by a story the listener dismisses as "nonsense" or "ridiculous."

Where does the reader (or listener) stand in relation to these fictions? To use Coleridge's famous phrase, what induces "the willing suspension of disbelief" that allows the reader to enter a world he or she knows to be quite false? This is an old and very searching question that has complex answers. Wolfe's concept of the rendering of status life by the modern novel is one of these, which must be seen in conjunction with the analysis of the power of words, phrases, and isolated sentences presented later in this chapter. In chapters 4 and 10, we look at another important element in the answer; namely, the special kind of absorbed attention that narrative can command because of the heavy consciousness demands it makes, and the ease with which such absorption maintains reality awareness while allowing what appears to be complete involvement in the fantasy experience. (We say "appears" because, as we shall see in chapter 10, the quality of the entranced reader's reality awareness, like that of the subject in hypnosis, is such that disbelief is willingly suspended because it is not really suspended at all but, in the form of alert critical consciousness, remains aware that the fantasy world is never more than a wind-up toy.) Finally, we willingly enter the world of fiction because the skepticism to which our adult sophistication condemns us is wearying: we long for safe places—a love we can entirely trust, a truth we can entirely believe. Fiction meets that need precisely because we know it to be false, so that we can willingly suspend our reality-testing feedback processes.

SCHEHERAZADE AND THE SULTAN: SUSPENSE IN NARRATIVE

Nothing seems clearer than the role of suspense in our enjoyment of narrative. "Don't tell me how it ends!" we plead with friends who recommend a movie or lend us a thriller. The trick short-story endings of O. Henry and his imitators, radio and television serials, and whodunnits in which on the last page it is the heroine who is discovered, blood-stained dagger in hand, all reinforce this view; and we remember the weekly adventure comics we read as children: "Will John Hogan die in Sly Symes' snake-filled cage? Read on in next week's *Hammer and Tongs!*"

The suspenseful serial has ancient origins. Here is the ending of the first tale in *A Thousand and One Nights* (which dates back to the eighth century) in Sir Richard Burton's translation:

> Quoth she: By Allah the Most Great, the Compassionating, the Compassionate! there is no help for it; thou must kill him on this holy day, and if thou kill him not, to me thou art no man and I to thee am no wife. Now when I heard those hard words, not knowing her object I went up to the calf, knife in hand—and Shahrazad perceived the dawn of day and ceased to say her permitted say. Then quoth her sister to her, "How fair is thy tale, and how grateful and how sweet and how tasteful!" And Shahrazad answered her, "What is this to that I could tell thee on the coming night, were I to live and the King would spare me." Then said the King in himself, "By Allah, I will not slay her, until I have heard the rest of her tale" (1897, p. 26).

In true cliffhanger style, the narrative breakpoint interrupts a decisive action sequence: will the merchant slaughter the calf or discover in time that it is his bewitched son? Here we must note a paradox that is more fully explored below in the context of formulaic storytelling, namely, that neither the Sultan, King Shahryar, whose dreadful revenge Scheherazade's narrative art is calculated to thwart, nor Burton's modern readers have any doubt about the outcome. We do not await the second night's tale in order to discover if the calf was slaughtered because we know that the storyteller must spare its life. The listener's need is to know how this is achieved rather than whether it will happen.

Accordingly, we would expect the breakpoints in sophisticated storytelling to occur where story development is unpredictable rather than within an action sequence. Television viewers are aware that episodes in serials do not end with the hero about to strike an antagonist: breakpoints are more subtly placed within or between elements of the narrative macrostructure in order to maximize audience anticipation. Indeed, we find that in many of the thousand-and-one tales, the long dash (—), indicating the point at which Scheherazade perceives the dawn and interrupts her narrative, does not recur in the cliffhanger position it occupies in the first tale. On the second night, for example, the story ends at the conclusion of the third Shaykh's story, at a point when the doomed merchant is certain to be granted a reprieve; on the fourth night, as the king is about to begin the tale of King Sindibad and his falcon; and so on.

Contrary to the belief that suspense is an essential component of the enjoyment of narrative, there is a great deal of evidence that it is not. For example, Labov's young storytellers are too absorbed in their account of a personal experience to monitor their own language production. Now, nothing could be more familiar and therefore less suspenseful than a dangerous personal experience, etched into one's memory and relived on countless occasions in dreams, daydreams, and narration. Nonetheless, this autogenic trance is the prototype of much other internal storytelling, which, though it fascinates us, can certainly not be considered suspenseful.

This strange conjunction of endless repetition and undiminished enjoyment is not restricted to individuals. Every family has its favorite amazing experience (finding a long-lost relative in the foyer of a hotel, or how a cat left home and returned six months later with a litter of kittens). Such tales are told with undiminished zest to such new audiences as become available, but not only the teller is zestful—spouse and children, who have heard the anecdote dozens of times, hang on every word. Indeed, our pleasure at a story a friend is telling for the fourth time is certainly different from the pleasure we felt the first time we heard it, but not necessarily less: on the contrary, our participation in its unfolding may render our enjoyment even keener. The favorite-anecdote phenomenon at once brings to mind the child's bedtime story routine, in which the parent endlessly repeats the same tale, whether it is "Little Red Riding Hood" (how the child thrills every time the wolf leaps ravening out of grandmother's bed!) or a personal anecdote. Strangely, though the parent may offer token protest ("Not how the watertank burst! Not again!"), he or she seems to enjoy the oft-repeated tale no less than the child-listener.

This tell-me-the-story-again bedtime phenomenon has another adult parallel in that class of reader who repeatedly returns to the same book, rereading it at short intervals with evidently undiminished enjoyment. Such readers sometimes keep a pile of these old friends on their bedside table and select one of these rather than a new book for the most delectable reading time of the day, the hour that merges quietly into darkness and sleep.

From the family to the tribe and nation: in Jordan's description (1966, p. 36) of audience participation in the Xhosa *ntsomi* (called "fattening the narrative") we have confirmation, if any is needed, that folktales are very well known to their audiences, since knowing a story well is a prerequisite for "fattening" it. This knowledge evidently adds to audience enjoyment rather than detracting from it. Jordan describes an occasion he witnessed in which six members of the audience joined the narrator, contributing "dialogue, mimicry, birdcalls, graphic descriptions," with the original narrator being most delighted of all (1966, p. 36). The best-loved stories are likely to be the most familiar, as they are for the child. The widely held view that popular folktales and legends (such as the Homeric myths) spread by word-of-mouth diffusion rather than re-invention implies that these stories were widely known and often repeated.

Another striking but little remarked indication that suspense is not an essential part of narrative pleasure is the way news is written: "An alert traindriver stopped just in time to avoid crushing to death a 15-year-old . . . youth who had been handcuffed to the railway track. The incident, which left the youth foaming at the mouth with fright, happened on Thursday" (*Rand Daily Mail*, November 28, 1981). In conventional narrative, the storyteller might have begun by alluding to the climax; for example, "Did you hear about this kid who was handcuffed to the railway line?" He would certainly have kept his audience in suspense for the resolution. In the news version, however, we know as we start that the youth survives, yet we read on with undiminished interest.

What explanatory mechanisms may be invoked to explain this continued enjoyment of the most intimately familiar material?

Formulaic Storytelling

Audiences apply different standards to private and public storytelling. For example, the media, for which we pay, are obliged to be continually fresh (news, we recall, derives from *noveles*). The worst sin an editor can commit is to run a news item or feature article that has appeared before. But private storytellers (friends and family) are allowed, even expected, to repeat themselves; and, under suitable safeguards, so may public storytellers. The most common of these safeguards is an appeal to the past: retelling folktales is culturally sanctioned, and this license may be made to apply to other kinds of material. The most powerful of the literary devices that sanction a disguised form of repetition is the formula story, which endlessly repeats what Freud called the triumph of "His Majesty the Ego" (1908, p. 180).

This is the third of our paradoxes: in many ways, stereotypes give stories more force than subtlety does. In his study (1976) of formula stories as art and popular culture, Cawelti notes that the child is prepared to listen endlessly to a story he loves, "and as he hears again the often-heard, his eyes glaze over with pleasure, his body relaxes, and the story ends in peaceful slumber. The recurrent outlines of a familiar experience have returned" (p. 1). For the adult, he suggests, the formula story offers what the same story offers the child; security through the fulfillment of conventional expectations by using highly predictable structures in "a well-known and controlled landscape of the imagination." This structure allows the reconciliation of two apparently contradictory needs: on the one hand, for intense excitement permeated with the symbols of violence and death; on the other, for order, peace, and security in a predictable world (p. 15). Within this framework, characterization and suspense are not abrogated but take on a radically altered form. Characters are drawn by stereotype (the schoolmarm from the East, the tycoon with a heart of gold) and freshened by unexpected combinations (Shane is both shy and violent, Sherlock Holmes is the dreamy poet and also the supreme man of reason), so that the stereotypic aspect of the character heightens audience response "through the recognition that comes from many previous encounters with these characters and situations" (p. 11).

In this secure landscape, suspense operates by evoking a temporary sense of fear and insecurity. We know that the hero is invulnerable, but here he is, handcuffed and locked into a stainless-steel safe at the bottom of the Mariana Trench. As with Scheherazade's bewitched calf, we know perfectly well that the hero will escape: but how? This certainty actually heightens the suspensefulness of formulaic literature, argues Cawelti, because in real life, which mimetic literature imitates, nothing is certain: in that genre, the hero in the safe will certainly die, so that suspense vanishes.

Here, then, is the resolution of the third paradox: if a lack of taste and subtlety is the price some kinds of reading ask us to pay for the safe and stereotyped landscape of the formula story, we do so willingly; nor do ludic readers have any sense that there has been a possibly disadvantageous trade-off. As long as the story conforms to the narrative requirements of assertability, tellability, and relevance, as specified by Paul Grice (in Pratt, 1977, chap. 4), it can deeply move even the most cynical reader. Wolfe records that "even the impeccable Lord Jeffrey, editor of the *Edinburgh Review*, had cried—actually blubbered, boo-hooed, snuffled and sighed—over the death of Dickens' Little Nell in *The Old Curiosity Shop*" (1972, p. 50). Oh dear: disbelief has unwillingly been suspended! Notwithstanding the whisperings of our critical sensibilities, our subjective perception of a narrative that conforms to minimal narrative rules is that it's a jolly good story, not that the same tired theme has been re-enacted. However, the nature of our enjoyment, like that of the child listening avidly to the hundredth repetition of a bedtime story or of the autogenic trance of Labov's young raconteurs, still eludes us.

Form and Attributes

We might be able to come nearer to a resolution of this recalcitrant problem if we conceive of narrative as a form with numerous attributes, none of them essential, but which, alone or in combination, enhance listeners' enjoyment. Suspense would be one such attribute; appositeness—for example, a deluge story told or read on a night of torrential rain—might be another; or the evocation of beauty of persons or landscapes; or manifest importance, such as a cosmic cataclysm, or the creation of a new world. These general attributes would be more or less evocative for particular listeners, depending on individual dispositions and current concerns.

This formulation seems useful in explaining why suspense, far from being essential to narrative, is so readily dispensed with: it is an attribute of narrative and not its essence.

INTERNAL NARRATIVE

The self-induced trance of Labov's adolescents has an important parallel in the experience of an author, who may also feel that he has been taken over by the plot and characters of his own story. Borges, for example, writes (1976, p. 101): "Walking down the street or along the galleries of the National Library, I feel that something is about to take over in me. That something may be a tale or a poem. I do not tamper with it; I let it have its way." This is the fourth paradox: although "we spend enormous amounts of conversational time exchanging anecdotes" (Pratt, 1977, p. 50), we spend more time telling ourselves stories than exchanging them with others. Fantasy gains its unique flavor—and its adaptive value— from its narrative quality. Like the informal storytelling between intimates, fantasy is governed to a greater or lesser extent by the autistic logic and disregard for reality that characterize primary-process products: dreams and daydreams are informal narratives we tell ourselves. Indeed, Singer defines a daydream as "an unfolding sequence of private responses made to some internal stimulus" (1976, p. 3). Here the narrative speech act, a sequence of clauses matched to a sequence of events, is entirely internalized, but without losing its narrative quality. The consequence of this fourth paradox is that a narrative continues to exercise its fascination if teller and audience are condensed into one person and the act of telling is reduced to silence.

WORD MAGIC

We have reached the innermost of our nested boxes now: it is so small that it can hold only a word or two. Yet even single words exert a strange power. In *Don Quixote*, Cervantes (1614) tells us that he came to read the story of his hero's adventures because "I have a taste for reading even torn papers lying in the streets" (p. 76). More than three hundred years later, Lord Eustace Percy, then British minister of education, told the following story: "Discomfort and exhaustion seem only to increase the need for the printed word. A friend, in describing the advance of one of the columns in East Africa during the war, has remarked how his men, sitting drenched and almost without food round the campfire, would pass from hand to hand a scrap of a magazine cover, in order that each man might rest his eyes for a moment on the printed word" (in Leavis, 1932, p. 56). A torn scrap of newsprint cannot be said to offer narrative satisfaction: there is simply not enough of it. The magic we have hitherto assigned to narrative is now seen to be exercised by a few words, having neither beginning nor resolution nor any point at all. We are therefore driven to conclude that it is in words alone, printed or spoken, without any narrative form, that the power to capture, carry off, and transport us resides. Indeed, we know this: we breakfast-cereal-box readers and bathroom soap-wrapper browsers are reading words, not stories, yet avidly. Let us examine the claim that narrative magic is word magic by listing some random examples of sentences, phrases, and words:

Sentences: (1). For a delicious and nutritious dessert add to a bowl of fruit
  salad some whipped cream topped with Honey Crunch. (2) The Chinese never sleep. (3) You git back there and git that duck!
Torn scrap of newspaper: . . . y occasion on record the accused failed to talk
  himself out of a tricky situation w . . .
Phrases: (1) screams of pain; (2) silk evening shirts
Single words: (1) enchanted, (2) skyscraper, (3) endless, (4) delectable

  The pupil bolting a hasty breakfast reads the cereal-box recipe with delight: a pleasant vision of an after-supper treat floats into consciousness, pushing away thoughts about the sum of the angles of a quadrilateral; a tired commuter, reading the sentence about the Chinese over the shoulder of the man in front of him, will be distracted for a little while at least: all Chinese? some Chinese? is it something about Hong Kong? Similarly with a phrase or a word (delectable? who's delectable?) heard as a scrap of conversation or read as portion of a headline.

  Gass (1972) offers some evocative thoughts about words: "a word is a concept made flesh . . . the eternal presented as noise" (p. 29). Concepts take up no space: "they take up us. They invade us as we read" (p. 32): "Concepts have no physical properties. . . . 'Five' is no older, wider or fatter than 'four'; 'apple' isn't sweeter than 'quince,' rounder than 'pear,' smoother than 'peach.' To say, then, that literature is language is to say that literature is made of meanings, concepts, ideas, forms . . . and that these are so static and eternal as to shame the stars" (p. 28). He notes wryly: "That novels should be made of words, and merely words, is shocking really. It's as though you had discovered your wife were made of rubber: the bliss of all those years, the fears . . . from sponge" (p. 27). Perhaps it is this "eternal" symbolism, the incarnation of a concept, that gives each word its power. Not all words: we distinguish between content words (nouns, verbs, and their descriptors) and deictic words (prepositions, pronouns, and conjunctions), which have no meaning out of context. A scrap of newsprint containing the typing exercise of the day (long lines of "buts" and "fors") would not be passed from hand to hand by the soldiers in East Africa but tossed angrily into the fire. But content words are not noise, they are life, perhaps even more vivid than life. The fiction reader, writes Gass, turns from the real world to the pages of a book "like a philosopher liberated from the cave". The reference is of course to Plato's *Republic* (book 7), which suggests that since we are unable to observe true reality, we spend our lives watching shadows projected as if onto a screen. Gass, like Plato, claims greater reality for words, through which we pass "to the clear and brilliant world of concept," than for the world around us (1972, p. 54).

It is this brilliant world, liberated from the constraints of narrative, that awaits the readers of non-narrative text—lyric poetry, prose poems, and the intricate wordweaves that make up all of some works and entire chapters of others. The world into which these readers pass is neither real nor safe, but as vivid and treacherous as a dream, created and held erect entirely by the magic of words.

Cognitive-process models of behavior change (for example, Bandura, Adams, and Beyer, 1977) now acknowledge the power of symbolically mediated processes to effect lasting alterations in behavior; and behavior therapy (Walker et al., 1981), especially desensitization through the construction of verbal hierarchies of increasingly aversive stimuli, similarly uses the symbolic power of words to evoke an anxiety-provoking stimulus in order to overcome the subject's fear of that stimulus. For example, in Wolpe's death-phobia hierarchy, the subject is asked to imagine seeing an ambulance, seeing a hospital, being inside a hospital, seeing a funeral, driving past a cemetery, and, finally, seeing a close relation in a coffin (in Walker et al., 1981, p. 86). Clearly, desensitization, which is now an important mode of psychotherapy, is able to function because, although the verbally mediated situation is entirely symbolic, it nonetheless has the affective content of the reality it mimics. Word magic is precisely this power words have to create symbolic equivalents of real-world experiences.

WORDS AND THE FEAR OF EMPTINESS

Let us now arrange our boxes in sequence, from largest to smallest, each with its contents, and see what progress we have made toward understanding, in psychological terms, how stories cast their spell.

We began our inquiry by asking where our appetite for news came from. Now we know that news is more usefully considered to be a kind of story, and a newspaper an assemblage of short fiction (Aneurin Bevan once remarked: "I read a newspaper avidly. It is my one form of continuous fiction" [*Observer*, December 9, 1953]). Our appetite for reading full-length novels is energized by what appears to be a universal love of narrative, attested to by the huge folktale literature and the still vigorous profession of storytelling. However, if an unfolding sequence of events can grip a person's attention as it happens inside his own head as a dream or daydream, or even when it is a personal anecdote told by the protagonist himself, the conventional framework of a speech act collapses, since there is neither storyteller nor audience. The framework crumbles entirely under the impact of the torn-scrap-of-newsprint argument, since narrative magic is shown to be word magic. Words, even a single word, take us out of emptiness into a momentarily fascinating otherness. But we do not yet know why this promise to take us somewhere else, to transport us, made even by a scrap of newspaper, like a conversation that drifts through the bars of a prison cell, should be so alluring. Most attempts to answer the question beg it, and we can do no more than speculate.

We turn once again to Gass. Empty consciousness, he writes (1972, pp. 268–69), is like a mirror reflecting itself, "a terrifying endlessness and mockery of light," while consciousness, "the whole of all we are at any time," is perceived as infinitely worse than "simple black oblivion," so that "nothing seems more obvious to me than the fear, hatred, and contempt men have for it." Accordingly, we trail the entertainer, ever ready to take a book, turn a dial, buy a ticket—pay any bribe to hold consciousness at bay. There may well be an existential problem at the root of our entertainment hunger, and it is tempting to speculate that this variant of ontological anxiety, which assails us when we are alone with our consciousness of ourselves (because it is self-consciousness that Gass means), has its root in that most primitive fear, separation anxiety (Bowlby, 1973). If the terror Gass describes is indeed rooted in infant fears, hearing a voice from outside ourselves, affirming that we are not alone, would be deeply comforting. For persons who are prey to such anxiety, spontaneous daydreaming, which, because of the weight of their current concerns, offers no escape from self-consciousness, cannot offer a similar comfort.

A STORY TREE

In this chapter we have reversed the perspective adopted elsewhere in this book. We have been concerned thus far with the reader's work of decoding the narrator's messages; here, as in most literary criticism, our emphasis falls on the narrator's encoding processes. These are diagramed in the story tree in figure 3.1, which is presented as a decision

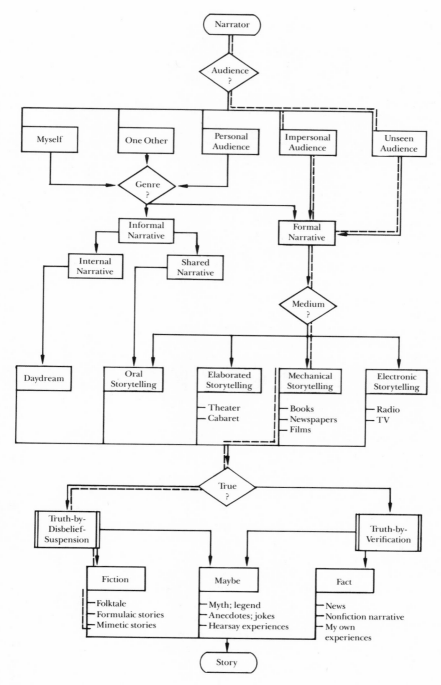

Figure 3.1. A Story Tree

flowchart (although standard flowchart process symbols are used, the diagram does not pretend to be programable). The diamond-shaped decision nodes indicate the points at which the narrator must take decisions about the nature of his or her product ("narrator" is a generic term that covers all tellers of tales: authors, scriptwriters, traditional storytellers, and so forth). In some cases, the presence of a prior condition (for example, an unseen mass audience) constrains the following decision without allowing choice options; sometimes, however, many options are open. Not all options are open to each kind of narrator; tribal storytellers, for example, are restricted to the oral medium and do not write books or scripts. Use of the flowchart convention, which requires a top-to-bottom temporal progression, has one strange consequence, which is to turn our story tree upside-down: the roots (the narrator) are in the air, and the branches appear to be underground. In the final paragraphs, we shall turn the tree the right way around again.

The four decision levels represented in figure 3.1 take note, respectively, of audience size, the genre options that certain audiences allow, story medium, and the stance the storyteller adopts in relation to truth criteria. We briefly consider these four decision nodes in turn below.

Audience size may vary from zero, in which case I tell stories to myself, through one other, as when I tell my spouse about the day's events or recount a joke to a friend, to the unseen mass audience reached by the mechanical and electronic media. Intermediate between the dyad and the unseen audience are personal audiences, groups in which each member is known to the narrator, and impersonal or anonymous audiences, as in a theater, in which the audience is physically present, though without individual identities. Informal storytelling, as defined earlier, may take the form of internal fantasy, as in daydreams, or be shared with others. The internal form is usable only in the zero-audience condition; informal storytelling may also be used in dyadic or, rarely, in personal group situations. Impersonal and unseen audiences tolerate only formal narrative (the secondary-process requirements imposed by ludic reading matter are considered in chapter 9), so that no genre decision node applies; in addition, formal narrative is frequently selected for dyadic and personal audiences and may also appear in stories I tell myself.

All mediums except daydreaming are open to formal narrative: indeed, as noted in chapter 2, there is convincing evidence that natural narratives, which by definition use the oral medium, exhibit the same structural characteristics as literary narratives. Informal narrative, however, has access only to the oral and daydreaming media. Elaborated and oral storytelling are not always easy to distinguish. The typical marks of elaborated storytelling are a demarcation, such as a stage between audience and narrator; the use of more than one storyteller; and the use of dramatic aids such as costumes, scenery, and externally provided sound effects (as distinct from the narrator's own mimicry of the calls and voices of the protagonists). However, some theatrical presentations lack all adjuncts, and some storytelling spills over into theater.

The relationship-to-truth decision is taken in all genres and across all media. We have already reviewed these options and note now only that the narrator must either offer sufficient proof of the truth of the story (dates, times, and witnesses, as in a news story) or else, by application of literary devices that help the reader define his relation to the truth (such as internal consistency, limitation of the supernatural, and others), convince the audience that, through disbelief suspension, the reinforcements offered by narrative products will be made available. The "Maybe" category, though it may draw on verification, operates largely through suspension strategies.

The route followed by the authors of popular romances (of whom Freud's "Poet," described in chapter 10, is the archetype) is traced from the first terminal through to the end product by the heavy broken line: the elaborated context provided by figure 3.1 shows that the ludic vehicle—that is, the work of fiction (bottom left)—is in a real sense defined as much by rejected options at the levels of audience, genre, medium, and truth as by those that are selected.

Developmental pathways. There is a final and rather unexpected use to which our story tree may be put: to delineate some of the developmental pathways the child follows in arriving at the conviction that narrative inputs in general, and reading in particular, offer positive reinforcements. In chapter 11, we note that this conviction is one of the necessary antecedents of ludic reading. In order to use figure 3.1 for this purpose, we again, as elsewhere in this book, focus on encoding processes, but this time we begin with the story as the topmost branch of the tree and work to its roots in the narrator. What follows should be regarded as speculations rather than theoretical formulations.

We suggest that the child's first experience of narrative is through stories told by a parent, an older sibling, in a peer group, or as internal fantasy through the medium of daydreaming. It will not be easy for developmental studies to resolve which of these genres occurs first or most frequently in the children of a given culture: the concrete and nonverbal character of fantasy (see chapter 10) imposes particular difficulties on verbal reporting, and in childhood fantasy, these problems are likely to be compounded.

The circumstances of the child's first experience of interactive storytelling are likely to be determined by an interplay of cultural norms and family circumstances. In the nuclear-family Western culture, the first story experience is almost invariably a one-to-one parent-child interaction which is often ritualized for time, place, and teller, as in the bedtime story. In the extended-family systems of Africa, on the other hand, the child's first stories are likely to be heard round a fire after dark, often in the company of only the women of the tribe (for example, Marivate, 1973).

In terms of truth relations, we have noted that the young child operates in a truth mode; the reality testing that allows the developing child to distinguish between reality and fantasy is, we suggest, a second stage that may be conceptualized in terms of Hilgard's evocative description of the development of reality testing as the creation of a safe and well-trodden path from the real world to fantasy and back again.

Let us attempt to trace some of these developmental routes from the bottom of figure 3.1 to the top: to avoid confusion, however, these routes have not been indicated on the figure. In the first developmental stage that we have hypothesized, the child proceeds from the story through the fact and verification blocks, and then to oral storytelling and formal narrative. In Western society, the interactional setting is likely to be dyadic; in tribal societies, to be a personal audience. The next developmental stage takes the child-listener to the left from the story node, through disbelief suspension; from the "True?" decision node, the story route follows the same course in both Western and tribal societies. We hypothesize further that concurrently with or soon after the child's first comprehended exposure to interactive storytelling at about the age of three (but seldom before), the daydreaming medium will become operative, leading to internal, informal, zero-audience narrative.

Let us turn now from these hypothetically universal processes that establish the reinforcement value of storytelling to electronic society, and inquire what routes a contemporary child is likely to follow in arriving at the conviction that ludic reading is pleasurable. Once the pleasures of interactive stories have been established, the child turns naturally to the flickering television screen and follows the adventures of Kermit or Little Noddy in the children's programs. This supplementary electronic narrative input reinforces pleasurable earlier interactive narrative experiences. Illustrated books (in which pictures rather than text predominate) are likely to make their first appearance in the child's life at about this time, probably during the fourth year. First parents read them aloud; later, the child may "read" to him- or herself by telling the remembered story of each picture. Accordingly, two new pathways to narrative pleasure are opened at about the time the child begins nursery school, or even before: one route passes through electronic and the other through mechanical storytelling.

A long latency now ensues until the child acquires independent reading at about the age of six or seven. During this period, no further inputs are added to those we have reviewed, although the child's verbal abilities and the available number of narrative frames (reviewed in the next chapter) show a sharp increase. Arguably, the most critical moments in determining lifelong reading habits, and whether or not ludic reading will develop, occur during the child's early attempts at independent reading: here, the three antecedents of rewarding ludic reading interact to determine the outcome. Much of this book is concerned with a detailed examination of these antecedents; the positive expectations we have been examining, a minimum level of reading ability (chapter 5), and correct book selection in terms of reader interest and text difficulty (chapters 7 and 8).

For the beginning child reader, as for the mature adult, deficiency in any one of the three antecedents will abort the reading enterprise; however, for the child, each failed attempt to transduce reading into narrative sets up negative reinforcers that may ultimately combine to ensure that reading is passed over in favor of other entertainment inputs. (Such is the position of the functionally illiterate adult considered in chapter 1.) However, we hypothesize that the positive value of narrative itself is never compromised by the failure to develop ludic reading: as in preliterate societies, it remains an important and time-consuming input throughout the lifespan.

The Component Processes
of Ludic Reading

4
Absorption and Entrancement

Among the mysteries of reading, the greatest is certainly its power to absorb the reader completely and effortlessly and, on occasion, to change his or her state of consciousness through entrancement.

Near the turn of the century, these and similar issues formed part of the study of consciousness, which, in the laboratories of Wundt and his American pupil E. B. Titchener, was a major concern of early scientific psychology. For fifty years, consciousness studies were largely neglected, until, in 1958, Broadbent suggested that attention is analogous to an electromechanical switching device and might therefore be studied within an information-processing paradigm. The effectiveness of this paradigm brought new vigor and respectability to cognitive psychology, and through the study of attention, the study of consciousness—or at least important aspects of it—once again became a legitimate research area (Lachman, Lachman, and Butterfield, 1979, p. 186).

Studies of attention are indeed of great assistance in elucidating the ludic reader's absorbed concentration and entrancement. If these states can be related to attention, we shall have succeeded in bringing one of reading's larger mysteries into the clearer light of experimental method. In order to do so, we shall have to trace at least part of the complex route the reader follows from attention to perception to comprehension, and thence to the creation of the world of the book. Fortunately, an exhaustive study of attention and comprehension can be avoided because our objective is phenomenological rather than cognitive. In other words, it is the reader's subjective experience, rather than the thought mechanisms that allow the experience to take place, that is of most interest to us.

ATTENTION

The most important issue in attention studies as they relate to reading is whether attention is unitary or divisible. Of course, we can do many complex things two or more at a time, such as talking while driving a car or, among surgeons, daydreaming while sewing up incisions (Singer, 1977). However, one member of each of these pairs of behaviors is highly automatized, so that only the other makes demands on conscious attention. On the other hand, it is impossible to carry on a conversation or do mental arithmetic while reading a book. This suggests the image of a bottleneck in attention, and there have been conflicting theories about its location in the human information-processing system (Broadbent, 1958; Deutsch and Deutsch, 1963). A way out of the problem is to regard attention as a resource which is allocated in part by unconscious rules, in part by conscious decisions, and in part by task difficulty (Kahneman, 1973).

It seems obvious that complex tasks use more attention than simple ones, and many studies support this view (Spelke, Hirst, and Neisser, 1976, on divided attention; and Zelniker, 1971). But this seemingly trivial conclusion is forcefully contradicted in a study by Britton, Piha, Davis and Wehausen (1978), who asked subjects to read three passages of increasing difficulty; at the same time, they had to press a button each time they heard a click sound. The result, counterintuitively, was that reaction times decreased significantly as passage complexity increased. In other words, the more difficult the passage they were reading, the more promptly subjects were able to respond to the sound. The explanation proposed by the authors is that the easy passages fill more "spaces" in short-term memory than the difficult ones, because memory space is not used for material that is not understood.

Though these results run counter to the commonsense expectation that we need more attention for hard tasks than for easy ones, they have a good fit with our own experience as readers. The more effortful the reading task, the less we are able to resist distractions and the more capacity we have available for other tasks—such as listening to the birds in the trees or other forms of woolgathering.

A more forceful analogy comes to mind. The reader of a text in an unknown language, like a tourist listening to a radio news broadcast in a foreign country, understands nothing. Since there is no comprehension, no demands are made on conscious attention, leaving the whole of that aspect of capacity available for other tasks. Thus with Britton's readers: as the text became more difficult, less of it was understood, leaving more conscious attention available for the monitoring task.

Attention and Effort

One of the most striking attentional characteristics of ludic reading is that it is effortless. Karl Pribram (1977, p. 227) remarks that the word *attention* derives from the Latin *tendere*, "to hold," in the sense of holding to one control program rather than another. There is of course a clear subjective distinction between what attention holds and what holds attention. The student who with furrowed brow reads and rereads a passage on the difference between classical and operant conditioning, despairingly trying to keep his mind on the saliva that drips and the pellet that drops (or does the pellet drip and the saliva drop?), exemplifies the state of holding fast to attention.

The second condition, in which attention takes hold of us, is that of the ludic reader, whose effortless concentration multiplies the demands made on attentional theory. This is because it is difficult to reconcile the reader's subjective perception of effortlessness with the known fact that all attention requires arousal. Kahneman's (1973) distinction between arousal, which is involuntary, and effort, which is volitional, clarifies the issue but does not solve the problem, since the reader's subjective effortlessness may be misreported effort (Nisbett and Wilson, 1977). The ludic reader is not only subjectively relaxed but is also able to resist outside distractions, as if the work of concentration (the teacher's "Pay attention!") is done for him by the task.

A final observation about effort in ludic reading is that response demands (replying to a question, doing a comprehension test) increase one's sense of effortfulness. Entertainment industry inputs, including leisure reading materials, have in common the absence of any response demands. Like fantasy (which is free because it is not subject to feedback control from the real world: Klinger, 1971, p. 10), ludic reading is also sovereign, subject to no evaluation or censure by any person other than the reader. Indeed, the moment evaluative demands intrude, as in the case of an absorbed reader suddenly told that he or she is to produce a critical review of the book, ludic reading, in obedience to a variety of mechanisms (Apter, 1979; Deci, 1976), at once becomes work reading: the response demand triggers a perceived effortfulness.

In conclusion, it should be noted that attention can be focused on the self or on the environment (Carver and Scheier, 1981). What kind of focus does reading require? On the one hand, the story I am reading does not exist except in my head; on the other, the book is an external stimulus. The latter is the more correct view, since the use of cognitive structures that are part of the self does not mean that focus is internal if the point of origin of the stimulus is outside the self (p. 36). In fact, a frequent use of ludic reading is to mask unpleasant mood states and to draw the reader's attention away from self-concern to the world of the book, thus confirming reading's status as an environment-focus activity (see chapter 11).

Reading and Consciousness

Attention and consciousness are not synonymous. With practice, cognition can become so routinized that most information processing takes place unconsciously. It may therefore be useful to regard consciousness as a processing bottleneck reserved for special tasks (Lachman et al., 1979). Skilled reading is an amalgam of highly automated processes (word recognition, syntactic parsing, and so on) that make no demands on conscious processing and the extraction of meaning from long continuous texts by the application of discourse-processing strategies (see chapter 5). The latter do indeed make heavy demands on conscious attention. Logan (1980) remarks that most studies have focused on "pure" cases of attention or automatic processing "and have relatively little to say about tasks that require a coordinated mixture of both modes of processing" (p. 253). However, he continues, studies of mixed processing are important, since many interesting tasks, such as reading, typewriting, and arithmetic, are of this kind.

In terms of the distinction between attention as consciousness and attention as processing capacity, it seems possible that although reading uses only a fraction of available processing capacity, it does use up all available conscious attention; and furthermore, that ludic reading, which makes no response demands of the reader, may entail some arousal, though little effort.

In this context, there are some interesting differences between reading a book and watching a television program. Reading imposes a demand that television does not—namely, the conversion of written text to a language analogue, followed by meaning extraction. Television, on the other hand, provides the viewer with ready-made language and a pictorial representation, which together function as an immediately available meaning structure. We would therefore expect the reader to have less conscious attentional capacity to spare than the viewer, and I can offer a personal observation that has some bearing on this issue. South African television broadcasts began in 1974, at about the same time that my son learned to read. Most evenings between 6 and 8 he would watch television with a book on his lap; electronics won the first round, but Gutenberg won the war. His eyes would stray to the book's cover, then to a page, and he would soon be sunk in the book, so that only a great noise and flurry on the screen could win his attention back again. "To an adult or a child who has tasted the delights of reading, the printed page seems to have greater power than even the most glamorous of the media" (Nell, 1978a). Below, we argue that this "power" of the book derives from the heavier demands reading makes on attention.

An Attentional Model of Reading

Most models of the reading process begin with visual perception and then work upward to the highest-level processes, such as sentence and text comprehension (see chapter 5). Many of the apparent paradoxes and contradictions in the ludic reader's state of attention can be accounted for by suggesting, first, that it is the upper-level comprehension processes that make demands on conscious attention. Consciousness is a processing bottleneck, and it is the readily comprehended messages (whether spoken or written) that fully engage the receiver's conscious attention. This full commitment of conscious attention gives rise to the ludic reader's absorption.

Are we not, however, exaggerating the cognitive load imposed by the notably uncomplex task of reading a James Bond story or listening to "The Three Bears"? The findings of Britton et al. (1978) are once again apposite: the simpler passages fill cognitive capacity more completely than the difficult ones. Indeed, the richness of the structure the ludic reader creates in his head may be inversely proportional to the literary power and originality of the reading matter (what Cawelti terms the mimetic force), and vice versa. The processing demands made by James Joyce may require frequent pauses and regressions, whereas the even pace of Wilbur Smith, and the well-practiced ease with which the reader can image his stereotyped characters and settings, may impose a heavier continuous load on attention.

This model of the nature of absorption frees the term *reading trance* for another use—to describe the extent to which the reader or listener has become, through the narrative, a temporary citizen of another world, has "gone away" in the sense we shall explore in chapter 10. This is undoubtedly part of the reading experience, easily distinguished from mere attentional absorption: the latter causes me to do a double take as I emerge from the book, while the former give me gooseflesh at the victorious hero's triumphant entry into the city he has liberated from the grip of Sauron, Lord of Evil; or at the sight of Pegasus, gleaming white and wisest of the beasts. Attention holds me, but trance fills me, to varying degrees, with the wonder and flavor of alternative worlds. Put differently, attention grips us and abstracts us from our surroundings; but the otherness of reading experience, the wonder and thrill of the author's creations (as much mine as his), are the domain of trance.

In terms of attention theory, therefore, the ludic reader's absorption may be seen as an extreme case of subjectively effortless arousal which owes its *effortlessness* to the automatized nature of the skilled reader's decoding activity; which is *aroused* because focused attention, like other kinds of alert consciousness, is possible only under the sway of inputs from the ascending reticular activating system of the brainstem; and which is *absorbed* because of the heavy demands comprehension processes appear to make of conscious attention.

This formulation allows us to view the ludic reader's absorption as a state no more mysterious than that of the clerk adding a row of figures, of the child engaged in imaginative play, or of the driver negotiating a busy intersection. But the ludic reader's entrancement, thus far characterized as a greatly deepened form of absorption, with analogues in other altered states of consciousness (see chapter 10), retains its mystery.

COMPREHENSION

For most adults, comprehension is rapid, automatic and effortless. But despite its apparent simplicity, comprehension includes a myriad of subprocesses, each of which by itself constitutes a formidable computational task. . . . Because of the sheer speed of comprehension, it is difficult for the reader to explain how he came to understand a passage. That task is left to those who study comprehension (Just and Carpenter, 1977, p. ix).

The product of the reader's attention is comprehension—the automatic and effortless process that transforms words, sentences, paragraphs, and chapters into inner worlds. Comprehension thus mediates whatever rewards the book offers, and we need to look more closely at comprehension processes.

Though the question of what meaning is, and how it becomes known, is central to cognitive psychology, it has until recently had little appeal for psychologists; it is a murky area (Lachman et al., 1979, p. 389) bordering on the metaphysical and burdened with the dangers of solipsism. Indeed, the recursiveness of definitions of comprehension and meaning (comprehension is understanding is apprehending a meaning) is their most striking characteristic.

Meaning was important to the nineteenth-century psychologists who studied consciousness, but this field lay dormant from about 1900 until the mid-1950s, when it re-emerged as a central issue for both experimental psychology and linguistics. *The Measurement of Meaning* (Osgood, Suci, and Tannenbaum) appeared in 1957 and described the semantic differential technique that, through factor analysis, allowed an individual's attributions of meaning to a concept to be placed within a three-dimensional space. Chomsky's *Syntactic Structures* was published in the same year. Meanwhile, in much the same way that the question of consciousness has been taken up within the more manageable study of attention, the investigation of meaning has been assimilated by studies of comprehension. This area also has its difficulties, which are keenly felt by reading researchers. Ronald Carver remarks that "the measurement of comprehension is a continual nemesis because it is impossible to know what comprehension tests measure" (1976, p. 381).

The ludic reader's comprehension process can be described using the familiar metaphor of a pebble striking a pond. For each individual, comprehension is an associative and therefore memory-enriched process; the enrichment derives from autobiographical episodic memory rather than from verifiable semantic memory (Tulving, 1979). Accordingly, comprehension may be seen as a set of concentric circles. The central point, where the sentence-pebble strikes the pond, is in large measure common to all speakers of the language, because it is the literal content based on syntactic rules and lexical conventions derived from and verifiable by semantic memory. But the first of the ripples taps aspects of the listener's episodic memory, with each successive ripple drawing on a wider circle of idiosyncratic associations dislodged from the listener's autobiography. The number of ripples and their richness depend on two factors: for how long attention is given to the sentence, and how effectively it cues the listener's own memory structures. If zero-cue conditions are met (for example, if attention is withdrawn immediately, or if for the listener in question the sentence is quite indifferent), no ripples develop.

For an attentive reader with a rich memory store that cues many related associations, the farthest of the ripples may be a long way indeed from the point where the sentence-pebble struck the water. Freud's interpretation (1907) of the "artificial dreams" in *Gradiva,* a short story by Wilhelm Jensen published in 1903, is a case in point. Freud sent a copy of his essay to Jensen, and in the exchange of correspondence that followed, notes Freud (1907, p. 97), Jensen "confirmed the fact that he had no knowledge of my theory of dreams": here is a striking example of how far beyond an author's conscious intentions the interaction between reader and book may move.

The ripple metaphor is useful, first, in clarifying exactly what we mean when we say that in the interaction between book and reader, there is no book. We now know that at the central point, where the pebble strikes the water, comprehension is indeed bookbound and universal, and the fact that readers asked to reproduce the gist of the text do so in almost identical terms (Lachman et al., 1979) shows this to be so. But because a ludic book does hold the attention for long periods and is by definition evocative for the reader in question, a large book-related structure arises that is quite idiosyncratic and therefore different for each reader. It is in this sense that there is no book.

Second, this metaphor focuses attention on an important aspect of the comprehension "nemesis," namely, that comprehension questions must always refer to the "central point" of comprehension, whereas what is often of the greatest interest to the educator is the idiosyncratic structure an individual reader has created, which, because of the great rapidity of the associative processes involved, is largely inaccessible even to the reader in question.

Comprehension can be studied at the sentence level, which has been the traditional domain of psycholinguistics, or at the level of discourse processing—that is, the extraction of a gist or macrostructure (Van Dijk, 1977) from long continuous texts. It is of course this second kind of comprehension, which has become an area of interest to psychologists only in the past decade, that is of greatest relevance to the understanding of ludic reading.

Discourse Processing and Global Models of Comprehension

Large-scale models of comprehension deal with data reduction: in order to comprehend a continuous text, "large and highly complex amounts of information must be organized and reduced in appropriate ways, without which processing (storage, control, retrieval) would be impossible" (Van Dijk, 1977, p. 30). Like other forms of perception, text comprehension involves the inhibition of impulses (Von Bekesy, 1967) judged to be irrelevant to the meaning-extraction task at hand. Telling a story clearly involves suppression of many possible propositions because they fail to meet relevance or interest criteria (Pratt, 1977). Thus, in telling a rescue tale, I include a description of the mountain peak but omit references to the texture of the gravel on the approach road and the state of the tires on the ambulance.

Macrostructures

Since text comprehension is a data-reduction process, the question that models of large-scale comprehension must answer is what the differences are between the input to a reader or listener and the material placed in store after comprehension has taken place: "in other words, what are the differences between the text on the page and the 'text' in the reader's head?" (Just and Carpenter, 1977, p. ix).

A text can be defined as the abstract structure of a discourse consisting of an ordered sequence of propositions mapped onto a series of sentences. Sentences are the microstructure of a text; these in turn are the inputs for the macrorules, which transform one level of discourse, microstructures, into another, *macrostructures*. For example, "Peter is laying bricks. Peter is sawing rafters. Peter is plastering walls. Peter is . . ." may be assigned to the macrostructure "Peter is building a house." If the context is founding a pioneer settlement in a new area, a further macrostructure may be generated. Recursiveness is held in check by defining the superordinate macrostructure as the most general macrostructure possible for the given discourse as a whole.

There are only four macrorules, which Van Dijk states as propositions in formal logic. *Generalization* is a reductive rule (dog, cat, parrot → pets). *Deletion* is "semantic tree pruning" (p. 11), which removes material irrelevant to the discourse topic. *Integration* allows us to replace "John took a cab to the station. He bought a ticket to Paris. He took his seat on the train . . ." with "John went to Paris." *Construction* is an inductive procedure that would allow us to say that John took the train even if the previous sentence set terminated at "bought a ticket to Paris."

In addition to macrostructures, discourse can express a second kind of global structure, namely, *superstructures*. For example, a discourse in story form expresses a narrative superstructure, which is examined in detail below. Other examples of superstructures are newspaper reports, arguments, psychological papers, and advertisements.

The third and last component of Van Dijk's organizational triad is the *frame:* "frames define units or chunks of concepts which are not essentially but *typically*, related. . . . There is no essential or immediate relation between the concept of 'table' and the concept of 'cereal,' nor between 'soap' and 'water.' . . . Yet, they are organized by the frames of breakfast [and] washing . . . respectively" (1977, p. 21). Frame information may be highly complex ("giving a party") and is therefore itself organized in various levels and subunits by the macrorules.

Narrative as a superstructure. In chapter 3 storytelling and story-hearing were analyzed in phenomenological terms. Now that we have reviewed the attentional components of absorption and the elements of comprehension processes, we can add some psychological sophistication to what we there called "the witchery of a story."

Kintsch (1977, pp. 38–42) defines narrative structure as a set of episodes, each of which contains an exposition, a complication (which is required to be non-trivial—that is, surprising, absorbing, or interesting), and a resolution, to which a moral may or may not be attached. Embeddings are frequent, so that the complication of one episode may contain a further episode with its own complication, and so on recursively. The complication is the central event in a narrative episode and is signaled by a frame change (for which there are typographical cues such as a new paragraph, propositional cues, or such macroconnectors as "but," "however," and the like) which renders the exposition frame redundant and replaces it with a new one. The relationship between these two frames, he suggests, is the source of much of the reader's interest in a story.

The operation of these rules is clarified by an analysis Van Dijk (1977) offers of a story by James Hadley Chase: A friend introduces a pretty reporter to a local gambler with a bad reputation. They meet in a bar, and the two cannot take their eyes off one another. In this example, which demonstrates the utility of Van Dijk's approach, the reader activates certain frames in order to comprehend the discourse. These are Meeting, Introduction, Falling in Love, and Bar. Since the gambler is a clean-cut, steady-looking fellow, thus disconfirming the reporter's (and the reader's) presuppositions, another frame is activated, namely, Good Guy/Bad Guy. Once the frames have been identified, the four macrorules given earlier operate on the passage to create macrostructures.

The macrostructure-superstructure model of discourse comprehension has considerable intuitive appeal and, unlike other models, appears to take adequate account of the interaction between readers' world knowledge and expectations, on the one hand, and text input, on the other. But it is in precisely these respects that macrostructuring has been found wanting. Beaugrande and Colby (1979) argue that because of the trend in current comprehension theory to abstract out units, the theories cannot account for the fact that some stories are considered more interesting and enduring than others, or that narrators select some stories over others from the vast repertory available to them. Finally, these theories cannot account for the psychological and social implications of narrating and understanding stories.

The *interactive model* proposed by Beaugrande and Colby is based on two sets of rules, one for telling stories and the other for comprehending them. The seven storytelling rules closely conform to the elements of exposition, complication, and resolution already examined. The second set of rules consists of nine processes for story understanding (some of which may be traced back to elements such as frames and macrorules). The significance of this approach is that it links the author's work of encoding and the reader's of decoding in a formal system (an input to the story understander, for example, is awareness of storytelling rules). This introduces new dynamic elements into the comprehension situation, approaching the richness and flexibility of the reader's response to a story more closely than other theories. For example:

> All the participants in narrating—the narrator, the audience, and the narrated characters—are probably engaged much of the time in complex activities of planning and predicting. The narrator must (a) plan out plausible state-action tracks for each main character, (b) relate narrated actions to recoverable plans of a character, and (c) anticipate and monitor how the audience recovers or reconstructs the character's plans and predicts further actions (Beaugrande and Colby, 1979, p. 49).

The Psychological Reality of Macrostructures

The macrostructure theory of text comprehension generates a number of hypotheses about the ways in which macropropositions are formulated, stored in memory, retrieved and lost. With the help of titles, thematic statements, and so forth, the reader hypothesizes an appropriate macrostructure (Dooling and Lachman, 1971, showed that recall for untitled ambiguous passages improved significantly when appropriate titles were provided) and assigns additional macrostructures recursively as soon as the complexity of the current level exceeds comfortable capacity. Additional cues in the formation of macrostructures are derived from the context and from propositional density. For example, our world knowledge enables us to reconstruct the major topics of most conversations about the Lebanese crisis, even if we have heard only the tail end of the conversation, illustrating contextual cueing. Cues deriving from propositional density arise because we do not relate all we know. The reader or listener has therefore come to expect that when the propositional representation of an event in discourse increases, the complication of the story will shortly ensue.

Storage in episodic memory is organized around macrostructures. This, as Kintsch (1977) has noted, accounts for listeners' and readers' ability to produce the gist of a discourse. Retrieval from memory is by inverse macrorule application, recovering from the high-level macrostructure lower-level macrostructures and, possibly, some components of the text base. Forgetting, suggests Van Dijk, has two phases. In the first, the text base and propositions not relevant to the frame are lost though the top-level macrostructure is still available; in the second, successive infractions of this macrostructure itself take place. In chapter 11, we shall see that readers' enjoyment in rereading well-known stories can be explained by reference to this model of narrative forgetting.

Kintsch (1977) reports data on the testing of some of these hypotheses which confirm that macrostructures do have psychological reality. For example, subjects sort story paragraphs into groupings that closely conform to theoretically derived macrostructures. Bartlett's early work (1932) is extended to show that subjects produce more informative story summaries when an appropriate or conventional schema is available. Finally, although scrambling sentence order rendered stories incomprehensible, Kintsch showed that subjects could summarize scrambled-paragraph stories as well as correctly sequenced stories. The reason, he suggests, "is that comprehending such a story involves filling in waiting slots in a fixed story schema according to certain well known rules and strategies" (1977, p. 50; see also Whaley, 1981). Kintsch's finding explains why news stories can begin with the resolution instead of the account or setting without losing comprehensibility.

5
Reading,
Reading Ability,
and Reading Habits

Reading is only one of a large number of symbolically mediated processes in which prolonged practice makes us proficient. Of these, spoken language is the first, both for the human race and for each individual. It seems remarkable that although every normal person learns to speak, not everyone learns to read. Why is it that speech is universally and automatically acquired while other symbol systems (reading, gestural language, Morse code, musical and mathematical notation) are acquired laboriously or not at all? Since Wundt's studies of reaction times to letters and words in the 1880s, reading research has persistently sought the answer to this question. Successive generations of researchers have adopted the same strategy—to tease out the component processes of reading skill by more and more clearly focused studies, and to relate these processes to one another by constructing increasingly sophisticated models of the reading process.

Reading research has an uneven history. The two decades after 1890 were a golden era, notes Venezky (1977), culminating in the publication of Huey's famous study in 1908. But from then until the mid-1950s, psychologists contributed virtually nothing to this area, largely because of "the domination of behaviorism in psychology, and the preoccupation with assessment within education" (p. 342). In the 1950s, renewed interest in cognitive processes and generous funding policies in the United States created the climate and opportunity for psychologists to re-enter the area of reading research.

Both the quantity and progress of research indicate that the period beginning in the late 1970s may be another golden era. For example, Carroll (1981) cites six studies bearing on the component skills of reading dated 1979 or later, while models of the reading process appear to be proliferating even more rapidly, with nine major models dating from 1977 or later (Beaugrande, 1981; Brown, 1981). Venezky's contention that current psychology-based research on reading processes is "not motivated by an interest in reading per se but . . . [in] the construction of information processing models for visual processing" (1977, p. 343) is thus no longer valid. On the contrary, seldom in the history of psychology has a multilevel cognitive process received such holistic treatment as current studies afford to reading (Brown, 1981; Frederiksen, 1980; Jackson and McClelland, 1979; and many others).

But whether or not current research is converging toward an adequate account of reading, with a full specification of its component skills and their hierarchical integration, is a matter of some controversy. Carr, for example, after reviewing nine recent articles on reading comprehension, comments that they "are disappointing because they make clear the tremendous intellectual distance that has yet to be travelled before anything like a scientifically complete description of the reading process will be achieved" (1981, p. 601). Carroll, on the other hand, argues that we are approaching both a complete catalogue of the components of reading skill and a statement of their hierarchical interaction (1981, p. 18). Although the indications are positive, then, the final assessment of the present flood of reading-process studies has yet to be made.

MODELS OF THE READING PROCESS

The vigor of current reading research is perhaps best captured in the proliferation of models of the reading process (reviewed in Beaugrande, 1981, and Stanovich, 1980). A scientific model describes not only how something works but also the interdependence of its structural elements; a successful model will thus predict how a change in one element will change another (Gephart, 1970). These models are in turn based on elegant studies of the component skills of reading (Carroll, 1981; Frederiksen, 1980; Jackson and McClelland, 1979).

Models of the reading process are of two kinds: bottom-up and top-down. In the former, the reader applies only knowledge from his own memory store to the understanding of letters, words, phrases, and sentences. In the top-down models, readers also make use of integrative hypotheses to confirm their best guess at the meaning of the text, derived from their reading of the text to that point, as well as from their own previous knowledge and experience (Frederiksen, 1980; Stanovich, 1980).

The most effective model will be the one that is closest to the way real readers in the real world do their reading, which is by a judicious mix of both data-driven, bottom-up processes and ongoing hypothesis-driven interpretations of the semantic content of the text. A model that matches these specifications quite closely and has many advantages for the study of ludic reading is Eric Brown's neuropsychological theory of reading, in which "all levels of explanation . . . represent spatio-temporal physiological events within the central nervous system" (1981, p. 443).

READING ABILITY

Is a high degree of reading skill a prerequisite for ludic reading? Like other complex activities, such as remembering or high jumping, reading can be described either in terms of its component processes, each of which is independently specifiable and measurable, or as a final, integrated performance to which one summating measure may be applied. The first option has its dangers. For example, memory is associated with structural and chemical changes in individual cells, and these changes may ultimately be specified at the level of individual molecules. On the other hand, memory summates in a measurable performance, as all students and examiners know. Similarly, once we know the height an athlete has cleared, we can ignore the almost uncountable components of this performance, such as the athlete's running speed, thigh circumference, cerebral lateralization, and make of running shoe, and cite one criterion performance—height cleared—in which all the component skills summate.

In this chapter, we shall endeavor to determine whether such a summating measure can be found for reading ability,* which is certainly no less complex an activity than high jumping. In order to develop such a measure, problems in measuring comprehension and computing reading-comprehension speed must first be solved. We then examine the relations between reading ability and ludic reading in order to determine whether an individual's reading ability determines how often and how much he or she reads for pleasure. Finally, we relate reading-speed flexibility to reading ability.

The Measurement of Reading Ability

A first step toward seeing reading as an integrated performance is to specify the minimum requirements for reading. Plug (1978, p. 3) suggests

---

*In the literature, reading ability is variously referred to as reading skill, reading attainment, reading efficiency, reading competency, reading maturity, effective reading, and so forth. Reading speed is sometimes used as a synonym for all these terms, and sometimes as one of their components. In fact, these descriptions are far from synonymous. To avoid confusion, we shall use the term *reading ability*, of which reading skill is a synonym, and avoid the others unless specifically defined.

three: the reader should recognize all (or nearly all) the words of the reading matter; they should be recognized in the order in which they appear in the text; and the reader should understand what the author wanted to say (or what he or she thinks the author wanted to say). However, this is not an ability construct since it fails to specify a skill or group of skills that progresses from the state of the struggling pupil who says "Teacher, I was too busy reading to understand" (Carr, 1981) to skilled reading. This latter condition, the possession of reading ability, is defined by Carroll: "Good readers are those who have attained high levels of automaticity in a large proportion of these components of reading skill, while poor readers are those who may have attained automaticity in only a few of these skills, and are far from mastery in others" (1981, p. 18). Implicit in Carroll's definition is the suggestion that the measurement of this automaticity will distinguish between skilled and unskilled readers; furthermore, it seems likely that a summating measure of reading ability will have to focus on whatever the end goal of reading is thought to be.

Every account of reading, from the earliest to the present day, converges on the view that its essence is the extraction of meaning from graphic symbols. In the fourteenth century John Barbour used *read* in this sense: "Auld storys that men redys, Representis to thaim the dedys of stalwart folk" (Oxford, 1933b); the dictionary definition of *read* emphasizes its function, "to inspect and interpret in thought [any signs which represent words or discourse]" (Oxford, 1933b), and modern reading research has the same emphasis. Tinker puts the matter elegantly: " 'reading' without understanding is not reading" (1963, p. 27). Jackson and McClelland confirm this: "The goal of the proficient reader is to understand the material as efficiently as possible in the shortest amount of time. . . . An appropriate measure of reading ability should jointly depend on both speed and comprehension" (1979, p. 155). It seems likely, therefore, that the summating measure we seek is reading-comprehension speed. How useful such a measure will be depends, to some extent, on whether the problems associated with comprehension measurement can be satsifactorily resolved.

Measuring Reading Comprehension

All measures of reading comprehension tap the central point of comprehension: that is, the most direct literal meaning of the text. The difficulty with questions about the literal meaning of a text is that it is often easy for the subject to guess the correct answers even without reading the text on which the questions are based. Carver and Darby (1971) report a blind comprehension rate of 33 percent. In a later paper, Carver (1972) reports a mean comprehension score of 57 percent for a group of readers (he does not say how many) who had not read the text in question.

And on similar material, Plug (1978) reports that his own blind comprehension score was 56 percent.

In establishing an accurate measure of reading—comprehension speed for ludic readers, the need to ensure that reading really is reading and not skimming must be balanced against the danger of burdening subjects with complex comprehension tasks that form no part of normal ludic reading. Indeed, one of the delights of reading for pleasure is that it is a truly response-free activity, pursued in the quiet certainty that no authoritative voice will call me to account for passages I skimmed or from which my attention wandered. One way of steering a middle path between ensuring that the reading-test passage has been read rather than scanned and the response-free character of natural ludic reading is to calculate a score that is a composite of both reading and comprehension attainment (Jackson and McClelland 1979; Tinker 1963, p. 21), giving only minimal weight to the comprehension component.

How Fast Do People Read?

Before moving on to consider reading ability in relation to ludic reading, it is useful to examine how fast various classes of readers do in fact read.

It is important to realize that there is an absolute upper limit to reading rate, if reading is understood to mean perception of most of the printed words. The limit is physiological and arises because reading requires two kinds of eye movements: saccades, or rapid sweeps of the eye from one word group to the next, and fixations, in which gaze is focused on one word group. This neuromuscular limit is 800–900 words per minute (w.p.m.; Harris, 1968, p. 208). Carver (1972) maintains that intelligent readers cannot fully comprehend even easy material at speeds above 500–600 w.p.m. The average college student reads at 280 w.p.m., and superior college readers at 400–600 w.p.m. (Harris, 1968). Among fifty-two otherwise unselected student subjects in the Jackson and McClelland study, the twelve slowest readers had a mean speed of 216 w.p.m. and the twelve fastest 396 w.p.m. on a long comprehension-controlled popular scientific text. We may therefore conclude that for college-level adults reading scientific texts of moderate difficulty, the range of reading speeds is from 200 to 400 w.p.m.; the former is slow reading and the latter fast. Though no data on fiction reading speeds could be traced in the literature, it seems unlikely that ludic readers would read more slowly than the 200 w.p.m. reported for slow college readers on scientific material.

Reading and Speaking Rates

There are clearly relations between reading and inner speech. The learner reader's progress from speech-aided phonemic decoding to fluent silent reading of word and phrase units seems to indicate that the speech component of reading withers away as higher degrees of silent reading skill are attained. It must, however, be noted that subvocalization (electrophysiologically detectable movements of the speech apparatus which produce no audible sound) is invoked under distracting conditions or when reading difficult material; Pauk (1981) argues that comprehension without subvocalization is impossible.

A comparison of reading and speaking rates throws additional light on the relation between silent reading and speech. Pimsleur, Hancock, and Furey (1977) report that fifteen French radio announcers had a mean speech rate of 177 w.p.m. (S.D. = 32.4) and fifteen American announcers a mean of 182 w.p.m. with much lower variability (S.D. = 7.5); the difference between the means is not significant. On the basis of this and previous studies they suggest that a moderate speech rate is between 160 and 190 w.p.m.; fast speech is above 220 w.p.m. and slow speech below 130 w.p.m. (orators on solemn occasions speak very slowly indeed: Charles de Gaulle's farewell to the French nation was delivered at 70 w.p.m.). The maximum rate at which spoken language can be comprehended was investigated by Carroll in 1967 (in Pimsleur et al., 1977), who established that time-compressed speech, recorded normally but played back with speech pauses electronically deleted, was well comprehended at a rate of 475 w.p.m., while some comprehension of words and isolated phrases was preserved at 700 w.p.m. Skilled readers thus read faster than they talk; it is possible that the reading rates of unskilled readers (for example, the less-educated persons whom Szalai, 1972, and Cole and Gold, 1979, report as reading newspapers and magazines but not books) very closely approximate speech rates. Maximum listening rates are especially interesting because of their close correspondence to maximum reading rates (that is, reading that recognizes most of the words in the order in which they appear, as distinct from the various part-reading techniques). A curious further connection between reading and speech rates is the phenomenon of "person-particular recoding" reported by Kosslyn and Matt (1977): when reading aloud, subjects read prose they knew had been composed by fast talkers (234 w.p.m.) significantly more rapidly than the prose of slow talkers (96 w.p.m.).

The close correspondences between maximum speech-comprehension and reading-comprehension rates and the possible match between the silent reading rate of non-college populations and speech rates point toward a closer correspondence between reading and speech than is generally acknowledged. Should a replication of the Kosslyn and Matt study (1977) show that, using slightly different instructions, person-particular recoding does indeed persist in silent reading, indicating that speech mechanisms play the same kind of role in silent reading as they do in reading aloud, further evidence for this connection would be available. The major implication of such findings would be that reading could be investigated as a special kind of speech rather than as a separate phenomenon which shares only a set of linguistic symbols with speech.

Reading-Speed Improvement

One other issue inextricably linked with the question of reading speed is reading-speed improvement, for which giddy claims have been made, such as being able to teach twelve-year olds to read at speeds up to "210,000 words a minute with good to excellent comprehension" (McBride, 1971).

Although the debunking of the speed-reading industry proceeds apace (Carver, 1972; Mendelsohn, 1977; Plug, 1978), many universities continue to offer study-skills courses which include a strong speed-reading component. Major determinants of reading speed, and hence the focus of those who seek to improve it, are eye-movement patterns, fixation duration, and perceptual span. Recent findings on these aspects of reading shed light on the techniques skilled readers use when reading for their own enjoyment and serve as a warning for those who offer reading-improvement courses based on assumptions that research has shown to be incorrect. Strategies based on faulty assumptions are unpro-.ductive and will demoralize the readers they purport to aid. If, as everyday observation suggests, ludic reading is rapid reading, readers (and teachers) are likely to assume that increasing reading speed will enhance reading enjoyment.

Jackson and McClelland caution that "individual differences in the ability to read depend more on central cognitive processes than on peripheral sensory processes" (1979, p. 152). Thus, on the issue of perceptual span, they note that there is no evidence that fast readers have a larger sensitive area around the fovea (the part of the retina with the highest visual acuity). If faster readers report more information from a single fixation, it is because they form the appropriate higher-level representations more quickly. This suggestion is echoed by Frederiksen (1980), who proposes that skilled readers are able to use contextual information to increase the amount of information encoded on a single fixation.

However, this process is independent of actual perception span. Rayner (1978, p. 623) notes that even skilled readers pick up information from at most eight or nine character spaces to the right of the fixation and four to the left. More important is the evidence Rayner reports on the question of fixation duration, which supports the hypothesis that fixations cannot be shorter than the time required for the cognitive processing that must take place before the next fixation. This hypothesis is strongly supported by a sophisticated study (Just and Carpenter, 1980) that used a computer-linked television monitor to calculate student readers' point of regard sixty times a second while they read scientific texts written by journalists. During ordinary reading, almost all content words were fixated, with an average of 1.2 words per fixation; second, under no-regression instructions, gaze durations (that is, the total time in milliseconds that a word is fixated) "reflect the time to execute comprehension processes . . .; the eye-mind assumption is that the eye remains fixated on a word as long as the word is being processed" (1980, p. 330).

These findings discredit the widely held view that the saccades and fixations of good readers are of approximately equal length and duration, or that reading ability is improved by lengthening saccade span and shortening fixation duration. Skilled readers in fact show substantial differences in the saccade and fixation strategies they apply. Moreover, the eye movements reported for speed readers are similar to those during skimming or scanning; readers who showed the greatest tendency to move down the center of the page had the poorest comprehension scores, and most speed readers resort to normal reading strategies when warned that their comprehension will be tested (Rayner, 1978, pp. 638–39).

The confusion that results from coupling speed reading with techniques for "better learning" is reported in a provocative study by Pauk (1965) that deserves to be better known: a six-session study-skills course in which students were advised to ignore reading rate produced grade-point- average gains three times higher than those produced by a four-session course in which the first two sessions were on speed reading. Pauk concludes that combining reading-rate training with study-skills training sets up a conflict that diminishes the value of study-skills training. In a later article, Pauk (1981) attacks another of the sacred cows of reading-efficiency training; namely, the need to extirpate subvocalization. His view is supported by current reading models, which invoke subvocalization as an essential part of the comprehension process (for example, Brown, 1981; Huey [1908] makes frequent references to "the inner speech of reading").

Traditional, perceptually based approaches to the improvement of reading speed (increasing fixation span and thus decreasing saccade frequency, acquiring regular eye movements, reading down the center of the page, eliminating subvocalization, and so forth) are therefore unsupported by recent studies, which, on the contrary, demonstrate that skilled readers do not use these techniques on scientific texts. Those concerned with teaching study skills might be well advised to exclude reading-speed-improvement strategies from their curricula until the most recent advances in studies of the reading process have been fully evaluated.

Reading Speed and Ludic Reading

Though it seems self-evident that ludic readers are skilled readers, very little empirical evidence relates reading ability and reading habits or determines the degree of reading skill required for ludic reading. Greaney and Quinn (1978) found that 920 Irish fifth-graders spent an average of sixty minutes a week in leisure reading (which included books, comics, and newspapers), and that the strongest predictors of leisure reading were gender and reading attainment. However, these variables accounted for only 23 percent of the variance in book-reading time, which indicates that their study failed to tap other important predictors. In a study of 2,731 Canadian seventh-graders, Landy (1977) showed that of one hundred variables, the most important predictors of amount of reading were gender, reading ability, and the number of books the child owned. Related findings are reported by Howden (1967) and Lamme (1976).

Some other kinds of evidence point to a link between reading ability and habits. For example, the time-budget data reviewed in chapter 1 show that the leisure reading of books increases sharply with increased education in both the United States and Europe, and that this is true whether book reading is expressed as a percentage of reading time or as a percentage of respondents. But this is indirect evidence, since it rests on the plausible but unproved assumption that reading ability increases with increased education. A similar conclusion, similarly indirect, may be drawn from Cole and Gold's (1979) finding that all book readers also read newspapers and magazines, although the contrary does not apply. As we have seen, this finding in turn relates to educational level, since the 30 percent of their respondents who read only newspapers and magazines have a lower educational level than the 55 percent who read both books and newspapers.

There is also direct evidence in the form of anecdotes and observations. For example, in a survey of adolescent readers, Fisher (1961) notes that fast readers enjoy books more than slow readers: one respondent reports that "being a slow reader, I usually take my eyes off the book if anyone enters the room or makes any noise" (p. 54). Another remarks that he has no time for books, "and even when I do start a book, I never get round to finishing it. . . . I lose interest and concentration." These slow readers are very likely distractible because comprehension has failed to take hold of their conscious attention; in a sense, therefore, their attentional status is that of the tourists listening to a news broadcast in a foreign language.

The observational data are of the kind cited in the introduction (ludic readers are proud of the rapidity of their reading, and the speed at which they devour books often surprises parents and friends), to which some additions can be made. For example, my late father, whom I knew to be a very slow reader, read two newspapers a day every day of his life, but only one novel in his last thirty years, and that under protest when he was bedridden for some weeks. His resistance to reading a book until a sea of empty time loomed ahead of him recalls another of the Cole and Gold findings: those who do not habitually read books are not prepared to start a book unless they have a long open period available. This would also be consistent with the hypothesis that non-book readers are slower readers who regard reading an entire book as a daunting task. If this is true, the slower, less fluent readers would restrict themselves to smaller reading "parcels," such as those provided by newspapers and magazines.

The most compelling item of observational evidence on the link between reading ability and ludic reading is, however, to be drawn not from our mother-tongue experience of learning to read, which for most of us is too remote (and at too low a level of language proficiency) to be well remembered, but rather from the experience of learning a second language and, at some point, of settling down to read what looks to be an exciting novel in this newly acquired tongue. We then forcefully become aware of the difference between being able to read and reading skill, between the possession of a technical literacy that allows us to decipher a newspaper headline or read a menu and the effortless fluency that opens the way to pleasure reading. The final and most stringent test of mastery in reading a foreign language (which is not the same as speaking it: we all know foreigners who read nothing but English novels, yet speak the language execrably, and, of course, of fluent speakers who cannot read) is to willingly assign one of the day's precious reading times (just before going to sleep, for example) to a novel in that language, and not to lay it aside for mother-tongue reading if one is feeling especially tired or out of sorts. Many Americans and others born to the use of the Latin alphabet (myself among them) have had this experience with Hebrew, in which the terrors of an entirely new syntax and a strange vocabulary are compounded by the need to master an alien right-to-left orthography from which vowels are usually absent. As a result, few of those who come to Hebrew late in life become true ludic readers in that language.

READING ABILITIES AND HABITS

Because so little is known about the links between reading ability and reading habits, I carried out a number of studies with 129 subjects who were first- or second-year students (that is, in their thirteenth or fourteenth year of education) either of English literature at a university or of building science at a technical college. Their mean age was 20.7, with a standard deviation of 2.7.

The reading-comprehension speed of this sample was tested using a passage from Wouk's *Caine Mutiny* (1951), to which I gave the title "Willie Keith and May Wynn." It read, in part, as follows:

> May's time between shows was monopolized by Willie Keith. Usually they sat in the dressing room, smoking and talking—Willie, the educated authority, May half respectful and half satiric as the ignoramus. After a few evenings of this, Willie persuaded her to meet him by day. He took her to the Museum of Modern Art, but that was a failure. She stared in horror at the masterpieces of Dali, Chagall, and Tchelitchew, and burst out laughing. At the Metropolitan Museum they did better. She found an immediate deep pleasure in Renoir and El Greco. She made Willie take her there again (p. 19).

The strong story line and Wouk's easy and uncluttered style (the passage had a Fog Index of 10.21, in the bestseller range; see chapter 7) made this an appropriate text for assessing ludic reading speed.

The comprehension test was deliberately kept simple; for example:

May Wynn's feeling about modern art was
a. deep pleasure
b. respect
c. horror
d. don't know   a   b   c   d

This, and the use of only three substantive multiple-choice distractors, probably had the effect of inflating the scores of guessers. Percentage correct on the comprehension test was calculated on only that number of questions applicable to the amount read by each subject. Since ludic reading is response-free, an overcorrection for comprehension failure seemed undesirable. Raw speed was thus allowed to play the major role in determining the reading-comprehension-speed score, correcting this only marginally for comprehension by subtracting half the percentage error on the comprehension test from the reading speed in words per minute. Because of this correction, reading-comprehension speed is a quotient and not a reading speed in words per minute.

The Reading Habits Questionnaire began by defining pleasure reading—"the kind we do for fun and relaxation. Work reading, on the other hand, is done not for fun but for some purpose. So in the answers you give below, make sure you talk only about your own pleasure reading—the books you read for enjoyment." Then, respondents were asked to say how long they read at different times and in various places—after lunch, after dinner, in bed before going to sleep, or even in the bathroom, and to indicate at which of these times they most enjoyed their reading.

Then came a question which yielded some interesting correlations with book reading:

> Suppose that your favorite reading time has arrived—but you're staying at a strange hotel. Suddenly, you discover you have nothing to read.
> a. How would you feel?
> b. What would you do about it?

The two parts of the question were scored and summed to give what was termed a Frustration Index. Some of the answers to "a" were strongly emotive, such as "absolutely terrible" or "completely lost" and were scored 4. A score of 3 was given for moderate affect ("frustrated"; "disappointed and at a loss"); 2 for weak affect ("disappointed"; "bored"); and 1 for "don't care" answers. Question 3b, asking what the respondent would do to remedy the deprivation, was scored 3 for a determined search for reading matter ("scour the shops till I found a book"); 2 for some effort ("try to buy a book"); and 1 for doing nothing. In practice, these proved to be unambiguous criteria for converting a wide range of answers to numerical values.

Next came questions about book-reading quantity and about newspaper- and magazine-reading quantities and times. The last question was about the phenomenology of reading and generated the important self-report data reviewed in chapter 11:

> Think back to some books you have enjoyed very much. What kind of enjoyment do you get out of books like that? Write a few honest sentences about the rewards this kind of pleasure reading offers you. (Remember that this kind of reading has nothing to do with learning or improving the mind.)

Reading Speed and Reading Quantity

Table 5.1 shows that reading-comprehension speed is related to book-reading time and quantity, but not to non-book materials; it is also related to the Frustration Index.

The hypothesis that reading ability and the ludic reading habit are co-occurrences (without necessarily having a causal relationship) is confirmed by these findings. Certainly, the relatively high values of the correlation coefficients between ludic reading speed, book quantity, and especially book time indicate that reading-comprehension speed and book reading co-occur with such regularity that they may be considered to be predictors of one another. Since this may take place through an unidentified intervening variable, we cannot infer any causal relationship such that reading-comprehension speed leads to ludic reading. In-

Table 5.1. Reading Ability and Reading Habits

	Reading-comprehension speed	Frustration index	Total reading time	Book time	Magazine time	Newspaper time	Total reading quantity	Number of books	Number of magazines
Reading Accompaniments									
1. Reading-comprehension speed	1.0								
2. Frustration index	32**	1.0							
READING HABITS									
Reading time									
3. Total reading time	28**	29**	1.0						
4. Book time	37**	34***		1.0					
5. Magazine time	08	09		27**	1.0				
6. Newspaper time	01	11		30**	15	1.0			
Reading quantity									
7. Total reading quantity	33***	20*	57***	57***	36***	11	1.0		
8. Number of books	33***	21*	53***	59***	28**	05		1.0	
9. Number of magazines	08	−01	42***	17	55***	−01		26**	1.0
10. Number of newspapers	12	09	14	09	06	42***		20*	26**

Note: Decimals omitted; empty cells indicate the deletion of spurious correlations between variables with a large common variance.

*p < .05 **p < .01 ***p < .001.

deed, in Western society, in which reading is a common and early acquired skill, it is almost impossible to conduct a study in which age, education, and intelligence are held constant while reading ability is manipulated as the independent variable. Accordingly, it is necessary to make inferences about the likely consequences of greater or lesser reading ability by extrapolating from studies that are methodologically rather less than ideal.

To confirm the view that slower readers read newspapers and magazines rather than books, significant negative correlations between reading-comprehension speed and newspaper and magazine reading are needed. Instead, we have near-zero correlations which do not support this conclusion. Nonetheless, the possibility that newspapers and magazines are the refuge of slower readers cannot be dismissed in view of the lower intercorrelations between newspaper and magazine times and quantities than between either of these and book reading. This pattern suggests that book reading is not practiced by the same group of readers as non-book reading.

Frustration Index

The Frustration Index, as anticipated, is related to time spent reading books (though less strongly to book quantity) but is quite unrelated to newspaper and magazine reading. This may be interpreted to mean that newspaper and magazine readers are less dependent on their reading matter than book readers, who feel reading deprivation more keenly and take more vigorous action to end it. Perhaps the eighteenth- and nineteenth-century critics were correct when they compared novel-reading to tippling: novels are habit-forming while newspapers are not. The desolation some ludic readers feel when deprived of their reading matter is reviewed at the end of chapter 11.

An interesting speculation arises with regard to the somewhat higher correlation between frustration and book time (.34) than between frustration and book quantity (.21). This seems to indicate that slower readers, who need more time to read fewer books, are more heavily dependent on their reading than faster readers. This in turn brings to mind the observations made in chapters 6 and 11, that involved readers, who savor the text, are likely to be slower readers than reading addicts, who bolt their reading matter. Although the evidence is tenuous, the possibility that involved rather than addictive readers have a higher degree of dependence on their reading is intriguing.

6
Reading as Eating

In the course of his psychoanalytic study of literature, Norman Holland remarks that "of all the different levels of fantasy in literature, the oral is the most common" (1968, p. 38). Indeed, the metaphor of reading is replete with the imagery of mastication and ingestion: "I rolled a phrase on my tongue and it tasted better than the wine," writes Somerset Maugham (1934, p. 337), who, at that moment, was drinking a vintage red. Books can also taste bad: 'In some ways it's a horrible little book, like overbrewed tea" (T. E. Lawrence, in Cohen and Cohen, 1971). Critics have described themselves as "tasters to the public," in the course of which occupation they encounter "many a nauseous mess" (Taylor, 1943, p. 41). Novel-writing is likened to the making of "intellectual gingerbread," and novelists to pastry-cooks: "Whether they are in the shape of a king, a queen, or a cuckold, they still consist of flour, water, brown sugar or treacle" (Taylor, 1943, pp. 45–46).

As books taste, so are they eaten: Hilgard (1979, p. 33) remarks that the involved reader savors the text, moving slowly to get its full richness. My own observation is that hungrier readers may bolt their reading as a dog does its food, tasting little but enjoying the sensation of fullness. Readers' self-descriptions, as well as the language of critics, abound with oral-incorporative imagery: readers are said to devour books, to consume them, to gobble them up greedily, to swallow them whole, and, perhaps, to digest them.

Readers themselves describe their reading in oral terms (see chapter 11). Indeed, the greed and avidity attributed there to Type A readers calls to mind the unkind metaphor of a glutton at a gourmet meal, cheeks bulging with successive mouthfuls of caviar, rare roast beef, and crème caramel, too busy eating to taste the food. However, swallowing chunks of text whole is by no means restricted to one kind of reader; the freedom reading offers to skim the duller passages and to savor the crises may be enjoyed as much by involved as by escapist readers. Within-text flexibility makes skimming, bolting, gobbling, and savoring possible.

A curious observation comes to mind in this context. Savoring a phrase to get its flavor involves a substantial reading-rate reduction. Perhaps as reading rate drops, subvocalization routines appear, as in Brown's (1981) model of the reading process, or as an aid to comprehension (Pauk, 1981). This motor activity of the articulatory-masticatory apparatus (that mimics eating) may further heighten the reader's enjoyment. As with a morsel, so with a phrase: rolling it on the tongue for longer than mastication requires extracts its full flavor and nutritive value.

READING-RATE FLEXIBILITY

Flexible reading is sometimes used as a synonym for reading maturity, which can mean almost anything, and sometimes to denote a reader's voluntary variation in reading rate in response to a change in either the readability level of the text or the reader's purpose in reading. Clearly, both circumstances may apply to a single text by the same author or to different texts: the former is called within-text and the latter between-text flexibility (or internal and external flexibility). Some of the problems in defining flexibility arise from failure to specify what kind of flexibility is in question. There are also methodological problems. Converse (1978) writes that although reading flexibility is a term that has been used in the literature for over fifty years, no satisfactory test has been devised to measure it.

Although readability levels may change dramatically within a text (for example, when an author moves from the concrete to the abstract, as in the transition from description to conceptualization), readability-level changes are more usually associated with movement from one text to another, and we shall consider between-text flexibility as the adaptation to differing levels of readability, abstraction and so forth. Tinker, for example, describes the mature reader as one who passes easily from one reading task to another, "almost automatically choosing the proper attack in each of the content subjects" (1965, p. 49).

For the student of ludic reading, rate variations within the same text are of considerably greater interest than between-text variations because the vehicle for most ludic reading is long continuous texts, often produced by formula writers who pride themselves on maintaining a uniform level of stylistic ease (even among mimetic writers, marked readability variations within a single composition are unusual). Accordingly, rate variations in ludic reading are likely to be purely voluntary adjustments, unconstrained by textually imposed processing requirements. If the within-passage reading rate of ludic readers shows spontaneous variation, these changes are in some way likely to be related to reading enjoyment.

Reading-rate flexibility does in fact enhance the hedonic value of the ludic reader's experience. First, spontaneous rate variations—lingering over the hero's arrival at police headquarters, racing through a beautiful sunset after the murder—are likely to increase the reader's sense of internal control. Reading is after all the only mass media entertainment input that is wholly user-controlled, whereas the presentation pace of storytellers, audiotapes, and movies is controlled by the producer of the material.

Moreover, the vocabulary many readers use to describe their reading experience is strongly oral—savoring a sentence or paragraph, relishing the flavor of prose, and returning to a delightful passage to digest it more fully. With reading rate flexibility, this kind of enjoyment (whether it be regarded in terms of psychoanalysis or locus of control) would not be possible.

Second, because slow reading is incompatible with ludic reading and comprehension processes are severely impaired at speeds above 800 or 900 w.p.m., it seems likely that reading rate is related to reading enjoyment by the inverted U-shape familiar from motivational studies. In other words, reading enjoyment peaks at moderate speeds and drops off as reading rates approach the very low and very high extremes.

A convenient method of expressing the degree of flexibility attained by a given reader is as a ratio, calculated by using the slowest speed as the denominator and the fastest as the numerator. A useful study along these lines was undertaken by Thompson and Whitehill (1970), who derived flexibility ratios for a group of sixty-four students by asking them to scan a passage of fiction (numerator) and then to read a different fiction passage (denominator). Low flexibles were then defined as those with ratios of 2:1 or less, and high flexibles as between 6:1 and 9:1. The latter were then shown to have the highest percentage of speed gains in a reading-improvement course, leading the authors to suggest that flexibility is a better measure of reading efficiency than speed. These results are not inconsistent with Carver's recent findings (1982, 1983) in support of his rauding theory, which states that when task demands are held constant, reading rate is constant for readily comprehended material at varying levels of difficulty. Although these flexibility ratios are interesting, scanning is not reading, and flexibility ratios derived from scanning speed should not be generalized to other reading situations.

However, there are few studies of within-passage flexibility by skilled readers reading under natural conditions (three essential conditions if comparisons are to be made with ludic reading). Eanet and Meeks (1979) claim to have studied three proficient readers in a natural setting, finding that on textbook material, internal flexibility ranged from 17 to 69 percent with a mean flexibility for the three subjects of 23 percent on a history passage and 55 percent on a science passage (no readability figures are quoted in the abstract). Even the highest of these flexibilities (69 percent) converts to a ratio of less than 2:1, which appears to be low.

The requirement for naturalistic observation of within-text reader behavior seems to be most elegantly met by eye-movement studies. Rayner's (1978) finding that reader purpose affects fixation duration and saccade length has already been noted. Moreover, for the same reader on a single text, "saccade lengths often range from 2 to 18 character positions and more, and fixation duration values from 100 to over 500 milliseconds *for a single reader within a single passage*" (p. 620; my emphasis). These data support a 9.1 flexibility ratio for natural reading. Just and Carpenter's (1980) gaze-duration data show that content words within a single sentence are fixated for between 267 and 1,566 milliseconds, a ratio of 6:1. Although caution is clearly required in extrapolating from data at this level of microanalysis to reading rates measured in words per minute (and not in milliseconds per word!), it seems likely that the origins of whatever within-text flexibility ludic readers are shown to have is at the individual letter and word level of processing.

These findings run counter to Huey's observation that a group of readers "showed a strong rhythmic tendency. Each would fall into a reading pace that seemed most natural to him, and would then read page after page in almost exactly the same time. Quite usually the differences from page to page would not be over three or four seconds" (1908, p. 175). Indeed, it seems more likely that skilled readers reading under natural conditions vary their attack so radically that in some sections of the same passage they literally savor their reading, dropping to very low rates, and in others they spontaneously move over to skimming at rates in excess of the 800 w.p.m. maximum for true reading. Fortunately, there are some data to support this prediction.

READING-RATE VARIABILITY DURING NATURAL LUDIC READING

How fast do ludic readers read during natural ludic reading—that is, when they are reading purely for their own pleasure—and how much rate variability is there during natural ludic reading? The laboratory experiment described in chapter 9 provided an ideal opportunity to answer these questions—that is, of course, if we can show that reading in the laboratory was experienced by the ludic readers as equivalent to natural ludic reading situations.

Most of the thirty-three subjects in the laboratory study responded to a small, single-column advertisement that appeared in a local newspaper:

BOOKWORMS REQUIRED

If you read a lot of light fiction and enjoy it very much, please volunteer to advance the cause of science! We need additional subjects for a laboratory study we are making of the effect fiction has on people to whom reading is an important pleasure.

If you are a fiction addict, please telephone us. We'll ask you to come to our laboratory in the Unisa Building for two sessions. You'll read a book of your choice while we record your reactions. Moreover, you'll be paid R6.00 a session. Applicants must be between 20 and 50 years old.

Seventeen subjects were chosen from the forty-nine who responded—with enormous eagerness—to this advertisement. I recruited sixteen others among colleagues, friends, and friends of friends. There were nineteen women and fourteen men, all of whom read at least a book a week for pleasure and relaxation. The mean age of subjects was 37.2 with a standard deviation of 9.7. No criteria were set for the language spoken at home, educational level, or reading preferences, on the ground that individuals who read a great deal for pleasure must find reading in English a rewarding experience. This in turn, as our ludic reading flowchart (figure 12.1) makes clear, presupposes adequate reading skills in English and a high level of positive reinforcement from reading.

Most subjects exceeded the minimum pleasure-reading criterion by a wide margin. The owner of a book exchange said she read two books a day and more on weekends, giving a total of some sixteen a week, or seventy a month. Another volunteer claimed that he, his wife, and their two daughters each read one book every weekday and two a day on weekends, giving a weekly total of nine, or thirty-nine per month for each of the four (this extraordinary family is discussed in some detail in chapter 11).

The purpose of the payment to subjects (which worked out at the derisory sum of about $1.25 per hour) was not so much to remunerate them as to give them the role of laboratory employees. In fact, the letter of instruction to subjects served as an appointment to the laboratory "job":

Thank you for volunteering to be a subject in our study of reading.

In volunteering, you undertake to make yourself available to us at the times stipulated below for two to three hours per session. Please withdraw now if you feel unable to give us this much time, since data from single-session subjects will be useless to us.

Your payment cheque will be posted to you after the experiment.

Only two of the subjects failed to appear during the forty-day period over which testing took place, and one canceled. The others arrived promptly for both sessions, armed with their carefully selected books and considerable enthusiasm. In the same letter, the important question of book choice was dealt with as follows:

Please come to the first laboratory session with THREE English-language fiction books you have not read before and that you are enjoying very much. In the laboratory, we'll ask you to continue reading these books, and it is important that they be:
- very enjoyable for you
- of the same kind of fiction that you normally read for relaxation.

If you read a lot of detectives or Westerns, bring three of them with you— *NOT* a tome on Minoan civilisation or a novel you've been trying to read for years!

In order to choose these books, please follow the procedure below:

Please go to your library or to a big book exchange on, or as near as possible to, the following date [seven days prior to the first laboratory session]. Choose five English-language fiction books of the kind you usually read and that you think you will enjoy reading very much. Don't rush!—give yourself enough time to choose carefully.

Take the books home and start reading. If you come to a section after the first 50 pages that you find very satisfying (gripping, exciting, relaxing or strongly rewarding in some other way), STOP READING! Mark the place carefully and bring the book with you to your first session.

If you find the book dull or disappointing, put it aside and try another. Carry on till you have stopped somewhere after page 50 in THREE books that you regard as offering the best reads you have had for some time.

Natural Ludic Reading and Reading in the Laboratory

During the intake interview, a Reading Mood Questionnaire that contained a detailed set of questions about reading enjoyment was administered. Subjects gave each of the three books they had read an enjoyment rating that was anchored to a "best book" question:

Think of the most enjoyable reading experience you've had during the past year or two. Take your time, and when you feel ready, tell me the title of the book. Don't answer till you feel sure you have identified the book that gave you your most enjoyable reading experience.

I then asked subjects to tell me about an especially vivid episode in the book that they still remembered with particular clarity; that episode in the specified book was given an "enjoyment rating" of 100 percent. In this way, generalizations were avoided, and reading pleasure was linked to very clear and specific memories. The enjoyment-rating scale was then elaborated by asking subjects to give the average enjoyment rating for their reading over the past year and then to rate a very recent much-enjoyed book.

For example, a twenty-four-year-old laboratory technician at a veterinary research institute picked James Herriot's *All Creatures Great and Small* as her most enjoyed book and gave her 100-percent rating to an episode in which the vet "finds it's true that the car has no brakes." Her most-enjoyed recent book was *Crimson Chalice* by Victor Canning, in which she gave a 70-percent enjoyment rating to the description of King Arthur's birth. Another subject rated an episode in Mary Stewart's *Nine Coaches Waiting* in which the heroine is sewing a dress when the hero walks in at 100 percent, and gave a 75-percent enjoyment rating to Dorothy Sayers' description of the discovery of a body crawling with cockroaches at the foot of a stairway.

With this rating system in mind, subjects could predict their enjoyment of each of the three books they had brought to the laboratory. For example, the yound lady who loved animals read *Vet in Harness*, to which she had given an anticipatory 90-percent rating, in the first laboratory session, and Peter Brown's *Uncle Whiskers*, from which she expected 95-percent enjoyment, in the second. In fact, after the second laboratory session, she increased this to 100 percent for the passage she liked best, in which the feline hero proudly brings its first rat kill to its master. Her next-most-enjoyed episode was Whiskers' victory over a rabbit twice its size; the response of many of my readers to these peak experiences in a cat's life is not likely to be enthusiastic, bearing out the view that one reader's ludic vehicle is likely to end up in another's garbage pail.

The lowest-rated of the three books was returned to the subject, the most highly rated was put aside for reading during the second laboratory session (which was recorded for later data analysis), and the book with the middle rating was used in the first, unrecorded session. The place the subject had stopped reading while "trying out" the book—usually about page 50—was marked in pencil, and the book was kept open at that page.

One of the striking differences among subjects was in how easy or difficult they found it to give examples of books and episodes in each of the five categories specified in the Reading Mood Questionnaire (best book, best recent book, book read under distracting circumstances, dull book, and book read for work). For some readers, this information was so accessible that they hardly knew whether to give episode or title first; others could scarcely remember the content, let alone the title or author, of books they had read a week or two before. The former are probably the involved savorers and the latter the escapist readers—or, to use the terms proposed in chapter 11, Type B and Type A readers, respectively. These two kinds of reader also differ quite markedly in their memory strategies (see chapter 12).

Next, the intriguing question of reading effortlessly while engulfed in tumult was explored:

> Here is a method of rating how distracting your surroundings are while you are reading. 0% means complete absence of distracting outside influences, while 100% is the level of distraction you would experience if you were trying to read in a boarding school dormitory on a rainy Sunday afternoon with children shouting and fighting in every corner.
>
> What distractibility rating would you give to the reading location you have just described? (Please remember that the question refers to what was going on around you, not inside your head, because some readers are able to concentrate absolutely even in the worst conditions.)

The mean distractibility rating of all subjects for this setting was 62.5 percent (S.D. = 24.8). Subjects were then asked to specify a book they had recently read under dreadful conditions (one subject said two cats had been mating on a tin roof just above her head!) and to give an enjoyment rating to a remembered episode in that book.

After the second laboratory session, subjects were asked:

> How do you rate the laboratory setting for distractibility as it was today during your 30-minute reading period—not before it or after it? You remember the scale we used? Nil percent was complete absence of outside distractions, and 100% was a crowded boarding school dormitory on a rainy Sunday afternoon, with children fighting in every corner.
>
> Remember two things: you are rating distractions in the environment, not your awareness or unawareness of them; secondly, you are rating the laboratory *only* during your reading period.

Surprisingly, the laboratory, at 15.2 percent (S.D. = 14.1), was rated much less distracting than the bad setting outside the laboratory ($t = 9.52, p < .001$), despite the television cameras, mirrors, observation windows, electrodes, and noisy loudspeakers that were part of the lab environment. Similarly, in rating their *awareness* of distractions in the laboratory and outside it there was a signficant 4.2 difference ($t = 2.83, p < .01$) in favor of lesser awareness of the distractions in the laboratory. To a significant extent, these favorable laboratory ratings may arise from the fact that the laboratory was rated for the second of the two laboratory sessions (see chapter 9), by which time a great deal of habituation to the novel setting had taken place.

These and other comparisons the subjects made between reading in the laboratory and under natural conditions indicate that ludic reading in the laboratory was perceived as natural ludic reading. For example, the book read in the laboratory was enjoyed an average of only 3.4 percent less than the most-enjoyed book that had been recently read and 9.7 percent more than the book read under distracting circumstances (all differences are statistically non-significant). Perceived involvement in the laboratory book was marginally higher than it had been in the book read under distracting circumstances. Accordingly, despite the unusual and apparently stressful circumstances in the laboratory, reading was nonetheless experienced as equivalent to natural ludic reading. To paraphrase a sentence from Klinger (1971, p. 7): if different activities feel the same, they are the same. Furthermore, there are no methodological reasons for questioning the comparability of laboratory reading to natural reading, since instructions to the subject emphasized reading for pleasure, reading was response-free, and the book was freely chosen by the subject as a ludic vehicle.

Measuring Laboratory Reading Speed

During the thirty-minute ludic reading period in the laboratory (and indeed for the duration of the ninety-minute laboratory session), the subject was alone in the laboratory, reclining against pillows on a bed in the laboratory so that his or her body was at an angle of approximately 45 degrees to the bed. The subject's back was to a one-way observation window, through which the page numbers of the book being read were clearly visible. At the beginning of the session, a mirror was placed to the subject's left and adjusted so that the experimenter was able to see the subject's eyes reflected in the mirror. The completion of a left-hand page was signaled by an unmistakable upward eye movement that brought the subject's gaze from the bottom of the left-hand page to the top of the right-hand page; completion of right-hand pages was of course indicated by page-turning. It was accordingly possible to monitor the subject's page-by-page progress by noting the times of left- and right-hand page completions. The time of each page turning was recorded by noting the reading on the electronic tape counter on the sixteen-channel tape used in the laboratory. This very accurate counter gave a resolution of 6.4 seconds, rather better than the ten-second resolution available from the pulse generator also in use during recording. However, because of this fairly wide resolution, an error factor of some 10 percent should be allowed for in the mean speeds cited for laboratory reading. Because ludic reading is response-free, it was not possible to test for comprehension, which would have created an attentional set incompatible with ludic reading. Accordingly, all laboratory reading speeds are uncorrected and expressed in words per minute.

Table 6.1.   Reading Speed across Subjects, Time, and Conditions

Group	Reading-comprehension speed (w.p.m.)	S.D.
On Reading-Comprehension-Speed Test		
1. 129 student subjects	238	71
2. Fastest students (34 university English females)	254	
3. Slowest students (19 college Afrikaans males)	175	
4. 29 ludic readers	387	121
Longitudinal stability		
6. 27 student subjects in 1976	277	83
7. Same subjects in 1978	321	117
Ludic readers in the laboratory		
5. 28 readers' mean speed on 837 pages	412	
6. Fastest laboratory reader	921	
7. Slowest laboratory reader	174	

Reading-Speed Variability across Subjects

Table 6.1 gives the reading speeds of various subject groups and individuals, either as reading-comprehension-speed quotients or as speeds in words per minute.

Several matters of interest emerge with regard to the Reading Comprehension Speed Test. The first is that it does a good job of predicting mean natural reading speed. On the test, the twenty-nine ludic readers read at a mean speed of 387; in the laboratory, they read at 412 w.p.m. (r (27) = .65, p < .001). Indeed, had the laboratory speed been corrected for comprehension, it would quite likely have been nearly identical to the test reading-comprehension speed of 387. Next, the ludic readers read significantly faster than the student subjects (t (156) = 6.38, p < .001). Finally, it is interesting that reading-comprehension speed appears to be quite stable longitudinally. Though the reading-comprehension speed of the twenty-seven follow-up students is higher after two years of university study by some 17 percent, the difference is not significant (t (52) = 1.60). This finding is in itself of interest, and, though no claims can be made on the basis of a single small-scale study, there is an indication here that reading skills may, at least for some students, be quite fully developed at the university-entrance level.

Table 6.2 indicates that there are substantial differences among individual ludic readers; the laboratory reading speed of the slowest reader stands to that of the fastest in a 5:1 ratio. The curious fact that the slowest reader read at only 60 percent of his tested reading-comprehension speed

Table 6.2.   Reading-Comprehension Speeds, Laboratory Reading Speeds, and Flexibility Ratios

Subject[a]	Reading-comprehension speed	Mean lab speed	N (pages)	w.p.m. High	w.p.m. Low	Ratio high/low
202	281	345	19	420	229	1.83
203	521	543	39	735	396	1.85
204	340	289	22	430	215	2.00
205	314	267	23	394	201	1.96
206	—	456	30	868	261	3.32
107	378	375	24	463	304	1.52
208	348	344	25	697	246	2.83
209	493	420	28	714	293	2.43
111	—	492	32	922	189	4.87
112	582	598	47	1,071	363	2.95
113	283	397	28	593	312	1.90
214	314	356	22	486	181	2.68
215	331	329	22	424	238	1.78
116	388	312	28	485	198	2.44
118	695	794	58	1,824	234	7.79
119	399	350	19	442	294	1.50
220	472	921	62	2,214	457	4.84
221	261	316	25	489	269	1.81
222	364	365	26	606	243	2.49
223	247	386	27	655	202	3.24
124	536	427	28	1,033	283	5.08
226	310	380	20	536	306	1.75
127	412	550	48	835	361	2.31
228	—	294	19	461	210	2.19
129	290	174	9	211	129	1.63
230	244	384	16	283	656	2.31
132	537	376	32	232	589	2.53
133	203	366	20	258	516	2.00
234	311	439	25	470	320	1.46
236	201	216	17	196	115	1.70

[a]Complete reading speed data are available for 30 subjects. The first digit of the subject number indicates sex (2 for females, 1 for males). The second and third digits give laboratory sequence. Thus, subject 101, a male, was the first to be run, and 236, a female, the last (3 subjects canceled after they had been allocated numbers).

in the laboratory whereas most of the other ludic readers read faster in the laboratory (table 6.2) has a straightforward explanation. The book that subject chose was *The Master of Go,* a complex account of a tournament between two masters of this extraordinarily protracted Japanese game of skill. Under the circumstances, his reading speed is quite high!

Some of the permutations of reading speed and reading rate variability are shown in figures 6.1 and 6.2. Figure 6.1 shows strikingly high flexibility coupled with high reading speed. Indeed, the 5:1 ratio between the mean speed of the slowest and fastest readers (table 5.1) reappears in the within-passage flexibility of this reader, who moved between a speed of 2,214 w.p.m. for p.87 and 457 w.p.m. for one of the pages he liked best, page 114 (4.84:1). Figure 6.2, on the other hand, shows a far lower variability ratio (2.95:1), though the mean reading speed of 598 w.p.m. is high, showing that high variability is not a necessary accompaniment of high speed. On the other hand, slow readers do show less within-text flexibility than fast readers. Thus, for the five subjects who read at speeds lower than 300 w.p.m., the mean flexibility ratio is 1.89, well below the sample mean of 2.63.

The mean flexibility ratio of 2.63 for the thirty-three readers is considerably below the 6:1 to 9:1 ratio suggested by the eye-movement studies of Rayner (1978) and Just and Carpenter (1980) cited above. But there is a great deal of difference between word- and phrase-fixation times, on which their findings are based, and per-page reading times, in which these differences are absorbed and will tend to average out. Though only one of the readers fell into the 6:1 to 9:1 range, twelve ratios are between 2 and 3, and six are more than 3, indicating flexibility ratios in excess of 2:1 for most ludic readers in our sample.

Most-Liked and Other Pages

Do readers in fact read most-liked passages more slowly than other passages in order to savor them? A question in the Reading Mood Questionnaire asked the reader to identify the most-liked passages in the book read in the laboratory, so that a reading speed for most-liked and all other pages could be computed for each subject. To avoid contamination, both most-liked and next-most-liked pages were excluded from computation of the mean of the remaining pages.

For the twenty-nine subjects for whom complete data were available, mean reading speed on the 113 pages they specified as most liked was 394 w.p.m. (S.D. = 140), and on the 634 other pages (excluding both most-liked and next-most-liked pages) their mean reading speed was 479 w.p.m. (S.D. = 245). In other words, most-liked pages were read, on average, at 85 w.p.m. more slowly than all other pages; this difference is significant (t (56) = -3.55, $p < .01$). Though enough self-report data is available to determine whether or not savoring occurred, the precondition for savoring—that is, slowing down significantly on passages one especially enjoys—was demonstrated. Again, because of data-gathering limitations, it is impossible to say whether this slowing takes place because of regressions (in which the favored passage is reread

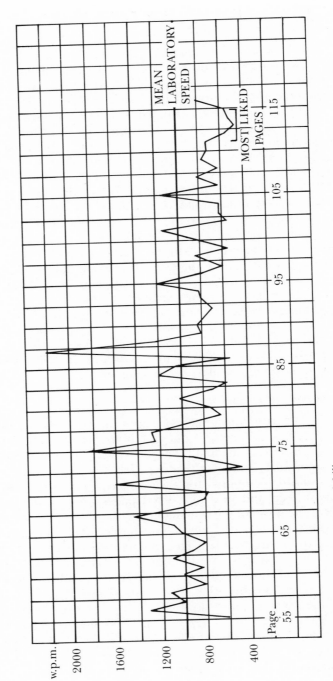

Figure 6.1. High Speed, High Variability

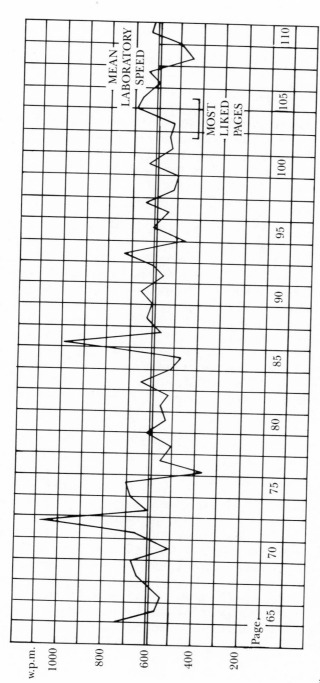

Figure 6.2. High Speed, Low Variability

once or more), an actual slowing of reading speed, or a mixture of the two.

Finally, the standard deviation reported for the most-liked pages (140) is almost half that for the other pages (245). It seems possible that much of the ludic reader's within-passage flexibility arises from moving into skimming or near-skimming for less-enjoyed passages. If, as seems likely, this ceased when savoring, the lower variability of reading speed in most-liked passages would be explained.

CONCLUSIONS

Self-report evidence suggests that despite the physical constraints and the intrusive novelty of the apparatus, television cameras, and background noise in the laboratory, ludic reading in this setting was perceived as equivalent to a natural reading experience. Since everyday observation indicates that ludic reading can take place under the most unlikely circumstances of discomfort and distraction, it seems reasonable to accept the subjects' self-reports as accurate and to regard laboratory reading as natural reading.

Second, the high variability in natural reading speed allows us to conclude that there is now at least prima facie evidence for the view that pace control is one of the reader's reward systems, and that such terms as savoring, bolting, and their equivalents are not only metaphors for the way text is consumed but also accurate descriptions of how skilled readers read.

The third broad conclusion relates to the validity of our Reading Comprehension Speed Test. We have found that this test does effectively predict mean speeds during natural reading and that it has a degree of stability over time. However, in view of the reading-speed-flexibility evidence we have produced, we are forced to conclude that measures of reading speed are poor predictors of how fast a reader will read a given page or paragraph during ludic reading: our group of subjects shows that this speed may vary by a mean factor of 2.63:1 during a half hour of reading and go as high as 5 or 7 to 1 for some readers.

Although the usefulness of statistical means arises, at least in part, through the obscuring of individual differences, this usefulness must be called into question when what is obscured, in the individual or a population, is very striking: this failing is only partially redressed by giving the standard deviation. For example, we would be startled to discover that an athlete ran the 100 meters at an average time of 9.3 seconds over four races if he completed two of them at 200 miles an hour and two at a slow walk. The performance of Subject 118, who read a page at 1,800 w.p.m. and another at 200 w.p.m. for an average speed of 794 w.p.m., is also extraordinary. We must conclude, therefore, that the validity claims of reading-speed measures should be tempered by including statements of natural speed variations. Moreover, effective reading certainly does not mean reading a passage at a steady pace: both here and in chapter 5, we have produced considerable evidence that a steady pace is most uncharacteristic of skilled or enjoyable reading.

7
Matching Books
to Readers

Now that we know something about reading skill and comprehension processes, we can return to the unanswered question raised earlier: what is the outcome of the conflicting forces acting on the reader's choice of reading matter? On the one hand, elite culture (supported by other powerful social forces) propels the reader toward the selection of "a good book," while readers themselves seem rather to be inclined toward "a good read." Publishers stake their fortunes on predicting reader preferences; at the same time, the entire ludic reading enterprise rests on the reader's success in selecting a book that will in fact prove to be ludic for that reader.

Two sets of experiments were conducted to find out more about the ways in which publishers and readers make these choices. First, 187 subjects from many different walks of life were asked to rank extracts from books in sequence from the one they would most like to curl up with and read to the one they would least like to read for pleasure. Then, the readability of the same thirty extracts was ranked by using two representative kinds of readability measure.

THE READABILITY CONSTRUCT

Readability measures try to match texts to readers by determining reader interest, on the one hand, and text difficulty, on the other: it is the interplay of these two variables that determines the reader's choice of ludic vehicle. A successful choice sets in motion an interaction rewarding enough to be sustained for long periods. The constraints operating on this choice are partly social (values) and partly cognitive (comprehension). Accordingly, it is important to know whether or not readability measures can predict reader interest and text difficulty and can there-

114

fore enable us to match texts to readers. As we shall see, the effort is great but the illumination scant. But we shall have to devote a good deal of space to showing that this is indeed so—because of the promise held out by the early readability enterprise, the great body of research relating to issues that concern us, and the links between readability and comprehension studies.

These concerns are reflected in the widely quoted definition of readability by Dale and Chall (1949): "In the broadest sense, readability is the sum total (including the interactions) of all those elements within a given piece of printed material that affects the success a group of readers have with it. The success is the extent to which they understand it, read it at an optimum speed, and find it interesting" (p. 23). At the heart of this construct is the matching of texts to readers. To determine how successfully the match has been made, this particular definition requires us to measure the reader's comprehension, reading rate, and interest. "Success" is the outcome of readability, not readability itself.

This technical sense of readability is very close to its original dictionary sense; since 1570, it has meant capable of being read or legible, and since 1826, it has been used in the sense of something that one reads with pleasure or interest (Oxford, 1933b). Klare (1963) notes that readability is used to mean *legibility*, due to either the interest value or the pleasantness of the writing, *ease of reading* and *ease of understanding* or comprehension due to the style of writing. These are of course commonsense requirements for any kind of successful reading, and reading researchers generally agree that these are the bases both of reading and of readability measurement (Chall, 1958; Gilliland, 1972; Tinker, 1965). Until recently, readability studies were more concerned with ease of reading (pleasantness) than with ease of understanding (comprehension).

The study of readability was an outgrowth of the spread of education, of reading, and, ultimately, of democracy. Propagandists and educators wanted their written messages to make the greatest impression on intended audiences and seized on whatever means were available in psychology and pedagogy to predict the likely impact of a particular message on a given audience (Harris and Jacobson, 1979). The term *readability* in its technical sense cannot be located in the literature until the 1930s (see Dale and Chall's bibliography, 1949, pp. 175–89); but although early studies of readability do not go under that name, they cast a useful light on the topics of interest to us.

Rubakin's Bibliopsychology

The most important early study is that of Nikolai Rubakin (1862–1946), a hugely erudite Russian revolutionary and propagandist who has been described as "the last of the encyclopaedists" (Simsova, 1968, p. 61) and who quotes extensively from Wundt, Ebbinghaus, and Jung. In the 1920s, Rubakin launched an extraordinary psychological enterprise: through his own creation—the science of bibliopsychology—he planned to achieve a classification that would perfectly match books and readers:

> We are certain that all printed books will eventually bear on their title page an indication of their bibliopsychological classification. A parallel classification of books and readers ensures a compatible book for everyone. . . . It follows, then, that libraries should offer each reader in each subject a selection of books corresponding as nearly as possible to his psychological type, and make them easily accessible (Rubakin and Bethmann, 1937, p. 20).

The impetus for this project derived from Rubakin's life work, the education of the Russian peasantry, 80 percent of whom were illiterate in the late nineteenth century. He himself wrote 280 books and pamphlets on every branch of science, in a style of exemplary lucidity that became known as "Rubakin's language," and reportedly prepared individual reading programs (based on his 24,000-title booklist, *Among Books*) for 15,000 correspondents (Simsova, 1968, pp. 61–62).

Rubakin's work has not been assimilated in Western studies of readability; he gains passing mention, as compiler of a word-frequency list, in Klare (1963), and none in other reviews (Dale and Chall, 1949; Harris and Jacobson, 1981). Both because he is so little known and because the goals he set himself were so lofty, his method deserves examination.

Reading is an interaction among author, reader, the book itself, and the environment (Rubakin and Bethman, 1937). Accordingly, the book is perceived differently by every reader: "In our view, when the book is being read *it is a subjective psychological phenomenon* based on impressions which the reader's psychophysical organism receives from it as an external object. Should the reader's organism undergo some change (through illness, aging, etc.) the same book would seem very different to him. Therefore, the book in itself, as a phenomenon independent of the viewer, is an unknown entity" (1937, p. 11; italics in original). Rubakin's position in assigning sovereignty to the reader rather than to the text is no less radical than that of Stanley Fish's reader-centered criticism (chapter 2). Indeed, a contemporary attacked Rubakin's relativism as undermining his own valuable contributions to "scientific methods of agitation and propaganda": "You deafen the reader with innumerable proofs that the book is in general a myth, a fiction, that cognition of the book is an absolute impossibility, . . . that the human "I" is doomed to absolute solitude" (Karpinskii, 1923, in Simsova, 1968, p. 54).

In describing the processes by which the reader attributes meaning to the book, Rubakin develops a model of comprehension closer to current cognitive psychology than to the behaviorism that dominated experimental psychology in the 1920s. Perceptions, argues Rubakin, leave traces called *engrams* in our organic matter, the sum total of which becomes our *mnema,* or memory store. Primary engrams are the mark left by reality while secondary engrams are fictitious constructions, which comprise the great bulk of each person's knowledge. Bringing an engram back to life from the mnema is called *ecphory,* from the Greek, meaning to draw out (Rubakin and Bethmann, 1937, pp. 11–12): "It is obvious that if some engrams are lacking, their ecphory is impossible. . . . Readers lacking certain engrams cannot appreciate a book which to others would seem remarkable, interesting and clear. A lack of essential primary and secondary engrams in the reader's consciousness is one of the greatest obstacles to the spread of knowledge and the development of intellect" (p. 13). This is Rubakin's core statement on comprehension, from which he proceeds to an analysis of reader interests based on a psychological classification of readers by type, "defined by a set of mental states called up more easily than others by a given text" (p. 15). This typology draws heavily on Jung's *Personality Types* (1923) and classifies readers as analytical or synthetic, rational or irrational, subjective or objective, and so on.

The final step, accurately matching books to readers, is achieved through the "special method of bibliopsychology" (Rubakin, 1921). From the seven "elementary formations" which he attributes to Ebbinghaus (ideas, images, sensations, emotions, volitions, instincts, and actions), Rubakin derives detailed descriptions. Under "images," for example, he lists general images of concrete ideas, psychological phenomena of the inner world, material objects, individual representations, and so forth. The reader then reads a given text and, for each word, records every category evoked by that word. "Powerful," for example, evokes a category under the head of volitions, another under emotions, a third under ideas. By totaling the category scores of every word in the passage the reader has read and repeating this for a number of readers of the same text, Rubakin is able to produce the result shown in figure 7.1. The broken line gives the mean category scores for a number of readers, showing that this particular reader (solid line) responds most to ideas and rather less to images; though he is emotional, the book has not stimulated his volition. "Further study will enable us to measure bibliopsychological coefficients and the variations in their amplitude within each type more accurately" (Rubakin, 1921, p. 46), and to this end Rubakin compiled an eighty-item questionnaire called "Reader Know Thyself" (Simsova, 1968, pp. 47–53), from which preliminary profiles of a reader's interests could be compiled.

Modern comprehension theory, as we have seen, operates at the sentence or discourse level rather than at the word level, which, probably influenced by Ebbinghaus' work on memory and Jung's association stud-

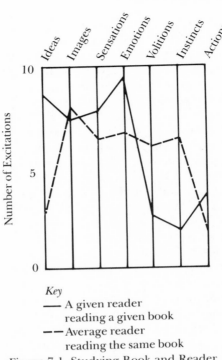

Key

—— A given reader
    reading a given book
– – Average reader
    reading the same book

Figure 7.1. Studying Book and Reader
Simultaneously

ies, Rubakin preferred for his analyses. The reductionism this engenders makes the value of his contribution doubtful. It is however unfortunate that his work, with its important emphasis on reader needs and interests, has until recently, when translations became available, been unknown in the West. Whether his enterprise is fundamentally feasible or is condemned to failure, both because of the relativism he himself emphasized so strongly and by virtue of his now untenable associationist view of comprehension, are questions we shall try to resolve in the discussion that follows.

We now consider in turn the three areas that constitute the domain of readability: legibility, reader interest, and comprehension.

LEGIBILITY

A type-specimen page produced by Erhard Ratdolt and dated Augsburg, April 1486 (Steinberg, 1955, plate 3) shows how very little the appearance of printed books has changed during the five centuries since the invention of printing. Ratholdt's roman type (as distinct from the gothic style) is still with us today, unchanged except for the shape of the letter *s* and the use today of fewer ligatures (a stroke connecting two letters, such as *fi*, or two letters combined as one, as *ae*). Lettering has always been black on white, lines have always marched down the page between white margins in orderly left-and-right-justified form, and letter spacing has been proportionate, with *m* and *w* occupying far more space than their emaciated fellows *i* and *l*. These conventions have survived both the nineteenth-century typesetting revolution that saw the introduction of mechanized composition and the twentieth-century revolution in printing techniques, in which photographically prepared lithographic plates have almost entirely supplanted the traditional letterpress printing developed in Gutenberg's day, which uses raised wooden or metal type. This extraordinary stability of print conventions, when considered together with the unchanging nature of perception physiology, combined to make Tinker's *Legibility of Print* (1963) appear to be the last word on the subject.

However, the technological innovations of the past decade or two have raised a multitude of new issues in legibility. These include new typesetting and reproduction methods within traditional printing, cathode-ray-tube displays in conjunction with word-processing systems and data banks, non-traditional type styles consequent on computer-generated printing, and the design requirements of magnetic and optical character recognition systems. All, in some measure, have affected the legibility of ludic reading matter or are likely to do so in unpredictable ways in the foreseeable future, thus creating new and urgent priorities for this area of readability research.

Lithographic printing has encouraged the development of typewriter-based typesetting. Ordinary typewriters, producing unjustified material (that is, copy with a "ragged" right-hand margin), can be used to "typeset" entire books (for example, Riesen and Thompson, 1976), but more typically proportional-spacing machines that produce right-justified text are used. Spacing between letters and words is less finely controlled by the typewriter than in traditional typesetting, so that letters may be fractionally displaced to the left or right to create the illusion of a word space, thus compelling the reader's eye to make an unnecessary regression; corrections (pasted in by hand) may be misaligned or leave page-wide shadows, causing additional regressions. Cheap printing masters produced by photocopying techniques produce poorly defined and low-contrast copy, more closely resembling the gray-on-gray appearance of some photocopies than the high-contrast black on white of traditional printing. Indeed, photocopies, which have an increasing role in today's work reading, cause numerous legibility problems resulting from low contrast, poor letter definition, and the distortion of letters and words at page edges. The ready availability of photocopying machines and the wide distribution of material in photocopied form has given rise to the problem of the *n*th-generation Xerox. This is often a document containing especially important or humorous material, the original of which is unavailable; a new set of copies is made from a copy, then another set from the copy of the copy, and so on to the *n*th generation. Each new set of copies is progressively less legible.

Computer-controlled word processing has within two decades profoundly changed relations between all those whose job it is to give words written form—authors, journalists, secretaries, academics—and their traditional media, typewriter or pen and paper. Computer terminals reverse usual figure-ground relations by showing luminous type on a dark ground, and the writer's direct contact with his or her medium (paper that can be marked, torn, or crumpled into an angry ball) is replaced by keys for cursor control and deletion. At home, monitor screens linked to data banks display not only stock market prices but also narrative-rich news reports, thus bringing display-terminal legibility problems into the domain of ludic reading.

The third area in which new technologies are increasingly affecting traditional legibility standards is in computer-linked print generation. In mainframe-computer environments, excessively long lines of upper-case type, produced by hammer-activated line printers, in which letter alignment and definition are poor, have greatly degraded legibility; moreover, ascenders and descenders make lower-case lettering inherently more legible than upper-case (Brainard, Campbell, and Elkin, 1961; Tinker, 1963). Other legibility problems arise from the use of fast dot-matrix printers which produce poorly defined gray letters, sometimes in distorted forms; the taxing task of proofreading is further burdened by the generation of proof material in this form. In addition, the constraints imposed by computer-based typesetting have had an impact on traditional typesetting norms and legibility standards in a variety of ways.

In the wake of these onslaughts on ease of reading, the once dormant area of legibility has once again become a vigorous research field (Nilsson, Ohlsson, and Ronnberg, 1983; Riley and Barbato, 1978; Van Nes and Bouma, 1980).

INTEREST

Gilliland (1972), quoting McLaughlin's 1968 proposals for British readability measures, suggests that comprehension and interest are closely linked; readability, suggests McLaughlin, is "the degree to which a given class of people find certain reading matter compelling, and, necessarily, comprehensible." This attractive assumption, which would greatly simplify the task of assessing reader interest, is unfortunately incorrect. For each of us, there is much reading matter that we understand perfectly well but fail to find compelling, such as a manual on the rules of the road; on the other hand, there is material that we understand imperfectly and yet, because of high motivation, find quite engrossing, such as the first sex manual we perused, or a pathology text about a disease we suspect we have contracted. The indisputable fact that some degree of comprehension, however imperfect it may be, is necessary before interest can develop should not be taken to establish an identity between comprehension and interest. Most studies of readability do recognize the distinction between reader comprehension and reader interest, so much so that "when the first studies appeared showing readability and readership (that is, popularity) to be related, they caused a considerable stir" (Klare, 1963, p. 143).

In this post-bibliopsychological age, how is reader interest in a given text to be predicted? At first sight, the simplest answer seems to be to ask readers themselves. Indeed, the most telling argument against the bibliopsychological apparatus called for by Rubakin is that ludic readers are able to select an appropriate ludic vehicle with great speed and accuracy by scanning the dust jacket and title page and sampling a few lines of text here and there. Though simple, this approach is unsatisfactory because it fails to meet the needs of reading teachers, who would like to be able to offer interesting reading matter to disadvantaged and unskilled readers; also, it fails to identify any of the factors that determine reader interest.

An equally direct but rather more promising approach is to ask writers. Though the nature of bestseller formulas has attracted a great deal of speculation, it is a curious fact that readability research has ignored both the speculations of critics about what makes a bestseller and the introspections of authors who have mastered the technique. This is evident both in early studies of reader interest (see, for example, Chall's bibliography: 1958, pp. 189–90) and in the most recent call for a valid predictor of reader interest by Harris and Jacobson (1979), who write that the development of a formula to predict reader affect should receive high priority in readability research.

It does not seem very likely that mechanistic formulas will predict reader interest. Content analysis and the new methods developed by the information-processing approach to cognitive psychology would probably yield richer dividends. Some more recent studies do embody these principles. For example, Beyard-Tyler and Sullivan (1980) show that adolescents prefer own-gender protagonists, while both genders prefer positive themes—that is, stories in which "the central problem was resolved successfully through the cooperative actions of the protagonists" (p. 108). The authors note that this kind of content analysis is likely to produce findings of higher validity than post-hoc determinations based on reader lists of favorite or recently read books. Such lists are of dubious accuracy, reflect the composition of available book collections as much as reader interest, and, finally, leave unresolved the issue of "whether the interest categories into which the books are classified by researchers actually reflect the attributes responsible for their selection and popularity among adolescents" (p. 106). Another study along these lines is by Owens, Bower, and Black (1979), who have explored the "soap opera effect" in fiction; namely, that readers have better recall for characters whose motives and problems are made to account for their behavior than for characters for whom no such information is provided.

However, the very small number of studies relating to reader preference (an issue that falls squarely within the domain of readability) is striking. One of the difficulties is that "reader interest" means many different things. Material may be "interesting" because it meets my need for knowledge, or awakens my curiosity, or grips and enthralls me. Only studies that address the multidimensionality of the reader-interest construct are likely to produce valid measures. The approach adopted in chapter 8 defines one of the interest dimensions—consciousness-change efficacy—by asking readers to decide which book they would most like to relax with. For textbook material, another dimension might be tapped: for example, "which of these books would you most like to have as your assigned history text, and which would you least like to have?" As shown in chapter 8, brief extracts are likely to be adequate representatives of the complete books.

COMPREHENSION

Although the term *comprehension* is much used by readability researchers, they avoid coming to terms with this construct. They speak of "ease of reading" or "ease of understanding" rather than comprehension, and, when comprehension is analyzed, it is lumped together with other concepts, such as learning and retention (as in Klare, 1963, chaps. 8 and 11) or treated as if it were one of a number of equally important reading ability factors and not, as argued in chapter 5, pre-eminent among them. It is certainly noteworthy that both the formula developers and Wilson Taylor, in the 1953 article in which he first described the cloze procedure, studiously avoid the term *comprehension*. As we shall see, both "black box" cognitive psychology and the psychometric movement have contributed to this neglect.

Formula Measures

The commonplace observation that sentence length, word length, and word difficulty are often associated with the reader's difficulties in comprehending a text led to efforts to formalize these relations. The first readability formula appeared in 1923 (Klare, 1963, p. 37) and calculated "vocabulary burden" by reference to Thorndike's *Teacher Word Book,* which, using a sample pool of 4.5 million words, listed the 10,000 most frequently used English words in frequency order. Formulas proliferated, so that by 1963 Klare was able to list thirty-nine separate formulas, most of which made their appearance in the decade following World War II. It seems likely that a major impetus for this development was the spread of the psychological-testing movement, which emphasized the value of precise measurement in the field of education and at the same time provided readability researchers with a convenient rationale. Since intelligence could not itself be defined within the behaviorist tradition of cognitive psychology, in which "mind" was a philosopher's aberration, it was instead described as being whatever the intelligence tests measured. If the measurement of intelligence could rest on this tautology, readability could clearly do the same, and the underlying issue of what readability formulas were measuring (namely, the nature of comprehension) could be ignored, as indeed it was.

The formula measure chosen for application here is the Fog Index (Gunning, 1952); its name is a reference to "foggy" writing in general and especially to "the professional jargon that clogs the paths of communication and fogs understanding" (Gunning, 1964, p. 2-2). This decision was based on the attractive simplicity of the method and the availability of copious normative data relevant to popular literature (Kwolek, 1973). In retrospect, the choice seems to have been as good as any, both because of the high intercorrelations of the formulas, as shown by table 7.1, and because the sophistication of formulas seems to have very little to do with their efficacy in measuring readability.

The method column in table 7.1 indicates that the formula measures operate by computing word difficulty and sentence length in words. Difficulty is measured either by counting syllables or by word frequency, determined by such lists as Harris and Jacobson's (1981), which is based on a sample of 56 million words. Zipf's principle (1935), which holds that higher-frequency words are shorter, accounts for the fact that word-length and word-frequency measures produce very similar results. It is noteworthy that despite the greatly increased sophistication that psycholinguistics has attained since the 1920s, when the first formulas were developed, the intuitive judgment of the readability pioneers in attributing ease of reading to vocabulary and sentence difficulty is confirmed by Hittleman (1978), who reports that those factors have the highest loadings on comprehension regression equations.

The robustness of the sentence-length and word-length factors, and the small additional contribution made by far more sophisticated approaches, is confirmed by an enlightening exchange in *The Reading Teacher* between Harris and Jacobson (1980), on the one hand, and Fry

Table 7.1. Intercorrelation of Readability Measures

Measure and Date	Method			Intercorrelations[a]							
	Word frequency	Words per sentence	Syllable count	Dale and Chall 1	Flesch 2	Fog 3	Smog 4	Spache 5	Fry 6	Cloze 7	Comp. 8
Dale and Chall, 1948[b]	x	x		—				83[c]	94[d]	67 to 90[e]	
Flesch, 1948		x	x	64 to 90[e]	—					68 74[f]	
Fog (Gunning, 1952)		x	x			—	99[g]		62[h]		
SMOG (McLaughlin, 1969a)			x				—				
Spache, 1953	x	x		71[h]				—		90[i]	
Fry, 1968		x	x	44[j]				90[i]	—		
Cloze (Taylor, 1953)		Delete words			-12[j]					—	95[k] 90[k] to 96
Comprehension tests										-22[l] -04 57[f] 61 68[m]	—

[a] All Pearson rs unless otherwise noted. Decimal points omitted. Significance levels reported in the notes to this table. To accommodate the data, both available cells in the matrix have been used.

[b] References for all measures are located in the reference list or in Klare, 1963.

[c] Bradley, 1973; rho is significant.

[d] Johns and Wheat, 1978. p < .001.

[e] Miller, 1976. Figures give range of rs derived from five criterion passages. All ps < .001.

[f] Entin and Klare, 1978. Upper figure for standard-blank cloze, and lower for dash-line cloze. p < .05 for both values in row 2, and p < .001 in row 8.

[g] Author's calculation, 1982, based on six ten-sentence samples.

[h] McLaughlin, 1969b, p < .01 for both values.

[i] Harris and Jacobson, 1980.

[j] Taylor, 1953.

[k] Bormuth, 1967. Figure above the diagonal for cloze with multiple-choice comprehension-test scores; lower figures are rhos giving range of correlations of cloze with comprehension-score ranks of four sets of paragraphs. All values significant.

[l] Entin and Klare, 1978. Cloze ranks with comprehension-score ranks. Rhos not significant.

[m] Rankin and Culhane, 1969. p < .05.

(1980), on the other. Fry's approach to readability is informal in the extreme: "I must confess that when I first developed the readability graph in Africa in about 1961, I had no idea that anyone would take it very seriously. . . . If I had, I might have put more care into its development. . . . If the truth be known, I'm amazed that my graph works as well as it does" (1977, p. 243; 1980, p. 926). The Fry Graph (1968, 1977) plots sentences and syllables per hundred words in order to read off grade level. Harris and Jacobson (1980), on the contrary, list the criteria on which the adequacy of readability formulas should be judged: in comparison with the Spache and Harris-Jacobson formulas, Fry's procedure is shown to be inadequate in the materials on which it is based, its statistical procedures, its utility for primary-grade materials, and so forth. Fry (1980) vigorously defends his procedure, remarking that a regression equation "is fine if you happen to have a computer handy or you like to count letters and look up words on lists" (p. 925).

We need to answer a very simple question: does the Fry formula rank materials in the same order as its more sophisticated counterparts? Fry (1980) reports grade-level scores on the same material for his measure and the Harris-Jacobson: $r (9) = .99$. This is as nearly perfect a correlation as one can get; in the clash between intuition and methodology, intuition, for once, emerges with flying colors.

Clearly, the sentence- and word-length variables tap fundamental psycholinguistic factors, and the formulas that use these elements are likely to enjoy a similar level of accuracy and reliability. Indeed, efforts to isolate other predictors of text difficulty have had equivocal results. Among them are syntactic complexity or density, transformation difficulty, and the effects of paragraph organization (Hittleman, 1978). Fry's kernel-distance theory suggests that distance within the sentence kernel (noun-verb-object) makes sentences harder than distance outside the kernel (Fry, 1977); the theory has been partially validated (Fry, Weber, and Depierro, 1978).

If the sentence- and word-length (or difficulty) formulas do tap the same underlying linguistic factors, the Fog Index can be expected to share whatever strengths the other formulas possess. This is indeed so: in the first five rows of table 7.1 correlation coefficients are all high and significant. The SMOG, which correlates with the Fog at an r value of .99 over six passages (values calculated by the present author), also correlates highly with the Fry, which has repeatedly been shown to agree well with other formulas.

Equally, the Fog shares the deficiencies of the formulas, vividly described by Taylor (1953): "Respectability" is easier for the average reader than "erg," and seven-year-olds, though they know all the words in "I came like Water, and like Wind I go" (from the *Rubaiyat*), will make little sense of it. So much for word length as an indicator of difficulty! Sentence length is equally misleading: "He came in smiling and sat down" is *not* approximately two to three times as difficult as "He came in. He was smiling. He sat down" (Taylor, 1953, p. 417). Since some very difficult authors, such as Gertrude Stein, use easy words, and others like Joyce use short nonsense words, it is quite easy to select passages that will "fool" the formulas: that is Taylor's phrase (p. 425), and he shows that both the Flesch and Dale-Chall produce absurd results on this kind of material. Davies (1973) gives the example of a fairy tale that scored 14.8 on the Fog Index and a philosophical discourse that scored 3.3 (p. 26) (unfortunately, he does not identify them).

However, these absurdities should not be overgeneralized. Both older (Chall, 1958; Klare, 1963) and numerous more recent papers (some cited above) have produced copious confirmation that in most applications the formulas are both valid and reliable.

The formula for the calculation of the Fox Index (Gunning, 1964) is to select three hundred-word samples. The average number of complete sentences per hundred words is added to the percentage of "hard words" and the sum is multiplied by .4. The resulting index is equivalent to the grade level for which the difficulty of the material is appropriate. The first difficulty in using the Fog relates to the definition of "hard words." This is somewhat vague, notes Kwolek (1973), but may readily be operationalized, he suggests, as words of three syllables or more, excepting syllabic plurals(-es), verb inflections (-ed, -ing) 2nd combinations of easy words (bookkeeper). However, hard words are not equivalent to abstract words, which are important in determining text difficulty (Harris and Jacobson, 1979). A second problem arises with regard to sentence length, since "longer sentences are generally handled with less difficulty in understanding than are hard words. . . . There was some evidence that words per sentence should be given less weight than hard words" (Kwolek, 1973, p. 262).

In order to determine the Fog Index for a wide variety of sources, Kwolek (1973) samples 1,440 pages drawn from 144 different sources, taking eight pages from each of eighteen categories. The mean Fog Index per category is therefore based on ten pages from each of eight different sources. Index figures for some of the categories of concern to us are as follows:

Great books (Darwin, J. S. Mill,
Dostoevsky, William James
St. Augustine, etc.):   21.84
Women's magazines: 11.37
Men's magazines: 10.97
Biology journals: 18.05
Bestsellers: 9.68

Kwolek concludes that a Fog Index of about 11 seems to be acceptable to most adults; if the index is over 14, he adds, the material will probably be ignored unless the reader has special motivation.

Cloze Procedure

By the time Chall (1958) and Klare (1963) published their authoritative reviews, formula development (with the single exception of the Fry Graph, 1968) had ceased. In 1953, however, Taylor's cloze procedure revolutionized readability studies by proposing a way of measuring readers' actual interaction with a text instead of attempting to predict it, as readability formulas do (Hittleman, 1978). Cloze procedure gets its name from the Gestalt concept of closure, because the subject's task is to fill in the gaps in a text that has been mutilated by the deletion of every fifth word; the first sentence (or sometimes paragraph) of the passage is left intact. All precise matches (misspelled words are accepted as correct) are scored, but not synonyms, changed tenses, and so forth. The subject's task is therefore to reproduce the author's original language. Taylor's paper touched off a new surge of interest in readability research centered on the cloze that has not yet abated. However, as with readability formulas, almost all of the very large cloze literature deals with the measure itself rather than the construct, leaving almost untouched the question of what exactly the cloze does measure.

In the thirty years since its introduction, the cloze has undergone numerous modifications in deletion and scoring techniques. Regarding deletion frequency, Taylor (1953) found that deleting every fifth word discriminated between passages better than other deletion patterns, and 20-percent deletion is now accepted as standard (though for children, an every tenth-word deletion pattern is recommended: Gilliland, 1972). Taylor also recommended that equal spaces be left for all deletions, regardless of the length of the missing word. Leaving a blank the size of the deleted word does not increase scores significantly, but a dashed-line technique, in which the dashes are equal to the number of letters of the deleted word (----), produces significantly higher scores. For example, Entin and Klare (1978) report that the mean percentages of correct insertions are 40 for standard-length blanks and 59 for dashed-line blanks; Rush and Klare (1978) confirm the significance of the difference between the results obtained by these two techniques.

The major modification with regard to scoring is the *clozentropy* technique proposed in 1974 by Lowry and Marr (cited in Hittleman, 1978); for each blank, the response frequencies of a criterion group are noted. A subject's response is then not matched to the original material but "deemed correct to the extent that members of the criterion group agree it is correct" (Hittleman, p. 120). This method broadens the lexical base for correct answers without reverting to synonym scoring, which, as Taylor showed, fails to improve discrimination between passages or change their ranks. However, in their review of the synonym-scoring issue, Panackal and Heft (1978) suggest that the successful replications of Taylor's finding were conducted in the lowest grades. At higher levels, students have a larger vocabulary and are more familiar with a range of synonyms.

The optimism with which readability researchers welcomed the cloze continues unabated. Cloze procedure is seen as a better indicator of readability than the formulas and as a radically different way of assessing it. For example, Davies (1973, p. 26) writes that the cloze "covers in effect all possible reading formulae." Hittleman (1978) maintains that the formulas predict the difficulty of a passage by placing it within a continuum of texts, the readability scores of which have already been established, while cloze procedure *measures* readability by quantifying the reader's interaction with the text. In order to determine what the cloze does measure, we shall have to analyze the task demands made by the cloze in some detail. As we shall see, these task demands, which are largely in the domain of language production, have to be placed in a general language-competence framework. This is arcane territory, and we shall once again have to be content with the erection of signposts rather than the provision of completed maps.

COMPREHENSION, PRODUCTION, AND THE CLOZE

Talking and listening are analogues of language production and comprehension. Production requires the expression of concepts in words, and comprehension requires that words be united with their conceptual significance. If, as Neisser's (1967) theory of analysis by synthesis suggests, we comprehend an utterance by covertly producing it, we can conclude that talking and listening are mediated by the same processes. In that case, the cloze procedure, which measures comprehension by scoring a production task, is eminently sensible. If, on the contrary, talking and listening do have some processes in common but are in other respects independent, our model of talking and listening changes radically, and supplying the missing words in mutilated text becomes a questionable way of measuring comprehension.

As we shall see, there is a good deal of evidence to support the latter view.

Evidence from Aphasiology

Considerable evidence suggests that the processes of language production and comprehension occupy anatomically distinct areas of the brain.

Lesions of the posterior part of the inferior left frontal gyrus appear to affect language production, giving rise to an expressive aphasia, the syndrome originally identified by Broca in 1861. Pure motor aphasia is associated with lesions that are restricted to the cortical surface; it involves dysprosody and decreased fluency with unimpaired reading, writing, and auditory comprehension. Usually, however, there is also subcortical involvement, giving rise to the more familiar expressive aphasia syndrome (or efferent motor aphasia: Luria, 1973), in which fluency is greatly reduced, confrontation naming is impaired or absent, and, though copying is possible, writing spontaneously or to dictation is impaired. On the other hand, comprehension of spoken language and often reading comprehension either are not lost or are soon recovered (Hecaen and Albert, 1978).

Language comprehension, on the other hand, largely spared by frontal-lobe lesions, is grossly impaired in receptive aphasia (also called sensory or syntactic aphasia), which Wernicke in 1873 identified with lesions of the posterior third of the left superior temporal gyrus (Luria, 1973). The syndrome is marked by the fluent or hyperfluent production of incomprehensible speech, made up of neologisms and paraphasias, often delivered with correct gesture and intonation, and great authority. The hallmark of the syndrome is comprehension defect for both auditory and written language which may vary from mild to total (Hecaen and Albert, 1978).

The diametrically opposed effects of these widely separated lesions appear to indicate an anatomical base for the notion that language has separate production and comprehension processes.

Evidence from Psycholinguistics

Reviewing evidence from a variety of sources, Lachman et al. (1979) note that comprehension and production processes can no longer be seen as analogues of one another; or, more concretely, that the cognitive structures involved in verifying a sentence are not the same as those used to speak or write it. Comprehension uses a word in order to identify a concept, while production uses a concept in order to access a word in the lexicon. Indeed, studies of the functioning of the lexical system produce results that are astonishingly different from those found in studies of the conceptual system (Lachman et al., 1979, p. 336). For example, the concept *bird* is not the word *bird*. Words are located in a lexicon, say Collins and Loftus (1975), which is organized not semantically but phonologically (Coltheart, 1980, has suggested that there is a right-hemisphere lexicon, and that it is semantically organized). Each name in the lexicon is linked to one or more concepts in semantic memory. The ability of aphasics to use objects appropriately even though they cannot name them, and the tip-of-the-tongue phenomenon, in which I am unable to name a concept that I have clearly in mind, seem to argue for the separateness of concept and word stores. Moreover, the literal paraphasias that characterize tip-of-the-tongue episodes (for example, in trying to remember a word invented by Hofstadter, I said "quirk? quark?—no, quine": 1979, p. 435) support the notion of a phonologically organized lexicon.

The nature of the cloze task is most usefully analyzed in terms of Chomsky's (1965) standard theory, which would hold that replacement of the missing words is a linguistic operation at the level of surface structure; the requisite words are derived from the deep structures by the application of transformational rules. This formulation can readily be rephrased in various ways—for example by reference to Frederiksen's (1980) hypothesis-driven model of the reading process, in which lexical accessing may be driven either by perceptual data or by conceptual schemes derived from a semantic model of the text. A curious example of the interplay of these processes arose recently in my university's cafeteria, where I was shocked to read on the distant menu display that the dish of the day was "Braaid* Bulldog": Though renowned for its innovative cuisine, this seemed an unlikely delicacy even for the cafeteria in question, and proved, on closer inspection, to be "Bread Pudding." Perceptual cues contributed to my misreading, since the incorrect version contains nearly the same number of letters in each word; moreover, there is a good orthographic match between the letters of the stimulus and those of the misperception. Conceptual cues arising from the cafeteria setting and the South African locale, in which barbecue dishes are common, determined the final form of the product. Had the words "Bread Pudding" appeared beneath a landscape painting in an art gallery (and the same degree of myopia been present), the misreading might have been Broad Paddock; another context might have produced Bored Hugging, and so on. In each case, orthographic consonance is preserved, with contextual cues determining interpretation.

Both these approaches to the cloze task—transformational grammar and perceptual-contextual cuing—suggest that the insertion of content words in a mutilated passage cannot begin until a set of semantic (or deep-structure) hypotheses about the text has been formed. In other words, gist recovery must take place in the absence of the missing words.

The reader will find it easier to follow the argument if he or she conscientiously tries to replace the missing words in the following passage before turning to the key at the foot of the page:

*"Braai" is a South African term for barbecue.

We reproduce here a _____ cloze passage from which _____ fifth word has been _____ . Replacing the missing words _____ a linguistic operation at _____ level of surface structure. _____ terms of Chomsky's standard _____ , the requisite words are _____ from deep structures by _____ application of transformational rules.*

This task cannot be attempted until the passage has been skimmed or otherwise previewed at least once, because gist recovery must necessarily precede the insertion of content words (function words—prepositions and articles—may be inserted automatically).

Even more instructive is our response to everyday experiences with mutilated texts, such as newspapers with tightly creased folds that obscure a word or two on every line, *n*th-generation photocopies, or slurred photocopies, in which considerably more than 20 percent of the text may be obscured. Readers persevere in reading such texts despite their irritation and often attain a fair measure of gist comprehension (Kintsch, 1977) without making any attempt to insert missing words.

We are therefore compelled to suggest a unidirectional interpretation of cloze scores. Although correct word insertion does indeed reflect good comprehension of the mutilated passage, the obverse does not apply. Failure to insert the correct words cannot be taken to mean that the subject has failed to comprehend the passage. All it means is that the subject's word-finding and context-matching abilities are lower than those of subjects who correctly replace the missing words. It does not mean that the subject's comprehension of the passage is lower.

The Cloze as a Comprehension Measure

Nonetheless, the cloze does purport to be a measure of comprehension, as the following statement of purpose in the introduction to a cloze workbook for schoolchildren indicates:

> *Cloze Connections* has been developed primarily to improve reading comprehension. The pupil's task is to identify the exact words that have been deleted. In identifying the correct deletions the pupils must relate the whole to the part and the part to the whole. The pupils depend upon their insight into the interrelationship of ideas. They must blend semantic and syntactic clues in order to choose the most appropriate responses. The deletion of words from a passage requires the pupils to pay more attention to the message of the passage as conveyed by the remaining cue words (Boning, 1981).

*Complete text: We reproduce here a *specimen* cloze passage from which *every* fifth word has been *deleted*. Replacing the missing words *is* a linguistic operation at *the* level of surface structure. *In* terms of Chomsky's standard *theory*, the requisite words are *derived* from deep structures by *the* application of transformational rules.

The implication is clear: the more accurately the missing words are replaced, the higher the comprehension level (we prudently close our eyes to the suggestion that practice on the cloze will, mysteriously, "improve reading comprehension").

Intuitively, high cloze scores could be expected to correlate positively with comprehension scores, since both draw on a common verbal-ability factor. In much the same way, scores in *Scrabble* (a lexical access game that has word-finding facility in common with the cloze) or on general-knowledge tests are likely to generate low and fluctuating positive correlations with comprehension scores, simply because *Scrabble,* general knowledge, the cloze, and comprehension tests all draw on this common underlying verbal-ability factor.

At first sight, there are ample data that cloze scores do in fact predict passage comprehension. Bormuth's original data (1967; column 8 of table 7.1) gave a correlation of .95 between a multiple-choice comprehension test, in which subjects were not allowed to look back at the passage, and cloze scores obtained three to four days earlier. Rankin and Culhane (1969), under the same conditions, produced a much lower but still significant correlation of .68; Entin and Klare (1978) obtained r values of .57 for a conventional cloze and .61 for a dash-line cloze with a multiple-choice comprehension test ($p < .001$).

A related set of studies examines the ability of the cloze to rank passages in the same order of difficulty as comprehension tests—a seemingly modest requirement. Bormuth (1967) reports *rho* values ranging from .90 to .96 for cloze ranks with comprehension-test-difficulty rankings; but Entin and Klare (1978) report near zero correlations: $-.04$ for the dash-line cloze-difficulty rankings with comprehension-test difficulties and $-.22$ for the conventional cloze. Comprehension, as before, is an untimed, open-book measure. The authors are unable to account for these "most suprising results" (p. 429); they note that the passage the cloze showed to be the most difficult produced the highest mean score on a multiple-choice comprehension test.

Entin and Klare's finding, though isolated, has a good fit with our theory-based predictions—indeed, where we had anticipated that cloze scores would generate unstable but generally positive correlations with comprehension scores, we see that some of these correlations are near zero and negative.

We may also anticipate that other aspects of lexical accessing, which cloze procedure fails to take into account, will further weaken the relations between cloze performance and reading comprehension. For example, the nth-word-deletion pattern fails to take into account such matters as the differing effectiveness of words as prompts, which is determined by their deep-structure salience (Blumenthal, 1967). Success in identifying missing words that fall just before or after effective prompts is likely to be significantly higher than if the prompt word itself is deleted. A closely related issue is verb primacy, which suggests that verb deletions are likely to have larger effects on deep-structure reconstruction than the deletion of other parts of speech (Fillmore, 1968). Neither can *n*th-word deletion take into account the higher error rates likely to be expected at phrase-structure transition points; nor can it allow for the differential effects of deleting marked and unmarked words (Lachman et al. 1979, chap. 10). Clearly, if *n*th-word deletion is repeated *n* times, beginning with word *n*, then with word *n*-1, *n*-2 and so on, and the mean result for these *n* tests is calculated, these lexical effects will cancel one another out; however, since the preparation, administration, and scoring of even one form of the cloze is considerably more time-consuming than the application of a formula to several passages of the same length, this exhaustive (and exhausting!) procedure is unlikely to be used in publishing or classroom situations. As one might expect, however, two variants of *n*th-word deletion in the same passage (for example, starting with word *n* and with word *n*-1) produce non-equivalent results. Meredith and Vaughan (1978) found significant differences among the mean scores for five different every-fifth-word deletions on the same passage. Porter (1978) reports similar non-equivalence for two cloze tests, identical except that in one, deletions began one word earlier than in the other.

On the other hand, there is considerable evidence that cloze procedures which minimize the word-finding problem enhance the reliability and validity of the test. For example, Panackal and Heft (1978) report substantial advantages for what they term the empirical key technique ("clozentropy"), which admits the correctness of synonyms selected by a criterion group, thus broadening the lexical base for cloze success. Similarly, Cunningham and Cunningham (1978) report that a limited cloze procedure, in which the deleted words are placed above the passage in random order, equaled or surpassed the conventional cloze in validity and reliability. Another kind of cueing that enhances reliability is the dashed-line technique reviewed earlier.

CAN READABILITY MEASURES PREDICT READER PREFERENCES?

Neither the Fog Index nor cloze procedure claims to be a valid measure of legibility or reading interest, but both do claim to measure "ease of reading." We would thus expect a correspondence between the order in which these readability measures rank the thirty passages in the Reading Preference Test (Appendix A) and the order in which readers rank the same passages. This expectation arises from the finding, reported in chapter 8, that readers' preference rankings are inversely related to their rankings for difficulty and merit, so that the most difficult passages were the least preferred, and vice versa. Since "ease of reading" is presumably equivalent to text difficulty, readability scores on both these measures should predict readers' difficulty, merit rankings, and, indirectly, also their preference rankings.

The vehicle for the readability rankings reported below as well as for the reader rankings reviewed in the next chapter was the thirty-item Reading Preference Test (Appendix A), which contains a few classics, a good deal of trash, and much material that hovers uneasily between these two poles of the merit continuum.

Before inspecting these rankings, which necessarily reveal the authors and sources of the extracts, readers of this book might like to try an illuminating little experiment. In the manner of I. A. Richards' famous exercise in *Practical Criticism,* see whether by close study of the words on the page you are unerringly able to detect in which of the thirty anonymous texts in Appendix A the quality of literariness resides. While you are doing so, try also to determine the order in which you think the Fog Index and the cloze test will rank twenty-six of the extracts (for this and the previous exercise, exclude the four nonfiction textbook items: 17, 23, 53, 83) for readability; see if you can pick the three most difficult and the three easiest. Decide if these are likely to be the same for the Fog, the cloze, and the readers who ranked the passages for difficulty. At the same time, ask yourself which of these extracts (pick two or three) you'd most like to relax with after a hard day's work.

Though by now this many-layered exercise may seem overwhelming, you will in fact find that is quite easy to hold questions about merit ("literariness"), difficulty, and preference separately in your mind as you work through the anonymous texts.

While you are making these decisions, you might like to introspect about the criteria you use in making these merit, difficulty, and preference rankings. The exercise is enlightening because of the vivid insights it offers about the usually covert value-attribution processes we use in assigning or denying literary merit to texts.

The Fog Index

Fog Index scores are usually computed by scoring three hundred-word samples (Gunning, 1952), but our briefer extracts accommodated only two such specimens. The sequence in which the Fog Index ranked the thirty passages used in the Reading Preference Test (Appendix A) is shown in the right hand half of table 7.2. Because the Fog ranks readability by the face-valid criteria of word and sentence length, your predictions about the Fog Index sequence in this table were probably pretty accurate.

Table 7.2.   Extracts Ranked from Most to Least Readable by the Cloze and the Fog

	Cloze Ranks				Fog Ranks		
Author	Cloze score	S.D.	Book code	Rank	Book code	Fog Index	Author
Charles Dickens	14.08	1.94	20	1	51	5.20	Peter O'Donnell
Somerset Maugham	13.77	1.19	52	2	46	5.84	Henry James
Louis L'Amour	12.69	2.02	38	3	30	5.90	Agatha Christie
Loren Fessler	12.08	2.30	63	4	44	6.64	Graham Greene
Henry James	11.92	2.59	46	5	62	6.76	Essie Summers
Wilbur Smith	11.85	1.88	98	6.5	66	6.88	Djuna Barnes
Jane Austen	11.85	1.66	14	6.5	16	7.10	Denise Robins
David Ogilvie	11.69	1.98	77	8	86	7.26	Ian Fleming
Ayn Rand	11.54	1.60	29	9	71	7.55	James Michener
H.S. Thompson	11.31	2.61	43	10	13	7.66	Gavin Lyall
Richard Gordon	10.92	2.02	36	11	85	7.96	Arthur Hailey (torture)
Graham Greene	10.35	2.07	44	12	76	8.13	Joseph Conrad
Ian Fleming	10.46	3.20	86	13	29	8.80	Ayn Rand
Essie Summers	10.31	2.40	62	14.5	36	9.08	Richard Gordon
Denise Robins	10.31	1.14	16	14.5	22	9.52	James Joyce
Agatha Christie	10.23	1.76	30	16	38	9.68	Louis L'Amour
James Joyce	10.23	2.12	22	17	49	9.80	Saul Bellow
Franklin Moore	9.85	1.75	17	18	98	10.00	Wilbur Smith
James Michener	9.62	2.40	71	19	20	10.04	Charles Dickens
Arthur Hailey (torture)	9.54	2.79	85	20	17	10.48	Franklin Moore
Gray's Anatomy	9.46	2.40	83	21	77	11.03	David Ogilvie
Peter O'Donnell	9.38	2.37	51	22.5	11	12.05	Herman Melville
Gavin Lyall	9.38	1.21	13	22.5	55	12.52	Arthur Hailey (fraud)
Saul Bellow	8.38	1.50	49	24	43	12.84	H.S. Thompson
Djuna Barnes	7.31	1.14	66	25	52	14.34	Somerset Maugham
Joseph Conrad	7.15	2.45	76	26	63	14.80	Loren Fessler
Nathan Rotenstreich	7.08	2.30	73	27	14	15.79	Jane Austen
Arthur Hailey (fraud)	6.69	2.02	55	28	23	18.72	Nathan Rotenstreich
Herman Melville	5.46	1.86	11	29	83	20.25	Gray's Anatomy
Harrison Gough	4.77	1.80	53	30	53	20.72	Harrison Gough

Cloze Procedure

All thirty items in the Reading Preference Test were prepared as cloze tests, using Taylor's (1953) procedure. The first five lines of each extract were left intact, the fifth word of the first new sentence commencing on or after the sixth line was deleted, and each fifth word thereafter, until a total of twenty words has been deleted. Because the deletions were made by painting out each fifth word with white opaque correction fluid, the blank spaces were proportional to the length of the missing word. A subsequent validation study with five extracts retyped with ten-space blanks for each missing word showed that this procedural variation had a non-significant effect on cloze scores, and none at all on rank order.

The blanks were numbered from 1 to 20 in each extract, and the instructions to subjects were to "write the number of the extract at the top of each answer sheet, and then fill in your best guess at what the missing word is. Please don't leave any blanks. If you can't work out what the word is, guess. This is not a speed test and there is no time limit. All the same, you should try to work fairly quickly." One point was awarded for each correct word. Spelling and number errors (for example, singular for plural) were accepted as correct, but other deviations from the original were not credited. Cloze rankings are given in the left-hand half of table 7.2. These ranks are the mean scores of thirteen subjects, all with twelve years of schooling and nine with three- or four-year university degrees or two-year diplomas. Ages ranged from 25 to 45.

Appendix B contains three specimen cloze items (in equal-space form), these ranked easiest and hardest by the cloze, and midway between the two. How do your guesses at the cloze sequence compare with these results? The coaching in the first part of this chapter may have given you the clues you needed to determine which extracts would make the greatest word-finding demands, and which the least.

Readability Rankings

Table 7.2 shows the rank order of the thirty extracts, from most to least readable, as determined by the Fog Index and the cloze scores. There are startling discrepancies between the rankings. Dickens, the most readable according to the cloze, is only nineteenth on the Fog. Somerset Maugham, second most readable according to the cloze, is near the bottom of the Fog list. Indeed, the rank order correlation coefficient (*rho*) between Fog and cloze ranks is .01, which is about as low an agreement between two rankings as one can get, equivalent to throwing each set of extracts up into the air and catching them as they come down.

The poor agreement between Fog and cloze fails to indicate which of the two measures does better at determining reader preferences and, inversely, at predicting reader rankings of merit or difficulty. Accordingly, we know that, at best, only one of them can predict preference, merit, or difficulty. As table 7.3 shows, it is in fact the Fog that shows significant positive relations with difficulty, merit, and preference.

These results indicate, first, that these three rankings have many factors in common (or, in statistical terms, share a large common variance) with the elements of lexical and syntactic complexity tapped by the Fog Index; second, that ludic reading preferences can be predicted with some accuracy by reference to this factor; and, third, that the word-

Table 7.3. Fog and Cloze Rankings in relation to Difficulty, Merit, and Preference

N	Subject groups[a]	Items in array	Fog rho	Fog p	Cloze rho	Cloze p
Difficulty Rankings						
(Easiest to hardest)						
21	Library assistants	30	.68	.001	.33	n.s.
5	Non-BBib graduates	30	.59	.001	.36	.05
Merit Rankings						
(Worst to best)						
23	Graduate librarians	25	.49	.01	.00	n.s.
10	Unisa lecturers	25	.35	n.s.	.05	n.s.
9	Experienced assistants	25	.54	.01	.19	n.s.
Preference Rankings						
(Most to least preferred)						
129	Students	30	.60	.001	.12	n.s.
44	All librarians	30	.61	.001	.14	n.s.

[a]The subject groups in this analysis are fully described in chapter 8.

replacement skill measured by the cloze is unrelated to readers' perceptions of text difficulty, and therefore to ludic reading preferences. Indeed, table 7.3 offers even stronger confirmation than we would have dared expect for the prediction that cloze scores would correlate weakly and unpredictably with comprehension scores, replicating the "surprising" results reported by Entin and Klare (1978). Since ranking for comprehension is in large measure synonymous with ranking for difficulty, the failure of the cloze scores to correlate with difficulty ranks confirms our view that the cloze is a poor measure of comprehension, and therefore of "ease of reading."

However, the claims made on behalf of the cloze as a comprehension measure are so entrenched in the literature that a further small study was undertaken, the results of which are reported in table 7.4. Six of the cloze subjects carried out preference sorts, and their preference ranks were then compared with the rank sequence of their own cloze scores. Here the direct interaction of the reader with the text during the cloze, which purports to measure comprehension difficulty, is pitted against the same reader's preferences, and the results in four out of six cases were found to be non-significant. This result cannot be attributed to idiosyncratic preference rankings, since each subject's preferences correlated at a statistically significant level with the mean preference rank for all six subjects.

The failure of the cloze to relate to most reader ratings of passage

Table 7.4.   Correlations between Subjects' Preference Ranking and the Same
Subjects' Cloze Ranking (Spearman's *rho*)

Subject's Preference Ranking *Same Subject's Cloze Ranking*	Subject						*Mean preference ranking for all 6 subjects*
	511	*512*	*513*	*514*	*515*	*516*	
511	.49**						.51**
512		.30					.66***
513			.12				.58***
514				.32			.70***
515					.32		.46**
516						.52**	.66***

p* < .01*p* < .001

difficulty, merit, or preference casts serious doubts on its appropriateness as a measure of readability and suggests that it is measuring an
unknown and as-yet-undefined construct in the domain of language
production.

AN OVERVIEW

Hirsch (1977) argues that there is an irreversible evolutionary tendency in
the language toward greater readability. Word-order choice becomes
more limited, spelling and punctuation become standardized, printed
letters acquire greater uniformity and clarity (though this trend is currently being undermined by electronic typesetting, and prose conventions
acquire greater force. The contribution made to this movement by readability studies is unclear. Certainly, the myth that shorter words and sentences make for easier reading is pernicious. The writer's easiest course,
say Lachman et al. (1979), is to use the most frequently occurring words as
often as possible, which "would require the receiver to work harder to
extract subtleties of meaning, because the sender's vocabulary would be
small and impoverished." With regard to school materials, Harris and
Jacobson (1979) complain in similar vein that overzealous application of
reading measures has tended to render "the subtle simplistic."

There can be little doubt that the readability enterprise has failed to
live up to the expectations embodied in its own early program. In large
measure, this must be attributed to its failure to erect a theoretical frame-

work within which the cognitive structures that mediate language comprehension can be accommodated. Part of the price exacted by this omission is, for example, the inability of one of readability's most favored instruments, the cloze, to measure comprehension reliably and the absence of any prediction of this failure in the readability literature.

Formula measures, as we have shown, can match texts to readers, but only crudely, by assigning age-level scores to texts. The definitive and fine-grained matching that Rubakin advocated is as far beyond our reach as it was beyond his: his project for a comprehensive bibliopsychological classification of books and readers was indeed doomed by what we now recognize to be the enormous richness and complexity of comprehension processes (and the reward they mediate) that would make even the partial bibliopsychological classification of just one book and one reader far longer than the book itself.

In embarking on these investigations of readability measures, we had hoped to throw some new light on the ways in which ludic readers so successfully match themselves to psychologically rewarding texts. At this point, we know little more about ludic readers' choice patterns than we did before—though we do know a great deal more about readability measures and how they work. The burden of this knowledge is that they are not of much use in reaching an understanding of how readers pick their books. To find out how real readers choose books in the real world, I carried out the separate series of studies reported in the next chapter.

8
How Real Readers Choose Books: Rankings for Pleasure Reading, Literary Merit, and Text Difficulty

It was earlier suggested that readers would show substantial agreement with one another in ranking books on a ludic continuum, and in this chapter, this and other predictions about the ways in which readers rank books are tested. Readers of this book who conscientiously performed the Practical Criticism exercise will be more perceptive observers of the ways in which our subjects carried out the tasks described below.

The concept of a ludic continuum asserts the hypothesis that taste is universal. In other words, if the same 10 or 30 or 100 books were translated from their original languages into perfect English, Hebrew, Japanese, Russian, and French, and were ranked on a ludic continuum by the citizens of London, Tel Aviv, Tokyo, Moscow, and Paris, these rankings would show statistically significant agreement with one another—despite the rather different meanings that the bearers of these distinct cultures would assign to the content of each book. In Western industrialized societies, we would also expect rankings of literary merit or quality to correlate at significant negative values with preference rankings. This prediction arises from our review of the effects of the social value system and especially the Protestant Ethic, leading us to expect that in these societies, literary quality and unpleasantness would often be seen as synonymous.

Over a three-year period, 219 subjects participated in the testing of these hypotheses. Among these were 129 students and 33 ludic readers, in addition to 44 librarians and 13 literary critics.

There were two major groups of librarians. Twenty-three were professional librarians in such areas as book selection, cataloguing, and reference librarianship. Of these, eighteen were Bachelors of Library Science (BBib), three held the Higher Diploma in Librarianship, and only two, though holders of a B.A., had no professional qualification in librarianship. A particularly interesting subgroup among these twenty-three professional librarians were the five graduates who were book selectors, whose job it was to place book orders, relying both on their own judgment and on reports from readers employed by the library service.

Because of their seniority and comfortable rear-line status, these selectors can be called "generals" and contrasted with the "privates"—the five front-line soldiers who had served an average of seven years at the lending desks of branch libraries. These privates formed part of the second major group—twenty-one branch library assistants. Though ten were B.A. graduates in a variety of fields, none held a librarianship qualification; the eleven others had only high school education. The privates were unique in that none had a university degree, and all were veterans of library service, having worked far longer at the circulation desks of branch libraries than the other sixteen assistants.

These differences aside, however, there was considerable homogeneity among the librarians: all forty-four were female, and all but two were Afrikaans-speaking and had been educated in the Calvinist fundamentalist tradition of the Afrikaans-language schools and universities of the Transvaal Province of South Africa.

Among the subjects there were also fourteen English lecturers, three from the small coastal University of Port Elizabeth (UPE) and eleven from the University of South Africa (Unisa). By training and experience, these lecturers were professional critics, trained to distinguish between "literature" and "trash" and to make fine qualitative distinctions within the domain of literature.

THE UNIVERSE OF READING MATTER

The thirty items in the Reading Preference Test (Appendix A) were selected as representative of the universe of reading matter. Of course, the number of dimensions along which reading matter can vary is practically infinite: in length, from single words and mutilated sentences to the lucid length of *War and Peace;* in difficulty, from the easy through the cryptic to the unintelligible; also in subject matter and affective tone and diction and purpose—the possible variations are too numerous to name. Although the compilation of a manageably brief sample that is fully representative of the universe of reading matter is a manifestly impossible task, a sample that seems to reflect its outlines with some faithfulness was compiled by restricting the choice to English-language materials and by making use of major superordinate concepts. To do so, a number of objective judgments that distinguish different categories of reading matter were applied, and then three other dimensions were specified. The *categories* we propose are fiction or nonfiction, genre, and date of production. The *dimensions* are difficulty, merit, and either trance potential (for fiction) or perceived usefulness (for nonfiction). Finally, we consider the issues of sample variability and anonymity.

The items in the Reading Preference Test are listed in tables 8.1 and 8.2, first the twenty-nine sources from which they are drawn in alphabetical author sequence, then in the sequence in which they were presented to subjects, according to the random number allocated to each extract. Of these items, twenty-two are from full-length works of fiction and one from a volume of short stories, two are narrative nonfiction (one of these is a free-standing essay), three are from textbooks, and one is a scientific paper.

Three Categories

Fiction and nonfiction. The distinction between fiction and nonfiction is useful and generally clear. It becomes fuzzy when New Journalism techniques fictionalize reality to produce the narrative nonfiction category described in chapter 2, but the ambiguity is resolved by following the author's intention, which is the creation of companion rather than utensil books (Escarpit, 1966). We shall therefore treat narrative nonfiction material, such as *Confessions of an Advertising Man,* as if it were ordinary ludic reading matter. Nonfiction is included in the sample to provide an anchor point for our hoped-for ludic continuum, since the utensil books can be expected to occupy the least-favored positions.

In terms of market share, nonfiction should have comprised 84 percent (twenty-five items) of our sample, but since fiction is the primary vehicle for ludic reading, nonfiction was limited to seven items, of which four were utensil books (Gough, Gray, Moore, and Rotenstreich). Narrative nonfiction, which has acquired considerable importance in the leisure reading market, is represented by three extracts: Ogilvie's autobiography, Fessler's *China* (hovering rather uneasily between didactics and entertainment), and Thompson's "strange and terrible saga" of Hell's Angels.

Genre. Genre is used in the sense of a style of art or literature; the style is in turn defined by subject matter and treatment. Nonfiction genre is determined by content area (travel, biography, childrearing, chemical

Table 8.1.   Extract Sources in Author Sequence

Code	Source
14	Jane Austen. *Pride and Prejudice*. London: Collins, 1973 (1813).
66	Djuna Barnes. *Nightwood*. London: Faber and Faber, 1963 (1936).
49	Saul Bellow. *Herzog*. London: Weidenfeld and Nicholson, 1965 (1961).
30	Agatha Christie. *Ten Little Niggers*. London: Collins, 1968 (1939).
76	Joseph Conrad. *Lord Jim*. Dent, 1955 (1900).
20	Charles Dickens. *Pickwick Papers*. New York: Dell, 1964 (1837).
63	Loren Fessler. *China*. New York: Time-Life International, 1968 (1963).
86	Ian Fleming. *Thunderball*. London: Jonathan Cape, 1961.
36	Richard Gordon. *The Captain's Table*. London: Michael Joseph, 1955 (1954).
53	Harrison G. Gough. A Leadership Index on the California Psychological Inventory. *Journal of Counselling Psychology*, 1969, *16*, 283–289.
83	*Gray's Anatomy: Descriptive and Applied*. London: Longmans, 1958 (1858).
44	Graham Greene. *The Power and the Glory*. Harmondsworth: Penguin, 1962 (1940).
55/85	Arthur Hailey. *The Moneychangers*. London: Michael Joseph, 1975.
46	Henry James. *The Portrait of a Lady*. Harmondsworth: Penguin, 1963 (1881).
22	James Joyce. *A Portrait of the Artist as a Young Man*. London: Jonathan Cape, 1954 (1916).
38	Louis L'Amour. *The Skyliners*. London: Transworld, 1967.
13	Gavin Lyall. *Midnight plus One*. London: Pan, 1973 (1965).
52	W. Somerset Maugham. *Ashenden, or The British Agent*. London: Heinemann, 1967 (1928).
11	Herman Melville. *Moby Dick or The Whale*. London: MacDonald, 1952 (1851).
71	James Michener. *Hawaii*. London: Corgi, 1964 (1959).
17	Franklin G. Moore. *Production Control*. Tokyo: McGraw-Hill, 1959 (1951).
51	Peter O'Donnell. *The Impossible Virgin*. London: Pan Books, 1975 (1971).
77	David Ogilvie. *Confessions of an Advertising Man*. New York: Dell, 1964 (1963).
29	Ayn Rand. *Atlas Shrugged*. New York: Random House, 1957.
16	Denise Robins. *Dark Corridor*. London: Hodder and Stoughton, 1974.
23	Nathan Rotenstreich. *Between Past and Present: An Essay on History*. New Haven: Yale, 1958.
98	Wilbur Smith. *Eagle in the Sky*. London: Heinemann, 1974.
62	Essie Summers. *Sweet Are the Ways*. London: Mills & Boon, 1965.
43	Hunter S. Thompson. The Hell's Angels, a Strange and Terrible Saga. In Tom Wolfe and E.W. Johnson (eds.) *The New Journalism*. London: Picador, 1975 (1966).

Note: Dates of first publication appear in parentheses if they differ from the date of printing.

engineering) and application (for example, primary school, university textbook, self-help). The number of fiction genres is very large, including such diverse kinds of reading matter as comics, picture stories, hardcore pornography (in turn subdivided into numerous categories of perversion), specialist fiction magazines (science fiction, true confession),

Table 8.2.   Extract Sources in Code-Number Sequence

Code	Author	Code	Author
11	Herman Melville	49	Saul Bellow
13	Gavin Lyall	51	Peter O'Donnell
14	Jane Austen	52	Somerset Maugham
16	Denise Robins	53	Harrison Gough
17	Franklin Moore	55	Arthur Hailey
20	Charles Dickens	62	Essie Summers
22	James Joyce	63	Loren Fessler
23	Nathan Rotenstreich	66	Djuna Barnes
29	Ayn Rand	71	James Michener
30	Agatha Christie	76	Joseph Conrad
36	Richard Gordon	77	David Ogilvie
38	Louis L'Amour	83	*Gray's Anatomy*
43	Hunter S. Thompson	85	Arthur Hailey
44	Graham Greene	86	Ian Fleming
46	Henry James	98	Wilbur Smith

and many others. Since ludic readers are book readers, many of these categories were eliminated by restricting ourselves to general-market book publishing. Commercially important categories are, among others, Westerns (the authors who dominate the field are Louis L'Amour and Zane Grey), historical romances (Georgette Heyer is pre-eminent), science fiction (Arthur C. Clarke), humorous novels, and, of course, that most important category, crime-and-violence, which encompasses such subcategories as espionage (Fleming, Le Carré), gang welfare (O'Donnell), gun-for-hire (Forsythe), sex-and-sadism, and so on.

Most of these categories are represented on our list: Fleming, Hailey, Lyall, O'Donnell, and Smith for crime-and-violence; one Western (L'Amour); two romances (Robins and Summers); a humorous novel (Gordon); a whodunnit (Christie); and the three narrative nonfiction items. Science fiction is an unfortunate omission.

The complex processes by which readers match themselves to the kinds of book that give them greatest pleasure may have a constrictive result; some readers read nothing but Westerns, or science fiction, or romances. Perhaps such constriction of the reading field arises because even the same landscape of formulaic fiction is not safe enough for these readers; the distance between the reader and the book must be maximized and the fictional terrain known in the finest detail. We suggest that genre publishing has developed to meet such needs. Each genre category has its giants, who tower over their competitors, and rigid conventions determine the bounds of the permissible with regard to setting, character, plot, and resolutions.

Period. Most books produced more than fifty or sixty years before one's own date of birth, or very long after it, are dismissed by ludic readers as "old-fashioned," "ultra-modern," or, in general, "strange." Tastes in fiction in particular change from one generation to the next; Rafael Sabatini and Marie Corelli have little appeal to readers brought up on Ian Fleming and Peter O'Donnell). There is necessarily more "old-fashioned" than "ultra-modern" material in existence, and we need to ask why the writing of previous generations is strange. This is so largely because the diction and conventions of prose and poetry reflect the manners, values, vocabulary, and syntax of the society in which they are produced. Since the conventions of one's own society are most easily understood, literary tastes change continually, and fiction readers seldom turn to the work of earlier periods unless it has been designated a classic by critical consensus. Nonetheless, non-contemporary prose forms as important part of the ludic reading universe. Indeed, the great success of historical novels, which deliberately emulate archaic prose conventions (such as Georgette Heyer's Georgian romances), indicates that readers do not experience alien diction as aversive in itself.

The sample includes five nineteenth-century works (Austen, 1813; Dickens, 1837; Melville, 1851; James, 1881; and Conrad, 1900), all classics. Nineteenth-century trash (of which there is an abundance) has little appeal to current readers and is excluded from the sample.

Having considered three categories of reading matter, we turn now to the dimensions along which it can be ranked: merit, difficulty, and trance potential.

Three Dimensions

Merit. Merit judgments are often dichotomous, with "literature" or "good stuff" opposing "trash." In our sample, material at these two poles is readily identified. The twentieth-century items by Conrad and Joyce can be added to the list of five nineteenth-century classics. At the other pole, the five formula bestsellers would be widely regarded as trash, and at least one of these has also been called evil—which is how Holbrook, in his *Masks of Hate* (1972), characterizes Fleming's work, and one of the literary critics in our sample fervently applied the same description to the torture passage in Hailey's novel. The two romances (Robins and Summers) can be added to the trash category.

Between these two poles is a large gray area. High on the merit list are the works by Barnes and Bellow, which are nearly classics, but not quite.

The former is little known to the general public (though Barnes' stature among critics is high), while Bellow is perceived by many readers—despite his Nobel Prize—as too recent (and perhaps too alive) for apotheosis. Greene and Maugham, both master craftsmen who produce highly readable narratives, hover uneasily in a twilight world: many carping voices suggest that they are no more than first-rate second-raters. Even more ambiguity—though here the negative pole dominates—surrounds Ayn Rand and James Michener: both are enormously successful, and both have pretensions to literary excellence. Greatly admired by their devotees, they are summarily dismissed by establishment critics. Finally, closer to the trash pole, are three genre authors, all acknowledged masters of their chosen fields: Christie, L'Amour, and Gordon.

Difficulty. Literary merit and difficulty are in principle independent, but in practice they are intertwined and sometimes even mistaken for one another. Some critics believe that merit and difficulty are equivalent, and readability measures certainly find most "literature" to be more difficult than trash, though great writing may of course be simple writing, as shown by the easy lucidity of Borges or Gide. On the other hand, it is frequently difficult writing: great minds usually command large vocabularies, and complex thoughts are more readily accommodated by long sentences than by short ones. As vocabulary burden and sentence length increase, so does readability level. Generally, but not necessarily, literary quality and difficulty are close companions.

The difficulty range in our sample is substantial at the two poles, with the nonfiction at one end and the bestsellers at the other. Between the poles, most of the items span a moderate range of difficulty, and the Fog scores in chapter 7 tend to confirm this (table 7.2).

Trance potential. The most important of the subjective judgments readers make about books is the third, trance potential, defined as the perceived capacity of the book to exercise dominion and superiority. In chapter 11, we argue that these are the two components of reading sovereignty and that the reader's assessment of a book's trance potential is probably the most important single decision in relation to correct book choice and the most important contributor to the reward systems that keep ludic reading going once it has begun. Quite often, readers' judgments of trance potential will override judgments of merit and difficulty. Thus, although Tolkien's *Lord of the Rings* (1954) is a relatively difficult book, many readers prefer it to easier ones because of its great power to entrance; or, for readers who usually avoid trash, a new Wilbur Smith, promising a rollicking good read, may be an irresistible temptation.

Though the term *trance potential* is new, the construct is not; it parallels the quality so avidly sought by nineteenth-century publishers, the creation of a pleasant atmosphere for the reader (Leavis, 1932). The instructions given to the subjects in this study follow Somerset Maugham in suggesting that the effective ludic vehicle is a felicitous interlocutor, a conversationalist able to engage the reader in pleasant chatter that takes one out of oneself.

Bestsellers are presumably entrancing to large numbers of readers and are well represented in the sample. At the other end of the scale are utensil books that lack even the capacity to absorb the reader and which cannot therefore entrance. The three narrative nonfiction works and the various classics and near-classics present an adequate range of intermediate trance potential. Readers' judgments of merit, difficulty, and trance potential are of course interactive; difficulty is likely to influence trance-potential judgments and itself be determined at least in part by perceived merit.

Variability

Within each class of reading matter, there are substantial differences between the high and low poles on each of the three merit, difficulty and trance potential dimensions. Difficulty may range from the near-impenetrability of the *Ulysses* monologues to the simplicity of books in the Silhouette library, and there are similar extremes for merit and trance potential. The dilemma we face is a familiar one in experimental design: if our sample represents the full range of variability along any of these dimensions, all our subjects will rank the materials in the same sequence (all readers will agree that Charles Dickens is easier than Djuna Barnes but more difficult than Ian Fleming). Agreement in rating widely differing items will tell us little about the ways real readers choose books. If, on the other hand, we limit the range of difficulty (or merit or trance potential) to less than what is typically represented on the fiction shelves of a public library, we may find that we are asking our subjects to make distinctions that are much finer than those called for in the real world, with the result that they have to distinguish among items that are almost entirely indistinguishable.

In our sample, there are extremes of difficulty-easiness and merit-trashiness, but the variability of the midrange twenty items is moderate. We predict (perhaps optimistically) that whatever findings emerge are likely to be modified but not overturned by replications with larger, more comprehensive samples of reading matter.

Anonymity

Should we present our sample in book form, complete with dust jackets, or anonymously, as I. A. Richards did? If we use anonymous extracts, it will be for a different reason. Richards wanted to prove that the quality of literariness could unerringly be detected by trained minds in anonymous texts, while we want to show that both trained and untrained minds share the same ludic reading tastes. To do so, we must as far as possible emulate the conditions on the desert island we described in chapter 2 by removing all indications of the taste culture to which the materials are directed, including their authors and publishers.

Of course, presenting real books would be much closer to real life, but anonymous extracts will yield more information about reader choices, reflecting more enduring choice mechanisms than rankings aided by numerous extrinsic cues. To ensure anonymity, "he" or "she" was substituted for names like Miss Marple, Mr. Pickwick, and James Bond. But was the price paid for this method unduly high? To answer this question, we need to know whether the extracts used in the ranking tasks were valid representatives of the books from which they were taken.

Four sets of twenty-one of these books (five were unavailable in multiple copies) were assembled, and thirty-nine of the librarian subjects took turns in ranking these according to the probable frequency with which they would be borrowed by readers. The contrast between the austerity of the anonymous extract sheet and the evocative, richly illustrated covers is striking. The cover of Michener's *Hawaii* shows a scantily clad couple embracing against a background of palm trees and mountains. The cover of *Eagle in the Sky* declares that "A new novel from Wilbur Smith promises excitement, action and adventure . . . a superb story." The austere intellectualism of Joyce's *Portrait* is emphasized by the dust jacket, which carries a line drawing of intense young men in clerical collars; in large print under the title we are told that this is "the definitive text, corrected from the Dublin Holograph." In other words, a good cover at once establishes a book's tone, quality, and intended market (in Petersen, 1975, there is an intriguing review of the role of the cover in book sales). Nonetheless, if our extracts are good representatives of their sources, a skilled reader will be able to infer from the twenty lines of the extract all the information made instantly available by the cover.

The results of this study show that the extracts were indeed valid representatives of the books (see table 8.3). Further, it appears that the extrinsic cues provided by the book's cover were interpreted by the librarians in a direction consistent with actual text content. The most stringent test of this skill is to compare subjects' book rankings with their own rankings of the extracts. Table 8.3 shows that those who fare best are the book selectors, suggesting that their job has taught them special skills in correctly relating extrinsic cues to texts.

Despite this encouraging validation, no single brief extract can be fully representative of a complete book. Though the passage selected

Table 8.3.   Correlations between Librarians' Rankings of Extracts and of Books

Ranking Extracts		Ranking Books		No. of items compared	rho	p (two-tailed)
N	Subject groups	N	Subject groups			
44	All librarians	10	Senior graduates	19	0.52	0.05
44	All librarians	21	Branch assistants	21	0.74	0.001
5	"Generals": graduate book selectors with themselves			19	0.65	0.01
5	"Privates": experienced branch assistants with themselves			21	0.53	0.05

from *Thunderball* does indeed convey the flavor of Fleming's writing, the James Bond books also contain many descriptions of weapons, cars, and cities that out of context seem like didactic writing and might be taken by subjects to be extracted from a different kind of book and ranked accordingly. Does this internal variation invalidate our expectation that a single extract will reliably represent a book? To examine this question, two extracts from Hailey's *Money Changers* were selected. One (Item 55) describes the detection of a fraud; the second (Item 85), an act of torture. Though outwardly dissimilar, these passages are by the same author and relate to central themes in the same novel. In fact, both students and librarians ranked these passages almost identically, further supporting the view that extracts can reliably represent books (see table 8.6).

RANKING INSTRUCTIONS

Preference

Instructions to the 129 student subjects were as follows:

> You have in front of you a pack of pages from many different books, identified only by random numbers.
>
> Now, imagine the following situation:
>
> You have just come home after a long and difficult day. You have an hour or so free before supper. There's nothing you would rather do than curl up with a good book, have a good read—and forget your troubles.
>
> From the pack, choose the book you would most like to relax with—and the book you would least like to relax with. Then arrange the other pages in the order of your preference.

To facilitate this rather cumbersome ranking task, a method adapted from Q-sorting (Stephenson, 1967) was used:

To make your job easier, it is divided into two parts:
a. First arrange the pages into four piles, like this:

LIKE MOST	LIKE	DISLIKE	DISLIKE MOST

Try to get a few sheets into every pile.
b. Next, arrange each pile in sequence, with those you like best on top and those you like least at the bottom. Put the piles on top of one another in the same way, so that all the pages run in the order of your preference from top to bottom.

Finally, subjects were reminded of the nature of the task:

1. This is *NOT* a speed test. Work at a comfortable pace.
2. Remember *NOT* to sort the pages into good and bad books. You are not concerned with literary quality or informativeness but with choosing books to relax with.

For the librarians, the task was presented in terms of lending frequency rather than personal preference ("please rank these books in the most likely order of *issue frequency*—i.e., the most likely borrower demand for each of these books"). Because of the special place librarians occupy in the social value system, their perceptions of borrower behavior are especially interesting. In asking the librarians to reflect lending frequency judgments, we may of course be setting up a projective test which will reflect each librarian's personal preferences. This is not the case, since one's perceptions of public preference may differ widely from one's own ("I can't stand Westerns, but the kids take out nothing else").

Merit

We have already noted that the merit criteria applied to utensil books (such as the four in our sample) are not the same as those applied to companion or "literary" books. Accordingly, these four, together with Fessler's *China*, were removed from the sample for the merit rankings (though fewer than twenty-five items were available for some comparisons). Instructions to the 129 student subjects were as follows:

The literary quality of the 25 extracts in front of you varies considerably. Some are of the highest literary quality, and others are absolute trash. Your task is to sort these 25 extracts into a merit sequence, with those of the highest merit on top and the trashiest trash at the bottom of the pile you make. To make your task easier, please first sort the extracts into four piles. Put the very best literary quality on your left and the very worst on the right. Second from the left will be fairly good extracts, and second from the right, fairly trashy ones.

As with all the ranking tasks, subjects were then asked to arrange the sheets in a single sequence, from highest ranked on top to lowest ranked at the bottom of the pile. For the librarians, the task was again framed in terms of their professional rather than their personal judgments; they were asked to shelve the twenty-five items in a graded sequence from "rubbish" to good literature, in order "to lead adult readers away from trash and toward the enjoyment of good books." This procedure is indeed projective in the sense discussed above, since the task of arranging a hypothetical library's book stock in merit sequence necessarily reflects the librarian's own judgments about literary excellence.

Difficulty

This task was presented to twenty-one of the librarians as follows:

> The thirty extracts you have in front of you vary considerably in difficulty. Some are very easy to read and others are very hard. Please sort these extracts into a difficulty order, so that the easiest are on top and the most difficult at the bottom. To make your task easier, first sort the extracts into four piles [as before].

PREFERENCE PATTERNS

Within-Group Consistency

The ludic-continuum construct suggests that readers will rank reading matter in a more or less consistent order. The most sensitive test of whether this is true is the extent to which individual readers' rankings agree with one another. Kendall's coefficient of concordance (W), which assigns a value of one to rankings that agree perfectly and zero to perfect disagreement, was computed for a variety of different groups. Table 8.4 gives the result for both preference and merit rankings by students, librarians, and professors of English.

The internal consistency for all these groups is statistically significant (chi-square values are all significant at the .01 or .001 level). Clearly, the members of each group of readers rank books and extracts in the same general pattern. At the same time, the frequently low absolute values of W indicate that there is a good deal of room for idiosyncratic choice patterns, which is consistent with the observations made about the publishing industry in chapter 1: bestsellers are drawn from both fiction and nonfiction genres and show a wide range of variability.

Table 8.4.   Concordances of Preference and Merit Rankings

N	Subject Groups		No. of items ranked	Kendall's W	χ^{2a}
Preference Rankings	*Students*				
129	All Port Elizabeth students		30	0.29	1067.7
34	University female English		30	0.39	389.4
10	University female Afrikaans		30	0.42	124.1
14	University male English		30	0.30	122.4
5	University male Afrikaans		30	0.50	86.2
3	College female English		30	0.65	56.5**
36	College male English		30	0.39	407.8
19	College male Afrikaans		30	0.33	184.0
27	University students in 1976		30	0.35	277.5
27	University students in 1978		30	0.36	284.8
	Librarians				
44	Ranking of extracts		30	0.52	670.2
21	Ranking of extracts		30	0.54	334.0
21	Ranking of books		21	0.73	295.5
10	Ranking of books		18	0.89	151.2
	Lecturers				
11	Unisa English lecturers		30	0.58	187.91
Merit Rankings					
10	Unisa English lecturers		25	0.52	126.16
27	English students	x	25	0.63	411.04
23	Graduate librarians		25	0.40	221.96
21	Library assistants	x	22	0.34	150.95

[a]All χ^2 values are significant at $p < .001$, except ** $p < .01$.

Across-Group Consistency

Mean ranks were computed for each of the groups shown in table 8.5. In addition, Spearman's rank order correlation coefficents (*rho*) were calculated between all student groups and some of the librarians. With some notable exceptions, correlations within this matrix are high and positive, indicating that there is wide agreement about what constitutes a good read across language, career choice, and gender differences. This is especially striking in the higher correlations between the predominantly English-speaking students and the Pretoria librarians, a conservative Afrikaans-speaking group. There are also some striking non-agreements. The two

Table 8.5. Correlations between the Preference Rankings of Various Groups (Spearman's *rho*)

			N	Whole Sample	University Female Eng	University Female Afr	University Male Eng	University Male Afr	College Female Eng	College Male Eng	College Male Afr
Whole sample			129	100							
University	Female	English	34	50**							
		Afrikaans	10	37**	81***						
	Male	English	14	86***	50**	45*					
		Afrikaans	5	83***	23	18	76***				
College	Female	English	3	81***	56**	49**	60****	54**			
	Male	English	36	88*	18	08	74****	87***	61***		
		Afrikaans	19	92***	27	19	75***	84***	78***	92***	
Librarians											
All librarians			44	89***							
Book selectors ("Generals")			5	77***							
Library assistants ("Privates")			5	74***							

Note: Decimals omitted.
*p < 0,05   **p < 0,01   ***p < 0,001

groups of university women are especially idiosyncratic, agreeing with one another's choices but not with the Afrikaans-speaking university males or with either group of college males. Both female university groups agree more strongly with the college females than with the English-speaking university males, suggesting that gender differences may override language-culture differences.

Preference Clusters

What can we learn from these figures about the ways in which readers make their choices? The two major groups of readers who carried out preference sorts were the 129 students and the 44 librarians: the mean ranks and standard deviations for these groups throw some light on choice and preference patterns.

Table 8.6 presents the authors of the thirty extracts in the sequence of the mean rank order assigned to each by these two groups of subjects. A brief characterization of the work of each is also given. These are self-explanatory except perhaps for "human drama" and "human nature": By the former is meant a character study carried by a strong narrative line, allowing the work to be read on two levels, as an adventure and as a study of behavior. In the latter, however, the focus is on character itself rather than on narrative, so that the story-seeking reader is soon disappointed.

Reference to the "mean rank" column indicates that the progression from one rank to the next is uneven: in some cases the difference is as little as .03 and sometimes it is as much as 5.1 (see ranks 12–13 and 26–27 in the student sample). By observing where the relatively larger steps from rank to rank occur, it is possible to divide the thirty extracts into rank clusters that are clearly separated from one another. Data on the formation of these clusters are given in the "step to next column," which indicates by how much the mean rank is incremented between that cluster and the next. For the students, these increments are 1.1; 1.5; 2.6; and 5.1. For the librarians, they are 1.1; 2.1; 2.0; and 3.5. For both groups, these steps are considerably larger than the other rank-to-rank increments in that section of the rank order in which they occur.

Among the students, the first and second clusters encompass eighteen extracts, including all the bestsellers, genre works, and even two twentieth-century classics, Conrad and Joyce. There is then a sharp step of 1.5 down to the next cluster, which takes in all the nineteenth-century fiction plus Bellow and Barnes, whom we classified as near-classics. Narrative nonfiction is separated from this heavy-fiction cluster by a step of 2.6: despite Ogilvie's racy style and the bestseller performance of his *Confessions*, it is lumped together with Fessler's *China*. The largest step down (5.1) is to the nonfiction. Here, it is interesting to note that the concrete material (such as anatomy) appears to have been marginally more acceptable to readers than the abstract (such as philosophy).

Turning to the librarians, we note first that the nonfiction choice pattern (ranks 27 to 30) exactly follows that of the students and is indeed considerably clearer, with a step of .9 separating the concrete from the abstract. The narrative nonfiction appears in the same lowly position (though Fessler now does better than Ogilvie), and above these, the classics now form a clear cluster, including every author we assigned to this category except Henry James. Incongruously, Gordon's seafaring humor falls squarely among the classics, indicating that the librarians feel dubious about the popularity of humor. It is striking that the first two clusters formed by the librarians' rankings almost exactly parallel the students' selections: of the sixteen items falling into this category for the librarians, all but one are the same as the students' first sixteen choices.

This analysis clarifies a previously puzzling aspect of the choice mechanisms readers may use in selecting reading matter. Instead of attempting to differentiate among all the items in an array (in a bookshop or a library), readers may assign books to discrete classes of desirability; this means that the members of each class are by and large undifferentiated, whereas classes are clearly distinct from one another. Indeed, there is an indication that for both groups, this clustering operation is essentially dichotomous: books that are desirable for leisure reading (namely, the first sixteen to eighteen items) and, on the other hand, those that are undesirable (namely, all or nearly all the classics, some of the narrative nonfiction, and all the didactic nonfiction). This latter class of undesirables is itself clearly separated into clusters representing a stepped sequence of undesirability.

A final interesting finding, briefly considered earlier in this chapter, relates to the two passages from *The Money Changers* (Items 55 and 85). Table 8.6 shows that the student sample ranked the two extracts within three places of each other—the torture extract was in sixth position and the fraud extract in tenth place (the mean ranks are 1.21 places apart). The librarians, with the clarity of vision given to those who judge others rather than themselves, found the two passages to be virtually equivalent, placing the torture extract in the sixth position and the fraud extract seventh. (The greater clarity of the librarians is also reflected by the fact that for the students, but not for the librarians, there was a great deal of ambiguity in ranking the torture extract: see below.)

Rank Ambiguity

The standard deviation of the ranks awarded to each book is a measure of the variability with which it was ranked by subjects in a particular

Table 8.6.   Stepwise Clusters in the Preference Rankings of 30 Extracts

129 Students

Rank order	Mean rank (N = 129)	SD	Cluster no.	Step to next	Range within cluster	Book code	Author and genre	
1	8.81	6.9	1	1.1	—	98	Wilbur Smith	War and love
2	9.97	6.7	2	1.5	4.5	29	Ayn Rand	Human drama
3	10.43	6.4				44	Graham Greene	Human drama
4	10.88	7.2				51	Peter O'Donnell	Crime and violence
5	10.95	6.8				86	Ian Fleming	Crime and violence
6	11.77	8.1				85	Arthur Hailey (Torture)	Crime and violence
7	12.22	9.1				13	Gavin Lyall	Crime and violence
8	12.34	7.2				30	Agatha Christie	Detective
9	12.82	7.7				52	Somerset Maugham	Human drama
10	12.98	6.6				55	Arthur Hailey	Crime and violence
11	13.22	7.2				71	James Michener	Human drama
12	13.34	7.5				62	Essie Summers	Romance
13	13.37	7.8				43	Hunter Thompson	Narrative nonfiction
14	13.93	8.2				38	Louis L'Amour	Western
15	14.08	7.1				76	Joseph Conrad	Human nature
16	14.11	8.6				16	Denise Robins	Romance
17	14.40	6.6				36	Richard Gordon	Humor
18	14.44	8.9				22	James Joyce	Human Nature
19	15.95	6.4	3	2.6	0.7	66	Djuna Barnes	Human nature
20	16.16	6.8				46	Henry James	Human nature
21	16.22	8.8				11	Herman Melville	Human nature
22	16.33	8.9				14	Jane Austen	Human nature
23	16.53	7.7				49	Saul Bellow	Human nature
24	16.66	7.2				20	Charles Dickens	Human drama
25	19.27	7.2	4	5.1	0.6	77	David Ogilvie	Narrative nonfiction
26	19.87	7.8				63	Loren Fessler	Narrative nonfiction
27	24.90	6.3	5	—	1.4	83	Gray's Anatomy	Text: concrete
28	25.05	5.6				17	Franklin Moore	Text: concrete
29	25.16	5.6				53	Harrison Gough	Text: abstract
30	26.31	5.1				23	Nathan Rotenstreich	Text: abstract

						44 Librarians	
Rank order	Mean Rank (N = 44)	SD	Cluster no.	Step to next	Range within cluster	Book code	Author
1	6.3	4.7	1	1.1	2.2	13	Gavin Lyall
2	7.2	5.3				98	Wilbur Smith
3	7.9	5.0				51	Peter O'Donnell
4	8.2	7.2				16	Denise Robins
5	8.5	6.3				30	Agatha Christie
6	9.6	7.0	2	2.1	4.3	85	Arthur Hailey (Torture)
7	10.2	7.1				55	Arthur Hailey
8	10.3	5.2				44	Graham Greene
9	10.3	6.4				86	Ian Fleming
10	11.3	5.7				29	Ayn Rand
11	11.6	7.8				38	Louis L'Amour
12	12.1	6.6				43	Hunter Thompson
13	12.2	7.2				62	Essie Summers
14	12.5	6.9				71	James Michener
15	13.5	6.6				46	Henry James
16	13.9	7.8				52	Somerset Maugham
17	16.0	7.7	3	2.0	3.8	14	Jane Austen
18	17.2	6.0				66	Djuna Barnes
19	17.2	6.9				22	James Joyce
20	17.5	6.3				49	Saul Bellow
21	18.2	5.9				36	Richard Gordon
22	18.2	5.4				76	Joseph Conrad
23	18.8	7.3				11	Herman Melville
24	19.8	5.6				20	Charles Dickens
25	21.8	6.2	4	3.5	0.8	63	Loren Fessler
26	22.6	4.9				77	David Ogilvie
27	26.1	5.0	5	—	2.1	17	Franklin Moore
28	26.5	3.3				83	Gray's Anatomy
29	27.4	2.6				53	Harrison Gough
30	28.2	2.2				23	Nathan Rotenstreich

group. A low standard deviation (or, more appropriately, variability score: see chapter 9) means that subjects agreed fairly closely on the rank of an extract, whereas a high variability score means that some subjects liked the passage very much (for themselves or for library users) while others disliked it. In figure 8.1, variability scores are plotted for the students and for the librarians for each of the thirty extracts, which are presented in the rank order sequence of the larger sample, the 129 students.

This point is clearly illustrated by comparing the variability scores for Rotenstreich (ranked thirtieth) and the torture passage in Hailey (ranked sixth). All the student subjects agreed that Rotenstreich's was one of the least desirable of the extracts; the low variability score of 5.1 on a mean rank of 26.3 indicates that this judgment was nearly unanimous. On the other hand, some readers felt that they would enjoy reading the book from which the torture passage was taken, while others ranked it much lower, giving it a variability score of 8.1 on a mean rank of 11.7. If we turn now to the librarians' rankings, based on their estimate of what the public would prefer, we note that the torture passage is no longer ranked with less certainty than the other passage from the same book (Code 55), as it was by the students. When preference and values conflict (as they may when I choose reading matter for myself) there is likely to be more variability than when I am judging the preferences of others, and this is what our data show.

In summary, there is an impressive stability of choice patterns across such important moderator variables as age, gender, home language, and value systems. Because of the limited cultural and linguistic diversity of our sample, no conclusions can be drawn about the wider, cross-cultural stability of the ludic continuum—though our findings suggest that such a study would be rewarding.

MERIT RANKING

The availability of preference, merit, and difficulty rankings for the same thirty extracts by a variety of subject groups allows us to explore questions about the impact of the social value system (and especially the Protestant Ethic) on readers' perceptions of literary merit, and the ways in which such merit judgments are related to preferences, on the one hand, and perceived difficulty, on the other.

Reliability of Merit Rankings

If our instructions to subjects performing the merit ranking were clear, and if merit criteria (of whatever appropriateness) were available to them, the coefficients of concordance for these rankings should be sig-

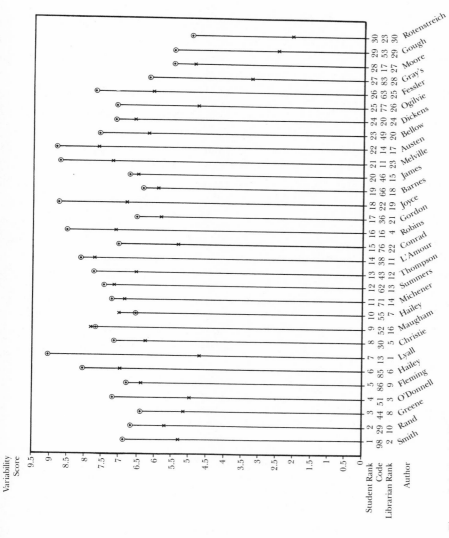

Figure 8.1. Variability Scores of Mean Ranks of 30 Extracts for 129 Students (⊙) and 44 Librarians (x)

nificant. The merit section of table 8.4 indicates that significant values of W were obtained by all four groups. The absolute levels of W are consistent with those obtained by the same and other groups for preference rankings, indicating that merit judgments were neither more nor less ambiguous than preference judgments, and that both professional and lay judges appear to use similar criteria in making merit judgments.

Another indication of the existence of such a shared set of literary value judgments would be wide agreement between diverse groups within a culture on merit rankings. The most striking result in table 8.7 is the high level of agreement between the two groups of English lecturers (*rho* [24] = .88), whom we have by virtue of their training called the professional critics. This very high rank-order correlation coefficient is open to a number of interpretations. One is that the critics' agreement is the product of their long education in literary criticism, the fruit of that heightened sensitivity to textual qualities that Practical Criticism strove to develop. Another is that we are dealing here with a cultural universal— in other words, that a sense of literary quality runs as deep as the sense of narrative quality (and hence the ability to form a ludic continuum).

Table 8.7 appears to support the second of these alternatives. Of the eight other comparisons we offer with the University of South Africa and the Port Elizabeth lecturers, none fails to reach significance, and six reach *rho* values exceeding .6. The present results may therefore indicate that the professional critics are not the possessors of an arcane gift but that, on the contrary, their judgments of literary excellence are closely emulated by lay readers. This impression is strengthened by the last two merit comparisons in table 8.7 showing that the most diverse groups of librarians also show high levels of agreement with regard to literary merit.

These high correlations raise puzzling questions about the criteria adopted by the less literate subjects in arriving at rankings that agree significantly with those of the experts. Below, we show that some readers were able to perform "merit" rankings without needing to consider literary excellence at all.

The Best Medicine Tastes the Worst

Having established the reliability of merit rankings, at least in the restricted sense that professional and lay judges appear to interpret the merit construct in congruent ways, we turn our attention to the suggestion that social value pressures constrain both critics and readers to view merit and preference as inversely related. The second part of table 8.7 provides unequivocal evidence that as the Protestant Ethic requires, the best medicine tastes the worst. All ten coefficients are in the negative direction, and of these, eight are significant, indicating that items judged to have more literary merit by professional critics or by the subjects themselves were considered to be less desirable for ludic reading.

How do subjects rate the merit of their own relaxation preferences? Only one valid comparison is available, which is for the twenty-seven follow-up students in 1978; this *rho* value is −.63. Here, the conclusion is inescapable: these students at best regard the material they prefer to relax with as devoid of merit and, at worst, as trash. The librarians, who were asked to rank lending frequency, take a pessimistic view of the public, seeing preference as the inverse of merit.

Merit and Difficulty

We return now to the puzzling questions raised by the high merit-ranking agreements reported above. The members of some of the groups involved in these comparisons (such as the library assistants) are unlikely to have made first-hand acquaintance with authors such as Austen, Conrad, James, or Joyce, both because of their limited education and because English was a second language for nearly all these subjects. It is therefore unlikely that a comparative evaluation of the literary merits of *Portrait of the Author as a Young Man* and *Thunderball* would have drawn on a store of experience with early twentieth-century English writing, or indeed on any direct knowledge of elite style. Nonetheless, these groups were able to arrive at rankings that agreed significantly with those of the professional critics.

It seems likely that in order to do so they drew on extrinsic criteria, and the difficulty-ranking task points to the kind of criterion that might have been used. Only three computations of rank correlation coefficients between merit rankings and the same subjects' difficulty rankings are available: the values of *rho* in these three cases are .78 ($p < .001$) for the library assistants; .60 ($p < .01$) for the non-BBib graduates; and .47 ($p < .05$) for the "privates." In all cases, twenty-two items were compared, giving twenty degrees of freedom. Equating merit with difficulty would indeed appear to have been an eminently practical strategy for subjects unversed in the subtleties of literary criticism: our society believes that pain and virtue are constant companions, and in reading, difficulty is one way of incurring pain. There may therefore be a purely artifactual reason for the wide agreement we have observed on the meaning of the merit construct, which appears to present no difficulties at any level of education or literacy. This artifact may be the substitution of the readily accessible difficulty construct for the more abstract and sophisticated concept of literary merit.

In order to complete the argument, we now need to demonstrate that

Table 8.7. Correlations between Merit and Preference Rankings

	N	Subject group	N	Subject group	No. of items compared	rho	p
Merit rankings compared	10	Unisa lecturers	3	UPE lecturers	25	0.88	0.001
	10	Unisa lecturers	23	Graduate librarians	25	0.75	0.001
	10	Unisa lecturers	21	Library assistants	22	0.51	0.05
	10	Unisa lecturers	27	English students	25	0.68	0.001
	3	UPE lecturers	5	"Generals": the selectors	25	0.66	0.001
	3	UPE lecturers	5	"Privates": branch librarians	25	0.51	0.05
	3	UPE lecturers	23	Graduate librarians	25	0.62	0.001
	3	UPE lecturers	10	Senior graduate librarians	25	0.64	0.001
	3	UPE lecturers	27	English students	25	0.80	0.001
	13	BBib graduates	9	Non-graduates	22	0.71	0.001
	5	"Generals"	5	"Privates"	22	0.61	0.01
INTERGROUP COMPARISONS. Merit and preference rankings compared	Merit rankings		Preference rankings				
	3	UPE lecturers	129	Port Elizabeth students	25	−0.58	0.001
	3	UPE lecturers	34	University Female English	25	−0.18	n.s.
	3	UPE lecturers	10	University Female Afrikaans	25	−0.11	n.s.
	3	UPE lecturers	14	University Male English	25	−0.57	0.001

3	UPE lecturers	5	University Male Afrikaans	25	−0.72	0.001
3	UPE lecturers	3	College Female English	25	−0.52	0.01
3	UPE lecturers	36	College Male English	25	−0.84	0.001
3	UPE lecturers	19	College Male Afrikaans	25	−0.73	0.001
23	Graduate librarians	44	All librarians	25	−0.69	0.001
21	Library assistants	44	All librarians	25	−0.46	0.05
13	Library science graduates: merit ranking with own issue-frequency ranking			25	−0.64	0.001

INTRAGROUP COMPARISONS. Merit ranking with own preference ranking for:

5	"Generals" (Graduate selectors): merit ranking with own issue-frequency ranking	25	−0.43	0.05
	Graduates without BBib: merit ranking with own issue-frequency ranking	25	−0.03	n.s.
5	"Privates" (experienced non-graduates): merit ranking with own issue-frequency ranking	25	−0.08	n.s.
10	Unisa lecturers: merit ranking with own preference ranking	25	0.90	0.001
27	English students (1978): merit ranking with own preference ranking	11	−0.63	0.001

this substitution is improper and will lead to the absurd consequence that a Chevrolet workshop manual and the poetry of T. S. Eliot are judged to be of equal worth. One way of doing so is to show that increased literary sophistication, presumably obtained by those with an education in the liberal arts, attenuates the relationship between merit and difficulty, and that the lack of such sophistication makes it stronger. Though difficulty and merit rankings were performed only by a small number of subjects, we do have Fog Index scores for each of the thirty extracts. As noted in chapter 7, the Fog, like other measures of word and sentence length, can claim to be a valid measure of difficulty. This is confirmed by our data. Nine non-graduate library assistants had a *rho* of .71 ($p < .001$) between their difficulty rankings and the Fog Index. For twenty-one library assistants, the coefficient was .68 ($p < .001$), and for five graduates without a BBib degree, the *rho* was .59 ($p < .001$; twenty-eight degrees of freedom throughout). In order to enlarge the number of groups for which merit and difficulty rankings can be compared, it therefore appears legitimate to use rankings by the Fog Index as a substitute for subjects' own difficulty rankings.

The results of this exercise are set out in table 8.8, in which the various groups are arranged in ascending order of years of education, which may be considered as a rough and approximate guide to level of literary sophistication. Though not decisive, the pattern of these results is consistent with the view we have advanced: namely, that increasing education attenuates the spurious link between merit and difficulty.

In summary, we have produced considerable evidence that for all our subject groups, as predicted, merit and preference rankings are inversely related. The close association that has been demonstrated between difficulty and merit rankings supports the notion that the value systems of many readers will be under the sway of Protestant Ethic convictions, such as that pain and virtue are constant companions. For some groups—notably those with library science degrees—this conviction seems to be supplemented by a social pessimism which holds that mass taste is depraved and that literary-merit judgments may therefore be derived from a mirror image of mass taste.

These issues lie within the obscure and complex domain of the processes by which cultural value attributions are made and become attached to cultural artifacts. Though our investigation of the socially mediated interactions of difficulty, merit, and preference judgments in the domain of reading barely scratches the surface of the issues that remain to be explored, it does cast some light on the psychological processes governing the consumption of entertainment inputs and the value placed on these inputs.

Table 8.8.   Correlations between Fog Index Ranks and Subjects' Merit
Rankings

N	Years of education	Subject group	rho	p
9	12	High school assistants	0.53	0.01
5	15	University graduates (BA and BAHons)	0.43	0.05
23	16	BBib graduates	0.49	0.05
3	19	UPE lecturers	0.46	0.05
10	19	Unisa lecturers	0.35	n.s.

Note: 23 degrees of freedom throughout.

Table 8.9.   Effects of Education on Preference Rankings

N	Subject group	N	Subject group	Items	rho	p
Preference rankings						
27	English students (1976)	129	Port Elizabeth students	30	0.56	0.01
27	English students (1978)	129	Port Elizabeth students	30	0.37	0.05
Preference rankings		Merit rankings				
27	English students (1976)	3	UPE lecturers	25	0.19	n.s.
27	English students (1978)	3	UPE lecturers	25	0.39	0.01

THE EFFECT OF EDUCATION ON MERIT AND PREFERENCE RANKINGS

The data available on the follow-up sample of English students throw an
interesting light on an issue of the greatest interest to educators; namely,
the effects of a liberal arts education on leisure reading preferences and
judgments of literary merit. First, the preference patterns of twenty-
seven students were internally consistent in both 1976 and 1978, with
concordances of .35 and .36 ($p < .001$ for both) in each of these two
years. Second, the rank correlation coefficient between their 1976 and
1978 preference rankings is .85 ($p < .001$).

However, behind this depressing finding, which seems to indicate that
two years of expensive education have left reading preferences untouched, lie some subtle changes (table 8.9). The agreement of these
English majors with the 1976 student body from which they are drawn
generated a *rho* of .56 in 1976; this fell to .37 by 1978 (a substantial
movement away from the views of their peers, even allowing for contamination of the 1976 result by the presence within the larger sample of our
twenty-seven subjects). A clue to the origin of this movement is provided
by comparing the 1976 and 1978 preference rankings of the twenty-
seven students with the merit ranking of their teachers, the three UPE

English lecturers. In 1976, this agreement produced a non-significant *rho* of .19, but by 1978 this was .39—again a substantial difference, and statistically uncontaminated. These figures provide interesting evidence that appears to point to the internalization of cultural value judgments, which may well represent an effect of the educational process. If this is indeed so, further studies along these lines could provide useful information about the ways in which social values are propagated among adults and internalized by them.

9
Excitement and Tranquility:
The Physiology of
Reading Trance

Up to this point, our investigation of the reinforcements available to the ludic reader has concerned itself with what happens inside the reader's head—with the origins of his or her reading preferences in the social value system, the delights of absorption and the possibility of entrancement, and the parallels between the reader's state of mind and those prevailing under other conditions of intense and focused attention. But the reader has not only a mind: there is a brain too, with a body attached to it, and the purpose of this chapter is to describe some of the things one's body might do when reading for pleasure and then to look briefly at some of the things it does do.

Indeed, the laboratory study, for which reading addicts were recruited to serve as subjects*, was the largest, the most complex, and certainly the most intriguing of the studies undertaken for the present project. Its purpose was to test the hypotheses deriving from the third part of our motivational model of ludic reading (Figure I.1), which suggests that some of the reinforcements available to the ludic reader are mediated by physiological change mechanisms. During some 200 hours of subject time and 50 hours of psychophysiological recording, 2,905 million bytes of digitized raw data were generated. Dealing with this mass of data—reduced by a long series of computer operations to some 148,000 scores—consumed large time and energy resources in both myself and my sponsors: the results are more fully reported in Nell (1988).

*A picture of a subject wired up to the recording apparatus is shown in figure 9.2.

VITALISM AND MATERIALISM

Searching for the physiological components of the rewards of reading may seem to be a retrograde step, coming as it does against the background of the evocative cultural and cognitive issues that have occupied us until now. In the first place, the movement from cognition to physiology appears atavistic, a return to the behaviorist tenet that the province of psychology is restricted to measurable responses, not black-box mental constructs. Second, the reader's physiological responses seem trivial when compared to the richer and more revealing material available through direct observation and self-report: the stimuli of the real world are rich and ambiguous, while clicks and flashes are often the best the psychophysiologist can offer (Gale, 1981, notes that many EEG experimental designs, which are not untypical of psychophysiological research in general, produce a state bordering on sensory deprivation in the subject). Moreover, this trend toward the trivialization of stimuli applies with even greater force to responses. For example, to report that a reader's pupil contracts when reading each of three different distasteful passages suggests that the reader's experience is invariant, whereas in fact the reader's subjective emotional responses to each of the passages may vary widely and be described quite differently by that reader.

Underlying these issues is a wider question, which is as much philosophical as psychological, since it concerns the relations of brain, mind, and consciousness. These in turn relate to a fundamental tension within science in general and psychology in particular. In the history of science, this is the tension between vitalism and materialism (Brazier, 1979), and, in psychology, between behaviorism and mentalism.

The vitalist critique of psychophysiology as "reductionist" emerges from the current revolt in psychology against the behaviorist excesses of the last several decades. Reductionism is a stirring slogan, suggesting that the wonders of creation are to be ground down into the primeval ooze from which they were fashioned, and we shall have to show that physiological precision does not rule out phenomenological richness and that a psychophysiology of cognition need be neither reductionist nor naive. We begin this review by examining the behaviorism-mentalism issue, then consider the relations between temperament, personality, and endogenous arousal levels, on the one hand, and specific thought-arousal connections, on the other; these in turn suggest a rationale for the monitoring of arousal during cognitive activity.

This review clears the way for consideration of whether the arousal that accompanies reading can be distinguished, quantitatively or qualitatively, from arousal during other mental activities; whether a specification of the nature of arousal during reading can be extended to clarify the distinctions between absorption and entrancement; and, finally, whether physiological measures are likely to throw any light on the reality status of the reading experience to the reader.

BRAIN, MIND, AND CONSCIOUSNESS

Twenty-five years ago, the relations of brain to mind and consciousness were a very real issue in psychology: brain and behavior were widely held to be real, whereas mind and mental events were at best their by-products. In current psychology, the mind-brain dilemma has lost much of its urgency, largely because of the explosive growth in the understanding of higher cortical functions since the 1950s (for example, Lezak, 1983; Walsh, 1985). An important contribution to this process of integration has been made by Roger W. Sperry, recipient of the 1981 Nobel Prize in physiology and medicine for his studies of information processing in animals and humans who had undergone commisurotomy (that is, the surgical separation of the brain's two hemispheres). The unique contribution each hemisphere makes to cognitive processing and emotion can then be studied in these split-brain subjects. Sperry suggests that we regard "consciousness as an emergent property of brain activity," while, reciprocally, "mind can rule matter in the brain and exert causal influence in the guidance and control of behavior, on terms acceptable to neuro-science and without violating . . . principles of scientific explanation" (1977, p. 239). Sperry explicitly describes this view as "a midway compromise between the older extremes of mentalism on the one hand and materialism on the other" (1969, p. 534). This in turn allows him to suggest that the chasm between the "is" of science and the "ought" of values (1977, p. 241) might be bridged by recognizing the directive role of consciousness in determining "the flow pattern of cerebral excitation" (1969, p. 533).

The intimate relations between the higher cortical functions and neural activity in discrete parts of the brain are strikingly demonstrated by the elegant correlations that have been established between "brain work" and cerebral blood flow. Even at rest, the brain is a prodigal consumer of bloodstream nutrients, with different metabolic rates for its various functional areas in direct proportion to their level of neural activity. By using a rapid washout radioactive isotope, the pioneers in this field showed that during silent reading, metabolism rises in the visual-association area, the frontal eye fields, the premotor cortex, and in the classic speech centers of the left hemisphere, Wernicke's and Broca's areas. (Lassen, Ingvar, and Skinhøj, 1978, p.57). The more recent positron emission tomography studies, which draw on new techniques in computerized tomographic brain scanning and nuclear medicine, amplify and confirm these findings (Brown & Kneeland, 1985; Yamamoto et al., 1984).

Within the context of such studies, physiological psychology need no longer serve as arbiter in a metaphysical dispute about the reality of mental events, to which behaviorism consigned it, and instead occupies a central position in determining the processes through which cognition takes place. These perceptions have made it easier for psychologists to move back into some holistic black-box areas that have long been avoided, such as mind, consciousness, and values. Reciprocally, many traditionally mentalist areas of psychology are actively strengthening their links with physical processes. A major force in current personality theory is the view that the organism's central tendency is the achievement of an optimal level of arousal, an essentially physiological concept. Other traditionally "soft" areas that increasingly seek physiological foundations are developmental psychology (reviewed in Griesel, 1981), psychopathology (Pincus and Tucker, 1974), and cognitive psychology (see chapters 5 and 6).

Within psychology, investigation of the physical processes that underly thought is undertaken by three related disciplines. The oldest is *physiological psychology*, which is based on animal research and has traditionally proceeded by observing the effects on behavior of destroying various parts of the central and peripheral nervous systems (Stern et al., 1980); its history is co-extensive with that of psychology itself, and the approach it adopts is exemplified in Lashley's classic article, "In Search of the Engram" (1950). *Psychophysiology*, in contrast, usually works with human subjects and therefore makes use of non-destructive (and usually noninvasive) techniques, such as recording heart rate and monitoring the electrical activity of the skin or the brain. Its formal history dates from 1960, when the Society for Psychophysiological Research was founded, and the experimental study reported later in this chapter is a fair example of its goals and methods.

The third member of this physically focused triad of psychological disciplines is *neuropsychology*, which dates its "definitive establishment" as a specialty from Broca's 1861 identification of the motor speech area named for him (Hecaen and Albert, 1978, p. 3). Neuropsychology, despite the "highly differentiated knowledge of the nervous system and its pathology" (Korchin and Schuldberg, 1981) that distinguishes it from other areas of psychology (Nell, 1985), is perhaps most usefully conceptualized as a subspecialty not of physiological but of cognitive psychology. The current definition of neuropsychology as a science that proposes a model relating brain dysfunction to observed behavioral deficits (Crockett, Clark, and Klonoff, 1981) does not appear to encourage this view. However, the actual clinical content of this specialty suggests that correct diagnosis may be elusive unless the neuropsychologist's knowledge of neuroanatomy and central nervous system functioning is accompanied by equivalent skills in cognitive psychology.

THE BIOLOGY OF PERSONALITY

There have been recurrent attempts to determine the biological bases of personality, the earliest of which focused on the ancient notion of temperament, which, in current psychology, is defined as the speed and intensity of emotional reactions (Eysenck, 1971). The search for a physiological basis for such traits is very old. Following Hippocrates, Galen proposed that the proportions of which the four bodily humors are mixed determines whether one's temperament will be predominantly sanguine, phlegmatic, choleric, or melancholic. This idea may be traced through Gall's essentially psychological theory of phrenology in the early nineteenth century to its re-emergence in modern psychology in the work of Gross (reviewed in Biesheuvel and Pitt, 1955). Gross suggested in 1902 that primary and secondary functioning were a dimension along which individuals might be ranged, thus, for example, accounting for the differences between mania and depression. By secondary function he meant the hypothesized continuance of brain activity for a brief time after its function has been fulfilled (Biesheuvel and Pitt, 1955), or "the aftereffect [a mental event] is capable of exerting after receding from consciousness" (Mundy-Castle, 1956, p. 95; S. Biesheuvel, personal communication, August 13, 1985). The finding by Zuckerman, Murtaugh, and Siegel (1974) that cortical excitability is reliably predicted by a measure of a personality trait (Zuckerman's Sensation Seeking Scale: 1979) gives interesting support to the early hypotheses put forward by Gross and extended by Heymans (1929).

Arousal is a basic concept in psychophysiology and is the dependent variable in most psychophysiological studies (including the laboratory study of ludic readers reported later in this chapter). Yet, although arousal is "one of the best candidates for the unification of psychology" (Gale, 1981, p. 187), its explanatory power has been weakened by imprecise use: it has a number of synonyms, at least eight senses (Gale, 1981), and three forms (cortical, autonomic, and behavioral), each with its own complexities (Lacey, 1967). Fundamental to the study of arousal is Sokolov's (1963) definition of the orienting response as the organism's "non-specific response to novelty in the environment"—for example, a dog's raised head and pricked ears. The sympathetic (or activating) branch of the autonomic nervous system, stimulated by adrenaline secretions, can rapidly convert this alerting response to a full-blown alarm reaction: the organism is poised to flee or to fight. But when the stimulus is perceived to be non-threatening, the alerted organism quiets again; in psychological terms, it has habituated to the stimulus. This restoration of homeostatic balance is often helped along by the calmative parasympathetic branch of the autonomic nervous system.

It has long been believed that the variations in an individual's excitability that occur from time to time are an imbalance in homeostasis, the direction of which can be determined by measuring the reactivity of these two branches of the automic nervous system. This view makes an early appearance in the proposal by Eppinger and Hess (1915, in Stern et al., 1980) that individuals deviate from a presumed norm in the direction of either *vagotonia* (parasympathetic dominance or placidity) or sympathicotonia (sympathetic dominance or excitability). The work of Kretschmer (1925) and Sheldon (1954) represents further attempts to isolate physical predictors of temperament. The leading current proponent of the homeostatic view of temperament is Marion Wenger, who made the first large-scale effort to determine predictors of individual autonomic responsiveness. His index of autonomic balance, which he called Ā (reviewed by Wenger and Cullen 1972), is a numeric index, arrived at by measuring seven different autonomic variables. The value of Ā indicates whether the individual is placid, dominated by the parasympathetic branch of the autonomic nervous system, or excitable, dominated by the sympathetic branch. Elizabeth Duffy (1972) has suggested that these two classes of individuals might be called *stabiles* and *labiles*.

Through a variety of channels, arousal is heir to these recurrent attempts to determine the biological bases of personality. The first of these has its origins in the historical developments just reviewed—the concepts of vago- and sympathicotonia, and their development in the work of Kretschmer, Sheldon, and Wenger.

A second major channel contributing to current arousal research may be traced to the discovery by Moruzzi and Magoun in 1949 of the reticular activating system of the brainstem, a non-specific system that mediates generalized cortical arousal (and hence a desynchronized EEG). The sensory deprivation studies that began in the 1950s (Zubek, 1969; re-evaluated in Reed, 1979) gave rise to the view, first formulated by Daniel Berlyne, that boredom is an unpleasantly high arousal level (1960, p. 189). Citing evidence in support of this hypothesis, Tushup and Zuckerman (1977) suggest that daydreaming is an attempt "to maintain a normal level of arousal by internal self-stimulation" (p. 292). Such theories suggest that the organism seeks moderately arousing experiences (the ambiguity of "moderately" is reconsidered below, in the context of reversal theory) in order to maintain positive hedonic tone. As we shall see, the more recent of these theories are robustly grounded in physiological findings.

This second channel is currently the more fertile. It has given rise on the one hand to the striking advances that have been made over the past fifteen years in the measurement of cortical arousal, especially through averaged evoked responses. On the other hand, findings on the differential activity of the reticular activating system have further encouraged a trend that began much earlier (for example, McClelland, 1951); namely, the development of personality theories that individuals differ markedly in the level of central nervous system activation they experience as optimal and in consequence develop characteristic strategies to augment or damp down experienced arousal so that it will conform to their personal threshold requirements or, to use the more usual formulation, approximate the individual's optimal level of arousal. The number of such theories is now substantial, and their indebtedness to a common origin is not always appreciated. The course adopted here is to present what is arguably the prototypical optimal-level-of-arousal theory, that of Hans Eysenck, and, at unequal length, three cognate theories (those of Zuckerman, Mehrabian, and Berlyne) that contribute to our ability to measure arousal during ludic reading and to determine its hedonic value.

Extraversion, Sensation Seeking, and Dominance

Eysenck's two-dimensional account of personality began with his studies of non-combatant enlisted men in World War II, which led him to the view that those suffering from neurotic disorders were of two main types, dysthymics and hysterics. Dysthymia is a syndrome with despondency as its central feature, and in this class were phobics and obsessionals; the other group suffered from "hysterio-psychopathic disorders" (Eysenck, 1947, in Kendrick, 1981). The depressives-dysthymics seemed to correspond to Jung's (1923) introverts and the hysterics to his extraverts. While Jung allowed admixtures of personality types and disorders, Eysenck showed by factor analysis that neuroticism and extraversion are mutually exclusive (Kendrick, 1981).

The first of the three key constructs that Gale (1981) identifies in Eysenck's theory of personality is that the extravert-introvert dimension is largely determined by genetic factors: extraverts have an endogenously lower level of excitation of the ascending reticular activating system than introverts (Gale, 1981). The second is the existence of a person-specific optimal level of arousal, which may be interpreted as an inherent drive state—that is, a motivation to achieve the optimal level—or, alternatively, as consciously experienced hedonic need.

The last of the three constructs is that introverts and extraverts develop differing strategies in order to match endogenous to optimal arousal. Extraverts are stimulus seekers, enjoying "interaction with others, novel experiences, stimuli of greater complexity, variety and intensity" (Gale, 1981, p. 184). Introverts, on the other hand, are dedicated to the reduction of incoming stimulation: they prefer old friends to new and the familiar to the novel.

Eysenck (1971) explicitly relates his own position to "the ancient Galen-Kant-Wundt scheme of the four temperaments" (Eysenck and Eysenck, 1964). In the light of the historical review offered above, it is clear that Eysenck's theory is rooted in what we have described as the homeostatic view of arousal. There are especially striking parallels with Gross' primary functioning, as Eysenck's definition of extraversion makes clear. He writes (1963) that extraversion is a pattern of behavior based on a largely inherited tendency of the central nervous system to generate rapid and lasting inhibitory potentials: this is also an acceptable description of the "vagotonic" temperament.

Zuckerman's (1979) sensation-seeking construct has illuminating parallels with Eysenck's theory. First formulated in 1964, the Sensation Seeking Scale has now appeared in its fifth revision (Zuckerman, 1979). In reviewing the antecedents of his own work, Zuckerman (p. 143) notes that sensation seeking and extraversion are highly correlated. For example, Eysenck's (1967) work on sex and personality found that extraverts get high scores on a promiscuity factor, are hedonists and happy philanderers, with an appetite for frequent sex contacts. Similarly, Zuckerman (1979) shows that high sensation seekers of both sexes report a greater variety of heterosexual activities with a greater variety of partners than low sensation seekers and also have an interest in visual and auditory erotic stimuli. There are furthermore striking similarities between the questions loading the extraversion factor on the Eysenck Personality Inventory (EPI) (Eysenck and Eysenck, 1964) and many of the items on the Sensation Seeking Scale (SSS) (Zuckerman, 1979, appendix G). In table 9.1, parallels from the Sensation Seeking Scale are given for five of the twenty-four extraversion items on the Eysenck Personality Inventory.

A second set of parallels between extraversion and optimal-level-of-arousal personality theories is found in the environmental psychology of Mehrabian and Russell (1974). They propose three emotional dimensions (pleasure, arousal, and dominance). The arousal dimension is later elaborated by Mehrabian (1976) as a predictor of the ways individuals manipulate their use of environments (a discotheque or a deserted beach) to raise or damp down endogenous arousal levels and thus increase their inner feelings of control or dominance. This model is readily applied to reading inputs. In this chapter, we examine the arousal consequences of reading; in the next, we take note of the reader's dominance or "sovereignty."

Table 9.1.   Parallels between the Eysenck Personality Inventory (EPI) and the
Sensation Seeking Scale (SSS)

	EPI		*SSS*
1.	Do you often long for excitement?	25B.	I like to have new and exciting experiences.
10.	Would you do almost anything for a dare?	10B.	I would like to try some of the new drugs that produce hallucinations.
		23A.	I would like to try parachute jumping.
25.	Can you usually let yourself go and enjoy yourself a lot at a gay party?	1A.	I like "wild" uninhibited parties.
		30B.	Keeping the drinks full is the key to a good party.
27.	Do other people think of you as being very lively?	24A.	I prefer friends who are excitingly unpredictable.
46.	Would you be very unhappy if you could not see lots of people most of the time?	5A.	I get bored seeing the same old faces.

Berlyne's Experimental Aesthetics

These relatively somber issues leave untouched an issue of the greatest importance to us; namely, pleasure. Indeed, psychophysiology's remarkable failure to accommodate the pursuit of pleasure might raise serious doubts about its applicability to the study of ludic reading, of which pleasure is the most essential attribute. Fortunately, however, at least one system of experimental psychology does accommodate hedonic value, Daniel Berlyne's "new experimental aesthetics" (the old began with Fechner in the late nineteenth century and died, impoverished, not long after: Berlyne, 1973).

Berlyne's models of aesthetic processes are deliberately reductionist but offer strong links with laboratory empiricism and mainstream psychological theory. From the 1950s until his death in 1976, Berlyne developed a psychobiological theory of aesthetics that has been profoundly influential in studies of intrinsic motivation, the hedonic consequences of arousal, and environmental perception (Berlyne, 1969, 1971, 1974; Konečni, 1978). The empirical base of this theory derives from the study of the conflict-producing stimuli he named *collative variables;* these, he writes, "seem to constitute the crux of the aesthetic phenomenon" (1973,

p. 9). The term *collative* derives from the Latin *collatum,* meaning collected or compared; and by collative properties, Berlyne means such elements as novelty, complexity, surprisingness, ambiguity, and puzzlement. In other words, to decide how novel, ambiguous, or puzzling a stimulus is, we need to collate information about it from two or more sources. Indeed, Berlyne proposes that experimental aesthetics be "identified with the study of motivational effects of collative variables" (1972, p. 305).

The pleasurableness of an aesthetic stimulus does not lie on the same dimension as its interest value or complexity. Berlyne has demonstrated that pleasure reaches its peak at moderate levels of complexity, whereas very uniform stimuli, and those that are highly complex, tend to be aversive. It is therefore easy to understand why chocolate-box art, with its facile beauty and moderate complexity, is rated as more pleasing than modern or abstract art, with its high level of complexity. "That's a fascinating piece you have there, but how can you live with it?"

The pleasurableness of arousal, central to Berlyne's aesthetic theory, must now be considered in relation to motivation theory, on the one hand, and as a consequence of exposure to collative variables, on the other. He argues that "our view of motivation will be broadened considerably if we are obliged to accept conflict as an additional source of drive" (1966, p. 86) because by so doing we are better placed to explain just what it is that reinforces intrinsically motivated behavior. When we say we do something "for its own sake," we are, as Berlyne points out, begging the question. If the reinforcement does not come from some external consequence, "it must come from some inner consequence, and in particular from some effect on the central nervous system" (1969, p. 841).

At the core of Berlyne's system is the proposition that arousal is the "inner consequence" that is rewarding to the central nervous system. We have already reviewed a good deal of evidence that supports this proposition, to which Berlyne adds both experimental evidence (1967) and observational support—for example, that "pleasant or rewarding events seem virtually always to produce observable changes in arousal level" (1971, p. 81), such as the quiescence of a hungry animal that has eaten or the elation of a child unwrapping a gift. The two-factor theory of hedonic value (1971, p. 136) rests on the complementary mechanisms of *arousal boost* (moderate arousal increments pursued because they are satisfying in themselves, such as a baby's play with a new toy) and *arousal jag* (in which a temporary rise in arousal is sought "for the sake of the pleasurable relief that comes when the rise is reversed"). That butt of countless jokes, the man who banged his head against the wall because it felt so good when he stopped, must be pleased to learn that he has now been immortalized in a psychological theory. The operation of the two-factor theory is most clearly set out in Berlyne's adaptation (1973, p. 20) of the curve Wundt developed in 1874 to accommodate the emotions (figure 9.1a).

Reverting to the previous distinction between "pleasing" and "interesting," we may now add that stimuli which are judged to be "pleasing" appear to be associated with the arousal-boost mechanism and to remain within the individual's range of positive hedonic value, while stimuli rated as "interesting" have an arousal potential within the aversive range but permit relatively prompt arousal reduction through cognitive and perceptual processing (Berlyne, 1973; and the same arousal-jag reduction mechanism, he argued in 1969, accounts for our pleasure in seeing the point of a joke).

Reversal Theory

Berlyne's theory, like other optimal-level-of-arousal versions of behavior, is formulated within a paradigm that draws extensively on the principles of operant conditioning, on the one hand, and homeostasis on the other. Apter's (1979) reversal theory, in contrast, is phenomenological, taking account of the way experiences feel. But, surprisingly, it is compatible with Berlyne's theory, and the effect of superimposing Apter's metamotivation on Berlyne's arousal-jag mechanism is to gain a richer understanding of the ways in which we enjoy aesthetic stimuli.

Apter distinguishes between behavior ("running") and action, which has a conscious intention ("running to catch a train"); to interpret an action, we need to know both what an individual is doing (his behavior) and why. This knowledge may not be easy to come by, since a goal may change during a single behavior sequence (one starts eating because one is hungry and continues eating in order to savor the food; starts reading to allay boredom and continues in entrancement). As we shall see, reversal theory is able to accommodate these alternations without strain by distinguishing between telic and paratelic activities.

For example, if I decide to cycle to work today, either the goal or the behavior may have priority. If my car won't start, my behavior is telic (from the Greek word for *goal*); if it's a beautiful day and I have time to spare, my cycling behavior is paratelic. Apter elaborates: "An example of someone in a paratelic state of mind . . . would be someone reading a novel, where the goal of completing the novel was not seen by him as an essential one, but the behaviour itself and the stimulation related to that behaviour were felt as enjoyable and in need of no further justification" (1979, p. 52).

Telic and paratelic states are bi-stable, like a light switch, which will return to the "on" or "off" position from any intermediate position.

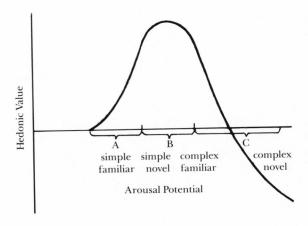

a. Effects of novelty and complexity on arousal
(from Berlyne, 1971, p. 193)

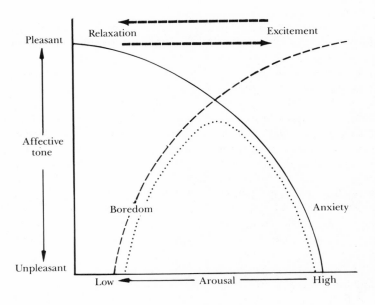

b. Perceived arousal and affective tone (from Apter, 1979, p. 56)

Figure 9.1. Two Approaches to the Measurement and Interpretation of Arousal

The second leg of Apter's theory relates these two states of mind—the goal-directed and the activity-centered—to states of arousal, namely, relaxation and excitement. However, relaxation can edge over into boredom, and excitement can run into anxiety.

The rock climber, suspended from a cliff face by his harness, is an excitement seeker; the same individual, relaxed that night beside the campfire, is likely to find high arousal aversive and even anxiety-provoking. Some of these distinctions are set out in figure 9.1b: high arousal (at the right) is perceived as pleasant in one metamotivational state and unpleasant in another; similarly, low arousal can be perceived either as relaxation or as boredom.

One cannot be sure about the individual's metamotivational state either by observing the behavior or by knowing what the underlying goal is unless one has "inside information": the telic-paratelic distinction rests on the nature of the act which the individual sees himself performing (see, for example, Apter and Smith, 1978, on excitement-anxiety reversals in sexual behavior). Apter also sees these as personality states in that people are predisposed to be in one rather than the other—though "one point which the whole reversal theory analysis underlines is that individuals are inherently inconsistent."

Implications. The advantages of Apter's bi-stable relaxation-excitement curves (the reversals between these two stable states are indicated in figure 9.1b by broken-line arrows between them) are readily apparent in accounting for many aspects of everyday life. A visitor to a resort hotel, for example, may start the evening at six with cocktails, move on to the more exciting setting of a musical show, and then spend several hours in a casino, the most exciting setting of all. In terms of optimal-level-of-arousal theory, it is difficult to account for these many consecutive hours of freely chosen elevation of sensory input to "aversively" high levels—and, for that matter, for the very low level of arousal the same individual may display on leaving the casino for a long stroll in a moonlit garden or an hour in a quietly decorated and deserted lounge before retiring.

This perfectly usual kind of behavior places considerable strain on the arousal-jag concept. The traditional inverted U of the Wundt curve (represented by a dotted line in figure 9.1b) suggests that both very high and very low arousal states are unpleasant, although this is in conflict with everyday experience. But the pleasure we take in protracted excitement and relaxation is readily accommodated by Apter's concept of metamotivational switches.

Sudden switches from arousal to relaxation, in which both states are perceived as pleasurable, are of interest because reading in bed before falling asleep is especially prized by ludic readers. It seems likely that reading induces a state of some arousal, succeeded, as the book is laid down and the light switched off, by relaxation and sleep. Sexual intercourse seems to offer an analogue: orgasm terminates a very high arousal level, and postcoital relaxation very rapidly takes over (figure 9.3 shows this parallels the arousal-relaxation sequence of the ludic readers in the laboratory). Apter's metamotivation offers a framework in which not only the high reward value of the excitement-relaxation switch but also the prolonged enjoyment of each can be explained.

Reversal theory also seems to offer an explanation of an otherwise puzzling phenomenon (which also occurs in other domains), namely that a given book and reader may interact quite differently at different times. On one occasion, as I return from a wrestling match, I read *Thunderball* with mounting excitement; later that day, after an hour's work in the garden, I find the same book pleasantly relaxing. As Apter suggests, "a given piece of behaviour may be performed to achieve various different goals at different times" (1979, p. 47).

Phenomenology and set. The phenomenological states that Apter calls "metamotivational" have long been known in psychology by a different name, "cognitive set." For example, Lazarus has shown that autonomic responses to frightening films of pain and genital mutilation are modified by differing soundtracks that emphasize, deny, or intellectualize the film's trauma (Lazarus and Opton, 1966). These findings have an analogue in Tannenbaum's mass communication analysis of indexing effects: a picture of a couple embracing on a station platform loaded to the "sad" side of the semantic differential when captioned "Parting" and to the "happy" side when captioned "Reunion." Tannenbaum (1971) has demonstrated similar effects for headlines and newscast leads.

In fact, the recent ascendancy of cognitive psychology has eroded earlier convictions among psychophysiologists about stimulus-response specificity, which holds that different stimuli (fear and anger, for example: Ax, 1953) produce distinctive arousal patterns. Lang (1979) notes the recent general acceptance of the view that "the physiological responses of subjects are . . . undifferentiated, a kind of bubbling physiological soup, which is stirred up and given its distinctive taste by the subject's cognitive appraisal" (p. 507). This is in fact the rather radical view taken by Apter: arousal level is interpreted in terms of the individual's regnant needs. This suggests that the use the organism makes of reading inputs may be determined by its needs at the time; in other words, that the autonomic responses associated with reading trance may be patterned either toward arousal or toward relaxation.

A Synthesis

Figure 9.1b shows that Berlyne's principles can be transposed into the reversal paradigm not only unscathed but considerably enriched. For example, the point at which high interest dips into aversively high arousal is placed under phenomenological rather than autonomic control. The obvious answer to the question, "That's a fascinating piece, but how can you live with it?" is "Because I like it." Within Apter's paradigm, this answer can as readily be attributed to an introvert as to a sensation seeker. The optimal-level-of-arousal systems, on the other hand, all assume that this level is stable for each individual, while metamotivation suggests that it fluctuates within individuals under their own cognitive control. The synthesis certainly makes it easier to understand the arousing and relaxing pleasures of ludic reading.

THOUGHT AND AROUSAL

The relations between brain and consciousness, on the one hand, and personality and arousal, on the other, point to the possibility that thought is also anchored in physical processes. We can develop a rationale for the selection of physical response systems that are related to cognitive activity only if we can demonstrate that mental activity has physical correlates—in other words, we need to show that there is such a thing as a cognitive psychophysiology, and that it rests on an adequate experimental basis. Two perspectives on this issue are possible. One is the moderate view that cognitive processes have physiological accompaniments; the other, more radical, holds that covert physiological processes (those that can be observed only with the help of special apparatus) are not merely an accompaniment of cognition but are themselves an essential part of cognition. For example, this radical view holds that language comprehension is bound up with the neuromuscular codes generated by each position of the lips, tongue, and larynx: when a stimulus impinges, it is transduced and transmitted so that eventually a verbal code is generated with the intimate involvement of the skeletal musculature. This neuromuscular processing results in phonetic coding that is neurally transmitted from the speech muscles to the central nervous system; arrival of the afferent neural volleys leads to the central evocation of phonemes, and to lexical and semantic processing (McGuigan, 1978, p. 378–79).

The more moderate view is associated with the work of Peter Lang, who has shown that events in the cortex and the viscera are different when an interesting stimulus is presented than when a dull one is used (Lang, Ohman, and Simons, 1978) and that imaginary activity has physical consequences. There are both old and recent findings that support this view. Lang (1979) cites Shaw's 1940 evidence that as imagined weights increased in imagined heft, so did arm muscle tension, and that the amplitude of eye movements in subjects imagining a recently seen rotating drum correlated with reported image vividness. Lang also notes the effect of the specific imagery instructions given to subjects. For example, in one of Jacobson's classic series of seven studies on "neuromuscular states during mental activities" (1930–31; references in McGuigan, 1978), subjects told to "muscularly" imagine bending their arm showed increased muscle tension in that arm but no increase in eye movements, whereas when they were told to visually imagine the same movement, the electromyogram remained unchanged but eye movements increased.

More important, Lang (1979) has demonstrated that emotional imagery does not produce changes in heart rate while action imagery does: "Heart rate accelerates in a situation where there are action-instigating elements, and not where there are not, even when both kinds of situation could be described as emotion provoking or arousing" (Elliot, 1969, p. 222).

Though this approach promises to relate to many aspects of the ludic reader's experience, Lang's work in fact emphasizes the distance between natural reading and the elaborate training procedures that are needed to produce significant physiological responses to imagery (1979). The trend of his data is therefore to reinforce the negative conclusion suggested by the literature to be reviewed in chapter 10, namely, that imagery is by no means essential to the comprehension or enjoyment of the ludic reader.

The Primacy of Muscle Activity

We have already noted McGuigan's contention that physiological activity, especially muscle activity, is not merely an accompaniment but an essential constituent of cognitive processes. However, there is wide support for McGuigan's ostensibly radical position regarding the major role played by muscle activity in thinking. For example, Sperry says that neuropsychologically, it is readily apparent that "the sole product of brain function is muscular coordination" (in Malmo, 1972), echoing the Russian physiologist Sechenov cited by McGuigan (1978, p. iii): "All the endless diversity of the external manifestations of the activity of the brain can finally be regarded as one phenomenon—that of muscular movement."

The intimate connection between cognitive activity and muscle activity is further illumined by Malmo's (1972) observation that subjects performing a tracking task under high-incentive conditions showed more elevated heart rate, respiration, skin conductance, and muscle tension than in a low-incentive condition, even though the effort required under the two conditions is identical. The high incentive, suggests Malmo, sets in motion neurophysiological mechanisms that prepare the subject for greater muscular exertion than is required. Moreover, these indicators rise steadily for the duration of the task, though EEG records show that brain activity remains constant. Malmo speculates that the increasing muscle tone may be the input "that keeps certain brain functions on a level course. . . . Feedback into the brain from tensed muscles is essential for staying alert" (1972, pp. 971–72). McGuigan (1978) speculates that "sustained tonic muscle activity functions to maintain general bodily arousal" by inputs to the brain's reticular activating system (p. 357).

Cognitive Psychophysiology

The major thrust of McGuigan's work is toward a theory of symbol-system processing, and especially of language comprehension. He shows, for example, that there is heightened covert behavior in the preferred arm while reading, memorizing, and listening and covert finger responses in the deaf while thinking (1978, p. 351). McGuigan argues that oral, nonoral, and neurophysiological responses all contribute to the processing of language: an "alternative code" is generated by the *non-oral musculature* (thinking "bicycle riding" causes symbolic non-oral responses—leg muscle contractions—to occur almost simultaneously with oral responses: p. 382).

McGuigan (1978) also cites evidence that during reading, activity of the *oral musculature* increases with increasing textual and environmental demands (such as when reading under adverse conditions): the amount of information generated and transmitted is proportionate to the amount of covert oral responding. Of course, if these muscle codes are to be used by the speech centers of the brain, they will have to be in binary form. McGuigan does in fact show that the speech stream can readily be converted to binary codes (1978, pp. 332, 367). Such coding is in turn compatible with the speech muscles, since neuromuscular processes can also be represented as single on-off events (single nerve impulses; single muscle-fiber contractions). This digital binary model of speech perception (p. 359) is fully compatible with processing modes in the central nervous system. It is interesting that McGuigan's model of language processing supports the importance Brown (1981) and others ascribe to subvocalization in the comprehension of difficult material or in reading under difficult circumstances. His suggestion (p. 369) that experimentally produced decreases in covert speech muscle activity may reduce reading proficiency is of particular interest.

Response System Selection

We must now decide which covert responses to measure during ludic reading. Thus far we have established that mind and brain are inseparable, that personality is powerfully influenced by biology, and that thought does indeed produce arousal. Accordingly, the elementary bodily processes that give rise to thought and arousal are of concern to psychologists. Knowledge in this area remains so meager that even the discovery that, among neurologists, covert extensor activity in the big toe invariably accompanies articulation of the word "Babinski" would represent a significant advance. Although thought has no consciousness of its biological constituents, a specification of these constituents will undoubtedly advance our understanding of thought and behavior and our ability to control them, in the same way that the discovery of muscle-action potentials led to the development of biofeedback techniques. Control is certainly not a synonym for understanding, but it is often its precursor.

Within the domain of reading, the work of Berlyne, Lang, and McGuigan indicates that the reader's physical responding and its possible patterns during ludic reading, though themselves largely unconscious, feed back to the reader's conscious perceptions, and that knowledge of these responses is likely to tell us more about the rewards ludic reading gives the reader than we knew before.

This rationale requires that we select the physiological response systems most closely related to the ludic reader's experienced pleasure in reading. Ideally, all such systems should be monitored. These would include those specified in McGuigan's taxonomy (1978, p. 77), such as muscle activity of the oral areas (tongue, lips, larynx, jaw) and non-oral areas (finger, arm, leg); audiometric measures; salivation measures and electrogastrograms; pupilometry; cardiovascular responses; electrodermal measures; and such neurophysiological measures as the EEG, evoked potentials, and so forth. In addition, biochemical assays of serum endocrine levels would be useful. In practice, the response systems available for use in the present study were electromyograms at three sites on the head and neck, heart rate, electrical activity of the skin, and respiration rate.

LUDIC READERS IN THE LABORATORY

In chapter 6, there was evidence that our thirty-three ludic readers greatly enjoyed their thirty minutes of reading in the laboratory despite the intrusive novelty of the laboratory situation and the twelve electrodes fixed to each reader's neck, arm, leg, and foot (some of which can be seen in figure 9.2). A great deal of planning went into inducing a relaxed state of mind compatible with true ludic reading. Habituation during the first, unrecorded, laboratory session certainly helped subjects feel at ease during the second, when all data gathering was done. Another contribution to reading pleasure was made by the tape-recorded instructions played to subjects at the start of each session. They are reproduced in part below to illustrate the mental set subjects were encouraged to adopt and to give a brief overview of the laboratory procedure:

Thank you for volunteering as a subject for our study of reading. This tape recording explains just what will be happening during both the first and the second sessions. When you hear it for the second time at the beginning of the second session, you will pick up many little items of information you missed during your first hearing of the tape. So please listen carefully the second time also!

The noise you heard as you entered the laboratory is there to mask out other sounds from outside the laboratory that may distract you during the experiment.* It has no other purpose, and you will hear it throughout the procedure, except when you are receiving instructions.

The electrodes I am attaching will record such things as heart rate, muscle

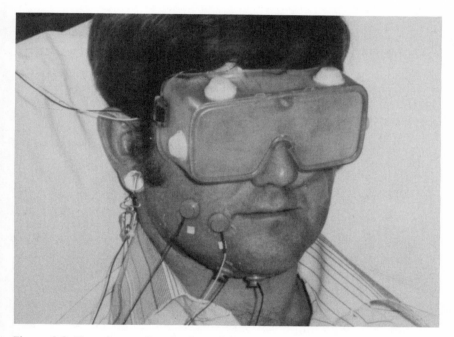

Figure 9.2. Translucent Goggles in Position
One of the laboratory subjects during the 25 minutes of mild sensory deprivation (Periods G and H), wearing a pair of translucent goggles and hearing only white noise over the laboratory loudspeaker. Leads to the forehead electrodes emerge from under the goggles, and two other pairs of muscle-activity electrodes can be seen at the corner of the mouth and under the chin. The thermistor used to monitor respiration is visible under the left nostril, and an earth electrode is clipped to the right ear.

*White noise—a sound like the hiss of escaping compressed air—was used for this masking effect.

activity, skin potential and respiration. The electrodes are fixed in position with adhesive collars. Although they are easy to remove, the collars hold the electrodes in position very firmly: you can even swim vigorously without dislodging them! So you can really forget about the electrodes and pay them no attention at all after they are fixed in position. They'll look after themselves! To give better contact, we put a little salty paste in the form of a jelly into the electrodes where they touch the skin.

These are standard, harmless laboratory procedures of the same kind that a doctor uses when he records a cardiogram. None of the electrodes penetrate the skin, nor do they carry any electrical current except for the minute voltages generated in your own body.

You are also probably curious about the purpose of the study. It is designed to find out what physical effect reading has on people. Some reports say people read a lot because books excite them, others claim that books relax them, while there is also some evidence that reading neither excites nor relaxes, but simply takes people's minds off their worries.

You can best help us by reading the book you have brought with you exactly as if you were at home, so that whatever usually happens to you when you read will happen here too. Of course, the more relaxed you are, the more likely this is to happen.

Each of your two sessions in the laboratory will follow an identical pattern. [Here the laboratory tasks reviewed in the next section were described.]

There are two key points I want to emphasize. First, this is not a reading test, and I'll ask you no questions about what you have read. Secondly, the key word in the whole procedure is relaxation. In order to relax, feel free to wiggle and move your head, to laugh and frown and smile. On the other hand, don't move unnecessarily. I know that this is a contradiction, but there's no avoiding it: move your body as much as you need to for comfort, but no more than you must to keep relaxed.

Activity Periods and Response Systems

Each laboratory subject engaged in eight separately timed activity periods chosen to provide a variety of tasks that could usefully be compared with ludic reading. During Period F subjects relaxed for five minutes with eyes shut: response levels in this period served as a comparative baseline. In Periods G (10 minutes) and H (15 minutes) subjects kept their eyes open while wearing translucent goggles (figure 9.2) and listening to white noise. Following Berlyne's suggestion that boredom is an unpleasantly aroused state (1960, p. 189), arousal was expected to rise during this period of mild sensory deprivation. During Period I, subjects read a book of their own choice, and for Period J, they laid the book aside, closed their eyes, and relaxed for five minutes. In Period K, they read a difficult book for three minutes, and in Period M, subjects were asked to do some mental arithmetic. In Period Q, they were asked to visualize someone they knew well, what they had done on their last vacation, and how a red apple looks when it is cut into sections.

During each of these periods, seven separate sets of data were collected and later analyzed. In order to understand figure 9.3, which sums up the results of the laboratory study, some information about the seven response systems monitored in the laboratory is necessary.

EMG stands for electromyogram, which is a recording of the tiny electrical potentials generated by contracting muscles; the more vigorous the contraction, the greater the amplitude of the recorded waveform. Three sets of muscle-activity data were collected. The top pair of electrodes (EMG1 in figure 9.3), just above the eye and concealed behind the goggles in figure 9.2, detected overt activity of the forehead muscle—a frown, raised eyebrows—and also more subtle indicators of psychic tension (Goldstein, 1972). Smiling and pouting are mediated by a pair of muscles (levator and depressor anguli oris) that cross near the corner of the mouth, and the second pair of EMG electrodes (EMG2) was located at this point. The third pair (EMG3) was placed on the platysma muscle just under the chin to detect such oral activity as subvocalization, movements of the masticatory apparatus, swallowing, and so on.

Respiration rate (RR in figure 9.3) was measured by a thermistor taped under a nostril (figure 9.2). This is a device that measures temperature changes by almost simultaneous changes in its electrical resistance. The warmth of each exhalation thus generated a measurable electrical potential, except for subjects who breathed through their mouths—either habitually or because they had colds—whose respiration records had to be discarded.

Measurement of the electrical activity of the skin, pioneered by Féré in 1888, was historically one of the first psychophysiological signals to be monitored and became known as the "psychogalvanic reflex," which gained notoriety because of its inclusion in lie-detector tests. Because autonomic arousal reliably produces increases in skin moisture, thus lowering electrical resistance (Edelberg, 1972), we also used a measure of skin electrical activity, the skin potential response (SPR). The two most active electrodermal sites on the body are the palms of the hands and the soles of the feet. We recorded from the foot because movement disrupts the SPR record and the hands are continually active during reading (gripping the book, turning pages).

Heart activity, routinely measured by the physician's electrocardiograph (ECG), is a robust signal that has the great advantage of being comparable from one laboratory to another (Elliott, 1969). It is sensitive to the orienting response and to information processing (Lacey and Lacey, 1978) and, directly or through other variables, to emotional experience (Jones and Johnson, 1978). Heart rate is the number of beats per

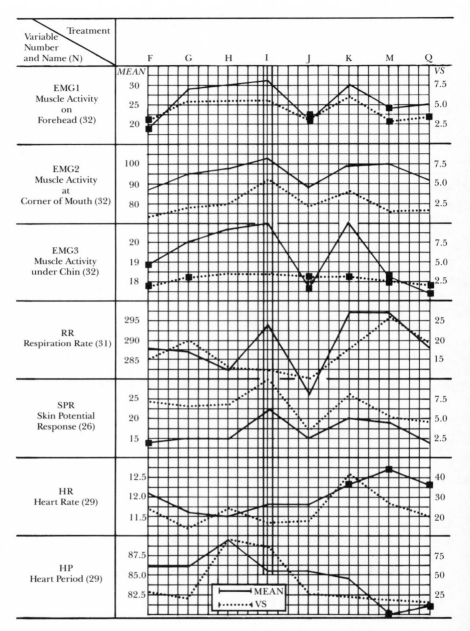

Figure 9.3. Mean and Variability-score (VS) Trends for All Subjects Pooled across 7 Variables and 8 Treatments

Note: Number of subjects pooled for each of the variables is indicated in parentheses on left. Squares on the plot indicate significant Dunnett's *t* values (see "Significance of Differences," p. 194 below.)

time period—in our study, per ten seconds. Heart period, the last of the variables plotted in figure 9.3, is the interval from one beat to the next, and provides a rather more sensitive indicator of second-by-second fluctuations in cardiac responding. Very roughly, these measures are reciprocals, since the more rapid the heartbeat, the higher the *rate* score, and the lower the *period* (or interval between heartbeats). This reciprocal relationship is illustrated in the last two rows of figure 9.3: as heart rate drops, heart period rises, and vice versa. However, this is clearly an imperfect reciprocality, because heart period can vary markedly even though rate remains more or less constant (Heslegrave, Ogilvie, and Furedy, 1979). We used the ECG Lead II configuration—that is, left arm and right leg—which gives larger and more prominent peak or R-waves than other configurations.

Arousal Trends

An enormous amount of data has been consolidated into each of the 112 points plotted in figure 9.3. For example, Treatment F (five minutes' relaxation with eyes shut) is one of the briefer of the laboratory activities. In the first row, for EMG1, the original analog recording was converted to 1,204 digital data points per second, giving 3,072,000 data points for the five minutes. Since the graph consolidates all subject data, this figure must be multiplied by the number of subjects (the figure 32 appears in parentheses under "EMG1") for whom data were entered into this cell, yielding a grand total of 98,304,000 data points for EMG1 in Treatment F. The sixteen mean scores plotted in each row of figure 9.3 thus represent mean standard score data based on an initial pool of 1,395,916,800 data points per row. The complex series of operations by which the raw data were coded by time block, cleaned of artifact, and standardized, is documented elsewhere (Nell, 1983).

In each activity period, two kinds of data interest us: average arousal level across all subjects, shown in figure 9.3 by solid lines, and also the extent to which arousal fluctuated in this period. Statistically, variability is measured by computing the standard deviation around the mean. To make it clear that this measure—broken lines in figure 9.3—reflects the subjects' response lability during each task period, we refer to these as "variability scores."

Period I, the thirty minutes of ludic reading, was of course the point of the laboratory study and the criterion treatment with which the others were compared. Perhaps the most important single decision in planning this experiment was to allow each subject to bring a book of his or her own choice to the laboratory rather than have all subjects read the same book. The latter course, masquerading as "standardization," would in fact have destandardized the experimental manipulation, in which our interest is focused on the reader's response to ludic reading. This will be comparable across readers only if the stimulus is equivalent, which means that each reader must bring a book he or she thoroughly enjoys. Accordingly, the comparability of our experimental manipulation across readers rests on the fact that each subject used a different freely chosen (and therefore equivalent) stimulus.

There were enormous variations in the kinds of books selected, ranging from *The Eye of the Storm* (Subject 205) to a neo-Nazi epic attributed to Adolf Hitler (Subject 107). A complete list of the books subjects read in the laboratory, the pages they read, and their most liked pages appears in Appendix C.

Does ludic reading differ from other waking states? This is a question that can best be answered by briefly considering the effect of each of the treatments, which were chosen to provide a variety of states that can usefully be compared with pleasure reading. In making these comparisons, we deal first with muscle activity, respiration rate, and electrical activity of the skin, shown in the first five rows of figure 9.3, and defer for the moment consideration of cardiac activity.

The steady rise in arousal from Period I through Periods G and H, during which subjects could see nothing through the translucent goggles and heard nothing except white noise, seems to confirm the view that boredom is an unpleasantly activated state, becoming more activated as it is prolonged.

Ludic reading is substantially more activated than baseline responding across all five response systems. Moreover, as predicted by experimental aesthetics, it is also substantially more labile than other activities on all the variables except respiration rate. For skin potential and muscle activity at the mouth, variability is substantially more elevated during reading than in other conditions. The two remaining muscle channels do not disconfirm the hypothesis: in the forehead muscle, the variability score is as high during reading as in two other conditions, and lower than only one; and on the throat, the variability during reading is one of the two highest scores. Also of interest is the fact that the same response pattern, on the same variables, is discernible for work reading (Period K). We can generalize and say that the two kinds of reading investigated both show greater lability than other activities.

Relaxing after reading. The single most striking feature of the graph is the precipitous decline in arousal in Period J, in which subjects responded to the instruction, "Lay the book aside, close your eyes, and relax completely for five minutes. Go to sleep or stay awake, just as you feel inclined."

It seems likely that the delight readers take in bedtime reading is linked to this marked drop in arousal as reading ceases, which, as reference to RR and SPR variables indicates, is not restricted to skeletal muscle but occurs also in the emotion-sensitive respiratory system and in the autonomic nervous system, as shown by the fall in skin potential. The powerful reward value associated with a sudden drop in activation level (after sex, or when a climber reaches a mountain peak) discussed earlier now also seems applicable to the ludic reader.

The three cognitive tasks (Periods K, M, and Q) that followed the eyes-shut relaxation in Period J were, respectively, hard reading, mental arithmetic, and visualizing. When the study was planned, it was hoped that including these tasks would help determine which kinds of mental activity elicited responses similar to ludic reading and which did not: again, the rather gross measures and simple analyses employed did not allow such a fine-grained distinction to be made. Probably for this reason, neither the mental arithmetic nor the visualizing task periods produced anything of psychophysiological interest.

Work reading. The distinction between ludic and work reading is an important one. The response-bound hard reading task in Period K emulated a work-reading task since subjects were told as they began that they would be asked "to sum up the content of what you have read in a few sentences at the end of the session." The text used was a cognitive psychology book by Jerry Fodor called *The Language of Thought* (1975). Beneath the disarming simplicity of Fodor's style is a great deal of abstract complexity. The first few sentences read as follows:

> There used to be a discipline called speculative psychology. It wasn't quite philosophy because it wasn't concerned with empirical theory construction. It wasn't quite psychology because it wasn't an experimental science. But it used the methods of both philosophy and psychology because it was dedicated to the notion that scientific theories should be both conceptually disciplined and empirically constrained.

Few subjects reached the end of the first page during the three-minute reading period. Our review of attention (chapter 4) leads us to expect that the effort invested in this task and the response demands it imposed would result in a notably higher level of arousal than during ludic reading.

Though arousal is certainly elevated during hard reading, the most striking feature of Period K in figure 9.3 is that with only one exception (respiration rate), these peaks are all equal to or lower than those for ludic reading. This finding is in conflict with Kahneman's well-supported view that increased effort entails increased arousal (chapter 4). It is also counterintuitive, in that I feel relaxed during ludic reading but under stress with a book such as *The Language of Thought*, especially if I am to be examined on it. However, the recurrence of the same pattern across five variables can hardly be due to chance and indeed suggests the interesting possibility that the ludic reader's perceived relaxation is in fact misperceived arousal. In other words, physiologically substantial arousal may occur during perceived effortlessness, and perceived effort may entail less physiological arousal than the individual imagines to be the case.

The high levels of Variable 39 (activity of the platysma muscle) during Period K is interesting. It is tempting to attribute this level to subvocalization, which various sources (reviewed in chapter 4 and earlier in this chapter) have led us to associate with the reading of difficult texts. However, our electrode placement renders this variable as sensitive to swallowing as to subvocalization, so that we are now unable to determine whether the high level of this variable during Period K is because hard reading encourages subvocalization or salivation! Since swallowing can be a stress reaction, this could account for the otherwise surprising finding that the platysma record (EMG3) generated the largest number of significant relations with reading.

Heart rate and information processing. The interpretive principles that apply to cardiac responding are rather more complex than those hitherto used and are also more sensitive to the cognitive processes involved in reading. Over the past two decades, the Laceys and their associates have demonstrated that the relations between heart period (beat-to-beat interval) and attention give rise to what they term the "bradycardia of attention" (Lacey and Lacey, 1978, p. 99)—that is, a slowing of heart rate as a result of the intention to note and detect external stimuli. This slowing immediately follows the stimulus and is delayed at most to the next cardiac cycle if the signal occurs late in diastole. Why, ask the authors, are "the pathways from brain to vagus [the parasympathetic nerve that mediates cardiac slowing] so promptly opened to these significant stimuli?" (p. 107). There is now evidence that stimulation of the pressure receptors in the carotid sinus produces widespread inhibitory effects on the central nervous system: "by inference, sensorimotor functions can be facilitated by decreases in baroceptor activity" (p. 107). The Lacey hypothesis thus suggests that attention is enhanced by a slower heart rate and that decreases in heart rate also occur in anticipation of the need to respond overtly to stimuli.

Acceleration, on the other hand, occurs while responding and also during cognitive processing (when it acts to shield the organism from outside stimuli); increases in heart rate are also elicited by the activity-instigating rather than by the emotional elements of stimulus materials.

With regard to *heart rate during ludic reading*, the best prediction we can make is, "It depends." It depends in the first place on how real the reading experience is to the reader. There are two possibilities. The first is that changes in the reader's imagination have the status of changes in the real world, so that each narrative conflict and resolution, each passionate embrace and mortal blow, will elicit the rapidly changing autonomic and postural events associated with the orienting response (Lacey and Lacey, 1978, p. 202). In other words, the printed page is to the reader as a flower to a bee. The second possibility is that the page is not at all like the real world and stands to the reader in the same relation as a picture of a flower stands to a bee—flat, odorless, and unchanging: the reader gazes at a succession of printed pages, each of which looks exactly the same as the others.

Apart from these unresolved questions about the reality status of reading, there are a number of other "it depends" provisos about how heart rate will respond to reading. It also depends on whether the cognitive processing associated with reading is automatized to an extent that renders the protective mechanism of heart-rate acceleration superfluous or whether the cognitive load requires such deceleration. And, finally, it depends on the content of the reading matter, in that action episodes are more likely than non-active emotional episodes to elicit acceleration—if, that is, the action imagery does in any way affect the reader, which Lang's findings, reviewed earlier, lead us to doubt.

Figure 9.3 shows that during ludic reading (Period I), heart rate shows a very slight deceleration of .27 beats per ten seconds, or 1.64 beats per minute. In other words, the various accelerative forces that might arise from cognitive processing, action elements in the reading matter, and so on, have had no effect on cardiac responses during reading: indeed, we may conclude that during the thirty minutes of ludic reading, decelerative forces (which may be associated with information intake) appear to have won out over accelerative forces. This in turn seems to suggest that ludic reading has at least some reality status since it produces the bradycardia of attention, which is how the organism responds to real stimuli in the real world. The cardiac deceleration also indicates that the cognitive processing demands made by ludic reading are not high.

Is reading a more labile condition than relaxing? Heart rate and heart period offer very different answers to this question. Heart period is certainly more sensitive than heart rate to moment-by-moment fluctuations in cardiac responding, and heart period does in fact show greater response lability during reading than in any other period except H. This high lability seems to reflect the multitude of conflicting accelerative and decelerative pressures on phasic cardiac responding during reading, among which are response instigators in the text and cognitive processing, on the one hand, which are opposed by information intake and passivity, on the other. As one or the other of these demands gains ascendancy, it will be accompanied by momentary accelerative or decelerative responses, resulting in the high level of lability measured by heart period.

Relaxing after reading (Period J), which mimics sleep onset, should show a deceleration relative to reading and indeed decline to a lower than baseline level. In fact, though response lability in this period is markedly lower than in reading, the anticipated deceleration does not take place. Both rate and period remain exactly as in reading. The explanation may lie in the deceleration induced by ludic reading. Hord, Johnson, and Lubin (1964) show that heart rate conforms more closely to the Law of Initial Values* than other systems, so that little additional slowing can be expected against the background of a rate that is already slightly below baseline.

Again, because of their passivity, the sensory deprivation periods (G and H) show the gradual decline in heart rate that might be anticipated, while processing-dominated hard reading (Period K) shows the theory-predicted acceleration relative to ludic reading.

Significance of Differences

Are the differences figure 9.3 shows between ludic reading and the other treatments merely trends, or do they have statistical significance? In this repeated-measures study, significance was determined by applying Dunnett's t test (1955) only if there was significant variance between all treatments combined (Abt, 1979). In figure 9.3, significant differences between ludic reading and the other treatments are indicated by the solid squares.

Reading is significantly different from 22 of the 98 other points plotted in figure 9.3. Nine of these differences occur on the two treatments of greatest theoretical interest, namely, baseline responding and relaxing after reading. Clearly, mean scores were a more useful measure than variability scores, with five of the former and only two of the latter showing significant variance; no variability score was significant unless coupled with a significant mean. The most fertile of the variables in generating significant differences with reading was the under-throat platym muscle, EMG3, which has ten significant t values on mean and VS scores combined. It is followed, in sequence, by the forehead muscle (EMG1), with seven significant t values, heart rate with three, heart period with two, and skin potential with one.

---

*This law, formulated by Wilder in 1967, holds that the higher the pre-stimulus level of a response system, the smaller its increase to further stimulation will be, and vice versa.

Enjoyment and Arousal

Were ludic readers more aroused when they read the pages they most enjoyed in the laboratory than during the reading of other pages? We already know the most-liked pages were certainly read differently, because readers savored these by reading them significantly more slowly than other pages (see chapter 6).

On each of the six variables, both mean response level for all subjects pooled and mean variability score were compared during the reading of most-liked pages and all other pages. On five of the six measures (the exception was for skin-potential response), mean responding was elevated during the reading of most-liked pages, but the variability score was lower on four of the six variables (the exceptions were muscle activity at the corner of the mouth and heart rate). The trend of the means suggests that heightened physiological arousal contributes to perceived pleasure during most-enjoyed reading, which is in good agreement with the predictions of experimental aesthetics. However, the failure of the variability score on four of the six measures to increase as pleasurableness increases is countertheoretical.

Conclusions

Placing bookworms under the laboratory microscope has led to some intriguing findings about ludic reading, even though the physiological measures have not shed further light on the differences between absorption and entrancement. Nevertheless, we have shown both theoretically and empirically that arousal does play an important role in reading; that both ludic and work reading give rise to more labile responding on most variables than the other activities we investigated—with the implications we have noted for the reality status of ludic reading; and that the cessation of ludic reading produces a profound deactivation of covert responding in five of the six response systems that were monitored.

PART THREE

The Capture of Consciousness

"The purpose of a literary work is the capture of consciousness, and the consequent creation, in you, of an imagined sensibility, so that while you read you are that patient pool or cataract of concepts which the author has constructed. . . . The will is at rest amid that moving like a gull asleep on the sea."

—Gass, 1972, p. 32

10
Reading, Dreaming, Trance

P sychologically, when different states feel different, they are different.
—Klinger, 1971, p. 7

Absorption, as we saw in chapter 4, is a necessary by-product of comprehension. But neither attention studies nor psychophysiology have been able to distinguish between absorption and entrancement or to show why some reading merely absorbs us while other kinds of reading matter work the far stronger spell of entrancement, transporting us to other places and transfiguring our consciousness to make other people of us. Entrancement exercises this power not only through reading but through many other everyday experiences, such as dreaming, being lost in one's waking thoughts, going to a movie, or listening to a story.

To find out why entrancement is a stronger form of consciousness change than absorption, we need to construct a phenomenology of fantasy—that is, a description of what readers actually experience when they are absorbed and entranced. This phenomenology in turn has to be related to established psychological theory. Fantasy is an enormously complex field, and to make the task easier, we shall follow a chronological sequence, beginning with Freud's *Interpretation of Dreams* (1900). The principles Freud uses there still mold the ways in which we approach other fantasy products, though in the course of time these principles have been formalized and extended to cover larger areas than sleep and near-sleep. In our search for psychological parallels to reading trance, we look at fantasy, daydreaming, and hypnosis. The role of visual imagery in problem solving, in fantasy, and in trance has always generated controversy, and we need to establish how important this kind of imagery is likely to be to the ludic reader. Then, because reading is a form of consciousness change, we look at some recent attempts to develop organizing principles for the confused area of "altered states of consciousness" (Pribram, 1977; Fromm, 1977a and b)—a term that entered our usage in the wake of Huxley's *Doors of Perception* (1954) and the drug culture of the 1960s. By the end of the chapter, we should be able to formulate a set of psychological criteria that distinguishes between readers who are merely absorbed and those who are in the grip of reading trance.

FREUD'S SALIENCE

We are all Freud's children. His influence on the way we see ourselves and others has been so pervasive that we forget how much our perceptions owe to him. For example, the principle of somatic conversion, which Freud established in his cures of hysterics, has been so thoroughly accepted by Western medical culture that patients suffering from impotence or loss of appetite find it difficult to convince their physicians that their symptoms are not psychogenic and that a physical examination is required. It is thus possible that "psychic conversion," the attribution of a false psychological origin to a physical complaint, is as common today as errors in the diagnosis of somatic conversions were in Freud's time. Yet physicians making such misattributions would hotly reject the suggestion that they were in this way demonstrating the strength of their Freudian convictions.

Freud himself was aware of the revolutionary significance of his work. In 1931, in the preface to the third revised edition of his *Interpretation of Dreams*, he writes: "It contains, even according to my present-day judgment, the most valuable of all the discoveries it has been my good fortune to make. Insight such as this falls to one's lot but once in a lifetime" (p. 1).

In June 1900, Freud rather whimsically asks in a letter to Fliess whether he supposes that one day a marble tablet will be placed at the entrance to the Freud home: "In This House, on July 24, 1895, the Secret of Dreams was revealed to Dr. Sigm. Freud" (Freud, 1900, p. 121). This tongue-in-cheek megalomania is more readily overlooked if we recall that by 1895, Freud had in his interpretation of Irma's dream shown that "a dream is the fulfilment of a wish" (1900, chap. 2); had taken the revolutionary step of placing responsibility for dream interpretation on the dreamer rather than the interpreter; had produced an account of the dream-work that for the first time made it possible to identify and recover the latent content of dreams; and had also specified the reinforcement processes operating within the "dream economy." Edelson (in Starker, 1977) has suggested that Freud and Chomsky were engaged in the analogous tasks of uncovering the transformational rules of dreams on the one hand and language on the other, which may be seen as two related semiologic systems.

A second reason for the continued salience of psychoanalytic concepts is not the "universality" of Freud's theories, but rather the striking similarities between turn-of-the-century Vienna and present-day Western societies; values in such major life areas as work, family, children, and sex might have more in common with those prevailing in Freud's time than we care to admit. Thus, although the developmental stage of orality might have little to do with a Trobriand Islander's later personality traits, it retains considerable explanatory power in the analysis of child and adult behavior in Western society. Accordingly, the use of psychoanalytic formulations expresses not allegiance to the dogma but acceptance of Freud's continued relevance to the study of fantasy processes.

The state of consciousness of the ludic reader has two principal parallels in the domain of fantasy: dreaming and hypnotic trance.

DREAMING AND READING

In his book about dreams, which Freud cites with approval (1900, pp. 9, 67), Hildebrandt (1875) writes that when we fall asleep, our whole being, with all its forms of existence, "disappears, as it were, through an invisible trapdoor". This, quite precisely, is the experience of the ludic reader who sinks "through clamorous pages into soundless dreams" (Gass, 1972, p. 27). Clearly, dreaming, especially daydreaming, is in certain ways an analogue of reading (Freud notes that dreams and daydreams have many essential features in common: 1900, p. 491). The dreamer knows that even if his dreams do not come from another world, they "had at all events carried him off into another world" (Freud, 1900, p. 7). Moreover, ludic reading shares its absolute effortlessness with dreaming and daydreaming. Whatever work takes place in reading and dreaming (and we have already established that for reading, substantial work is done), it is subjectively effortless. The cognitive passivity reading and dreaming share is markedly different from the closely related activity of fantasy production as in storytelling, and we shall return to this distinction.

The Dream-Work

Despite these striking parallels, reading is not dreaming. In chapter 6 of the *Interpretation* (1900), Freud specifies the four agencies of dream production: condensation, displacement, representability, and secondary elaboration (or revision). Through *condensation,* the dream itself, when fully written out, may occupy only half a page, but "the analysis, which contains the dream-thoughts, requires six, eight, twelve times as much space" (1900, p. 279). There are clear parallels between condensation and the gist-extraction powers of comprehension, which in chapter 4 we characterized as a data-reduction process; accordingly, condensation should not be seen as unique to the dream-work. On the contrary: consciousness, which Freud defines as a sense organ for perceiving data that arise elsewhere (1900, p. 146), is essentially reductionist in its operation, and full elaboration of any single conscious thought ("how happy you look") would stand in the same 12-to-1 relationship as elaboration of a dream thought.

Displacement means that there is frequently a misalignment between the dream thoughts and dream content: "the dream is . . . centered elsewhere" (1900, p. 305). The structure of the dream, notes Freud, may chiefly be ascribed to "these two craftsmen," condensation and displacement (p. 308).

Representability means that "whatever is pictorial is capable of representation in dreams" (pp. 339–40); concrete terms, notes Freud, are richer in associations than abstract terms. This most characteristic aspect of the dream-work therefore operates by the intrusion of concrete images which repress the abstract ideas from which they originate. Freud reports Silberer's tenacious investigation of this phenomenon, which he carried out by setting himself intellectual puzzles as he was falling asleep: "I lost the thread in a train of thought. . . . Symbol [concrete image]: Part of a [printer's] form of type, the last lines of which have fallen out" (pp. 344–45).

The dream thoughts arise in an agency Freud later identifies as primary process; a second agency, which has a defensive rather than a creative role, selects and censors these primary-process thoughts (1900, chap. 4). *Secondary elaboration* refers to the role of this censoring agency, which cannot be differentiated from waking thoughts, in shaping the dream content. The tendency of this agency is therefore to construct a content that is compatible with waking consciousness. For this reason, and because the dream economy is as sparing of energy as other parts of the psyche, this aspect of the dream-work "prefers to make use of ready-made phantasy instead of putting one together out of the material of the dream thoughts" (p. 495). The source of such fantasies is daydreams, and their ready incorporation into dreams is a further indication of the same "primary process laziness" that willingly makes use of somatic and external stimuli in the construction of dreams (the tickling of a feather, thirst, a blow on the cervical vertebrae). Hildebrandt's famous "backwards dreams," in which the ringing of his alarm clock appears at the end of a long series of events with a subjective timespan of many hours, is elucidated by Freud by means of this fantasy mechanism (pp. 495–98).

The creative and control processes in dreaming, elaborated as primary- and secondary-process thinking, constitute one of Freud's major contributions to the study of fantasy processes (1900, chap. 7). *Primary-process* thought (its name indicates its primacy in the development of ego structures) has four distinguishing marks. Through condensation, its ideas are endowed with great intensity; intermediary or compromise ideas abound; thought connections are associative rather than logical; and contradictory ideas exist side by side as if there were no contradiction. *Secondary process* thought, on the other hand, is logical, goal-directed, and subject to reality-testing feedback.

Freud's well-developed attention theory allows volition to play a limited but nonetheless important role in determining the extent to which secondary processes modify primary-process output: "The act of becoming conscious depends upon a definite psychic function—attention—being brought to bear. This seems to be available only in a determinate quantity, which may have been diverted from the train of thought in question by other aims" (1900, p. 593).

If one releases attention-cathexis completely, thoughts drop out of consciousness, but a partial relaxation produces a very different result. Through suspension of the critical faculty, involuntary ideas emerging from the first agency may be made available to consciousness. Indeed, the process of creative writing requires a distribution of attention similar to that of a patient in psychoanalysis recalling dreams, or a person about to fall asleep. But in the latter state, the involuntary thoughts readily lose their abstract quality and are transformed into concrete, usually visual, images. The onset of these hypnagogic hallucinations is encouraged "by a relaxation of the strain of attention" (1900, p. 31), supporting the view put forward in chapter 4 on the absence of attentional effort in ludic reading: "I have observed in my psychoanalytic work that the whole frame of mind of a man who is reflecting is totally different from a man who is [passively] observing his own thought processes. . . . This is shown among other things by the tense looks and wrinkled forehead of a person pursuing his reflections, as compared with the restful expression of a self-observer" (1900, p. 101).

The Poet and Daydreaming

Freud's most important statement about the psychology of literary creation and of reading is his essay "The Relation of the Poet to Daydreaming" (1908), in which "poet" means "the less pretentious writers of romances, novels, and stories, who are read all the same by the widest circles of men and women" (p. 179). Sterba (1939) casts an interesting light on this rather good-natured characterization of authors who cater to popular tastes; the method Freud followed "was to observe the effect of cheap novels on the minds of uneducated people" (p. 335). Sterba was a member of the Vienna Society and personally close to Freud (Jones,

1957, vol. 3, p. 236), so that this stigmatizing remark may accurately reflect Freud's intention. In that case, "The Poet" must take its place among other elitist condemnations of mass culture; however, it also relates to exactly that aspect of fiction writing that interests us, the investigation of "the secret of popularity in art."

In this densely argued little essay, Freud undertakes to relate dreaming to fiction reading and to account for the mystery of how "that strange being, the poet, is able to carry us with him in such a way and to rouse emotions in us of which we thought ourselves perhaps not even capable. . . . The knowledge that not even the clearest insight into the factors conditioning the choice of imaginative material, or into the nature of the ability to fashion that material, will ever make writers of us does not in any way detract from our interest" (1908, p. 173). The advantages of three quarters of a century enabled us to show in chapter 3 that this mystery is not so impenetrable as it appeared to Freud. But first let us see how he sets about answering the question.

Freud relates authorship to the child at play and to the ambitious or erotic wish-fulfillment of daydreaming. The writer's skill lies in overcoming the feeling of repulsion daydreams have for others by using disguises and aesthetic bribes "in order to release yet greater pleasure arising from deeper sources in the mind . . . , putting us in a position where we can enjoy our own daydreams without reproach or shame" (pp. 183–84). Here is the key to Freud's explanation of the power of fiction to carry us away. Robert Holt, commenting on Freud's essay, interpolates at this point that the author's strategems "enable us to obtain vicariously the deeper pleasure of daydreaming" (1961, p. 21)—vicariously, because we are, so to speak, riding on the author's back and therefore are liberated from the task of creating our own daydreams.

An important extension of Freud's system is made by David Rapaport (1951), who suggests three "economic and structural" dimensions along which fantasy differs from directed thought. As an individual passes from the latter to the former, there is a diminution in reflective awareness or self-consciousness, and then in the ability to exert effort or to will; third, there are four differences in the formal characteristics of thought. Though these items parallel Freud's primary-process qualities in some respects, Rapaport's formulation is especially useful to us. In the first place, he notes that words are replaced by images, which differ from the images of secondary-process thought in that hypnagogic or dream images are qualitatively very different and much closer to hallucinations. Second, conclusions and transitions become implicit. Third, rational logic is replaced by autistic logic, in which syncretic and animistic forms are possible, as well as *pars pro toto, post hoc ergo propter hoc,* and so forth.

Fourth, primitive, infantile, and incorrect syntax characterizes the language used in fantasy.

Passive and active fantasy. A directly related set of issues is explored by Robert Holt (1961) in his consideration of Thematic Apperception Test (TAT) stories as cognitive products. Fantasy production is effortful, notes Holt (as shown by the long latency before a TAT story is told), while dreaming is "a passive cognitive product [which] arises spontaneously with a feeling of drifting rather than one of responsible effort" (1961, p. 22). We shall use the terms *active fantasy* and *passive fantasy,* of which storytelling and dreaming are respectively the prototypes, in order to distinguish between these two modes of fantasy production, which, Holt suggests, take place at different levels of consciousness. Dreaming, as might be anticipated, is nearer to primary process and therefore syntactically primitive, illogical, and unreal, whereas active fantasy is produced by an act of conscious will in response to an externally imposed task, with full reflective awareness. Other distinctions are that passive fantasy is often unavailable to conscious recall. It has little plot, a loose structure, and only slight resemblance to literary forms; it is blatantly wish-fulfilling and, in terms of Freud's theory of defensiveness, may or may not carry negative-affect defenses, as nightmares do; it is obviously self-relevant, openly featuring the dreamer as hero, regarded as private, and seldom communicated. Finally, Holt suggests that daydreaming lies midway between waking and dreaming and may easily shade off into one or the other.

Reading Is Not Dreaming

We are now in a position to say why reading is not dreaming despite the striking parallels between these two cognitive activities. In the first place, because of the idiosyncratic and changeable nature of the interaction between book and reader, in which the reader may be more or less bookbound, reading must be defined in a way that clearly distinguishes it from other book-related activities. Let us describe two hypothetical cases. First there is the reader who follows George Smiley from London to West Berlin and waits with him in the shadow of the Wall (Le Carré, 1969), rapidly uprooting the lines of print to discover the messages beneath, leaping from sentence to sentence, not pausing to fantasize. On the other hand, there is the reader who is transported to Narnia to witness Aslan's creation of the world (Lewis, 1968), who moves his eyes over the page but perceives no type. Wholly taken up by book-induced fantasy, this reader has ceased for the moment to attend to book inputs. Smiley's reader is bookbound, Aslan's is not, and we are unable to specify

whether the transition from book-related inputs to book-related fantasizing, during which reading processes cease, takes place instantaneously,
as in a reversal (Apter, 1979), or whether each reader experiences a
continuum of states from absorption through successively more distracting thoughtful or fantasizing pauses during which reading processes
stop momentarily and are then continued until, finally, a full-blown
daydream takes over from the book. Fortunately, a study of ludic reading is necessarily restricted to that part of the reader's activity during
which reading processes are more or less continuously under way; when
reading ceases, so does our inquiry. Thus reading—though it may encourage fantasy, especially in the moments after the book is put down—
must be clearly distinguished from fantasy.

A second group of arguments indicating that reading is not daydreaming arises from our review of the dream-work. In relation to Rapaport's
fantasy indicators, we note that the reader's volitional ability is unimpaired, and all the formal characteristics of primary-process thought are
absent. Thought is verbal rather than imaginal, and images lack the hallu-
cinatory qualities of dream images; transitions are explicit, logic is rational, and syntax sophisticated. Applying the more stringent criterion of
the four aspects of the dream-work, it is clear that neither condensation,
displacement, representability, nor secondary elaboration play a part in
the ludic reader's reading—though they may certainly do so when book-
induced fantasy takes over, especially in the drifting hypnagogic state
before sleep.

Vicariousness. Another kind of comparison between reading and daydreaming can be made. In one of his last published papers, Freud remarks on "the mild narcosis induced in us by art" (1930, p. 81). Our
analysis thus far suggests that the agent of this narcosis is the mechanism
of vicarious daydreaming that Freud describes in "The Poet" (which
Holt calls "the best case I know of for parallels between fantasies and
stories": 1961, p. 19). Moreover, the 1930 formulation suggests that this
narcosis is not unique to a particular input but that other art forms
(painting, music, dance) may also induce this effect. But what is "vicarious daydreaming," and why does Freud regard it as so pleasurable?

In terms of Holt's analysis, the book is an active fantasy product,
logical and with explicit connections, reflective, and publicly available.
But the story unfolding in the reader's mind is a passive product, making
use of what Freud calls "ready-made phantasy." The reader's experience
is therefore that an active-fantasy product produces a passive cognitive
experience which may be described in exactly the terms that Holt uses
for reverie or daydreaming—effortless, dreamy, abstracted, drifting—
and yet, paradoxically, continually under the sway of an active input. We

may now say that vicarious daydreaming is peculiarly pleasurable because, while fully conscious, the reader is able to enjoy the "mild narcosis" of a passive cognitive product without the expenditure of any perceived attentional or critical effort. To this may be added the invaluable safeguard provided by consciousness; namely, that the terrors and negative emotions of some dreams and daydreams are held at bay. Nothing in the book can threaten the reader for longer than the instant it takes to raise his or her eyes from the page.

Transmutations. If the foregoing analysis is correct, the reader's satisfaction will clearly be better served by material that is easily transmuted from its active-product forms to a passive-product process, and the psychoanalytic analysis of dreaming and fantasy suggests three additional elements of the pleasurableness of ludic reading inputs. The first of these may be derived from Freud's remark in *The Poet* that the author's fantasies "would repel us, or at least leave us cold. . . . The essential *ars poetica* lies in the technique by which our feeling of repulsion is overcome" (1908, pp. 102–03). What is repulsive is the marks of primary process—for example, that fantasy is illogical and autistic, blatantly wish-fulfilling and self-referent, and so forth. Although both formulaic and mimetic literature are clearly active- and secondary-process fantasy products, the most difficult and taxing reading matter is the kind of mimetic literature that is in many respects closest to primary-process material—such as Joyce's *Finnegan's Wake* (1939), Barnes' *Nightwood* (1937), and most works by Gertrude Stein. In these and similar literary products, connections are implicit, word use is neologistic, and the logic is more autistic than rational. In formulaic material, on the other hand, with its stereotyped characters and immediately accessible narrative frames, the origin of the tale in the writer's fantasy is completely disguised, drives and wish-fulfillments are neutralized, and the reader's passivity—his or her ability to daydream vicariously—is heightened. In other words, there are some reasons to think that a work of art's proximity to primary process reduces its utility as a ludic reading input.

The second element is closely related to the first. Freud notes that the author places the hero under the protection of "a special providence," so that the reader enjoys a feeling of security as he follows the hero's dangerous adventures: "this significant mark of invulnerability very clearly betrays . . . His Majesty, the Ego, the hero of all daydreams and novels" (1908, p. 180). Freud's central argument in *The Poet* (1908) is that if a story grips or hypnotizes me, it does so at a regressed and childlike level. His Majesty the Ego delights, from the moment of his emergence, in ambitious and erotic wish fulfillments; neither education nor experience changes this fundamental requirement, which may well span all ages and cultures. Freud here partially explains why there is such a lamentable disjunction between critical excellence and reader enjoyment, why a good read and a good book are often not the same thing. If Arthur Hailey writes stories that grip and hypnotize me, it is because they appeal to the child in me. When Lord Northcliffe described newspaper readers to his reporters ("They are all 10,") it was to this regressed and childlike taste, which is truly universal, that he was referring.

The third element is the link between reading and sleep, of which ludic readers are keenly aware, and which many exploit by making reading the day's last waking activity. In other words, the passivity of the reader's experience, which so closely resembles the passivity of the hypnagogic state, may literally bridge reading and sleep by inducing a sleep-related state. The most famous hypnagogic state in literature is probably that described by Marcel Proust in *Swann's Way:*

> For a long time I used to go to bed early. Sometimes when I put out my candle, my eyes would close so quickly that I had not even time to say "I'm going to sleep." And half an hour later the thought that it was time to go to sleep would awaken me; I would try to put away the book which, I imagined, was still in my hands, and to blow out the light; I had been thinking all the time, while I was asleep, of what I had just been reading, but my thoughts had run into a channel of their own, until myself seemed actually to have become the subject of my book: a church, a quartet, the rivalry between François I and Charles V (1913, p. 3).

The experience Proust so evocatively describes is very common, and introspective readers regard the gentle continuation of the quintessentially safe and non-threatening subject matter of their reading into the hypnagogic state, which itself fades into the perceived safety of sleep, as one of the great pleasures that reading offers. Newall (1980) relates that Ivan the Terrible was unable to fall asleep unless he had first listened to a tale told by one of his three blind storytellers; there is a similar anecdote about Josef Stalin.

The Organization of Fantasy

A notable restatement of the organizing principles of fantasy is offered by Eric Klinger (1971), who defines fantasy as "verbal reports of all mentation whose ideational products are not investigated by the subject in terms of their usefulness for some immediate goal extrinsic to the mentation itself" (pp. 9–10). We spend a great part of every day in fantasy, notes Klinger, while resting, waiting, driving, walking, going to sleep, and getting up. Indeed, "interstitial fantasy forms the matrix for reasoned thought" (p. 4). The phenomenological continuities between fantasy and play, on the one hand, and fantasy and dreaming, on the other, lead Klinger to suggest that these activities "all form phases of a common continuous stream of activity, a kind of baseline activity to which organisms return when not engaged in scanning or acting upon their environment instrumentally" (p. 348). Klinger further notes that fantasy is segmented by content and hierarchically ordered, in that each segment is elicited by something in the previous segment, which it then interrupts. In a sense, therefore, each segment is a subcategory of its immediate predecessor (overt behavior is also perceived as a segmented sequence of action units bounded by breakpoints: Carver and Scheier, 1981, p. 90). But what laws determine the content of the fantasy segment that replaces the one now ending? Klinger's answer has the singular effect of linking psychoanalytic formulations to learning theory: he notes that under primary process, thought is unconcerned about its possible impact on the environment ("the behavior feels non-volitional and relatively effortless"; 1971, p. 351), while under secondary process, feedback from the real world is used fully in securing the intended effect, and thought often feels effortful. These two kinds of behavior correspond rather closely to one of Skinner's constructs, the chaining of operant and respondent responses. Respondent acts, like fantasy segments, "are elicited rather than emitted, are controlled by antecedent events rather than reinforcements at their termination, and entail relatively little sense of effort" (p. 351).

A single startling insight thus explains one of ludic reading's greatest attractions, its effortlessness, which, in terms of Klinger's formulation, arises because passive fantasy is a respondent chain, in which each successive event is as effortless as the salivation of Pavlov's dogs. Perhaps the difficulty of the task Silberer set himself in recalling his hypnagogic fantasies, and the lethargic unwillingness of a wakened dreamer to recover and recount a vanishing dream, are connected with this operant-respondent distinction. Reading and dreaming are effortless respondent acts, whereas telling a dream is operant: like throwing a moving truck into reverse, the awakened dreamer, asked to tell his dream, goes through a wrenching change of mental gears.

Daydreaming

Dreaming is a subcategory of fantasy. "Dreams and fantasy seem to be continuous phases of an individual's diurnal cycle, fantasy melting imperceptibly into dreaming," writes Klinger (1971, p. 347), who goes on to propose a control mechanism for this transformation: a meaning complex operating on an integrated response sequence. Such overlearned sequences account for the smooth and rapid flow of certain fantasies which, like language, are hierarchically organized by means of a preexisting plan. The power of a meaning complex to govern an unfolding fantasy sequence is diminished by sleepiness and fatigue. Just as the duration of control over non-fantasy sequences is reduced by such conditions, so are fantasy sequences subject to "a kind of lawful degeneration," with dream symbolism seen "as a limiting case of severe degeneration" (1971, pp. 349–51; quotation from p. 351). Singer (1976) also emphasizes the continuity of waking fantasy and nocturnal dreaming, in that non-anxious and introspective subjects reported considerable dreaming within the first five minutes after sleep onset without any electrophysiological indications of eye movements. But not all fantasy is daydreaming, which Singer defines as "a shift of attention *away* from some primary physical or mental task . . . *toward* an unfolding sequence of private responses made to some internal stimulus" (p. 3; his italics).

"Unfolding" can be taken to mean "narrative," and the view that daydreams tell a story is confirmed by Singer's factor-analytic study of daydreaming styles among over 1,000 subjects (sees also Blum and Green, 1978). The four principal patterns of daydreaming are anxious distractibility, guilty daydreams, positive-vivid daydreams, and controlled thoughtfulness; the last two are non-pathological and serve a useful purpose. In view of the continuities previously noted among the various forms of fantasy, daydreaming style can be expected to predict the affective tone of nocturnal dreams. Positive-vivid daydreamers, for example, are less prone to nightmares than other kinds of daydreamer, although, because of the semiological problems posed by dreaming, the actual content of current concerns is less readily traced from daydreams through to nocturnal dreams (Starker, 1977).

The adaptive role of daydreaming. Despite the stress Western culture lays on directed thought, a growing body of evidence, reviewed by Gold and Cundiff (1980), indicates that frequent daydreamers are better able to cope with boredom, better communicators, more spontaneous in their play, and possess greater potential for creative thinking. The view that daydreaming is therapeutic and should be encouraged is certainly a far cry from sweeping condemnations of escapism. Similarly, fantasy and daydreaming may function as covert rehearsal processes for actively seeking solutions to current problems (Klinger, 1971, p. 140; Singer, 1976).

Hypnosis

Our search for an analogue of reading trance now leads us to consider an especially promising avenue—hypnotic trance. Like reading, it is a condition of cognitively mediated consciousness change; it is the most fully researched of the reading analogues we have thus far examined; and its scientific history, from mystery to normal science, parallels the course we have set ourselves in elucidating reading. In 1843, James Braid rejected Mesmer's "animal magnetism" in favor of a theory of "nervous sleep," and this trend toward embedding hypnosis more and more firmly both in the everyday and within the fabric of established psychological theory continues to the present.

Today, a number of competing theories attempt to account for the phenomena encountered in hypnosis (Hilgard, 1973), and of these, two have special relevance for ludic reading. *Trance theory* argues that in the hypnotic state, reality orientation disappears and the subject's behavior changes. The leading exponent of this view is Shor (1970), who maintains that "the reader's fantasy world is an encapsulated unit and it seems totally real. . . . The reader is completely oblivious at the conscious level to the true reality about him" (pp. 92–93). Since the reader's fantasy world owes much of its appeal to the reader's continued awareness of its unreality, we must take issue with Shor. A better fit with the nature of the reader's world is offered by *psychoanalytic ego theory,* notably in Rapaport's formulation (1967), which holds that hypnotic induction fragments the ego, which then restructures itself at a partially regressed level, with a regnant ego remaining as an observer and in this way maintaining the individual's reality orientation. Josephine Hilgard (1979) develops this view in relation to imaginative involvement in general, and reading in particular.

Imaginative Involvement

Hilgard (1979) argues that hypnotic susceptibility, as measured by the *Stanford Hypnotic Susceptibility Scale* (Weitzenhoffer and Hilgard, 1959), has repeatedly been shown (see Fellows and Armstrong, 1977) to predict the capacity for absorption in non-hypnotic situations: "What we found out was that the hypnotizable person was capable of deep involvement in one or more imaginative-feeling areas of experience—reading a novel, listening to music, having an aesthetic experience of nature, or engaging in absorbing adventures of body or mind" (Hilgard, 1979, pp. 4–5). Hilgard goes on to distinguish involvement and addiction, define the reality status of the imagined experience, and describe the antecedents of imaginative involvement.

For the involved subject, the distinction between the subject and the object of the experience breaks down: there is a total immersion in the experience, which, for the reader, means being "transformed or transported by what he reads . . . swept emotionally into the experience described by the author" (p. 23). Hilgard draws a parallel between deep imaginative involvement and the "fascination" and "complete absorption" that Maslow (1962) attributed to peak experience. Holt's formulation is similar: "We are at the peak of conscious awareness when we are so deeply committed and fully absorbed in some cognitive activity that we have no self-consciousness, no immediate reflective awareness" (1961, p. 11).

There is, however, an important distinction between this kind of total involvement or immersion and the kind of reading that is merely absorbed, like that of Hilgard's subject Richard, for example, who cannot hear himself being called and whose close attention could mislead the observer into seeing him as an involved reader (Hilgard, 1979, p. 41). However, he does not continue the story in his head after he stops reading, and, like Ruth, whose reading "has a voracious quality" and who failed her first year at college because she would read for days at a time, neglecting classes (p. 42), he does not savor the story, it leaves no residue, and it awakens no deep feelings. This kind of reading, says Hilgard, is addictive rather than involved: it produces a kind of escape, but the content is evanescent.

Hilgard's formulation has some interesting parallels. In the first place, our distinction between attentional absorption and entrancement is closely paralleled by her distinction between absorption (though she does not link this state to the demands of attention) and imaginative involvement. Second, there is an extraordinary correspondence between the incapacity for entrancement that Hilgard remarks on and an observation made by Jerome Singer, who writes that "addictive behavior grows not so much out of excessive involvement in private fantasy, as out of a desire to seek some novel experience because one has failed to develop such an inner capacity" (1977, p. 111). Addictive behavior, in other words, predicts an underdeveloped capacity for private fantasy. We shall return to this issue in chapter 11, when we consider the relation between reading addiction (or escapist reading) and reading quantity.

A second issue clarified by Hilgard's characterization of imaginative involvement is an aspect of the strange duality of the entranced reader's experience, which grants imperative internal reality to the imaginary world while at the same time—even at the height of the reader's involvement—never lays claim to an external reality (as dreams so often do). This extraordinary phenomenon has a parallel in hypnosis, in which, in the words of one of Hilgard's subjects, one "might explore the possibilities inherent in something that doesn't really exist. . . . Nothing's really wrong because some part of you is always aware that it's hypnosis. . . . It's like dreaming when you know you're dreaming" (p. 36). For example, Sarah was told that her hands had been amputated; she felt the pain of her loss, could not see her hands, "yet I know I am still whole" (pp. 37–38).

Hilgard's explanation is formulated in terms of ego psychology, and is obviously of great relevance to understanding the reality status of the ludic reading experience. She writes that the observing and participating egos coexist, so that the subject is able to maintain "a continued limited awareness" . . . that what is perceived as real is in some sense not real" (pp. 27, 36). This disjunction, allowing the reader both to be involved and to maintain a safe distance, is neatly captured by her subject Robert, who comments on a movie scene in which a monster enters a cave, trapping a group of children: "I'm not one of them but I'm trapped with them, and I can feel the fright they feel" (p. 31).

A third important issue explored by Hilgard is the development of reading involvement. On the basis of interviews with her subjects, she notes that reading involvement commonly develops before the onset of adolescence, often as an identification with parents who read or as a way of dealing with loneliness in childhood. Echoing Ernest Hilgard's formulation, she writes that the capacity for involvement is founded on the easy passage from reality to fantasy and back again as the child listens to a parent's tale of ghosts and princesses and castles: the passage from the animistic to the objective is on a well-worn path, and the gateway between them is swift and safe in either direction. However, this capacity may be lost as the result of altered thinking patterns or a change in circumstances, and once lost it cannot be recaptured: "once reality testing processes have taken hold, they may predominate over areas of imagination and feeling" (p. 32).

Absorption: Trait and State

There are clearly similarities between the state of being lost in hypnosis and lost in reading; as one of Hilgard's subjects remarks, "the intense concentration is the same in a book . . . as it is in hypnosis" (1979, p. 24). Tellegen and Atkinson (1974) carried out a factor-analytic study of hypnotic-like experiences in everyday life. They report that "openness to absorbing and self-altering experiences" is a major factor and correlates significantly with measures of hypnotic susceptibility and found that subjects who were open to self-altering experiences could be absorbed in both real and fantasy experiences. For example, subjects would endorse such reality-absorption items as "The sound of a voice can be so fascinating to me that I can just go on listening to it," as well as such fantasy absorption items as "If I wish, I can imagine or daydream some things so vividly that they hold my attention in the way a good movie or story does" (p. 270). Tellegen and Atkinson argue that this absorption factor indicates "a special attentional object relationship . . . , a state of "total attention" during which the available representational apparatus seems to be entirely dedicated to experiencing and modelling the attentional object" (p. 274). This kind of attention is a state (a transient condition) arising from the absorption trait (a stable characteristic). The subject's attentional state has three major manifestations. The first is a heightened sense of the reality of the attentional object; in other words, an effect of concentrated attention (characteristic both of hpynosis and of reading trance) is to endow its object with a peculiar vividness and intensity. The full commitment of attention leads in turn to the second correlate, imperviousness to normally distracting events. The third correlate is "an altered sense of reality in general and of the self in particular" because "the vivid subjective reality experienced during episodes of absorbed attention may . . . during more 'decentred' normal states of wakefulness impress one as 'altered,' 'unreal,' or 'imaginary' " (p. 274). This sense of altered experience may occur whether the object of attention is the self or a part of the self, another person, or any other animate or inanimate objects which, by the quality of the attention bestowed on them, "acquire an importance and intimacy normally reserved for the self" (p. 275).

This densely argued extension of attention theory suggests parallels between the reader's absorption and the strange "otherness" encountered in alternate states of consciousness. One of the most famous descriptions of such an altered state is Aldous Huxley's account of looking at a flower arrangement some ninety minutes after he had taken mescalin: "I was not looking now at an unusual flower arrangement. I was seeing what Adam had seen on the morning of his creation—the miracle, moment by moment, of naked existence . . . , a bunch of flowers shining with their own inner light and all but quivering under the pressure of the significance with which they were charged" (1954, p. 17). There is obviously a very good fit between this description and Tellegen and Atkinson's account of focused attention—for example, the vividness and intensity of the attentional object, the altered subjective reality, and the absence of "metacognitions," such as "these are only flowers after all." In other words, the reader's absorption and entrancement, the hypnotic subject's trance, and the drug-user's altered state of consciousness can be explained within this single paradigm of intensely focused attention.

Another important aspect of Tellegen and Atkinson's argument is that the trait of absorption has two components. The first of these is *cognitive,* the complementary operation of diverse representational modalities ("syngnosia") reminiscent of the Freudian mechanism of condensation. We can link this component to Huxley's work by noting that when the doors of perception are cleansed, pharmacologically or by book-induced absorption, syngnosia changes the way the world looks. The *motivational-affective component* of the absorption trait is "a desire and a readiness for object relationships, temporary or lasting, that permit experiences of deep involvement" (p. 275). This second component neatly accommodates individual variations among readers: all who can read well enough will experience absorption, but not all readers will have the "desire and readiness" for the reality-changing experience of total attentional commitment.

In suggesting that absorption is a trait that both predicts hypnotic suggestibility and has state-like manifestations closely resembling our description of reading trance, Tellegen and Atkinson (1974) offer a powerful way of conceptualizing reading trance within a normal-science framework. This conceptualization allows us to propose a phenomenology of reading trance within a cognitive frame of reference, since it links absorption to attention and shows how totally committed attention may heighten the reality of the cathected object so as to transfigure both the object and the observer. It also describes the relation between the entranced reader and the book in terms that have an excellent fit with the observations reported earlier: the reader feels that he or she has been transported to another place, which, though real, is known to be false, since there is still an observing ego, distinct from the participating ego (Hilgard, 1979).

IMAGERY

Imagery is a pervasive form of experience, notes Pylyshyn (1973): "we cannot speak of consciousness without, at the same time, implicating the existence of images" (p. 2). Yet there are great individual variations in the clarity and detail of mental images, which Kosslyn (1981, p. 46) defines as "quasi-pictorial representations . . . supported by a medium that mimics a co-ordinate space."

At one extreme is Luria's mnemonist (1965), who may well be the most remarkable visualizer in psychological literature. This pathetic figure, "a Jewish boy, who, having failed as a musician and a journalist, had become a mnemonist" (p. 12), was able to remember immensely complex pseudo-formulas or letter arrays not merely for the duration of a stage performance but for as long as fifteen years, reproducing perfectly what he had memorized so long ago, even though he had no prior warning that the task would be repeated (pp. 42–43). Indeed, to forget anything at all was for many years an almost insuperable problem for him. He achieved these prodigious feats of memory with the help of a remarkable synaesthesia (by which he transformed sounds to images), but principally through extraordinarily vivid imagery, which enabled him to convert even senseless words or figures into intelligible images.

At the other extreme Koffka found (in Kosslyn and Jolicoeur, 1980, p. 142) that many subjects had imagery so vague and indeterminate that they were readily able to perform feats that seem beyond human capacity, such as imagining a coin of no particular denomination or an animal of no given species. This latter feat is an interesting comment on Descartes' observation in his *Discourse on Method:* "Painters themselves, even when they study to represent sirens and satyrs by forms the most fantastic and extraordinary, cannot bestow upon them natures absolutely new, but can only make a certain medley of the members of different animals" (1641, p. 81). Descartes is right, of course: to sketch or paint an entirely new animal (or to construct one for a science fiction movie) is as impossible as imagining a new color. But the indeterminacy of much mental imagery makes it possible to imagine even such impossibilities.

The substantial individual differences in imaging proficiency pose a number of problems. I. A. Richards (1929) remarks on the difficulties connected with the place of visual imagery in reading poetry because of "the incurable fact that we differ immensely in our capacity to visualize. . . . Some minds can do nothing and get nowhere without images" (pp. 14–15), while others get everywhere without them. The problem for psychology is that these individual differences have proved remarkably resistant to measurement, so much so that Sommer (1980) has suggested that studies of individual visualizers should replace investigations that strive for generality. However, such pessimism is unwarranted because of recent substantial advances (reviewed in Kossyln and Jolicoeur, 1980, and Kosslyn, 1981) that make it possible to develop a theory-based measure of individual differences in the clarity of imagery and the frequency of its use.

Reading Imagery

A measure of this kind is important in order to decide whether vivid imagery is a prerequisite for ludic reading. On the one hand, there is evidence that the ability to form images correlates well with comprehension, so that imagery contributes to comprehension success (Jacob, 1976). In view of the previously noted links between hypnotic suggestibility and reading trance, it is also significant that "lack of vivid imagery is an almost invariant accompaniment of insusceptibility to hypnosis" (Perry, 1973, p. 219); White, Sheehan, and Ashton (1977) review further evidence to this effect. Moreover, an essential part of reading enjoyment is sinking through the page into the world of the book, and it seems possible that without imagery, this world-creating process might be greatly impeded.

The alternative view seems to be equally well supported. On the basis of his own investigation of the nature of meaning, Huey approvingly quotes G. F. Stout's comment in *Analytical Psychology* that the work of Hobbes, Berkeley, Hume, and others "bore unequivocal testimony to the fact that the flow of words is for the most part unattended by a parallel flow of mental imagery" (in Huey, 1908, p. 160). Huey remarks on these and similar findings with his customary vigor: "Consciousness is not a picture gallery, or a magic lantern exhibition with slide displacing slide in rapid succession" (1908, p. 161).

Ideas and sensations. Our imaginings are imprecise and misty, writes William Gass (1972), and characters in fiction are "mostly empty canvas. I have known many who passed through their stories without noses, or heads to hold them" (p. 45). Henry James' Mr. Cashmore, for example, "would have been very red-headed if he had not been very bald." Cashmore is simply impossible as a set of sensations, notes Gass, though "as an idea he is admirably pungent and precise" (p. 46). One need not look far to confirm that fiction characters are more canvas than paint: the appearance of that bestselling righter of wrongs, Modesty Blaise, is not described by so much as a single phrase in one recent volume devoted to her exploits (O'Donnell, 1973), while of the hero, Dr. Giles Pennyfeather, we are told only that "he was thirty but looked younger, all hands and feet, incredibly clumsy" (p. 10). Yet I as the reader feel in no way cheated by this slighting of the visual; I want to know what Modesty and Giles do, not what they look like. Of a richly descriptive passage in *Under the Volcano* (Lowry, 1947), which names the trees, bushes, and flowers growing beneath a timber house that stands on "wide girthed legs of pine," Gass asks, "Do you have all that? I'm afraid you'll be all day about it" (1972, p. 43). Constructing images takes time, adds Gass, and slows the reader's flow; we cannnot, while imaging, keep up with the intricate conceptual systems that the author may spin like a spiderweb in a single sentence. In a phrase that brings Luria's mnemonist to mind, Gass remarks that "to imagine so vividly is to be either drunk, asleep, or mad" (1972, p. 40).

We are now able to return to some of the issues about "the willing suspension of disbelief" raised in chapter 3. In the context of the wider psychological canvas now available, we are better able to appreciate the impact on the novel of the literary devices that Tom Wolfe described as equivalent to the introduction of electricity in the machine age. If readers are reluctant imagers and prefer to have ideas about characters rather than sensations, we are better able to understand why the introduction of realism (especially through the description of status life) is such a powerful device. Tolkien's Hobbits become real to us not because we see them clearly but because we know where they live, how they speak, and what they do. James Bond entrances us because we have been to his London flat, have met his secretary and his housekeeper, and know that he keeps his hand-rolled cigarettes in a gunmetal cigarette box (though we do not much enquire whether gunmetal is blue, black, or silver). In other words, propositions liberate the reader from the vagueness of imaginings and allow the use of propositional thought modes, which, for reasons that psychology has yet to explore (but which are bound up with comprehension processes), are more readily evoked and more richly evocative than the often colorless and wispy pictures we are able to make in our heads.

Poe's animal. Some of these issues can be brought to a focus by analyzing a passage in Borges' *Book of Imaginary Beings* (1969), which quotes a description of an Antarctic creature in Edgar Allen Poe's *Narrative of Arthur Gordon Pym of Nantucket* (1938):

> We also picked up a bush, full of red berries, like those of the hawthorn, and the carcass of a singular-looking land-animal. It was three feet in length, and but six inches in height, with four very short legs, the feet armed with long claws of a brilliant scarlet, and resembling coral in substance. The body was covered with a straight silky hair, perfectly white. The tail was peaked like that of a rat, and about a foot and a half long. The head resembled a cat's, with the exception of the ears; these were flapped like the ears of a dog. The *teeth* were of the same brilliant scarlet as the claws.

Dutifully, I visualize this singular beast: dead in the narrator's arms, long body and short legs (a dachshund?), red-clawed (aha! the claws are translucent), white-haired and cat-headed . . . but the body, not yet clothed in white hair, has faded from my mind before I see the legs, which vanish in a mist as the red claws appear (shocking, that!); and so the beast passes through my mind piece by piece, a leg, a claw, a coat, each a momentary and independent essence. Aha, I say, it's a cat-headed dachshund!—and at once the metaphor resurrects the creature whole: but no, the dachshund's coat must be whitened, its claws crimsoned—and look now: it's got a doggy head again! If metaphor, as Gass suggests, brings an entire system of meanings to bear on a concept, not serially "but wholly, totally, and at once" (p. 65), then, at least for this reader, it is conceptual rather than visual metaphor he is referring to.

In order to bring clarity to this mass of conflicting claims about the role of imagery in reading (in which the weight of evidence thus far cited seems to favor the view that imagery is not an essential part of the reader's experience), we need a theory that can cast some light on the amount of effort needed for imaging, on whether or not image formation is time-consuming (as Gass alleges), on the circumstances in which people seem to prefer imaginal to propositional thought, and on a method of measuring individual differences in the clarity and frequency of images. Finally, in view of the important distinctions between language production and comprehension systems (chapter 7), the theory should distinguish quantitatively and qualitatively between the imagery processes of the storyteller and the story listener.

A Theory of Imagery

A theory that meets most of these requirements is offered by Kosslyn and his associates. On the basis of an elegant series of studies beginning in 1975, Kosslyn and Jolicoeur (1980) propose that images are "surface representations generated from more abstract 'deep' level representations" (p. 149). In the "deep" representation, the name of the object accesses two parallel files, one containing propositional information and the other imagery information stored as coordinates of angle and distance. This information is used to achieve transformations of the surface-structure image, such as scanning (which moves parts of the image under the sharply focused center), rotating, and expanding or contracting the image, as when the image is searched for a specified part ("is the car's right rear tire smooth?"). In fact, some of the most ingenious studies reported by Kosslyn and Jolicoeur relate to diverse properties of the surface structure, such as "the angle of the mind's eye," focus, and grain. Of particular interest is the finding that the surface representation is a short-term memory structure that must be continuously regenerated to prevent fading. This is confirmed by studies showing that more complex images (as of the cat-headed dachshund) are more difficult to maintain, thus explaining why many readers seem to resent the "work" involved in dealing with complex descriptions. A telling example of this kind of difficulty is in readers' responses to *The Poseidon Adventure,* described in chapter 11.

Which of these two files—one propositional and one imaginal—is an individual likely to access? This depends on whether or not the propositional information is readily available. For example, if I am asked whether an elephant is bigger than a mouse, I draw on overlearned propositional information and require no image. However, if I have to say whether a mouse or a hamster is larger, I must generate an image, because propositionally both mouse and hamster belong to the same category, "small." Similarly, there are questions for which the proposition file has no answer at all, such as "Is a horse's knee or the tip of its tail higher off the ground?" If we translate this information back to the reading process, there are clearly narrative frames for which no images are necessary, such as the hero's good-natured face or the flash of his blue eyes. On the other hand, there are descriptions of new and unusual creatures or machines for which the reader must generate an image in order to understand the narrative. Again, the implications of these concepts for ludic reading are explored in the light of actual readers' experiences in chapter 11.

In this connection, another series of studies by Kosslyn and Jolicoeur

(1980) shows that images are in fact constructed and that construction takes time, which increases with the amount of detail included, the subjective size of the image, and the degree of overlearning of the image in question (a zebra is imaged more rapidly than Poe's strange creature). Hence, Gass' "You'll be all day about it" (1972) is indeed fair comment on the imaging of a uniquely constructed house and its garden.

We have now found answers to most of the questions raised in our specifications for an adequate theory of imagery generation and use. On the basis of the Kosslyn model, we can conclude that image generation will seldom form part of ludic reading (though for the reader of an anatomy text, it is likely to be an essential part of the comprehension process). First, ludic reading is response-free, and image generation often takes place in order to find the answer to a specific question. Second, formulaic reading matter is highly stereotyped, so that both characters and situations are overlearned and therefore readily accessible in propositional form. To these conjectures, a third may be added: some readers (myself among them) find it unpleasant to read a book after they have seen a film based on it because normal reading patterns are buffetted by the upsurge of movie-based imagery, which is perceived as distracting and stressful.

If we can show that the construction of images is stressful, a fourth factor can be added to our list of indications that ludic reading is more likely to be a propositional than an imaginal process. Though Kosslyn does not address this question directly, his findings appear to indicate that imaging is subjectively more effortful than propositional operations. First, images are generated only if the propositional file fails to yield the requisite information. Second, information available with equal readiness in both image and propositional formats is more rapidly accessed in its propositional form; in cognitive processes, time and effort are often equivalent.

Another question of interest to us is whether the author's imagery processes differ from the reader's. There are some grounds for assuming that imagery is more important for the storyteller than for the audience. It is probably impossible to tell a plausible story without access to an ongoing stream of imagery. How else is the storyteller to describe the clothing, gait, and facial expressions of the protagonists, to ascribe sounds to their actions ("Pow! she hit him under the chin, lifting him a few inches off the ground") and even to preserve plausible spatial relations between them? This is not to claim that all authors are vivid imagers (C. S. Lewis, 1968, is certainly a better visualizer than J. R. R. Tolkien, 1954); but rather that, in general, authors are likely to make greater use of imagery than readers, who may remain as propositional as they please with no loss of comprehension or enjoyment. Indeed, the perceived stressfulness of telling a story may arise at least in part from the requirement it imposes to generate and continually renew an imagery stream.

Individual Differences

Finally, we need a way of measuring imagery use that will distinguish vivid from misty imagers and individuals who use imagery a great deal from those who make little use of it. By relating imagery vividness and use to reading quantity and enjoyment, we will be able to determine whether high-imagery readers read more and with greater enjoyment than low-imagers. Kosslyn and Jolicoeur (1980) review some traditional instruments and suggest a new one. In chapter 11, we review evidence gathered in this study that addresses the relations between imagery and ludic reading.

ALTERNATE STATES OF CONSCIOUSNESS

There is nothing new about alternate states of consciousness (ASCs) except the name, which is even newer than the more familiar "altered states." Zinberg (1977) prefers the term *alternate,* which "makes it clear that different states of consciousness prevail at different times for different reasons" without implying that these states represent a deviation from the way consciousness ought to be (p. 1). The first recorded alternate state is probably Noah's drunkenness (Gen. 9:21). William James' *Varieties of Religious Experience* (1902) reflects early psychology's concern with the study of consciousness. For example, mystical moments are "states of consciousness of an entirely specific quality" (p. 389), and "the deliciousness of some of these states seems to be beyond anything known in ordinary consciousness" (p. 403). One of the first edited volumes to use the term *altered states* is Tart (1969), which explores some of the issues that came into prominence in the 1960s, such as Zen meditation and psychedelic drugs. ASCs once had a raffish air, and they continue to occupy an uneasy position between the respectability of cognitive psychology and what for many is still the outer darkness of parapsychology.

Despite the confusion surrounding ASCs, they may be useful in providing an organizing principle for the permutations of consciousness-change. A convenient starting point for this survey is table 10.1, which offers four listings of alternate states. A definitive list is by definition impossible because of the widely accepted view that ASCs are not discrete, qualitatively different states but rather are ranged along a continuum (Block, 1979, p. 198). Nonetheless, there is a degree of consensus about what constitutes an ASC, as the table indicates. Karl Pribram's list, which is the most comprehensive, is given first.

A number of attempts have been made to specify the dimensions on

Table 10.1.   Four Listings of Alternate States of Consciousness

Pribram, 1977	Fromm, 1977a	Simon, 1977	Tart, 1969
Ordinary perceptual awareness	Waking, normally alert and concentrated		
Self-consciousness	Waking, fascinated, entranced	'Aha' experience in psychoanalysis	
Dream	Daydreaming; nocturnal dreams	Dreaming	Dreaming
Hypnagogic	Hypnagogic or hypnopompic	Hypnagogic	Hypnagogic
Ecstatic (in orgasm)			
Trance (socially induced)	Relaxation	Relaxation response; biofeedback	
Drug-induced	Psychedelic		Minor psychedelic (marijuana, nitrous oxide); Major psychedelic (LSD; plant alkaloids)
Social role	Hypnosis	Hypnosis; yoga	Hypnosis
Linguistic			
Translational			
Transcendental (creative)	Inspirational phase of creative act	Artistic creation	
Transcendental (other)	Rapture, religious ecstasy	Mystical	Mystic
Meditational	Meditative	Transcendental meditation	Meditation
Dissociated	Dissociation; fugue states; psychotic states		
Psychomotor (epilepsy)			
Extrasensory	Sensory deprivation		

which these alternate states vary, and we focus on two of these. First, Pribram (1977) suggests that much behavior is state-dependent; that is, it may be engaged in only in a particular state of consciousness, which "by definition excludes for the time being all others" (p. 221). He adds that ASCs differ from one another not by virtue of unique sensory stimuli, physiological drives, or memory stores, which are used in common by all states, but by differing programs or control functions: "Alternate states of consciousness are due to alternate control processes exercised by the brain on sensory and physiological stimulus invariants and on the memory store" (p. 223). These control functions may be differentiated into feedback or homeostatic loops and open-loop feed-forward controls that are essentially information-processing systems. Pribram goes on to suggest that the feedback loops control associative primary-process-thought mechanisms, while the feed-forward controls, through the agency of the executive ego, control the volitional information-processing of secondary-process thought (p. 226).

Erika Fromm (1977a) offers a different (and phenomenologically richer) approach to defining the dimensions along which ASCs vary. She suggests that they may be ordered on a depth continuum: the deeper the ASC, the more there is of primary-process thinking, of fantasy rather than reality testing, of imagery rather than abstract concepts, and of unfocused, free-floating attention. In a formulation that parallels Pribram's notion of a control system, she suggests that these attributes of ASC depth are mediated by a single mechanism, ego state.

In *ego activity*, the individual is free to make choices; in *ego passivity*, this voluntarism is lost and the individual must accede to demands coming from the instincts or the external world and may indeed feel overwhelmed by excessive demands. In *ego receptivity*, the individual holds goal-directedness and critical judgment to a minimum and freely allows "unconscious and preconscious material to float into his mind" (p. 375). For example, in the hypnagogic state the ego is passive and the individual cannot voluntarily direct his flow of associations; the daydreamer is ego-receptive and can, at least to some extent, direct his imagery: "Now picture two children, one intently listening to a fairy tale, the other making up a story. In the child who is absorbed in listening to the fairy tale, the ego allows itself to be more receptive than active with regard to imagery. In the child who is making up a story, the ego is more active" (p. 378). Depth of ASC may therefore be correlated with the degree of ego receptivity the individual is able to tolerate—that is, the extent to which "regression in the service of the ego" (Fromm, 1977a, p. 377, quoting Kris), is allowed. Since this is an undefended state, it can be experienced as threatening unless the ego can cope successfully with the demands made upon it by the instincts and society. In ego receptivity, as in ego activity, coping can be creative rather than defensive—that is, the ego can handle impinging demands "masterfully at its own leisure and pace" (p. 375).

Finally, we must note Fromm's views on the psychodynamic structure of imagery: "bidden" imagery is ego-actively produced and stems from the preconscious; "unbidden" imagery stems from the preconscious and the unconscious and may be experienced either ego-passively, as in nightmares and hallucinations which "flood and overwhelm the ego" (p. 380), or ego-receptively, in which the ego allows imagery to rise from the unconscious or preconscious.

A further dimension along which consciousness varies is perceived time duration, and introspection tells us that one of the great attractions of ludic reading is that it shortens the passage of time. We settle down to a good read at four in the afternoon, and the rumbling of an empty stomach at seven may be the first indication that three hours have sped by. Block (1979) addresses the issue of duration perception by quoting William James: "In general, a time filled with varied and interesting experiences seems short in passing, but long as we look back. On the other hand, a tract of time empty of experiences seems long in passing, but in retrospect short" (p. 19). Block then reviews the cognitive mechanisms mediating perceived duration and proposes a contextual-change hypothesis, which suggests that our sense of duration is governed not so much by the task itself as by changes in the context in which the task is performed, such as environmental stimuli, internal sensations, affective reactions to the task, and so forth. Thus, an idle duration seems long in passing because of increased attention to contextual information but short in retrospect "because there are few retrieval routes to contextual information as a result of the relative lack of memories of stimulus events. Opposite effects are found for relatively busy, 'filled' duration for exactly opposite reasons" (Block, 1979, p. 197).

There are, however, some grounds for questioning the validity of these conclusions. A notably unpleasant aspect of standing a three-hour guard shift at a military base in the small hours of the morning is not only that minutes feel like hours but that in retrospect that empty time seems equally (and unendurably) long. A three-week vacation that rushes by in a flash seems in retrospect to have been governed by special clocks that condensed hours to minutes. Similarly, the ludic reader's perception of accelerated time also holds up in retrospect. It might therefore be profitable to re-examine concurrent and retrospective duration perception in order to resolve this anomaly.

Review

We must now endeavor to establish whether the concepts reviewed here add materially to our formulation based on the absorption-trait view of reading trance. Pribram's concept of separate control systems for each alternate state is adequately represented in Tellegen and Atkinson's notion (1974) of intense and focused attention. Fromm's proposal (1977a) that ASC depth is mediated by an ego activity-receptivity-passivity dimension adds significant clarity to a construct that we have encountered under a variety of names, including passive- and active-fantasy production, respondent- and operant-response chaining, the presence of a regressed and a regnant ego, the participating and observing egos, and so forth. Each of these pairs of opposites describes greater or lesser degrees of voluntary control, in which the first member of each pair is equivalent to some degree of ego passivity (and therefore unbidden thought and imagery) and the second to voluntary, reflective feedback control, in which only bidden imagery is tolerated. In addition, Fromm's use of the term *ego receptivity* clarifies the status of daydreaming and its reading analogue—vicarious daydreaming—which we have seen described as a state between waking and dreaming, or a state in which voluntary control of associations sometimes is and sometimes is not perceived. Ego receptivity, which allows both bidden and unbidden imagery and willingly relaxes reality feedback while retaining reality awareness, has a good fit with Hilgard's suggestibility (1979) and with the motivational-affective component of absorption specified by Tellegen and Atkinson, which determines the individual's degree of openness to involvement experiences.

The duration experiences of ludic readers, which might intuitively have been inferred from their attentional status, have in part been clarified by Block's perceived-duration model, which predicts that, for the ludic reader, whether absorbed or entranced, time spent reading will be short in passing; but we abandon Block at this point, arguing that a retrospective view does not alter this perception.

The thrust of this chapter has been to argue, with William James (1902), that consciousness change is eagerly sought after and that means of attaining it are highly prized—whether through alcohol, mystical experiences, meditative states, or ludic reading. Among these, ludic books may well be the most portable and most readily accessible means available to us of changing the content and quality of consciousness.

11
The Sovereignty of
the Reading Experience

Reading's airy bamboo-and-paper house is a marvelously safe place, a protection from many kinds of earthquake: this fragile dwelling allows readers to enjoy a kind of sovereignty over their lives and their worlds.

Dominion and Superiority

Sovereignty means two things: dominion and control, on the one hand, and unquestioned superiority, on the other. In this chapter, we examine the ways in which ludic reading renders sovereignty to its devotees.

Dominion. Dreams and daydreams may be so threatening that they lead to depersonalization (Shapiro, 1978). When I say, "I had a dream last night," I am denying that the dream had me, as it did; in telling a dream, I demonstrate control over it (Monchaux, 1978, p. 447). For the ludic reader, these acts of subterfuge are unnecessary. The most fundamental control the reader exercises over the book arises from the fact that although there may be a movie or a record or a theatrical presentation, there is no book: each reader creates the book anew. My dominion over the book is absolute because when I lift my eyes from the page, the book ceases to exist. But when I close my eyes, the movie or record or television program continues; when I am asleep, dreams have dominion over me.

Unlike dreams, book fantasy can never become overwhelming. Indeed, reading guarantees us the dreams of invulnerability, power, and desirability we would most like to have and would, if we could, summon up nightly. Moreover, the pace at which this bidden book-dream unfolds is entirely under the reader's control, something that no other entertainment input allows. It may be that for many readers reading aloud and being read to offer a pale shadow of the pleasure given by silent reading because pace control is to a large extent lost.

Superiority. The processing demands reading imposes on both automatized and conscious attention are heavier than those made by movies, television, and cognate media (chapter 4). Reading absorption, which results from a fuller commitment of the attentional apparatus than movie- or television-absorption, is thus likely to do a better job than the other media of blocking out environmental distractions and changing the focus of the reader's attention from the self to the book. Readers, however, are likely to express this superiority of the book to other media rather differently. They may say, for example, that reading traps the eyes, locking them to the page, in a way that even television does not; the television viewer is more aware of goings-on in the room than the reader, they would claim, because the viewer's eyes are more free to roam. We know, in light of the processes reviewed in chapters 4 and 7, that it is not the page that locks the reader's eyes in place but the cognitive demands made by reading and comprehension.

Another source of reading's superiority is that the novel can achieve things quite beyond the power of other media: "No film maker has ever brought the audience inside the mind . . . of a character, something that even bad novelists are able to accomplish as a matter of routine" (Wolfe, 1973, p. 64). Words alone allow us to make the novel's people our own, which we cannot do if they are created for us.

THE USES OF READING SOVEREIGNTY

Reading may be used to heighten consciousness or to dull it. Though the boundaries are shifting and permeable, readers can very broadly be divided into what we term Type A, those who want to dull consciousness, and Type B, those who use reading to heighten it.

Let us imagine a busy physician's waiting room. Patients are seated in chairs round the walls, and there are magazines on a central table. Mr. A enters, book in hand. He looks at no one, goes directly to the magazine table, and selects a *Time* and a *Reader's Digest*. He opens *Time* and starts reading before he is properly seated. He glances up frequently, not to make contact with the people in the room, but to check the line of waiting patients. Soon he finishes the *Time* story and turns to his book, which he reads rapidly but expressionlessly. He does not return the magazines to the table; they lie unopened on his lap while he reads the book. Meanwhile, Mrs. B comes in. She looks at the seated clients, smiles at one and greets another, and sits down. Soon she is lost in reverie, quite relaxed. After a while she takes a *Cosmopolitan* from the magazine table, pages through it to a short story, and begins reading. She becomes quite absorbed, seems to be reading quite slowly, all the while smiling, frowning, nodding, and even laughing aloud. When she finishes the story she puts the magazine down, but the story-mood stays with her: again, she loses herself in reverie. When Mr. A's turn comes, he takes his book and both magazines with him, lest vacant time again assail him.

On the basis of the knowledge we have accumulated about reading and fantasy, we are able to offer some hypotheses about Type A and Type B readers with regard to their probable current concerns and their experienced quality of consciousness, the kind of sustenance reading offers them, their use of memory, their preferred reading matter, and, finally, the way literary critics see them. But throughout the typology that follows, we bear in mind a fundamental ambiguity; namely, that in response to maturational and environmental events, each type may, temporarily or permanently, turn into the other. The boundaries are permeable.

Current Concerns and Quality of Consciousness

Reading to dull consciousness. If consciousness is unpleasant, it seems likely that reading will be used to dull it. An individual in the grip of a deep and negatively toned current concern (after a separation such as a bereavement or a divorce, or during an ongoing personality disturbance) will experience negatively toned fantasy colored by pervasive anxiety or fear. This follows from the analysis of fantasy in chapter 10, in which current concerns were shown to have a potentiating effect on fantasy content and self-states to correspond in large measure to current concerns (Klinger, 1971; see also Blum and Green, 1978). Fantasy also develops spontaneously during unoccupied time, such as waiting, driving, and resting, periods when environmental feedback is attenuated (chapter 4). For an individual whose inner life is governed by fearfulness, anxiety, guilt, or other negatively toned affective states, empty periods during which fantasy can develop will be especially threatening. Aloud or to themselves, such individuals say, "I'm OK as long as I keep busy," and they will especially prize the shift of attentional focus from the self to the environment offered by a book (chapter 4). They are likely to fortify themselves against the threat of empty consciousness by accumulating books, by setting aside promising books to be retrieved when relief is especially needed, and by carrying a book or two with them wherever they go, especially on vacation, when they often take absurdly large supplies of reading matter with them.

It is to such Type A readers that the pejorative term *escapist* is most correctly applied. For them, the book is an island of tranquility in a sea of fearfulness, and in turning to the book, they are quite literally escaping from self-consciousness. It seems likely, however, that the very high levels of anxiety, as in some neurotic and psychotic conditions, will flood consciousness so that attention is fully occupied, comprehension processes cannot operate, and reading is blocked. This line of thought suggests that the mental hospital patients sunning themselves in the gardens, eyes darting and fingers twitching, would be unable to read even if they wanted to; similarly, it may be found that social isolates and other high-anxiety individuals are unable to read for pleasure.

For non-readers, who lack one or more of the antecedents of ludic reading (reading ability, positive expectations of ludic reading, and correct book choice), consciousness may be held at bay by alternative entertainment inputs in combination with lifestyle mechanisms. The most common of these is keeping busy. "I'm running late already, I must go now," says such a person, as if he or she were a train. For socially competent individuals, the day may be dotted with time-bound arrangements that stretch from early morning till late at night and do not leave the person alone or open to fantasy for more than a few minutes at a time.

Reading to heighten consciousness. Pleasantly toned current concerns and fantasy content concerned with positive expectations and the recycling of enjoyable experiences are likely to be characteristic of the healthy personality, such as Maslow's mature and fully actualized person (1962) or Rogers's fully functioning person (1961). Common to most such specifications of the healthy personality are self-acceptance, openness to experience, spontaneity and creativity, and a generous capacity for interpersonal warmth and intimacy (Maddi, 1976). Such individuals, like Mrs. B in the waiting room, welcome fantasy and are quite happy to lose themselves in it. A book therefore ceases to be primarily an instrument for shifting attention from the self to the environment in order to block out self-consciousness and becomes instead a vehicle for involvement with the characters and situations in the book (Hilgard, 1979); this involvement may in turn lead to self-exploration through the awakening of personal memories and aspirations. In self-reports, such readers are likely to say that reading enlarges experience, allows them to live more intensely, to solve problems, and so on. Type A readers, on the other hand, may be expected to say that reading takes their minds off their troubles.

Hatred of consciousness. This analysis suggests a corrective to Gass' judgment of humanity in general, namely, that "nothing seems more obvious to me than the fear, hatred, and contempt men have for [consciousness]" (1972, p. 269). It seems likely that hating consciousness is a function of negative current concerns, such as among those Singer (1976) found to have guilty and anxious-distractible daydreams. "Healthy" individuals, in the sense specified by Maslow or Rogers, on the other hand, are likely to welcome self-consciousness.

Trait or State

Are the characteristics of Type A or Type B readers sufficiently stable, enduring, and productive of other habitual behaviors to be classified as enduring personality traits? Perhaps current concerns and the quality of the fantasy they produce are not traits but states that change in a single individual from hour to hour. In the waiting room, it is possible that Mr. A is undergoing a transient anxiety reaction to a threatening life-event while Mrs. B, who has just learned that her husband has received a longed-for promotion, is in remission from a condition of chronic fearfulness; on the following day, Mrs. B might be a Type A reader and Mr. A a Type B. We would then be dealing not with types at all but with manifestations of passing states. Nonetheless, it seems likely that an individual's relationship to self-consciousness, though liable to sudden change, will exhibit many of the enduring marks of a personality trait and that books will be used either voraciously and anxiously to hold consciousness at bay or as one among many aesthetic inputs used to heighten consciousness. The view that ways of reading may be stable traits is strengthened by Hilgard's evidence (1979) that the capacity for reading involvement may be irrecoverably lost at a certain point in the life span, and that the capacity for involvement has specific developmental antecedents. Later in this chapter, the self-reports of our subjects will support the notion that reading is indeed governed by enduring traits.

Memory Utilization in Reading

The depth-of-processing hypothesis (Craik and Lockhart, 1972), which holds that deeper processing leads to better recall from episodic memory than shallower processing, has recently been extended to show that semantic processing may itself vary in depth (Lachman et al., 1979). It seems likely, therefore, that the involvement of readers who move slowly to savor the richness of a text means they will remember it better and longer than those who bolt their reading. For such readers, the global-local mechanism (Beaugrande and Colby, 1979) would operate through only the most general and highest level macrostructures (see chapter 4).

What memory and forgetting mechanisms can be used to elucidate this recall-free reading? Eric Brown (personal communication, March 20, 1982) describes a kind of automatic reading: "One reads material close to sleep, but has the singular impression of having read the material, but can recall nothing." I repeatedly had a similar kind of experience when working as a radio news editor listening half-asleep to an early morning news broadcast and fixing the content of the headline items in my mind, only to find, on rising, that the entire structure had vanished like a mist. It seems likely that certain readers will discover that recall-free reading is possible, perhaps through a late-night experience, and then will deliberately cultivate this ability.

This analysis leads to a further conclusion. We can extend the hypothesized relationship between reading and eating by arguing that for the reader who holds consciousness at bay, bolting down chunks of text will be even more satisfying if the reader feels that the text has not been consumed but is available for recycling. This end is achieved by the mechanism of keeping the text out of memory and forgetting it as rapidly as possible.

Entrancement

Type A readers seem to be strangers to entrancement, which is the position taken by Hilgard (1979), who clearly distinguishes between addictive and involved readers. Our own argument that Type A readers bolt their reading, thus precluding involvement, supports this view.

On the other hand, everyday observation indicates that there are voracious and very rapid readers who do seem, at times, to become deeply involved in their reading. For example, as a child and an adolescent, I often read a book or more a day, especially if I was lonely or upset. Yet despite this prototypical Type A behavior I recall many deep involvements: lying on my bed and kicking my bare feet against the wall in excitement as the hero cut a swathe through his assembled adversaries; or weeping copiously (but oh so secretly!) at Marjorie Kinnan Rawlings's sad tale of Jody and the yearling.

Escapism Reconsidered

Is it possible that the harsh judgments of ludic reading made by critics since the eighteenth century are in fact judgments of Type A readers only? Certainly, the sort of reading that is a killtime rather than a pastime seems to be the escapist or addictive kind that we have characterized as swallowing great mouthfuls of text whole in order to hold consciousness at bay. It also seems likely that Type A readers would select highly formulaic material, which best meets their needs for safety and predictability but which, in critical terms, is as near to the bottom of the literary heap as prose can get. If the critics have correctly discerned that there are different kinds of reader and have then selected Type A's for their sharpest criticism, are we to agree that these readers deserve the merciless roasting that has been their lot for the past two hundred years? That is, do Type A readers have a shallower level of involvement in their reading than Type B readers, and do they read worse books?

Our analysis suggests that although reading trance is possible for Type A readers, it may occur less often than for Type B readers; and, furthermore, that this lower trance frequency has something to do with the strength of the need to read and with the book choice this gives rise to. In other words, Type B readers, who seek a heightening of consciousness in their reading, will be inclined to lay aside books that offer little involvement and select alternative activities, including those that leave consciousness open for fantasy, such as jigsaw puzzles or walking. Type A readers, on the other hand, who are impelled to read, are unlikely to lay a book aside because it offers only absorption but not trance: absorption is what they are after.

Clearly, the criteria the two kinds of reader apply to the choice of books are very different. Type A's, who apply an absorption rather than an entrancement criterion, are considerably less exacting than Type B's, who seek not only absorption but also entrancement. The first set of criteria is based on a simple and undifferentiated need—to escape from one's own consciousness—and the second on a perception of oneself as a complex cognitive apparatus seeking a good fit with a particular author and the world he or she creates. The less exacting criteria lead naturally to that branch of formulaic fiction—romance, espionage, science fiction—that the reader has in the past found to provide absorption; the more stringent criteria take the reader rather toward differentiated writing in which doubt tempers certainty and shades of gray rather than stark black and white predominate.

The consequence of the interplay of reader needs and book selection criteria is that Type B readers will read fewer books but will experience some deep involvement in all or nearly all of them while Type A's will read many books and find involvement in only a few of them. We have, however, repeatedly emphasized that although the distinctions between Type A and Type B readers are real, the boundary between the two types is permeable. To show just how permeable it is, we quote at some length from the work of a remarkably perceptive (and unrepentant) escapist—W. Somerset Maugham. What he says is useful for what it tells us about escapism, about the experience of reading, and about the self-confessed book addict's capacity for reading trance:

> Some people read for instruction, which is praiseworthy, and some for plea-sure, which is innocent, but not a few read from habit, and I suppose that this is neither innocent nor praiseworthy. Of that lamentable company am I. Conversation after a time bores me, games tire me, and my own thoughts, which we are told are the unfailing resource of a sensible man, have a ten-dency to run dry. Then I fly to my book as the opium-smoker to his pipe. I would sooner read the catalogue of the Army and Navy Stores or Bradshaw's Guide than nothing at all, and indeed I have spent many delightful hours over both these works. At one time I never went without a second-hand bookseller's list in my pocket. I know no reading more fruity. Of course to

read in this way is as reprehensible as doping, and I never cease to wonder at the impertinence of great readers who, because they are such, look down on the illiterate. From the standpoint of what eternity is it better to have read a thousand books than to have ploughed a million furrows? . . . And like the dope-fiend who cannot move from place to place without taking with him a plentiful supply of his deadly balm, I never venture far without a sufficiency of reading matter (1932, p. 29).

So great was Maugham's dependence on his "deadly balm" that he traveled with a great leather-bottomed bag brimming with books:

There were books of all kinds. Volumes of verse, novels, philosophical works, critical studies (they say books about books are profitless, but they certainly make very pleasant reading), biographies, history; there were books to read when you were ill and books to read when your brain, all alert, craved for something to grapple with; there were books that you had always wanted to read, but in the hurry of life at home had never found time to; there were books to read at sea when you were meandering through narrow waters on a tramp steamer, and there were books for bad weather when your whole cabin creaked and you had to wedge yourself in your bunk in order not to fall out; there were books chosen solely for their length, which you took with you when on some expedition you had to travel light, and there were books you could read when you could read nothing else (1932, p. 33).

On the one hand, we have here the unmistakable marks of the Type A reader: first, reading is a need so imperative that it is explicitly compared to a drug addiction; Maugham is suggesting that withdrawal of a habitual reader's books threatens his sanity, indeed his life, no less seriously than withdrawal of an opium-smoker's pipe. Second, books are a fortification against consciousness that accompany one literally to the ends of the earth. On the other hand, the differentiated and selective use of reading matter characteristic of Type B readers is also evident. It is not so much a bag of books Maugham carries with him as a bag of people, each ready, at the opening of a page, to engage him in precisely the kind of conversation he longs for at that moment—fiercely intellectual, pleasantly discursive, informative, or vacuous.

But the most effective kind of escapism requires the exercise of imaginative faculties associated with Type B readers—namely, joining one's own imagination to the author's in order to escape not only self-consciousness but also the here-and-now. Again, Maugham is telling us that addictive readers, among whom he classes himself, are also capable of this exercise of imagination:

There are few books in the world that contain more meat than the "Sailing Directions" published by the Hydrographic Department by order of the Lords Commissioner of the Admiralty. They are handsome volumes, bound (very flimsily) in cloth of different colours, and the most expensive of them is cheap. For four shillings you can buy the "Yangtse Kiang Pilot," containing a description of, and sailing directions for, the Yangtse Kiang from the Wusung river to the highest navigable point, including the Han Kiang, the Kialing Kiang, and the Min Kiang. . . . These business-like books take you upon enchanted journeys of the spirit; and their matter-of-fact style, the admirable order, the concision with which the material is set before you, the stern sense of the practical that informs every line, cannot dim the poetry that, like the spice-laden breeze that assails your senses with a more than material languor when you approach some of those magic islands of the Eastern seas, blows with so sweet a fragrance through the printed pages. They tell you the anchorages and the landing places, what supplies you can get at each spot, and where you can get water. And it is strange when you think how sedately it is all set down, with no words wasted, that so much else is given you besides. What? Well, mystery and beauty, romance and the glamour of the unknown. It is no common book that offers you casually turning its pages a paragraph such as this: "Supplies. A few jungle fowls are preserved, the island is also the resort of vast numbers of sea birds. Turtle are found in the lagoon, as well as quantities of various fish. . . . A small store of tinned provisions and spirits is kept in a hut for the relief of shipwrecked persons. Good water may be obtained from a well near the landing-place." Can the imagination want more material than this to go on a journey through time and space? (1931, pp. 302–03).

This voyage into the spice-laden breezes of China is escapist, certainly; but to condemn it as "dysfunctional" or "narcotizing" (Katz and Foulkes, 1962, reviewed in chapter 2) is to condemn both fantasy and the deepest kind of enjoyment reading offers us, which is the creation of new worlds solely by the application of our own focused attention to the printed page. In this sense, escapism is the ultimate exercise of the sovereignty reading offers us.

Four Ludic Readers Talk about Reading

Self-reports by readers, especially introspective reports about ludic reading, are rare in the literature (Hansen, 1973, and Hilgard, 1979, are notable exceptions), so it seems appropriate to give a good deal of space and weight to the very vivid descriptive material available in the transcript of a two-hour tape-recorded discussion among four of the most introspective and articulate of the thirty-three ludic readers. This group discussion took place in November 1977, about a week after the laboratory study had ended. The complete transcript (Appendix D) is a rich mine of virtually undefended disclosures about the nature of the reading experience. Readers might find it helpful to read Appendix D in its entirety at this point before going on with this chapter.

The four subjects who participated in the group discussion, to whom fictitious names have been given, were:

Ockert Olivier (Subject 119), a 45-year-old Afrikaans-speaking clerical worker.

Sanette Olivier (Subject 206), his daughter; like her father (whom she emulated in many other ways), she is an office worker.

Wendy (Subject 215), a 52-year-old university lecturer, English-speaking but, like the other discussants, fully bilingual.

Mary (Subject 230), 35, an English-speaking businesswomen.

There were also two non-subject participants—myself (*Victor* in the discussion transcript) and *Psyche,* a clinical psychologist with a special interest in the psychodynamics of dreaming. Psyche attended as a facilitator who would be free to focus on covert processes and bring these to the attention of the discussants when it seemed appropriate to do so. My role as chairman was to introduce discussion topics and on occasion to curb irrelevancies. In addition, it was necessary to ensure that the quieter subjects (such as Wendy) were given a fair hearing by the more voluble participants. Indeed, the participants' press to self-disclosure, leading to frequent interruptions and overlapping speech, is one striking aspect of the discussion. Another is the dramatic raconteur style adopted by Ockert, Mary, and Sanette. Here, their desire to be center-stage is allied to a keen sense of the dramatic and the ability to present personal experience in a dramatic narrative form.

Subjects were encouraged to talk about themselves during the intake interview, and especially full self-descriptions were presented by the four discussants. Four members of the *Olivier* family participated in the study—the father (Ockert), mother, and two daughters (the younger is Sanette). Since their reading is an interactive family pursuit, which for the children is the outcome of social learning and parental pressure, some information about the family is helpful.

When he volunteered to participate in the study, Ockert said that he read nine books a week: one each weekday and two on each day of the weekend. (During the interview, he added, "When I find a book I really enjoy, I hide it away for the weekend.") He also indicated that the rest of his family read similar quantities. Their own claims were more modest. Ockert (whose laboratory reading speed was 350 w.p.m.) indicated a total of over 30 books a month, and Sanette (456 w.p.m.) a total of 18; her elder sister (Subject 220; 921 w.p.m.) claimed 28, and the mother (Subject 221; 316 w.p.m.) 25 books a month. In the course of his intake interview, Ockert gave the following description (translated from the Afrikaans) of himself and the family. He has just explained that he tries to forget what he reads even while he is reading so that he will be able to enjoy the same book again soon.

I try to forget because there are so few books that really give one the pleasure of reading. My wife remembers everything. She would be able to tell the children the story quite exactly. Then she stops and says, "Now you must read on yourselves if you want to know what's going to happen." I would also sit and listen to her, even if I'd read the book the day before, and I enjoy listening to the same story very much [makes a face of absorption and delight]. There's a crowd of kids that listen to her, the neighbors' children also. It's always puzzled me that she manages to remember the stories so well. . . .

We've got it worked out that the children must also read. One really wants them to read too but I think in the long run it becomes a kind of disease because all we do is read. Life passes us by. Normal people go to Fountains Valley [a park in Pretoria], just get into their car and go. But we just sit at home. The youngster [aged 15] doesn't read such huge quantities. He gets a reading bug, reads for a week without a break, then he stops and pesters all of us when we're trying to read. We tell him to find a book, but he just runs off somewhere. We don't want to own a TV set. I think it's a waste of time. We wouldn't have enough time for reading or for anything. We have a hard time bringing the children up. I never trade my books in, I never return a book, not even an expensive one. I buy books that are falling apart. Owning the books is important to me. I always want to be able to go back and read the book again. I just want more books all the time. . . .

The elder daughter (Subject 220) remarks: "Our whole lounge is full of books. When you come into our house, it's as if a reading fever suddenly grabs hold of you." She describes the symptoms of reading fever and indicates that she may be on the way to a cure now that she is no longer living at home: "If I don't read for a week or so, I get terribly restless. I'm irritable, it's a type of hunger, not to eat but to read. As soon as I touch a book, I feel better and it gets better as I read on. . . . Lately, since I left home [for a university hostel], I've half cooled off about books."

Sanette remarks that her preferred reading matter is a Western, especially those by Louis L'Amour. She dislikes love stories, which upset her. Sanette's graphic description of how she and her siblings were taught to read by the mother's cliffhanger technique is contained in the group discussion transcript.

Mary gives the following account of her weekly routine: she works in her own business, in which she and her husband are partners, from 6 A.M. to 7 P.M. Mondays to Fridays, and from 6 A.M. till noon on Saturdays and Sundays. By 8 P.M. she is in bed, where her children (aged about 8 and 10) often join her. She reads for about two hours before going to sleep and claims that she finishes 20–30 books a month. On Saturday before coming home she collects six feature-length movies and four shorts from a film rental shop which she and the children watch using family-owned projection-equipment. (In 1977, when these interviews were conducted, videotapes had not yet supplanted 16-mm. movies as the mainstay of home entertainment.) They spend Saturday and Sunday afternoons in this way till about 8 P.M. Her husband does not join them for the movies, preferring to work in the garden or play squash and tennis ("he can't soak up all this trash all the time," she adds spontaneously). She remarks that once she and the children saw thirteen half-hour movies in a single afternoon. Mary notes that television fails to absorb her; while watching television, she does painting by numbers or jigsaw puzzles.

When the family goes away on holiday to Durban (the coastal resort nearest Pretoria), her husband spends time with the children while Mary's routine is to look at the shops till 10 A.M., go to a morning movie until lunchtime, another movie at 2 P.M., and another in the evening at 8.

Her children, she notes, do not seem to mind the weekend movie routine at home. They have their own activities, and Mary feels she gives them as much love as she can. In her two years at home with them full-time when they were younger she spent more time scolding them than she does now. She remarks that when the children began watching movies with her they were upset by violence, but she was able to convince them that it was only playacting. Sometimes, there are still tears after a show. For example, after seeing *The Chalk Garden*, they both wanted to know if she felt the same way about them as the movie mother did about her children. When the elder child was seven or eight, they saw *Puppet on a Chain*, and "he was in hysterics." Now she makes a point of showing a comedy last, so that the children can go to bed on that and not wake up in the middle of the night asking questions.

Reflecting on her intake of books and movies, Mary remarks, "I enjoy it so much I can't really say it's trash." Talking about the kind of movie she enjoys, she says she prefers one in which the good guy wins or the lovers come together to "heavy" movies like *Deliverance* or *The Godfather*, which are "too gory and too sordid": "I like a nice lighthearted thing like *Ivanhoe* or *Prisoner of Zenda*. I cried from beginning to end of *The Chalk Garden* (I tend to cry very easily, especially when children are involved) and I enjoyed it very much, but I'd rather see something on the lighter side, I'd rather be entertained while watching and not have to get personally upset at what's going on."

It is ten years since I have seen Mary, and I often wonder what has become of her, her marriage and her children: pathology has a way of resolving itself, though at a price, and she—as well as our other subjects—is very likely living differently today than the way she was in 1977.

Wendy, the fourth discussant, an English-speaking university lecturer, reads four or five books a month and often becomes deeply involved. Describing the pleasure reading gives her, she concludes by writing that there is "a very special pleasure if I can 'live' in the book, be part of it, know the characters as well (often much better) than I would have known them if they had been alive."

THE READING EXPERIENCE

The material in this section presents themes and trends derived from the group discussion, from the spontaneous remarks subjects made about their reading during the intake interview or in the laboratory, and from their questionnaire responses. Two questions were especially useful. These were "Why do you enjoy reading in bed?" and:

> Think back to some books you have enjoyed very much. What kind of enjoyment do you get out of books like that? Write a few *honest* sentences about the rewards this kind of pleasure reading offers you. Remember that this kind of reading has nothing to do with learning or improving the mind.

Obviously, the thematic arrangement is arbitrary, reflecting my own perceptions of the pervasive concerns of these readers. This is especially true of the way the open-ended responses and spontaneous comments have been treated, and rather less so of the quantitative questions, such as those about attentional effort, rereading habits, and the percentage of trashy reading matter.

Reading Ability and Reading Gluttony

You have to be able to read well in order to enjoy Louis L'Amour, argues Ockert, and to those who say it's not good reading matter, he replies that they probably can't read well enough to enjoy it, that they are still at the stage of decoding letter by letter like children in school. The mark of the involved reader who is really enjoying reading is that awareness of the mechanics of reading drops away: "You get the feeling you're not reading any more, you're not reading sentences, it's as if you are completely living inside the situation." Subject 110 seems to be alluding to a similar phenomenon when he remarks on the "simple satisfaction of the process of reading itself."

Ockert is not an especially fast reader, and his flexibility ratio is low, especially in comparison with Sanette's (see table 6.2) Nonetheless, he lays great emphasis on smooth and effortless reading. He is attracted to the part-reading techniques taught in speed-reading courses ("You're supposed to read from the top down to the bottom") and seems unduly troubled by the information that one of his daughters reads faster than he does. Central to Ockert's interest in speed reading is his need to read fast so that he can forget fast. During the intake interview, he remarked:

> The more I enjoy a book the quicker I want to forget it so that I can read it again. Like *Fallon* [by Louis L'Amour], for example, I've already read it ten

times, and I enjoy it almost exactly the same each time. I read it as quickly as I can just to get the story. Some people can tell you exactly what they read a year or two years later. I try to forget because there are so few books that really give you the pleasure of reading.

Ockert is the model for a gluttonous reader, a text gobbler who swallows books whole, achieving that pinnacle of gluttonous security, the ability to eat the same dish endlessly, passing it through his system whole and miraculously wholesome, ready to be re-eaten again and again. The myth of the Cornucopia, the inexhaustible horn of plenty which Zeus presented to Amalthea, promising that it would supply in abundance whatever she desired, is here literally achieved: the book is the horn of plenty, an inexhaustible supply of nourishment.

Comparatively speaking, Ockert is a discriminating glutton. He knows what nourishment he likes, and despite his intention to forget a book he is enjoying, he was able to specify how much he had enjoyed books he had read two years previously and the episodes that had especially delighted him. Other subjects, however, had great difficulty recalling the content of even recently read books ("I read so many books that often I forget most of the plot," writes Subject 226) and were able to retrieve the titles and names of authors required by the Reading Mood Questionnaire only after extensive and time-consuming probing. Like the readers "who can turn around and take the same book off the shelf again and never notice," books appear to pass through their systems in great quantities but in an automatized and, paradoxically, partly conscious way.

Escapism

As we allow our four discussants and the twenty-nine other ludic readers to develop the escapism theme, it will become apparent that for many of them, escaping is synonymous with ludic reading and raises a series of questions that are central to their enjoyment of reading and the way they feel about it. As Ockert has told us, one needs to be a skilled reader before one can escape. Escaping in turn raises what for some of our readers is an existential issue: how does book reality relate for them to world reality, and is guilt an appropriate response to the desire they feel to move from the world to the book—especially if influential others regard the book as trash? Behind this is a larger question: do readers live the good life? if I read while my neighbor does the things that keep other people busy, which of us is living well? The reality status of the book in turn raises questions about the emotions that accompany reading: is it "real" pain that Mary (for example) feels when she weeps, real fear, real excitement?—or are these shadows of reality that instantly disappear in the even light of the real world?

In one way or another, most of the answers to the questions about

reading enjoyment in the Reading Habits and Reading Mood Question-
naires touch on the issue of escapism. Some of these replies have a
remarkable quality of pathos, describing a blighted life in which reading
is an island of delight. Subject 101 (a young man) writes:

> Reading removes me for a considerable time from the petty and seemingly
> unrewarding irritations of living—I did not choose to be born, and cannot say
> (in all honesty) that I get 100% enjoyment from life. So, for the few hours a
> day I read "trash" I escape the cares of those around me, as well as escaping
> my own cares and dissatisfactions. This is a selfish attitude, which I can justify
> only by saying that it contributes in no small measure to preserving what
> sanity I have. I'm not so sure, then, that I read for "reward" as much as for
> "escape."

A middle-aged woman, with a number of children and a high school
education, writes:

> When I feel sad and read an Afrikaans book, especially by Driecky Beukes, I
> have a good cry and can use the book as an excuse. The nursing stories give an
> insight into life in a hospital and I think they make up for the fact that I was
> unable to take up nursing as a career because of ill health.

In specifying the rewards of pleasure reading, the metaphor most often
used—though in a variety of guises—was that of switching off one world
and switching on another. It takes one's mind away from the problems
and pressures of life (Subjects 129), it switches one off from one's "other
life" and shuts one's mind to the tensions and worries of the day (223),
one forgets everything (202), it relaxes one and relieves tension by letting
one escape to a make-believe world (234; 230) and to a different life in
another place and time (203).

   When you escape into a book, do you go into the page, asks Psyche, or
does the page enter your life? There are not two separate worlds, Wendy
had said earlier, because the book world enters one's own life, and this
applies even to events in the century before Christ, in Michener's *Source:*
"Things happen there that are real as if they were happening in your
own life." For other subjects (such as 208 and 222) the book is a stage on
which they try out their own reactions to the situations faced by the
characters. A related question (again framed by Psyche) is whether the
book world is an extension of one's own real world or quite different
from it. It's quite different, say Sanette and Mary; earlier, Sanette had
related to this issue in a slightly different context: "A love story is so near
real life. When I want to escape, I don't want to escape into the same
world again. . . . I want to escape into a fiction world, a world that was."

   For the Oliviers, the question of whether the world is passing them by
or, on the contrary, whether they are passing by the rest of the world is
an unresolved and painful issue. In the intake interview Ockert said that

his family's reading was "a kind of disease . . . , life passes us by." In the group discussion, however, he took the view that the life that passes them by is not worth living:

> Like Mary said about her husband, I can't imagine how people keep themselves busy fishing and so on every weekend in a little world sixty miles around Pretoria. That's all their world consists of. He can get no escapism . . . , he's just busy with himself all day. If I had to be occupied with myself all day I'd go mad, crazy. I'd say our reading is like Sigmund Freud said, "Dreams are the means whereby we compensate for the harshness of reality." You can say "reading" instead of "dreams."

Ockert seems to be suggesting that the life of the reader is larger, deeper, and more satisfying than many real but impoverished lives, such as that of the weekend fisherman. Sanette, predictably, takes a similar view: the other girls in the dormitory where she lives are all pleasure seekers, she says, who go out while she enjoys herself reading in her room. They spend a weekend at a resort and bore her for hours with stories of what they did, while she would not spare more than a sentence for such pursuits but could talk for hours about a book she's read and would like to share with an unnamed "him." There is a pathos in both these readers, a gnawing uncertainty about the true value of the rich but shadowy world in which they have chosen to spend most of their leisure time. Of course, they are not alone: this is the plight of the constitutionally hyperexcitable introvert, who often turns his or her back on the bright lights and loud voices of the "real world," mourning the fun that has thus unwillingly been renounced. We produce some psychometric evidence later in this chapter to suggest that heavy readers are introverts and that the plight of Sanette and Ockert is at least in part shared with others who must retreat to quieter areas in which stimulus loads do not threaten to become overwhelming. As we argued earlier, reading is such a domain because of the easy dominion the reader exercises over it.

Escapism is often associated with guilt. Western society is oriented to work and recreation, and the long tradition of pejorative judgments about ludic reading undermines its claim to be considered recreational. These uneasy relations are neatly captured by Subject 127, who turns guilt to pleasure: "to be able to sit, relax with a book, is a time-wasting delight." However, though reading when one should be working is sloth (I may burn the food, but that doesn't mean I'm not living properly, protests Mary, though without great conviction), it is nonetheless preferable to complete idleness. When Mrs. Olivier saw her children sitting round doing nothing, recalls Sanette, she would tell them a story like *Fear is the Key* and leave them to read on. There is a suggestion here (albeit defensive) that reading is a kind of work, at least in the sense that it is to be preferred to idleness. Sanette, in a certain sense, also sees reading as a job. She cannot bear to leave a book unfinished, especially if her father has recommended it to her, as if an unfinished book, like an unfinished task, is a testament to one's sloth.

Trash and Guilt

The following question appears in the Reading Mood Questionnaire:

> If all the fiction I have read for pleasure only for the past 12 months were laid out for judgment by my high school English teacher and the head of the English Department at which I studied as an undergraduate, they would classify——percent as "trash" that was not worth reading.

For the thirty-two ludic readers who responded to this question, the mean percentage of their reading matter they rated as trash was 42.65, with a standard deviation of 26.42. It is a strange reflection on Western culture that these readers rate nearly half of their pleasure reading as aesthetically worthless in society's eyes if not their own. Trash ratings ranged from zero to 90 percent; twelve readers rated more than half their reading as trash (there were two ratings of 90 percent, four of 75 percent, and six of 60 percent), and twenty rated less than half of their reading matter as trash (two gave a percentage of 45, eleven gave 30 percent, five said 15 percent, and two gave zero ratings). The four discussants were all well below the sample mean. Sanette and Mary rated only 15 percent of their reading as trash, with 30 percent for Wendy and Ockert.

A number of difficulties surround this measure of trash. Ostensibly, the percentage reflects not the reader's own judgment of his or her reading matter but that of the bearers of socially approved literary values. At the same time, the figure is given by the reader, not by the external authority, and therefore reflects an internalized judgment (this is an ambiguity inherent in the voice of conscience, which is both my own and society's). These problems are exacerbated by two further issues. One is the unknown effect of the defense mechanisms for the resolution of dissonance (chapter 2), and the other is the extent to which readers in fact follow the instruction to judge their reading not personally but as it would be judged by an authority figure. The weight of all these biases is in the same direction, and their combined effect has therefore probably been to underestimate the trash percentage—though it is by no means clear that a direct question ("How much of your reading matter do you regard as trash?") would have produced more interpretable results.

Most readers in our study took the position that other people read more trash than they do. "I don't consider the books I read are trash," says Mary, readily admitting that there is indeed a lot of trash around, such as science fiction. Cowboy books aren't trash, says Sanette, but the other girls read cheap stuff like picture stories and women's magazines. Mary provokes general laughter when, tongue-in-cheek, she says the Westerns are trash, to which Ockert replies that for many readers they open a new world. Paradoxically, there is one way in which reading trash assuages guilt. The elder Olivier daughter, despite the self-disgust thus occasioned, reads a lot of Silhouette books "because they are so thin and go so fast. Where it's boring you just turn over and go on because in any case you know how it will turn out." Once again, in this unusual family, the guiltless skipping of whole pages (certainly a self-defeating way of reading) seems to be a learned behavior. Mrs. Olivier (Subject 231) says: "Mills and Boon [Silhouette books] has given me a standard [of enjoyment] to judge other books. And I can skip pages, read a line on a page and get finished quickly and I don't feel guilty. I'll finish reading perhaps at 2 A.M." In the same vein, the elder Olivier daughter quite happily admits that 60 percent of her reading would be regarded as trash: "I enjoy it very much for the moment I am reading it. Afterward I am sometimes disgusted with myself for reading books like Mills and Boon stories. I know it doesn't improve my mind, but I do absolutely nothing about it." For both mother and daughter, the "trash" judgment absolves them of the responsibility that Sanette feels to do her reading job properly: if it's rubbish you're reading, treating it like rubbish is not only permissible but also establishes your good taste, as if to say, "Sure it's trash I'm reading—and you won't catch me treating it with respect!" Hence the paradoxical statement by Mrs. Olivier: her reading matter supplies a standard of enjoyment, but it is also rubbish of which whole pages can be skipped. This license-to-disdain adds to the reader's sense of control and freedom.

Entrancement

Escapism successfully pursued results in entrancement, and many subjects indicate that they live completely inside the situation (Ockert) in the book (Subject 215), or in the characters (Subject 228): "I was so involved with the characters in this book they were like my own family and friends. I really got to know and feel for them." A possible mark of entrancement is being held by the book; for example, Wendy could not stop reading *The Fountainhead*, and Mrs. Olivier finds *Reader's Digest* condensed books extraordinarily gripping: "They're OK for most books. They have as much in them as I want to know. Oh, they're good! It's terrible to put them down."

Mood and Emotion

Our treatment of attention and absorption suggested that a much sought-after aspect of the sovereignty of the reading experience was its power to move the focus of one's attention from self to environment, thus changing the content of consciousness and mediating mood changes. Mrs. Olivier writes: "I often feel sorry for myself and a book can change my mood very quickly. . . . Books make me happy, books make me cry—after a good cry I feel a new person." The catharsis of a good cry (though not all crying is pleasurable) is frequently referred to by Mary, and other subjects: "a good old cry . . . a nice cry").

For three of the four discussants, fear is an especially salient emotion—fear of social and sexual rejection, of maltreatment, and of separation from the sources of security. For them, one of the principal uses of reading is for the fine control of fear, in order to master it by experiencing its gooseflesh but not its terror, to know that the fear is self-induced and under one's own entire control. They explore these issues indirectly, with little insight, but at length.

Sanette has learned from her father that twice-read material is doubly enjoyed, and she says she uses this method to help her visualize, but in fact to make sure that nothing will go bump on the page and startle her. In a fascinating disclosure, she describes this double reading, a preview first and then back again, more slowly the second time, "and suddenly the horse comes upon him and he sees the other man. . . . I always go back because then I know what to expect." For Sanette, the safest reading is a cowboy story that she has already previewed: "If it's a cowboy book it won't frighten me. But if it's not a cowboy I get so frightened I could die." Both father and daughter take a theatrical delight in describing how well they control their fear. Sanette says: "When I was small . . . I read an Afrikaans book about werewolves and I was so frightened I had to go and sit right next to my dad. I was scared to death especially when I read it at night." But so delightful is the fear, so well managed by the father's solid presence, that she reread the werewolf story three or four times! The father, from whom one may infer that Sanette has learned her fear-control stratagem, says: "I get so frightened [at Hitchcock, for example] I could die of fright. I get heart palpitations. . . . I get so scared I must sit next to someone." Both these readers vividly illustrate the truth of Hilgard's comment about the open gate between fantasy and reality in the development of fantasy life.

The control of fear also has a reality-testing aspect. Sanette's tongue-in-cheek remark that Ockert reads books about the frozen ice-world (although he gets cold very easily!) so that he'll know what to do if he lands there is nearer the mark than she thinks. There are many indications, from the discussants and the other subjects, that the covert rehearsal of real-life coping strategies is a significant aspect of ludic reading.

Mary practices a variant of Sanette's double-reading technique, directed to the neutralization not of text but of movies: in order to stop herself from closing her eyes and keep her fingers out of her ears during the terrors of the movie *Cassandra Crossing,* Mary first read the book very quickly "just to get an idea of who was going to die when so I could keep my eyes open."

We suggested in chapter 9—partly in the light of interactions with these readers—that reading-induced affect becomes unpleasant when it touches on non-neutralized current or childhood concerns. Thus love stories are painfully real for Sanette, though to other readers—Mary, for example—they are just one among many kinds of fiction. Mary's own area of sensitivity relates to child maltreatment: "I can take a murder story with ten dead bodies, but don't have a child involved, then I've had it." Thus, reading Dickens as a child, she wept so copiously that her mother (in a show of solicitousness that Mary may remember so vividly because it was unusual) took the books away from her "because I was a nervous wreck at that stage." Dickens remains "just too horrible" for her because it is not just history: "There are people who treat children like that today," and this present reality touches a raw nerve.

In psychodynamic terms, the distinction that both Sanette and Mary make between strong emotions they enjoy ("a good cry"; "I was scared to death") and those that flood them with unmanageable affect is an important one. An aspect of the mastery they exercise over their reading is that both have identified the kind of reading matter that releases non-neutralized emotions, which they carefully avoid (though we cannot choose our dreams, we certainly can choose our books). It seems likely that emotionally disturbing reading is so aversive that one-trial conditioning takes place. It is certainly striking that all our subjects tell of bad reading experiences that happened in the distant past, not in their current reading. In relation to his avoidance of painful material, Mary makes an interesting observation: in illustrated comic-book form, Dickens lost his power to hurt her (in chapter 3, we examined some of the mechanisms that may account for the greater emotional power of the novel).

Visualization

We suggested in chapter 10 that ludic readers were more likely to employ propositional strategies than to use visualization. The importance of imagery to ludic readers was indirectly explored by the series of questions about books, movies, and book illustrations in the Reading Mood

Questionnaire and more directly in the group discussion. Later in this chapter, we review evidence suggesting that imagery may be more important to ludic readers than we concluded in chapter 9. Some support for this evidence comes from the reports of all four of the discussants, which indicate that though readers' imaginal experiences of the same book may diverge widely, imagery is an essential aspect of the reading experience for all of them, good and poor imagers alike.

The discussion of *The Poseidon Adventure*, which three of the discussants had read, was especially illuminating. Mary, though a poor visualizer, was unable to enjoy the book because of the visualization problems presented by the upside-down boat in which floors had become ceilings and passengers ascended inverted stairways in order to reach the surface. Only after she had seen the movie was Mary able to "picture the whole thing and appreciate what it was like." The plight of the vivid visualizers was more acute and their solution more original: Ockert lay down on his back on the floor, holding the book above his head, while Sanette used a picture of a stairway turned upside down in order to orient herself. However, visualizing is time-consuming and stressful, and one suspects that for all three readers of this inverted epic, the need to align the ship with their mental images arose because of the vivid descriptions the author offered. Indeed, all three say quite emphatically that they do not like too much description in their reading matter. Mary reads for what people do, not for what they look like or the settings in which they move. Sanette objects to copious description because, "like my father says, you're so tied down you can't manage to think yourself into that situation."

Sanette, an acute observer of her own and her family's reading strategies, is in effect supporting the position taken by William Gass: to image in great detail and vividly is a kind of madness; moreover, one will be all day about it. She heartily agrees with Gass that characters in fiction are—indeed, should be—mostly empty canvas. L'Amour is a great writer, she says, because he does not burden the reader with description: the hero rides through thick bush, the Indians are silhouetted against the horizon, no more, and the reader, using a ready-made store of images, at once sees the whole picture—mistily, perhaps, but well enough.

Book illustrations. Of the twenty-three readers who responded to the question "Do illustrations in books ever irritate you?" fifteen said no, while eight (with considerably greater emphasis) said yes. It seems likely that the degree of dissatisfaction will be greater for more vivid imagers. Though this proposition was not tested, Subject 111, a lecturer in fine art and himself a painter, writes that he is "madly" irritated by book illustrations unless the book is history or biography: "The illustrated novel, even

Cruikshank's [illustrations for] Dickens, I suppose, specifies locality and character too much." Wendy and Ockert (both strong visualizers) have similar feelings. A curious aspect of the irritation they both feel with the illustrations for an Afrikaans series of children's books is that although one of them sees the character as delicate and curly-headed and the other sees the same character as plump and well-built, they are equally convinced that his depiction in the book is quite wrong. At least for some readers, the freedom to see things as one wants to, without being dictated to by the author's too-full descriptions or the illustrator's drawings, seems to be a much-prized aspect of reading sovereignty.

Movie versions of books. A complex set of questions in the Reading Mood Questionnaire asked readers to compare books and movies in a number of ways—reading a book first and then seeing the movie of the book, and vice versa; comparing a vividly remembered movie scene with the best book scene and saying which gave "deeper and more intense enjoyment"; and then comparing a television scene with the book and with the movie.

Two issues emerged from these comparisons: one is the question of control, considered below, and the other the conflict between two sets of images—those in the reader's head and those on the screen. Subject 111, the painter, comments on this conflict as follows: "The book is curiously better—this is a general comment. I would say that the acted character becomes too specific; the same character read is more agreeably framed in one's own mind. This applies also to the setting." Sanette, on the other hand, prefers to see a movie before reading the book, "because then I can take the character I've seen in the movie and put it into the book"; predictably, this reflects Ockert's view. He says he will not go to a movie if he's read the book, which means that he almost never gets to the movies. Even for Mary, the weakest visualizer, the conflict can be disturbing: she and Ockert join forces to dismiss *Murder on the Orient Express* as a wholly inadequate rendering of Agatha Christie's characters.

But answers to these questions about books, movies, and television programs did not prove very helpful in exploring the nature of the interference between internally and externally produced images. In comparing a book to the movie version of that book, about half the respondents enjoyed the movie more and half the book: in view of the previously noted pro-reading bias of the questionnaire and the respondents, this indicates that readers may in general prefer the film versions to the books they are derived from. Indeed, Sanette and Mary say so directly. This runs counter to our theory of dominion and may perhaps be attributed to the filmic potential of books that appeal to movie producers, which may render them rather less satisfying reading matter than the stereotyped staples of many ludic readers—the Westerns, romances, and undistinguished sex-and-sadism novels often specified as preferred reading. On the other hand, some readers do support our theoretical position. Ockert always prefers books to movies, and Subject 214 volunteered that she and her four children all read while they watch television, and that the book "far and away" is superior in holding their attention.

Finally, the four discussants speculated enthusiastically but naively about the origins of their visualizing ability: though the literature review in chapter 10 indicates that imagery vividness is most likely an innate ability, these subjects attribute it to learning. Mary thinks she is a poor visualizer because she has always taken the easy way out and watched movies; Sanette believes her mother taught her how to be a visualizer; while Wendy feels that she had to teach herself.

Control

We suggested earlier that the reader's control of the pace of reading is an important aspect of reading sovereignty and that in this respect the book is markedly superior to other entertainment inputs. Not even videotapes, played on one's own VCR in one's own living room, which one can start, stop, and freeze at will, can match the reader's control over a book, because the pace at which words and images are delivered on the screen is the producer's choice, not the viewer's. As we showed in chapter 6, ludic readers move often from skimming to savoring, reading some passages, on average, more than two and a half times faster than they read others; this variability is a constant accompaniment of reading and is quite beyond the reach of the VCR user.

Since I unwisely made my own views on pace control known to the discussants, evidence from this source cannot be cited except in cases where the subjects who reported similar views had not first been exposed to my own. An interesting and unprompted statement in this regard comes from the intake interview with Ockert, who, early in our interaction, gives the following response to a question in the Reading Mood Questionnaire: "I can read a book at my own pace, I can put it down whenever I like, and I can always go back to it. A movie can't be switched off, same with TV, but perhaps the most important of all, I can't replay the enjoyable parts—or see it at my pace." Ockert's elder daughter (Subject 220), also in response to Question 30, wrote: "I find a totally different type of enjoyment from books than from movies. . . . I savour the content of the book and can always go back and read it again; that you can't do with movies or TV programs." Mrs. Olivier, in response to the same question, wrote that if a book bores her she can put it down, but she has to sit through a boring movie: "what a waste of time!" Subject 101 writes: "I don't really enjoy movies—I feel I'm a captive audience; if I get bored I feel compelled to stay to the end, as I've paid. . . . The books one reads provide a pleasure that is entirely at one's beck-and-call. You read, stop . . . as the mood takes you." Subject 111, the artist, takes a similar view: "I feel that a movie has to be compellingly good if it is to overcome a resentment of its inexorable push—I can't drop a movie when I want to, and my long history of crap reading has, I'm sure, built up a resentment that a crap movie can't be stopped." Subject 223 presents another aspect of control (not unique to books), namely that books are to be preferred to movies because reading, unlike movie-going, can be done without any previous planning.

Prejudices

We noted in chapter 8 that readers varied widely in their rank-ordering of genre fiction—westerns, humor, romances (see figure 8.1). In the first place, our readers have stereotyped expectations, from which they resent any departure: our discussants express the view that Louis L'Amour should not set a novel in Canada and South African farmers should not act like cowboys. Subject 234 remarks that in selecting a book she relies on the author, and moves on to the second kind of prejudice readers have, to be strongly for or against particular genres. "I don't enjoy the simple 'Mills and Boon' type of book," she writes, adding that she avoids historical novels and especially Georgette Heyer.

Subject 226, an opinionated young lady with a sharp sense of humor and a neat turn of phrase, had an especially well-developed set of prejudices. For example, after once trying to read a Kurt Vonnegut novel, she won't touch science fiction:

> My personal opinion is that there are no little green men on Mars. It's highly unlikely that a spaceship is going to land in my backyard. Why should I waste time on something that's not going to happen?
>
> Mills and Boon? [makes a face]. That's one thing I'd never touch no matter how hard up I am. They always have a happy ending. I mean, let's be a little realistic. Louis L'Amour? I don't really like cowboys. If I want a cowboy I'll go to a movie.

I ask what she would do if she were on a desert island with a great stock of Louis L'Amour and Mills and Boon and nothing else. "I'd read the Louis L'Amour," she said. "And after that?" "I'd start a hockey team with the monkeys." This pride in prejudice is not uncommon among readers. Subject 111 found a Georgette Heyer he had not read before and delightedly read this novel in the laboratory session; many other readers said she was one author they'd never touch. Similarly, in the group discussion, Mary said Westerns are trash while Sanette and Ockert would be happy to read nothing else.

Reading in Bed

For most subjects, taking a book to bed is a distillation of the delights of reading, and little of the guilt that may accompany reading at other times attaches to bedtime reading. It is a private time, and, like play, it stands outside ordinary life. For many readers, it is the only time of day they can truly call their own (thus Ockert, in response to Question 34). Subject 236 writes that reading in bed "helps to keep me awake till the last child gets in and I do forget the hassles of the day for a while and it's really the only time I get more or less to myself." In the light of our findings in chapter 9 about the very deep relaxation that immediately follows the laying aside of a book by a reclining subject (see especially figure 9.3), we might expect readers to refer explicitly to the links between bedtime reading and sleep; it is surprising, however, that they do so in terms of "addiction." Wendy writes that she enjoys reading in bed "because it is part of life and a fitting way to end the day and also a habit which I certainly do not wish to break. Even if I read for only 5 minutes, I must do it—a compulsion like that of a drug addict!" Similarly, Subject 111: "My addiction to reading is such I almost can't sleep without a minimum of 10 minutes (usually 30–60 minutes) of reading." It is comfortable and soporific, remarks Subject 226: one is already undressed and must only switch off the light when reading ends. Subject 110, a teacher of English literature, enjoys his bedtime reading because it is response-free: "I can read exclusively for the pleasure of reading without critical demands being made on the book or on my responses." A recurrent theme in subjects' replies to Question 34 is the power of bedtime reading to shut out the day's activities and problems and to induce the relaxation essential for sleep. Subject 101, an English lecturer, writes: "I find it possible to relax and thus get to sleep easily. If I don't read, the 5 or 6 hours' work I've done in the study keep going through my mind in a series of images." Subject 223 writes that reading in bed "takes my mind away from the day's tension and sends me to sleep."

These themes return in virtually the same words in at least five other protocols. The role of reading in inducing relaxed and peaceful sleep is well known to all these readers, providing important support for the profound physiological relaxation after reading reported in chapter 9.

The quantitative data in response to the question "How often do you read in bed before going to sleep?" support the importance of bedtime reading: of the 26 respondents, 13 said "every night" or "always" and 11 said "almost every night" or "most nights."

Rereading Habits

Pilot-study interviews with ludic readers before the questionnaire was drawn up had indicated that for some, rereading well-liked and well-known books was an important part of their reading enjoyment, both in terms of hedonic value and in the daily reading time it occupied. Preliminary interviews with two readers, one of whom became a subject in the laboratory study, suggested that some keep a pile of these old friends on their bedside table for use during the most precious reading time of the day, in the minutes before falling asleep. Other readers, however, seldom reread, and then only a long time after the first reading.

The data indicate that rereading is the exception rather than the rule: sixteen readers report that rereading is 5 percent or less of their monthly reading, and nine of these specify 2 percent or less. The group mean of 9.96 percent is substantially exceeded by only two readers (Subject 202 with 50 percent and Subject 112 with 25). It seems likely that rereading old favorites renders the formulaic even safer and that readers who do a great deal of rereading have especially high needs for this kind of security. However, the group discussion brought to light a covert form of rereading which serves the same purpose; namely, to purge the formulaic of the unexpected. One method is Sanette's double reading, in which she first skims and then, having noted lurking dangers in the narrative, rereads the same material more slowly. Mary's pre-movie reading of *Cassandra Crossing* has the same goal. Rereading may therefore be more important than our figures suggest, but in disguised forms.

Reading Involvement

Reading involvement was scored by summing the answers to four related questions, each scored on a 6-point scale, from zero for no involvement in or commitment to the book to 6 for the greatest possible involvement and commitment:

1. I felt intimately involved with/rather distant from the characters in the book, their narrow escapes, their loves and their sorrows.
2. My mood and emotions while reading were determined exclusively by the book, so much so that the mood I brought with me when I started reading was forgotten/my mood and emotions were book-related, but only slightly so.
3. I found that I concentrated quite effortlessly on the book/my mind tended to wander to other things so that it was a considerable effort to concentrate.
4. The book had the effect of strongly intensifying and heightening my emotions/had very little effect on my emotions.

Before the first laboratory session, readers were asked to apply these questions to Book C (read under distracting circumstances) and, after the second session, to the book they had read in the laboratory.

The analysis presented in chapters 3 and 10 suggests that a deeply involved reader would indeed attain maximum or near-maximum scores. In fact, 12 of the 33 readers estimated their involvement at 22 or better on the 0–24 scale for the laboratory book. For the sample as a whole mean involvements in Book C and in the book read in the laboratory were 16.33 and 17.97, respectively, which is in the upper third of the scoring range, indicating that readers perceived themselves to be substantially involved.

Attentional Effort

Two paradoxical results troubled us in the laboratory study: ludic reading, which is subjectively effortless, is accompanied by a high level of physiological arousal, and work reading, which is subjectively effortful, is no more arousing (and often less so) than ludic reading. The following questionnaire item related directly to these paradoxes:

> In reading the following books, did you find you concentrated effortlessly (zero percent effort) or that your mind kept wandering to other things and you had to force yourself to concentrate as hard as you could (100 percent effort)?

The books subjects had to rate were those for which they had already supplied titles, authors, and well-remembered episodes: the most-enjoyed book read in the previous week or ten days (Book B); a book read with enjoyment but under very poor circumstances (Book C); "a book you found thoroughly dull, flat, and uninteresting, but that you nonetheless read quite a chunk of" (Book D); and, finally, "a work book of average difficulty you have read extensively in the last few weeks."

Of the 25 subjects who answered this question, 13 said their concentration effort while reading an enjoyable book was zero, with a sample mean of 5.40 and a standard deviation of 9.00. The very low standard deviation means that most readers were convinced that the effort required of them by ludic reading is indeed very low. This finding strongly supports the attentional model of reading (chapter 4), which suggested that fully engaged conscious attention would be perceived as subjectively effortless. Second, it supports the suggestion that there is a disjunction between the physiology of ludic reading (and, by implication, of many other cognitive tasks) and reader's perceptions of it, so that perceived relaxation is in fact misperceived arousal.

Substantially more effort is needed for a dull and boring book (67.28 percent, S.D. = 78.65) than for a work book (39.65 percent, S.D. = 51.59), though the very large standard deviations of these means require cautious interpretation. Here, not comprehension but interest is at issue; readers appear to be relating to the effort of forcing themselves to read something they would prefer to lay aside. Finally, it is interesting to note that a degree of attentional effort seems to be compatible with enjoyment: subjects ascribed a mean concentration effort of 26.80 percent (S.D. = 40.76) to reading Book C (under distracting circumstances), which is five times higher than the mean for Book B (5.40 percent), read under normal conditions. Nonetheless, the mean-enjoyment percentage readers gave for Book C was 67.42 percent.

In this light, the surprising laboratory finding that work reading is substantially less arousing than we had expected is at least partly explained by the sense readers have that work reading (at a mean 39 percent concentration effort) is not much more effortful than some kinds of successful ludic reading (26 percent for Book C) and needs a great deal less effort than failed ludic reading (67 percent for Book D).

READING AROUSAL AND READING IMAGERY

One of the most striking features of the laboratory study was the arousal drop between reading (Period I) and relaxing after reading (Period J). It seemed likely that the difference between these two periods would be most expressive of the physiological reinforcers of reading. The differences between the variability scores for Periods I and J generated only one statistically significant correlation with seven measures of reading behavior, namely a positive .35 correlation ($p < .05$) between the clarity and vividness of imagery while reading, on the one hand, and muscle activity at the corner of the mouth (EMG2), on the other. These are the muscles that control smiling and pouting, and the suggestion that vivid imagery is associated with expressive facial activity is an appealing one that has a good fit with McGuigan's position, outlined in chapter 9. Similarly, the frontalis muscle (EMG1), which is associated with tension as well as with other aspects of facial expressiveness, approaches significance ($p < .10$) in its correlation with imagery, as well as with perceived reading involvement.

The correlation matrix computed for this analysis also showed a strong positive relation (.47) between reading involvement and reading imagery. This runs counter to the theory-based predictions in chapter 10, where we found that propositional structures are more rapidly and less stressfully generated than imaginal ones, and that image generation is not therefore likely to be an essential part of ludic reading. Clearly, the .47 correlation coefficient between imagery vividness and profusion while reading the laboratory book, on the one hand, and emotional involvement in that book, on the other, supports the second set of predictions, suggesting that vivid imagery is indeed frequently associated with reading involvement.

THE PERSONALITY ATTRIBUTES OF LUDIC READERS

People who read a great deal for pleasure may share personality traits that set them apart from the rest of the population or that distinguish them as a group. To determine if this is so, subjects were asked to complete the Eysenck Personality Inventory (Eysenck and Eysenck, 1964) and the Cattell Sixteen Personality Factor Questionnaire (16PF; Cattell, Eber, and Tatsuoka, 1970; Madge, 1975).

The most striking feature of the subjects' performance was the low extraversion score on the Eysenck Personality Inventory. This reflects negative answers to questions such as those cited in table 9.1 ("Do you often long for excitement?" or "Would you do almost anything for a dare?"). Accordingly, low extraversion scores are characteristic of introverts, as our subjects most strikingly appear to be. This finding is confirmed by the 16PF results, on which three of the five scales (F$-$, M$+$, Q$_2$$+$) show loadings consistent with the second-order introversion factor.

In terms of the characterization of introverts we offered in chapter 10, which suggested that they would develop strategies for the reduction of incoming stimulation (such as preferring the familiar to the new), we note that there is an excellent fit between such strategies and those described by our four discussants. Formulaic fiction—especially if reread or previewed in the ways we have discussed—offers the reader dominion over an exceedingly familiar landscape, suggesting that avid readers prefer reading to doing because they prefer the familiar and the readily controlled to the unpredictable patterns of arousal offered by the real world. Insulation from the world and control over experience are achieved through a sufficient supply of formulaic fiction.

TYPE A AND TYPE B READERS

Books may be used either voraciously and anxiously to hold consciousness at bay, as with Type A readers, or to heighten it, as with Type B's. We suggested that the fundamental distinction between them lay in the tone of consciousness, with the inner life of Type A readers being governed by fearfulness, anxiety, guilt, and other negatively toned affective states and that of Type B's by positive expectations and the recycling of enjoyable experiences.

The most direct probe of the intensity of our ludic readers' needs to escape from unpleasant consciousness is Question 3a in the Reading Habits Questionnaire (scored in chapter 5 as part of the Frustration Index); namely, how one would feel to discover, alone in a strange hotel, that one had nothing to read. This question elicited a range of replies from the 129 students readily scored in terms of their affective tone and intensity. These dimensions are even more clearly discerned in the response of the 28 ludic readers who replied to this question. In approximate sequence of intensity, with headings selected on intuitive grounds to describe the tone of the response, these 28 replies are set out below (if more than one reader made a given response the number who did so is indicated in parentheses):

No emotion: nothing
Displeasure: restless (2), frustrated (5), annoyed, peeved, a bit hassled
Anger: bloody annoyed
Agitated: manic, bothered, a little upset, let down, disappointed, bad, bitterly disappointed, terrible
Anxiety: lost (2), quite lost, lost and miserable, really miserable, desolate! awful/dispossessed, desperate

The emotions grouped under "anxiety" are both more intense and qualitatively distinct from those in the "anger" and "displeasure" groups, bringing to mind the description Bowlby (1973) offers of the separation anxiety of early childhood. "Desolate," "desperate," and "dispossessed" describe a state of almost unendurable anxiety, and all for want of a book! If the eight individuals whose responses are noted under "anxiety" are, in fact, Type A readers (and, in the absence of additional behavioral descriptors, we cannot make a firm pronouncement on this question), their powerful reactions to reading deprivation support the view that Type A's read to retreat from unpleasant consciousness, and the desolation they anticipate is fear of confrontation with their own anxiety.

The status of the more intense terms in the "agitation" group ("bitterly disappointed," "terrible") is unclear. Though they may describe emotional states as desolate and abandoned as those in the "anxiety" group, they have been treated separately because anxiety is a necessary part of being lost or desolate, but not of feeling terrible or disappointed.

12
A Motivational Model of Ludic Reading

In this final chapter, we attempt to draw together the manifold threads of our inquiry and at the same time answer the question that has been our central concern: namely, how reading performs the prodigious feat of capturing consciousness. The most parsimonious way of answering this question is by presenting an elaborated version of the motivational model of ludic reading introduced in figure I.1 and relating our findings to its hierarchy of decisions and processes. At the same time, we shall be able to comment on a wider question, and say whether these conclusions relate to other aspects of the entertainment industry.

The elaborated model (figure 12.1) is cast in the form of a decision flow chart, indicating the sequence in which events take place and their hierarchical relations; it also plots the motivational forces that determine at each stage of the process whether reading will be pursued or supplanted by another activity. For clarity, the exposition that follows is numbered to conform to figure 12.1.

A. ANTECEDENTS OF LUDIC READING

Ludic reading is unlikely to be attempted or to succeed unless three antecedents are available to the intending reader.

A1. Reading Ability

We have argued that reading skill summates as reading-comprehension speed and have shown that a high degree of reading skill co-occurs with ludic reading. It would certainly have been more satisfying to show that reading ability predicts ludic reading, but the methodological difficulties

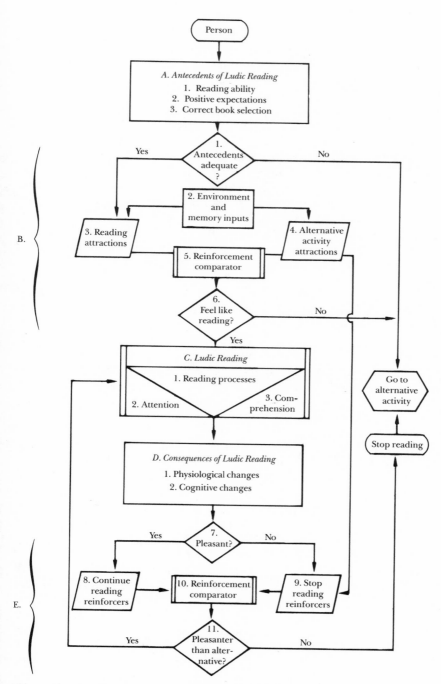

Figure 12.1. A Motivational Model of Ludic Reading

that stand in the way of demonstrating this causal relationship are formidable. Nonetheless, trivial as our finding may appear to be, it confirms the anecdotal and observational findings reported in chapter 5 that reading ability appears to be a prerequisite for ludic reading and bolsters the very meager empirical evidence in this area. In chapter 5, we were also able to produce some preliminary evidence that reading ability in adults is a fully developed skill that hardly changes over time, and that it does indeed vary substantially across individuals of similar educational attainment.

With regard to the minimum speed required for ludic reading, our theoretical prediction in chapter 5 that this is unlikely to be below 200 w.p.m. is upheld. Indeed, this estimate can be revised upward quite substantially. The mean natural reading speed of the thirty-three reading addicts in the laboratory study is 408 w.p.m., with a standard deviation of 153. If the distribution were normal, this would mean that 84 percent of the sample read at better than 255 w.p.m.

Of course, these laboratory subjects constitute a highly selected group, and for that reason we would do well to look at the student sample, most of whom are not ludic readers. Their mean reading-comprehension speed of 221 w.p.m. is therefore likely to be lower than the cutoff for ludic reading. However, the groups that spend most time reading books and read the largest number of books for pleasure are the university and college females, whose mean reading-comprehension speeds are 254, 227, and 228 w.p.m., which convert to raw speeds of approximately 273, 244, and 245 w.p.m., respectively. It appears then, that the minimum level of reading ability that constitutes an adequate antecedent for ludic reading is a reading-comprehension speed of between 227 and 387, the means, respectively, for the Afrikaans-speaking university women and twenty of the ludic readers. These convert to raw reading speeds of between 244 and 412 w.p.m. The lower figure is likely to be the minimum reading speed for the attainment of sufficient automaticity in a large proportion of the components of reading skill to free consciousness for comprehension processes, thus circumventing the difficulty of the pupil who was too busy reading to understand (chapter 5).

With regard to the upper limit of ludic reading speed, we cited evidence in chapter 5 that reading stops and skimming starts at about 800 or 900 w.p.m. It seems unlikely that savoring a text could take place at or above such speeds. Table 6.2 shows that only three of the speeds in the "Low" column are above 500 w.p.m., well below this ceiling. In fact, eighteen subjects (58 percent of the sample) savor their reading matter at below 300 w.p.m. The view that ludic readers would move freely between savoring and skimming is amply supported by the data in table 6.2. The most striking example is Subject 220, who skimmed at 2,214 w.p.m. and savored at 457 w.p.m.!

Other entertainment inputs. The skill demands made by ludic reading are far higher than those required for full enjoyment of most other entertainment inputs. The storyteller's art is accessible to the very young; so are most kinds of what we called "elaborated storytelling" (figure 3.1) and its modern electronic forms, radio and television.

These contrasting skill requirements arise from the odd circumstance that although every normal person learns to speak, not everyone learns to read, and that reading has this difficulty in common with other symbol systems (musical notation, Morse code), which are acquired laboriously or not at all (chapter 5). In other words, storytellers and movies make language for us by speaking to us directly. The reader, by contrast, must himself perform this creative act by the exercise of automatized but nonetheless complex symbol-transformation processes.

The superiority to other entertainment inputs that readers attribute to reading derives largely from the concentrated attention demanded by this act of symbol transformation. This is not to suggest that other entertainment inputs are unable to achieve an analogue of the transfiguring power of reading trance but rather that they must work harder for it. A movie encloses us in a darkened room facing a towering screen; in the theater, we are moved by the force and clarity with which the actors speak to us. The book needs only reading skill.

A2. Positive Expectations

Chapter 3, about story witchery, casts a wide net. This is reflected in the story-tree graphic (figure 3.1), which is in effect a phylogeny and an ontogeny of narrative. It is phylogenetic because it demonstrates that the storytelling arts (and therefore the appetite for hearing stories) can be traced back to the earliest human societies and ontogenetic in that we trace the likely path followed by the developing child in acquiring a lifelong taste for narrative. Indeed, our analysis of the five narrative paradoxes in chapter 3 showed that both children and adults delight in well-known, stereotyped, and essentially suspense-free tales which they hear others tell or endlessly tell to themselves, so that neither teller nor audience is necessary for the provision of narrative rewards. The propositions developed in chapter 3 have interesting confirmation in the readers' self-reports in chapter 11 and Appendix D.

The ontogenetic account in chapter 3 of the ways narrative reinforcers develop, when read together with the speculations about the origins of hypnotic susceptibility and reading involvement in chapter 10, leads to the conclusion that reading ability—and therefore reading habits— may vary in response to developmental events, and thus independently of educational level. It seems likely that a child to whom the doorways to fantasy are open (Hilgard, 1979) will find ludic reading a more rewarding experience than a child for whom fantasy is blocked. This may have two developmental consequences: the open-fantasy child is likely to develop a higher level of reading ability purely through practice and to be more attracted to literature and the tender-minded careers. For the child to whom fantasy has been closed, such tough-minded careers as engineering and the sciences are likely to have more appeal.

There is limited support for this prediction in table 8.2, which shows that college men who are students of building science spend between one-half and two-thirds less time reading books for pleasure than the liberal arts group with which they can be most closely compared, the university men.

A3. Correct Book Selection

Correct matching of book and reader is the foundation upon which ludic reading rests. The consequences of a mismatch, as we saw in chapter 11, are an inordinate expenditure of energy in order to maintain reading, which our ludic readers rated as a concentration effort of 67 percent, or thirteen times more than the effort required for reading a really enjoyable book. Clearly, the effort of reading a poorly chosen book is likely to lead to speedy abandonment of reading in favor of another activity.

Insofar as readability ratings are based on measures of text difficulty as determined by word and sentence length, such as the Fog Index, they offer a good guide to readers' ludic preferences. The cloze procedure, as we predicted in chapter 7, fails to measure text difficulty and is quite unrelated to the ludic continuum.

However, the scale of the publishing industry and the size of the mass reading habit indicate that ludic readers are able quickly, accurately, and with little effort to select appropriate vehicles. This was certainly the experience of our thirty-three ludic readers, who reported that they had enjoyed choosing three new books for reading in the laboratory and certainly did not find this an onerous task.

The ease and facility with which readers match themselves to books are in marked contrast to the somewhat higher failure rate among video watchers and movie- and theater-goers. Accordingly, an important but little recognized aspect of reading sovereignty is that we select books by directly sampling them ourselves while plays and movies are most often rated indirectly (and therefore less accurately) through the judgments of friends or reviewers.

Finally, we have shown (chapter 8) that book-selection preferences are culturally determined, and that within a given culture, book preferences within and across taste culture groups show substantial and statistically significant consistency. We were also able to cast some preliminary light on the formation and internalization of the values that give rise to these consistencies by showing that after two years of study, the changes in the preference patterns of a group of English majors led them to closer conformity with their mentors' views.

B. START-READING DECISION

If any one of the three antecedents of ludic reading is deficient, the "Antecedents Adequate?" decision node (Location 1 in Figure 12.1) leads via "No" to an alternative activity. If, however, reading is fluent and automatized, ludic reading has established a set of positive expectations, and a correctly selected ludic vehicle is available, the relative reward values of reading and available alternative activities are computed by the hypothesized reinforcement comparator (Location 5). Among the motivational forces operating at this location are the reader's current concerns, the strength of the desire to dull or heighten consciousness (chapter 11), and the strength of competing demands on the reader's attention. An important constituent of the latter forces is the reward expectancy that has been set up by previous reading experiences, especially by the remembered reward strength of the book the reader is currently reading. It is possible that this memory is in turn mediated by the decay-resistant higher-level macrostructures specified in chapter 4, which are memories for global rather than local events. The frequency with which readers return to the book they are reading in preference to alternative pursuits seems to indicate that these global-event memories offer substantial reward potential. In other words, my decision at bedtime on whether to continue reading *Thunderball*, to take up another book, or to read the newspaper is largely governed by a global recollection ("Bond's girlfriend is in danger again") rather than by a desire to attain closure on a local event ("Will Domino be tortured before Bond rescues her?").

C. LUDIC READING

C1. Reading Processes

The automatized reading skills, which require no conscious attention, are placed at this location in our motivational model. (Brown, 1981, offers a singularly useful neurophysiological specification of both automatized and conscious reading processes.) Logan's observation, cited in chapter 4, that reading is a mixed task containing both automatized and consciously controlled processes is apposite: the conscious aspects of reading are located at C2 and C3 below.

Events at C1 are not of much interest to us except for the remarkably large spontaneous adjustments of reading speed noted in chapters 5 and 6. These variations in within-text reading rate seem to be mediated by automatized processes; some support for this assertion comes from the fact that there was not much clarity among the ludic readers as to whether they had read the most-liked passages faster or slower than other passages.

Slowed reading rate—savoring—may arise from slowing of reading rate itself—for example, by longer fixations—or because of regressions (in other words, the most-liked passage is read as fast as the preceding material, but the reader then goes back over it again, at the same or a slower pace). Our data-collection method reflects both these strategies as a slower rate for the affected pages, so that no light can be cast on the mechanisms through which savoring is achieved.

C2. Attention

Reading is necessarily preceded by tonic activation (Brown, 1981, p. 446): following Kahneman, reviewed in chapter 4, we regard this attentional priming of the central nervous system as an autonomic event, unaccompanied by perceived effort, which we defined as a special case of arousal. In chapter 11, we produced strong support for these theory-based predictions: our ludic readers reported a concentration effort of near zero for ludic reading. This percentage climbed steeply through work reading (39 percent) to boring reading (67 percent).

On theoretical grounds, we argued further that conscious processing is a prerequisite for comprehension processes, but not for automatized reading processes. We noted that the demands comprehension makes on continuous attention are heaviest for readily comprehended material, such as ludic reading matter. These demands result in intense externally focused attention. This intense focus initiates reading absorption, which leads to two further effects. First, attention is removed from the self, thus holding unpleasant consciousness at bay. At higher levels of intensity, during which both the individual and the object of attention are transfigured (through the mechanisms reviewed in chapter 10), focused attention may initiate reading trance. Both absorption and trance are thus likely to have their origin in the full commitment of the attentional apparatus. Second, the reader is shielded from distractions, and the almost undiminished enjoyment our subjects report for the book they read under extremely distracting circumstances (Book C) is powerful confirmation of the protective effect of reading absorption.

In terms of Kahneman's attentional-effort theory, we would expect the subjective effortlessness of ludic reading to be accompanied by electrophysiological indicators of arousal. At D1 below, we shall see that this is in fact so.

C3. Comprehension

The sentence-level and global-comprehension processes reviewed in chapter 4, with their accompanying heavy demands on conscious attention, appear at this location. These processes mediate between the printed page and the inner worlds that readers construct through macrostructuring, to which sentence-level comprehension processes are the input.

D. CONSEQUENCES OF LUDIC READING

It is at this location in the model that consciousness is captured—by reading and by other entertainment inputs. All share the ability to change the content and tone of consciousness by an intense and highly energized state of concentrated attention. What is unique to reading is the economy of the means by which this feat is accomplished, requiring neither stage nor actors but a single small package of paper and cardboard.

Since the physiological changes are seldom perceived by the reader (and are misperceived if they are), the heart of the model is at location D2, where reading's sought-after modification of consciousness takes place.

D1. Physiological Changes

In chapters 4 and 5, we predicted on theoretical grounds that reading would require heightened arousal. This prediction is amply substantiated in chapter 9, where we show that on all five non-cardiac parameters, reading is more aroused than eyes-open relaxing, and significantly so on three of the five. Moreover, reading is more labile than baseline on four of the five parameters, and significantly so on two. The differences between reading and the eyes-shut relaxation period immediately after reading are even more striking. Both amplitude and lability drop markedly on all five non-cardiac variables, and significantly so on four of these ten parameters.

There is also some preliminary evidence that readers are more aroused when they are reading the pages they like most. This finding has an excellent fit with the predictions derived from experimental aesthetics in chapter 9 that fluctuating arousal is the "inner consequence" that is rewarding to the central nervous system (Berlyne, 1969, p. 841).

As we have seen, reading's arousal is misperceived by readers as relaxation (there is a parallel finding by Shapiro and Crider [1969] that subjective estimates of heart rate under varying stimulus conditions are notoriously inaccurate). It is unlikely that the physiological events during reading, or those that immediately follow the cessation of reading, are themselves directly reinforcing; indeed, readers never report these events in describing their reading satisfactions. It seems likely, therefore, that the reward value we have attributed to fluctuating arousal feeds back to consciousness as a generalized feeling of wellbeing and summates with the cognitive change mechanisms reviewed below.

D2. Cognitive Changes

We showed in chapter 10 that although reading resembles dreaming, it is not dreaming, for a number of reasons, of which the most salient is that while the dreamer's ego abdicates, the reader's does not. This is indirectly confirmed by readers' ability to control their reading to avoid emotionally overwhelming experiences, as shown by the absence of reports of such experiences in recent reading. Thus, the "mild narcosis" Freud ascribes to aesthetic experiences is no more than mild. Reading is closer to hypnotic trance than to dreaming, and we argue that, as in hypnosis, the reader's concentrated attention transfigures both the self and the object of attention. We suggested that this kind of attention—more common among Type B readers than Type A's—accounts for reading trance: absorption holds one, but trance fills readers with the wonder and flavor of alternative worlds. During both these conditions, the reader transmutes active secondary-process inputs to effortless, passive, and drifting cognitive products, a vicarious daydream which fully occupies consciousness. We argued that this daydream is especially pleasant both because of its content (which casts the reader in the role of triumphant hero) and because a regnant ego holds threatening experiences at bay by continually reassuring the reader that the imagined experience is only make-believe.

In the light of this analysis, we reject any claim that ludic reading should be seen as a new and discrete alternate state of consciousness. We adopt instead the more parsimonious view that the attention construct adequately accounts for reading's "otherness."

Another interesting item of evidence (chapter 5) about the consciousness-changing powers of reading is that book reading may give rise to greater consciousness-changes than newspaper or magazine reading. This conclusion arises from the finding that book readers feel far more distress when deprived of books than newspaper and magazine readers feel when they have nothing to read.

With regard to the personality attributes of ludic readers, the indication that they are anxious and fearful, but that this anxiety does not reach incapacitating levels, has a good fit with the theory developed in chapter 11. The much stronger evidence that ludic readers are introverts is particularly important. Though unanticipated, this finding is entirely congruent with the premises of the biologically based theories of personality described in chapter 9.

E. CONTINUE-READING DECISION

Ludic reading, like other intrinsically motivated (Deci, 1976) or paratelic (Apter, 1979) activities, is in ceaseless competition with other possible activities. Shall I read on or go to sleep? read a book or a newspaper? go for a walk, do the accounts, tell my spouse what happened on the way home from work today? Accordingly, positive reinforcements derived from reading are continually evaluated against at least two sets of criteria: whether the reader's book-induced cognitive product is itself rewarding (that is, is it judged to be pleasant, interesting, exciting) and whether the reward value of this cognitive product is more attractive than the rewards offered by available alternatives. Inputs from these two sources to the reader's hypothesized response comparator are shown at Location 10. The book fights alone against both outside competition and whatever negative resonances it may set up in a given reader. Let us examine these two sets of inputs.

Book-induced reinforcers (Locations 8 and 9). Since we have already considered the range of positive reinforcements books make available, we focus here on negative reinforcers that may arise because a dissonance is discovered between the sampling of the book in A1 and the product to which it gives rise on continuous reading. For example, a reader may find that the cognitive product arising from the book is uncomfortably close to current concerns—for example, a love story for a young reader who has just broken up with a boy- or girlfriend. Or the narrative may be found to be trivial and a so-what judgment passed: "It's such a stupid story, I couldn't be bothered." The reader may lack the narrative frames employed by the author and may accordingly have difficulty assigning content to macrostructures, so that the narrative quality is obscured. Readers' judgments in such cases are likely to be: "I just couldn't get into the book," or "It doesn't have a story." There are many other ways in which a given book, at a given moment, may fail a given reader so that "No" answers are given at decision nodes 7 and 11 and the "Stop Reading" location is reached. In such circumstances, in which the book itself rather than competing inputs leads to the cessation of reading, it is particularly likely that an alternative reading input will be sought. We must also note that although a book fails a reader on one occasion, the same reader, a little later and in a different state of mind, may again take up the book and continue reading it, but now with enjoyment.

Alternative activity attractions (Locations 4 and 9). We can now look again at two categories of such attractions, first considered under B above, namely, those of internal and those of external origin. The most common internal-origin alternative, and one of the most powerful, is sleep. As we have noted, reading in bed is particularly prized: often the book is laid aside as sleep intrudes and the reader's eyes begin to close. Other alternatives in this class are watching television, chatting, or reading the newspaper. External-origin alternatives are those imposed by the environment (Location 2 provides inputs to Location 9), such as leaving for work, a mother's command to bathe the dog, or the guilt that arises in many ludic readers that instead of wasting time reading they should be outdoors in the garden, indoors in the study, or generally elsewhere.

The reinforcement comparator (Location 10). The reinforcement comparator, a hypothetical cognitive structure in the reader, sums the positive and negative reinforcers and computes the resultant, which is the input to Location 11, the "Pleasanter than alternative?" decision node. The reader's decision on whether to continue reading or go to an alternative is under continual review: the balance is delicate, as we may infer from the observation that the "Stop Reading" decision may be taken at a paragraph end, at a page turning, or, indeed, in the middle of a sentence.

Epilogue

We have traveled a long road from a little question about newsworthiness in the introduction to the elaborated model of reading in chapter 12. It has been a circular route round a central point—consciousness, and how the sovereignty of the reading experience changes it. Reading sovereignty is a gift conferred on the skilled reader by the harmonious interaction of the myriad processes and subprocesses of reading: attention, decoding, comprehension through macrostructuring, and continually changing physiological arousal.

Skilled readers use sovereignty with the flair and precision of an old magician, achieving the most spectacular effects for the least effort: in the land of the dead or the country of the sleepless, the quiet spell cast by the reader shivers the corpses to life or plunges angry bodies into sweet dreams. Using a book selected for the purpose from among countless others, the ludic reader achieves the most startling changes of mood and consciousness—gloom explodes into delight, fear dissolves into power, and agitation becomes easy tranquility. Indeed, little in the study of consciousness is as striking as the economy of means and precision of outcome with which skilled readers are able to operate on their own state of mind.

Reading also means entertainment, and we have tried, in the interstices of the argument, to show what the relevance of our findings might be to other consciousness-changing activity.

But reading remains mysterious. That acme of a psychologist's achievements, the full analysis of what we do when we read, is still firmly beyond our grasp. So we end as we began, secure in the book's fragile world: a little wiser, perhaps, but still surprised at how very easily we sink through soundless pages into clamorous dreams to lose ourselves in a book.

Appendix A
Reading Preference Test

The thirty anonymous extracts from twenty-nine different books appear below in the random number sequence in which they were presented to the experimental subjects. The identifying information about the source of each extract is given in chapter 8 and should not be consulted before you have attempted the Practical Criticism exercise in chapter 7.

EXTRACT 11

As I sat there in that now lonely room; the fire burning low, in that mild stage when, after its first intensity has warmed the air, it then only glows to be looked at; the evening shades and phantoms gathering round the casements, and peering in upon us silent, solitary twain; the storm booming without in solemn swells; I began to be sensible of strange feelings. I felt a melting in me. No more my splintered heart and maddened hand were turned against the wolfish world. This soothing savage had redeemed it. There he sat, his very indifference speaking a nature in which there lurked no civilized hypocrisies and bland deceits. Wild he was; a very sight of sights to see; yet I began to feel myself mysteriously drawn towards him. And those same things that would have repelled most others, they were the very magnets that thus drew me. I'll try a pagan friend, thought I, since Christian kindness has proved but hollow courtesy. I drew my bench near him, and made some friendly signs and hints, doing my best to talk with him meanwhile. At first he little noticed these advances; but presently, upon my referring to his last night's hospitalities, he made out to ask me whether we were again to be bedfellows. I told him yes; whereat I thought he looked pleased, perhaps a little.

EXTRACT 13

Suddenly somebody stuck his head and gun up from the rocks on the bank above Harvey and loosed off two shots in my direction. Broken shale clattered down the rock wall behind me. I ducked, and grabbed for the Mauser, clipped the holster on as a butt, and switched the buttom to Automatic.

Another shot, from somewhere back up the road, slammed into the battered Renault beside me. And another. As if it were a signal—and it probably was—my first man jumped up from the rocks and starting pumping shots past my head.

I jammed the Mauser into my shoulder, clamped my left hand on the magazine, and fired.

It went off in one short brrap, trying to rip out of my hands. The man was hit by a sudden wind: his arms flung out sideways, then his head snapped up, and he pitched back out of sight.

Through the ringing in my ears I heard Harvey saying: "I keep telling you the war's over. Keep it single shots."

"I got him." I was trying to work out how many rounds I'd fired; I couldn't. The Mauser fires too fast for individual shots to echo in your brain. I guessed I'd fired ten—half the

EXTRACT 14

"Pardon me for interrupting you, madam," cried Mr. Collins; "but if she is really headstrong and foolish, I know not whether she would altogether be a very desirable wife to a man in my situation, who naturally looks for happiness in the marriage state. If therefore she actually persists in rejecting my suit, perhaps it were better not to force her into accepting me, because if liable to such defects of temper, she could not contribute much to my felicity."

"Sir, you quite misunderstand me," said Mrs. Bennet, alarmed. "Lizzy is only headstrong in such matters as these. In everything else she is as goodnatured a girl as ever lived. I will go directly to Mr. Bennet, and we shall very soon settle it with her, I am sure."

She would not give him time to reply, but hurrying instantly to her husband, called out as she entered the library, "Oh! Mr. Bennet, you are wanted immediately; we are all in an uproar. You must come and make Lizzy marry Mr. Collins, for she vows she will not have him, and if you do not make haste he will change his mind and not have her."

Mr. Bennet raised his eyes from his book as she entered, and fixed them on her face with a calm unconcern which was not in the least altered by her communication.

"I have not the pleasure of understanding you," said he, when she

EXTRACT 16

Three weeks ago he had thought up the plan for her to meet him in Madeira on the return journey.

"Even for a few days—let's have a sort of pre-honeymoon holiday."

At once Corrie agreed. "Super idea. I'll be waiting for you. People may think us mad but meeting you like that sounds so heavenly, I can't resist it. It'll be madly extravagant too."

"Then madly extravagant we'll be," he said. "And everyone will think we're an old married couple."

Then he had given her a wicked look from those sleepy handsome eyes of his—grey and darkly lashed. But the sleepy look was deceptive. Martin, as they all told Corrie at his office, was right on the ball. And so very goodlooking with his thick fair hair, not too short, not too long, his attractive mouth and boyish gay smile. He was not tall. Of medium height and with the broad, strong shoulders of an athlete. He played excellent tennis when he got the chance. Corrie played less well but they enjoyed a set or two together.

Thinking of their plans for Madeira she said, "The only thing I have against all this gorgeous madness is that I'm not allowed

EXTRACT 17

Production irregularities of the day-to-day type are responsible for a good bit of replanning and rescheduling. Sometimes a man gets a job done before you expected. Then his machine is freed sooner, maybe so soon that the job you'd planned next isn't ready yet so you have to shift things around. More often, however, you are dealing with jobs taking longer than you'd planned and again you have to change schedules. Materials or tools aren't ready, or the tools don't work well, or sub-par material takes longer to work, or other reasons make delays.

When you use piece rates and where the rates are very loose, workers, afraid that the rates might be cut, set a ceiling on their output. They peg it at a point considerably below what they can do.

From management's point of view, this is most unfortunate because it holds down production and holds down machine use to the worker's ceiling. Unfortunate though it is, it simplifies scheduling. You know how much output you'll get and can plan accordingly. Minor delays during the day don't cut output down any because the men can easily make up the loss in the ample time

EXTRACT 20

Just as the clock struck three, there was blown into the crescent a sedan-chair with Mrs. Dowler inside, borne by one short fat chairman, and one long thin one, who had much ado to keep their bodies perpendicular: to say nothing of the chair. But on that high ground, and in the crescent, which the wind swept round and round as if it were going to tear the paving stones up, its fury was tremendous. They were very glad to set the chair down, and give a good round loud double-knock at the street door.

They waited some time, but nobody came.

"Servants is in the arms o' Porpus, I think," said the short chairman, warming his hands at the attendant link-boy's torch.

"I wish he'd give 'em a squeeze and wake 'em," observed the long one.

"Knock again, will you, if you please," cried Mrs. Dowler from the chair. "Knock two or three times, if you please."

The short man was quite willing to get the job over, as soon as possible; so he stood on the step, and gave four or five most startling double knocks, of eight or ten knocks a piece: while the long man went into the road, and looked up at the windows for

EXTRACT 22

A messenger came to the door to say that confessions were being heard in the chapel. Four boys left the room; and he heard others passing down the corridor. A tremulous chill blew round his heart, no stronger than a little wind, and yet, listening and suffering silently, he seemed to have laid an ear against the muscle of his own heart, feeling it close and quail, listening to the flutter of its ventricles.

No escape. He had to confess, to speak out in words what he had done and thought, sin after sin. How? How?

—Father, I . . .

The thought slid like a cold shining rapier into his tender flesh: confession. But not there in the chapel of the college. He would confess all, every sin of deed and thought, sincerely; but not there among his school companions. Far away from there in some dark place he would murmur out his own shame; and he besought God humbly not to be offended with him if he did not dare to confess in the college chapel and in utter abjection of spirit he craved forgiveness mutely of the boyish hearts about him.

Time passed.

He sat again in the front bench of the chapel. The daylight

EXTRACT 23

The problematic nature of the validity of empirical knowledge is inherent in the fact that concepts render validity to a knowledge which is a synthesis of both concepts and percepts. The problematic nature of empirical knowledge lies therefore in the very fact that it is an *empirical* knowledge. It lies in the nature of the contact of the elements and in the impossibility of deducing one of the elements from the other, or of justifying the contact of them through some third element outside both. The problematic nature of this kind of knowledge lies in the fact that this knowledge which *demands validity* is based on a contact which in itself is *not validated*. Here the difference between mathematical and empirical knowledge becomes apparent. In mathematical knowledge the very fact that the object is constructed by thought guarantees the validity of that object, since validity is a feature of thought as such; in empirical knowledge it is thought which extends validity to a synthesis of both thought and percept.

Critical philosophy is based on the assumption that although the material or the percept is an indispensable element of valid knowledge, it is not *this* element which makes knowledge valid. The

EXTRACT 29

It was almost full daylight. A train went past the station, without stopping. In the purity of the morning light, the long line of car roofs melted into a silver string, and the train seemed suspended above the ground, not quite touching it, going past through the air. The floor of the station trembled, and glass rattled in the windows. She watched the train's flight with a smile of excitement. She glanced at Francisco: he was looking at her, with the same smile.

When the day operator arrived, she turned the station over to him, and they walked out into the morning air. The sun had not yet risen and the air seemed radiant in its stead. She felt no exhaustion. She felt as if she were just getting up.

She started toward her car, but Francisco said, "Let's walk home. We'll come for the car later."

"All right."

She was not astonished and she did not mind the prospect of walking five miles. It seemed natural; natural to the moment's peculiar reality that was sharply clear, but cut off from everything, immediate, but disconnected, like a bright island in a wall of fog, the heightened, unquestioning reality one feels when one is drunk.

The road led through the woods. They left the highway for an old

EXTRACT 30

Vera drew a deep shuddering breath.

She said:

"Do you really think—what you said at breakfast?"

"Be a little more precise, my dear. To what in particular are you referring?"

Vera said in a low voice:

"Do you really think that Rogers and his wife did away with that old lady?"

Emily Brent gazed thoughtfully out to sea. Then she said:

"Personally, I am quite sure of it. What do you think?"

"I don't know what to think."

Emily Brent said:

"Everything goes to support the idea. The way the woman fainted. And the man dropped the coffee tray, remember. Then the way he spoke about it—it didn't ring true. Oh, yes, I'm afraid they did it."

Vera said:

"The way she looked—scared of her own shadow! I've never seen a woman look so frightened . . . she must have been always haunted by it. . . ."

Miss Brent murmured:

"I remember a text that hung in my nursery as a child.

'Be sure thy sin will find thee out.' It's very true, that. 'Be

EXTRACT 36

"Perhaps you've heard the funny story. . . ." Ebbs began again, the determination of a lifetime at sea behind him.

"No, do go on!" the table exclaimed. They settled their eyes on him like schoolchildren with a new teacher.

"Well, it—it isn't hilariously funny really," Ebbs mumbled, his nerve faltering.

"Please! Please go on, Captain!"

"Well, you see." Ebbs swallowed. "There was once an old Captain I knew, trained in the days of sail . . . one of the old sea-dogs, in fact."

On his left. Mrs. Porteous burst into uproarious giggles.

"One of the old sea-dogs," Ebbs repeated warily, keeping his eye on her. "Trained in the days of sail. When ships were propelled by—ah, sail."

Seeing the funny point had not yet been reached, Mrs. Porteous immediately silenced herself and followed his words with exaggerated attention.

"And whenever he took his ship into port, this Captain, he always had his Quartermaster standing by to heave the lead. In the old-fashioned way, you understand. You see, he was an old-fashioned

EXTRACT 38

Slipping the rawhide thong off the hammer of my six-shooter, I put that pitch-fork down as easy as I could. Then I straightened up to listen. If he knew I was up here I'd best stir around a mite, or he'd be suspicious.

Many a cowpoke slept in a livery stable, and that was the idea I hoped to give him. What I figured on was getting him to come up that ladder, instead of him catching me coming down.

All the same, I started figuring. Seems to me a man can most usually take time to contemplate, and if he does it will save him a lot of riding and a lot of headaches.

Now, suppose I was down there and wanted to shoot a man on one of those ladders? Where would I take my stand so's I could watch all three to once?

It didn't leave much choice. Two ladders were on one side of the loft, opposite to him; the other ladder he knew of was on his side of the loft, up toward the front. If the man below wanted to keep all of them under cover, he had to be somewhere on the right side of the stable, toward the rear. If there was another ladder, which went up from that empty stall, one long unused, it would be

EXTRACT 43

Bass Lake is not really a town, but a resort area—a string of small settlements around a narrow, picture-postcard lake that is seven miles long and less than a mile wide at any point. The post office is on the north side of the lake in a cluster of stores and buildings all owned by a man named Williams. This was the Hell's Angels' rendezvous point . . . but the local sheriff, a giant of a man named Tiny Baxter, had decided to keep them out of this area by means of a second roadblock about a half mile from the center of downtown. It was Baxter's decision and he backed it with his three-man force and a half dozen local forest rangers.

By the time I got there the outlaws were stopped along both sides of the highway, and Barger was striding forth to meet Baxter. The sheriff explained to the Angel chieftain and his Praetorian Guard that a spacious campsite had been carefully reserved for them up on the mountain above town, where they wouldn't "be bothered." Baxter is six-foot-six and built like a defensive end for the Baltimore Colts. Barger is barely six feet, but not one of his followers had the slightest doubt that he would swing on the sheriff if things suddenly came down to the hard nub. I don't think the sheriff doubted it either, and certainly I didn't. There is a

EXTRACT 44

Maria plucked at him. "Get in. Quick. On to the bed." Presumably she had an idea—women were appallingly practical: they built new plans at once out of the ruins of the old. But what was the good? She said, "Let me smell your breath. O God, anyone can tell . . . wine . . . what would we be doing with wine?" She was gone again, inside, making a lot of bother in the peace and quiet of the dawn. Suddenly, out of the forest, a hundred yards away, an officer rode. In the absolute stillness you could hear the creaking of his revolver-holster as he turned and waved.

All round the little clearing the police appeared—they must have marched very quickly, for only the officer had a horse. Rifles at the trail, they approached the small group of huts—an exaggerated and rather absurd show of force. One man had a puttee trailing behind him—it had probably caught on something in the forest. He tripped on it and fell with a great clatter of cartridge-belt on gunstock: the lieutenant on the horse looked round and then turned his bitter and angry face upon the silent huts.

The woman was pulling at him from inside the hut. She said, "Bite this. Quick. There's no time . . ." He turned his back on the advancing police and came into the dusk of the room. She had

EXTRACT 46

"I'm sorry I waked you," Isabel said; "you look too tired."

"I feel too tired. But I was not asleep. I was thinking of you."

"Are you tired of that?"

"Very much so. It leads to nothing. The road's long and I never arrive".

"What do you wish to arrive at?" she put to him, closing her parasol.

"At the point of expressing to myself properly what I think of your engagement."

"Don't think too much of it," she lightly returned.

"Do you mean that it's none of my business?"

"Beyond a certain point, yes."

"That's the point I want to fix. I had an idea you may have found me wanting in good manners. I've never congratulated you."

"Of course I've noticed that. I wondered why you were silent".

"There have been a good many reasons. I'll tell you now," Ralph said. He pulled off his hat and laid it on the ground; then he sat looking at her. He leaned back under the protection of Bernini, his head against his marble pedestal, his arms dropped on

EXTRACT 49

He thought what a fine achievement he had made of his life that—aging, vain,
terribly narcissistic, suffering without proper dignity—he was taking comfort
from someone who really didn't have too much of it to spare him. He had seen
her when she was tired, upset and weak, when the shadows came over her eyes,
when the fit of her skirt was wrong and she had cold hands, cold lips parted on
her teeth, when she was lying on her sofa, a woman of short frame, very full, but
after all, a tired, short woman whose breath had the ashen flavor of fatigue. The
story then told itself—struggles and disappointments; an elaborate system of
theory and eloquence at the bottom of which lay the simple facts of need, a
woman's need. She senses that I am for the family. For I am a family type, and
she wants me for her family. Her idea of family behavior appeals to me.

Aunt Tamara's clock began to chime. He went into her parlor to look at its
old-fashioned porcelain face with long gilt lines, like cat whiskers, and listened to
the bright quick notes. Beneath it was the key. To own a clock like this you had to
have regular habits—a permanent residence. Raising the window shade of this
little European parlor with its framed scenes of Venice and friendly Dutch
porcelain inanities, you saw the Empire State Building, the Hudson, the green,

EXTRACT 51

She was in the doorway now, stopping short, giving a little gasp and widening her
eyes as if in shock. Giles was sagging against the wall, grey-faced, hands clasped
to his stomach. Two men. One stood over Giles, gently rubbing his chin with the
knuckleduster fitted on his right hand. A compact, stocky man, bull-necked,
round-faced, straight black hair cropped short. Very strong. One of those quick,
heavy men. Rare. Dangerous. Full of bouncy muscle. A gun in his left hand,
hanging by his side. A Colt Python, she registered, with the barrel shortened, the
forepart of the trigger-guard cut away, the hammer-spur cut off. A professional's gun, modified for quick draw and quick fire. He wore a light jacket, and she
knew it must hide a fast-gun harness.

The other man was taller. He wore a tailored black shirt with short sleeves,
and close-fitting slacks, rust coloured. His hair was silver, carefully groomed.
Beneath it, a well-bred face, a little haughty, almost impassive. A young face.
Which was the true datum, old hair or young face? She checked the hands and
neck. He was thirty, thirty-five. The neck and hands never lied. He might be less
dangerous than the stocky man, but she would not have laid odds on it. He
carried no gun. She would have seen a shoulder-

EXTRACT 52

When Ashenden went on deck and saw before him a low-lying coast and a white
town he felt a pleasant flutter of excitement. It was early and the sun had not
long risen, but the sea was glassy and the sky was blue; it was warm already and
one knew that the day would be sweltering. Vladivostok. It really gave one the
sensation of being at the end of the world. It was a long journey that Ashenden

had made from New York to San Francisco, across the Pacific in a Japanese boat
to Yokohama, then from Tsuruki in a Russian boat, he the only Englishman on
board, up the Sea of Japan. From Vladivostok he was to take the Trans-Siberian
to Petrograd. It was the most important mission that he had ever had and he was
pleased with the sense of responsibility that it gave him. He had no one to give
him orders, unlimited funds (he carried in a belt next to his skin bills of exchange
for a sum so enormous that he was staggered when he thought of them), and
though he had been set to do something that was beyond human possibility he
did not know this and was prepared to set about his task with confidence. He
believed in his own astuteness. Though he had both esteem and admiration for
the sensibility of the human race, he had little respect for their intelligence: man
has always found it easier to

EXTRACT 53

A representative example of systematic work on attitude and disposition variables in leadership may be found in Fleishman's report on his Leadership Opinion Questionnaire. This instrument has two scores, one assessing "structure" (the
extent to which an individual is likely to structure his own efforts and those of his
subordinates toward goal attainment) and "consideration" (the degree to which
an individual stresses warmth and consideration in his dealings with others). In
studies with the questionnaire (Fleishman, 1960), the C scale correlated .29 and
.32 with criteria of leadership in samples of 53 industrial supervisors and 42 sales
managers; scores on the S scale were essentially unrelated to the criteria.

These validity coefficients are low, but they do not necessarily indicate that
the tests are without value. Prediction of leadership in any particular setting must
take account of the demands and circumstances of the situation (cf. Bass, 1960;
Fiedler, 1967; Vernon, 1953). Measures of intelligence, dominance, sensitivity to
others, etc., might serve to identify a pool or sample of subjects from which
leaders in most situations will be drawn, even though these variables will not yield
precise forecasts

EXTRACT 55

Once again the assistant, Gayne, began placing papers on the conference table.
. . . evidence of theft from the bank . . . this has now been found.

Edwina, scarcely listening any more, had her eyes riveted on the signature on
each of the cancelled cheques—a signature she saw each day, familiar to her,
bold and clear. The sight of it, here and now, appalled and saddened her.

The signature was Michie's—young James whom she liked so well, who was so
efficient as assistant operations officer, so helpful and tireless, even tonight, and
whom only this week she had decided to promote when Tottenhoe retired.

The Chief of Audit Service had now moved on. "What our sneak thief has
been doing is milking dormant accounts. Once we detected a single fraudulent
pattern earlier this evening, others were not hard to find."

Still in his lecturer's manner, and for the benefit of the FBI men, he defined a dormant account. It was an account—savings or checking, Burnside explained—which had little or no activity. All banks had customers who for varied reasons left such accounts untouched over long periods, sometimess for many years, and with surprisingly large sums

They parked the car in the lane, came up the path and round the house. What a charming garden . . . flowers blooming exuberantly as if they knew this was the last month of summer and there might never be another season as fragrant, as sweet . . .

The sound of laughing came from ahead of them and Elspeth's voice.

"Oh, Dougal, don't, don't! I'm so comfortable. I love reading in the crotch of this tree, but it takes an age to get the cushions right . . . I'll come over after tea and see your new fowl-house."

A man's answering laugh. "You'll come now . . . I've sweated and toiled this whole Monday and I want someone to ooh and aah over it. And you ooh and aah more delightfully than any other woman I've ever known. Down you come, Elspeth!"

Sounds of resisting, giggles, insulting remarks that meant nothing being bandied back and forth . . . they rounded the corner to see a tall broad-shouldered man reaching up into an ancient pear-tree and tugging.

There was a lilt in Elspeth's voice that neither of them had ever heard before. "Dougal, stop it! You're a mean, horrible, beastly man! You ought to be called MacCrab, not MacNab . . . Ouch, you brute, you're bruising me! Look out, I'm falling!"

She landed fair and square on Dougal, knocking him off his balance,

China is an ancient land of superlatives. Its western mountains, soaring to heights of 24,000 feet and more, share with the Himalayas the distinction of being the world's tallest; in the North-West, China possesses one of the lowest spots on earth, the Turfan Depression, which lies 505 feet below sea-level. For 1,500 miles across the country's northern provinces winds the longest structure ever made by man, the Great Wall, erected more than 2,000 years ago to slow the encroachments of peoples from the steppes of Asia. In areas, China is exceeded only by Canada and the Soviet Union, and it has by far the largest population in the world—considerably more than 700 million people. Behind that statistic lies the country's most overwhelming problem and its greatest challenge, for the most important fact about China is that it does not have sufficient superlatives. It lacks enough cultivable land to feed its constantly increasing numbers. Already so numerous are the people of this giant nation that at least one out of every five persons on earth is Chinese.

There is no sameness about them or their land, Chinese cities and towns are jammed with workers and bureaucrats, and on crowded plains and in river valleys peasants work elbow to elbow. Yet China

EXTRACT 66

The doctor, nodding, straightened his tie with two fingers. "The number of our days is not check rein enough to look upon the death of our love. While living we knew her too well, and never understood, for then our next gesture permitted our next misunderstanding. But death is intimacy walking backward. We are crazed with grief when she, who once permitted us, leaves to us the only recollection. We shed tears of bankruptcy then. So it's well she didn't." He sighed. "You are still in trouble—I thought you had put yourself outside of it. I might have known better, nothing is what everybody wants, the world runs on that law. Personally, if I could, I would instigate Meat-Axe Day, and out of the goodness of my heart I would whack your head off along with a couple of others. Every man should be allowed one day and a hatchet just to ease his heart."

She said: "What will happen now, to me and to her?"

"Nothing," the doctor answered, "as always. We all go down in battle, but we all come home."

She said: "I can only find her again in my sleep or in her death; in both she has forgotten me."

"Listen," the doctor said, putting down his glass. "My war

EXTRACT 71

Big Rafer Hoxworth kicked back his chair and grabbed Abner by the coat. "Is Jerusha Bromley aboard that brig out there?" he asked menacingly.

"Yes," Abner replied steadily.

"God Almighty!" Hoxworth cried, shoving Abner back into his chair. "Anderson! Lower me a boat!" With fury clouding his face he grabbed his cap, jammed it on the back of his head, and stormed aloft. When Abner and John tried to follow he thrust them back into the cabin. "You wait here!" he thundered. "Mister Wilson!" he bellowed at his mate. "If these men try to leave this cabin, shoot 'em." And in a moment he was on the sea, driving his men toward the brig Thetis.

When he swung himself aboard, refusing to wait for a ladder, Captain Janders asked, "Where are the missionaries?" but Hoxworth, dark as the night, roared, "To hell with the missionaries. Where's Jerusha Bromley?" And he stormed down into the smelly cabin, shouting, "Jerusha! Jerusha!" When he found her sitting at the table he swept all the other missionaries together with his giant arms and roared, "Get out of here!" And when they were gone he took Jerusha's hands and asked, "Is what they tell me true?"

Jerusha, with an extra radiance now that she was both recovered

EXTRACT 76

She told me, "I didn't want to die weeping." I thought I had not heard aright.

"You did not want to die weeping?" I repeated after her. "Like my mother," she added readily. The outlines of her white shape did not stir in the least. "My mother had wept bitterly before she died," she explained. An inconceivable calmness seemed to have risen from the ground around us, imperceptibly, like the still rise of a flood in the night, obliterating the familiar landmarks of emotions. There came upon me, as though I had felt myself losing my footing in the midst of waters, a sudden dread, the dread of the unknown depths. She went on explaining that, during the last moments, being alone with her mother, she had to leave the side of the couch to go and set her back against the door, in order to keep Cornelius out. He desired to get in, and kept on drumming with both fists, only desisting now and again to shout huskily: "Let me in! Let me in! Let me in!" In a far corner upon a few mats the moribund woman, already speechless and unable to lift her arm, rolled her head over, and with a feeble movement of her hand seemed to command—"No! No!" and the obedient daughter, setting her shoulders with all her strength against the

EXTRACT 77

Managing an advertising agency is like managing any other creative organization—a research laboratory, a magazine, an architect's office, a great kitchen.

Thirty years ago I was a chef at the Hotel Majestic in Paris. Henri Soulé of the Pavillon tells me that it was probably the best kitchen there has ever been.

There were thirty-seven chefs in our brigade. We worked like dervishes, sixty-three hours a week—there was no trade union. From morning to night we sweated and shouted and cursed and cooked. Every man jack was inspired by one ambition: to cook better than any chef had ever cooked before. Our esprit de corps would have done credit to the Marines.

I have always believed that if I could understand how Monsieur Pitard, the head chef, inspired such white-hot morale, I could apply the same kind of leadership to the management of my advertising agency.

To begin with, he was the best cook in the whole brigade, and we knew it. He had to spend most of his time at his desk, planning menus, scrutinizing bills, and ordering supplies, but once a week he would emerge from his glass-walled office in the middle of

EXTRACT 83

A typical vertebra is made up of two principal parts, an anterior or ventral, termed the *body*, and a posterior or dorsal, termed the *vertebral arch;* these enclose a foramen (aperture. Plural: foramina) which is named the *vertebral foramen.* The opposed surfaces of the bodies of adjoining vertebrae are firmly connected to each other by discs of fibrocartilage, termed *intervertebral discs.*

In the articulated column the bodies and the intervertebral discs form a continuous pillar, which constitutes the central axis of the body and, in man, supports and transmits the weight of the head and trunk. The vertebral foramina, placed one above another, constitute a canal in which the spinal medulla is lodged and protected. Between contiguous vertebrae two *intervertebral foramina,* one on each side, open into the canal and serve for the transmission of the spinal nerves and vessels.

The body of a vertebra is more or less cylindrical, but is subject to a wide range of variation in size and shape in different animals and in different regions of the same animal. Its upper and lower surfaces are flattened and roughened to give attachment to the intervertebral discs. In front, it is convex from side to side

EXTRACT 85

His legs and thighs were strapped tightly, cruelly together. His arms had been forced down on to a rough wooden table. His hands and wrists were being nailed to the table . . . nailed with carpenter's nails . . . hammered hard . . . A nail was already in the left wrist, two more in the wide part of the hand between the wrist and fingers, fastening it tightly down . . . The last few strokes of the hammer had smashed bone . . . One nail was in the right hand, another poised to tear, to hack through flesh and muscle . . . No pain was ever, could be ever . . . Oh, God, help me! . . . would be ever greater. Miles writhed, screamed, pleaded, screamed again. But the hands holding his body tightened. The hammer blows, which had briefly paused, resumed.

"He ain't yelping loud enough," Marino told Angelo, who was wielding the hammer. "When you get through with that, try nailing down a couple of the bastard's fingers."

Tony Bear, who was puffing on a cigar while he watched and listened, had not bothered concealing himself this time. There would be no possibility of Eastin identifying him because Eastin would soon be dead. First, though, it was necessary to remind him—and others to whom the news of what had happened here would filter

EXTRACT 86

The big jolly-boat was almost up with the plane. There were six men in it. Petacchi waved and shouted delightedly. One man raised a hand in reply. The faces of the men, milk-white under the moon, looked up at him quietly, curiously. Petacchi thought: these men are very serious, very businesslike. It is right so. He swallowed his triumph and also looked grave.

The boat came alongside the wing, now almost awash, and one man climbed up on to the wing and walked towards him. He was a short, thick man with a very direct gaze. He walked carefully, his feet well apart and his knees flexed to keep his balance. His left hand was hooked in his belt.

Petacchi said happily, "Good evening. Good evening. I am delivering one plane in good condition." (He had thought the joke out long before.) "Please sign here." He held out his hand.

The man from the jolly-boat took the hand in a strong grasp, braced himself, and pulled sharply. Petacchi's head was flung back by the quick jerk and he was looking full into the eyes of the moon as the stiletto flashed up and under the offered chin, through the roof of the mouth, into the brain. He knew nothing but a moment's surprise, a sear of pain, and an explosion of brilliant

EXTRACT 98

They piled the luggage into the Mustang and the girl's companion folded up his long legs and piled into the back seat. His name was Joseph—but David was advised by the girl to call him Joe. She was Debra, and surnames didn't seem important at that stage. She sat in the seat beside David, with her knees pressed together primly and her hands in her lap. With one sweeping glance, she assessed the Mustang and its contents. David watched her check the expensive luggage, the Nikon camera and Zeiss binoculars in the glove compartment and the cashmere jacket thrown over the seat. Then she glanced sideways at him, seeming to notice for the first time the raw silk shirt with the slim gold Piaget under the cuff.

"Blessed are the poor," she murmured, "but still it must be pleasant to be rich."

David enjoyed that. He wanted her to be impressed, he wanted her to make a few comparisons between himself and the big muscular buck in the back seat.

"Let's go to Barcelona," he laughed.

David drove quietly through the outskirts of the town, and

Appendix B
Cloze Blanks

1. EXTRACT 20*

Mean cloze score 14.08. Cloze rank 1.

Just as the clock struck three, there was blown into the crescent a sedan-chair with Mrs. Dowler inside, borne by one short fat chairman, and one long thin one, who had much ado to keep their bodies perpendicular: to say nothing of the chair. But on that high ground, and in the crescent, which the wind swept round and round as if it were going to tear the paving stones up, its fury was tremendous. They were very glad __1__ set the chair down, __2__ give a good round loud __3__ -knock at the street door.

__4__ waited some time, __5__ nobody came.

"Servants is __6__ the arms o' Porpus, __7__ think," said the short __8__ , warming his hands at __9__ attendant link-boy's torch.

"I __10__ he'd give 'em a __11__ and wake 'em," observed __12__ long one.

"Knock again, __13__ you, if you please," __14__ Mrs. Dowler from the __15__ . "Knock two or three __16__ , if you please."

The __17__ man was quite willing __18__ get the job over, __19__ soon as possible; so __20__ stood on the step, and gave four or five most startling double knocks, of eight or ten knocks a piece: while the long man went into the road, and looked up at the windows for

2. EXTRACT 62

Mean cloze score 10.31. Cloze rank 14.5

They parked the car in the lane, came up the path and round the house. What a charming garden . . . flowers blooming exuberantly as if they knew this was the last month of summer and there might never be another season as fragrant, as sweet . . .

The sound of laughing came from ahead of them and Elspeth's voice.

"Oh, Dougal, don't, don't! __1__ so comfortable. I love __2__ in the crotch

*Don't peek! You will not be able to do the exercise in practical criticism set out in chapter 7 if you identify the authors and sources of these extracts prematurely.

of this ___3___ , but it takes an ___4___ to get the cushions ___5___ . . . I'll come over after ___6___ and see your new ___7___ -house."

A man's answering laugh. " ___8___ come now . . . I've sweated ___9___ toiled this whole Monday ___10___ I want someone to ___11___ and aah over it. ___12___ you ooh and aah ___13___ delightfully than any other ___14___ I've ever known. Down ___15___ come, Elspeth!"

Sounds of ___16___ , giggles, insulting remarks that ___17___ nothing being bandied back ___18___ forth . . . they rounded the ___19___ to see a tall ___20___ - shouldered man reaching up into an ancient pear-tree and tugging.

There was a lilt in Elspeth's voice that neither of them had ever heard before. "Dougal, stop it! You're a mean, horrible, beastly man! You ought to be called MacCrab, not MacNab . . . Ouch, you brute, you're bruising me! Look out, I'm falling!"

She landed fair and square on Dougal, knocking him off his balance,

3. EXTRACT 53

Mean cloze score 4.77. Cloze rank 30.

A representative sample of systematic work on attitude and disposition variables in leadership may be found in Fleishman's report on his Leadership Opinion Questionnaire. This instrument has two scores, one assessing "structure" (the extent to which an individual is likely to structure his own efforts and those of his subordinates toward goal attainment) and "consideration" (the degree to which an individual stresses warmth and consideration in his dealings with others). In studies with the ___1___ (Fleishman, 1960), the C ___2___ correlated .29 and .32 ___3___ criteria of leadership in ___4___ of 53 industrial supervisors ___5___ 42 sales managers; scores ___6___ the S scale were ___7___ unrelated to the criteria.

___8___ validity coefficients are low, ___9___ they do not necessarily ___10___ that the tests are ___11___ value. Prediction of leadership ___12___ any particular setting must ___13___ account of the demands ___14___ circumstances of the ___15___ (cf. Bass, 1960; Fiedler, 1967; Vernon, 1953). ___16___ of intelligence, dominance, ___17___ to others, etc., ___18___ serve to identify a ___19___ or sample of subjects ___20___ which leaders in most situations will be drawn, even though these variables will not yield precise forecasts

Appendix C
Laboratory Books

Subject[a]	Book	Pages Read	Most-liked Pages
101	J. B. Priestley. *The Image Men*. London: Heinemann, 1976 (1968).	32–53	52–53
202	Lucien Nahum. *Shadow 81*. London: New English Library, 1976.	86–111	97–102
203	Morris West. *The Navigator*. London: Collins, 1976.	80–122	117–18
204	John Steinbeck. *Sweet Thursday*. London: Pan, 1974 (1954).	53–75	73–75
205	Patrick White. *The Eye of the Storm*. Harmondsworth: Penguin, 1975 (1973).	64–88	67–70
206	Louis L'Amour. *Fallon*. London: Corgi, 1972 (1963).	48–78	70–75
107	Norman Spinrad. *The Iron Dream*. St Albans, Herts.: Panther, 1974. (First published in 1954 as *Lord of the Swastika* by Adolf Hitler.)	76–103	83–95
208	Bernard Malamud. *A New Life*. New York: Dell, 1970 (1961).	58–85	75–77
209	Ellis Peters. *The Grass Widow's Tale*. London: Collins, 1968.	52–86	66–76
110	Richard Brautigan. *Willard and His Bowling Trophies: A Perverse Mystery*. London: Jonathan Cape, 1976.	126–67	141–42
111	Georgette Heyer. *The Unknown Ajax*. London: Heinemann, 1971 (1959).	69–106	84–88
112	John Harris. *The Mercenaries*. London: Arrow, 1976 (1969).	63–112	102–05

113	Ursula Le Guin. *The Dispossessed.* St Albans, Herts.: Panther, 1976.	59–93	76–81
214	Robert Ludlum. *The Osterman Weekend.* St Albans, Herts: Panther, 1977 (1972).	45–80	66–67
215	Neville Shute. *Pied Piper.* London: Pan, 1973 (1942).	65–92	86–88
116	Anthony Burgess. *Tremor of Intent.* London: Heinemann, 1973 (1966).	12–40	19–21
118	Len Deighton. *Spy Story.* St Albans, Herts.: Panther, 1974.	18–87	20–27
119	Alistair MacLean. *Fear is the Key.* London: Fontana, 1973 (1961).	52–77	67–68
220	Desmond Bagley. *High Citadel.* London: Collins, 1965.	50–119	113–16
221	Dick Francis. *In the Frame.* London: Readers Digest Association, 1976.	58–86	60
222	Gavin Lyall. *Judas Country.* London: Pan, 1976 (1975).	48–76	51–54
223	Peter Pook. *Gigolo Pook.* London: Robert Hale, 1975.	53–89	56–58
124	Agatha Christie. *The Hound of Death.* Glasgow: Collins-Fontana, 1977 (1933).	38–69	48–58
226	David Niven. *The Moon's a Balloon.* London: Hamish Hamilton, 1971.	80–104	101–02
127	Alfred Tack. *Return of the Assassin.* New York: Putnam, 1974.	57–114	92–94
228	Ernest Gann. *Fiddler's Green.* Manchester: Ensign, 1974 (1954).	63–83	68–73
129	Yasunari Kawabata. *The Master of Go.* Harmondsworth: Penguin, 1976 (1951)	30–44	42–44
230	Clive Cussler. *Iceberg.* London: Sphere, 1977.	34–52	45–46
132	Wilbur Smith. *Gold Mine.* London: Pan, 1974 (1970).	62–96	86–87
133	Allen Drury. *The Promise of Joy.* New York: Doubleday, 1975.	52–74	59–60
234	Louise Montague. *The Sand Castles.* New York: Putnams, 1974.	71–108	84–86
235	Philip E. Brown. *Uncle Whiskers.* London: Fontana, 1977 (1974).	50–91	72–75
236	Elizabeth Seifert. *Take Three Doctors.* Muttituck, NY: Aeonian Press, 1947.	108–26	109–11

[a]See note to table 6.2.

Note: Date of first publication given in parentheses.

Appendix D
Four Ludic Readers
Talk about Reading

The four participants are chatting quietly as the recording starts. They know they have been invited to today's discussion because they are all avid readers and they are curious to get to know one another. Sanette is talking to Mary about rereading books. Mary, speaking to the recorder, says she plans to speak partly English (her home language) and partly Afrikaans, in which she is fluent, and it is agreed that people will talk in whatever language they are most comfortable. In fact, all four participants switched readily between languages, sometimes several times in the course of one statement. Passages that have been translated from Afrikaans are indicated by an "A" in brackets; if a statement begins in Afrikaans and then moves into English, an "E" is used. Absence of a language note means the statement was made in English.

VICTOR: We're going to talk about what reading means to us and how we feel about it. What I really want, more than for me to ask questions, is for you to talk to one another. The reason I chose you is that of all the readers I had, there was a small group who were particularly articulate about their reading, who could particularly well put into words how they felt about their reading and what it meant to them. I thought to myself, if I got such very good material from each of you individually, then when you talked to one another it's probably going to get even better, and I thought it was an idea worth pursuing.

One of the things Mary remarked to me is that she reads a lot and also shows movies on weekends, and that her husband prefers sports and gardening to these things: "He's not prepared to come inside and soak up all that trash with me." All of you indicated pretty high percentages of trash in your reading—20 percent, 35, 50.* Now, there is obviously some sort of uneasy feeling. You enjoy reading, but you're not quite sure of the quality of what you read, and you feel a bit suspicious of yourselves for doing this. Another contradiction is that you [Ockert] object to TV because you feel it's a waste of time. So perhaps let's begin

*This was an exaggeration. Sanette rated 15 percent of her reading as trash, and the other three gave 30 percent.

287

by talking about this question. If you see your reading as trash, why do you do it? And if you see other things as a waste of time, then is your reading a waste of time too?

WENDY: I just want to say something. When you asked that question, you said, "Would your professor of English, or your teacher or something, consider what you read as trash?" That doesn't mean *I* consider it trash when I read it, but they would have considered it trash because it's not all of very high literary quality.

VICTOR: I selected that outside figure because I wanted someone that everyone would regard as an authority figure. Someone who really is in a position to pass judgment on your reading.

WENDY: The point is I don't think it's a waste of time because I don't think it's trash myself. If it's trash I stop reading it, but like the *Pied Piper* [Nevil Shute], it wasn't all that wonderful. Somebody else might have thought it was trash, but I didn't think it was. I'm sure the professor would have thought so.

MARY: With the books that I read, if it's bad I tend to stop reading it. In other words I don't consider the books that I read are trash. If I did, I wouldn't read them. I'm thinking of books like science fiction, which I don't consider a subject worth reading about unless it's based on fact, something like factual studies about UFOs or something like that. But the point is that the people who consider our activity as useless, like for instance my husband, who doesn't like movies or reading anything but biographical studies or things like that which I couldn't sit through—his interests in life and the things that he enjoys doing, like going out sailing and fishing, I couldn't do. I couldn't sit in the sun all day and get a headache every five minutes. I much prefer to sit inside in the cool and read a book. Perhaps I'm escaping. I don't know. He obviously considers it a waste of time in the sense that you're not getting on and doing things. You're in a fantasy world hiding yourself away from reality, which I don't really think is the case, but this is the sort of attitude that people seem to take to a great extent, that you're not getting on doing things that you ought to be doing.

VICTOR: And your feeling is that this kind of criticism can be quite safely ignored?

MARY: I think so, unless of course one does nothing else at all—I mean I burn the food every night because I'm sitting reading a book, but I don't consider that as terribly significant. It doesn't mean that I don't live properly.

SANETTE: When I read a book, it's the type of book—the type of world—I want to live in. I'm very fond of cowboy books. Now maybe, as I said, a love story is so near real life that when I want to escape, I don't want to escape into the same real world again. That's why I want to escape into a fiction world, a world that was. But still you can lose yourself in the book. Some books are trash, but by that we don't mean the type of books we read. Take for instance Alistair MacLean's *Puppet on a Chain*. He's written a lot of good books, but *Puppet on a Chain* wasn't as good as the others, so then you describe that specific book as trash. It's not really trash, but not as good as the others. In the circle I move in, the girls are all going out and pleasure seekers and I mostly enjoy myself reading in my room and that's what I can't understand. I get my newspaper daily. The person who brings my paper looks at me every day as if to say, "Yes, here's your paper, go and bury yourself in the paper." They just can't see why you read or the type of books you enjoy. Often the girls come into my room and ask, "Haven't you got something to read?" I'll say, "What'd you like to read?" "Well—let me see the books you've got," and she looks through my books—"Well, I don't think I'd read what you read." I don't really know what type of books they're really looking for. [Inaudible] Yes, but those people . . . sometimes I've got to hunt for a book for myself. The only books you can get from them are cheap stuff like you said, recipes and *Kyks* [picture stories] and *Keurs* [woman's magazine] and things like that. That's all. But you bury yourself—that's what they think, you live in a world of your own. When you read a thriller, it's because you like excitement and . . .

MARY: Your own life is pretty boring.

SANETTE: Yes, but for me that type of book is too violent to read so I much prefer to read a cowboy book. That's also violent, but like I said to you, I like the Sacketts. It's great when all these Sacketts come to help this one Sackett who's in trouble.

VICTOR: Something else that you said to me is that you know the love stories could be real and they are sort of nearer. The thing about the cowboy books is that they all take place a long way away.

MARY: [A] I don't read cowboy books. For me, that's trash! [Laughter].

OCKERT: [A] Let me tell you, the other day I met a woman at the book exchange that I go to evening classes with, and I persuaded her to try Louis L'Amour. The next time I saw her in class (it was Saturday we talked and Monday that I saw her again) she said she'd never known, that a new world had opened up for her [Laughter]. It depends, you must first find a good writer. There are cowboy books written by Australians, thin little books, you polish one off in half an hour or an hour, fantastic books. So it doesn't depend on who the writer is.

SANETTE: [A] Max Brand is also a good writer but he's not a good cowboy writer.

OCKERT: [A] You get Max Brand, you get J. T. Exner, you get hundreds of them, but you get fed up with them. You don't get fed up with Louis L'Amour. He's written about sixty books so far, but he writes too slowly for me. A new book by him comes out only every three or four months [Laughter]. Lots of people say it's not good reading matter but I don't see that. I argue with people who say that. I say to them, you haven't read the book yet, or your reading isn't good enough to allow you to read properly. Some people can't read, I'm convinced of that, and I think the big mistake is at school where they teach the child to read quite incorrectly, letter by letter. This is an *A*, this is a *B*, a *C* and so on. Then they learn words, thousands of words, and each word has a different meaning and a different emotional value, and in the end you see the child is still reading letter by letter or word by word. . . . You're supposed to read from the top down to the bottom.

VICTOR: [A] What's interesting is that you aren't a terribly fast reader. In my sample, which doesn't come from the general population, you were pretty average, and so was Sanette. (Your elder daughter) is exceptionally fast, one of the fastest readers in the study. When I watched her reading on the TV monitor, her eyes just went straight down the page, they hardly moved. Don't you feel sorry for her finishing a book in an hour or two? You enjoy a book for four or five hours.

OCKERT: [A] That really puzzled me because I know I actually read faster than (the elder daughter), so I checked what book she'd read. It was an Alistair MacLean [in fact, it was Desmond Bagley], and I also read an Alistair MacLean, but a softcover and smaller. It was *Fear Is the Key*, and I don't know, I just never got into it, and I know the more interesting a book is, the faster I feel I read (I don't know what your measurements show). The more interesting it gets, the more you get the feeling you're not reading any more, you're not reading words, you're not reading sentences, it's as if you are completely living inside the situation.

SANETTE: [A] Like a movie.

VICTOR: [A] I must tell you, you two are both really good visualizers. You see things very clearly. The apple I asked you about, for example—you [Mary] barely saw the apple, but he [Ockert] could describe every spot and blemish, and Sanette too. So when you say it's like a movie, it makes a lot of sense to me.

SANETTE: [A] I'm inclined to read a book as if it's a movie showing. I like to read very quickly, a word, a paragraph, till the end of the chapter, and then I take it up again because you know what's happened and I see it like a movie and I fill in the episodes. Then I'm ready to go, then I know what's going to happen. Then I take the whole passage and I see it like a movie and I fill it in, how the chap comes on his horse [talking very fast] and comes on this other guy, and the other guy's all scared and puts his hands up. Then I go back, and I see how that rider came along, all at his ease [talking slowly now], and he saw this, and that, and this, and the other chap is sitting making his coffee, and I can see how he pours his coffee into his cup, his old tin mug, and so it goes, and suddenly the horse comes upon him and he sees the other man and recognizes him. I always go back because then I know what to expect and I can color in my own picture.

VICTOR: Mary, you're not a visualizer.

MARY: I think the reason I'm not a visualizer is that I sit and look at movies and I'm used to taking them in visually, and taking the real thing in more mentally than visually. In other words, when I think about things I don't actually see them. If I think about the person that you asked me to think about [one of the visualizer tasks] I have a vague vision of them but it's not alive or a tremendous movement or anything. It may be because I spend a lot of time watching movies—that's when I use my eyes and actually take it in that way.

VICTOR: In a movie, the pictures are made for you, you don't have to make your own pictures. What Ockert was saying was very interesting. When you read a book you lose the feeling of reading. The whole mechanics of the process of turning the pages and looking at letters vanishes and it's as if you are in another world where things are being acted out in front of you and you are a participant. Either you are in it yourself or you're standing somewhere and you can get a good view and you can see it all happening in front of you.

OCKERT: [A] That's true.

VICTOR: You've sunk through the pages of the book [Ockert shows agreement] and you find yourselves in the world on the other side of the book, as if you walk through a mirror or something, as if you are there and you are participating. Now you [Mary] enjoy reading very much but your experience of reading must be very different from theirs. When you're really enjoying a book, how do you feel?

MARY: I have often rushed through a book, I must admit. I miss paragraph after paragraph for the story, but not chapter after chapter. As you say, I go through it for the story to end as one piece, and I explained to Victor about the one book which I read very quickly on the plane once—I read it because I wanted to see the movie, but it sounded from the trailer of the movie that it was a very thrilling, scary sort of a film, and then I sit with my eyes closed and my ears blocked because I'm scared all the way through the show.

VICTOR: What book was it again?

MARY: *Cassandra Crossing*, so I read the book first.

VICTOR: What was it about again? I've forgotten.

MARY: About someone who picked up the plague and was wandering about on a train with bubonic plague, and they had to seal off the train and divert it. Well now, from the trailer I thought, now this is my kind of movie—lots of action, exciting, love stories thrown in on the side—and so on. So I read the book as I say very quickly just to get an idea of who was going to die when, so that I could keep my eyes open, and then about a week later I went to see the film. Now when I have read a book before the film, I'm very often disappointed—the only ones I can say I have enjoyed the film after I've read the book are *Cassandra Crossing*, for instance, and *The Poseidon Adventure*, which to me was very complicated when the ship was upside down and I couldn't visualize what it was like for those people to work their way up the ship to the surface. . . .

OCKERT: [A] You know how I read that book? You'll be amazed. I know that book made me terribly . . . I just couldn't get a grip on it. I couldn't read it because the ship is quite upside-down, and in the end [great emphasis] I lay down on my back in the middle of the floor [laughter] to get my thoughts right, to get my images right, so I could see what was going on, because (and perhaps this is the difference) I can't read the words without seeing the images, that's how you get it right, I actually had to lie on my back with the book above so that I was like the passengers were.

SANETTE: [A] The steps were upside down. So I got hold of a picture of just ordinary stairs in a house and turned it upside down and then I could see how upside-down stairs were and I could go on reading . . .

OCKERT: [A] Because before I could really get into the book . . . because the ceiling is now underneath, they're walking on the ceiling, how can you do that, it doesn't make sense. The floor is now up on top, so I had to go and lie on my back and then I could read, I'd got the book right and I could read [laughter].

MARY: [A] I read it without really understanding what was going on, [E] I couldn't imagine what it was like for those people so I went to see the movie as soon as it came out and only then could picture the whole thing and appreciate what it was like. In other words, when [A] I read, I don't see it the way you see it, I don't see pictures at all. [E] I read the book more for what happens to the people, who lived and who died and who was brave and who wasn't. That's the kind of thing I'm reading the book for, not for the pictures it's giving me—I'll go and see the film in order to get those pictures.

VICTOR: What did you enjoy more—the book or the movie of *Poseidon Adventure?*

MARY: The movie.

VICTOR: And the book?

MARY: I didn't really enjoy the book. I found it too difficult to picture what was going on. But I enjoyed the personalities that were involved—how they reacted, which ones proved themselves to be extra brave, and so on.

SANETTE: I can't see how you can read a book without visualizing it. I read a book some time ago, *The Fountainhead* [Ayn Rand].

WENDY: Mm, lovely book.

SANETTE: Have you read it?—I spoke to my father about it . . . this man wanted to use his own style, not like other architects, and I just couldn't visualize how he wanted his things, his buildings, to look. [A] He wanted to build a house on a rock, so first you have to see the rock and then the house on top of it. Often I found I was drawing things from the book as they are described, but the descriptions aren't good.

VICTOR: [A] The very first thing he built was a filling station, and I can still picture it very clearly.

SANETTE: [A] The filling station was quite well described, but not the house or the rock. I couldn't visualize that. . . .

   I read *Campbell's Kingdom* [Alistair MacLean] four or five times—my mother said to me, "Read it, it's a lovely book."

VICTOR: [A] Did she just tell you that, or did she tell you part of the story and stop?

SANETTE: [A] My mother taught us to read. When she saw we were sitting around and not doing anything, she would take a book like Alistair MacLean, *Fear Is the Key* or *Night Without End,* and she would tell us the story. Now I see that's where we got our visualizing from. She can tell you a story so that you see it unfolding in front of you. We were so frightened—she would say, "something's there," and you'd be careful not to sit down on top of it [laughter], she'd tell us about people in the story and cut out pictures for us of each character—pictures of just anyone who happened to be in the newspaper—so you'd learn your characters because she'd say, "I'm talking about this one now, or this one." When we got bigger we were spoiled, and when a new book came we'd say, "Ma, tell us the story," and she'd tell us to about halfway and leave us at the most important part, so we'd fetch the English dictionary and read, one of us would read the book and the other would sit with the dictionary, and that's how we learned to read.

   We were still small when she told us the story of *Campbell's Kingdom,* and later I found the book in the library—I was school library prefect [monitor] then. It was in Afrikaans and I didn't like English all that much, so I read it in Afrikaans. Then some time later I came across the book in English and then I read it in English. Each time I got a different picture. When I read the Afrikaans I was more interested in the story. Then the second time, in English, it wasn't the same book because I visualized every detail, how he drove down the mountain, how the dam wall broke, and that type of thing. It was something completely different for me. I had to visualize absolutely everything. Sometimes I say, "Dad, give me something good to read." Then if I don't like it, I struggle and struggle because I feel terribly guilty if I start a book and don't finish it. . . .

When I was small I got very frightened reading. I read an Afrikaans book about werewolves and I was so frightened that I would go and sit right next to my dad. I was scared to death, especially when I read it at night. . . . I read it three or four times and every time I would go and sit next to my father. Sometimes I would scream, I could feel something waiting to get me, but I always finished reading. I couldn't visualize it. [Pause]. I was so frightened, I would just cry and cry bitterly [laughter].

VICTOR: Mary, you've been listening with fascination to this. When you were a kid, did you read this way too? What does it make you think of?

MARY: No. I can remember for instance reading Charles Dickens' books as a child, and lying in my room continuously crying and crying and crying over his books. I used to get terribly upset and my mother would take them away from me and I haven't read Charles Dickens since. I get very emotionally involved with people as such. I'm not visualizing it, I'm not seeing it happening, but just the thought that this poor kid is getting into trouble for asking for more [laughter] upsets me so much that I just can't watch it.

VICTOR: But did you enjoy it when you were a kid? Was it an enjoyable upset?

MARY: I must admit I don't enjoy having the upsets at all. I don't like Charles Dickens' books at all. I think they're just too horrible. I don't think I enjoyed that kind of a cry. I read *Oliver Twist* and started *David Copperfield* and that's when my mother took the books away from me because I was a nervous wreck at that stage. I read *Tale of Two Cities* as a *Classics Illustrated* comic, and from there on I read them all as *Classics Illustrated* comics and didn't get involved. . . .

OCKERT: [A] But *David Copperfield* I could never read properly because the setting in which it took place was so strange to me, the England of those times, that I couldn't visualize it—I couldn't think myself into the situation and I couldn't enjoy it.

MARY: I looked at it not so much from the historical point of view. I looked at it from the point of view that there are people who treat children like that today [sounds of agreement]. As I say, for me it has a lot more to do with personalities and the actions of the people than with pictures of the historical times—that doesn't bother me in the least.

The thing that puts me off is accents, for example in cowboy books, it's not written in proper English, they drop their aitches all over the place.

SANETTE: [A] I can't read a book with a tremendous lot of description in it because I visualize it. It's very nice for me to think myself into the setting in which it's taking place, but often I prefer to make my own interpretation of what it looks like; otherwise, like my father says, you're so tied down you can't manage to think yourself into that situation. He [the writer] sees it as he experienced it, but you can't see it that way, so I prefer a Louis L'Amour cowboy book because there it tells you he was riding through thick bush—that's all. He won't tell you there were monkey ropes hanging down from the trees or that it was a swamp, unless maybe the cowboy is lying in a swamp with water all round him. Because you read your Louis L'Amour you know his world, and that's why you enjoy it so much. When he talks about Indians, you immediately know how the Indian world looks—you've never been there but you know at once from Indian pictures that you've seen. Have you seen Indian movies? [Yes, yes]—the Indians suddenly rise up against the horizon. That's all he says, "Suddenly the Indians were on the horizon," and you see it immediately, it gives you a fright . . . you get a fright [no pause] I'm terribly scared of emotional books.

MARY: [Interrupts] Funnily enough I had to type the Afrikaans translation of *Oliver Twist* about a month or two back, and while I was sitting there and Nancy was dying I was having a good old sob and the tears were rolling down my cheeks in the office (can you believe it!). Everyone knows when I'm typing a school magazine and the children write their little [A] summaries and when I get to one of those sobby-wobby stories, and those Afrikaans children write terribly sobby-wobby stories, I sit there and I weep [on a dramatic falling note], it's terrible [laughs]. [E] It just mustn't have anything to do with children, that's what gets to me. I can take a murder story with ten dead bodies, but don't have a child involved, then I've had it, and I don't enjoy that sob. I enjoy my sob when the guy's eighteen years old and the woman's forty and they fall in love and you know . . . I'll have a good old cry, but that's a nice cry, that's not an unhappy sad cry.

PSYCHE: And do you sometimes read funny books and laugh out aloud?

MARY: Yes, I read one I thought was gorgeous.

VICTOR: Didn't you read a funny book in the laboratory?

MARY: Yes, I read my Edgar Wallace [during the first laboratory session]. I'm always very much amused at Edgar Wallace.

PSYCHE: So you laugh aloud as well?

MARY: I do. I cry too, I actually sob. Once at the movies my husband got up and walked out and pretended he didn't know who I was because I was still crying when the film ended and I was making such a noise it was most embarrassing. I couldn't control myself. I never go to a movie if I know it's a drama because I know I get too upset. . . .

VICTOR: Wendy, you also talked about getting into the character and intellectual involvement. Now when these people talk about sobby-wobby and crying and getting upset and having a mood change for the whole day, does it make sense to you?

WENDY: I think I read a book on quite a different level than they do. They read purely for the story and I don't. That's why I can't read books that are in my opinion not well written.

VICTOR: Forgive my saying so, but that sounds terribly superior.

WENDY: [Angry] No, it's not meant to sound superior. I don't mean I only read heavy books and not light books, but I mean there must be something in the style which grips as well, not only in the story. Now, I don't skim for the story, I read from the beginning . . . I get my visualization from what the man writes. Now, the cowboys I enjoyed were Zane Gray . . . he can describe the country and the characters in quite a different way. He's "literary" in comparison to L'Amour. *The Fountainhead* was one I enjoyed from the beginning right through, and it was one of the books that gripped me so much I couldn't stop reading it. I must have wasted plenty of time on that . . . the descriptive side is just as important as the actual story. . . . I could visualize his buildings because of his descriptions of his feelings about his architecture . . . the way Ayn Rand writes, the style is what makes the book. It's not a case of trying to be superior, I think it's the way you start learning to read.

I found it extremely interesting hearing the way she [Sanette] learned to read. I learned to read in quite a different way. There were always books in the house I could read when I went to school, and I grew up among books, but I had to do it for myself, I read my books myself. . . . [A] I think my approach to reading is different than yours. As a child I spent hours and hours on my back reading, English and Afrikaans both, from the beginning. I had to visualize everything without outside help, so you build up your picture differently. So long descriptions are very important, I fill in the details for myself. I enjoyed *The Poseidon Adventure,* the book and the film, in that order, first the book and then the film, and I could visualize that upside-down ship with no difficulty. . . . I can go back and remember certain books, [A] *Kobie-hulle* [Kobie and her friends] and *Patrys-hulle* [Patrys and his friends].

OCKERT: [A] I didn't read those. I was too old already.

WENDY: [A] Some had illustrations, some just on the dustcover, and they irritated me till I could scream, because Kobie didn't look to me like that picture . . .

OCKERT: [Interrupts; A] Yes, Kobie for me was a plump girl . . .

WENDY: [A] . . . to me she was a delicate child with curly hair . . .

OCKERT: [A] . . . a well-built girl . . .

WENDY: [A] . . . and so on.

OCKERT: [A] I've often read books with illustrations and finished the book and thought, that's not how he looks . . . I had another picture of him all through. . . .

SANETTE: [A] I prefer to see a movie first and then to read the book, because then I can take the character I've seen in the movie and put it into the book. But if I read the book I see the character differently and then the movie isn't the same as the book and that spoils the book.

OCKERT: [A] That Alistair MacLean, *Night Without End,* no, the one about the submarine . . .

SANETTE: HMS *Ulysses.*

OCKERT: [A] No, the other one . . .

SANETTE: *Ice Station Zebra.*

OCKERT: [A] Yes [laughter]. The hero of the story is a black man. But not in the book. I will not go to a movie if I've read the book, so I just about never go to the movies.

MARY: I have an idea what Jane Marple looks like in the Agatha Christie stories, and I have an idea what Hercule Poirot looks like, and the two of them . . . I have read all the books, and the movies of those two are . . .

OCKERT: [Interrupts. A] . . . are completely wrong.

MARY: Pathetic.

OCKERT: [A] Poirot, for example, I'll never go to another movie of Poirot.

VICTOR: Did you see *Orient Express?*

OCKERT: [A] Yes. It's noisy, it's repulsive, it's not Agatha Christie.

VICTOR: You [Wendy] were remarking that *The Poseidon Adventure* didn't bother you at all while you were reading, you didn't have to lie on your back in order to see it. The impression I have from the questions I asked you in the laboratory about visualizing is that you are much less of a visualizer than Ockert. So I think maybe he had to lie on his back because he was seeing things on a far higher level of detail than you were.

WENDY: Possibly yes. It's quite a different type of visualization, that's why it's so interesting.

SANETTE: [A] . . . in the movie you can't turn over [a page] and make the movie faster; the other people with you enjoy it, and I can't. . . .

PSYCHE: You [Mary] said your husband likes to be busy, and if you read a lot, he sees it as withdrawing into your own world, [A] and you [Sanette] said, people say your world is different from theirs because they don't read your books. I was wondering, is there a connection between the real world you live in and this other world? Is there a specifically different world that books create for you, or is it an extension of your own world?

MARY: [A] It's a completely different world.

SANETTE: [A] It's a different world.

MARY: [A] The situations and the people you meet are different. [E] You identify with them to a certain extent. I'd love to be a tall, beautiful blonde, thin, bla-bla. I've never been and am never likely to be . . . obviously the book I enjoy reading is not an extension of my own kind of life at all. I consider my life is in one little old rut all the time and have no way of getting out of it at all . . . and this is another world that I can imagine myself into . . . a fantasy world.

SANETTE: [A] Take my own environment. A girl comes back from a weekend at Buffelspoort or one of the other holiday resorts [near Pretoria] and she'll bore you for hours with stories of that marvelous weekend, how they swam and went walking. I can also have a weekend like that, I can also go to Buffelspoort and have a marvelous time and come back (I've been there) and perhaps tell that person of one funny incident—but about a book, I can talk for hours. It's worth a lot more to me.

PSYCHE: [A] More real?

SANETTE: [Pause; A] Yes. Look, if I've read an interesting book, I want to share it with someone who also loves reading, and that person understands my feelings and ideas, and he will be able in turn to tell me about another book that he's read. . . .

I was at a youth camp, mainly about religion, and the chap there said to us, "If you become a child of the Lord, it's such a wonderful experience, you want to share it with everyone." If you've read a fantastic book you want to tell, to share it with other people. If you've had a very bad experience, if you've been humiliated or had a heartbreak, you're not going to share it. But if I've seen a fantastic movie I'm going to say, "You must see the movie." For me, that happens more with books.

PSYCHE: [A] Can I chip in? [To Wendy] Your experience of these different worlds is very different, and [to Ockert] yours too.

OCKERT: [A] Yes.

WENDY: [A] It's difficult to express, but some kinds of books are far from your own life. But I feel that characters have qualities of people you know, you see yourself very clearly in the character, your own reactions, you see something in a situation that makes you think of something in your own life when your reactions were the same or different. There's a connection, definitely. There are a lot of things that are an extension of your own life.

PSYCHE: [A] It's a two-way exchange.

WENDY: [A] It's an exchange. There's not one world and another world. One influences the other. Definitely. But it depends what you read. There are things that don't touch you at all, strange things that you can think yourself into but without becoming involved in them.

PSYCHE: [A] Whereas you [Mary] would say, there wasn't a two-way interaction, what happens there doesn't influence what happens every day. Whereas to you [Wendy] it does.

WENDY: I want to give you an example. I'm now reading a book for the second time, it's *The Source* [James Michener]. Some of those situations have nothing to do with me. It's now the century before Christ, and things happen there that become as real as if they were happening in your own life.

PSYCHE: [A] And Ockert—how do you experience this?

OCKERT: [A] You read and every time it's as if you change. You get into situations, you go back, for example, to a thousand years before Christ. For example, I enjoy tremendously to read about the old Romans . . . and I can get into that situation, I can feel myself what they were feeling. Like Mary said about her husband . . . I can't imagine how people keep themselves busy, fishing and so on every weekend in a little world sixty miles around Pretoria. That's all their world consists of. He can get no escapism, he can't get into other things, he's just busy with himself all day. If I had to be occupied with myself all day I'd go mad, crazy. I'd say our reading is like Sigmund Freud said, [E] "Dreams are the means whereby we compensate for the harshness of reality." [A] You can say "reading" instead of "dreams" [laughter]. Because you feel you live in a tiny little world, you don't have the money to really get away . . .

SANETTE: [A] For a holiday on the French Riviera.

VICTOR: When he talks about getting into the ancient Roman world, into faraway places, what happens to you [Mary]?

MARY: Well, I read a lot of historical books. I went through a stage of reading historical novels, but when I read it's like when I studied history at university, I'm not living myself into that world, I can't imagine . . .

VICTOR: It's you here and the book there.

MARY: That's right . . . I don't live in those books. It's only when I'm reading a modern novel that I dream, I wish, that those things would happen to me. I don't actually get into it. . . .

VICTOR: What I'm getting at is whether you go through the page, whether you get into the book world, or you stay outside of it. . . . You [Mary] have a strong reality sense. The page is there and you're here, and you don't drop through the page. Is that right?

MARY: Yes. It's something that remains external to you.

PSYCHE: I think there's a third possibility here. Does the page get into your life?

WENDY: You can apply what's in there to your reactions and feelings rather than going into there. . . .

SANETTE: [A] You people that are readers, do you find that you're very curious? It's just an interesting point. Someone said it to me once. If you read it's because you want to know more. You read a historical book because you want to live in a bigger world, not because it's a good book. You read a love story and a doctor story and an adventure story.

WENDY: [A] You want a broader view of life. . . .

VICTOR: [A] Each of you has a favorite kind of book—Louis L'Amour, Arthur Hailey, [E] espionage. I just put a thought to you. You know that type of book pretty well, so you read not to find out what's going to happen. Why? Why go to the trouble of reading all that when you know what's going to happen? Is it because you like your familiar landscape? When you get out of your Westerns into love stories you're worried and anxious. How much sense does this make to you?

MARY: It's true. It is true. I can't take that drama at all, and I'm upset and I'm bothered all the way through and I'm expecting that the hero isn't going to win after all or that the poor child is going to die of disease and you're upset. You're more satisfied when you know the hero is going to win . . .

VICTOR: That's precisely what you said to me when we were chatting about reading, you want to know that the good guys are going to win, that the cops are going to get their man. . . .

OCKERT: [A] Now I'm wondering why is it that I'm so fond of stories about the ice-world, about Canada.

MARY: [A] Yes, I'm the same.

OCKERT: [A] I know I wouldn't survive half an hour there because of the cold, I get cold very easily. And I enjoy those stories very much, how they fight in the ice, all those expeditions.

SANETTE: [Giggling; A] I know. [E] You read everything about ice so that if you land there you'll know what to do [laughter] because you'll learn from other people's experience. [To Mary; A] You love thrillers. Are you a very scared person?

MARY: Yes, I am. I look under the beds [laughter].

OCKERT: [A] When I read a frightening book [stutters slightly] I get so terribly frightened I've got to go and sit next to someone . . .

PSYCHE: [Interrupts; A] What sort of book?

OCKERT: [A] . . . and if someone grabbed me, I think I'd die of fright. I get heart palpitations.

SANETTE: [A] He's not a frightened person.

OCKERT: [A] Scary books. Alfred Hitchcock, that sort of thing. I get terribly frightened. I see something standing behind me, I feel it, I look around.

SANETTE: [A] The ice thrillers don't scare you. I read a cowboy book, even if it's a thriller, if it's a cowboy book it won't frighten me. But if it's not a cowboy, I get so frightened I could die.

MARY: [A] Because you don't know what's going to happen.

VICTOR: I think we must stop now. I want to say thank you very much for participating.

SANETTE: I wish we could have it more regularly (laughter).

WENDY: [A] My subject is reader studies, and it was so interesting to hear about the effects of reading on people because I teach that to students and now I've seen it in the raw.

OCKERT: [A] How does it agree with . . .

WENDY: [A] Oh, here it's much more intimate and in more detail than the way you teach it to students. The reasons we give why people read, I could see them all, they're all true! [Laughter].

References

The date of the first known publication is given in parentheses when this differs from the printing date; the first publication date is cited in text references, for example, Auerbach, 1946.

Abelson, R. P. 1981. Psychological status of the script concept. *American Psychologist, 36,* 715–19.

Abt, K. 1979. Statistical problems in the analysis of comparative pharmaco-EEG trials. *Pharmakopsychiatrie Neuro-Psychopharmakologie, 12,* 228–36.

Adrian, E. D. 1954. The physiological basis of perception. In E. D. Adrian (ed.), *Brain mechanisms and consciousness.* Oxford: Blackwell.

Albee, G. W. 1977. The Protestant Ethic, sex and psychotherapy. *American Psychologist, 32,* 150–61.

Altick, R. D. 1963 (1957). *The English common reader: A social history of the mass reading public, 1800–1900.* Chicago: University of Chicago Press.

Anderson, J. R. 1976. *Language, memory, and thought.* Hillsdale, N.J.: Erlbaum.

Anderson, T. H. 1974. Cloze measures as indices of achievement comprehension when learning from extended prose. *Journal of Educational Measurement, 11,* 83–92.

Apter, M. J. 1979. Human action and theory of psychological reversals. In G. Underwood & R. Stevens (eds.), *Aspects of Consciousness* (vol. 1). London: Academic Press.

Apter, M. J., and Smith, K. C. P. 1978. Excitement-anxiety reversals in sexual behaviour. *British Journal of Sexual Medicine, 5,* no. 38, 23–24; no. 39, 25–26.

Arendt, H. 1963. *Eichmann in Jerusalem: A report on the banality of evil.* London: Faber and Faber.

Atkinson, J. W., and Raynor, J. O. 1974. *Motivation and achievement.* Washington, D.C.: Winston.

Auerbach, E. 1953 (1946). *Mimesis: The representation of reality in Western literature.* New York: Doubleday.

Ax, A. F. 1953. The physiological differentiation between fear and anger in humans. *Psychosomatic Medicine, 15,* 433–42.

Bailyn, L. 1959. Mass media and children: A study of exposure habits and cognitive effects. *Psychological Monographs, 71,* 1–48.

Bandura, A., Adams, N. E., and Beyer, J. 1977. Cognitive processes mediating behavioral change. *Journal of Personality and Social Psychology, 35,* 125–39.

301

Barker, R., and Escarpit, R. 1973. *The book hunger.* London: Harrap.

Barnes, D. 1963 (1936). *Nightwood.* London: Faber and Faber.

Bartlett, F. C. 1932. *Remembering.* London: Cambridge University Press.

Beaugrande, R. de. 1981. Design criteria for process models of reading. *Reading Research Quarterly, 16,* 261–315.

Beaugrande, R. de., and Colby, B. N. 1979. Narrative models of action and interaction. *Cognitive Science, 3,* 43–66.

Berelson, B. 1958. Who reads what books and why. In B. Rosenberg and B. H. White (eds.), *Mass culture: The popular arts in America.* Glencoe, Ill.: Free Press.

Berger, R. J. 1961. Tonus of extrinsic laryngeal muscles during sleep and dreaming. *Science, 134,* 840.

Berlyne, D. E. 1963. Complexity and incongruity variables as determinants of exploratory choice and evaluative ratings. *Canadian Journal of Psychology, 17,* 274–90.

———. 1966. Conflict and arousal. *Scientific American, 211,* 82–87.

———. 1967. Arousal and reinforcement. In D. Levine (ed.), *Nebraska Symposium on Motivation.* Lincoln: University of Nebraska Press.

———. 1969. Laughter, humor, and play. In G. Lindzey and E. Aronson (eds.), *Handbook of Social Psychology* (vol. 3). Reading, Mass.: Addison-Wesley.

———. 1971. *Aesthetics and psychobiology.* New York: Appleton.

———. 1972. Experimental aesthetics. In P. C. Dodwell (ed.), *New horizons in psychology II.* Harmondsworth: Penguin.

———. 1973. The vicissitudes of aplopathematic and thelematoscopic pneumatology (or The hydrography of hedonism). In D. E. Berlyne and K. B. Madsen (eds.), *Pleasure, reward, preference: Their nature, determinants, and role in behavior.* New York: Academic Press.

———. (ed.). 1974. *Studies in the new experimental aesthetics: Steps toward an objective psychology of aesthetic appreciation.* Washington, D.C.: Hemisphere.

Berlyne, D. E., Craw, M. A., Salapatek, P. H., and Lewis, J. L. 1963. Novelty, complexity, incongruity, extrinsic motivation and the GSR. *Journal of Experimental Psychology, 66,* 560–67.

Berlyne, D. E., and Lawrence, G. H. 1964. Effects of complexity and incongruity variables on GSR, investigatory behavior and verbally expressed preference. *Journal of Genetic Psychology, 71,* 21–45.

Berlyne, D. E., and McDonnell, P. 1965. Effects of stimulus complexity and incongruity on duration of EEG desynchronisation. *Electroencephalography and Clinical Neurophysiology, 18,* 156–61.

Berry, J. 1961. *Spoken art in West Africa: An inaugural lecture.* London: University of London.

Beyard-Tyler, K. C., and Sullivan, H. J. 1980. Adolescent reading preferences for type of theme and sex of character. *Reading Research Quarterly, 16,* 104–20.

Biesheuvel, S., and Pitt, D. R. 1955. Some tests of speed and tempo of behaviour as predictors of the primary-secondary function temperament variable. *Journal of the National Institute for Personnel Research, 6,* 87–94.

Binswanger, L. 1963. *Being-in-the-world: Selected papers of Ludwig Binswanger.* New York: Basic.

Blaas, S. A. 1975. *Manual for the SORT.* Pretoria: Human Sciences Research Council.

Block, R. A. 1979. Time and consciousness. In G. Underwood and R. Stevens (eds.), *Aspects of consciousness.* London: Academic Press.

Blum, G. S., and Green, M. 1978. The effects of mood upon imaginal thought. *Journal of Personality Assessment, 42,* 227–32.

Blumenthal, A. L. 1967. Prompted recall of sentences. *Journal of Verbal Learning and Verbal Behavior, 6,* 203–06.

Boning, R. A. 1981. *Cloze connections* (book 1). Baldwin, N.Y.: Barnell Loft.

Bonis, M. D., and Baqué, E. F. I. 1978. Diphasic electrodermal response, heart rate and moods. *Biological Psychology, 6,* 77–91.

Boorstin, D. J. 1964. *The image: A guide to pseudo-events in America.* New York: Harper and Row.

Booth, W. C. 1965 (1961). *The rhetoric of fiction.* Chicago: University of Chicago Press.

Borges, J. L. 1964. *Labyrinths.* New York: New Directions.

———. 1969. *The book of imaginary beings.* London: Jonathan Cape.

———. 1976. *Dr. Brodie's report.* Harmondsworth: Penguin.

Bormuth, J. R. 1967. Comparable cloze and multiple choice comprehension test scores. *Journal of Reading, 10,* 291–99.

Bowlby, J. 1973. *Separation: Anxiety and anger.* London: Hogarth.

Bradley, J. M. 1973. Extent of agreement of reading tests and readability measures. Ph.D. diss., University of Pennsylvania. University Microfilms no. 73–27,554.

Brainard, R. W., Campbell, R. J., and Elkin, E. H. 1961. The design and interpretability of road signs. *Journal of Applied Psychology, 45,* 130–36.

Brautigan, R. 1976. *Willard and his bowling trophies: A perverse mystery.* London: Jonathan Cape.

Brazier, M. A. B. 1979. Challenges from the philosophers to the neuroscientists. In Ciba Foundation Symposium 69, *Brain and mind.* Amsterdam: Excerpta Medica.

Britton, B. K., Piha, A., Davis, J., and Wehausen, E. 1978. Reading and cognitive capacity usage: Adjunct question effects. *Memory and Cognition, 6,* 266–73.

Broadbent, D. E. 1958. *Perception and communication.* London: Pergamon.

———. 1981. Introduction. In R. Lynn (ed.), *Dimensions of personality: Papers in honour of H. J. Eysenck.* Oxford: Pergamon.

Brown, E. R. 1981. A theory of reading. *Journal of Communication Disorders, 14,* 443–66.

Brown, R. P., and Kneeland, B. 1985. Visual imaging in psychiatry. *Hospital and Community Psychiatry, 36,* 489–96

Bryant, S. C. 1933 (1905). *How to tell stories to children.* Cambridge, Mass.: Houghton Mifflin.

Buckhart, R., and Grace, T. 1966. The effect of food deprivation and expectancy on heart rate. *Psychonomic Science, 6,* 153–54.

Bundy, R. S. 1974. The influence of previous responses on the skin conductance recovery limb. *Psychophysiology, 11,* 221–22.

Burton, R. F. 1897. *The book of the thousand nights and a night* (12 vols.). London: Nichols.

Buss, D. M. 1982. A paradigm for personality? (Review of *A model for personality*, ed. H. J. Eysenck). *Contemporary Psychology, 27*, 341–43.

Caillois, R. 1961 (1958). *Man, play, and games.* Glencoe, Ill.: Free Press.

Carr, T. H. 1981. Research on reading: Meaning, context effects and comprehension. *Journal of Experimental Psychology: Human Perception and Performance, 7*, 592–603.

Carroll, J. B. 1981. New analyses of reading skills. Paper presented at the 26th annual convention of the International Reading Association, New Orleans, April 27–May 1, 1981.

Carver, C. S., and Scheier, M. F. 1981. *Attention and self-regulation: A control theory approach to human behavior.* New York: Springer.

Carver, R. P. 1972. Speed readers don't read; they skim. *Psychology Today*, August, 22–30.

———. 1976. Measuring reading comprehension using the paraphrase test and the reading-storage test. *Journal of Reading Behavior, 9*, 381–89.

———. 1982. Optimal rate for reading prose. *Reading Research Quarterly, 18*, 56–58.

———. 1983. Is reading rate constant or flexible? *Reading Research Quarterly, 18*, 190–215.

Carver, R. P., and Darby, C. A. 1971. Development and evaluation of a test of information storage during reading. *Journal of Educational Measurement, 8*, 33–44.

Cattell, R. B., Eber, H. W., and Tatsuoka, M. M. 1970. *Handbook for the Sixteen Personality Factor Questionnaire (16PF).* Champaign, Ill.: Institute for Personality and Ability Testing.

Cawelti, J. G. 1976. *Adventure, mystery and romance: Formula stories as art and popular culture.* Chicago: University of Chicago Press.

Cervantes, M. de. 1966 (1604–1614). *The adventures of Don Quixote.* Baltimore: Penguin.

Chall, J. S. 1958. *Readability: An appraisal of research and applications.* Columbus, Ohio: Ohio State University Press.

Chandler, G. 1973. Research on books and reading in society in the United Kingdom. *International Library Review, 5*, 277–82.

Chang, S. S., and Hanna, G. S. 1980. Reliability of reading rate tests as a function of warm-up passage and time limit. *Reading World, 20*, 232–38.

Chomsky, N. 1957. *Syntactic structures.* The Hague: Mouton.

———. 1965. *Aspects of the theory of syntax.* Cambridge, Mass.: MIT Press.

Christie, M. J., and Woodman, D. D. 1980. Biochemical methods. In I. Martin and P. H. Venables, *Techniques in psychophysiology.* Chichester: Wiley.

Clark, H. H. 1978. Inferring what is meant. In W. J. M. Levelt and G. B. F. d'Arcais (eds.), *Studies in the perception of language.* Chichester: Wiley.

Cleland, C. J. 1980. Piagetian implications for reading models. *Reading World, 20*, 10–15.

Codlin, R. D. 1974. The fiction thing. *New Library World, 75*, 5–6.

Coetzee, J. M. 1986. *Foe.* Johannesburg: Raven.

Cohen, J. M., and Cohen, M. J. 1971. *A Penguin dictionary of modern quotations.* Harmondsworth: Penguin.

Coke, E. V. 1976. Reading rate, readability and variations in task-induced processing. *Journal of Educational Psychology, 68,* 167–73.

Cole, J. Y., and Gold, C. S. 1979. *Reading in America 1978.* Washington: Library of Congress.

Collins, A. M., and Loftus, E. F. 1975. A spreading activation theory of semantic processing. *Psychological Review, 82,* 407–28.

Collins, W. 1980 (1859). The unknown public. In Thomas, W. M. and Fouché, B. (eds.), *Historical readership: Development of the reading habit, a selection from the subject literature.* Pretoria: University of South Africa.

Coltheart, M. 1980. Deep dyslexia: A right-hemisphere hypothesis. In M. Coltheart, K. Patterson, and J. C. Marshall (eds.), *Deep dyslexia.* London: Routledge and Kegan Paul.

Converse, J. 1978. What is so difficult about measuring flexibility? Paper presented at the 23rd Annual Convention of the International Reading Association, Houston, Texas.

Craik, F. I. M., and Lockhart, R. S. 1972. Levels of processing: A framework for memory research. *Journal of Verbal Learning and Verbal Behavior, 11,* 671–84.

Crockett, D., Clark, C., and Klonoff, H. 1981. Introduction: An overview of neuropsychology. In S. B. Filskov and T. J. Boll (eds.), *Handbook of clinical psychology.* New York: Wiley.

Crompton, R. 1922. *Just William.* London: Newnes.

Cunningham, J. W., and Cunningham, P. M. 1978. Validating a limited-cloze procedure. *Journal of Reading Behaviour, 10,* 211–13.

Dale, E., and Chall, J. S. 1949. The concept of readability. *Elementary English, 26,* 19–26.

Davies, A. 1973. *Printed media and the reader.* Bletchley, Bucks: Open University Press.

Davis, C. M., Brickett, P., Stern, R. M., and Kimball, W. H. 1978. Tension in the two frontales: Electrode placement and artifact in the recording of forehead EMG. *Psychophysiology, 15,* 591–93.

Davis, E. 1973. Practical criticism. In *Study Guide for English Honours* (part 1). Pretoria: University of South Africa.

Deci, E. L. 1976. *Intrinsic motivation.* New York: Plenum.

de Grazia, S. 1962. *Of time, work and leisure.* New York: Twentieth Century Fund.

Descartes, R. 1949 (1641). *A discourse on method.* London: Dent.

Deutsch, J. A., and Deutsch, D. 1963. Attention: Some theoretical considerations. *Psychological Review, 70,* 80–90

De Wet, R. 1968. [A study of the leisure reading patterns and interests of undergraduates at the University of South Africa]. Pretoria: University of South Africa.

The concise Oxford dictionary (6th ed.). 1976. Oxford: Oxford University Press.

Donchin, E., and Israel, J. B. 1980. Event-related potentials: Approaches to cognitive psychology. In R. E. Snow, P. A. Federico, and W. E. Montague (eds.), *Aptitude, learning and instruction* (2 vols). Hillsdale, N.J.: Erlbaum.

Dooling, D. J., and Lachman, R. 1971. Effects of comprehension on retention of prose. *Journal of Experimental Psychology, 88,* 216–22.

Drummond, P., White, K., and Ashton, R. 1978. Imagery vividness effects habituation rate. *Psychophysiology, 15,* 193–95.

Duffy, Elizabeth. 1972. Activation. In N. S. Greenfield and R. A. Sternbach (eds.), *Handbook of psychophysiology.* New York: Holt, Rinehart and Winston.

Dunnett, C. W. 1955. A multiple comparison procedure for comparing several treatments with a control. *Journal of the American Statistical Association, 50,* 1096–1121.

Dutch, R. A. 1962. *Roget's Thesaurus of English words and phrases.* London: Longmans.

Eanet, M. G., and Meeks, J. W. 1979. Internal reading flexibility: A fact or an artifact of measurement? Paper presented at the 29th Annual Meeting of the National Reading Conference, San Antonio, Texas.

Edelberg, R. 1967. Electrical properties of the skin. In C. C. Brown (ed.), *Methods in psychophysiology.* Baltimore: Williams and Wilkins.

———. 1972. Electrical activity of the skin: Its measurement and uses in psychophysiology. In N. S. Greenfield and R. A. Sternbach (eds.), *Handbook of psychophysiology.* New York: Holt, Rinehart and Winston.

Edelberg, R., and Muller, M. 1981. Prior activity as a determinant of electrodermal recovery rate. *Psychophysiology, 18,* 17–25.

Elliot, R. 1969. Tonic heart rate: Experiments on the effects of collative variables lead to a hypothesis about its motivational significance. *Journal of Personality and Social Psychology, 12,* 211–28.

Empson, W. 1949 (1939). *Seven types of ambiguity.* London: Chatto and Windus.

English, H. B., and English, A. C. 1958. *A comprehensive dictionary of psychological and psychoanalytical terms.* London: Longman.

Entin, E. B., and Klare, G. R. 1978. Some inter-relationships of readability, cloze and multiple choice scores on a reading comprehension test. *Journal of Reading Behavior, 10,* 417–36.

Erlich, V. 1969. *Russian Formalism.* The Hague: Mouton.

Eron, L. D. 1980. Prescription for reduction of aggression. *American Psychologist, 35,* 244–52.

Escarpit, R. 1966. *The book revolution.* London: Harrap.

Evans, R. V., and Ballance, C. T. 1977. Cloze scores and writing criteria as predictors of instructional level. *Journal of Educational Research, 71,* 110–13.

Eysenck, H. J. 1963. Emotion as a determinant of integrative learning: An experimental study. *Behaviour Research and Therapy, 1,* 197–211.

———. 1967. *The biological basis of personality.* Springfield, Ill.: Thomas.

———. 1971. Temperament. In *Encyclopaedia Britannica,* vol. 21. Chicago: Benton.

Eysenck, H. J., and Eysenck, S. B. G. 1964. *Manual of the Eysenck Personality Inventory.* London: University of London Press.

Fellows, B. J., and Armstrong, V. 1977. An experimental investigation of the relationship between hypnotic susceptibility and reading involvement. *American Journal of Clinical Hypnosis, 20,* 101–05.

Festinger, L. 1957. *A theory of cognitive dissonance.* Evanston, Ill.: Row, Peterson.

Fillmore, C. J. 1968. The case for case. In E. Bach and R. T. Harms (eds.), *Universals in linguistic theory.* New York: Holt, Rinehart and Winston.

Filskov, S. B., and Boll, T. J. (eds.). 1981. *Handbook of clinical neuropsychology.* New York: Wiley.

Fish, S. 1980. *Is there a text in this class? The authority of interpretive communities.* Cambridge, Mass.: Harvard University Press.

Fisher, M. 1961. *Intent upon reading.* Leicester: Brockhampton.

Fodor, J. A. 1975. *The language of thought.* New York: Crowell.

Foster, D. 1983. Psychoanalysis is alive and generally quite well. (Review of J. Forrester, *Language and the origins of psychoanalysis*). *Unisa Psychologia, 10*(1), 34–35.

Fouché, B. 1972. [The leisure reading habits of adult Afrikaans-speakers in Johannesburg]. Ph.D. diss., Rand Afrikaans University.

———. 1981. [Social functions of the public library]. *South African Journal for Librarianship and Information Science, 49,* 4–9.

Fowler, G. L. 1978. The comparative readability of newspapers and novels. *Journalism Quarterly, 55,* 589–92.

Frazer, J. G. 1910. *The golden bough: A study in magic and religion* (3d ed.). London: Macmillan.

Frederiksen, J. R. 1980. Component skills in reading: Measurement of individual differences through chronometric analysis. In R. E. Snow, P. A. Federico, and W. A. Montague (eds.), *Aptitude, learning, and instruction* (2 vols). Hillsdale, N.J.: Erlbaum.

Freud, S. 1968 (1900). The interpretation of dreams. In *The standard edition of the complete psychological works of Sigmund Freud* (vols. 4 and 5). London: Hogarth Press.

———. 1985 (1907). Delusions and dreams in Jensen's *Gradiva.* In A. Dickson (ed.), *The Pelican Freud library* (vol. 14): *Art and literature.* Harmondsworth: Penguin.

———. 1957 (1908). The relation of the poet to daydreaming. In *Collected papers* (vol. 4). London: Hogarth.

———. 1984 (1909). Notes upon a case of obsessional neurosis. In A. Dickson (ed.), *The Pelican Freud library* (vol. 9): *Case Histories.* Harmondsworth: Penguin.

———. 1973 (1930). Civilisation and its discontents. *Standard Edition,* vol. 21. London: Hogarth.

Frisch, A. M., and Perlis, D. 1981. A re-evaluation of story grammars. *Cognitive Science, 5,* 79–86.

Fromm, Erika. 1977a. An ego-psychological theory of altered states of consciousness. *International Journal of Clinical and Experimental Hypnosis, 25,* 372–87.

———. 1977b. Altered states of consciousness and hypnosis: A discussion. *International Journal of Clinical and Experimental Hypnosis, 25,* 325–34.

Fry, E. 1968. A readability formula that saves time. *Journal of Reading, 11,* 512–16, 575–78.

———. 1977. Fry's readability graph: Clarifications, validity and extension to level 17. *Journal of Reading, 21,* 242–52.

———. 1980. Comments on the preceding Harris and Jacobson comparison of the Fry, Spache and Harris-Jacobson readability formulas. *The Reading Teacher, 24,* 924–26.

Fry, E., Weber, J., and Depierro, J. 1978. A partial validation of the kernel distance theory for readability. *27th Yearbook of the National Reading Conference,* 121–24.

Gale, A. 1981. EEG studies of extraversion-introversion: What's the next step? In R. Lynn (ed.), *Dimensions of personality: Papers in honour of H. J. Eysenck.* Oxford: Pergamon.

Gans, H. J. 1974. *Popular culture and high culture: An analysis and evaluation of taste.* New York: Basic.

Gass, W. H. 1972. *Fiction and the figures of life.* New York: Vintage.

Gephart, W. J. 1970. *Application of the convergence technique to basic studies of the reading process.* Bloomington, Ind.: Phi Delta Kappa.

Geyer, J. J. 1972. Comprehensive and partial models related to the reading process. *Reading Research Quarterly, 7,* 541–87.

Gilliland, J. 1972. *Readability.* London: University of London Press.

Ginzberg, L. 1954–59. *The legends of the Jews* (7 vols.). Philadelphia: Jewish Publication Society.

Gold, S. R., and Cundiff, G. 1980. Increasing the frequency of daydreaming. *Journal of Clinical Psychology, 36,* 116–21.

Goldstein, I. B. 1972. Electromyography: A measure of skeletal muscle response. In N. S. Greenfield and R. A. Sternbach (eds.), *Handbook of psychophysiology.* New York: Holt, Rinehart and Winston.

Gottlieb, A. A., Gleser, G. C., and Gottschalk, L. A. 1967. Verbal and physiological responses to hypnotic suggestion of attitudes. *Psychosomatic Medicine, 29,* 172–83.

Gough, H. G. 1969. A leadership index on the California Psychological Inventory. *Journal of Consulting Psychology, 16,* 283–89.

Gray, J. A. 1970. The psychophysiological basis of introversion-extraversion. *Behaviour Research and Therapy, 8,* 249–66.

Gray, W. S. Illiteracy. 1971. In *Encyclopaedia Britannica,* vol. 11. Chicago: Benton.

Greaney, V., and Quinn, J. 1978. Factors related to amount and type of leisure time reading. Paper presented at the annual meeting of the International Reading Association 7th World Congress, Hamburg, August 1978.

Greenfield, N. S., and Sternbach, R. A. (eds.). 1972. *Handbook of psychophysiology.* New York: Holt, Rinehart and Winston.

Griesel, R. D. 1981. *Neuropsychology since 1960.* Pretoria: Institute for Behavioural Sciences, University of South Africa.

Groves, P., and Schlesinger, K. 1979. *Introduction to biological psychology.* Dubuque, Iowa: Brown.

Gunning, R. 1952. *The technique of clear writing.* New York: McGraw-Hill.

———. 1964. *A new guide to more effective writing in business and industry.* Boston: Industrial Education Institute.

Guyton, A. C. 1971. *Textbook of medical physiology.* Philadelphia: Saunders.

Haney, C., Banks, C., and Zimbardo, P. G. 1973. Interpersonal dynamics in a simulated prison. *International Journal of Criminology and Penology, 1,* 69–97.

Hansen, I. V. 1973. *Young people reading: The novel in secondary schools.* Carlton, Victoria: Melbourne University Press.

Harris, A. J. 1968. Research on some aspects of comprehension: Rate, flexibility, and study skills. *Journal of Reading, 12,* 205–10, 258–60.

Harris, A. J., and Jacobson, M. D. 1979. A framework for readability research: Moving beyond Herbert Spencer. *Journal of Reading, 22,* 390–98.

Harris, A. J., and Jacobson, M. D. 1980. A comparison of the Fry, Spache, and Harris-Jacobson readability formulas for primary grades. *The Reading Teacher, 24,* 920–24.

Harris, A. J., and Jacobson, M. D. 1981. *Basic elementary reading vocabularies.* New York: Macmillan.

Hart, J. D. 1950. *The popular book: A history of America's literary taste.* Westport, Conn.: Greenwood Press.

Hecaen, H., and Albert, M. L. 1978. *Human neuropsychology.* New York: Wiley-Interscience.

Herr, M. 1978. *Dispatches.* London: Pan.

Heslegrave, R. J., Ogilvie, J. C., and Furedy, J. J. 1979. Measuring baseline-treatment differences in heart rate variability: Variance versus successive difference mean square and beats per minute versus interbeat intervals. *Psychophysiology, 16,* 151–57.

Hess, E. H. 1972. Pupillometrics: A method of studying mental, emotional and sensory processes. In N. S. Greenfield and R. A. Sternbach (eds.), *Handbook of psychophysiology.* New York: Holt, Rinehart and Winston.

Heymans, G. 1929. [Introduction to special psychology]. Haarlem: Bohn.

Hilgard, E. R. 1965. *Hypnotic susceptibility.* New York: Harcourt Brace and World.

———. 1973. The domain of hypnosis, with some comments on alternative paradigms. *American Psychologist, 28,* 972–82.

Hilgard, J. R. 1979. *Personality and hypnosis: A study of imaginative involvement.* Chicago: University of Chicago Press.

Himelstein, H. C., and Greenberg, G. 1974. The effect of increasing reading rate on comprehension. *Journal of Psychology, 86,* 251–59.

Hiraga, M. 1973. Senior high school students' reading interests and attitudes. *Science of Reading, 17,* 35–47.

Hirsch, E. 1977. *The philosophy of composition.* Chicago: University of Chicago Press.

Hirschowitz, R., and Nell, V. 1983. The relationship between need for power and the life style of South African journalists. *Journal of Social Psychology, 121,* 297–304.

Hittleman, D. R. 1978. Readability, readability formulas, and cloze: Selecting instructional materials. *Journal of Reading, 21,* 117–22.

Hobbs, J. R., and Evans, D. A. 1980. Conversation as planned behaviour. *Cognitive Science, 4,* 349–77.

Hoffman, J. V., and O'Neall, S. F. 1979. An investigation into the internal and external rate flexibility of proficient readers in relation to the difficulty level of the material. Paper presented at the 29th annual meeting of the National Reading Conference, San Antonio, Texas.

Hofstadter, D. R. 1979. *Gödel, Escher, Bach: An eternal golden braid.* Brighton: Harvester.

Hoggart, R. 1958. *The uses of literacy.* Harmondsworth: Penguin.

Holbrook, D. 1972. *The masks of hate: The problem of false solutions in the culture of an acquisitive society.* Oxford: Pergamon.

Holland, N. N. 1975 (1968). *The dynamics of literary response.* New York: Norton.

Holt, R. R. 1961. The nature of TAT stories as cognitive products: A psychoanalytic approach. In J. Kagan and G. Lesser (eds.), *Contemporary issues in thematic apperceptive methods.* Springfield, Ill.: Thomas.

Hord, D. J., Johnson, L. C., and Lubin, A. 1964. Differential effect of the law of initial values (LIV) on autonomic variables. *Psychophysiology, 1,* 79–87.

Howden, M. A. 1967. A 19-year follow-up study of good, average and poor readers in the 5th and 6th grades. University Microfilms, Ann Arbor, Mich., 68–9998.

Huey, E. B. 1968 (1908). *The psychology and pedagogy of reading.* Cambridge, Mass.: MIT Press.

Huizinga, J. 1950 (1938). *Homo ludens.* Boston: Beacon.

Hull, C. L. 1952. *A behavior system: An introduction to behavior theory concerning the individual organism.* New Haven: Yale University Press.

Huxley, A. 1960 (1954). *The doors of perception.* Harmondsworth: Penguin.

Ireland, O. I. 1973. *Index to fairy tales, 1949–1972, including folklore, legends and myths in collections.* Westwood, Mass.: F. W. Faxon.

Irwin, R. 1971. Library. In *Encyclopaedia Britannica,* vol. 13. Chicago: Benton.

Iser, W. 1978. *The act of reading: A theory of aesthetic response.* London: Routledge and Kegan Paul.

Jackson, M. D., and McClelland, J. L. 1979. Processing determinants of reading speed. *Journal of Experimental Psychology: General, 108,* 151–81.

Jacob, S. H. 1976. Contexts and images in reading. *Reading World, 15,* 167–75.

Jacobson, E. 1927. Action currents from muscular contractions during conscious processes. *Science, 66,* 403.

James, W. 1950. *The varieties of religious experience: A study in human nature.* New York: Modern Library, date unknown (1902).

Johns, J. L., and Wheat, T. E. 1978. Newspaper readability. *Reading World, 18,* 141–47.

Johns, W.E.\1934. *Biggles flies again.* London: Hamilton.

Johnson, L. 1979. *The cultural critics: From Matthew Arnold to Raymond Williams.* London: Routledge and Kegan Paul.

Johnson, L. C., and Lubin, A. 1972. On planning psychophysiological experiments: Design, measurement and analysis. In N. S. Greenfield and R. A. Sternbach (eds.), *Handbook of psychophysiology.* New York: Holt, Rinehart and Winston.

Jones, E. 1980 (1957). *Sigmund Freud: Life and work* (3 vols.). London: Hogarth.

Jones, G. E., and Johnson, H. J. 1978. Physiological responding during self-generated imagery of contextually complete stimuli. *Psychophysiology, 15,* 439–46.

Jones, R. 1978. The third wave. In A. Pines and C. Maslack (eds.), *Experiencing social psychology* (2d ed.). New York: Knopf.

Jordan, A. C. 1966. Tale, teller and audience in African spoken narrative. In J. Berry, R. P. Armstrong and J. Povey (eds.), *Proceedings of a conference on African languages and literatures held at Northwestern University, April 28–30, 1966.* Evanston: Northwestern University Press.

Joyce, J. 1977 (1914). *Dubliners.* London: Granada.

Joyce, J. 1939. *Finnegan's wake.* London: Faber and Faber.

Jung, C. G. 1949 (1923). *Psychological types.* London: Routledge and Kegan Paul.

Just, M. A., and Carpenter, P. A. 1977. *Cognitive processes in comprehension.* Hillsdale, N.J.: Erlbaum.

Just, M. A., and Carpenter, P. A. 1980. A theory of reading: From eye fixations to comprehension. *Psychological Review, 87,* 329–54.

Kahneman, D. 1973. *Attention and effort.* Englewood Cliffs, N.J.: Prentice Hall.

Kahneman, D., and Beatty, J. 1966. Pupil diameter and load on memory. *Science, 154,* 1583–85.

Katz, E., and Foulkes, D. 1962. On the use of mass media as an escape: Clarification of a concept. *Public Opinion Quarterly, 26,* 377–88.

Kendrick, D. C. 1981. Neuroticism and extraversion as explanatory concepts in clinical psychology. In R. Lynn (ed.), *Dimensions of personality: Papers in honour of H. J. Eysenck.* Oxford: Pergamon.

Kintsch, W. 1977. On comprehending stories. In M. A. Just and P. A. Carpenter (eds.), *Cognitive processes in comprehension.* Hillsdale, N.J.: Erlbaum.

Klapper, J. T. 1965 (1960). *The effects of mass communication.* New York: Free Press.

Klare, G. R. 1963. *The measurement of readability.* Ames: Iowa State University Press.

Klinger, E. 1971. *Structure and functions of fantasy.* New York: Wiley-Interscience.

Kochman, T. (ed.). 1972. *Rappin' and stylin' out: Communication in urban Black America.* Urbana: University of Chicago Press.

Konečni, V. J. 1978. Daniel E. Berlyne: 1924–1976. *American Journal of Psychology, 91,* 133–37.

Korchin, S. J., and Schuldberg, D. 1981. The future of clinical assessment. *American Psychologist, 36,* 1147–58.

Kosslyn, S. M. 1981. The medium and the message in mental imagery: A theory. *Psychological Review, 88,* 46–66.

Kosslyn, S. M., and Jolicoeur, P. 1980. A theory-based approach to the study of individual differences in imagery. In R. E. Snow, P. A. Federico, and W. E. Montague (eds.), *Aptitude, learning and instruction* (2 vols). Hillsdale, N.J.: Erlbaum.

Kosslyn, S. M., and Matt, A. M. C. 1977. If you speak slowly, do people read your prose slowly? Person-particular speech recoding during reading. *Bulletin of the Psychonomic Society, 9,* 250–52.

Kretschner, E. 1925. *Physique and character.* London: Kegan, Trench and Trubner.

Kuhn, T. S. 1962. *The structure of scientific revolutions.* Chicago: University of Chicago Press.

Kundera, M. 1984. *The unbearable lightness of being.* London: Faber and Faber.

Kwolek, W. F. 1973. A readability survey of technical and popular literature. *Journalism Quarterly, 50,* 255–64.

Labov, W. 1972. *Language in the inner city.* Philadelphia: University of Pennsylvania Press.

Lacey, J. I. 1967. Somatic response patterning and stress: Some revisions of activation theory. In M. H. Appley and R. Trumbull (eds.), *Psychological stress.* New York: Appleton-Century-Crofts.

Lacey, J. I., Kagan, J., Lacey, B. C., and Moss, H. A. 1963. The visceral level: Situational determinants and behavioral correlates of autonomic response. In P. H. Knapp (ed.), *Expression of the emotions in man.* New York: International University Press.

Lacey, B. C., and Lacey, J. I. 1978. Two-way communication between the heart and the brain: Significance of time within the cardiac cycle. *American Psychologist, 33,* 99–113.

Lachman, R., Lachman, J. L., and Butterfield, E. C. 1979. *Cognitive psychology and information processing: An introduction.* Hillsdale, N.J.: Erlbaum.

Lacroix, J. M., and Camper, P. 1979. Lateralisation in the electrodermal system as a function of cognitive hemisphere manipulations. *Psychophysiology, 16,* 116–19.

Lakoff, G. 1971. Presupposition and relative well-formedness. In D. D. Steinberg and L. A. Jakobovits (eds.), *Semantics.* Cambridge: Cambridge University Press.

Lamme, L. L. 1976. Are reading habits and abilities related? *Reading Teacher, 30,* 21–27.

Landy, S. 1977. An investigation of the relationship between voluntary reading and certain psychological, environmental and socioeconomic factors in early adolescence. M.A. thesis, University of Regina.

Lang, P. J. 1979. A bio-informational theory of emotional imagery. *Psychophysiology, 16,* 495–512.

Lang, P. J., Ohman, A., and Simons, R. F. 1978. The psychophysiology of attention. In J. Requin (ed.), *Attention and performance VII.* Hillsdale, N.J.: Erlbaum.

Lashley, K. S. 1967 (1950). In search of the engram. In T. K. Landaver (ed.), *Readings in physiological psychology.* New York: McGraw-Hill.

Lassen, N. A., Ingvar, D. H., and Skinhøj, E. 1978. Brain function and blood flow. *Scientific American, 239* (4), 50–59.

Lazarus, R. S., and Opton, E. M. 1966. The study of psychological stress: A study of experimental studies and theoretical formulations. In C. Spielberger (ed.), *Anxiety and behavior.* New York: Academic Press.

Leavis, Q. D. 1965 (1932). *Fiction and the reading public.* London: Chatto and Windus.

Le Carré, J. 1965. *The looking-glass war.* London: Heinemann.

———. 1979. *Smiley's people.* London: Hodder and Stoughton.

Leedy, P. D. 1963. *Read with speed and precision.* New York: McGraw-Hill.

Letson, C. T. 1958. Speed and comprehension in reading. *Journal of Educational Research, 52,* 49–53.

Lewis, C. S. 1968. *The magician's nephew.* London: Pan.

Lewis, G. H. 1978. The sociology of popular culture. *Current Sociology, 26,* no. 3.

Lezak, M. D. 1983. *Neuropsychological assessment* (2d ed.) New York: Oxford University Press.

Logan, G. D. 1980. Attention and automaticity in Stroop and priming tasks: Theory and data. *Cognitive Psychology, 12,* 523–53.

Lowry, M. 1947. *Under the volcano.* London: Jonathan Cape.

Lubbock, P. 1957. *The craft of fiction.* New York: Compass.

Luria, A. R. 1970 (1947). *Traumatic aphasia.* The Hague: Mouton.

————. 1975 (1965). *The mind of a mnemonist.* Harmondsworth: Penguin.

————. 1973. *The working brain: An introduction to neuropsychology.* London: Penguin.

MacCulloch, J. A. 1905. *The childhood of fiction: A study of folk tales and primitive thought.* London: John Murray.

MacKay, C. J. 1980. The measurement of mood and psychophysiological activity using self-report techniques. In I. Martin and P. H. Venables, *Techniques in psychophysiology.* Chichester: Wiley.

MacLean, P. D. 1973. *A triune concept of the brain and behaviour.* Toronto: University of Toronto Press.

Maddi, S. R. 1976. *Personality theories: A comparative analysis* (3d ed.). Homewood, Ill.: Dorsey.

Madge, E. M. 1975. [*A review of existing knowledge of the primary personality factors measured by the PQC, HSPQ, and the 16PF*]. Pretoria: Human Sciences Research Council.

Mailer, N. 1971. *A fire on the moon.* London: Pan.

Malmo, R. B. 1972. Overview. In N. S. Greenfield and R. A. Sternbach (eds.), *Handbook of psychophysiology.* New York: Holt, Rinehart and Winston.

Mann, P. H. 1971. *Books: Buyers and borrowers.* London: Deutsch.

Manzo, A. 1979. Toward defining and assessing reading maturity. Research report, University of Missouri, Kansas City, November.

Marivate, C. T. D. 1973. Tsonga folktales: Form, content and delivery. M.A. thesis, University of South Africa.

Maslow, A. 1962. *Toward a psychology of being.* Princeton, N.J.: Van Nostrand.

Mason, J. W. 1972. Organisation of psychoendocrine mechanisms: A review and reconsideration of research. In N. S. Greenfield and R. A. Sternbach (eds.), *Handbook of psychophysiology.* New York: Holt, Rinehart and Winston.

Maugham, W. S. 1970 (1931). The vessel of wrath. In *A second baker's dozen.* London: Heinemann.

————. 1970 (1932). The book bag. In *A second baker's dozen.* London: Heinemann.

————. 1970 (1934). The human element. In *A second baker's dozen.* London: Heinemann.

McBride, V. G. 1971. The fastest readers in the world. *School and Community, 57,* 29, 32–33.

McClelland, D. C. 1951. *Personality.* New York: William Sloane.

————. 1977. The impact of power motivation training on alcoholics. *Journal of Studies on Alcohol, 38,* 142–44.

McGuigan, F. J. 1978. *Cognitive psychophysiology: Principles of covert behavior.* Englewood Cliffs, N.J.: Prentice Hall.

————. 1979. *Psychophysiological measurement of covert behavior: A guide for the laboratory*. Hillsdale, N.J.: Erlbaum.

McKellar, P. 1980. Between wakefulness and sleep: Hypnagogic fantasy. *Journal of Mental Imagery, 3,* 189–97.

McLaughlin, G. H. 1969a. SMOG grading: A new readability formula. *Journal of Reading, 12,* 639–46.

————. 1969b. Clearing the SMOG. *Journal of Reading, 13,* 210–11.

McLuhan, M. 1967 (1951). *The mechanical bride: Folklore of industrial man*. London: Routledge and Kegan Paul.

McQuilkin, J. A. 1980. An investigation of the reading flexibility of graduate students. *Dissertation Abstracts International,* 41, 1925A.

Meehan, J. 1977. TALE-SPIN: An interactive program that writes stories. *Proceedings of the Fifth International Joint Conference on Artificial Intelligence*. Boston, 91–98.

Mehrabian, A. 1976. *Public places and private spaces*. New York: Basic.

Mehrabian, A., and Russell, J. A. 1974. *An approach to environmental psychology*. Cambridge, Mass.: MIT Press.

Mendelsohn, L. R. 1977. Jetting to Utopia: The speed reading phenomenon. *Language Arts, 54,* 116–20.

Meredith, K., and Vaughan, J. 1978. Stability of cloze scores across varying deletion patterns. *Yearbook of the National Reading Conference, 27,* 181–84.

Milgram, S. 1974. *Obedience to authority: An experimental view*. London: Tavistock.

Miller, P. D. A. 1976. The effect upon reading rate of variations in purpose, familiarity and difficulty: An investigation of reading flexibility at the community college level. Ph.D. diss., University of Minnesota.

Miron, M., and Brown, E. 1971. The comprehension of rate-incremented aural coding. *Journal of Psycholinguistic Research, 1,* 65–76.

Monchaux, C. de. 1978. Dreaming and the organising function of the ego. *International Journal of Psychoanalysis, 59,* 443–53.

Morse, S. J., and Orpen, C. (eds.), 1975. *Contemporary South Africa: Social psychological perspectives*. Cape Town: Juta.

Moruzzi, G., and Magoun, H. W. 1949. Brain stem reticular formation and activation of the EEG. *Electroencephalography and Clinical Neurophysiology, 1,* 455–73.

Mott, F. L. 1960. *Golden multitudes: The story of bestsellers in the United States*. New York: Bowker.

Mulder, J. 1976. Reading motivation and the role of interest. *Mousaion, 2* no. 3. Pretoria: University of South Africa.

Mundy-Castle, A. C. 1956. The relationship between primary-secondary function and the alpha rhythm of the electroencephalogram. *Journal of the National Institute for Personnel Research, 6,* 95–102.

Murray, H. A. 1938. *Explorations in personality*. New York: Oxford.

Myers, J. L. 1979. *Fundamentals of experimental design* (3d ed.). Boston: Allyn and Bacon.

Mynhardt, J. C. 1980. Prejudice among Afrikaans- and English-speaking South African students. *Journal of Social Psychology, 110,* 9–17.

Myslobodsky, M. S., and Rattok, J. 1977. Bilateral electrodermal activity in waking man. *Acta Psychologica, 41,* 273–82.

Neisser, U. 1967. *Cognitive Psychology.* New York: Appleton-Century-Crofts.

Nell, O. 1968. Value development and identification in 10 to 15 year old Afrikaans and English speaking children. M.A. thesis, University of Port Elizabeth.

Nell, V. 1977. A nose for news and a stomach for whiskey: Speculations on the psychology of the entertainment media. Unpublished paper.

———. 1978a. Kinds of reading and kinds of motivation: Reflections on the psychology of the reading habit. *Mousaion, 2* (5),

———. 1978b. News value rankings and power motive scores. *Communicatio, 4,* 40–43.

———. 1980. The structure of aesthetic judgments: Perception, arousal, motivation, and values. *Communicare, 1,* 3–9.

———. 1981. At the heart of darkness: Eichmann and *Apocalypse Now, Critical Arts, 1* (4), 28–40.

———. 1983. The psychology and physiology of reading trance. Unpublished doctoral dissertation, University of South Africa.

———. 1985. Proposals for the training and credentialling of clinical neuropsychologists in South Africa. In K. W. Grieve and R. D. Griesel (eds.), *Neuropsychology II: Proceedings of the second South African neuropsychology conference.* Pretoria: University of South Africa.

———. 1988. The psychology of reading for pleasure: Needs and gratifications. *Reading Research Quarterly, 23,* 6–50.

Neuberg, V. E. 1971. *Literacy and society.* London: Woburn.

Newall, V. 1980. Tell us a story. In J. Cherfas and R. Lewin (eds.), *Not work alone.* London: Temple Smith.

Nilsson, L.-G., Ohlsson, K., and Ronnberg, J. 1983. Legibility of text as a function of color combinations and viewing distance. *Umea Psychological Reports,* no. 167.

Nisbett, R. E., and Wilson, T. D. 1977. Telling more than we know: Verbal reports on mental processes. *Psychological Review, 84,* 231–79.

Norman, D. A., Rumelhart, D. E., and the LNR Research Group. 1975. *Explorations in cognition.* San Francisco: Freeman.

Obrist, P. A. 1963. Cardiovascular differentiation of sensory stimuli. *Psychosomatic Medicine, 25,* 450–59.

O'Donnell, P. 1973. *The impossible virgin.* London: Pan.

Ohmann, R. 1971. Speech acts and the definition of literature. *Philosophy and Rhetoric, 4,* 1–19.

Osgood, C. E. 1963. On understanding and creating sentences. *American Psychologist, 18,* 735–51.

Osgood, C. E., and McGuigan, F. J. 1973. Psychophysiological correlates of meaning: Essences or tracers? In F. J. McGuigan and R. A. Schoonover (eds.), *The psychophysiology of thinking.* New York: Academic Press.

Osgood, C. E., Suci, G. J., and Tannenbaum, P. H. 1957. *The measurement of meaning.* Urbana, Ill.: University of Illinois Press.

Owens, J., Bower, G. H., and Black, J. B. 1979. The "soap opera" effect in story recall. *Memory and Cognition, 7,* 185–91.

Oxford. *Oxford English dictionary* (13 vols.). 1933a. London: Oxford University Press.

———. *Shorter Oxford English dictionary.* 1933b. London: Oxford University Press.

———. *The concise Oxford dictionary* (6th ed.). 1976. Oxford: Oxford University Press.

Panackal, A. A., and Heft, C. S. 1978. Cloze technique and multiple choice technique: Reliability and validity. *Educational and Psychological Measurement, 38,* 917–32.

Pauk, W. 1965. Scholarly skills as gadgets. *Journal of Reading, 8,* 234–39.

———. 1981. You haf'ta vocalise to comprehend. *Reading World, 20,* 225–26.

Pearce, M. 1974. Put down that cornflake packet. *New Library World, 75,* 213–14.

Perry, C. 1973. Imagery, fantasy and hypnotic susceptibility. *Journal of Personality and Social Psychology, 26,* 217–21.

Petersen, C. 1975. *The Bantam story: Thirty years of paperback publishing.* New York: Bantam.

Picton, T. W., Campbell, K. B., Baribeau-Braun, J., and Proulx, G. B. 1978. The neurophysiology of human attention: A tutorial review. In J. Requin (ed.), *Attention and performance VII.* Hillsdale, N.J.: Erlbaum.

Pimsleur, P., Hancock, C., and Furey, P. 1977. [Speech rate of radio broadcasts: A comparative study of French and American announcers]. *Études de Linguistique Appliquée, 27,* 12–18.

Pincus, J. H., and Tucker, G. J. 1974. *Behavioural neurology.* New York: Oxford University Press.

Plug, C. 1978. *Speed reading: An evaluation.* Pretoria: Reports from the Psychology Department, University of South Africa.

Poe, E. A. 1838. *The narrative of Arthur Gordon Pym of Nantucket.* New York: Harper and Brothers.

Port Elizabeth Municipal Library Service. 1973 and 1974. *Annual Reports.* Port Elizabeth: The City Librarian.

Porter, D. 1978. Cloze procedure and equivalence. *Language Learning, 28,* 333–41.

Pratt, M. L. 1977. *Toward a speech act theory of literary discourse.* Bloomington: Indiana University Press.

Pribram, K. H. 1977. Some observations on the organisation of studies of mind, brain and behavior. In N. E. Zinberg (ed.), *Alternate states of consciousness.* New York: Free Press.

Pribram, K. H., and McGuiness, D. 1975. Arousal, activation, and effort in the control of attention. *Psychological Review, 82,* 116–49.

Proust, M. 1928 (1913). *Swann's way.* New York: Modern Library.

Pylyshyn, Z. W. 1973. What the mind's eye tells the mind's brain: A critique of mental imagery. *Psychological Bulletin, 80,* 1–24.

Rank, O. 1929. *The trauma of birth.* New York: Harcourt, Brace.

Rankin, E. F., and Culhane, J. W. 1969. Comparable cloze and multiple-choice comprehension test scores. *Journal of Reading, 13,* 193–98.

Rapaport, D. 1951. States of consciousness, a psychopathological and psychodynamic view. In H. A. Abrahamson (ed.), *Problems of consciousness: Transactions of the Second Conference.* New York: Mercy.

———. 1967. A historical survey of psychoanalytic ego psychology. In M. M. Gill (ed.), *The collected papers of David Rapaport.* New York: Basic Books.

Rayner, K. 1978. Eye movements in reading and information processing. *Psychological Bulletin, 85,* 618–60.

Reed, G. F. 1979. Sensory deprivation. In G. Underwood and R. Stevens (eds.), *Aspects of consciousness.* London: Academic Press.

Richards, I. A. 1956 (1929). *Practical criticism: A study of literary judgment.* London: Routledge and Kegan Paul.

Riesen, A. H., and Thompson, R. F. 1976. *Advances in psychobiology* (vol. 3). New York: Wiley Interscience.

Riley, T. M., & Barbato, G. J. 1978. Dot-matrix alphanumerics viewed under discrete element degradation. *Human Factors, 20,* 473–79.

Robeck, M. C., and Wilson, J. A. R. 1974. *Psychology of reading: Foundations of instruction.* New York: Wiley.

Rockwell, F. A. 1975. *How to write plots that sell.* Chicago: Henry Regnery.

Roessler, R., and Engel, B. T. 1977. The current status of the concepts of physiological response specificity and activation. In Z. L. Lipowski and P. C. Whybrow (eds.), *Psychosomatic medicine.* New York: Oxford University Press.

Rogers, C. R. 1961. *On becoming a person.* Boston: Houghton Mifflin.

Rokeach, M. 1971. Long-range experimental modification of values, attitudes and behavior. *American Psychologist, 26,* 453–59.

———., (ed.). 1979. *Understanding human values: Individual and societal.* New York: Free Press.

Rubakin, N. 1968 (1921). The "special method" of bibliopsychology. In S. Simsova (ed.), *Nicholas Rubakin and bibliopsychology.* London: Clive Bingley.

Rubakin, N., and Bethmann, M. 1968 (1937). The psychology of the public library. In S. Simsova (ed.), *Nicholas Rubakin and bibliopsychology.* London: Clive Bingley.

Rumelhart, E. D. 1980. On evaluating story grammars. *Cognitive Science, 4,* 313–16.

Rush, R. J., and Klare, G. R. 1978. Re-opening the cloze blank issue. *Journal of Reading Behavior, 10,* 208–13.

Russell, E. W. 1981. The pathology and clinical examination of memory. In S. B. Filskov and T. J. Boll (eds.), *Handbook of clinical neuropsychology.* New York: Wiley.

Ryan, R. P. 1982. The Geneva School: In search of other minds. In R. P. Ryan and E. S. van Zyl, (eds.), *An introduction to contemporary literary theory.* Johannesburg: Ad Donker.

———. 1985. Pathology of epistemology in literary studies. *Journal of Literary Studies, 1,* (1), 3–42.

Sassenrath, J. M. 1972–73. Alpha factor analyses of reading measures at the elementary, secondary, and college levels. *Journal of Reading Behavior, 5,* 304–16.

Scholderer, J. V. 1971. Incunabula. In *Encyclopaedia Britannica,* vol. 12. Chicago: Benton.

Schramm, W. 1949. The nature of news. *Journalism Quarterly, 26,* 259–69.

————. 1964. *Mass media and national development.* Stanford: Stanford University Press.

————. Communication in crisis. 1965. In B. S. Greenberg and E. B. Parker (eds.), *The Kennedy assassination and the American public: Social communication in crisis.* Stanford: Stanford University Press.

Schramm, W., Lyle, J., and Parker, E. B. 1961. *Television in the lives of our children.* Stanford: Stanford University Press.

Schreiner, S. A. 1977. *The condensed world of the Reader's Digest.* New York: Stein and Day.

Schroeder, J. K. 1981. Studying popular culture in the public library: Suggestions for cooperative programs. *Drexel Library Quarterly, 16,* 65–72.

Sersen, E. A., Clausen, J., and Lidsky, A. 1978. Autonomic specificity and stereotyping revisited. *Psychophysiology, 15,* 60–67.

Shagass, C. 1972. Electrical activity of the brain. In N. S. Greenfield and R. A. Sternbach (eds.), *Handbook of psychophysiology.* New York: Holt, Rinehart and Winston.

Shapiro, D., and Crider, A. 1969. Psychophysiological approaches in social psychology. In G. Lindzey and E. Aronson (eds.), *Handbook of social psychology.* Reading, Mass.: Addison-Wesley.

Shapiro, S. H. 1978. Depersonalisation and daydreaming. *Bulletin of the Menninger Clinic, 42,* 307–20.

Sharon, A. T. 1974. What do adults read? *Reading Research Quarterly, 9,* 148–69.

Sheldon, W. H. 1954. *Atlas of men.* New York: Harper and Row.

Shera, J. H. 1965. *Foundations of the public library.* Chicago: University of Chicago Press.

Shor, R. E. 1970. The three-factor theory of hypnosis applied to book-reading fantasy and to the concept of suggestion. *International Journal of Clinical and Experimental Hypnosis, 18,* 89–98.

Siddle, D. A. T., and Turpin, G. 1980. Measurement quantification and analysis of cardiac activity. In I. Martin and P. H. Venables (eds.), *Techniques in psychophysiology.* Chichester: Wiley.

Simon, J. 1977. Creativity and altered states of consciousness. *American Journal of Psychoanalysis, 37,* 3–12.

Simora, F. (ed.). 1980. *The Bowker annual of library and book trade information* (25th ed.). New York: Bowker.

————. (ed.) 1986. *The Bowker annual of library and book trade information* (31st ed.). New York: Bowker.

Simsova, S. (ed.). 1968. *Nicholas Rubakin and bibliopsychology.* London: Clive Bingley.

Singer, J. L. 1976. *Daydreaming and fantasy.* London: George Allen and Unwin.

————. 1977. Ongoing thought: The normative baseline for alternate states of consciousness. In N. E. Zinberg (ed.), *Alternate states of consciousness.* New York: Free Press.

Smith, H. R. (ed.) 1963. *The American reading public: What it reads, why it reads.* New York: Bowker.

Sokolov, A. N. 1972. *Inner speech and thought.* New York: Plenum.

Sokolov, Y. N. 1963. *Perception and the conditioned reflex.* Oxford: Pergamon.

Sommer, R. 1980. Strategies for imagery research. *Journal of Mental Imagery, 4,* 115–21.

Spanos, N. P., and McPeake, J. D. 1975. Involvement in everyday imaginative activities, attitudes towards hypnosis, and hypnotic suggestibility. *Journal of Personality and Social Psychology, 31,* 594–98.

Spelke, E., Hirst, W., and Neisser, U. 1976. Skills of divided attention. *Cognition, 4,* 215–30.

Sperry, R. W. 1969. A modified concept of consciousness. *Psychological Review, 76,* 532–36.

———. 1977. Bridging science and values: A unifying view of mind and brain. *American Psychologist, 32,* 237–45.

Stanovich, K. E. 1980. Toward an interactive-compensatory model of individual differences in the development of reading fluency. *Reading Research Quarterly, 16,* 32–71.

Starker, S. 1977. Daydreaming styles and nocturnal dreaming: Further observations. *Perceptual and Motor Skills, 45,* 411–18.

Stein, M., and Luparello, T. J. 1967. The measurement of respiration. In C. C. Brown (ed.), *Methods in psychophysiology.* Baltimore: Williams and Wilkins.

Steinberg, S. H. 1955. *Five hundred years of printing.* Harmondsworth: Penguin.

Stephenson, W. 1964. The ludenic theory of newsreading. *Journalism Quarterly, 41,* 367–74.

———. 1967. *The play theory of mass communication.* Chicago: University of Chicago Press.

Sterba, R. A. 1939. The significance of theatrical performance. *Psychoanalytic Quarterly, 8,* 335–37.

Stern, J. A. 1972. Physiological response measures during classical conditioning. In N. S. Greenfield and R. A. Sternbach (eds.), *Handbook of psychophysiology.* New York: Holt, Rinehart and Winston.

Stern, R. M., Ray, W. J., and Davis, C. M. 1980. *Psychophysiological recording.* New York: Oxford University Press.

Strang, R. 1942. *Exploration in reading patterns.* Chicago: University of Chicago Press.

Szalai, A. 1972. *The use of time: Daily activities of urban and suburban populations in twelve countries.* The Hague: Mouton.

Tannenbaum, P. H. 1971. The indexing process in communication. In W. Schramm and D. F. Roberts (eds.), *The process and effects of mass communication.* Urbana, Ill.: University of Illinois Press.

Tart, C. T. (ed.) 1969. *Altered states of consciousness.* New York: Wiley.

Tawney, R. H. 1958 (1926). *Religion and the rise of capitalism.* New York: Mentor.

Taylor, J. T. 1943. *Early opposition to the English novel: The popular reaction from 1760 to 1830.* New York: King's Crown Press.

Taylor, W. L. 1953. Cloze procedure: A new tool for measuring readability. *Journalism Quarterly, 30,* 415–33.

Tellegen, A., and Atkinson, G. 1974. Openness to absorbing self-altering experiences ("absorption"), a trait related to hypnotic susceptibility. *Journal of Abnormal Psychology, 83,* 268–77.

Thayer, R. E. 1970. Activation states as assessed by verbal report and four psychophysiological variables. *Psychophysiology, 7,* 86–94.

Thompson, M. 1979. *Rubbish theory: The creation and destruction of value.* Oxford: Oxford.

Thompson, M. R., and Whitehill, R. P. 1970. Relationships between reading flexibility and speed gains. *Journal of Educational Research, 63,* 213–15.

Thompson, S. 1955. *Motif-index of folk-literature: A classification of narrative elements in folktales, ballads, myths, fables, mediaeval romances, exempla, fablieaux, jest-books and local legends* (2d ed., 6 vols.). Bloomington: Indiana University Press.

Tinker, M. A. 1963. *Legibility of print.* Ames: Iowa State University Press.

———. 1965. *Bases for effective reading.* Minneapolis: University of Minnesota Press.

Tolkien, J. R. R. 1954. *The lord of the rings* (3 vols.) London: Allen and Unwin.

Trevarthen, C. 1979. The tasks of consciousness: How could the brain do them? In Ciba Foundation Symposium 69, *Brain and mind.* Amsterdam: Excerpta Medica.

Tulving, E. 1979. Memory research: What kind of progress. In L. Nilsson (ed.), *Perspectives on memory research.* Hillsdale, N.J.: Erlbaum.

Turpin, G., and Siddle, D. A. T. 1979. Effects of stimulus intensity on electrodermal activity. *Psychophysiology, 16,* 582–91.

Tursky, B., Schwartz, G. E., and Crider, A. 1970. Differential patterns of heart rate and skin resistance during a digit transformation task. *Journal of Experimental Psychology, 83,* 451–57.

Tushup, R. J., and Zuckerman, M. 1977. The effects of stimulus invariance on daydreaming and divergent thinking. *Journal of Mental Imagery, 2,* 291–302.

Ullman, A. D. 1952. The psychological mechanisms of alcohol addiction. *Quarterly Journal for Studies of Alcohol, 13,* 602.

UNESCO. 1957. *World illiteracy at midcentury.* Paris: Author.

———. 1981. *1980 Statistical yearbook.* Paris: Author.

———. 1985. *Statistical yearbook.* Paris: Author.

Van Dijk, T. A. 1977. Semantic macro-structures and knowledge frames in discourse comprehension. In M. A. Just and P. A. Carpenter (eds.), *Cognitive processes in comprehension.* Hillsdale, N.J.: Erlbaum.

Van Nes, F. L., and Bouma, H. 1980. On the legibility of printed numerals. *Human Factors, 22,* 463–74.

Varley, D. H. 1958. The lighter reading of our English South African ancestors. *Quarterly Bulletin of the South African Library, 13,* 22–29, 52–58.

Venables, P. H., and Christie, M. J. 1980. Electrodermal activity. In I. Martin and P. H. Venables (eds.), *Techniques in psychophysiology.* Chichester: Wiley.

Venables, P. H., and Fletcher, R. P. 1981. The status of skin conductance recovery time: An examination of the Bundy effect. *Psychophysiology, 18,* 10–16.

Venezky, R. L. 1977. Research on reading processes: A historical perspective. *American Psychologist, 32,* 339–45.

Von Bekesy, G. 1967. *Sensory inhibition.* Princeton, N.J.: Princeton University Press.

Walker, C. E., Hedberg, A., Clement, P. W., and Wright, L. 1981. *Clinical procedures for behavior therapy.* Englewood Cliffs, N.J.: Prentice Hall.

Walsh, K. W. 1978. Neuropsychology: A clinical approach. Edinburgh: Churchill Livingstone.

———. 1985. *Understanding brain damage: A primer of neuropsychological evaluation.* Edinburgh: Churchill Livingstone.

Walter, W. G., Cooper, R., Aldridge, V. J., McCallum, W. C., and Winter, A. L. 1964. Contingent negative variation: An electric sign of sensori-motor association and expectancy in the human brain. *Nature, 203,* 380–84.

Waples, D., Berelson, B., and Bradshaw, F. R. 1940. *What reading does to people.* Chicago: University of Chicago Press.

Warwick, R., & Williams, P. L. (eds.). 1973. *Gray's anatomy* (35th ed.). London: Longman.

Watt, I. 1971. Novel. *Encyclopaedia Britannica,* vol. 16. Chicago: Benton.

Weber, M. 1965 (1904). *The Protestant Ethic and the spirit of capitalism.* London: Unwin.

Wechsler, D. 1958. *The measurement and appraisal of adult intelligence* (4th ed.). Baltimore: Williams and Wilkins.

Weintraub, S., Smith, H. K., Roser, N. L., Rowls, M., and Hill, W. R. 1980. *Summary of investigations relating to reading.* Newark, Del.: International Reading Association.

Weitzenhoffer, A. M., and Hilgard, E. R. 1959. *Stanford hypnotic susceptibility scale.* Palo Alto, Cal.: Consulting Psychologists Press.

Welleck, R., and Warren, A. 1955. *Theory of literature.* London: Cape.

Wenger, M. A., and Cullen, T. D. 1972. Studies of autonomic balance in children and adults. In N. S. Greenfield and R. A. Sternbach (eds.), *Handbook of psychophysiology.* New York: Holt, Rinehart and Winston.

Westra, P. E. 1981. [Public lending right in theory and practice, with special reference to South Africa]. Pretoria: State Library.

Whaley, J. F. 1981. Readers' expectations for story structure. *Reading Research Quarterly, 17,* 90–114.

White, K., Sheehan, P. W., and Ashton, R. 1977. Imagery assessment: A study of self-report measures. *Journal of Mental Imagery, 1,* 145–70.

Wickens, C. D. 1980. The structure of attentional resources. In R. S. Nickerson (ed.), *Attention and performance VIII.* Hillsdale, N.J.: Erlbaum.

Wilder, J. 1967. *Stimulus and response: The law of initial value.* Bristol: Wright.

Winer, B. J. 1971. *Statistical principles in experimental design* (2d ed.). New York: McGraw-Hill.

Winograd, T. 1972. Understanding natural language. *Cognitive Psychology, 3,* 1–191.

Winter, D. G. 1973. *The power motive.* New York: The Free Press.

Wolf, K., and Fiske, M. 1949. The children talk about comics. In P. F. Lazarsfeld and F. N. Stanton (eds.), *Communication Research, 1948–1949,* New York: Harper.

Wolf, S., and Welsh, J. D. 1972. The gastrointestinal tract as a responsive system. In N. S. Greenfield and R. A. Sternbach (eds.), *Handbook of psychophysiology.* New York: Holt, Rinehart and Winston.

Wolfe, T. 1975 (1972). *The new journalism.* London: Picador.

Wouk, H. 1951. *The Caine mutiny.* London: Cape.

Yamamoto, Y. L., Thompson, C. J., Diksic, M., Meyer, E., and Feindel, W. H. 1984. Position emission tomography. *Neurosurgical Review, 7,* 233–52.

Zaaiman, R. B. 1981. Light or enlightened reading? *South African Journal for Librarianship and Information Science, 49,* 47.

Zeigarnik, B. 1927. [On memory for complete and incomplete tasks]. *Psychologische Forschung, 9,* 1–85.

Zelnicker, T. 1971. Perceptual attenuation of an irrelevant auditory verbal input as measured by an involuntary verbal response in a selective attention task. *Journal of Experimental Psychology, 87,* 52–56.

Zinberg, N. E. (ed.). 1977. Alternate states of consciousness. New York: Free Press.

Zipf, G. K. 1965 (1935). *The psycho-biology of language.* Cambridge, Mass.: MIT Press.

Zubek, J. P. (ed.). 1969. *Sensory deprivation: Fifteen years of research.* New York: Appleton-Century-Crofts.

Zuckerman, M. 1979. *Sensation seeking: Beyond the optimal level of arousal.* Hillsdale, N.J.: Erlbaum.

Zuckerman, M., Murtaugh, T., and Siegel, J. 1974. Sensation seeking and cortical augmenting-reducing. *Psychophysiology, 11,* 535–42.

Index

SQUARE-SHOOTER

Center Point
Large Print

Also by William MacLeod Raine and available
from Center Point Large Print:

The Black Tolts
Clattering Hoofs
Courage Stout
Gunsmoke Trail
Long Texan
The Trail of Danger

SQUARE-SHOOTER

William MacLeod Raine

CENTER POINT LARGE PRINT
THORNDIKE, MAINE

This Center Point Large Print edition is published
in the year 2017 by arrangement with
Golden West Literary Agency.

The text of this Large Print edition is unabridged.
In other aspects, this book may vary
from the original edition.
Printed in the United States of America
on permanent paper.
Set in 16-point Times New Roman type.

ISBN: 978-1-68324-318-2 (hardcover)
ISBN: 978-1-68324-322-9 (paperback)

Library of Congress Cataloging-in-Publication Data

Names: Raine, William MacLeod, 1871–1954, author.
Title: Square-shooter / William MacLeod Raine.
Description: Center point large print edition. | Thorndike, Maine :
Center Point Large Print, 2017.
Identifiers: LCCN 2016056207| ISBN 9781683243182 (hardcover :
alk. paper) | ISBN 9781683243229 (pbk. : alk. paper)
Subjects: LCSH: Large type books. | GSAFD: Western stories.
Classification: LCC PS3535.A385 S37 2017 | DDC 813/.2—dc23
LC record available at https://lccn.loc.gov/2016056207

CONTENTS

SQUARE-SHOOTER

Chapter I

A Peaceable Citizen

Cole Sanborn sat in a tiptilted chair on the porch of the Jonesboro House, the worn heel of one boot hooked in a rung. His long, lean body was slack, apparently relaxed, but its ease was like that of a coiled spring which might be released at the touch of a trigger. Chill gray eyes set deep in a hard, reckless face swept the dusty road with indolent vigilance. In them lay a cynical audacity, no apprehension. Yet he knew he was a temptation to itching fingers. His presence was a challenge— to perplexed and dubious law which knew much and guessed more, to the anger of many whose vanity and rights he had flouted, to the vengeance of enemies powerful and entrenched.

He was as nearly motionless as one could be who rolled, lit, and smoked cigarettes at spaced intervals. For an hour he had not left the porch, and every instant of that time he had been watched. That there was menace in the air Cole knew. He had seen a lifted head in the window-casing of the new store being built farther down the street. Eyes had glittered at him from Pete Casey's Haven of Rest. The man knew the chance he was taking. Someone in a flush of anger might take a shot at him. To sit there in the

9

center of the little town's stage, so contemptuously unconcerned, was a jeer at good, law-abiding citizens—and others not so good. For Cole Sanborn was wanted on many counts, the latest of which was the murderous robbery of a K. & J. express car less than a week ago.

Tacked to the wall back of Cole's head, so close that his thick black hair brushed the edge of the paper, was a poster advertising a reward for the capture of the robbers. Attention was given to a short, heavy-set man dressed in the leathers of a cowpuncher, to a lank fellow in jeans; but the authorities showed more concern about the leader. He was a big, rangy, black-haired man wearing corduroy trousers stuffed into the tops of boots, a gray cotton shirt with a blue polka-dot bandanna round the neck, and a broad Stetson decorated with a band of rattlesnake skin. For information leading to his arrest and conviction the railroad would pay one thousand dollars, the state five hundred.

And on the porch of the Jonesboro House sat a man who fitted the description even to the polka-dot bandanna and the bedecked Stetson. What Cole banked on was that faint line which lay between moral certainty and absolute evidence. The train-robbers had been masked. A hundred men might feel sure Cole Sanborn led them, but none of them could swear it.

A small man, sun-tanned and wrinkled, came down the plankwalk toward the Jonesboro House.

He wore the high-heeled boots of a cowboy and walked gingerly, the weight of his body on the toes. In front of the hotel porch he stopped.

'So you're back,' he said harshly.

Sanborn's eyes danced. 'I'm back, sheriff. Can't stay away, I reckon. Got so many good friends here.'

'What's your business here?' the officer demanded abruptly.

The brows of the other man lifted, but the grin did not leave his face. 'You asking me or telling me, Magruder?'

'I don't aim to have any unnecessary killings in this town. Jonesboro don't want you here, unless—'

'—unless I put up at your hotel.'

'My advice is for you to light a shuck outa here.'

'After I've finished my business,' Sanborn concluded for him with drawling correction.

'Which is?'

'Thought I'd have a look at that gather of beeves n the mesa. If I could buy at a whack-up, I'd take a bunch of them.'

'You paying cash?'

'Right interested in my business, aren't you, sheriff?' Sanborn suggested, gentle sarcasm in his voice. 'You'll want to know next whether I'd settle with gold or greenbacks.'

The black, beady eyes of Magruder rested on the

indolent figure in the chair. The little man had no clear course of action mapped in his mind. He had been elected because he was known to be game, but this was not a question of nerve but of judgment. His fingers rubbed the criss-crossed lines that scored deeply the back of his neck. His opinion was that Cole Sanborn was guilty as hell, but a man could not take opinions to court.

'Come into money, have you, Cole?' he asked guardedly.

The big man ignored this and trod with cheerful effrontery on dangerous ground. 'I'll tell you, Magruder, man to man. I came back to help you hunt the robbers of the K. & J. express.'

The sheriff did not share the other's levity. His black eyes were hard as jade.

'You'll go too far one of these days, Cole— soon,' he predicted.

'I wouldn't go far to find the scalawags that did this job,' Sanborn replied hardily. The clatter of horses' hoofs crossing a wooden bridge had drifted to them and his eyes were on the advancing cavalcade. 'I'd look right near here.'

'So would I,' Magruder agreed darkly. 'What's eatin' you, Cole? Haven't you got any sense a-tall? Don't you know there are men in this town who wouldn't ask better than to shoot you down on sight?'

'Only they don't do it,' Sanborn murmured, his eyes still on the dust-cloud of riders.

'You can drive 'em too far.'

Five riders swept past to the Haven of Rest, the other two drew aside and reined in at the hotel.

Cole answered with light derision, his mind no longer on the conversation. He watched the two who were dismounting. One was a big rawboned cattleman, his companion a girl in her teens.

'Friends like you are far and seldom, sheriff,' the soft drawl of the man in the chair went on. 'You'd hate to see me bumped off, wouldn't you?'

'I don't give a dawg-gone when they get you if it ain't on my range,' Magruder flung back with swift emphasis. 'I'm sheriff of Boone County.'

He, too, had his eyes on those who had just arrived. A pulse of excitement beat in his leathery throat. For the man who had swung down from the sorrel was Jerry Haskell, foreman of the Circle 3 T outfit, and between that brand and Sanborn there was bitter warfare.

Haskell straddled forward, then stopped abruptly. His glance had fallen on the man in the chair.

'Of all the damned fools,' he commented aloud.

The gazes of the two big men locked unwinkingly. Haskell was the first to speak.

'So you decided to give yoreself up,' he said.

'Guess again,' Sanborn advised quietly.

Haskell swung on the sheriff. 'You arrestin' this outlaw, Magruder?'

The officer shifted a cud of tobacco from one

13

cheek to another. 'No-o. Can't say I am, Jerry. Not yet.'

'What you mean—not yet?' Haskell wanted to know angrily. 'You waiting till he's hid in the brush again before you make a move?'

'I want more evidence.'

'Evidence! What the blue blazes!' exploded the foreman. 'Do you expect a photograph of him took on the spot? Read that poster back of his ugly head. Then take a look at him. He's the spit'n' image of that description, ain't he?'

'In a way.'

'Goddlemighty! Can't you read and see for yourself, Magruder? Big black-haired guy in corduroy trousers—blue polka-dot bandanna—hatband of rattler's skin. Why, he hasn't even took the trouble to change his clothes.'

'Which ain't reasonable, Jerry. Looks like before he held up the express he'd have made himself less conspicuous. Looks like—'

'Thought he'd get away with it in the dark. You scared of him because he claims to be a killer and has a rep as a bad man? If so, say the word, and I'll do the job for you.'

Magruder flushed angrily. 'I don't need any help from outsiders unless I call for it, Jerry. If you'll prove to me he held up the train—'

'Prove! Doesn't every man in town know it? Are you a plumb fool?'

Sanborn broke in with a lazy question. He still

14

lounged in the chair. Only the glint in his steady, narrowed eyes showed that every nerve and muscle of him was keyed for instant action.

'When you arrest me, Haskell, who do you aim to get help you—that bunch of warriors that's just trailed into Casey's?'

'Gimme a deputy's star, Magruder,' blurted out Haskell. 'I'll show him.'

'I'll do what showing is necessary,' the sheriff said bluntly. 'I'm not askin' help of the Circle 3 T to run my business.'

'Which seems to be to protect train-robbers.' Haskell looked at the officer poisonously. 'Look out, Magruder. Don't get swelled up on yoreself. You're not the big boss here.'

'Who is?' cut in Sanborn.

The question was surplusage. Everybody in Boone County knew who ran it.

Samson Magruder was an honest man. His election had been a surprise, to nobody more than to Chet Radbourne, the man who pulled wires and gave orders to subordinates. The little cowman had upset the cut-and-dried ticket of the machine by defeating the politician selected for the job. But he had no desire to measure strength against the Circle 3 T because of a campaign accident. He would be swept away like a chip in a flood.

Haskell remembered the young woman with him. 'Go into the house and get a room for yourself, Miss Mary.'

15

The girl looked at the foreman with sullen resentment. 'That's an order, is it?' she asked.

'This is no place for a girl,' he said, still watching Sanborn. 'There's going to be trouble—soon.'

'I'm used to it,' she answered bitterly. 'I've seen nothing else since I came here.'

'Did you hear me?' warned Haskell curtly. 'Get into the house. I'm responsible for you.'

Sanborn looked at her for the first time. She was slender, trim, and young.

'Better go, Miss,' he advised. 'Big Chief Heap Much Talk has got notions.'

The girl was aware of an electric tenseness in the air. She looked at Haskell, at Sanborn, then turned sharply on her heel and went into the house.

Magruder spoke hastily. 'Get this right—both of you. If there's any killing here, I'm in on it. I'll jump the first man draws a gun.'

The foreman did not look at him. Not for an instant did his gaze lift from the enemy sitting there at careless and alert ease. As he looked, the white heat of his anger burned out. His native caution reasserted itself. No use taking a chance, not with all the cards stacked against Sanborn. All he had to do was to wait—take his time. The fellow had ridden into a trap. Perhaps he had not expected to meet any Circle 3 T men, though he must have known he had enemies in town. Willfully he had run the risk. Now he was caught

16

unless he moved very swiftly, and apparently he had no intention of leaving. For Cole Sanborn's audacity was colossal. Danger was the breath of life in his nostrils. He seemed to ignore rather than defy the enemies who ringed him about. Haskell could count four or five of these, not including Circle 3 T riders. There was Lauret, professional gambler, dealer at the Arcadia, who had been forced to take water during a difficulty with Sanborn. He was dangerous and vindictive. The proprietor of the place, Jim Maxon, had been drawn into the trouble, and he too had given way rather than press the matter to an issue, which had involved more than five hundred dollars as well as the prestige of the house as a square-shooting concern. Also, there was Lutz, who had tried to skin Sanborn on a cattle deal. And Harley—and Preston, bully puss gunmen from the Nation. On Main Street Cole had killed a horsethief in a duel. It was known the fellow had brothers quick on the trigger.

Haskell hated Sanborn, always had from the first hour of meeting. They had been in a poker game at Summit. The foreman was strong and masterful. Most men stepped around him rather than oppose his temper. But Cole had completely disregarded it. Later Haskell cursed himself for not having seen that this quiet, cool stranger was dangerous. As usual, Haskell had begun to bull the big pots. Smoothly and efficiently Sanborn had relieved him of three hundred dollars, cashed in, and sauntered out of the saloon. Haskell knew that a dozen men were snickering in their sleeves at him. He hated it. Rage boiled in him. But there had been something in Sanborn's cold, steady eyes that had quelled his impulse to shoot it out.

Since then Haskell had met the man occasionally, and never without anger surging in him. There was something about the fellow's look and manner, something careless and contemptuous, that stirred the bile in him. He had taken the trouble to learn what he could of Sanborn. The young man had once been a Circle 3 T rider, but even then was a rebel. An hour had come when he had publicly slapped Chet Radbourne's face and left the ranch.

That had not hurt him any with the public, but his subsequent wildness had affronted Jonesboro. The town had been a rendezvous of bad men, and he had faced down the worst of them. He had broken into the jail to release a friend of his charged with rustling by the Circle 3 T. Radbourne's warriors had dry-gulched him, and he had got away after being wounded. A wiser man would have capitalized his courage, but Sanborn let his name become anathema to God-fearing men and women. Though his strong, sardonic face was far from handsome, the eyes of many women had followed his light-stepping trail with reluctant fascination. No mother ever introduced her daughter to him. His friends were devoted, but his foes outnumbered them. With scornful derision he moved among them, knowing that he was marked for death.

Now he sat on the porch of the Jonesboro House, in the heart of the enemy country, with a devil-may-care negligence amazing in its effrontery. Haskell was not afraid of him. He would not admit that. But why take a fifty-fifty chance when it was not necessary? Sanborn could draw like a streak of lightning and fling accurate bullets with a speed incredible. He had shot Buck Travis, a notorious gunman, through the heart, though Buck had been pumping lead before Sanborn's fingers had closed on the butt of his forty-five.

'I'll give you an hour to get out of town,' Haskell said hoarsely. 'An hour. If you're here then—'

'If I'm here, maybe you'll give me another hour,' Sanborn scoffed.

'If you're here, you'll go to hell on a shutter, fellow,' the foreman warned.

'Why an hour, Jerry? Why not now?' Cole asked, smiling hatefully. 'You got to go and get those nice Circle 3 T boys ready for to entertain me? That the play?'

'One hour, Sanborn,' his enemy warned furiously. 'You hear me.'

Haskell turned and went straddling down the walk to the Haven of Rest.

Magruder was the first to speak. 'Better burn the wind outa this burg, Cole,' he said. 'Soon as you can fork your bronc.'

'I'm so dad-gummed forgetful,' Cole drawled. 'I'd meant to mention to you I had business here.'

The little man snorted. 'Business! You heard Haskell. He's done served notice on you. Right now it may be too late. An' you sit here chinnin'.'

'Don't you reckon he was joshing, maybe? With the sheriff here to protect me—'

'You know dawg-gone well I can't protect you,' Magruder broke in impatiently. 'Unless I take you to jail. Not then likely, with the Circle 3 T riders here egging on the boys to a necktie party they figure is considerable overdue. They'd bust through the jail like it was a doll house. You know it.'

'Ain't there any law in this town, Magruder?' Sanborn asked plaintively. 'Here I am, a peaceable citizen, attending to my own affairs, not interfering with anybody—'

'Peaceable hell!' the exasperated officer yelped. 'Dog my cats, you raise more cain than any other son-of-a-gun I ever saw. You're so ornery you get even yourself in trouble to see the fur fly. This minute you've got yore tail in a crack, and all you do is sit there whittling away yore slim chance. Fellow, Haskell is on the prod. He'll cut loose his dog in no time a-tall. If I was

20

your friend, I'd tell you to slap a saddle on the nearest broomtail and make dust.'

Cole pointed to the reward poster. 'You throwin' in with a train-robber like Haskell said, sheriff?' he asked with a grin.

'If I knew you'd robbed that train, Cole, hell an' high water wouldn't prevent me from arresting you. I've a good mind to do it, anyway,' Magruder said quietly.

Sanborn rose and stretched himself with a yawn. He looked at his watch. 'I reckon your advice is good medicine, sheriff,' he said. 'Gave me an hour, eh? A whole hour. Think of that. I'll be saying "Adios"!'

The big man walked into the house with the springy tread divorced a thousand miles from fear.

Magruder's gaze followed him. The sheriff frowned in puzzled uncertainty. He had not the least idea whether the man meant to play safe and hit the trail or stay and fight. To stay would be suicide, but to leave at Haskell's order, like a cur with its tail between its legs, would be the last course one would expect of Cole Sanborn. He was no hell-roaring braggart. When he started a play, he made it stick. Yet it stood out like a sore thumb that if he did not get out, hell-for-leather, he was a gone coon.

The officer shrugged his shoulders and turned away.

Chapter II
An Offer is Made and Accepted

The high-heeled boots of Cole Sanborn clumped up the stairs to the upper hall. On both sides of the dark passage were the doors of bedrooms. One of these was partly open.

He caught sight of a figure and pulled up abruptly. A slim form moved forward.

'You're Cole Sanborn,' a young vibrant voice said.

'Right, first guess,' the owner of the name admitted.

'I'm Mary Landis.'

She gave the information shyly. He guessed an imperative urge behind this unexpected introduction.

'Pleased to meet you, Miss,' he said formally.

'You know who I am?'

'Jed Burrows was your uncle.'

'And I suppose you know I inherited the Lazy B Ranch from him?'

'Yes.'

'And that Mr. Radbourne is my guardian?'

'Everybody knows that.'

'Yes, they know he got himself appointed by the

court because he wants to run my affairs,' the girl cried passionately. 'Because my range lies next to his and he needs the water my cows drink and the grass they eat if he is to be God Almighty in this country.'

'Correct,' Cole agreed.

'Everybody kowtows to him. He stands in with the court. When I spoke to the judge, he told me not to worry because Chet Radbourne would be a good friend to me if I didn't make trouble.' She stopped, anger flashing in her eyes.

'He doesn't stand in with the court,' demurred Sanborn. 'The court stands in with him. He's got the law buttoned up in his pocket.'

'Isn't there any justice in this country?' she demanded.

'I haven't bumped into any lately, Miss Landis.' A sardonic humor danced in the gray eyes. 'But I'm supposed to be biased on what justice is.'

'You know what kind of a friend he'll be to me, the same kind a wolf would be to a lamb,' she went on urgently. 'I don't want his friendship. I want him to let me alone. I don't want his riders drifting Circle 3 T stock over my range as if they owned it.'

'Better make a deal with him,' Cole suggested. 'Sell out for what he'll give. Of course he'll skin you something terrible, but it will be better to take anything he says rather than try to oppose him. His say-so goes in this country.'

23

'Does it go with you?' she asked, eyes fixed in his. 'I heard his man Haskell give you an hour to leave. Are you going? What will he do if you stay?'

'I wonder,' he murmured.

'I've heard about you ever since I came into this country three months ago. They say—'

'They say—' he prompted.

'That you're a bad man and a killer,' she blurted out. 'But that you're afraid of nothing and that if you give your word you'll keep it.'

'Maybeso.'

He waited. Her troubled eyes searched his weather-beaten face.

'Could I make it worth your while to fight for me? I'd pay you well to be my foreman.' She hurried on, impetuously: 'There's nobody else I can go to for help. Everybody is afraid of him. Perhaps you are too.'

If he was surprised at her offer, his impassive face did not show it.

'How can I be your foreman? Read that poster on the wall downstairs. I'm not only a killer. I'm an outlaw. I robbed the K. & J. express. Anyone can tell you that. It's common gossip. I'll be lucky if I can crawl into the brush alive. Say I made my getaway and you took me on as foreman. You'd be buying trouble. And it wouldn't do any good, because Chet Radbourne is sitting up there at the Circle 3 T like a fat spider with the law sewed up in his jeans.'

'So I've got to let him rob me! If I stay, I've even got to marry the man he picks out for me,' the girl lamented, torn between anger and self-pity.

'Looks like,' Sanborn agreed. His hard eyes narrowed in thought. 'Yes, I reckon Chet would play it that way, pick as a husband for you a putty man, one under his thumb, who would jump when he gave the high sign. Safer than to let you get away and try to make trouble for him.'

'He doesn't intend to let me go,' she said, fear shaking her low voice. 'I'm as much a prisoner as if I were locked up.'

He saw terror in the deep violet eyes uplifted to his. 'It's come to that, has it?'

'Yes. *Only he's not going to pick a putty man.*'

Cole read in her cry the despair that flowed like a river of woe through her bosom. He was oddly moved by her young desperation, and from a detached distance was cynically amused at his sympathy. What did it matter to him if Chet Radbourne had picked this girl to be his wife? As Magruder had said, his own tail was in a crack. The chances were he would not get out of town alive. If so, he would have to fight his way through enemies. For he knew Haskell was not giving him any hour, but was busy already setting the trap.

Yet she was such a child, so young and slim and vivid, that he could not ignore her plight. To his mind there jumped a picture of Chet Radbourne, gross and shapeless and middle-aged, humped up like a big toad, using this clean sweet girl as a pawn in his foul schemes. Even the touch of his fat hand would soil her, and she was entangled beyond escape in the net he weaved so patiently. To marry him would be the end of life for her. That was what he saw in her stricken face. She would go on living, in a physical sense, but her soul would be violated, all the zest of her ardent youth forever quenched.

Swiftly his mind reviewed the possibilities. No, he could not take her with him. To try to reach the brush country, with her by his side, would be to attempt the impossible. Moreover, the success of such a forlorn hope would defeat the purpose of it. She could not spend a week with him alone in the chaparral, while trying to reach a railroad, without losing every shred of reputation; not with Cole Sanborn, a man notorious for his wildness with women.

'There's nobody to help me,' she went on. 'The men who ride for him—you know what they are like. Even if one wanted to help me he would not dare lift a finger. Something terrible would happen to him.'

'Yes,' Sanborn agreed.

'Why do I come to you, who have your own troubles?' she asked, and at her own question wakened up to the immediate danger pressing on him. 'What are you going to do? Don't let them kill you. Get away now, before your hour is up. Hurry . . . hurry!'

He smiled sardonically. 'I haven't any hour. That was talk, a stall to duck a showdown right there. Haskell has his men posted for me.'

'Then you must send for the sheriff and surrender to him. He will protect you.'

Sanborn shook his head. 'Magruder would if he could. But he can't. The calaboose is a shack. Tonight it would be torn to pieces.'

'But—'

She paused, horror-stricken, her fear-filled eyes in his cold, steady gaze. Did he mean that he was lost, already as good as dead? If it was as bad as that, how could he stand there with not a hint of panic in his bearing?

'I'm a mighty live dead man, if that's what you mean,' he told her cheerfully. 'I've been in worse jams than this.'

'You must do something—soon,' she urged.

'What's the hurry? Haskell is figuring that I'll try to make a break and then he'll get me. Why play his game for him? Let his lads do some worrying while they nurse their guns. It won't help their nerve any. I'll make the riffle. Don't you worry about that. I never have thrown down on myself yet. Let's get back to your worries. I'll ask your own question, Miss Landis. Why did you come to me? I'm a bad man, a killer, an outlaw. What makes you figure I'm any better than Radbourne?'

'He's a horrible man. And you—you look clean.' She went on swiftly, to justify herself: 'I heard one man say you'd never killed anybody who didn't need killing. And anyhow you are his enemy.' She flung out her hands in a little despairing gesture. 'I had nobody else to go to.'

Cole was moved by her helplessness, more than he wanted to admit to himself. He was one hard, tough *hombre*, with as harsh an exterior as the stinging desert plants. For him the price of life was a wary and suspicious alertness. He could survive only if he was as instant in attack as a rattler, as swift to melt into the chaparral as a coyote. Yet his thoughts clung to her problem. If there was any way to rescue her . . .

He could find none. The half-formed ideas that jumped through his mind he rejected. They were one-way pockets, like a rabbit's burrow. To get her into more trouble would be easy, to get her out quite another thing. Why start something he couldn't finish?

'That foreman idea is no good,' he told her. 'You've got to have color of law with you in any fight you make. Chet will claim he's appointing any foreman you need. How long until you'll be of age?'

'Fifteen months. It might as well be that many years. I can't stand out against him that long. He's giving me a little time to get used to the idea of—of marrying him. Just as a concession to public opinion. Not that he gives it much weight.'

'There's one way . . . maybe,' he reflected, aloud. 'If you could marry some decent young fellow—'

'How shall I find him—put an ad in the paper?' she asked.

'The hills are full of nice lads.'

'Good enough for me, at least,' she flashed, with a flare of resentment at his casual manner.

'Don't know about that,' he answered, unstirred by her protest. 'I'm not acquainted with you. But by your own say-so you're not fixed to be too particular. It's neck meat or nothing. Chet's sitting up at the Circle 3 T, hunched up in his chair, waiting till you quit struggling. You're roped and ready to brand. It's Chet for you—unless someone else beats him to it.'

'Do you think anyone else would dare marry me, knowing he had to fight my guardian, even if I were willing to take him?'

His hard gaze swept her slim figure, her immature bosom, the dainty head poised gallantly above a slender throat. A heat wave stirred in him. She was, he thought, the loveliest thing in human flesh he had seen in many a day.

'I reckon you could find a man—if Chet didn't have you roped,' he drawled. 'But with you rounded up and in his corral, that's another story again.

He's poison, sure enough. It's a fool notion, maybe. But a husband—if he was man enough—could throw a monkey wrench in Chet's steam-roller and knock his guardianship higher than a kite. He'd have a right to run your business for you if you wished. Of course, that would just be the start of it. Chet would be in his wool right off and he wouldn't likely last long.'

'No,' she agreed. 'He'd have to be strong enough to hold his own against the Circle 3 T killers. And who is?'

In the man's eyes a light kindled. In imagination he was looking at some picture which pleased him. 'He'd have to be some curly wolf himself to make the grade.'

'Yes. Someone as savage and ruthless as Radbourne himself—and with brains enough not to let himself get trapped,' she said.

'And with luck enough to bull through when he got in a jam. Send out a call for a Wild Bill Hickok or a Jesse James, ma'am.'

A flood of color swept the cheeks of Mary. 'Someone—like you,' she murmured.

He stared at her with fixed surprise. That he had thought of and rejected himself because of his bad record was one thing. That she had thought of and accepted him was much more amazing.

The long dark lashes of the girl fluttered to the hot cheeks, then lifted bravely. Her eyes held to his.

'You're crazy,' he cried roughly. 'Hell's bells, girl, have you forgot who I am—Cole Sanborn, outlaw, killer, professional gambler? I'm the bogey man of this country here. Chet is a fine respectable citizen beside me. Mothers use my name to scare their kids when they are troublesome. I'm put up as a text by preachers to warn wild young fellows back into the fold. Me, I'm out, for a girl like you.'

'Are you as—bad—as all that?' she faltered.

'Ask the first man or woman you meet.' He bowed with ironic mockery. 'Much obliged for the compliment, but I won't do. 'Soon as you married me you'd be damaged goods. Anybody but me.'

'Even Chet Radbourne?' she asked.

'No, by Heaven, I'm better than he is, no matter how bad I am. But I'm the dog with the bad name. Like I just said, I won't do.'

'You're human, at least,' she replied unsteadily. 'And he's not. I'd be paying only for—the use of your name. I'd have to take my chance that you'd play fair, that you'd be . . . just my foreman. Any money you ask, in reason, I would give.'

'I see,' he said slowly. 'The only privilege I'd have would be that of getting dry-gulched—at so much a month.'

'The Circle 3 T men are hired to fight. This would be the same, wouldn't it?'

'Not quite,' he said dryly. 'They're hired to kill. Your husband-in-name-only would be hired to get killed. It's some different.'

31

'Would they kill you for sure?' she asked.

'Would they eat cherry pie like mother used to make?'

'And the law—it wouldn't help you?'

'No, I'd have to rely on Judge Colt.'

'Why ask, since I know the answer already?' she said, her voice gone dead. 'You're right. It's a crazy idea. I don't know you, and you don't know me. I thought—since you are his enemy too—perhaps—But there's nothing to it. You'd get killed, as you say. And nothing would be changed. I take back what I said.'

She turned to walk into her room. Cole followed her.

'Here we can see each other,' he said, mockery in his sardonic face. 'You can look for my cloven hoof, and I'll take a long look-see my own self.'

'What for?' she asked. 'I told you I'd taken it back. For just a moment I was mad, I guess.'

'Don't take it back yet, Miss Landis. We're both up against a situation that calls for desperate remedies. There are points to this thing. It would be a pleasure to me to get a foothold from which I could annoy Mr. Chet Radbourne. And I know a few willing lads who would throw in with me if they thought we had a chance.'

'Which you have just finished telling me you wouldn't have,' she reminded him.

'Maybe—and maybe not. I've been known to use a gun myself. Would I have full power to do what I decide is best? Or would you wilt as soon as the band began to play?'

'You mean—war?'

'That's just what I mean.'

'I'll not be responsible for starting anything. I wouldn't stand back of you while you shoot down riders from ambush, if that's what you're thinking of doing.'

'I'm not thinking of that,' he said, his eyes filled with a moving light that surprised her. 'We're in a position where we want public opinion to support us. We'd have to let him make the attack, then we'd yelp loud as we could about it. The trouble wouldn't be of our making, but there would be plenty of it. Don't get any other notion.'

It was what she had wanted, a valiant defender of her rights. But woman-like she drew back.

'No, I can't start anything like that.'

'It's coming, anyhow. Do you think this country is going to lie down to Chet Radbourne while he runs over everybody like he's a czar? Not on your life. Someone has to lead. I'll take a chance if you will. It's not so much of a chance for me. I'm first on Chet's dead list anyhow. He means to get me. This way I'll get a run for my white alley.'

'Would you stick to our bargain?' she flung at him, her cheeks drenched by new waves of hot color. 'Or would you think . . . afterward . . . that since I . . . had taken your name and you were fighting for me . . . ?'

'You told me that one of the things you heard about me is that if I give my word I keep it,' he said, looking steadily at her. 'That happens to be true. I'll loan you my name, because I want a good crack at Chet. It's a good name. I come of a good family, though I'm a black sheep myself. I've got the rep of a hell-roaring devil. But in my own way I'm a square-shooter. I don't rue back from any bargain I make. You'd be Mrs. Cole Sanborn to the world. To me you'd be Miss Mary Landis.'

Mary looked into the sardonic face of this outcast from society, and it did not seem to her a bad one. It was hard and reckless, but in the steel-gray, youthful eyes was the light of an audacious candor. Somehow he had contrived, in spite of the wreckage he had left in his wake, to keep his own self-respect. At the worst he was neither a sneak nor a coward, but a man ready to walk unafraid into desperate peril.

Yet she drew back for a moment, appalled at the necessity of having to make so momentous a decision. It would be a terrible risk, but if she rejected it, Chet Radbourne would be no risk but a horrible certainty. She had tried to escape from the Circle 3 T and had been taken back to the house by a cowpuncher who had evidently been detailed to watch her. Chet was taking no chances.

'Three months ago I was finishing school—in America, where people are free,' she cried, a sob in her throat. 'Now I'm in some horrible country ruled by a devil-man who doesn't recognize any of my rights.'

'I've heard of revolutions,' he said, with a swift smile. 'If we win, I'll be a patriot. If we lose, I'll be a dead dog of a rebel. I'm a poker player, Miss Landis. Chet holds all the aces in a stacked deck, but at that he might not win. I'm ready to sit in.'

The heart of the girl beat furiously. Bad man though this Cole Sanborn was, he stirred in her an excitement she could not escape. The situation made for drama. In different ways both of them were doomed. Why not take a fighting chance with the outlaw in an attempt to escape?

'All right,' she said quietly. 'When do we get married?'

'Soon as we can get the county clerk here with a license and a preacher to do the job. And that'll be right now, inside of an hour.'

Inside of an hour. The words gave her a shock. They reminded her that Jerry Haskell had given Sanborn an hour to live. Was she to be maid, wife, and widow all in the same day?

This was a mad adventure on which she was embarking, with the most notorious bad man of the district as a partner. It was probably a sin for her to marry someone whom she did not love, whom she intended to know only as her foreman. But she had to save herself if she could from the biting jaws of the trap which had gripped her.

'Send for the minister,' she said. 'I'm ready.'

He wrote a note to the county clerk and another to a minister. While they waited, the man she was about to marry discussed business with Mary Landis. She was confirmed in her opinion that he was no scatterbrained fool. The suggestions he made seemed to her pertinent and wise. They drew up papers and she signed them.

'We're crossing the Rubicon,' she said, fear in her eyes. 'I hope—'

'Keep on hoping, partner,' he replied cheerfully. 'Most of our worries scare us half to death and never happen. We're going to give Chet a run for your money.'

Chapter III
Mary Marries
a Dangerous Man

The Reverend Calvin Brown was a plump, rubicund little man who always gave an impression of being out of place on the lawless frontier. He was soft and genial and emotional, but at bottom he did not lack stamina. The proposed marriage shocked him. He looked at Sanborn, hard-bitten, bronzed, with well-packed muscles rippling beneath the skin like those of a panther. The man was strong as steel and apparently as emotionless. What Brown saw was the brand of Cain written on his forehead. The troubled gaze of the minister passed to the girl, so young and dainty and harassed. In her soft dark eyes he read stark fear. It made her loveliness more poignant without quenching it.

It seemed to Calvin Brown that this marriage had been hatched in hell. His soul recoiled from it.

'I can't marry you without having a private talk with this young lady,' he told Sanborn quietly.

'Suits me,' agreed Cole promptly, a satiric smile on his lean face. 'Let's not have any bully-ragging, Reverend. Stomp on it if you find any snake sticking up its head. It's up to Miss Landis. If she doesn't want to get married, of her own free will, there will be nothing doing. And while you're at it, you better warn her I'm a hellion, and that if she marries me decent folks won't have anything to do with her.'

The minister gulped. It took courage for him to answer this notorious killer as he did, but he looked straight at the big man as he spoke.

'I shall. I'll advise her not to go on with this.'

'Do,' Sanborn replied, with his sardonic smile. 'But be quick about it. It's got to be yes or no. We've got no time to shilly-shally.'

Cole strode out of the room and closed the door behind him.

'My dear young lady, you can't know what you are doing,' the rosy-cheeked little man began. 'This Sanborn is a ruffian of the worst type. He's supposed to have held up the K. & J. Flyer only last week. He's a desperate fellow, dangerous—'

'That's why I'm marrying him,' Mary interrupted.

'I beg your pardon,' the preacher exclaimed.

'It's his chief merit, that he's dangerous. I want someone to fight for my rights. You needn't waste time warning me about him. I know what a ruffian he is.'

The Reverend Calvin was startled. 'But, God bless my soul, if you know that—'

38

'I know it, and still I'm going to marry him,' she said doggedly.

'But marriage is a holy institution ordained of God. My dear, you must not—'

'What kind of a husband would Chet Radbourne make me?' she broke in. 'If I married him, would our marriage be ordained of God?'

Her mind, it seemed to him, hopped about like a restless bird pecking at grain. 'We're not talking about Chet Radbourne, but about this man Sanborn.'

'I've got to marry one of them, and I've made up my mind which one,' she explained. 'Chet is my guardian. I'm his prisoner. He means to make me do what he says. You haven't answered my question.'

Brown was appalled. He had no illusions about Radbourne. The owner of the Circle 3 T was evil, a menace to the county and the town. His deeds were conceived in darkness and woe followed their execution.

'I'd rather see you in your grave than married to him,' he said bluntly. Yet he spoke in a low voice, for in Boone County the walls had ears when Radbourne was mentioned.

'And I'd rather be there,' the girl answered. She was white to the lips, but she did not falter. 'I've made up my mind. You don't know all the facts, Mr. Brown. I want to marry Cole Sanborn.

It's the only way out for me. Please don't refuse to help me.'

'Of course I'll help you, but don't be precipitate. You said yourself he is a ruffian. Let me talk with Mr. Radbourne. I'll explain to him how you feel.'

'He doesn't care how I feel,' she said. 'He knows I'd as soon touch a snake as his clammy hand. It will please him to break my pride and my spirit. When you talk with him he'll "Te-he," with that cackle he uses for a laugh, and soft-soap you with a lot of lies. Then he'll grin at me and gloat over me and make me do what he says. Is this Cole Sanborn so very bad? I know he has killed men and is wild, but I've heard he keeps his word. Don't you think, if he makes a promise—?'

Mary left her question suspended in air, but voice, manner, eyes, all pleaded for a favorable verdict from him.

'I don't know how bad he is,' the minister answered. 'He's aboveboard, at any rate. They say he's faithful to his friends, but don't let that—'

'I'm going to marry him—now!' she cried.

Mary walked quickly to the door and flung it open. Sanborn was just coming up the stairs followed by the hotel waitress and the cook.

'Witnesses,' he mentioned. 'Unless you've changed your mind.'

'I haven't,' the girl replied. 'I'm ready to go

40

on—at once.' Her clear complexion was without a stain of color, but her bearing was undaunted.

They were married in the little bedroom, the two witnesses staring at the principals with wide-open eyes of startled wonder. They thought they had never seen a bride so lovely and with such tragedy in her eyes.

Sanborn did not kiss the girl who had just become his wife. Not a flicker of feeling touched his cold, hard face.

Calvin Brown shook hands with the girl. 'I hope I've not done wrong,' he said, still troubled.

'You haven't done wrong,' Mary answered him tremulously. 'No matter how it turns out.'

'It's an even steven bet, Rev., as to how it turns out,' the new husband said, imps of deviltry dancing in his eyes. 'If Mrs. Sanborn is lucky she won't be a widow until I've finished a job I've got to do.'

This was Greek to Calvin Brown. What that job was he had no idea, though he guessed it was connected with Chet Radbourne.

'I'll pray you may be happy,' he said to the bride.

A twisted, ironic smile touched Mary's pale lips. 'I'm sure I shall be,' she returned. 'As happy as I deserve.'

To the minister Cole spoke, with a disarming smile: 'I hate to hand you your hat right off, Reverend, but there are reasons why we're in some hurry. You'll hear later what they are. Both Mrs. Sanborn and I are very much obliged to you for what you've done.'

Cole followed Brown into the corridor and pressed a gold piece into the hand of the preacher. The latter rejected it, abruptly.

'No. I don't want money for what I did. I wouldn't feel right about taking it, under the circumstances. I'll ask you to treat her well. I'm disturbed about this marriage. Remember she's a young girl, sweet and good and unused to men like you. Be kind to her, no matter how harshly you treat the rest of the world. Protect her— guard her—from your own evil ways as well as from others who would harm her. Do that, and God may forgive you your sins.'

'I aim to do just that,' Cole said simply.

Something in the way he made his simple promise lifted a load from the heart of the minister. After all, while the light holds out to burn, the vilest sinner may return, he reflected.

Chapter IV
'Can't a Husband be a Friend Too?'

Sanborn walked back into the room and shut the door. Mary's gaze followed his light-footed movements. As he came forward, his muscles seemed to ripple with the easy, sinuous grace those of a panther have.

Panicky fear was in her shining eyes. Through them he read her skittery emotions. She had rushed to impulsive action. Now that it was too late, she realized the madness of it. This killer and train-robber was her husband. What folly to have thought that such a man would keep the promise he had made her.

He did not try to reassure her with pledges, but came to business in a matter-of-fact voice.

'We've got to make plans,' he said. 'Chet will be on the prod 'soon as he learns this, and I've got to light out. Can't take you with me. That's sure. There's going to be heap much war in the hills. Can't hide you anywhere in this country where he won't find you. Question is, What are we going to do with you?'

Cole thought he knew the answer, but he felt it more courteous to let her join in the decision.

'If you can't take me with you and if you can't hide me—'

'Nothing left for you to do but run away until Chet and I have finished our rumpus. I'll get you to Red Circle and you can take a train back home.'

Mary had forgotten her fear of him. It was swallowed up in disappointment. Had it come to this already, that the only result of her mad marriage was to leave two wolves to fight over her property? If she left the country, it would be as good as forfeiting her rights.

'I'm not going,' she said bluntly. 'The Lazy B Ranch is mine. I thought you meant to try to save it for me.'

'Sure enough,' he assented. 'You ought to be here on the ground. It would look a lot better. That's a fact. If it were safe. But I can't protect you from Chet. Not yet. I've got to gather what men I can. It will take time. We'll be on the dodge till I get ready to make my play.'

'I can see that,' she agreed. 'But I can see another thing too. If I run away, everyone will think I've abandoned my claim to the ranch. I have to stay here and let people know you represent me. Don't you see that's necessary to make your cause a good one?'

He saw it, plainly enough. If she ran away, the public would regard the quarrel merely as a dog-and-cat fight between him and Radbourne. To build up opinion on her side and his she had to stay. But could she do this without being gathered in again by the long arm of her guardian? If he put her in the care of good people in Jonesboro, if she gave it out that she wanted to stay there and not at the Circle 3 T, would Chet Radbourne dare take her away by force? The man controlled the county politically. He dominated the range. Fear of him reached the most distant nester. But after all this was a country which respected good women. That was branded into the unwritten code of the out-door West. How far could even the owner of the Circle 3 T outrage this sentiment?

'I'm not going back home,' Mary went on, sharp decision in her voice. 'That would be to give up the fight. Maybe you're sorry you went into this. Maybe you want to back out. If you do, say so. You can have the marriage annulled and tell Mr. Radbourne you're sorry.'

He smiled at the challenge flung at him so flatly. She was so young and slim, so full of spirit. And she had cut through to the essential fact that they could not win unless she stayed on the ground. There was a risk for her if she remained within reach, but Cole thought he knew a way to minimize it. Moreover, there was no use ignoring the fact that she could not fling down a defiance to Radbourne without running some risk. That was in the cards.

'You're sure you want to stick it,' he said. 'You know Chet and his hellions. I'll protect you all I can, but it won't be possible for me to be staying around town all the time.'

'With whom can you leave me?' she asked, brushing aside his protest.

He gave that consideration. The office-holders at Jonesboro were Radbourne men. His mind eliminated them. The Reverend Calvin Brown had not enough force in his personality, and anyhow he was a bachelor. There was Hal Peters, a lawyer, an honest man with courage enough openly to disapprove of Radbourne's venal clique. His wife was a lady much respected in the best circles of the town. Cole had never met her. He was barred from meeting women of her kind because he was a semi-professional gambler and a bad man. But she was known to be generous and might respond to an appeal from a helpless girl. It would be worth trying.

He told Mary what was in his mind. At his suggestion she wrote a note. The small son of the landlord carried it.

'I'm not so sure we won't have Chet checkmated 'far as you are concerned,' Cole said cheerfully. 'I wouldn't trust him any more than I would a rattler. He's poison. In the hills there are graves of several men he has dry-gulched. But a young lady, under the care of Mrs. Peters, if she will take you, would be different. Very likely he would lay off until he had got me.'

'What are your plans for yourself?' Mary asked.

It came to her with an odd sense of strangeness that the movements of Boone County's leading desperado now intimately concerned her—and an hour ago she had never seen him.

'I'll gather what wild devils are footloose in this country,' he said easily. 'Chet has made enemies. Plenty of 'em. I'm expecting two lads here tonight. They'll do to ride the river with, both of 'em. Before we leave town I'll make a play before Haskell. I want word to travel through this country that I'm on the warpath against Chet. I want it known I've called his bluff that he's the big boss.'

'Is it a bluff?' the girl asked. 'Isn't what you are doing really the bluff?'

'Maybeso. We'll see if I can make it stick. No use fooling ourselves. I don't claim I can. It's heavy odds I can't. But I aim to take a whirl at it. 'Soon as I can, if things break my way, I'll call for the showdown.' He stopped, frowning at her. 'There's another thing. If we play a game, we've got to play it so as to fool our enemies. You'll have to call me Cole and I'll call you Mary. Before I leave town I'll fix it so as to kiss you before folks.'

'Will that be necessary?' she asked, in a small voice.

'Yes. We're aiming to pull public opinion our way. Love at first sight, and all that sort of thing.' He added dryly, 'I won't like it any better than you do.'

His curt manner, so entirely divorced from

47

sentiment, relieved her apprehensions and at the same time stirred feminine resentment. She had been kissed before, but never by one who told her it was an unwelcome duty. The two or three lads who had won the privilege had not seemed to so regard it.

'All right,' Mary said, as indifferently as she could. 'If it has to be. A stage kiss.'

'That's right. If I act like I meant it, you'll understand. It will have to be done right.'

'From what I have heard I'm sure you know how,' the girl replied, a sting in her voice.

'When I hit the grit on my way out of town I'll likely be in a hurry,' he said, ignoring her sarcastic thrust. 'If I give a yell, come out onto the porch a-running. I won't call for you unless it looks safe. We won't fool with the love and kisses if guns are popping.'

'Shall I hear from you, about how you are getting along? I'll want to know, now that we are business partners in a way.'

'You'll hear,' he told her grimly. 'Plenty. Especially if Chet bumps me off. Don't forget that no news is good news. And don't worry. Keep yore head high, like you wasn't a bit scared of this sidewinder.'

'Yes,' she murmured, with mock humility. He was giving her orders already, and she was taking them as though he were really the head of the family. But she could not keep back an ironic fling. 'Every day will be a year till I see you again, my lord.'

A sudden boyish grin warmed his harsh face. 'I reckon you're sore as a toad on a skillet now you've got yore way. You want me hard enough to whop Chet and his Circle 3 T outfit of gunmen and soft enough to say, "Thank you kindly, ma'am," for the chance. Now ain't that a woman for you?'

'You wouldn't expect a woman to know enough to think straight, would you?' Mary asked, eyes flashing.

The laughter died out of his face. 'Girl, we're in a tight. Till we get out of it I'm boss. It's a job that has been wished on me, but I aim to handle it. You'll do like I tell you. Understand?'

She met the cold, hard light in his eyes and read there the rigor of a spirit virile and inflexible. Whatever else he might be, he was a dynamic personality. A pulse of excitement beat in her throat, stirred less by fear than expectancy. A queer exultant dread fluttered in her bosom. Her gaze shifted. She looked out of the window at the mountain peaks, crags of fire in the sunset.

'I understand,' she said in a low voice.

He swung from her toward the door, wary, motionless, brown hands resting on hips close to the butts of the revolvers in his belt. Feet were moving in the passage outside the room.

Mary's heart died under her ribs. A weight

pressed on her chest so that she could not breathe. Was this Haskell, backed by his men, ready to strike?

There came a knock on the door, a cheerful voice raised in profane greeting. The door swung open, to admit two men.

'Fellow, we're here,' the first broke out. 'With half the dust of Boone County in our throats. A li'l' drink—'

His words ceased, abruptly. He stared at Mary, his eyes amazed question marks. For he recognized her. He had seen her in town once with her guardian. What she was doing here he did not dare to guess.

'Mary, this slabsided guy who looks like a rail upended is Dave Pope. He's long as a snake, and he drags the ground when he walks. The hammered-down runt is Pete Daggett. Boys, meet Mrs. Cole Sanborn.' The voice and manner of Cole were casual.

Dave Pope's lank, unshaven jaw dropped. If he had heard aright—But of course Cole was joshing. Dave looked at his friend reproachfully.

'You hadn't ought to drap around jokes with dynamite in 'em, fellow,' he remonstrated.

'No joke,' Sanborn corrected, eyes dancing. 'Gospel truth, boys. Ask the lady.'

'But you said only yesterday you hadn't ever met up with this young lady,' Dave reminded him, still suspicious.

'That was yesterday,' Cole said. 'This is another day. Right off, we knew what we wanted, this young lady and I.'

The squat cowpuncher who had been introduced as Pete Daggett stammered out what was in his mind. 'B-but C-chet Radbourne—where's he at?'

Cole looked at Pete with mild interest. 'I don't know. You looking for him?'

'I—t-thought—'

'I don't reckon he's in town, Pete, but Jerry Haskell is here. I expect he can tell you where Chet is. What say we mosey over to the Haven of Rest and ask Jerry?'

Pope scratched his red head and looked at Mary for information. 'This fellow Sanborn is such a dad-gummed josher, Miss, you got to check up on everything he says. I reckon the old horned toad is just trying to put something over on us, but—'

'We were married not fifteen minutes ago,' the girl interrupted.

'I'll be teetotally flabbergasted,' Dave ejaculated.

'That all you got to say?' Sanborn asked, lights dancing in his eyes. 'No good wishes for the young lady? No congratulations at getting so good a man?'

The lank man ducked his head in a kind of bow, scraping his right foot back along the floor as he did so. 'I hope you'll be plumb happy, Miss.

51

It's a surprise, you might say. We didn't know Cole was a marrying man, but—'

'Didn't know it myself till an hour ago, boys,' Sanborn cut in. 'You want to look out, boys.'

He found himself intrepidly light-hearted, for no reason he could have precisely defined. Of late he had been low in his mind, dissatisfied with himself and his part in life. A monotonous vista of meaningless years had stretched ahead. That was why he had come to town and sat on the porch of the Jonesboro House inviting battle. He had wanted to drug his discontent with an adventure. Now one had come to seek him, the greatest one of his life, a hazard from which he would probably not emerge alive. He could not remember when he had been so keenly exhilarated before. Why? Was it because this crazy venture had some meaning to it, because he had gone into it for reasons not wholly selfish. He did not know, and just now he did not care.

The long, lean cowpuncher found a warm little hand in his. 'I'm very glad to meet any friend of my husband,' Mary said. 'We're going to need friends, I think.'

Dave looked into the deep, soft eyes and was lost. He was from that moment sealed to the service of this girl whose beauty, tempered like a blade, held a fire imperishably live. In spite of her delicacy there was a swift eagerness in her. He liked the tiny freckles powdered over the impudent little nose. They made him think she might be good fun if a fellow knew enough to keep his place.

'You've got one, ma'am,' Dave said promptly.

'M-make it two, Mrs. S-sanborn,' Pete Daggett stuttered when it came his turn.

'Thank you both—very much,' Mary answered, and her white teeth, strong and even, gleamed in a swift smile. 'A little while ago I had no friends. Now I have two. That's fine.'

'Two—or three?' drawled Cole. 'Can't a husband be a friend too?'

Mary answered without looking at him, an overlying pink flushing the smooth brown skin of her cheeks. 'Sometimes they are,' she said lightly.

Her nonchalance was fraudulent. What had occurred had established a relationship with this grim stranger. She might come to hate or despise or fear him. Time alone could answer that. But their lives had become interlaced and indifference was not possible. Already he stimulated excitement in her.

'Put me down as one on trial,' he suggested. 'Maybe I'll do to take along.'

'He s-sure will, ma'am,' Pete promised.

'If he don't treat you right, Mrs. Sanborn, you tell us,' Dave said, grinning. 'We'll work him over for you.'

Mary nodded, cheerfully. Already this wild adventure began to seem less crazy than it had at first.

Chapter v
More Friends

Again came the sound of footsteps in the passage, followed by a knock on the door.

'Mr. and Mrs. Peters to meet you, ma'am,' a boyish voice sang out.

Cole moved noiselessly to the door and swiftly flung it open. He was taking no chances.

A man and a woman stood there. The boy had vanished. The man was a long-legged, awkward man in a shiny coat known then as a Prince Albert. The woman beside him was in her late thirties, well-dressed and graceful but not pretty. In her thin face character was stamped.

The rough-hewn countenance of Hal Peters registered surprise and resentment. He knew Sanborn by sight and by reputation.

'What does this mean, sir?' he asked stiffly.

Mary came forward timidly. She felt shy and embarrassed at being found alone in a bedroom with these men.

'Please come in,' she invited. 'I'm Mary Landis, and I'm in trouble. Mr. Sanborn thought you might be willing to help me.'

'What has Mr. Sanborn to do with this?' His swift glance swept over the three hillmen and came

54

back to her. 'In your note you didn't mention—'

'I know,' she interrupted. 'We were afraid you wouldn't come if you knew he had anything to do with it. Maybe it wasn't candid, but I need help so badly. You will come in and hear my story, won't you?'

Peters hesitated. There was something strange and sinister about this. He had heard about this girl and been sorry for her, but no good woman had anything to do with Cole Sanborn.

Mrs. Peters took the decision out of his hands. She walked past him into the room and shook hands with the girl. 'Of course we'll listen to it,' she said warmly. This young woman needed friends, especially one of her own sex. That was all Jessie Peters needed to know.

Tears misted the eyes of Mary. It had been so long since she had met kindness from such a woman.

'You are good to me,' she said simply. 'Will you and Mr. Peters sit down, please?'

Mary told her story, as briefly as she could, beginning with the time when she had come to Boone County to take over the property left her. She made clear the hopelessness of her condition and then mentioned the desperate remedy at which she had jumped.

Peters cried out, amazed. 'Good God, you don't mean that—you have married this man Sanborn?'

'That's what she is telling you, sir,' Cole

55

answered. 'Out of the frying-pan into the fire.'

'But—but—if you knew—'

'I know,' Mary said quietly. A tide of color was flushing her cheeks, but she held her head up and her eyes were steady. 'I've heard all the stories. Mr. Sanborn himself warned me. He said it wouldn't do. He tried to dissuade me. But—there was nothing else ahead of me except something worse than death. I made my choice, of my own free will. I married the only man I know who will fight to save me. Whatever he has done—I believe in him.'

She continued to look at Peters, but her hand went out to meet that of the man she had just married. The gesture was wholly impulsive, and it set a wild song singing in the veins of Cole Sanborn. She trusted him to keep faith. He would do it until the crashing guns sounded faint in his ears as he sank into death.

Cole spoke, in a voice tutored to dryness. 'This is the point, Mr. Peters. I can't take Mrs. Sanborn with me, for I'm up against the guns of forty killers. She won't leave and go back to her old home, even if I could get her through to the railroad. Where will she be safe from Chet Radbourne?'

'In our house,' Mrs. Peters said swiftly. 'He wouldn't dare take her back to his ranch against her will if the whole town knows she wants to stay here. Even Mr. Radbourne couldn't do that.'

'I'm not so sure,' Peters demurred cautiously. 'He's a wily fox. Probably he would appeal to the law. In any case, this is a serious matter, not one to be jumped at hurriedly. There are several angles to it.'

Sanborn looked straight at the lawyer. 'One of them is that he will consider it an unfriendly act for anyone to shelter her against his wishes. It may not be a safe thing to do.'

The attorney flushed. 'I have never claimed to be a friend of Chet Radbourne. In this town that is well known. If Mrs. Peters and I decide it is right to ask this young lady to our house, you may be sure we shall do so.'

'And of course it is right,' his wife said quickly. 'You agree with me about that, Hal, do you not?'

Peters hesitated a fraction of a second. 'Yes, we shall be glad to have Miss Landis as our guest.'

'Mrs. Sanborn,' the girl corrected quietly.

'It was a slip. I meant to say Mrs. Sanborn.'

None the less, Cole knew Peters was against him just as he was against Radbourne. The lawyer would welcome Mary in her own right, not as the wife of an outlaw.

Mary thanked Mrs. Peters and her husband. 'It is a great deal for you to do. It may bring you trouble, and you do not know me at all. I am very, very grateful.'

'Nonsense,' answered Mrs. Peters briskly. 'It will do us good to have a young person in the house.'

'I shall never forget your kindness,' Mary insisted. 'Never as long as I live. I wish I didn't have to impose on you, for it isn't a light thing to make an enemy of Mr. Radbourne.'

'Better wait here until you hear from me,' Cole told Peters. 'I'm going over to Casey's to have a talk with Haskell. Likely the house is watched now. I'll arrange with him to call off his boys.'

'How will you arrange that?' the attorney asked bluntly.

Cole smiled, but there was no softness in the smile. 'We'll have a little talk.' He turned to the cowboys. 'Let's drift and find out for Pete where Chet is.'

'I d-don't care a billy-be-damn where C-chet is,' Pete said. 'I ain't looking for him none.'

'All right,' Cole said gaily, 'we'll go over and ask Jerry what time it is.'

'If you want to know the time, I can tell you,' Dave put in. 'No need to ask Jerry.'

'He gave me an hour quite a spell back,' Cole replied cheerfully. 'I've got to find out if it's up yet, haven't I?'

'What do you mean to do?' Mary asked, in a low voice.

'Surprise Mr. Haskell.'

'You'll be very careful, won't you?'

'Careful is my middle name,' he told her.

With which he led the way out of the room followed by his two men.

Chapter VI
Cole Says 'Adios'

The fire had died in the hill crotch and left a lake of deep purple with edges of glittering crimson. Soon night would flow over the valley.

Dave Pope stood on the porch of the Jonesboro House and looked up and down the street. A man was standing among the horses at the hitch-rack in front of Blossom's Emporium. Another was in the doorway of the Haven of Rest. A third sat in a window-frame of the new store that was going up. None of them moved. No casual loafers were on the street. Tensity gripped the atmosphere. It was as though time stood still, waiting for the ticking of a clock that would signal death's entry.

A squat figure lounged out of the hotel and joined Dave. They stood on the porch a minute, unhurried, apparently undisturbed. Pete rolled and lit a cigarette.

The two separated. Pete sauntered across the road and joined the motionless figure at the door of the Haven of Rest. Dave moved toward the hitch-rack at Blossom's. Neither of them hurried. As he passed the unfinished store, Dave cocked an eye up to the window-frame.

'Just watching the stars come out, aren't you, Hank?' he taunted.

Cole Sanborn walked into the picture. He strode lightly across the road, looking neither to right nor left, straight for the Haven of Rest. He did not linger. Nor did he hasten. Though his friends protected flank and rear, a bullet might come flying out of the night at him. That was a chance he had to take. Dave and Pete, by their silent presence, said 'Check!' to the men posted for the attack. This might be enough, since the victim was walking to the place where Jerry Haskell waited and was not trying to escape. Cole was betting high stakes that it would, but he could not be sure.

He reached Casey's place and passed through the swing door. Pete did not at once follow. He did not want the guard stationed there to shoot Sanborn in the back. Cole would have to play a lone hand, for the moment at least.

Those in the Haven of Rest saw Cole the instant he came into the room. There was a faint murmur, as though the wind had swept through the place. The dealer at a poker game stopped, cards sus-pended in air. Roulette players forgot to place their bets. The bartenders stared, their eyes fixed on the newcomer.

Haskell was at the bar, his back to the door. Aware of the sensation, he slowly turned his broad shoulders and stared at the man moving toward him. Not until his enemy had reached the bar and was facing him did he speak.

'So it's you,' he said slowly, rage in his throat.

'Nobody else, Jerry,' Sanborn answered cheerfully. 'You gave me an hour to leave town, you remember. Haven't forgotten my time's up, have you?'

'I haven't forgotten,' Haskell replied heavily.

'Afraid you had, so I came to remind you. I've been so busy I didn't think to go. Otherwise, of course, I'd have lit out like the heel flies were after me.'

Haskell glared at him. The thick neck of the foreman was suffused with angry color. This fellow's insolence always had that effect on him.

'You're a damn fool, Sanborn,' he said.

'Not news, Jerry,' the other responded lightly.

Cole's roving glance had swept the room as he came forward. Most of those present were innocuous citizens. Three or four perhaps bore him ill-will, but would not be likely to carry this to the point of hostilities. Lutz, playing poker, would not fight unless pushed. Lauret might, given enough backing. Except Haskell himself there did not appear to be any Circle 3 T men present. The other riders were on guard outside. Probably one of them was galloping into the hills to report to Chet Radbourne a piece of news he would not like.

'This country won't stand for a minute to have a nice young lady marry a man like you,' the foreman announced loudly.

'You mean Chet won't like it, Jerry,' Sanborn corrected.

'Don't twist my words, fellow,' growled Haskell.

Cole's white teeth flashed in a broad smile. 'You scare me when you talk savage thataway. 'Makes me all jumpy. By and by, like enough, you'll land on me all spraddled out. Why didn't I cut dirt for the brush country instead of foolin' away my hour getting married?'

'You're talking yourself into a coffin,' the Circle 3 T man said blackly. 'One of these days—'

'Now ain't that generous of you,' Sanborn drawled. 'You've done extended my time free gratis. Here I was all whipped out because my hour was up and so plumb terrified I drapped in to ask for an extension, and right off you let me know you've postponed the fireworks.'

'I told you to shove,' Haskell flung out, slamming a fist on the bar.

'That's right,' agreed Cole. 'And you're the venomous kypoote, a walawahoo from the mal pais. Fact is, I'm so blamed frightened, my legs won't track. If I didn't have nigger luck, I reckon you'd be eating me up right now. Well, I'll shove, Jerry. But first you call in those willing warriors of yours you've got stationed up and down the street to bushwhack me.'

'That's a lie,' the foreman roared.

'*Call 'em in,* Jerry.' Sanborn's voice was almost a whisper, but a bell of warning rang in it loud as a cathedral chime.

Haskell's swift glance slid around the room. A

score of fascinated eyes were watching the drama. This was a frontier town. All present knew that a challenge had been given. If it was accepted, the roar of guns would fill the room. A body— perhaps two—would crumple up and slowly slide to the floor. In that deadly silence Haskell found no help. He had to make his own choice.

Again the foreman's instinct warned him to evade the issue. What was the sense in letting the outlaw fling bullets into his stomach, even though in turn he killed the fellow? At the right time he would get him without risk.

'If you're afraid of my boys, I'll tell 'em to let you alone,' he jeered.

'Good of you, Jerry. I'm scared of them almost as much as I am of you. Call 'em in and say your little piece to them.'

Haskell turned and hooked his elbows on the bar. Sullenly he spoke to a man at the poker table.

'Jim, run along and bring the boys in. They're hellin' around somewheres outside.'

'You'll find them where Jerry posted them to bump me off,' Cole added.

The man named Jim left the room hurriedly. Tension relaxed. The croupier spun the wheel. The dealer at the poker table resumed distribution of the cards. Someone ordered a drink. For there was to be no trouble, at least not immediately. Haskell had made his choice, and that choice had been to decline his enemy's challenge to a fighting finish.

Lauret moved forward from the faro table and joined Haskell at the bar. He was a neatly built man, well-dressed, with the cold, impassive face of the professional gambler. That he was serving notice he stood with the Circle 3 T against Sanborn was apparent to all.

With characteristic insolence Cole took occasion to insult him at once. From experience he had learned that the best way to meet danger was to challenge it rather than to run away from it.

'Thought you were a capper for the Arcadia, Lauret,' he said scornfully. 'Does the tenderfoot money drift to this joint now?'

'Any objections to my being here, Mr. Sanborn?' the gambler asked crisply. 'Do I have to ask you where I may hang out?'

'Nary an objection, if you don't run on me just because Jerry has got me scared.'

A man walked into the place through the side door. He was Butch Preston, a bad man from the Nation with whom Cole had had a difficulty.

Sanborn accosted him instantly. 'Well—well, if Butch isn't among us, too. A meeting of all my friends, looks like. Come up to the bar and have a drink, Butch, along with Haskell and Lauret. My treat.'

The man from the Indian Territory declined the invitation. 'I don't like a hair of yore head, Sanborn, and I'm not drinking with you.' His wall-eyed stare took in the situation accurately.

'Looks to me like you might be right busy soon, with one thing and another. I'll tell you something, fellow. I'm not sitting in on this play. If I ever get on the prod, I won't need any help. I'll play a lone hand.'

Cole looked at him, a long, lean man with a clean brown jaw, and he knew at once that Preston's declaration was on the level. He was not going to join Haskell and Lauret if guns were drawn.

Into the Haven of Rest men trickled. First, foul riders of the Circle 3 T; close on their heels Dave Pope and Pete Daggett. At sight of Sanborn's friends, Haskell knew why his men had not obeyed the order to kill Cole when he left the hotel.

The foreman spoke to his men sourly. 'This fellow here, Sanborn, is scared some of you boys might jump him, so he crawled in here and asked protection. He gets it, for tonight only. I'm giving him time to hightail it outa town.'

'Jerry being so fond of me he'd hate to see any harm come to me,' Cole drawlingly explained.

One of the men, a black-haired, graceful fellow, looked at Cole, at the foreman, and laughed aloud. 'So that's the way of it,' he said.

Haskell turned on him, eyes blazing. 'What you mean by that, Slim?'

The black-haired man grinned at his boss with cool hardihood. 'I'm wondering, Jerry. Just a private little thought of my own.'

'Don't get funny with me,' Haskell warned.

'It's yore say, Jerry. You can change yore mind if you like. Only—'

'Got any kick coming?' Haskell demanded angrily.

'Nary a kick,' Slim answered evenly. 'But that wasn't the way you talked awhile ago. Maybe he hasn't got you buffaloed. Maybe you're just long-lost brothers. It's all right with me—if it is with Chet.'

'Keep your trap shut,' the foreman ordered, with a poisonous look.

The narrowed eyes of Sanborn rested on Slim. 'Too bad you don't get a crack at me,' he said.

Slim returned his gaze, steadily. 'If I don't,' he added.

'I reckon you was born high up on the Guadaloupe, raised on prickly pear, quarreled with alligators, and played with grizzlies,' Cole said pleasantly. 'Too bad you couldn't get along with the sheriffs in that country. But of course its loss is our gain.'

'If you'd like to read my pedigree, begin soon as you're ready,' Slim suggested, very gently, black eyes fixed on Sanborn.

Cole shook his head. 'Not now, Slim, if that's your present name,' he said. 'I'm taking things in the order of their importance tonight. Likely I won't get down to you.' He let his glance range over the other Circle 3 T punchers. 'Funny what gets swept up into this neck of the woods. About what you'd expect that double-back action four-flusher Chet Radbourne would find to do his dirty work. Ugly as galvanized sin, every last one of you. I don't know how you rank as gunmen, but you'd ought to be good if Chet's to get his money's worth, for there ain't one of you could chouse a longhorn on the prod.'

The Circle 3 T warriors stirred uneasily. They waited for Haskell to give the word, and he did not give it.

'Big business you're in, all of you,' Sanborn went on, his voice not raised, but biting clear. 'Helping that thief Radbourne steal the ranch and cattle from a girl who can't protect herself. A nice bunch of flop-eared curs you are. Keep your hand away from that gun, Mex, or I'll drill you through. I'm talking, and you'll listen. Tell Chet from me he can't cut it. He's up against a man now, not a kid girl. From now on, as the husband of the owner, I'm running the Lazy B. I'll come up right soon and relieve him of his guardian-ship of my wife's property.'

'If you don't go to the state penitentiary first,' Haskell cut in.

The cold, hard gaze of Sanborn swept to the foreman. 'Tell your slimy boss, Haskell, that my wife is the guest of Mrs. Peters by her own wish. That's where she is going to live. He's to lay off and not hound her. My orders. Tell him I've got hell in the neck, and that if he just looks at her cross-eyed I'll hunt him to his hole and pour lead in him. I'll do it, if it's the last thing I ever do in this world, so help me God. He'll get it when he's least expecting it. Tell him that.'

'You talk like you was the angel Gabriel,' jeered Slim. 'If I was running this shebang I'd call yore bluff right now. Maybe I came from the Guadaloupe like you say. Wherever it was, we'd never have let a sandy like yours ride without a showdown.'

'The showdown's coming,' Haskell said, hoarse with anger. 'Things have changed since we came to town. It's up to the old man to decide what he wants done. I don't aim to take the play outa his hands. He'll call the turn on this scalawag. Don't worry.'

'I'll not worry,' Cole said cheerfully. 'Come on, Pete—Dave, we'll be drifting.' He looked round with cool effrontery. 'Unless anyone feels hostile and can't wait. Glad to accommodate any urgent gent.' His cold, sardonic gaze ranged from one to another of the Circle 3 T men. 'No takers? In that case I'll say "Adios." '

He turned his back and walked out of the room. It was a risk, but not too big a one. For his companions still faced the enemy. Another moment, and the three friends stood together outside.

As they moved toward a hitch-rack down the

street, Cole let out a yell. The three men found their horses and swung to their saddles.

'Wait here a minute,' Cole said.

He rode back to the Jonesboro House. A slight figure ran down from the porch to meet him. He leaned down, caught Mary by the arms, and swung her to the saddle in front of him. From the door of the Haven of Rest he saw men pouring as seeds are squirted from a squeezed lemon. The stars were out, and he knew that what he did could be seen by anyone watching.

'I'm on my way, girl,' he said.

A tumult of excitement beat in her. 'Don't let them kill you,' she begged.

'Bet your life I won't.'

He held her warm, slight body in his arms and drew her close. When his lips met hers, Mary felt herself sinking in waves of emotion. She did not know how long that clamor of the blood lasted. She felt herself being lowered gently to the ground.

Sanborn swung his horse as on a dime. The animal jumped to a gallop and pounded down the street.

A shot rang out—another—and another.

The man she had married vanished in a cloud of dust.

Chapter VII
Partners in a Deal

The stars were over the flat tops when Bud Calloway reached the Circle 3 T with a message.

'Where's the boss at?' he asked of a puncher who lounged out of the stable to meet him.

'Up to the house. Where the other boys?'

'Still in town.'

Bud did not volunteer any further information. He swung from the saddle, hitched up his chaps, and bowlegged toward the house.

The ranch-owner was in the bare little room which served him for an office. Radbourne sat in front of a desk, his heavy rounded shoulders hunched, his huge body slumped in the chair. As usual he appeared to be doing nothing. When Bud came into the room he looked up, a question in his small black eyes. He knew there must be news. Otherwise Haskell would not have sent a messenger. But he said nothing. Only his jaws moved. He was chewing tobacco.

Bud did not waste words. 'Cole Sanborn was in town when we got there—on the porch at the Jonesboro House. Jerry had words with him. He gave Sanborn an hour to leave town, but he posted the boys to prevent a getaway.'

Still Radbourne waited, silently. He knew the gist of what Calloway had to tell was still to come.

'Jerry left Miss Landis at the hotel,' the cowpuncher went on. 'I dunno how it happened, but she an' Sanborn got together.'

'He broke through and took her with him? That what you're trying to tell me?' Radbourne asked, a danger signal in the beady eyes.

'No, sir. Jerry has got him penned up. The point is that Miss Landis and Sanborn got married.'

'They—what?'

Menace rumbled in Radbourne's deep voice.

'Sent for Reverend Calvin Brown and he up and married them.'

The black eyes of the Circle 3 T boss were pinpoints of fury.

'What was Jerry doing—and the rest of you?'

'We didn't know a thing about it till afterward, then right off Jerry sent me here to tell you. He aims to bump Sanborn off soon as he shows his nose.'

A dull color rose in Radbourne's pallid cheeks. 'Numbskulls and dolts! All of you. Not an ounce of brains anywhere in the lot. Why do I pay wages to such blundering fools?' He finished with venom-dripping oaths.

Calloway shifted uneasily on his feet. He found it difficult to sustain that malevolent look.

'Jerry thinks—'

'He never thought in his life. Or he would have known better than to leave the girl and Sanborn alone together. The fool will probably slip up now and let the ruffian get away.'

'He's got every door covered,' Bud said. 'Cole ain't got a chance.'

'They're only five to one against him,' jeered the fat man. 'He can fight his way out, since you're not with the boys.'

'I can hold my end up, Mr. Radbourne,' the puncher protested mildly. 'I don't aim to let Sanborn or anyone else run on me.'

'Meaning me?' asked the ranchman silkily.

'No, sir, not meaning you a-tall. You're my boss. I expect to take orders from you. That's what I'm paid for.' Calloway spoke hastily. The last man in the world he wanted to get a down on him was the owner of the Circle 3 T. He had heard stories whispered that sent a scunner through him. Men had disappeared when Chet had given the word, and echoes of their fearful exits had drifted back as a warning to others.

Radbourne showed his teeth in an evil grin. 'Don't forget that,' he advised gently.

At his gesture of dismissal, Calloway departed. Little beads of perspiration stood on the puncher's forehead. It was not what Chet said but the way he said it that left a fellow's throat dry, Calloway thought. He had not done a thing to be blamed for. Not a thing. Yet it gave him a sick feeling to have those snake eyes fixed on him, always with a veiled threat in their glittering depths.

As Bud was leaving, Radbourne flung an order after him. 'Send Jordan to me.'

Chet's shapeless body slumped down in the chair. He sat there motionless, absorbed in thought, even the restless jaws clamped.

A man came into the room. 'Calloway said you sent for me,' he remarked in a voice peculiarly flat.

'Yep.' Radbourne barked out the monosyllable and said no more. He stared at the inkstand, but that was not what he saw.

The newcomer slid into a chair and waited. He was in no hurry. Eyes cold and dead as those of a mackerel on a fish stall fastened on the great mass of huddled flesh in the seat at the desk. Jordan was a man slightly below middle height, hard as nails, tight-lipped, with a face leathery and seamed. He had the rippling muscles of an athlete. His movements were rhythmic and easy. A manner of perpetual wariness rested on him.

'What d'you think that lunkhead Haskell has gone and done?' Radbourne asked angrily.

'I wouldn't have a guess,' Jordan murmured.

'The Landis girl had to sign a paper before a notary. I sent her down to Jonesboro with Jerry—and five of his warriors. Six husky fatheads to look after one little girl, all of 'em garnished with guns. Was that enough?'

'I'd say plenty, Chet.'

'You're wrong,' the owner of the Circle 3 T barked. 'That devil Cole Sanborn was in town. He met up with the girl—and married her—all inside of an hour.'

For just an instant the dead eyes came to life. 'Someone must have been right busy,' Jordan drawled.

'Not Haskell or any of his loafers,' Radbourne snarled. 'Jerry sent Calloway up to break the glad news and to say he'd got Sanborn trapped.'

'Which makes everything nice,' Jordan mentioned in his ironic, colorless monotone.

'If Sanborn doesn't break through,' Radbourne corrected.

'Out of a trap the great Haskell fixed for him?' jeered Jordan.

The ranchman's stubby fat fingers drummed on the desk. 'We'll know about that soon, Curt. Sanborn's slippery as a fox. Jerry ought to get him, but—'

'Betcha a golden eagle to a dollar Mex he don't,' Jordan interrupted, with a thin-lip smile.

Radbourne beckoned the other man to come closer. Chet leaned forward, so that a heavy fold of his great stomach rested on the edge of the desk.

'That's where you come in, Curt,' he wheezed.

'Oh, that's where I come in, is it?'

Just as there was something catlike in the lithe, gliding movements of Jordan, so there was in

74

the patience with which he could bide his time. He would not have been a killer with so formidable a record if he had not known when to strike and when to lie in wait. Now his dead-fish eyes rested on those of his employer. Any talking that was necessary he could do after Chet had stated his proposition.

Radbourne whispered, lips close to the ear of the other man. Curt Jordan listened, his mouth a straight, cruel line. Once or twice he spoke, a terse, crisp sentence, but for the most part he held to a wary silence.

When at last he carried the talk, it was to object to the terms proposed by the man with the rounded, hunched-up shoulders.

'You've always wanted something for nothing, Chet,' he sneered. 'Most usually you get it, because the other galoot is scared of you. This time you pay full value, or I don't deliver the goods. This bird Sanborn is poison. Look what he did to Buck Travis and to that Texas man Sanderson. He's one fighting fool. Anyone who goes up against him takes a big chance. I'm right fond of my hide. If I risk it, there will be real mazuma in it for me. Quit talking as if a hundred bucks was big money. It will cost you just one thousand.'

Radbourne gave a yelp of pain. It always hurt him to spend money except when he could see a financial return for it. He began to explain how easy the job was.

'If it's so easy, why don't you do it yourself?' derided the killer.

'Haskell may have done it already.'

'If he has you've saved just a thousand bucks.'

'Five hundred,' pleaded Chet.

'You hard of hearing?' asked Jordan. 'I said a thousand. What's eating you, Radbourne? With this fellow outa the way you get the Lazy B, the girl, her money, and her cattle. Yet you try to beat me outa my measly pay. You're a lousy son-of-a-gun, Chet.'

'Don't you suppose it costs any money to run this shebang, Curt?' snapped Radbourne. 'I'm paying wages to thirty good-for-nothings who don't do anything but sit around and eat up the ranch. I have to scrabble to get my monthly payroll together. Be reasonable. Five hundred spot cash 'soon as I know the job's done, and on top of that I'll try fix it so as you get the reward offered for the fellow who pulled off the K. & J. express robbery. I can't say fairer than that, can I? There won't be any comeback from the law afterward. You'll be a public benefactor for getting rid of this scoundrel.'

'That wouldn't interest me,' Jordan said callously. 'I'm out for the dough. But I'll be fair. Get me the reward and I'll do the job for nothing. But don't try to slip anything over on me. I wouldn't stand it for a holy minute.'

'What's the sense of talking thataway, Curt?' the ranchman demanded irritably. 'My word's good as the wheat. You know that. I never in my life threw down on anyone who was square with me.'

'Don't begin with me then,' the killer advised.

The fat man slammed a fist on the desk. 'You act like you were locoed, Curt,' he cried, with an oath. 'Here we are partners in a deal, and you start off loaded with suspicions I'm trying to rim you.'

Jordan laughed hardily, without mirth. 'I know damn well you would if you could, Chet. You sit there like a fat toad figuring out ways to sweat dollars out of everyone you meet. Yeah, I've heard your smooth talk, heap much of it, but it don't fool me one little bit. I'd trust you just as far as I could throw a bull by the tail. You're a sink of iniquity, and I've helled around considerable myself. I'll just mention that I'll be watching you every minute.'

'And I thought you were my friend.'

The killer looked at the fat man, a curious contempt in his shallow, cold eyes. 'Ain't you ever honest even with yourself, Chet?' he asked. 'Don't you play the good respectable church deacon with me. I know you.'

If Jordan had been a timid soul, the look that his employer slid at him would have daunted. There was murder in it—for a fraction of a second. Then the threat was veiled, curtained by a film of wariness.

'We're talking the way crazy kids do, Curt,' the rancher said. 'No sense to it. Let's get to brass tacks.'

'Suits me. Sanborn held up the express. So you say.' There was a flare of ironic humor in the flat voice. 'And I reckon you ought to know. Can you prove it and get the reward for me when I bring him in—dead?'

'What do I run the politics of the county for? I'll see the commissioners vote you the money.'

'Good enough. I'll sleep on the trail till I get this bird.'

'How do you aim to set about it?'

'I'll go to Jonesboro, stick around there, and keep my eyes and ears open. Presently I'll find out where Sanborn is holing up. Then I'll go get him. If Jerry hasn't done it already.'

'Jerry hasn't.'

The voice came from the door.

Both men at the desk slewed around hurriedly.

Chapter VIII
Four Hands on the Desk

The fat face of Radbourne took on an expression of ludicrous dismay. Cole Sanborn leaned indolently against the door jamb, thumbs hitched in his belt close to the butts of the revolvers. He was smiling, but Chet found no reassurance in that smile.

'Hands on the desk, gentlemen,' the visitor ordered quietly.

Neither of the Circle 3 T men made the mistake of discounting his vigilance. No liberties could be taken with that manner of negligent ease. The deep-set eyes in the strong brown face were like half-scabbarded steel.

Radbourne's soft plump hands moved to the top of the desk.

'Talking to you too, Jordan,' Sanborn said crisply.

The dead eyes of the gunman did not lift from the uninvited guest. 'If I had an even break,' he said slowly.

'But you haven't. Not this time. Better luck some day . . . maybe. Put 'em up.'

Jordan looked longingly at this man whom he had just been commissioned to kill. It was in his mind to go through with it now. The fellow's insolence got under his skin. By rights Haskell's warriors ought to have filled him full of lead. But here he was, in the stronghold of the enemy, a dozen men within call, standing before them as though he were monarch of all he surveyed. There was something superb about his arrogance. He was a grim, strong fighting man. The cool, sardonic eyes were those of one who did not know fear and would not admit defeat. They suggested the wisdom of surrender. The guns so close to the competent hands would roar instantly if Jordan made a false move. No, it would not do to force an issue yet.

'You can't do a thing to us,' the Circle 3 T killer made answer. 'The boys are in the bunkhouse. If a shot was fired—'

'They would come on the jump,' Cole interrupted. 'And what would they find? Two dead men on the floor. The live man loping into the darkness they might hear, but they wouldn't see. No, Jordan, that bet is coppered. You'd never make it as easy for me as that. Put 'em up, like I said. I'll not mention it again.'

'Do as Cole tells you, Curt,' Radbourne snarled. 'Don't you see it's his say-so? No use getting het up and talking fight. We'll talk this over the way neighbors should.'

Reluctantly Jordan's hands slid along the desk and came to rest.

Sanborn shut the door with his foot. He did not lift his gaze from the two at the desk. One instant of carelessness would be fatal.

'We can talk more comfortably with the door shut,' he said. 'You wouldn't want for us to be interrupted, Chet.'

'Just before you came in, we were mentioning you, Cole,' the ranchman said, from a dry throat.

'Saying nice things about me,' Sanborn drawled derisively. 'Don't quit just because I drapped in. But I don't need to hear you talk to know how fond of me you are.'

'You figure me wrong, Cole,' replied Radbourne, with unctuous heartiness. 'I never did have a thing against you. Trouble is, you're one of these impatient lads who get notions and stick to them through hell and high water.' The Circle 3 T man tittered, on a note of simulated friendliness, palpably false.

'Good old Chet, I've been doing you a wrong,' Sanborn murmured. He saw the rancher only out of the corner of his eyes. His attention was on the other man. He read the thought behind the shallow, stony eyes. 'You did right, Jordan, in putting up your hands. No chance of beating me to the draw—*then or now.* You'll have to wait till you can get me from the brush.'

The vanity of the bad man was aroused. 'I don't need to get you from the brush. I'll take a chance with any man alive,' he boasted.

'If you have to,' Sanborn answered contemptuously. 'I know your kind.'

Again Radbourne cut in. 'Don't be a fool, Curt. He came here on business, Cole did. We'll listen to his proposition.'

'Good of you,' Sanborn said, with his thin, sardonic smile.

'You and I don't always see alike, Cole, but I aim to be reasonable. I reckon a talk will clear things up. It's been quite some time since we met up, and we've both listened to a lot of lies whispered by busy-bodies. I'm right glad you came.' Chet managed a reciprocal smile, but it was not a very convincing one.

'It's been a year since we met—in person,' the visitor said. 'But I've had messages from you since then. A few months ago I stopped a Circle 3 T bullet. By the way, Chet, you'd ought to make your warriors demonstrate before you hire them. No use dry-gulching a man unless you're thorough about it.'

Radbourne shook his head sadly. 'That's no way to talk, Cole. If any of my boys fired at you, it was without instructions from me. I did hear about one of my riders, when he was crazy with drink, pulling a gun and firing at you. I gave him his time right off.'

'Then his name wasn't Jordan?'

The bleak gaze of the owner of that name met that of Sanborn.

'I'm thorough,' he said hardily. 'When I shoot a man he stays dead.'

'So I've heard. No hospital for those you drop. Better get Jordan next time, Chet.'

The gross body of the ranch-owner shifted uneasily. 'You're barking up the wrong tree, Cole. I done told you there's nothing but a misunderstanding between you and me. Anyhow, I'm a law-abiding citizen.'

'And Mr. Jordan is here for ornament?'

The boss of the Circle 3 T brushed this aside impatiently. 'What's the use of jawing? I'm not a kid with a chip on my shoulder. And you're no fool, Cole. You came here to tell me something. Spit it out.'

'I came here to get your blessing, Chet,' Sanborn said, with a satiric lift of the upper lip. 'I've just married your ward, though I don't reckon that is news to you. Of course you'll be glad not to be worried with her affairs any more. I'm taking them over.'

Radbourne did not say what he would have liked to say. It would not do to try too far the patience back of that bitter, insolent smile. Had Sanborn come to devil him into making a false move as an excuse for killing him? That was likely. This strong, virile devil of a fellow was thorough. He had given his proofs.

'We'll have to talk that over, Cole,' he said smoothly. 'I had other plans. But no use going into that now. Spilt milk, you might call it. You and missy have certainly put the kibosh on them. Well, we got to make the best of things as they are. Can't any of us stand out against love's young dream.' He stopped, to give a cackle of splenetic laughter. 'You're certainly a young man in a hurry, Cole. I don't recollect ever having seen faster work. Some of these other lads oughta take lessons from you. You always were a knockout with the ladies. Boy, you'll have to quit hellin' around now.'

'Yes,' agreed Sanborn. 'I'm going to settle down now, Chet—on the Lazy B.'

'That's fine,' Radbourne said promptly. 'I'm too busy with my own affairs to have much time left to look after those of other folks. I felt it was my duty to see Miss Landis got a square deal, but now she's married I can step out with a clear conscience. I'll admit I was some riled when I heard she had taken so important a step without letting me know. But the more I think of it, the better I like it. You're no Montgomery-Ward cowboy, Cole. You know cows.'

There was a hint of ironic derision in the weather-beaten face that looked down at the Circle 3 T owner. All this talk was a lie, designed to put Cole off his guard. Sanborn knew that, and it got exactly nowhere.

'Much obliged for your endorsement, Chet,' he drawled. 'I was worried for fear I was a four-flusher. I reckon then you'll push your stock back off our range right away?'

Radbourne chewed his quid. 'Sure. If any of my stuff have drifted over. We won't quarrel none about that.'

'If you've got private business with Chet, I reckon I'll be going,' Jordan announced. He did not lift his hands from the desk, but a ripple passed through his lithe body, as though he were about to move.

'Don't you!' warned Sanborn, with deadly evenness.

The ripple died down. 'I'm to stay here, am I?' Jordan inquired sullenly.

'Couldn't get along without you.'

'I'll get along without you, one of these days.'

Sanborn spoke to Radbourne. Over his eyes a film had come, a shutter which left them opaque and without warmth. The muscles of the brown face were rigid, the voice cold as wind blowing across an ice-covered lake. 'Listen, Chet. I sent a message by your man Haskell, then decided to deliver it myself. I'm here to lay the law down. My wife will stay with Mrs. Peters, as a guest, until I'm ready to take over the Lazy B and run it. That will be right soon. From now on, it will be hands off. You'll not bully her. You'll not crowd her. It was up to her to make a choice, and she's done that. I've come here to tell you just one thing. If you annoy or mistreat Mrs. Sanborn, or if you harm Mr. or Mrs. Peters, I'll put you where you'll never trouble another woman. I could do that tonight, but I'm giving you one chance. Don't make a mistake. You can't hide in your hole deep enough so that I won't drag you out. Understand?'

Chet understood, but at the moment the question was put, his mind was not wholly centered upon what his visitor was saying. His face had the absent look of one who is listening intently. Through the open window had come the sound of horses' hoofs.

A man called, 'That you, Jerry?'

For answer came a raucous curse.

Voices, the stamping of horses, the creak of saddle leather, drifted to those in the room. Someone was striding toward the house.

Swiftly Cole drew a revolver. 'You don't want to be interrupted just now, Chet,' he warned.

The lean muscles of his jaw had tightened and his deep-set eyes had narrowed to shining slits, but there was not the faintest hint of panic in the cool voice.

Neither of the men at the desk spoke. Neither of them moved. But both knew the equation had changed. Sanborn had stayed too long and was now on the defensive. In another moment, with any luck . . .

The footsteps came close.

Sanborn leaned against the door. He was trapped, and as always when danger came close, he felt the lift of the spirit only dare-devils know.

'Say your piece now, Chet,' he murmured.

The beady eyes of Radbourne gloated, but he did not intend to make a mistake. He did not want to pass out with his enemy when the guns roared.

'I'm busy,' he called hoarsely to the approaching man.

'It's me,' the answer came harshly. 'Got to see you, Chet.'

Fingers turned the doorknob, but Sanborn's weight prevented the man from entering.

'Get him, Jerry,' shouted Jordan. 'It's Sanborn.'

He reached for a weapon and flung his body to the floor, and at the same time Radbourne's great bulk slid under the desk. The man outside put his shoulder to the door and pushed it open.

The noise of the guns filled the room. The kerosene lamp went out. Flashes stabbed the darkness. There was a crash of glass.

Haskell yelled an order. 'Get him, boys! It's Sanborn! He went outa the window.'

The foreman ran around the house, in time to see a man flinging himself into a saddle. He fired wildly. The answering shot plowed into his shoulder.

Sanborn lifted his mount to a gallop. Men were running across the open to cut off his retreat. Others were climbing back into the saddles they had just left.

A Mexican vaquero clutched at the bridle of Sanborn's claybank and was bowled over like a tenpin. Two others were closing in on him. One of them, on horseback, was the man Slim.

'Here's where I get that crack at you, fellow,' the black-haired cowpuncher called, and simultaneously the roar of his revolver sounded.

Voices, shots, confusion, filled the night. Half a dozen men were between Sanborn and the road. He could not run with any chance of escape such a gauntlet. Abruptly he pulled his mount round, gave it a touch of the spur, and sent it straight at a closed gate opening into a pasture.

The claybank gathered itself for the jump, rose beautifully, and sailed across without touching the top plank. Horse and rider disappeared in the darkness, untouched by the random bullets flung after them.

Chapter IX
Harmony at the Circle 3 T

When Slim walked into the office the victims of Sanborn's visit were examining their casualties, the foreman with raucous profanity, Jordan in a grim silence. The latter had a shattered ankle, Haskell a punctured shoulder. Radbourne sat slumped at the desk. The black-haired puncher guessed that rage was boiling in him.

'Mex has got a busted collar bone,' Slim mentioned. He added, a devil of mischief dancing in his eye: 'Looks like we'll have to turn the Circle 3 T into a hospital. That hell-a-miler Sanborn 'most ruined our outfit.'

'I hired a fine bunch of buzzard heads,' Radbourne burst out, an ugly rasp to his voice. 'How many chances at the fellow you want? First, down at Jonesboro, where you were only six to one; then here, with about twenty of you sitting in.'

'Including the boss, under the desk,' Jordan said viperishly.

'Six to one, Jerry, and you figured it too dangerous,' Chet went on, disregarding Jordan's thrust. 'What kind of odds you looking for?'

The bull-necked foreman glared at his employer angrily. 'I told you he had two guys with him, and I told you, too, why I didn't bump him off. After he'd married the girl, I thought you might want to figure out some other play. If you want him so bad, Chet, you had a chance to get him your own self. Why didn't you plug the scalawag?'

'Buzzard head is right for me,' Slim said cheerfully. 'I took a crack at him in town and another here. No damage. His bronc was moving right lively both times. I'll say that for myself.'

'Chet didn't plug him because he never did have a thing against Sanborn,' explained Jordan ironically, his cool, flinty eyes on Radbourne. 'They're good neighbors, only busybodies have been telling them lies about each other. I was expecting Chet to kiss him.'

'He had the drop on us from the moment he stepped into the room,' Radbourne said, a dull flush suffusing his heavy face. 'If you'd had your way he would have finished us both right here. I use my head, Curt.'

'You sure do,' agreed Jordan. 'You'll never hear me say again a fat man is slow-moving. The way you slid for cover! You didn't aim for to stop any bullets, did you, Chet?'

'Take me for a fool?' the ranch-owner demanded. 'Think I wanted to sit there and be killed?'

Jordan looked at his ankle with disgusted resentment. 'Well, I'm climbing a horse to go see a doc at Jonesboro,' he announced. 'Any other buzzard head going with me?'

'You've got my company,' the foreman said sourly.

'I reckon Mex will trail along with you,' Slim said, decorously suppressing a grin. 'But you boys want to be careful about meeting this hell-a-miler. If he jumps you with only three of you present, no tellin' what all he'll do.'

Jordan looked at the graceful, black-haired puncher out of opaque, stony eyes. 'I wouldn't make any more funny cracks like that, Slim,' he suggested, almost in a murmur. 'My ankle hurts like hell, and I'm sorta irritable right now.'

Slim was reckless, but he was no fool bent on suicide. 'Take it back, Curt,' he apologized promptly. ' 'Course I know Sanborn got a lucky break. I was only joshin'. No offense meant.'

Snarling, Haskell turned on the Texan. 'Where I come from a thirty-dollar waddy don't horn in with advice like he was boss of the outfit. Myself, I've had about enough of you. Maybe you're one bad *hombre* down in the brush country where you was raised, but that line don't go up here. You're just a dog-goned cowpoke here.'

'Did I claim I was a bad *hombre*, Mr. Haskell?' asked Slim silkily. 'If I did, I reckon I'll have to demonstrate any time you call my bluff.' The man from the Lone Star State did not raise his voice, but the last six words were spaced, evenly and deliberately.

With an oath Radbourne brought a fist down

91

heavily on the desk. 'What do I pay you scalawags for?' he snarled. 'If you're on the peck so big, quit fussin' with one another and go get Sanborn. I ain't interested in listening to your quarrels. 'Far as I can see I haven't got a rider worth a barrel of shucks. Gimme results. I'm the big auger here 'long as I pay the bills. Understand? Swelling up and claiming you are big chiefs don't explain away the fact that Sanborn makes you all look like plugged nickels. You rock along to the bunkhouse where you belong, Slim. I'll have a private word with you, Jordan, before you go.'

'Looks like I'm being handed my hat,' Slim said coolly, and forthwith departed.

The foreman followed him sulkily. He did not know why there should be close conference between the boss and Jordan which excluded him.

'I'm in a hurry, Chet,' Jordan told his chief shortly. 'Get it off yore chest, whatever it is.'

'Stick around Jonesboro till your ankle heals up, Curt,' said Radbourne meaningly.

'What I aim to do,' Jordan answered, looking straight at the fat man.

'Sanborn will come slipping in to meet his new wife. They're all alike when it comes to a woman. She's a good-looking little wildcat, and he'll buzz around her the way a bee does around clover blossoms. The poor fool has framed himself for you. Just keep an eye on the Peters place.'

Jordan meant to kill Sanborn before he returned to the ranch. The lust for revenge burned savagely in him. But he was in no humor to give Radbourne the satisfaction of knowing it.

'I'll please myself about that,' he said dourly.

'A sure thing,' the owner of the ranch said persuasively. 'Candy from a baby.'

'That's what you were telling me just before you dived under the desk.'

'Don't you see how easy he has made it, Curt? He'll be crazy about this wench. He doesn't know the little devil married him just to take a slap at me. I'd like to give her a good quirting, and one of these days I will.'

'That all you've got to tell me?' Jordan asked sourly.

'That's all.' Chet leaned forward and whispered. 'Fifteen hundred *dolares* waiting for one little crook of your finger.'

'Have someone bring my bald-faced roan round here,' the gunman ordered. 'I don't aim to do any unnecessary stepping on this ankle.'

'That's right,' Chet agreed. 'I'll go tell one of the boys to rope and saddle for you.'

Radbourne waddled out of the room. Anger surged in him, but he did not dare to show it. After all, no matter what Jordan said, the man would never let Sanborn get away alive after what he had done.

Chapter X

Hotter Than Hell
with the Lid On

The blast of the last gun died away as Cole rode rapidly across the pasture. His heart was high in him, lifted by the elation that often came after passing through danger. His enemies might follow him a little way, but not for far. No profit for hired warriors was to be found in pressing a dangerous foe too closely. A Circle 3 T man could save his face with Radbourne by the plausible excuse that night had swallowed the fugitive.

At the pasture boundary Cole swung from the saddle, cut the wire with his nippers, and rode into the rough country beyond. It was a night of pale suffused moonlight. To his left he could make out dimly the barranca running almost parallel to his line of travel. In the shadowy gloom the desert had taken on the magic charm of mystery. Details were blurred. One did not notice that the vegetation was gray with alkali dust, that the sahuaro had the desiccated look of extreme old age and were not glorious candelabra. The sunbaked plain, scene of a million fights for survival against drought and other extinguishers of life, did not show its teeth as it did in the untempered atmosphere of day.

Expertly the claybank wound a path among the mesquite and the cholla. It dropped down a steep bank into a wide dry wash. Here Sanborn guided to the left, following the bed of the old river in its devious way to the mountains.

Before him rose a castle formation, left standing stark against the sky by ages of erosion. As he came closer, its architecture became more visible. Ramparts and bastions stood out above the sheer cliff of the lower wall.

He drew up his horse and gave a hail. From the foot of the precipice a voice shouted answer. Two horsemen loped out to meet him.

'You durned old alkali, I'm sure plumb glad to see you,' Dave Pope cried joyfully. 'I was scared you never would come back from that crazy trip. We been restless as a pair of toads on a hot skillet.'

'D-did you s-see Radbourne?' Pete Daggett stuttered.

'Yes, I saw him,' Sanborn replied. 'Had a nice little chat with him.'

'Well, fellow, hop to it,' demanded Dave. 'Yore story moves like a snail climbing a slick log. What happened?'

Sanborn showed his white teeth in a gay grin. 'Nothing much. I told him where to get off, took a crack at him, and said "Adios, amigo." '

'What you mean—took a crack at him? Did you have trouble?'

'Me? No, I didn't have any trouble. I left some at the Circle 3 T, I reckon, because some of the boys got on the prod.'

'You kill someone?'

'No. They got to kinda crowding me and my old Tried and True stopped a couple with a pair of pills. Haskell and Jordan. Only winged 'em.'

'Haskell and Jordan!' Excitement blazed in Dave's pale blue eyes. 'You're not just a-loading us, Cole? You did get those sudden-death artists?'

'Nothing permanent about it,' Sanborn apologized. 'Didn't stop their clocks for keeps. Fact is, I was in quite some hurry at the time. The Circle 3 T boys were buzzing around me like angry bees. I hadn't time to be thorough.'

'S-sounds like it might have been h-hotter than hell with the lid on,' Pete suggested. 'T-tell us more.'

'You're so dad-gummed tight you never give another guy a chance to get in on the fun,' the lank puncher complained querulously. 'It would have cost you nothing Mex to have taken me an' Pete along. But no, you gotta play a lone hand. Serve you right if those buzzing bees had stung you proper.'

'You know why I didn't take you, Dave,' his chief said amiably. 'My only chance was to drop in on Chet unexpected. If I took an army with me,

I couldn't do that. Besides, I wanted him to know his bunch of warriors didn't scare me any. As it turned out, my luck stood up fine. I saw Chet and we had our talk. 'Seems I've done him wrong. He's quite a friend of mine, by his way of it.'

'You don't say.'

'Yes. He's plumb glad I married his ward, because now he won't have to spend his time looking after her affairs.'

'Fine. Now tell us all about it. Begin at the start.'

Cole told his story as the three rode side by side into the cañon which cut like a sword cleft through the hills. They moved up a dry arroyo until it pinched out, after which they clambered up a steep rock chimney, loose rubble sliding down under the hoofs of the horses. This brought them among the hilltops. They turned south, struck a ledge trail, and dropped down into a pocket wooded with live oaks.

Here they found a camp, and in it a man just aroused from sleep. He jumped for the shelter of a tree before asking any questions.

Cole hailed him a second time. 'Don't get busy with that scatter-gun, Dunc,' he added. 'We ain't after your scalp. Friends. Dave and Pete and Cole.'

Duncan McCoy emerged from cover. 'Might as well kill a fellow as scare him to death. I was sleeping awful sound when you woke me. Thought maybe it was old Magruder with a posse. You never can tell.'

'If you'd live a good life the way I do, you wouldn't have to roost 'way up here where a fellow had orta have hooked horns to reach,' Dave reproved the camper.

McCoy was a blue-eyed man, with red hair and sandy complexion, somewhere between thirty-five and forty. He was bull-necked and heavy-set, but he had moved with extraordinary rapidity when he had jumped for the tree. There was not an ounce of fat on his thick body.

He spoke with the faintest brogue. 'I've admired your good life, David man,' he said. From his pocket he drew a poster which could not be read in the dim light. 'Now this tall man in jeans, wanted for robbing the K. & J. express. It wouldn't be David Pope by any chance, would it?'

The Scotchman's pawky smile robbed the question of offense.

'No, Dunc,' Dave answered cheerfully. 'And the rangy black-haired bird in corduroy trousers and polka-dot bandanna wasn't Cole. I'm wondering if the heavy-set one in leathers was that well-known hoot man, Dunc McCoy. 'Course you don't have to confess, old oat-meal-and-scones, if you've been holding up trains as seems likely.'

Cole was no longer in corduroy trousers, so far as could be seen by the naked eye. If he wore them, a pair of well-worn shiny chaps hid the incriminating fact. But the polka-dot bandanna and the decorated Stetson were in evidence.

'You looking for the K. & J. holdups, Dunc?' he asked. 'If you are, there's no reason why you can't go back to Jonesboro and join Magruder's posse. I've brought you good news. That fellow Gildea that you plugged is going to make the grade. You didn't shoot straight enough. Also, those present when the fracas took place say Gildea was reaching for his gun when you cut loose. So all's well along the Potomac. Except, of course, that some of the other Circle 3 T warriors may not like what you did.'

Relief showed plainly on the rugged face of McCoy. This was better news than he had dared to expect. But he chose to comment on the sentence of Sanborn that was of the least importance to him.

'You're damned whistling they won't like it,' he admitted. 'I'll have to roost a long way from their range.'

'Unless you throw in with us, Dunc,' Cole said. 'We've declared war against the Circle 3 T. One of these days hell's going to pop.'

'It started popping tonight,' Dave put in. 'Cole went up to old Chet's bailiwick and read him the riot act. Haskell and Jordan crowded him and he gave 'em hail Columbia.'

'M-made 'em step high as a blind dog in a field of stubble,' Pete grinned.

The cold blue eyes of McCoy glittered. 'Tell

me about this war, Cole. I might be interested.'

Sanborn told him what had taken place in the past eight hours. Before he had finished the tale, McCoy had made up his mind.

'Count me in,' he said quietly. 'There'll be no peace in Boone County until the claws of this wolf are cut.'

Cole told him of his plans, as far as he had made any. He was going to gather a bunch of riders he could trust, after which he meant to try to force Radbourne into a position where he would be forced to attack.

The four men rolled up in their blankets and slept till the first gray gleams of dawn began to sift into the sky. One of them brought in the horses while the others made coffee and cooked steaks from a *ladino* beef McCoy had killed the day before. Breakfast finished, the camper packed the sawbuck saddle cinched to his spare mount and threw a diamond hitch expertly so as to take up all the slack.

The world was still mysterious in the dim morning light when they set out. From the summit of the ridge, after a long climb, they looked down on a caldron of opaline mist which filled the valley into which they were about to descend. The crystal light of dawn began to lose its magical radiance as the sun rose and the desert stars vanished.

An hour later they were crossing a mesa

quivering with heat. Lizards clung to the rocks. Dust eddies whirled in spirals. The soapweed and the cacti were stunted and parched. Even the mesquite leaves were shriveled.

'Dry as a cork leg,' Dave commented. 'Not a sign of filaree. Betcha there hasn't been a rain in a year.'

All of them were glad to escape from the burning heat into the shadows of the box cañon beyond.

Chapter XI
'I'll Ride You with Spurs'

As a killer, Curt Jordan had only one defect. He was a swift and deadly shot. He was as ruthless and as patient as an Apache. His assassinations were staged with a minimum risk to himself. But he was subject to sullen depressions, during which he bolstered his spirit by heavy, steady drinking. Until he had wiped out Sanborn this moodiness would be riding him hard. He spent a great deal of time at Casey's Saloon staring in front of him, a bottle and glass on the table.

Gildea was in town. The bullet from Dunc McCoy's gun had put him in bed for weeks, and only during the past few days had he been up and around. Since the man was still on the Circle 3 T payroll, Jordan used him to scout the neighborhood around the Peters house. Ten days had passed, and as yet there had been nothing seen of Cole Sanborn. If he had been in town, he had slipped in and out very quietly. Neither Gildea nor Jordan had learned of anybody who had seen him.

Twice Jordan had seen Mary Sanborn on the streets with Mrs. Peters. The sight of her, so light-footed and so carefree, so unaware of him when they came face to face, stirred the rage in him. She was a reminder of the fact that the man he was waiting to get still rode the hills unhurt. The more he drank, the stronger became his desire to send her back to the Circle 3 T. Radbourne had not given orders to that effect, but the wishes of the boss did not weigh heavily with Jordan. By capturing and removing the girl, Curt would score against Sanborn. Very likely, as soon as Cole heard of it, he would head for town bent on a rescue.

Jordan came to an abrupt decision to play this game his own way. His brain muddled by drink, he let his grudge outweigh discretion. To Mexico with Chet's caution! He would send this girl back where she belonged.

Gildea was reluctant, but he had not the nerve to stand out against the implacable gunman. Protesting that this was no responsibility of his, the man at last consented to do as he was told.

They knew that every morning Mary took a long walk, usually up the hill trail back of the Peters place that led to the summit of old Bald Knob. Gildea watched her start, then rode to Casey's Haven of Rest and notified his companion.

The bald-faced roan was tied to the hitch-rack in front of the saloon. Jordan swung to the saddle and the two men rode away.

Half an hour later, Mary came face-to-face with

them at a bend in the trail. At sight of them the stomach muscles of the girl collapsed and she went cold inside.

'Morning, Missy,' Jordan said, with a cold, evil grin. 'You're going for a little ride.'

'No,' she protested faintly. 'You can't—you've got no right—'

The dead mackerel eyes of Jordan held to hers steadily as he moved forward. They held her motionless.

'Don't touch me!' she cried.

He caught her by a wrist and dragged her to one of the horses, then lifted her to the saddle.

Fear swept her in waves. 'Where are you taking me?' she asked.

'You'll find out,' Jordan told her. 'Get going, Gildea!'

The cowboy led the way, holding the bridle of her horse. Jordan watched them go until the two riders had disappeared around the side of the hill. He limped back toward town.

The riders struck the hill road that ran parallel to the main one in the valley below.

'We're going to the Circle 3 T,' Mary said.

'You've done guessed right,' Gildea said, chewing tobacco stolidly.

'If you don't let me go at once, my husband will settle with you for this.'

'Yore husband who is on the dodge?' he asked impudently.

'I have friends in Jonesboro. They won't let you do this to a woman.'

'Let 'em talk to Curt Jordan—or Chet Radbourne. I'm only an escort to see you get home safe. You ain't any of my responsibility.'

'Then if I'm not you can let me go,' she urged. 'I'll pay you well.'

He shook his bullet head stubbornly. 'No use talking, Miss. I've got my orders. I aim to carry them out.'

Mary tried to talk him out of this, but the fear of Jordan and of Radbourne was too heavy on him. Defeated, she fell back into silence.

The windmills of the Circle 3 T heliographed to them the rays of the sun. After a time they rode up to the office of Radbourne.

By this time Mary had recovered her courage. She walked straight into the little room where the owner of the ranch sat hunched in a chair behind the desk. Gildea followed.

Chet looked up. His little pig eyes stared at her in astonishment. 'What you doing here?' he demanded.

'That's what I've come to ask you. This man, and that other ruffian of yours—the one they call Jordan—caught me while I was taking a walk and forced me to come.'

'Is Curt here?' Radbourne asked of Gildea.

'No, sir. He had me bring her on his horse.'

'Why?'

'I dunno why. He sent you this-here note.'

Radbourne read the note and grunted. 'All right, Gildea. *Vamos*!' To Mary he said, snarling: 'You did a fine day's work, Missy, when you married this scoundrel Sanborn. The killer came up here and tried to murder me. He wounded three of my boys.'

Mary had heard the story. It was common talk around Jonesboro.

'That's not true, that he tried to kill you,' she said.

'Don't talk to me thataway. I've a mind to wear you to a frazzle with a blacksnake,' he growled.

The pulse in her throat beat fast, but she looked at him level-eyed. 'My husband told me if you ever hurt me he would settle with you. Didn't he say the same to you when he called a little while ago?'

'He's not your husband. I won't stand for it. Not for a minute. You're under age and can't marry without my consent.'

'But I did.'

'I'll have it annulled. He's a notorious character —a gambler, a dissolute ruffian, a killer, and an outlaw.'

'You can't have it annulled without my consent, and I'm not going to give him up.'

He slammed his fat fist on the desk. 'What's the matter with you? Looks like you gone crazy, to marry a fellow you'd never seen before, and

106

then to pick the worst bad man in this country.'

'I picked a man, anyhow,' she said, and for a moment fire gleamed in her eyes. 'He's not afraid of you and all your men. I'm not afraid of you now. I know if you do me any harm, he'll make you pay for it.'

'Don't you think it,' he told her venomously. 'He's skedaddling into the brush country fast as he can go, not daring to stay put more than a few hours, scared to death for fear I'll get him.'

Mary laughed, mocking him, looking down at him with a touch of contemptuous defiance. 'He must have been terribly frightened, or he wouldn't have come here and stood your whole ranch on its head.'

'Listen, girl.' The jet eyes in the fat, pallid face fastened to hers. 'Men have got in my way before, and they're buried in the desert without a slab over 'em to mark the spots. Nobody can interfere with my plans and not rue it. This fellow Sanborn is not one-two with me. If he'd 'a' had a lick of sense he would have killed me an' Jordan when he had a chance. Instead of which he sloshed around bragging what he was going to do until his chance was gone. He'll never get another break like that. I'll hunt him down like I would a wolf. Your friend the killer ain't thorough enough to stand up against me.'

He looked more like a swollen toad than ever. His clammy, unwholesome face and hands sent a shudder through her. They seemed to her an expression of almost reptilian personality. Everything about him was repellent to her. His thoughts, she felt sure, were slimy. Even the way he shuffled across the room was gross and earthy.

To her mind there jumped in contrast the picture of another man. If the stories told about him were true, he too was beyond the pale. But out of him was born something vital and clean that challenged the facts. The light ease of his tread, the sinuous strength of the arrogant shoulders, the indomitable courage back of the recklessness, even the sardonic insolence of the eyes, somehow carried reassurance to her troubled soul. That he was tough as hickory and hard as steel she knew. His lawlessness had become a proverb. In his turbulent life he had done evil. Men and women looked at him askance. Yet she was convinced, regardless of his bad reputation, that there was in him a residuum of clean decency. That was what differentiated him from this fat slug whose gloating gaze sent shivers up and down her spine. He had a code of his own by which he lived, and because of it he would do to ride the river with, to use his own phrase.

'Perhaps your men will kill him.' A faint tremor passed through her slight body, but her voice did not quaver and her steady eyes did not fall.

'If so, it will be because there are many of them and only one of him. None of you would face him on even terms.'

He shrugged his shoulders. 'You mean that he's a fighting fool. That kind is the easiest to trap.'

In spite of her fear there was a momentary burst of song in her. She saw him, strong and confident, breaking through the nets spread for him. 'Jerry Haskell didn't find it easy at Jonesboro. You and your twenty men didn't find it easy here.'

Chet looked at her in black anger. 'You talk like a besotted idiot. It sounds like you've gone off your head about this ruffian. Don't you know what he's like, that you'd have to share him with every paid woman in the cowtowns?'

At his brutality she flushed scarlet. 'You wouldn't say that if he were here!' she cried.

'Everybody will say it and snicker at you. The fellow's a no-'count scalawag.'

'He's my husband,' she answered.

'You poor fool, d'you think you can make me the laughing-stock of the country?' he broke out, in a sudden fury. 'Why, I'll break you like I would an obstinate colt. I s'pose you thought you were doing something big, getting Sanborn to go cahoots with you in interfering with my plans. I've been too easy with you. That's the trouble. You'll walk a straight line from now on, girl. 'Soon as I've collected his scalp I'll put my brand on you. Don't think anything else. And, by

Gad, I'll ride you with spurs, you li'l' wildcat. I'm through humoring your airs. When I snap my fingers you'll come running, or you'll get a taste of the whip. Now get outa here and go to your room. If I see any more of you, I'll start the quirting tonight.'

'You're not going to send me back to Jonesboro,' Mary said.

'No. I'm going to keep you here, where you belong, on your guardian's ranch.'

'If you do, you will be sorry. I promise you that.'

It was strange, but she was no longer afraid of him. She had met a man, and some of his iron nerve had flowed into her. She looked at Radbourne out of eyes hot and hard. The nails of her fingers bit into the palms of her clenched hands.

'I'll never, never do as you say,' she said, with a flare of feminine ferocity. 'I'd rather die.'

She turned and walked swiftly out of the room, the hot color of defiance still in her cheeks.

Chet followed her, to make sure she was securely locked in.

Chapter XII
A Respectable Married Man Goes to Town

Five men were camped in the wooded pocket between two hills far up on the range. The night was chill and they were taking it easy before the fire. Wind soughed through the tops of the pines.

One of the men was a wrinkled little oldtimer. He picked up a live coal in his leathery fingers, dropped it in the bowl of his pipe, and leaned back against a saddle, his star-topped boots stretched toward the flames. That some of the younger men were 'running on' him good-naturedly because of the tall tales he was telling did not disturb him in the least. A large part of his life had been spent before campfires swapping lies.

'That's the worst of meeting up with a lot of one-gallus young squirts like you-all,' Rusty Hunter said placidly. 'Tell 'em the truth, and they know so dog-goned much they won't believe it. This bronc Sage I'm tellin' you about was ten years old. That's the best age for a cutting horse. Gentlemen, hush. I could read a list of brands to him and he'd go into a herd and cut out the beef steers I wanted. It got so when the critters saw him coming, they would go out of their own accord.'

'Y'betcha!' corroborated Dave Pope. 'They got a gold statue of that bronc on the state capitol grounds. The brass plate below it says, "Talked to death by Rusty Hunter." They claim that bronc druv a trail herd to Roswell all by its lone. The boss said to take 'em to old man Chisum, and, by jolly, this here Sage up and done it.'

Hunter turned reproachfully to Cole Sanborn. 'Didn't I tell you? Just a bunch of pilgrims that don't know rattleweed from grama grass. All they can do is sit on their spurs and cackle at what a fellow who knows says is so. Not a lick of sense. Me, I was taking a trail herd to Dodge when these pore plugged nickels were in diapers. I recollect onct on the trail we had a tenderfoot along looked just like this fence rail who calls himself Dave Pope. We had just crossed the Brazos in flood. We swum the herd, and you could just see the tops of their horns and the ends of their noses. Well, the boss didn't know what in time to do with this no-'count young rooster that had been wished on him, so finally he sent him out to grease the chuck-wagon. By and by this bird comes back plumb full of smiles at himself. That hairpin had greased the whole wagon—sides, back, spokes of wheels, the whole durn thing, except the axles, which he claimed he couldn't get at. Like I said, he was the spit'n' image of Dave here.'

Dave grinned. 'I ain't claiming you're not old, Rusty. Folks say you came out here skinning a mule team when these hills were holes in the ground. An oldtimer done told me once you must be two years older than God because you looked like Methuselah when he was a kid. Naturally I got a lot of respect for age and—'

Hunter snorted. 'Old! Who said I was old? I could ride out a blizzard today long after you had turned up yore toes to the daisies. I can throw and hogtie a three-year-old quicker'n you any day in the week. There's twenty dollars in my jeans says so.'

Cole stretched his long body in a yawn. 'I'm not so young as I once was myself. Anyhow, I'm going to roll up and get some sleep. Don't forget we hit the trail by daybreak.'

Amiably Dave jeered at him. 'Yeah, Cole, you're so wore down you don't hardly throw a shadow. The old gray mare ain't what it used to be. When a man or a dog or a horse gits stove up onct it's fare-you-well to the frolicsome days of youth. You're not fit for much any more except to wrangle Mary's little lamb on the sage flats. I reckon if we got into a rookus you couldn't hardly handle more'n three or four of us lads now simultaneous. You an' Rusty get yore blankets and we'll tuck you in nice.'

'Hmp!' snapped Hunter. 'I'll do you, fellow, like I done a tenderfoot at Wamsutter, Wyoming, onct.

We was at the hotel, him an' me and a fellow called Jimmy Bounce. We was sidekicks, Jimmy and me. There was only one bed, so I says to the tenderfoot, real generous, "You take it." He looked kinda surprised, but he took it. After he got sound asleep, Jimmy and me lifted him, nice and tender, to the floor, and we had a comfortable night in the bed.'

The pack-horses were loaded and lashed while a pale moon was still riding high in the gray morning sky. The cavalcade dropped swiftly down through deep gorges filled with mist to the flats leading to the mesquite desert.

From the top of a high mesa they looked down into a deep well of space, the bottom of which was shrouded in the obscurity of fog.

'Looks like some giant a million years ago plugged the earth's rind and druv the plug in a ways,' Rusty remarked.

They wound down to the desert through a manzanita cañon. Before they reached it the sun had swept away the last of the mist. The riders fell into a road gait and jogged across the shimmering plain. The desert showed its teeth. White bones of cows met the eye. Every bit of scant vegetation carried spines for defense. In the sting of reptiles lurked death. The struggle for existence here was a continual fight. Even the plants strove incessantly, sending roots far down for the scanty supply of water necessary to keep them alive. What was true of the desert products applied in varying degrees to the men now moving swiftly toward the hills so illusively near. Of some of them at least it could be said that they had survived because of the toughness of their fiber and the sharpness of their sting.

The day was still young when the party reached a cottonwood arroyo above Jonesboro.

'Throw off here, boys,' Sanborn said. 'Rusty and I are going down to have a powwow with some of the respectable citizens of Jonesboro. I aim to look like a reasonable gent sticking up for his rights against a scalawag who has done me and mine dirt. You'll understand why I can't take you rapscallions with me. I'd get the horse-laugh.'

His smile was one of friendly derision.

'Are you claiming you got a better reputation than we 'uns?' Dave demanded, grinning at him. 'If so, you're certainly loading yoreself, young fellow.'

'I'm a reformed character, Dave, and a fat chance I'd have of getting anyone to believe it if I rode in to town surrounded by a lot of tough *hombres* like you, every last one of you bristling with guns.'

'You got a consid'rable nerve,' Dave demurred. 'Me, I'm a preacher's son. But the point that sticks out like a sore thumb is that you're liable to get into a rookus down there with no friends present except Rusty. We could drap in, kinda accidental, and clutter up the scenery while you have yore powwow. That sounds to me like good medicine.'

'No, Dave. I'm not going down there looking for trouble. The idea is that I'm a humble hillbilly, as they call them in Tennessee, trying to make a stand against the great mogul who is robbing Mrs. Sanborn. I've got no friends. I'm playing a lone hand, and I've come to get advice from smarter men.'

'Who are these smart galoots, Cole?'

'I thought I'd talk with Hal Peters and Judge Fairley and James K. Cross, all of them props of the community.'

'You'll play a lone hand onct too often,' grumbled Dave. 'S'pose you meet up with Jerry Haskell—or Lauret—or Butch Preston, say?'

Cole smiled. 'I've met them before, Dave. They didn't molest me. I'm not expecting to visit any palace of sin. Don't you worry. Rusty will look after me.'

'Rusty, hmp! About the time she busts wide open, Rusty will be busy telling a windy.'

As usual Rusty had the last word. 'If there was two of you, Dave, you would be a pair of buzzard heads; if there was three, you'd be a passel of 'em.'

An hour later, Sanborn and the oldtimer drew up at the hitch-rack in front of the Peters house.

Chapter XIII
Judge Fairley
Gives an Order

Mrs. Peters opened the door for him. 'Good morning, Mr. Sanborn,' she said. 'Mary is out walking. Will you come in and wait?'

'No, thank you,' Cole replied. 'I'll call later in the day. Is Mr. Peters at his office?'

'I think so. I'll tell Mary you were here. She has been anxious about you.'

Cole had come to town partly on legal business. He and Rusty dropped in to see Peters.

The lawyer greeted them stiffly. He had been retained to protect the interests of Mary, but he did not intend to show any friendliness toward this gunman she had married. He liked the young woman very much, but it did not follow that he must like this outlaw whom she had attached to her cause.

'How is it going, Judge?' Cole asked.

'I have prepared the papers, but Judge Fairley declines to terminate the guardianship. He says the young lady must be protected against the consequences of her folly.'

Cole smiled grimly. 'I reckoned he would say something like that. I'm in favor of you and me having a li'l' talk with him. Maybe he would see the light and change his mind.'

Peters looked at him steadily. It took courage to say what was in his mind, but he did not intend to be intimidated by the reputation of this man.

'Where do you stand in this matter, Mr. Sanborn?' he asked. 'Are you trying to get the rights of your wife established? Or are you starting a feud with Radbourne? I don't intend to be anybody's cat's-paw.'

'I'm doing both,' Cole admitted frankly. 'What's the use of saying anything different? He'll jump anybody who stands up for her.'

Still the lawyer hesitated. Sanborn read his mind.

'You hate to have me for a client, don't you?' he went on, with a sardonic grin. 'I expect you're afraid one of these days I'll be asking you to keep me out of the penitentiary on account of the K. & J. express robbery.'

'I wouldn't take any case for one whom I believed to be a law-breaker guilty of a pre-meditated crime,' Peters said firmly.

'That's fine,' Cole drawled. 'I wouldn't want a lawyer who didn't believe me innocent. Now we'll get down to cases.' He took a chair and sat down. 'What I want to know is the legal way to get possession of Mrs. Sanborn's ranch and cattle. Neither she nor I want any trouble with Radbourne, though we are going to get plenty.

How do we end this guardianship and take over the property?'

The lawyer answered at once. 'You've asked two questions, not one. I can tell you how to terminate the guardianship, subject to the decision of Judge Fairley that it ought to be terminated. After that, taking over the property ought to be automatic. Whether it will be is another matter. Chet Radbourne doesn't always follow the letter of the law.'

'So I've been told,' Cole answered dryly. 'I'm asking you only for the legal angle of this matter. The recovery of the Lazy B I'll attend to personally, but I want to be clear about the law. Where do we start from here?'

From his desk Peters produced a paper. This the lawyer read. It was a petition, written by Mary Sanborn, née Landis, asking the court to end the guardianship and turn her property over to Cole Sanborn, now her husband. The signature at the bottom was attested by the county clerk.

'Fairley can't by rights get away from that, unless he claims it was obtained by duress,' Cole said. 'He's holding court now. What say we drift over and ask for action?'

Hal Peters knew there was danger in taking this case. Radbourne would resent it bitterly. The owner of the Circle 3 T would probably win out by hook or crook in the end, and he might think it advisable to punish as an example a lawyer who had espoused the cause of his enemy. But Peters had in him a substratum of stark courage. His father had been a Union die-hard in Kansas during the days of border warfare, and the son was proud of the family record. He was convinced that Radbourne was a menace to the community, that his domination of Boone County was subversive of all American principles. The man's influence had to be fought and defeated before law and order would again obtain. It was true that Sanborn also had been an element of disorder, but he was not engaged in corrupt politics and in this case was clearly within his rights.

'It is not likely that Fairley will reconsider and decide this in our favor,' the lawyer mentioned. 'I don't like to say it about a member of my own profession, but the man is corrupt.'

'He's a lowdown scalawag,' Rusty said, lighting his pipe.

'I expect Judge Fairley to do Mrs. Sanborn justice,' Cole said grimly.

Peters looked quickly at him, frowning. 'No violence—no threats. Or I'm out of this.'

Cole nodded agreement, a sardonic gleam in his eye. 'That's right. We're peaceable citizens asking for fair play.'

The three men walked to the old courthouse, a square two-story brick building set in a plaza dotted with cottonwoods. In the courtroom were two lawyers, a bailiff, and half a dozen other men. The judge was about to dismiss court when Peters presented the petition of his client.

Judge Fairley was taken completely by surprise. He was a Radbourne man, elected by the edict of the owner of the Circle 3 T, and he had no wish to offend his boss. But Radbourne was fifteen miles away in the hills, and Cole Sanborn, killer, was sitting in the room not fifteen feet from him. The cold, menacing eyes in the strong harsh face daunted him.

'I'll take this under advisement and give a decision later,' Fairley said, and hastily adjourned court.

He rose to leave, but Sanborn's big bulk stood in the way.

'Just a minute, Judge,' Cole said very gently. 'Like to have a little talk with you before you go.'

Fairley was a plump, soft man. He looked round, hurriedly and helplessly, to see the other lawyers and the spectators leaving the room.

'I'm in a hurry just now, Mr. Sanborn,' he quavered. 'Got an appointment.'

'With me,' Cole drawled. 'I wouldn't want to be in contempt of court or anything, Judge. Everything has got to be proper and legal. But I reckon we've all got to be courteous to ladies. I wouldn't like to feel that anyone had slighted Mrs. Sanborn.'

Sanborn's gaze drilled into the politician. The stomach muscles of the judge tightened. He felt a chill run down his spine. For he had been on the street the day this man had killed Buck Travis. It had been a clear case of self-defense, but Fairley saw again, as sharply as though etched before his eyes, the swift efficiency with which Sanborn had rubbed out the bad man. Travis had stepped out of a gambling-house and fired at his enemy. Three times his revolver had barked, that of Sanborn once. The one bullet had been enough.

'I'll let you know my decision tomorrow,' Fairley promised. 'I want to look up the law.'

'Hadn't you better look it up now, Judge?' Cole asked still with silky softness.

In the hard, unblinking eyes the judge could find nothing soft. He tried to summon courage to stand out. He told himself this man dared not kill him, but could find no conviction in his assurance. Out of the corner of his eyes Fairley saw Peters and Rusty Hunter. Neither of them spoke. They were awaiting the course of events. From them no help was to be had. He gave way, because he had not the nerve to stand out.

'All right. All right.' His voice was sharp and irritable. 'If it has to be done in such an infernal hurry. Just what do you want, Peters?'

The lawyer explained in detail, and the judge gave the necessary order.

'Two other little points, Your Honor,' Peters went on. 'We would like an order restraining Chet Radbourne from disposing of any of the cattle, horses, or other property of his ex-ward pending the time we receive an accounting from him. I understand a sale of her stock is now being negotiated with a buyer from Jefferson County. Also, if Your Honor pleases, an order to the First National Bank of this town instructing its officials not to honor any checks drawn on my client's account by Radbourne.'

Still under the compulsion of that stark, bleak look, Judge Fairley did as requested. It was in his mind that later he could find some excuse for repudiating his actions.

'He'll send a message to Chet hot-foot,' Peters said as the three left the courthouse.

'So he will,' agreed Cole calmly. 'But we've got him on record. Like to drop into the bank and say "Howdy" to Mr. James K. Cross, if you don't mind, gents.'

'Might as well see this out,' Peters assented. 'I've stuck my big foot in it too far to escape from annoying Chet. You've heard the proverb about the sheep and the lamb.'

On the way to the bank they met a cattleman emerging from Blossom's Emporium. Cole promptly hailed him.

'Glad to meet up with you, Mr. Perry,' he said cheerfully. 'Want to talk over a little business with you. D'you mind coming to the First National with us? We're going to see Mr. Cross.'

Fred Perry hesitated, trying to figure out in his

123

mind what the business could be. It probably had to do with the bunch of Lazy B beef steers he was buying from Radbourne. Sanborn looked so uncompromisingly sure he would go that the cowman assented. He was a little curious, anyhow, to discover what was in the air. He nodded assent.

They found James K. Cross at his office in the bank. He was a middle-aged man with a hearty manner and eyes cold enough to freeze the blood of some poor debtor caught in the toils.

If there was truth in the first flash of his eyes, before he called into service his good-fellow manner, he was not pleased to see Sanborn.

'Well—well, boys!' he exclaimed. 'It's certainly nice to see you-all. What can I do for you? Or is this a social call? For pleasure, as you might say.'

'Both business and pleasure, Mr. Cross,' Sanborn told him, with an air as genial as his own. 'I've been making a round of leading citizens today. First Mr. Peters, then Judge Fairley, and last of all you. I'd like to include Mr. Perry, but unfortunately he is from Jefferson County and not a resident here. I reckon that's his loss and ours too.'

'Yes, we would like to claim Mr. Perry as our own,' agreed the banker, his mind on a more important matter. This fellow Sanborn had something up his sleeve. What was it?

124

'Jefferson is a good county too,' Cole admitted. 'How's the grass on your range this year, Mr. Perry?'

'Never saw it better. I'm taking back a bunch of feeders with me.'

'What brand?' asked Sanborn casually.

'Lazy B stuff. Getting them from Chet Radbourne. They're on the thin side right now, but they will put on tallow fast in our country.'

'Made your deal yet, Mr. Perry? Paid for 'em?' Cole asked lazily.

'We've agreed on a price. I'm to pay tomorrow.' Perry was surprised at the question. It was not customary to make inquiries into the business of other people. Moreover, Sanborn knew him only slightly.

'I wouldn't,' Cole advised.

'Wouldn't what?' the cowman asked.

'Wouldn't buy Lazy B stuff from Radbourne. He can't deliver title. The Lazy B Ranch belongs to my wife, Mrs. Sanborn. I've just got an order of court restraining Radbourne from selling any of her stock.'

Perry was an innocent buyer. A gleam of anger flickered in his eyes. 'Radbourne didn't mention this to me. He said he was the guardian of the lady who owned the ranch.'

'He was, but he ain't now,' Cole told him. 'Anyone buying Lazy B stock from Radbourne will be throwing his money away. He can't touch a hoof of one of them. Mr. Peters will explain the facts to you.'

Peters did, briefly and lucidly.

'Much obliged,' the cowman said. 'You've saved me money. I'll let Radbourne know the deal's off.'

'Talk some more, Mr. Peters—to Mr. Cross this time,' Cole suggested, rolling a cigarette.

The lawyer explained to the banker that he had a court order restraining the First National from honoring any checks made out by Radbourne against the account of Mrs. Sanborn.

Cross smiled thinly. 'Very well, gentlemen. As long as this order stands, the bank will pay no money belonging to Mrs. Sanborn to the order of Mr. Radbourne.'

'What is the amount of Mrs. Sanborn's deposit at present?' Cole asked.

The banker rang for the cashier, found out the amount, and told Sanborn.

Cole looked at Cross, very steadily. 'I'll hold you personally responsible if any of my wife's funds are turned over to Radbourne, even if the court order is withdrawn. Chet is a rascal, but I'm going to protect Mrs. Sanborn from his crookedness.'

James K. Cross was hand in glove with Radbourne. To their mutual advantage they had worked out a dozen dubious deals. But Chet and his warriors could not protect him from this man Sanborn except by rubbing him out.

'You understand that, I hope, Mr. Cross?' Cole persisted.

Cross was between the devil and the deep sea, but his guess was that Sanborn would be likely to erupt more violently than Radbourne. He could explain the situation to Chet and perhaps they could between them cook up some scheme to thwart this scamp.

'I understand, Mr. Sanborn,' he said. 'I shall do nothing not legal and proper.'

'And nothing crooked,' added Cole bluntly.

The banker bridled. 'Was that necessary, Mr. Sanborn?'

'If not necessary, I withdraw it,' Cole said, a satiric smile on his sardonic face. 'If necessary, *you'd better remember it.*'

He rose and led the way out of the bank.

Chapter XIV
Not Looking for Trouble

Peters stood on the sidewalk in front of the Haven of Rest. 'Got to go in and see Pete Casey about a lease,' he said to Cole.

But he did not go in at once. He stood looking at Sanborn, a curious reluctant admiration in his seamed face. 'Young man, you've got me guessing,' he went on. 'I thought you were a bad egg, all the worse because you're a fighting fool with guts. I've heard plenty of stories about you. Wherever you go you seem to leave trouble behind you. The other night Doctor Burns was busy mending three of your victims. They claim you robbed the Flyer. You're supposed to be in all the deviltry that takes place within forty miles of here.'

'I'll know who to come to for a recommend when I need one,' Cole drawled with a grin.

'I don't go to church myself, but the good people who do make a text out of your life. You're a warning to all young people.'

'Go ahead and finish the sermon,' Cole said. 'I'll listen real attentive.'

'By Gad, that's the point, I don't know how to finish it,' the lawyer said. 'Until a few days ago I never met you except to pass the time of day, and I don't mind telling you I didn't want ever to meet you. But I see I've got to revise my ideas. You're not just a fighting fool with a vicious streak. There's more to you than that. You may be bad, but you're strong.'

Cole smiled derisively, not at the lawyer but at himself. 'I'm turning respectable now I'm married. No more helling around for me.'

'I give you up,' Peters said, with a wave of the hand. 'You don't look like a train-robber to me, but then I've never been acquainted with one.'

'And you're not now. I didn't rob the Flyer.'

'Glad to hear it. I don't want train-robbers for clients.' Peters turned away abruptly and walked into the Haven of Rest.

Cole walked down the street with Rusty. The two men turned in at the office of the *Boone County Beacon*. Tim Alderson, the editor, was setting type. He was a bright-eyed midget of a man. At sight of Sanborn the color receded from his face. The *Beacon* had been urging insistently that the robbers of the Flyer were known to the officers and ought to be arrested. Though the paper had mentioned no names, everybody knew who was meant.

'We dropped in to tell you we're with you in yore law and order campaign, Tim,' drawled Cole amiably. 'The sooner those scalawags are arrested and hanged, the better it will be for Boone County.'

Alderson was not reassured by the genial manner of Sanborn. He had a vision of the swift flash of revolvers, could almost hear the impending roar of guns. More than once he had criticized this gunman severely.

Dry-lipped, he offered his defense. 'An editor of a paper has to speak out for the public, Mr. Sanborn.'

'Y'betcha. I've got no complaint, Tim. I'm here to set myself right with you. If you've got time I'll tell you how things shape. First off, I didn't rob the K. & J. Had nothing to do with it. The fellow who led the miscreants rigged himself up like me so that I'd get the blame. You don't have to believe me, but it's true. Say anything you like in the *Beacon*. But that's not what I came to talk with you about. You're a square-shooter, and not one of Radbourne's lick-spittles. I'd like you to know exactly how it is between me and Chet. There's going to be war, and I'm going to tell you my side of it. I need public opinion back of me.'

The chill waves passed from the editor's spine, the dry tightness from his throat. His tense nerves relaxed.

'I'm listening,' he said. 'I'll say to begin with that I'm no friend of Chet Radbourne. I think this county never will be free and prosperous until his evil influence has been destroyed.'

'It's because you think that out loud I came in to talk with you.'

Cole told the story of his relations with the owner of the Circle 3 T and of his intention to stick up for the rights of his wife.

'This is a private fight in one way, Tim, and in another it's not,' he concluded. 'If Chet wipes me out, he'll be boss here for a long time; if I can hold out against him, his power will be broken. Forget that I've got a rep as this county's worst character. I'm entitled in this struggle to the support of all good citizens. I don't ask you to get yoreself in trouble by coming out actively on my side. All I ask is for you not to line up with Radbourne.'

'I'll not do that,' Alderson promised. A light flamed in the bright eyes looking into those of Cole. 'Maybe I've been wrong about you, Sanborn. Some of the boys have told me so. If you didn't do this K. & J. job, and if you're going through with this fight against Radbourne, you've got a great chance to serve this town and county. I won't countenance violence, except in self-defense. Understand that. But if what you do seems right to me, I'll support you till the cows come home.'

'Fair enough. It will be Chet that starts the trouble. The other night I had a chance to bump him off and I didn't do it, though I know his gunmen are laying for me.'

'I heard about that,' the editor said dryly. 'You shot up some of his men, the way it was told me.'

'Those two beauties Jerry Haskell and Curt Jordan, after both of them had their guns out blazing at me. I can't prove what I say. You'll have to take it or leave it. But it's like I say.'

'Curt Jordan is in town today,' Alderson mentioned. 'At least he was here an hour ago. A man told me he was making threats against you. I saw him on the street. He still limps some. Better look out for him.'

'Much obliged. I will. Be seeing you later.'

Sanborn and Hunter walked out of the office and turned down the street toward the Jonesboro House.

Rusty began to tell a story, but Cole stopped him.

'Not now, Rusty,' he warned. 'I've got a notion we're likely to be in a tight. If that fellow Jordan is still in town, he must know we're here. He's bad medicine and he'll shoot from cover if he gets a chance. We'd better keep our eyes peeled.'

'You got eyes in the back of yore head?' demanded Rusty irritably. 'What you mean if he gets a chanct? Can't he plug us after we're past from any door or window on the street? All he's got to do is to whang away at us. We're a pair of the dog-gondest idjits I ever met up with. Right now he's got the dead wood on us, betcha. I wisht I was anywheres but here. Me, I feel as goosey as a tenderfoot climbing aboard a bucker. What say we duck into the Arcadia and take cover our ownselves? We can sashay outa the back door and along the alley.'

'You're shouting, Rusty,' Sanborn agreed.

He pushed open the door and the two walked into the gambling-house.

As yet the place was doing only a perfunctory business, though after dark it would roar with life. Two cowpunchers were drinking at the bar. There was a stud game at the far corner of the room. In the dealer's seat, back of a faro table, Lauret sat smoking a cigar. Jordan was not present.

The cold, shallow eyes of Lauret had picked up Cole at once. They did not waver from him. The faro dealer shifted, almost imperceptibly, to get his revolver into better position. He was not looking for trouble, but if it was looking for him he wanted to be prepared.

'Evening, Lauret,' Cole said, and his white teeth flashed in an ironic grin. 'The flies not buzzing around the honey-pot yet?'

Lauret did not answer. Cole had spoken as he was passing and had not stopped.

From the stud game Sanborn beckoned a man with the slightest lift of the head. The man threw his cards into the discard, rose, and came toward them. He was the little sheriff, Samson Magruder.

' 'Lo, Cole,' he said gruffly. 'Don't forget this

ain't any honkatonk town. You can't come here and paint it no gaudy color.'

'Law and order still flourishing in Jonesboro?' Cole asked lightly.

'Yes, Cole,' the sheriff countered. 'You been out of town, haven't you?'

'Roosting in the hills.'

'Yeah, I heard about you. Up at the Circle 3 T one night, weren't you?'

'For a short visit, to see my old friend Chet Radbourne. I'm a reformed character, Magruder. A married man has to settle down.'

'Did you settle down before you visited the Circle 3 T or afterward, Cole?' the sheriff asked dryly.

'I wasn't responsible for that rumpus up there, if that's what you're hinting at. Some of Chet's boys got to picking at me. That's what I want to talk with you about. One of 'em is in town now, or was an hour ago. Curt Jordan. I understand he's been looking for me. Now I don't want to see him. Rusty and I came to town on business and we've finished it. We want to hit the trail without trouble. Do you know where Jordan is hanging out?'

'I reckon I can find out. You're not loading me, Cole. You aim to sidestep him if you can?'

'If there's a difficulty he'll make it, not me,' Cole promised.

'All right. You and Rusty sit tight here and I'll

scout around. I'll let you know what I find out about Jordan.'

The sheriff left the room. A few minutes later, Lauret rose and sauntered toward the door. Cole intercepted him.

'Like to talk with you a while,' Sanborn said.

'What about?' Lauret asked coldly.

'About the weather,' Cole said cheerfully. 'And crops—and the state of the country.'

'Did you come in here to make trouble for me?' the faro dealer asked evenly.

'No, Lauret. I'm not looking for trouble with you, now or any other time. Anything that has happened in the past between you and me is in the discard, unless you rake it out.'

'Then what's this play you're making about keeping me here?'

'It won't hurt you to sit down and talk things over, will it?'

'I've got nothing to talk over with you, Sanborn. Put your cards on the table. You're trying to hold me here. Why?'

Cole explained quietly. 'There's a man in town looking for me. If you were to go out of here, and then right soon he was to drift in to the Arcadia, I might think you had sent him here. But if you stay and talk with me, I'll know you're not responsible for anything that happens—if anything does.'

'I don't care what you think,' Lauret said curtly.

He looked blackly at Sanborn, hung for a moment in hesitation, then turned sharply and resumed his seat. 'But I'd as lief stay here. I'm not running to anyone with information about you. I have more important matters on my mind.' He began to shuffle a deck of cards and deal a game of solitaire.

The sheriff returned and drew Cole aside. 'Jordan is at Pete Casey's place. He is sitting in a chair near the window with his eye on your horses. Pete tells me he has been drinking and has made threats against you. I'm having a Mexican boy bring your mounts here to the back door. 'Soon as they show up I'll give you the high sign and you boys can hit your saddles and get out. That suit you?'

'Fine.'

'Jordan claims he has proof you held up the K. & J. express. His story will be that he tried to arrest you and you resisted. I wish I knew whether you did that job, Cole. My business is not to help criminals escape.'

'I didn't do it, Magruder, but if Jordan gets me, you can bet Chet will work up evidence to prove I did, so this killer can get the reward. I was on Dead Horse Mesa the night of the robbery.'

'Who says you were there—except you, Cole?'

'Dave Pope will tell you he was with me.'

'And you'll tell me Dave was with you. Makes a nice alibi for you both, only it's not worth a billy-be-damn, since everyone knows that if you were on this K. & J. job, Dave was with you.'

'It's the only alibi I have, but you can bet your saddle that if I was guilty I'd be fixed up with a nice airtight one. Like to ask you a question, sheriff. Did you ever make any inquiries to find out where Jerry Haskell was that night?'

Magruder stared at him. 'Jerry Haskell. What you mean, Cole? Can you prove——?'

'Not a thing. And I'll bet if you ask Jerry he's got an ironclad A1 alibi. Likely you'll find he was playing cards with two-three Circle 3 T riders, one of 'em a short, heavy-set guy and another a tall hairpin.'

'Have you boys plumb forgot we're allowin' to make a getaway from this burg?' Rusty interrupted impatiently. 'Don't you reckon that Mexican boy of yours is about due, Magruder? Unless he's taking a siesta or something. I dunno about you, Cole, but I'm kinda anxious to get outa here while my skin hasn't any holes in it. I'm peculiar thataway.'

Cole laid a hand on his shoulder. 'No need for you to get mixed up in this, Rusty,' he said. 'Jordan isn't looking for you. Stay around here with Magruder. I'll make my break for a getaway. After a while you can mosey out to camp unmolested.'

The oldtimer shook the hand from his shoulder. 'Say, young fellow,' he snarled, 'from where I come from a man don't run out on his partner.'

'You won't be running out on me, Rusty. I'm not fighting, but ducking trouble. One can slip away more inconspicuous than two.'

Hunter shook his head vigorously. 'No, sir, you don't fool me worth a cent. Being as I'm drug into this jackpot, I aim to stay till the call. But I ain't throwin' up my hat and cheering. Not none. Like as not this scalawag Jordan will have a whole passel of gunmen with him. Dawged if I wouldn't give four bits to be safe on my old broomtail in the hills. Reminds me of onct when I was down in Santone—'

Rusty was destined never to finish that reminiscence. The side door of the Arcadia opened swiftly, as though blown in by a blast of wind. A bullet whistled past Cole's head and flung a splinter from the wall where it struck. In the doorway stood a man, a smoking revolver in his hand. The man was Curt Jordan. He moved a step or two forward, with wary, catlike litheness, body swaying slightly. The face was venomous, the mouth a thin cruel slit. His eyes were fixed on Sanborn. He came shooting, scabrous epithets dripping from his mouth.

Cole whirled to meet him. The young man's arm swept up, dragging a forty-four from its scabbard as it rose. From the barrel of the weapon death leaped.

The force of the bullet flung Jordan out of

line, so that one of his shots struck an unlighted wall-lamp. The Circle 3 T killer stood in his tracks, distorted face shocked and bewildered. Then his knees sagged and he sank to the floor.

Cole leaned slightly forward, every nerve and muscle keyed to instant response. He watched his enemy intently, a cold, fierce eagerness shining in his eyes.

Jordan made a desperate effort to lift his revolver, managed to raise himself on an elbow, then collapsed into a huddled heap.

Chapter XV
Self-Defense

Silence followed the crash of the guns. Men emerged from the shelter of the tables and chairs behind which they had dived.

Cole stood as motionless as the crumpled form on the floor. Not until he was sure Jordan was dead did he lift his eyes from the body of the gunman.

Tongues began to buzz with excitement, released from the fear that had stilled them.

'Curt made a mistake coming after he'd been drinking hard . . . He made a mistake coming at all. Cole was that cool and easy . . . Never fired but once . . . Well, Jordan sure asked for it . . . Me, I was almost in the line of fire. I sure took a running jump lickety-split . . .'

Sanborn pushed his revolver back into the holster. 'I call you all to witness,' he said evenly. 'Jordan came in here shooting. I fired in self-defense. Nothing else I could do.'

'That's right,' the sheriff agreed. 'Cole was trying to get out of town without trouble, though he knew Jordan was threatening him. I'd just had his horse brought to the back door so he could slip away. He was noways to blame.'

A chorus of those present approved this verdict.

Cole looked down at the still body of the man who had been hired to kill him. After the fashion of the time the black hair of the dead desperado was plastered across the forehead in a quarter-circle with an absurd little curl at the end. On the little finger of the hand that still clutched the sixshooter was a plain gold ring. Sanborn found himself wondering if once the man's mother or sweetheart had put it there. Not many years ago Jordan had been a little boy playing at marbles. Now . . .

Abruptly Cole plucked his thoughts back to the cold fact that the man had tried to murder him.

'Send for Alderson,' he told the sheriff. 'I want to make sure the *Beacon* gets this right.'

Doctor Burns arrived and examined the victim. Presently he rose. 'He's past any help from me,' he said. 'Better send for the undertaker.'

The undertaker was also the coroner. He was a Radbourne man.

'I want an inquest,' Sanborn told him. 'Right now while all the witnesses are present.'

The coroner looked at him sulkily. 'What for? You claim it was a fair fight, don't you?'

'I claim I killed him in self-defense after he was firing at me. But what I say doesn't go in this town. I want the facts brought out by unprejudiced parties.'

Magruder spoke up. 'Yes, let's have an inquest, Holt. Fair for both sides.'

Under pressure from others Holt reluctantly consented.

Alderson came hurrying into the room as the jury was being chosen. He looked at Sanborn accusingly.

'Wait till you hear the evidence,' the latter advised.

'Nothing to it, Alderson,' blurted out Rusty. 'Jordan came in with his gun smoking. Cole let him have it onct. That ended the fireworks. Would you want Cole to stand there and let this scoundrel plug him?'

The jury listened to the evidence. Even Lauret was forced to testify that Jordan had been the aggressor, though he did it with bad grace. There was not a shred of testimony against Cole until Holt put Sanborn himself on the stand.

'Ever have any trouble with Jordan?' the coroner asked.

'He tried to make trouble for me at the Circle 3 T not long since,' Cole said. 'Drew a gun and attempted to kill me.'

'What were you doing at the Circle 3 T, Mr. Sanborn?'

'I went there to talk with Chet Radbourne about my wife's property and to warn Chet not to hurt a hair of her head.'

Cole had not raised his voice, but in the

crowded room his words rang like a bell. There was a murmur of sympathetic accord. The general opinion in Boone County was that the owner of the Circle 3 T intended no good to his ward.

'Isn't it a fact, Mr. Sanborn, that you knew your presence would not be welcome at the Circle 3 T and that you went to make trouble?' Holt asked.

'I didn't expect to have any fatted calf killed for me,' Cole drawled. 'But nobody except a locoed fool would go alone looking for trouble with more than thirty men against him.'

'Wasn't it your idea that maybe you might get a chance to kill Mr. Radbourne unnoticed and slip away? And when you were discovered, didn't you try to get Mr. Radbourne? And didn't you shoot the foreman of the ranch and this man Jordan when they interfered to protect him?'

'No—to all three questions. Radbourne told me he was glad I had come. Jordan and Haskell drew and fired on me. I wounded them in self-defense.'

'That's your story. Have you any witnesses to back it?'

'None. But anyone using his brains could guess I wouldn't start trouble with thirty Circle 3 T men against me. I told you that before.'

'Haven't you hated and been jealous of Mr. Radbourne for years?' Holt demanded sharply.

'No. I have despised and loathed him because he is what he is.'

The coroner hesitated before he asked the next question. 'Have you not been accused of robbing the K. & J. express car, Mr. Sanborn?'

'No.' Cole looked steadily at the man. 'Are you accusing me, Mr. Holt?'

'Not at all,' the coroner said hastily. 'But there are stories going round. Probably you have an alibi?'

'If I have I won't offer it here—unless you are trying me for the robbery,' Cole said coolly.

'By jacks, you ought to be tried and hanged for killing poor Shrader,' a voice from the crowd called excitedly.

Shrader was the express messenger who had been shot down by the bandits at the time of the train hold-up.

Cole looked in the direction from which the voice had come. 'Ought I to be hanged for a crime I didn't do?' he asked evenly.

'Who does the description on that poster fit?' someone else demanded.

'It fits me too well,' retorted Cole instantly. 'If I were robbing a train, I'd have to be crazy with the heat before I would leave so perfect a description. Any fool can see the miscreant was trying to shove the thing on me because I have a bad name—and because he has a personal grudge at me.'

'Might be thataway, Cole,' a cattleman agreed. 'I'll say you don't seem to me like the kind of a fellow would shoot down a man for doing his duty when there wasn't any need a-tall of killing him.'

The coroner brushed aside the interruptions impatiently.

'Ever have any trouble with Jerry Haskell before you shot him at the Circle 3 T, Mr. Sanborn?'

'No.'

'Something about a poker game at Summit.'

'Oh, that. I wouldn't call it trouble. We sat in a game together.'

'Didn't you beat him out of four-five hundred dollars?'

'I don't like the way you put it, sir,' Cole said curtly. 'I quit three hundred winner, if that's what you mean.'

The coroner decided to drop the matter of the poker game.

'Isn't it true that you had a difficulty with Haskell at Casey's place not long ago?'

'We exchanged compliments,' Cole said, with a smile.

'He ordered you out of town, didn't he? And you went?'

'Yes. He gave me an hour, and I was so busy I couldn't go right then. So he gave me another.'

Someone laughed. The coroner rapped angrily for order.

'I suppose you'll claim that you and Haskell are good friends,' he said, with obvious sarcasm.

'No, sir.' Cole spoke lightly, but his words dripped with contempt. 'I don't make friends with coyotes.'

'Do you deny you hate him?'

'I don't like a thing about him,' Cole admitted promptly. 'But I don't see where you're going. It wasn't Haskell who came in here to kill me just now, was it? Are you aiming to prove I had to shoot Jordan because I don't like Haskell?'

Again there was a ripple of laughter.

'I'll ask you one more question,' the officer said, his face flushed with annoyance. 'Didn't you send someone to tell Jordan you were here so that when he opened the door you could kill him?'

'No. I was trying to leave town without trouble as Mr. Magruder has told you. If I ever lay a trap for anyone, Mr. Coroner, I won't give him three free gratis shots at me before I get my own forty-four into action.'

The jury did not leave the room. Within a few minutes the foreman announced the verdict. Curtis Jordan had come to his death from a bullet in the heart fired from a revolver in the hand of Cole Sanborn. The latter had shot in self-defense.

Rusty flung up his hat with a yell. 'You're damn whistling, boys! He's one straight-up rider, Cole is. Drinks on me. Everybody in the house.'

The sentiment was divided. There were Radbourne

men present. Also there were good citizens not ready to accept Sanborn because in this instance he had not done wrong. Against him there was still the bad record of years. But there could be no doubt that his position with the public had been improved.

Alderson came up and congratulated him. 'I'm going to tell this exactly the way it happened,' he said.

As Cole walked along the dusty street of false fronts, Rusty and Alderson by his side, the change of atmosphere was like a fresh breath from the hills. A cowboy standing in the doorway of the Haven of Rest let out a yip at sight of Sanborn.

'Leave old King Cole to show these bully-puss killers,' he shouted. 'Boy, I was there and seen you do it. You was that cool and easy, but bingo! and it's Mr. Jordan gone to hell on a shutter with his boots on.'

'Sorry,' Cole told him. 'Had to do it. He had his neck bowed and wouldn't have it any other way.'

On the porch of the Jonesboro House sat Preston, the bad man from the Nation with whom Cole had once had a difference of opinion.

At sight of Sanborn a smile, sarcastic but not ill-natured, rested on the brown, clean-cut face of the man who had migrated under pressure of too much attention from United States marshals.

'You're certainly one hell-a-miler, fellow,' he

called to Cole. 'I reckon you 'n' I will have to bury the hatchet. You don't know it, but you've just done me a service. This bird Jordan was some overbearing, and yesterday it looked like he was getting set to run on me. What-say we call it quits?'

'Suits me fine,' Cole said, and shook hands on it. 'Fact is, just now I've bit off about all I can chew in the way of enemies. Glad to smoke the pipe of peace with you. I don't mind saying now that the crack I made about gents fagging it here from the Nation wasn't meant for you at all, but for another guy.'

'Well, it landed sock on my jaw,' Preston said, with a grin. 'But if it wasn't meant for me, that's all right. When a fellow is on the dodge he's some sensitive to remarks he wouldn't notice at another time. And all I did at that was to hide a friend who had shot up a deputy marshal.'

'Be seeing you one of these days,' Cole said as he swung to his saddle. 'Drift up to the Lazy B when you've got nothing else to do.'

'Would I find you there or some of Chet Radbourne's warriors?' Preston asked, with a chuckle.

'Don't push on your reins and you'll find me in possession,' Cole said coolly. 'Say in a week or so.'

'Y'betcha!' corroborated Rusty. 'We aim to cut loose our dog on Mr. Radbourne one of these-here days. And then, gentlemen, hush!'

'In a perfectly legal way,' Cole amended, with a bland smile.

The two riders moved down the dusty street at a road gait. To the man seated on the porch Rusty's cracked voice, lifted in exultant song, drifted back.

> 'Yes, we'll come to the table
> As long as we're able,
> And eat every damn thing
> That looks sorter stable,'

the oldtimer croaked.

Cole swung from the main street into the residence section of the town. He stopped in front of the Peters house.

Once more the wife of the lawyer came to the door.

'Mary isn't back yet,' she said. Perhaps she caught a disturbed look on the face of Sanborn, or she added: 'You needn't worry about that. She goes back into the hills and stays for hours—takes a book with her. If you would care to wait?'

Cole shook his head. He was disappointed. 'No, Mrs. Peters, much obliged. We've got to shove on. Will you tell her I'm sorry I didn't see her, and that what I did today I had to do? It wasn't my choice.'

Mrs. Peters was puzzled. What had he done today? But she asked no question. 'I'll tell her,' she said.

The two men on horseback rode out of town.

'Looks like you're safe on your old broomtail headed for the hills like you was wishing to be awhile ago,' Cole said cheerfully. 'By the way, you was starting to tell about once when you were in Santone and Jordan interrupted you. I'll listen now, if you like. I wouldn't want to say for sure, but my view is that your singing is worse than your story-telling.'

'No such thing,' Rusty denied with spirit. 'My singing has bedded down more trail herds than you ever saw, young fellow. Onct on the old Chisum Trail in a thunderstorm, when the lightning was so clost you could see it glancing off'n the horns of the cattle—'

Rusty was off on another windy.

Chapter XVI
'I'm Not Paid to Like Them'

Slim Calhoun sauntered forward to the porch where Radbourne sat slumped in a homemade armchair. Haskell was standing beside the boss engaged in talk with him. Evidently the foreman had just ridden up, for his big sorrel with the roached mane had not been tied to the hitch-rack, but had been left free, reins grounded.

Haskell looked sourly at the black-haired puncher in shining leathers. The slender body of the man was graceful as that of Apollo, his young brown face good-looking beyond question. The foreman did not like the fellow, never had. The Texan was too reckless and independent to kowtow to him.

It was the boss who spoke. 'I hear you're quite a lad with the ladies, Slim,' he said. 'If I set you to ride herd on one who came back to visit us today, do you reckon you could get her back to the ranch safe and innocent?'

'I'm just a country boy from Texas,' Slim answered. 'Maybe you'd better send an experienced man like Jerry here.'

'Jerry has got other business,' Radbourne said; and added, with an insulting giggle: 'Anyway,

Jerry is out; last time he chaperoned this lady she made a monkey of him.'

The foreman flushed angrily. 'I took her to the Jonesboro House, where you told me to leave her.'

'Did I tell you to fix up a marriage for her with that scalawag Sanborn?' Radbourne asked, with a bitter jeer.

'You talk like you expected me to be a mind-reader, Chet,' Haskell retorted angrily. 'She had never met the cuss. How was I to know she would marry him right off the bat?'

Radbourne ignored the defense, speaking instead to the cowpuncher. 'Miss Landis wants to go for a ride. You're to trail along and have her back here by noon. Don't go any farther than Dry Gulch. If you ride south, stay this side of the Fiddleback. Take a rifle with you, on the off chance that Sanborn may be hanging around. If you see him, don't forget there's an open season on that wolf. There's a reward waiting for the man that gets him. Dead or alive.'

'There's a reward for the fellow that held up the express,' Slim corrected. 'How am I going to prove Sanborn did it?'

'I'll have him sworn to by witnesses,' Radbourne promised. 'Don't worry about that. Not that you're likely to see him. He's on the dodge somewhere in the brush.'

'I reckon,' Slim said.

'You're a better-looking young squirt than that walleyed buzzard. If you put your mind to it, maybe you can beat his time. I shouldn't wonder but what the young lady is right hungry for some powwow with a scatter-brained young jackass with a good line of talk. You've got my permission to go as far as you like—within reason. Give yourself a good time, fellow.'

'Suits me,' the Texan said. 'Anyhow, it will be a change from high-tailin' after longhorns over the hills.'

'If I was running this show I wouldn't let her go galloping all over the country,' Haskell growled. 'I'd keep the little devil penned up and feed her bread and water. I would so.'

The little black eyes of Radbourne jeered at him. 'I reckon you would. Different here. She's my ward, not my prisoner. That's the story. So I treat her well. Give her all reasonable privileges. Let her ride every day. I could wring the little hellcat's neck, but I don't. Instead, I use my brains.'

Slim did not hurry to avail himself of the opportunity to flirt with the young woman in his charge. He rode beside her knee to knee, offering only the most desultory conversation.

Mary made note of one point. The other men who had accompanied her on the daily rides had called her Miss Landis, as they had evidently been directed to do. Slim Calhoun addressed her as Mrs. Sanborn. His manner was easy but deferential. He did not seem interested in making a good impression, nor did he rush into talk lest she might think he had nothing to say.

The girl asked questions about his experiences. He told her about Texas, of the long trail drives, of the wild frontier towns where Northern buyer and Southern seller met. Greatly daring, she ventured a remark about his home life. Instantly he became reserved.

They rode through the dancing heat of an alkali plain to the wooded uplands bordering the desert. Through the foliage a stream of morning sunlight dappled the forest carpet and filled the park with pools of fretted gold. Above their green-roofed fairyland they could see stretches of blue sky unflecked by clouds.

'It's lovely,' she said.

'Right pretty,' he agreed, smiling at her. Perhaps he was not thinking of the landscape.

He was a wild young fellow and had been in trouble. It was not hard to guess that he had come to this country because of something done in his turbulent past. But she could not understand why such a man, no matter how foolish and reckless he had been, was content to become one of Chet Radbourne's ruffians.

She flung a question at him bluntly. 'How do you come to be working for the Circle 3 T?'

'Jobs are right seldom these days,' he told her.

'I know, but—' She broke off, to ask another.

'Do you like Mr. Radbourne—or Jerry Haskell?'

Slim gave her a Yankee answer. 'Do you like them, either one of 'em?'

'No, I don't,' she cried. 'You know that. I think they're both hateful. I think they are terrible men—Mr. Radbourne especially.'

'Then why would you expect me to like them?' he drawled. 'I'm not paid to like them.'

'What are you paid for?' she demanded, looking directly at him.

'Right now I'm being paid to ride with the prettiest young lady I've seen since I left Texas,' he parried.

'You're being paid to be her jailer, to make sure she doesn't escape from a man who means to ruin her life if he can,' Mary accused. 'And I had heard that Southerners are chivalrous.'

'When he hired me Chet didn't mention any young lady,' Slim said gently. 'I don't reckon you could say I'm yore jailer.'

She pulled up her horse. Her eyes challenged his stormily. 'How can you say that? Do you mean that if I start to ride away, across the Fiddleback, you wouldn't stop me?'

'I couldn't let a young lady go off into the desert alone,' he parried. 'You'd never get out alive.'

'I thought so,' she said bitterly.

'If you don't want to be here, why did you come back?' he asked.

'Because your boss dragged me here an

155

hour ago. I didn't have a chance to get away.'

'Would you have a chance now?'

'No.'

'Well, then, what's the use of talking about running away? Since you've asked me, I'll say that Chet Radbourne is my idea of something spewed up from hell. But as long as I'm taking his pay I won't work against him.'

'For thirty dollars a month he has bought you body and soul, then?'

Slim Calhoun looked with cool eyes at this glamorous girl, caught so hopelessly in the net woven for her. If the desperation of her case touched him, he gave no sign of it.

'I wouldn't say that,' he replied lightly. 'But when my trail don't go the same way as his, I'll tell him so. That may be right soon, and then again it may not.'

'I've heard you quarreling with Jerry Haskell. I don't see why, if you don't like him—'

'I don't like a thing about him. He's a bully-puss kind of a fellow, and I don't aim to let him run on me. Not none. But I'll ask you a question, Mrs. Sanborn. If I get my time and go down the road, will it help you any?'

She shook her head. 'No. No, it won't. Nothing will help me, unless—'

'—unless yore husband whops Chet and the Circle 3 T, and you can see right off he has no chance to do that.'

'You think he hasn't,' she said, and her voice pleaded for a reversal of judgment.

'It's a fifty to one bet against him. Anyone with horse-sense will tell you that.' A sudden light gleamed in his eyes. 'But that rapscallion of yours is a sure-enough go-getter. He's liable to pull off a miracle, and, by jacks, I'd like to see him nail the old weasel's hide to a fence. For two bits I'd throw in with him.'

'Why don't you?' Mary asked, a glow running through her lithe young body. 'You don't belong with these . . . murderers.'

'Don't I? What do you know about me? And about where I belong?' The mask was on his face again. 'And I don't reckon we'd better call names, Mrs. Sanborn. Cole has the rep of being a killer just as much as Jordan has—or Chet himself, in a different way.'

The girl felt the warmth drain out of her. What this man said was true. The man she had married was known as a bad man too. But she defended him none the less.

'He doesn't kill for pleasure—or for money. If he has killed bad men, I'm sure he couldn't help it.'

'Maybeso,' the Texan assented. 'I've heard he's a square-shooter in his way.'

'Then why don't you join him? He can't be as bad as the men you are with now.'

'I'm lined up on the other side. A fellow can't jump around like a toad.'

Calhoun spoke with curt decision, but his mind was not so decided. He did not like his environment at the Circle 3 T. He was an outlaw from his native state. A wild young hellion, he had known the riproaring life of trail's-end towns. For months he had hung out in the brush on the edge of a big outfit's range and rustled the stock of absentee owners. While on a drunken spree he had helped hold up a gambling-house in San Antonio. But at the worst he had played his hand openly and aboveboard. There was something about the Circle 3 T atmosphere that got under his skin.

First, there was the old man. Radbourne was not a wholesome scoundrel. His methods were cruel and sinister. What Sanborn had said at the Haven of Rest was true. He was fighting to help the fat slug of a villain rob a defenseless girl of all she had. More than once Slim had been on the point of quitting the outfit. All he needed was a push from outside. But it had to come from Radbourne and not from this girl.

Yet she had given him impetus to start him on the way. There was a point about which he had been curious. Now he meant to find the answer if he could.

This determined upon, he at once moved the conversation back to a safer channel. He pulled up and pointed with his quirt.

'There's a big rattler. See. There by the bush. Hold yore horse steady.'

From its holster he drew a forty-four, took deliberate aim, and fired. The reptile collapsed.

'A good shot,' she said.

'Just a mite low, but it did the work.' He looked at the sun. 'Don't you think we'd better be heading for home, Mrs. Sanborn?'

'For *home*,' she echoed bitterly. 'All right. We might as well turn back.'

He disregarded her ironic comment. All the way to the ranch he was full of irrelevant and cheerful talk.

Chapter XVII
'I've had an Elegant Sufficiency'

Chet Radbourne shuffled out to the porch as the two young people drew up at the house after their ride. Slim lifted Mary to the ground.

In her soft curved cheeks pink was glowing. The eyes of the girl sparkled with life.

'Thanks for bringing me *home* safely,' she said, with a touch of almost gay malice.

Light-footed as a deer, she walked past Radbourne into the house, paying no attention to him.

The owner of the Circle 3 T lowered his bulk into a chair, overflowing in every direction.

'The young lady certainly has got a sunset in her cheeks,' he said to Calhoun, with his mocking te-he-he of a giggle. 'Maybe I hadn't ought to send a respectable married woman out with a wild rapscallion like you. We don't want a scandal on the Circle 3 T.'

'That young lady grades A1, Chet,' the cow-puncher said, looking straight into the jeering eyes of his employer. 'There won't be any scandal about her anywhere.'

'Not if I have her chaperoned by a model young

Christian like my Texas man, eh? I'll bet you'd like to take on the job permanent, and let my longhorns stray. Did she tell you how she'd feel about that?'

'She didn't mention it.'

'Well, she's surely made a complete recovery, whatever your treatment is,' Radbourne said. 'Here she was mooning like a sick calf. One ride with Doctor Calhoun, and she comes back pretty as a painted wagon. You'd ought to hang a shingle out, Slim. "Young lady specialist. Cures guaranteed." I'll bet you got a fine bedside manner, te-he.'

'I'll give you my recipe,' Calhoun said. 'Treat her decent. When she saw I was a white man, not looking for any personal advantage, she perked right up.'

'You wouldn't mean to imply I didn't treat her decently,' Chet suggested. 'Or that I'm not a white man.'

'I don't know how you treat her,' the Texan answered. 'She acts to me like she's scared. I don't know what of. Maybe of this fellow she married. I'd say she needed to be gentled, but it's none of my business.'

'You're right about that last, Slim,' his employer agreed pointedly. 'I don't recollect that when I hired you I mentioned needing advice from you.'

'And I'm not offering any,' Slim said coolly.

'You good as asked me how I treated her. I told you she forgot her troubles for a while and was happy, kinda.'

'She's got troubles, has she?' Radbourne asked, with silky malice.

Slim looked at the older man hardily. 'What's the use of picking at everything I say, Chet? You wanted me to be nice to her. I was. Have you got any kick at that? I'm not looking for trouble.'

The Texan may not have been looking for trouble, but inside of the hour he found it. After leaving Radbourne he went to the bunkhouse and left the rifle he had been carrying. The place was empty. Four or five of the men were down at the corral and one or two more at the stables. Of Jerry Haskell he had seen nothing. Someone had mentioned in his hearing that the foreman was riding out to see a bunch of stock on the north mesa.

Calhoun stood for a moment at the door of the bunkhouse, then stepped quietly to the cabin used by the foreman. After a quick look around to make sure he had not been observed, he stepped inside and glanced about the place.

The room was a litter of disorder. In one corner of the room, tossed on the floor, were a saddle, quirt, and sweat-stained blanket. Several pipes, tobacco ashes, an old boot, a soiled shirt, and a dozen other odds and ends had been flung on the table. The bed was not made, the floor looked as if it had never been swept. On the only chair were a pair of muddy boots and two Spanish spurs.

The Texan's lip curled with contempt. 'He's sure one prize hog,' he murmured disdainfully.

Close to one wall a trunk stood. The range rider threw open the lid. The tray was filled with a nondescript pile of shirts, ties, tobacco sacks, pictures of nude women, foul pipes, and papers. This he lifted to the floor. In the lower part of the trunk he found the articles for which he was looking—a blue polka-dot bandanna, a gray cotton shirt, a rattlesnake skin hatband.

'So you're the pilgrim that led the road agents when they robbed the express, Mr. Haskell,' he said to himself. 'And you wished the blame on Cole Sanborn, you dirty yellow coyote.'

He replaced the tray, closed the trunk, and moved toward the door. But before he got there he pulled up short. He heard footsteps, saw the shadow of a man in the doorway. Jerry Haskell stood at the entrance scowling, suspicion written large on his sullen face.

'What you doing here, fellow?' he demanded.

'Ran out of the makings and came to borrow some,' Slim said casually.

The foreman ripped out an oath. 'What you get is the best whaling you ever had. I'm gonna work you over, fellow, so's yore mother wouldn't know little Slim.'

Calhoun made no protest. For a moment he had

a fleeting regret that he did not have a gun with him. Then he gave his whole mind to the matter in hand. An unholy glee filled the face of the foreman. Haskell was a notorious rough-and-tumble fighter. He weighed thirty pounds more than the rider. Slim knew he was in for an unmerciful beating.

Haskell crouched, put up his fists, and moved forward. He lashed out with the right. Slim ducked, landed hard on the sneering mouth, and dodged out of reach. With a roar of rage the foreman rushed, broke down the defense of the other, and slogged at his brown good-looking face.

Slim fought back as best he could, but he took a savage mauling before he escaped from the corner into which his opponent had jammed him. He was still groggy when Haskell nailed him again and sent blow after blow crashing into him. Calhoun's arms fell and his knees sagged. He slid down the wall into unconsciousness.

The foreman flung a bucket of water over his head. The range rider came back to life and stared up at the cruel, vindictive face glaring down at him.

'And I've always been told Texas is a he-country in pants,' the foreman jeered.

A grin broke through the blood on the disfigured face of the man on the ground.

'You're damn whistling it is,' Slim said. 'Fellow, you pack a wallop like a piledriver. I've got no business putting my maulers up before you.'

'If you haven't had a bellyful, get up and take some more,' Haskell urged. 'I haven't started yet.'

'Me, I've had an elegant sufficiency,' Slim told him promptly.

'Say the word and I'll break you in two.'

'I ain't saying it,' the battered puncher announced.

'I'm the best fist and skull fighter ever showed his face in Boone County,' the foreman boasted. 'If you know any other Texas man who doubts it, shove him along.'

Slim sat up, then slowly rose to his feet. The room was still swimming before his eyes. 'By jinks, I'm not sure whether there are two or three of you there, Jerry,' he laughed, out of the corner of a disfigured mouth.

'Don't you try to gun me from behind,' Haskell warned. 'I'll be watching you every turn of the road.'

Calhoun looked at the big rangy fellow contemptuously. 'What's eating you? Think I can't take a whopping without yelping about it? You beat me fair and square. You haven't heard me kick, have you?'

'Better not let me hear it either, or I'll give you another where that came from.'

'Not if I see you first, Jerry. Well, if you're through with me, I'll rock along.'

Slim sauntered from the room, his battered head still up. He was a bit unsteady on his feet, but as he moved toward the bunkhouse he chanted jauntily two verses of a cowboy song.

'Roll yore tails and roll 'em high,
We'll all be angels by and by.'

At the door of the bunkhouse he came face-to-face with Bud Calloway and Hank. Bud stared at him. 'Holy smoke, Slim. What you been doing to yourself?'

Slim laughed, cheerfully but lopsidedly. 'Wrong guess, Bud. Another guy did it to me. Our beloved foreman handed me a few souvenirs to enforce discipline. Fetch me a bucket of water from the pump. I got to make repairs.'

Bud brought the water, then sat down on a bunk and asked questions. Slim answered some of them. He did not mention what he had been doing in the cabin of the foreman.

Chapter XVIII
Slim Goes Down the Road

The little black eyes of Radbourne fixed on Mary. His big body, slumped in the chair, was motionless. Only his jaws moved, as he chewed his quid of tobacco.

'Sit down,' he snapped.

'Is it worthwhile?' Mary asked. 'I won't be staying long.'

'You'll stay long as I like, Missy. Don't you try to be hoity-toity with me. I've got a recipe for taming hellcats. Listen. I sent to get you to sign this paper. It's a legal document asking the court to annul your marriage to that ruffian Sanborn.' He pushed the paper across the desk. 'You sign on this line.'

'Only I don't,' she told him. 'I'm quite satisfied. Why should I ask for an annulment?'

'Because he scared and trapped you into this marriage. That's why. This paper gives reasons a-plenty.'

Slender and vivid, with contempt in her deep violet eyes, she looked down at his swollen, unwholesome bulk. 'Reasons that aren't true, unless it says I married him because I was trapped by and was afraid of you. They say you own the courts here, but even you can't make them give me an annulment I don't want and won't take.'

'Makes no difference to me what you want. You're nothing but a crazy girl. If you think I'm going to let you interfere with my plans, you're 'way off. Not for a holy minute. You'll sign this paper. Understand?' He snarled his ultimatum savagely.

'I won't!' she defied, her eyes flaming. 'You can't make me. All you can do is threaten. But you daren't hurt me. If you did, my husband would stamp you out of existence just as he would a poisonous snake. You're afraid of him. You may pretend you're not, but it's a lie you feed to your vanity. As long as he is alive I'm safe.' She picked a phrase out of her memory. 'As safe as if I were in God's pocket.'

'I reckon your outlaw husband told you to say your prayers and you'd be all right,' he jeered. 'God doesn't function in this neck of the woods, Missy.'

'So you think. You're swollen with conceit, and some day soon you are going to be struck down for your sins.'

He showed his teeth in a derisive grin. 'By God's representative, Cole Sanborn, I reckon. Girl, you used a word just now. You said, *as long as Sanborn is alive.* I'll hand it right back to you. If you don't sign this paper, he won't be alive twenty-four hours. I'm telling you.'

The heart of the girl died under her ribs. Had he caught Cole in a trap? Was that why he had sent for her, to force her under pressure to sign this paper? It would be like him.

'You are so full of lies,' she answered. 'You'd like to kill him. I know that. But he's looking out for himself. He won't let you get him.'

'I know where he's roosting, and I aim to dig him out of his hole—unless you sign this paper. It's up to you to say whether he lives or dies. He don't mean a thing to me, except when he gets in my way. If this marriage is annulled, he can skedaddle out of this country soon as he's a mind to hit the trail. But one way or another, I'm putting an end to this fool marriage. Take your choice. If you want him dry-gulched, it's all the same to me.'

She tried to still the panic in her breast. It probably was not true that he knew where Cole was. Even if he did the attack on Sanborn's camp might fail. Moreover, she knew Radbourne could not be trusted. No matter what he promised, if he ever had her husband at his mercy he would kill. It would do no good to sign the paper, but would only rob her and Cole of the strategic advantage they had gained.

'When you have dug him out, as you call it, bring him here to the ranch,' Mary said, driving down her fear. 'If he asks me to sign this paper to save him, I'll sign it.'

Angrily he slammed a fat fist down on the desk. 'You'll sign it now.' He leaned forward, his pallid face filled with malevolence. 'Ever hear of Mr. Curt Jordan? He's a famous bad man with nine notches on his gun. Just now he works for me. When he starts on a trail, he rides it to a finish. Never fails. If I say the word he'll take after this fellow Sanborn. And I'll say it damn quick if you annoy me.'

Slim had told her about Jordan. She knew he had killed for pay, not once but many times. If Radbourne put this man on Cole's trail to assassinate him, her husband would not have a chance.

'You might say it anyhow,' she temporized. 'I don't trust you.'

'No need to burn that in like a brand,' he said harshly. 'You go too far, girl. If I give you my word, I'll keep it. I'm offering to make a trade with you. This fellow Sanborn's life for your signature on this paper. I don't give a continental cuss which you choose. I'd as soon have you a widow as an ex-wife.'

His little black eyes gloated. As she looked into them she shuddered. Neither honor nor mercy was in this man. She knew she could not trust any promise he made. He was a liar, and the truth was not in him.

Her resolution hardened. If Cole were standing here, she knew what he would tell her to do.

'I'll not sign,' she said swiftly.

Rage contorted his face, but before he could speak someone knocked on the door.

'What you want?' he snarled.

The door opened, to let in Slim. Mary stared. His face was terribly beaten and bruised.

'Just heard some news,' the cowpuncher said, ignoring the fact that he had interrupted a scene. 'Mex was coming down the road from Box Cañon and met a Rocking Horse rider who had just been to town. He says Jordan had a run-in with Sanborn at the Arcadia and got killed.'

Radbourne stared at the rider, his clammy face colorless. 'You mean—Jordan—got—killed?'

A flicker of enthusiasm crossed Slim's face and was instantly sponged out. 'Y'betcha! Curt went after him—fired two-three times and missed. He'd been drinking, it seems. Sanborn cracked down on him, once. That ended it.'

'Who told this?'

'They call the guy Yorky. Says he was at the inquest. Jury said Sanborn killed him in self-defense.'

Radbourne gasped like a fish out of water. This was a body blow over the heart. He had depended on Jordan to get the fellow. It had never occurred to him that his killer would fail.

'You're sure? This fellow couldn't have been loadin' Mex?'

'No, sir. Nothing like that.' Slim took pleasure

in handing his employer another jolt. 'It seems Jonesboro backs Sanborn every way from the ace. The best people are all with him.'

From ashen lips Mary murmured, 'Thank God.'

'How come they had trouble?' Radbourne asked. The thought that had jumped to his mind was that Jordan might have told the truth before he died.

Slim looked at his employer coldly. 'I dunno,' he said. 'Jordan claimed he was out to get him. 'Far as I know he didn't tell why.'

Chet could not get away from the stunning fact. Jordan was a hangover from the old days, a killer who usually set the scene for his murders before he moved to action. Yet Sanborn had rubbed him out as if he had been an amateur. The owner of the Circle 3 T was shaken. He had been top dog for so long. Had the luck turned on him? This girl had told him that soon he would be struck down for his sins. Was it a prophecy?

'Sure it was Jordan? Couldn't have been someone else?' he asked, his question almost a supplication.

'It was Jordan all right. Yorky saw him lying on a billiard table after the inquest. Sanborn got him right spang through the heart.'

Again Mary murmured her faint cry of thanks to God.

Radbourne turned on her with a snarling oath.

'Get out of my sight or I'll quirt you till your back is raw.'

As Mary turned to go, her eyes fell on the cowpuncher. The eyes in his rigid face had grown cold and steely. She realized he was her friend, and the thought of it warmed her forlorn heart. She walked from the room.

Slim, too, turned away, but his boss called him back.

'Want to talk with you,' Radbourne said abruptly.

'I'm here,' Slim said curtly.

'Sit down.'

The cowpuncher took a chair, but his spine was as straight as if there had been a poker in it. He knew he was not being invited out of friendliness. Radbourne wanted something from him.

'Looks like I haven't a man on the job who isn't a bungler,' Chet complained bitterly. 'This scoundrel Sanborn makes every last one of you look like three for a nickel. First there was Grat. All he could do was give him a flesh wound.Then Jerry fails me. Now Jordan.'

'If you want a thing well done, you have to do it yoreself, my dad used to say,' Slim mentioned, a flicker of derision in his eyes.

'Jordan came here with a rep as a bad man,' Radbourne went on, disregarding the sneer. 'Hadn't been another like him since the old days of John Wesley Hardin, I was told. And he turns out a false alarm. Starts drinking and throws me down without the least consideration.'

'He threw down on himself too,' Slim said. 'Don't forget that. And paid for his foolishness.'

'What's it matter about him?' Radbourne replied sourly. 'He needed killing anyhow. One of these days it was coming to him.'

The Circle 3 T owner's callousness revolted Slim. The young man looked at his employer as one does at some species of unpleasant reptile.

'Sure. His death was inconvenient to you. Outside of that—'

Chet interrupted his rider. Not sensitive to atmospheres, he did not feel the other's contempt. 'I'd ought to have known he wasn't dependable. That's the trouble with notorious killers. They get all swollen up with their own importance. Now a smart young fellow like you, Slim—'

'With nothing to get swelled up about,' Slim interpolated.

'You'd go about a business of that kind with some sense.'

'A business of what kind?' Slim asked coolly.

He was shaking tobacco into a cigarette-paper. Before Radbourne answered him he had rolled and lit his smoke.

'This fellow Sanborn is a bad citizen,' the ranchman said, watching the other. 'He's a killer, bad as Jordan was. On top of that he's a professional gambler, an outlaw, and an immoral character. His marriage to my ward, Mary Landis, is an outrage against decency. I'd be a traitor to my trust if I let him get away with it. But the fellow's slick. He has the law on his side, to a certain extent. Before I've got him beat, he'll have this young girl's life ruined—if I let him get away with it. I can't do it, Slim. I've got to protect her and her interests.'

'I'll bet it's a moral duty laid on you by yore conscience,' Slim said evenly. He guessed what was coming, but he would not forestall it. If Chet had a proposition to make, let him come out with it plainly.

'She's a young girl, and the court has put it up to me to see she gets a fair break. I aim to do that, Slim. Ain't I right?'

Slim looked at him out of level eyes which said nothing. 'I don't reckon a man can be criticized for seeing an unprotected girl gets a square deal,' he agreed.

'There's only one way to do it, Slim,' Radbourne told the young man, leaning forward and speaking in a whisper.

He waited for Calhoun to ask him what way that was, but Slim did not speak, only continued to watch him from black opaque eyes.

' 'Long as Sanborn is alive that girl is in danger,' the big man went on wheezily. 'If she's to be saved he's got to be stomped out.'

'And Jordan was a false alarm when it came to

stomping him out,' Slim suggested. 'He made a bad mistake—gave Sanborn an almost even Break and got rubbed out himself.'

'Exactly what the lunkhead did,' Radbourne cried irritably. 'I figured him sure-fire. He loaded me with how he would wait till he had this fellow right. Instead, he got himself bumped off, losing just fifteen—hundred—dollars thereby.'

The owner of the Circle 3 T fixed the gaze of the cowpuncher as he dragged the last words out, stressing the sum almost by syllables.

'And his life,' Slim added. 'Though I think you said that wasn't important.'

'A lot of money, fifteen hundred plunks,' Chet mused aloud. 'Waiting for the fellow who brings in the man that led the K. & J. express bandits.'

'Meaning Sanborn?'

'Yes, sir. If I was tackling that job, I'd bring him in dead and not alive.'

'It would be safer, don't you reckon?' Slim murmured. 'A tough guy is as easy to dry-gulch as any other kind. Yes, I expect he would pack better as pork. But after I'd done it, I'd be worried for fear I wouldn't get the reward. Some galoot would raise the point it wasn't proved Sanborn was the bandit. And the authorities would likely decline to kick in with the mazuma.'

'I would attend to that. I have some influence, you know.'

'I'll bet you have,' Slim assented.

'The money would be as good as in your pocket—after you had earned it,' Chet urged. 'It would give a young fellow a start in business, and if he was the right kind of a man he might marry Miss Landis and run her ranch.'

'So he might,' Calhoun nodded. 'But don't you reckon she might object some to marrying the bird who had killed her husband?'

'She'll do as I tell her. And you're a good-looking waddy, Slim.'

'Much obliged.' Slim rose from his seat and looked down at the hulk of a man back of the desk. When he spoke scorn etched his voice and contempt blazed in his eyes. 'You've made a mistake, you dirty double-crossing wolf. I'm no hired killer, if I have got outside the law off and on. I don't shoot men down from ambush, and I don't work for a cur who hasn't enough sand in his craw to do it himself, but gets another scalawag to do it for him. Nor for one who bullies women and talks about quirting them. I'll take my time, for I'm going down the road tonight. And every minute till I go I'll be watching to see that noneof your crooks empties his gun into me.'

The dark blood poured into the sallow face of Radbourne. He glared at the reckless cowboy, for the moment so choked with rage that words would not come.

'No waddy alive can talk to me like that,' he

ground out at last. 'Every word you've said is a nail in your coffin, fellow. The road you're going down tonight is a one-way trail. Get out of my sight right damned now.'

'Pleases me to death,' Slim said promptly. 'I'm hoping this will be farewell to you till you rattle yore hocks on the other side of Jordan. But don't bet too heavy on that one-way trail. My pinto is saddled in front of the house, and I aim to land in the saddle with the horse a-running. But first off I'll take my paycheck.'

Radbourne calculated the sum due and wrote a check. Slim pocketed it.

'I'll be drifting,' Slim went on. 'If I meet up with Cole Sanborn, I'll tell him how badly you're worried by him. So long, you damned side-winder.'

Slim backed to the door, watching him to make sure he did not reach for a gun. Without turning, he reached the knob and opened the door. Swiftly he slid through, jumped for the hitch-rack, pulled the slip-knot, and landed in the saddle without touching the stirrups.

The pinto gathered itself to a gallop and pounded into the darkness of the night.

Radbourne heaved his big bulk out of the chair and waddled to the porch. He gave the alarm by firing his revolver at the shadowy figure disappearing in the gloom. Savagely he cursed his folly. He had made a mistake—two of them.

The first was in sizing up the Texan wrong, the second in threatening him. The latter was the more serious. If he had let Slim go to the bunkhouse to pack up his roll, he might have had him shot down before he left the ranch. Now the fellow had got away. He would talk, of course. He would spread the story of the attempt to get him to kill Sanborn. All Boone County would have more evidence of what it already suspected, that Radbourne rubbed out the men who got in his way.

That could not be helped now. The thing to do was to draw the sting from Slim's testimony. He must come out in the open with the claim that he had given Sheriff Magruder clear proof Sanborn was the K. & J. bandit and that the sheriff would not lift a hand to arrest the criminal. Out of a sense of patriotism he was now posting a reward for the capture of this notorious bad man dead or alive. This he was doing as a public duty to free Boone County from the outlaws who infested the brush country.

Yes, that would be good medicine. He would make the reward a thousand dollars. For that sum it was reasonable to think that someone of Sanborn's enemies would take a crack at him.

Chapter XIX
Mary Writes a Letter

Mary heard the sounds of clattering hoofs, of shots, of strident voices. Softly she raised her window, trying to make out what had occurred. But though she listened intently she could not learn the cause of the disturbance. The speakers were too far away for her to hear what was being said. Only once did she catch a sentence, and that in a high-pitched shout of excitement. 'Betcha he's high-tailin' it to town like a streak of greased lightning.'

There had been a fight, of course, and someone had run away. Could it have been Cole? Was it likely he had come alone to the ranch a second time? Not probable, since she could think of no urgent reason for him to take such a risk. Unless he had come to kill Chet Radbourne because the owner of the Circle 3 T had hired Jordan to assassinate him. Or had in some way heard of her capture. That was possible, but it did not seem to her likely.

Her spirit was still riding the hilltops because of the news Slim had brought. In memory she could still see the shock of fear registered in Radbourne's sallow face. His enemy had struck home a jarring blow that had shaken the man's confidence. To kill a man was a terrible thing, but just now she could not think of the death of Jordan that way. Her husband, who was a stranger to her, whom she had met only for one hour vividly significant among months of stagnation, had been too much for the notorious killer attempting to take him at advantage. What he had done had been forced on him while he was defending her interests. Men called Cole Sanborn a killer, too, but she had an unshaken conviction that he had never killed from choice, but always of necessity. He was wild and reckless, scornful of public opinion, but she would not believe that he was bad. It was written on the hard, sardonic face that there burned in him a dynamic spark of self-respect which would not let him follow a path of shame.

The noise outside died down. Mary tried to read, but the words of the book meant nothing to her. Hours passed. She waited, for what she did not know. The lights in the men's bunkhouse went out, as did the lamp in the foreman's cabin. The two night guards must be awake, but except for them the ranch had gone to sleep. It was time for her to go to bed.

A light tap sounded on the window. It set her pulses drumming. She moved noiselessly to the casement.

'Who is there?' she asked in a whisper.

The answer came back in a murmur no louder than her own. 'Slim Calhoun. I had trouble with

Chet and lit out. Can I speak with you a minute?'

She moved back to the coal-oil lamp and blew it out. Very slowly, in order to make no sound, she raised the window higher. A dark form lifted itself and dropped lightly to the floor.

Her heart was beating wildly. Never before had she been alone with a young man in a dark bedroom at night. She felt sure that in his visit lay no amorous intent. He had never made the least effort to ingratiate himself with her. But all the training of a chaperoned life protested at such a situation.

'Don't be scared, ma'am,' he reassured. 'Nobody saw me come. I left my horse tied to the pasture fence quarter of a mile away. You know I don't aim to hurt you any.'

'I know,' she said, and could not keep the quaver out of her voice. 'The shooting I heard—Was it you and Chet Radbourne?'

'It was Chet. I never fired a shot. He wanted to hire me to kill yore husband. I let him make his proposition, then told him what a skunk he was. After that I lit out. That was when he got to burning powder. Here's the way of it, Mrs. Sanborn. I've been dragged into this feud. Looks like I'd better join up with Cole. But if I propose it, he'll shy off like a wild colt. I had words with him at Jonesboro that time, and up here we exchanged shots. He won't believe a thing I say. The notion that will stick in his craw is that Chet is trying to plant a spy with him. If you can give me a line to him, he'll know I'm all right.'

'Yes,' she assented, still in the whisper they were using.

'Providing you're satisfied in yore own mind about me,' he added.

What Slim had said was true. It would be a characteristic Radbourne trick to stage a pretended quarrel with one of his own men and send him into the camp of the enemy. But Mary felt sure that back of this man's recklessness was loyalty.

'I'm satisfied,' she said quietly. 'I'll write a note, well as I can in the dark.'

She moved to a table, sat down, found paper and pencil. A pulse of excitement beat in her throat. How should she address this man who was her husband and yet not her husband at all? What should she call him? Once he had said he must be Cole to her and she Mary to him, at least in public. She wrote, without any word of endearment from start to finish.

Cole, I am sending this by Slim Calhoun, until tonight one of Chet Radbourne's men. He is what you call square. I am sure of it. Today he fought with Jerry Haskell and has a badly wounded face from the battle. Later, he quarreled with Mr. Radbourne, who tried to kill him as he rode away. He has slipped back to see me, to take a message from me to you.

I must explain why I am here. Jordan and another of the Circle 3 T men caught me, and the other man made me come here with him. I am writing this in the dark, for there are guards outside. So that you may know this is not a forgery to bait a trap, I will remind you that once you promised, after our stage kiss, not to let your enemies and mine kill you. Every night I pray that they may not.

I am quite safe here. Do not worry about me. Mr. Radbourne treats me well, even though he is very angry at me because I will not sign a paper asking for an annulment of our marriage. As safe as in God's pocket. You once said that. Please—please do not do anything in a hurry. Take your time. Work out whatever plans you have.

For what you told me about Mr. Radbourne is true. As long as you are alive he will not harm me. He dare not. He is afraid of you. I was with him tonight when Slim came in with word that you had killed that dreadful man Jordan. Cole, I could see fear riding him. So, to protect me, you must look after your own safety.

I am sorry you had to do what you did tonight, but I do not blame you. I know it was self-defense. I am sure you would never kill for any other reason.

MARY

She folded the letter, sealed it in an envelope, and gave it to Slim. The cowboy put it in the pocket of his shirt.

'I hate to leave you with that wolf,' he said.

'It won't be for long,' she said confidently.

'I know, but—what he said tonight to you.'

'About quirting me till my back is raw? He'd like to do that, but he dare not. I have a husband, and he is afraid of him. Didn't you see his eyes tonight when you told him about Jordan?'

'Yes. It handed him a scare sure enough. If the scare lasts.' He added, with a touch of embarrassment: 'Wish I could help you.'

'It will last long enough. Slim, if you line up with my husband, try not to let him expose himself. They'll kill him if they can. That's the one way you can help me. Look out for him.'

'I'll certainly do that if I can,' he promised. 'I'll be saying "adios" now.'

He slid out of the window, after listening for a moment for the watchers. Mary waited, nerves tense, fearing every instant she might hear the sound of a shot. The minutes passed, with the silence unbroken. She measured in anxious thought the distance he had to cover. Now he would have reached the root house, now the blacksmith shop. He must by this time have crawled through the barbed-wire fence into the pasture. The guards had not seen him.

Chapter XX

A Recruit

Pete Daggett brought a prisoner into camp, a gun trained on him.

'C-claims he's got a m-message for you,' stuttered Pete.

Cole looked at the black-haired young fellow in plain leather chaps and recognized him at once.

'A message from Chet Radbourne?' he asked.

'Not from Chet,' Slim answered, and he handed Sanborn a letter.

Before looking at the letter, Cole made another remark. 'Last time we met you came a-shooting.'

'And the time before that,' Calhoun amended coolly, 'yore horse was on the jump and I didn't score a hit. Glad of it now.'

'How did you find our camp?'

'A nester gave me a line on it. I loaded him with a story I knew already and he kinda let slip where it was.'

'You're one of Chet's riders?'

'Was,' corrected Slim.

'I get it.' Cole's voice held an edge of sarcasm. 'You've had a quarrel with him and so you'd like to bury the hatchet with me.'

Slim smiled. 'I'm handing you a big laugh, Sanborn. That's exactly the way it is.'

'I must be a mind-reader,' Cole said evenly.

He read the letter, not without difficulty. In the darkness some of the words had run over the edge of the paper. Lines were crossed. His first impression was that it was a forgery, but the reference to the stage kiss convinced him of its genuineness. Nobody except Mary could know he had said this.

Cole flung a swift, abrupt question at Calhoun. 'When did Jordan send Mrs. Sanborn back to the Circle 3 T?'

'Yesterday morning. He sent Gildea back with her. It must have been only an hour or two before you killed him.'

'Is she safe at the ranch?'

'I'd say quite safe. Chet isn't fool enough to harm her.'

'He'd better not,' Cole said harshly.

After the first reading, he turned back and went over the scrawled sheets a second time. No man could have called this a love letter. She had not even begun with the conventional 'Dear Cole.' But between the lines he read an emotion that set his blood racing. *Every night she prayed they might not kill him.* His brown face reflected no feeling, but a bell of joy pealed in his heart. He saw her kneeling beside the bed, slender and dainty, a remote mystery in a white nightgown, and the picture filled him with awe.

Cole looked into the black eyes of the Texan and liked what he saw there. He liked, too, the fellow's cool and easy manner, his assumption that no apologies were necessary for past alignments. But Chet was a tricky devil. He would have sense enough to choose an emissary who looked frank and honest. Perhaps they had pulled the wool over Mary's eyes.

'So you had a rumpus with Chet,' Cole said. 'How-come?'

'I been on edge for quite some time,' Slim replied. 'More with Haskell than with the old man, though I never liked a hair of the old wolf's head. Yesterday Jerry beat the stuffing outa me. Whaled me till I couldn't stand.'

'Yes?' Sanford said, with a polite coolness that might have been incredulity.

'You might like to hear about that,' Slim continued, reaching for the makings. 'I got a leetle mite curious about something was none of my business, and Haskell worked me over real thorough on account of it.'

'Am I supposed to ask what you were curious about?' Cole wanted to know.

'Up to you as to that,' Slim said lightly. 'You'll be interested before I'm through. Got a match?'

Slim lit the cigarette he had rolled and went on with his story. 'I was camped near the mouth of Box Cañon the day before the K. & J. express robbery. Three fellows rode up the gulch. They didn't see me, but I saw them. One of the three was Jerry Haskell. I couldn't swear to the others account of the sun getting in my eyes.' The ex-Circle 3 T man stopped to flash a grin. 'Next time I saw Jerry was two days later. He was back on the job at the ranch. What kinda got my attention the day he rode up the cañon was that he was wearing corduroy pants, a blue polka-dot bandanna, and a rattlesnake skin band round his hat. I hadn't seen him in that get-up before, and I've never seen him in it since.'

The black-haired man had kept his promise to interest Cole. The latter looked at him, steadily, without speaking, but he could not repress the eager excitement in his eyes.

'Me, I put two and two together, and it added just four,' Slim explained casually. 'Like I said, it was none of my business, and I let it ride until Chet picked me to ride with Mrs. Sanborn. She took a smile to me, and we became friendly. I don't claim to be anything but a hell-raisin' young rooster. Still and all, I know a lady when I meet up with one. If I could do Mrs. Sanborn a good turn I was ready to be Johnny-on-the-spot. 'Course I knew there was war between you and the Circle 3 T, and I began to wonder if Haskell was handing you the burnt end of the stick in the K. & J. robbery matter. So I visited his hogan when he was out on a look-see expedition. In a trunk I found the corduroy pants, the polka-dot bandanna, and the rattlesnake band. I hadn't hardly more than closed the trunk when Jerry walked in on me. He was noways welcome. Before he got through socking me with his maulers I was plumb tired of him.'

'That why you quit the Circle 3 T?' Cole asked.

'No, sir. My system can absorb a licking when it's coming to me without any hard feelings. I'll tell you why I quit. It just happened I was the guy who carried Chet the news that you had rubbed out Jordan. It made him plenty sick. When he came out of that, he made me a proposition. I was to bushwhack you and get the K. & J. reward money. Seeing I was sore at the skunk, anyhow, for telling Mrs. Sanborn he'd like to give her a quirting, I up and told him where to get off. He threatened me. I hit my saddle and lit out, with the old toad pumping lead at me. But I wasn't satisfied to leave without seeing Mrs. Sanborn, since I had figured I'd try to fix things up with you. I know the Circle 3 T layout, and it wasn't much risk to sneak back, tap on her window, and have a talk. That was when she wrote me the letter to give you.'

The imperturbable face of Sanborn was hard as a rock wall. When he spoke his voice was ominously quiet.

'He said that—to Mrs. Sanborn?'

'After she'd cried "Thank God" when I spilled the news that you had got Jordan.'

'He said he'd—quirt her?'

'He threatened, but he won't do it. That old devil ain't anyways easy in his mind. He's plumb scared you'll get him. 'Long as you're alive and kicking he won't do Mrs. Sanborn any personal harm. That's my guess, for what it's worth.'

'She says in this letter you've been kind to her.'

Slim waved that aside lightly. 'Nothing to that. I claim to be a white man, and when I went riding with her I acted like one. If I wanted credit for that I'd be proving I wasn't.' He hesitated a moment before he carried on: 'That old skunk is full of tricks. He hinted if I bumped you off, it would be my turn with Mrs. Sanborn. My guess is I'd be dry-gulched inside of a week.'

The doubts of Cole had vanished. This Texan was not a spy from the camp of the enemy, unless his whole manner and appearance were lies. On the frontier character is etched upon the face and stamped into the bearing of a man. Slim was reckless and lawless, as Cole had always been himself, a rebel against the smug safety of conventions. He had followed joyously rough and crooked trails. But he would do to ride the river with when the stream was full and turbulent. More than once Sanborn's life had depended upon not making a mistake in his judgment of a man. He felt sure he was not making one now.

'Did you come here only to bring me this letter?' Cole asked. 'Or is it your idea to throw in with us?'

'That last would be up to you, don't you reckon?'

The hard eyes of the two men met and held. There was as yet no friendliness between them, but each felt a curious sense of kinship with the other. Both had strayed to the edge of that borderland beyond which a decent man may not go, and both had turned their backs forever on dishonor.

'This is no picnic we're starting on, Calhoun,' said Cole gravely. 'Some of us are liable to get bumped off.'

'Not me,' Slim grinned gaily. 'I was born lucky. I'll help do the bumping. Lead me to this war.'

'I'll lead you to it soon enough if you've made up your mind. No use telling you the odds are heavy against us. Chet may blast us off the map.'

'You're such a hell-a-miler I'd hate to sweat a game[1] when I can horn in beside you,' the cow-puncher said cheerfully.

Abruptly Cole flashed a question at him. 'How many men does Chet keep at the Lazy B?'

'Four. He changes them every three-four days.'

'Instructions are to kill, I reckon?'

'The season is open on you whether you attack or don't,' Slim said. 'Any Circle 3 T man who takes a crack at you will be the white-haired boy with Chet—if he shoots straight.'

'Will Chet's warriors go through?'

[1]Sweating a game is looking on without participating.

192

Calhoun gave this consideration before he answered. 'They're tough nuts. Pick of the riff-raff in this neck of the woods.'

'Loyal to their boss, you'd say?'

'There ain't a horse, dog, or man on the place loyal to Chet,' Slim said bluntly. 'Nothing in him that calls for loyalty. But I'm not saying they won't fight for him. They will. That's what they're paid to do. A man doesn't throw down his outfit.'

Cole knew this was true. These men regarded themselves somewhat as a soldier of fortune does. They hired out to the side that would pay them best. It would be a mistake to assume they would not fight as savagely for a bad cause as for a good one.

But they had to be kept well fed and comfortable. They would not endure hunger and thirst and cold nights among the rocks far up in the hills as Dunc McCoy and Dave Pope and Pete Daggett would because of friendship and loyalty. They were Circle 3 T men because of strictly business reasons.

Chapter XXI
On the Way to the War

Into Jonesboro from the hills dropped seven riders. They crossed the bridge at the lower end of town and stopped at the hitch-rack in front of the hotel. One of the group stayed with the horses, the others moved up the street of false fronts, their spurs jingling as they went. They made no pretense of not being heavily armed. All of them carried rifles. Some wore revolvers in belts. The rest, no doubt, had their small-arms in scabbards under their arms or in other convenient places.

In advance of the compact group word spread that Cole Sanborn had come to town with his gang. The news passed from one to another citizen, not without excitement. The presumption was that Sanborn was on his way to avenge the abduction of his wife. This display of force was taken as an open declaration of war against the Circle 3 T. In an incredibly short time saloons and honky-tonks buzzed with murmured conjecture.

Sheriff Magruder teetered down the walk in his high-heeled boots to meet the new arrivals.

'Morning, Cole—boys,' he said. 'Today Fourth of July or something?'

'News to me if it is,' Cole replied.

194

'Didn't know but what you lads were mixed on yore dates,' the little officer said. 'Haven't come to hurrah the town—or anything like that, have you?'

'We're here only for a short visit, sheriff,' Cole answered. 'On our way through to the Lazy B. I aim to take possession today.'

'Have you arranged that with Radbourne?'

Cole looked at Magruder coldly. 'Not yet. He didn't arrange with me when his scoundrels took Mrs. Sanborn to the Circle 3 T.'

'I don't blame you for feeling sore, Cole,' the sheriff said. 'All I want to know is that you're going to stay within the law.'

Sanborn laughed, bitterly, without mirth. 'Will the law reach to the Circle 3 T and bring my wife back here?'

Beneath the tan Magruder flushed. 'There's been no complaint made to me, Cole. 'Far as I know officially Mrs. Sanborn is on a visit to the Circle 3 T.'

'And there won't be any complaint made, Magruder. I'll attend to that as personal and private business of my own. But there's another point might interest you. One of my boys has a little information for you about the K. & J. robbery. Speak yore piece, Slim.'

Calhoun told the story of what he had suspected about Haskell and the confirmation he had later found in the foreman's trunk. The sheriff did not

195

show enthusiasm, though he did not reject the tale.

'How-come you recognized Jerry Haskell as he rode into the gulch and didn't know those with him?' Magruder asked.

'He was between me and them. Couldn't swear to them.'

'Funny. Mighty funny. I reckon you have no idea who they were.'

'Nary a notion,' Slim said cheerfully, his white teeth flashing in a grin.

The wrinkled little officer gave an incredulous snort. 'Yore evidence ain't worth a lick. If you recognized Haskell, you did the others. No two ways about that.' He added, resentfully: 'When-ever any mouthy guy wants to let off steam, he roasts me for not maintaining the law. How the heck can I get anywhere running down criminals when all you fellows hold back information it doesn't suit you to tell?'

'I wouldn't know about that, sheriff,' Slim said, shaking his head.

'Another thing. You're a Circle 3 T rider, I'm told.'

'Not now. I was.'

'Had a row with Radbourne or Haskell?'

'I told Chet he was a skunk. You might call it a row. He was pumping bullets at me as I left.'

'I heard some story about Haskell beating you up,' Magruder probed.

'Correct. He whaled the tar out of me.'

'So now you tell a story that ties him up with the K. & J. robbery.'

'You'd call me a prejudiced party, I reckon,' Slim admitted. 'But I got my info before I was worked over by Haskell, if that is important.'

'What you expect me to do about this?' Magruder asked, turning to Cole. 'Go up to the Circle 3 T and arrest Haskell on this man's story?'

'No, Magruder, I'd keep this under my hat if I was you,' Cole replied. 'Presently you'll pick up evidence to back what Slim says. When you have enough, it will do to talk about an arrest.'

The party broke up in front of the Arcadia. Sanborn and Calhoun walked down the street to the office of the *Boone County Beacon.*

Tim Alderson was scratching a news item on a pad of paper.

In a sing-song voice Cole recited another one for him.

Slim Calhoun and Cole Sanborn dropped into town from the rimrock country and paid a visit to the *Beacon* office. They report that the grass is good and cattle are taking on weight. Come again, boys. Jonesboro always has the glad hand out for visitors like you.

Tim Alderson grinned. 'What deviltry are you two boys up to now?' he asked.

'None,' Cole demurred. 'I'm on the way up to the Lazy B with a bunch of riders. Going to take over the place and run it for Mrs. Sanborn.'

'Does Chet agree to that?'

'He will, I reckon. When I mentioned I was aiming to do it, he didn't raise any objections.'

The editor's smile had vanished. 'You understand what this means, Sanborn?' he said.

'I have a rough idea.'

'I wish you didn't feel you had to do it,' Alderson went on gloomily. 'I don't like it a bit.'

'Neither do I, but it will make news for the *Beacon*,' Cole said sardonically.

'You know you're starting a war. There will be bloodshed. Bound to be. Radbourne won't quit now. He has gone too far. If he gave up, his prestige would be gone.'

'I'm not starting the war,' Cole corrected. 'If there's one started, it won't be by me or any of my men. When he took my wife to the Circle 3 T, he made it my move next. We're going on a legal errand. I'll say another thing. If everybody in Boone County lies down and lets Radbourne ride over him, there won't be any trouble, but it will pop when anybody stands up for his rights. That fellow would be looking for trouble if that's the way you view it. But I would think different. My opinion would be that Radbourne was to blame one hundred per cent.'

'Mine, too,' assented Alderson. 'I wasn't

thinking about blame, but about the fact that lives are going to be lost.'

'Every time an engineer builds a big bridge or a great irrigation dam lives are lost,' Cole reminded him. 'He can't stop for that.'

'I'll do the best I can to see that public opinion is with you,' the editor promised.

Cole nodded. 'I read your last editorial. Much obliged for it. I realize that one of Radbourne's plug-uglies might make you trouble, but I don't figure any of them will. There has been a change of sentiment in Boone County and Radbourne is too smart to try to buck it in too raw a way. There's an open season on me and my boys. We're supposed to be a bunch of wild hellions. But you represent the best sentiment of the good people of this section. Chet won't let his warriors ride roughshod over you.'

'I'm not afraid of that,' Alderson said.

Cole and Slim walked back up the street just as the rest of their group came jingling out of the Arcadia.

'Did you pass along the tip I gave you?' Cole asked Dave Pope.

The lank cowpuncher nodded. 'I mentioned in Lauret's hearing at the faro table that we were headed for the Lazy B to take possession. He finished the deal and excused himself for a minute. I saw him talking to a man who beat it on the jump. Dunc says he saw a fellow faggin' it outa town on a big roan not five minutes later.'

Cole turned to McCoy. 'Know the rider?'

'Aye, I know him,' the brindle-headed man answered. 'It was the man they call Mex. He's a Circle 3 T rider.'

'Gone to carry the good news to Ghent,' Sanborn said, with a memory of his McGuffey Reader days.

'My thought was that maybe he had gone to carry bad news to Chet and Jerry,' McCoy differed. 'Though only the Lord knows for which of us it's going to be bad and for which good.'

'If that weighs on you, now's the time to quit,' Cole said lightly as he swung to his saddle.

'I'll no' deny it weighs on me, man. I'm a person of experience and sagacity. But I'll thank you not to insult me by suggesting I'm a fair-weather friend.' The Scotchman found his horse and mounted.

The seven riders jogged soberly out of town. They might have been going to a prayer-meeting. But a hundred eyes watched them as they rode up the dusty road. They were going to make history.

Chapter XXII
Up Suicide Trough

The seven riders passed along a draw from the dusty baked plains into the foothills. In front of them was a cleft in the rimrock.

Rusty eyed it dubiously. 'Fine if they do what we're expecting them to do, Cole, but not so good if they don't try to ambush us at Big Pine Point and come on down to the mouth of the gulch instead.'

'They won't do that,' Cole replied. 'Big Pine Point is the best spot for a trap on the road. They'll figure we won't know they have heard we're coming. But I'm coppering my bet some. Slim and Pete, you two swing round the bluff and climb it from the rear. Give us the come-on signal if there's nobody up there. If you meet any warriors, don't stay to fight, but come back on the jump.'

Slim and Pete moved ahead rapidly. The others followed at a walk. It would be half an hour before the two scouts reached the summit of the bluff at the entrance to the gorge.

Sanborn was confident that Lauret had sent a messenger to warn the Circle 3 T men of his approach. Mex would stop at the Lazy B to tell those on duty there to be prepared and would then ride across country to the Circle 3 T. The men at the Lazy B would hold a consultation. It was an easy guess that they would not wait there to be attacked, but would decide on an ambush for the invaders at Big Pine Point. From the rocks above they could pick off Cole's party without exposing themselves. If they had luck, they could end the war in one brief battle. So they would reason.

While they were waiting for their victims, Radbourne's men would have to leave the Lazy B unguarded. Cole meant to slip into the ranch-house during that period. There was a chance the plan would not work, but he thought the odds were very much in its favor.

The five men loitered in an arroyo a few hundred yards from the rock wall. The heat waves played above the sand.

'I don't reckon there's anybody down the cañon this far,' Dave Pope surmised. 'Cole has got this figured out right. They're waiting for us up at Big Pine Point. Wouldn't be any sense to their doing anything else. We might as well save time and move on into the gulch.'

The faded eyes of Rusty rested on him as the old-timer drew a plug of tobacco from his pocket and tore off a ragged chew with his teeth.

'Nobody has got a holt of you. If you're so crazy to save time, by gum, you can start right damn now. Any last words you'd like conveyed to friends, if any, we'll pass along.'

'Me, I'll wait till we have information on the subject,' Dunc McCoy announced definitely. 'I'd hate to get jostled off my horse in that narrow cañon by any of you anxious lads trying to outrun bullets. There are no road laws in a stampede.'

Presently they made out two riders on the summit of the bluff. One of them made the signal that all was well.

'What did I tell you?' Dave jeered.

'It's not important what you told us, son,' McCoy answered. 'You might ram-stam in a hundred times and be right. Fine. And the next time, if you were wrong, it would be bury him out on the lone prairee.'

The cavalcade moved forward into the defile. Cole led the way, on the off chance that the enemy might be waiting for them at the first bend in the trail. They wound up in single file. A few hundred yards from the mouth of the gorge a rock slide had scorched a path down to the bottom.

Cole put his horse at this precipitous ascent. The other riders followed him. The cowponies clambered up like cats, ropy muscles standing out as they went. There was a good deal of rubble among the rocks. More than once a horse went to its knees, fought to its feet again, and sent stones clattering down on those behind.

The slide terminated in a chimney leading to the top of the wall.

Rusty looked up the narrow, dangerous pitch. 'Holy smoke! This is sure a rough road to heaven, boys. Better grab the apple with a strangle holt and say yore prayers.'

'Can do,' Cole called back. 'I once went up here on a bet when I was a crazy kid.'

'That don't make it noways safe if you did,' Rusty complained querulously. 'I recollect some of the boys figured yore head ought to have been examined. And now I've been drug into the same fool business. Right now I'm naming this spot Suicide Trough.'

'If it was easy we wouldn't be going up here,' Cole made cheerful answer. 'It's only because they won't imagine we're soft-headed enough to try it that we're taking this back door way to the Lazy B.'

'Well, get going, fellow,' Rusty snapped. 'Might as well get stove up now as later.'

The sides of the horses were pumping like bellows. 'We'll give the broncs a rest,' Cole said. 'Not far to the top. We're 'most there. Say forty or fifty feet.'

'Not far,' agreed Dave, squinting an eye along the trough. 'Only trouble is it's straight up. I wisht I had practiced old Baldy climbing the sides of houses.'

'My p-pegleg is p-plumb whipped already,' Pete Daggett stuttered. 'But he'll m-make it if any hoss here does.'

'You never had a lick of sense about that broomtail since you let Arapahoe Bill saw the wall-eyed critter off on you,' Dave reproved.

'S-say, if you ever had one as good—'

'Let's start, irregardless of consequences,' Rusty urged. 'We've done burned our breeches behind us, as the old saying goes. I'm gettin' goosey sitting here on the edge of nowhere.'

'All right,' said Cole, with a grin cheerful but meretricious. 'All we have to do is to keep going.'

'Yeah,' derided Rusty. 'He means up, boys, not down. If anyone gets started the other way, we can kiss that baby good-bye. There won't be enough of him left to collect.'

They watched Sanborn's roan take the finish with a rush of scrambling hoofs.

'Me next,' Rusty said. 'If Old Socks comes sliding down with me, remember the brake's done bust and get outa the way.'

Rusty reached the summit safely. The other horses clawed their way up, each with a clatter of falling rocks and rubble.

Cole drew a deep breath of relief. He had been dubious about taking this hazardous cutoff. Against all probability there was not a broken leg among the forty-two which had just come up the slide.

'Lady Luck is with us, boys,' he said.

'Yes, sir,' drawled Slim. 'All we got to do now is whop thirty or forty of Chet's warriors. Nothing to worry about after this.'

'We'll try to meet them a few at a time,' Cole said.

The riders cantered across the mesa to a cottonwood draw running parallel to the rimrock. They followed it, taking the shelter of the lower ground and the trees. The draw dropped down to a mountain valley in which the buildings of the Lazy B nestled against a green hillside. Smoke rose lazily from the chimney of the main house. There was no movement about the place.

'I don't reckon anyone is home, unless they're holed up waiting for guests,' Slim surmised aloud. 'What say I make a detour and investigate?'

'I'm doing that,' Cole differed. 'Wait here, boys. If the land is clear, I'll give you a signal.'

'And if it ain't clear, if they plug you like a sieve, that will be a signal not to come, I reckon,' Dave said. 'No, sir, I'm going with you.'

Cole nodded assent. 'All right, buckaroo. That will be fine. If they only get one of us, maybe it will be you.'

The two men made a wide circle, dropping back of a hill into an arroyo that fell gradually to the valley of the park. From a clump of live oaks they watched the house for a few minutes. It seemed to be entirely deserted.

'Filled with absentees, looks like,' Dave murmured.

Between the live oaks and the main house lay a stretch of two hundred yards of open ground.

Cole looked at his companion. 'Got to make a run for it, Dave. No other way.'

Their two horses came out of the timber on the run. The men reached the back of the house, flung their reins to the ground, and ran in the open door of the kitchen.

Unwashed dishes were piled everywhere. The stove, still lit, was grimy with grease. The floor had not been swept within the memory of man.

Dave motioned to the stove. 'Not away for long.'

'No,' agreed Cole.

They passed warily into the big living-room. Nobody was there, though there was plenty of evidence of recent habitation. Spurs, saddles, tobacco sacks, old boots, a pair of chaps, newspapers, and other odds and ends littered the place.

The two men made a tour of the bedrooms. When they were satisfied the occupants had departed, they signaled to their friends in the cottonwoods.

The five riders cantered down to the ranch-house.

'Better get the horses out of sight in the stable,' Cole said to Daggett. 'No need telling the boys they have visitors.'

Rusty dismounted stiffly. 'Well, you done got the hacienda, Cole. An' now you got it, can you hold it? Reminds me onct when I was in Abilene, after I had druv a herd there for Shanghai Pierce—'

'We're not aiming to hold it,' Cole drawled.

The men stared at him, surprised. 'Not hold it, man!' McCoy said. 'Did you take us up Rusty's Suicide Trough for exercise?'

'Not exactly. This will be the way of it.'

Cole explained in detail what he had in mind.

Chapter XXIII
Trespassers Warned

Five disgusted Circle 3 T riders trooped back from Big Pine Point. Mex had brought them a false alarm. He had said that Sanborn and his gang were on the immediate way to the Lazy B. They had waited up there among the big rocks for their victims until they were hot, hungry, and tired. All the way back to the ranch they had been quarreling with one another.

Straight to the ranch-house they rode and dismounted.

'Quit yore beefing, Hank,' Bud Calloway said, loosening the saddle cinch of his horse. 'You don't have to run on us because Cole Sanborn didn't ride up the cañon and ask to be shot. We're noways to blame.'

A figure stood in the doorway.

'Looking for me, boys?' a voice drawled.

Cole was leaning against the jamb. He had not drawn a weapon, though the butts of two revolvers were close to his capable hands.

Five pairs of amazed eyes stared at him.

'You—here!' Bud gasped. 'W-where did you come from?'

'From Jonesboro. Didn't Mex mention I was

on my way? No, don't you, Gray Shirt. It's not safe.'

Gray Shirt recognized the truth of this advice. A man had come round the end of the house, a rifle in his hands. A second one with a scatter-gun was sitting in an open window. Still a third had emerged from back of the root house. He carried a forty-four trained on the Circle 3 T men. Radbourne's riders were trapped.

'How did you get here?' Bud asked. 'We was guarding the pass.'

'You couldn't have come round by Hankins Fork,' another said. 'You didn't have time.'

'A balloon drapped us in here,' Slim said, in his soft, derisive drawl. 'What-say, boss? Hadn't I better collect the hardware off the boys? They're too young and tender to play with firearms.'

Cole invited his guests into the house. He told them where to sit.

'We've just finished dinner,' he explained. 'Sorry there isn't anything more cooked. It is too late to start fixing food now. You'll enjoy your supper more after missing a meal—if you get any.'

'What you aiming to do with us?' Hank growled unhappily.

'What were you going to do with me and my boys as we came up the pass?' Cole asked, his face hard and cold as a mountain lake in winter.

'We were going to warn you to go back,' the man mumbled.

'That's a lie,' Cole said harshly. 'You meant to shoot us down without a chance for our lives. Have you anything to say why we shouldn't do the same to you?'

'My God, you wouldn't do that, Cole!' Bud pleaded, tiny beads of perspiration all over his forehead. 'We wasn't fixing to harm you. Honest we wasn't.'

'Tie their hands in front of them,' ordered Cole. 'We'll take them back to Big Pine Point.'

The face of the man called Hank blanched. His mouth twitched. From one to another of his captors his skim-milk eyes darted, seeking help.

'What for?' he asked, in a whine. 'Goddlemighty, boys, you ain't aimin' to—to—'

The dry whisper died away. He could not put into words his fear. To do that would be to make it too real.

The twelve men got to horse, the five prisoners with their hands still bound.

Before they started, the frosted granite eyes of Cole bored into those of his captives. 'You'll go to sleep in smoke if any one of you makes a sound to warn Chet's riders when they come in.'

'We'll do like you tell us,' Hank promised.

Gray Shirt was a hardy ruffian. 'Radbourne will be pleased to find out what company you're keeping, Slim,' he said.

Young Calhoun looked at him, a challenge in his cool eyes. 'I'm worrying a lot about what Radbourne thinks,' he answered.

'The Circle 3 T hired you, didn't it?'

'Hired me and fired me, Jim. But it didn't take a mortgage on the rest of my life.'

'So you tie in with this fellow McCoy, the guy who almost killed Gildea of our outfit; and with Sanborn, who has shot up several of the boys.'

'Neither McCoy nor Sanborn dry-gulched the men they got, like you were going to do us, did they?' Slim asked pointedly.

Gray Shirt let his frozen, insolent eyes travel from Slim to Cole. 'This *hombre* whose dust you are eating, Slim, takes in too much territory when he gets on the prod with Chet. I'll give him a week before he's bucked out and cashed in.'

'You never can tell,' Slim retorted. 'I'll bet after Mex came in here a while ago, so fast his bronc was draggin' his belly in the sand, you wouldn't have given Cole an hour, let alone a week.'

'What's the idea in making them sore, Jim?' asked Hank, between a whine and a growl. 'The thirty dollars a month I get from the Circle 3 T don't keep me from being reasonable.'

'I'll bet it don't,' Gray Shirt said, contempt in his glance. 'You're plumb scared to death and look so bad yore ears flop. Fellow, get it into that buzzard head of yours that it doesn't matter a lick what we say. This bird Sanborn has his mind made up. 'Long as there's a button on Jabe's coat I'm not crawling to him. He knows damn well we were aiming to stop his clock. No use making a holler if he's fixing us up with a through ticket to Kingdom Come. But we don't have to act like we're three for a nickel.'

The trail divided, one branch dropping down into the cañon in front of them, the other rising to the rimrock above.

'I reckon I'll take that sign now, Cole,' said Slim. 'One of the other boys better go with me to keep a lookout while I stick it up.'

Cole passed to Slim the top of a small table from which the legs had been sawn. Upon it a legend had been neatly printed with a blue marking pencil.

TRESPASSERS WARNED!
COLE SANBORN'S PRIVATE ROAD
DANGEROUS

Daggett joined Calhoun. They took the right-hand trail.

Rusty shouted a warning after them. 'I don't reckon Chet's killers will be there yet, but you boys keep yore eyes skinned. Good men are right seldom, and yore mammies would miss you, if you still have them.'

'I never yet throwed down on myself,' Slim called back gaily.

Cole dropped back and rode beside the man called Jim.

'I'll say this for you, Gray Shirt,' Sanborn said. 'You're a game villain. I don't care much for you, but I prefer your kind to that of your friend Hank.'

Gray Shirt met him eye to eye. 'Am I supposed to say thanks?' he asked coolly. 'And who said this yellow dog was my friend? I'm some particular who I call by that name.'

He spoke loud enough for Hank to hear. That ill-visored specimen squirmed but said nothing.

'Apologies offered,' Cole replied. 'What I'm here to tell you is that I don't kill in cold blood. I'm not like Radbourne and his hired riff-raff. You're safe enough, unless you make a mistake.'

'Such as?'

'Attempting to escape, or trying to warn the Circle 3 T men as they come up the cañon.'

'Are they coming up the cañon?' Gray Shirt asked, almost too casually.

'You know it. A big bunch of them, soon as they can catch and saddle after Mex gets to the ranch.'

'Smart as a whip, aren't you?' jeered the prisoner.

'I'd be a fool not to guess that.' Cole's questioning gaze rested on him. 'Point is, must I gag you to keep your trap shut?'

'You aiming to dry-gulch the boys, if they come up the cañon?'

'It may surprise you, but I'm not. This property belongs to Mrs. Sanborn, and I'm here as her legal representative. I expect to order these intruders to keep off it. If they go, fine. There won't be any trouble. If they don't, I won't hold myself respon-sible for what takes place.'

Gray Shirt looked steadily from opaque eyes at the man riding beside him and came to a decision.

'If you're going to warn them, I'll sweat the game and not put any chips in the pot,' he promised.

Captors and captives rode up the ridge back of the rimrock. In a clump of live oaks they dismounted. The prisoners were fastened together. One man was left as a guard. The others climbed up the steep, rough ascent to Big Pine Point.

Chapter XXIV
'If Cole Wasn't so Damned Legal'

From the bed of boulders at Big Pine Point the pass below could be covered for a distance of two hundred yards.

Dunc McCoy let his glance sweep along the trail. 'A fat chance we would have had if we'd come up there, lads. I'll remember that when I cut loose at Radbourne's wolves.'

Cole looked at him. The Scotchman's blue eyes, mere slits, were drained of color. Anger was in his grim face.

'No, Dunc,' Cole said to the red-headed man. 'We're trying to stay inside the law. Unless they force it there won't be any shooting. We're here on our legal rights. I don't want to throw away that advantage.'

'Then what in Mexico did we come up here for if we ain't going to give this bunch of scalawags what their friends were fixing to give us?' Rusty asked sharply.

'Don't you reckon that if they go crawling back to Chet with their tails between their legs, Boone County is going to get a good laugh?' Cole answered. 'Here's how it shapes. Chet has been the big auger in this country. Whatever he has said has gone. Nobody stood up against him. If we can show that all his claims don't amount to a barrel of shucks, his power will be gone. The important thing isn't to bump off a lot of his warriors, but to show him up for a bluffer. If we do that, folks won't let him crowd them. What they need is confidence. With enough of that, a brush rabbit will spit in a rattler's eye.'

'Maybeso,' Dave Pope assented. 'I'm sure a whole lot less scared of Chet and his deviltry than I was before you began to call his hand, Cole. I'd like a crack at these killers he brought in to terrorize the country, but what you say goes with me.'

Below them they could see Slim Calhoun and Pete Daggett on the trail. Exactly in the center of it they were propping up the sign with big rocks.

'If there are a dozen or more of Circle 3 T riders, that sign won't stop them,' Rusty said. 'They will come pouring up like longhorns with their tongues hanging out when they smell water after a hot drive.'

'That will be their lookout,' Cole said. 'They will have had their warning.'

He gave his men explicit instructions. Nobody was to fire unless he gave the signal. He might have to drop a bullet in front of the invaders as a warning, but this would not mean that the battle had begun. Radbourne's men were to be given a chance to withdraw if they would.

Cole stationed his men among the boulders. Presently Daggett and Calhoun joined them.

'We d-done p-posted yore road for you, Cole,' Pete said. 'I r-reckon their eyes will b-bug out when they read the sign.'

Dave Pope chuckled. 'I hope these guys aren't going to disappoint us the way we did their friends,' he said.

'We'll know about that inside of half an hour,' Cole mentioned.

'They'll be here,' Rusty prophesied. 'Y'betcha! Don't buzzards always come when a cow critter dies on the desert?'

The oldtimer was right. They had not to wait long before sounds of approaching riders drifted up the cañon walls to them. Those posted in the rocks could hear voices, laughter, the striking of horses' hoofs against stones. The party below was making no attempt to conceal its approach. Evidently danger was the last thing in mind.

A man rode around a bend in the gulch trail. Others followed. Cole counted twelve. Jerry Haskell was in the lead.

At sight of the sign he pulled up with an oath. 'Look!' he cried.

An exploding bomb could not have been more unexpected. The men gathered in a huddle and discussed the meaning of the warning. Had

Sanborn broken through the ambush set for him? Had there somehow been a slip-up? Or was this Hank's idea of a joke? Everybody had a suggestion, but Haskell's heavy voice bore down the others.

'If Sanborn's fellows were here, they would be cutting loose at us right now,' he shouted. 'I'm going on. I don't scare worth a cent.'

Braggadocio was in his words and manner, but he flung a nervous glance up at the big boulders above. What he saw there riveted his gaze. The bulbous eyes of the foreman fixed on a figure that had risen from the rocks.

'Sanborn, by jacks!' broke from his lips.

In his hands Cole held a rifle, loosely, the end of the barrel pointed skyward.

'I've taken possession in my wife's name,' he called down. 'This road is closed, for the present.'

'How did you get there?' Haskell demanded. 'Where is Hank? And the other boys?'

'Don't get to worrying about them,' Cole advised. 'Keep your mind on Jerry Haskell and those with him. That ought to keep your thoughts busy.'

'You—killed them?' a Circle 3 T rider cried, almost in a gasp. He was thinking that in another moment the roar of guns would fill the gorge.

'First off, drop your weapons right where you are, every last man of you,' Cole ordered sharply. 'We've got you covered. You haven't a chance.'

There was one critical moment of hesitation. Someone in that party of hired gunmen might decide to fight it out, even with the odds heavily against them. Perhaps the men waited for Haskell to give the signal by drawing his gun and blazing away.

The face of the foreman twitched. Conflicting emotions surged in him. There was the venomous desire to throw away caution and fight it out with his enemy. There was the urgent fear of instant violent death. The men in the rocks had the drop on them. It was almost certain that they had been instructed not to let him escape if there came a clash. In racing brain flashes he decided against battle. The chances were not good enough.

'What you mean to do with us?' he asked, exactly as Hank had done less than an hour earlier.

'I'm not discussing that,' Cole answered, his harsh face expressionless as the spar of quartz on which he stood. 'My men will empty half your saddles first crack. We'll get the whole caboodle of you.' His voice took on the sharp accent of command. 'Drop those guns!'

Rifles and revolvers clattered to the ground.

'Move back into that rock pocket,' Cole ordered.

The disarmed men did as they had been told.

'Out of your saddles.'

Twelve men dismounted.

'Tie your horses together, in bunches of six.

Two of you move up far as that clump of Spanish bayonet with the broncs. No farther.'

Again the imperative in Cole's curt mandate gained obedient answer. Two Circle 3 T men moved the animals as directed.

'Looks like these boys have been slandered,' Dave jeered. 'They're good Sunday School lads who have been taught to say their little pieces proper.'

'Don't take any chances on them, Dave,' Cole advised. 'I'm asking you and McCoy and Pete to fork your broncs, ride down, and take charge of the beauties. Gather the weapons and make sure they haven't any concealed about them. I'll have you hold them till the rest of us can get down. Don't lift your eyes from them a moment. They're tough nuts.'

Not until the three riders came round a bend in the cañon trail did the prisoners realize the party above had split. It was too late to attempt a break now, even if any of them would have been fool-hardy enough to try it had they known in time.

McCoy lined the Circle 3 T men up with their faces to the rock wall.

'All right, Cole,' he called up. 'Everything pretty. We'll be responsible for these blackbirds till you get down.'

'You'd bump us off the way you did Gildea!' Haskell cried, with an oath.

'I'd do just exactly that any time you reach for a

221

gun to kill me as he did,' McCoy told him bluntly. 'So put that in your pipe and smoke it, man.'

'Don't l-look so cast down, boys,' Pete said cheerfully. 'Y-you're getting a g-great break, considering what you deserve. You'll be joshed a-plenty all the rest of yore lives, but, hell's bells, funning at yore expense won't break any bones. If C-Cole wasn't so damned legal he would start a little b-boot hill of his own right here.'

A cavalcade came round the bend in the cañon twenty minutes later. The five prisoners rode in advance, their hands still bound. Behind them came their captors.

Gray Shirt counted aloud the men lined up against the wall. 'Seventeen of us in all,' he summed up bitterly. 'Trapped—disarmed—and not a shot fired. Grab it from me, that's a nice story to spread around Boone County, Jerry. I'm damned if I don't almost wish I'd gone out in smoke. We'll never live it down.'

Cole ordered the hands of his latest batch of prisoners tied. Haskell resisted when McCoy approached him and took a swipe from a revolver barrel on the head.

After the red-headed Scotchman had knotted the rope fastening the foreman, Cole suggested carelessly that he had better bind up the bleeding head with a handkerchief.

'He's got quite a distance to walk,' Sanborn explained. 'We don't want him playing out on us.'

'I'm not walking a step,' Haskell said stubbornly.

'Suits me, Jerry. Just as you say. Anyone who doesn't want to walk will be dragged with a rope back of a bronc. Take your choice.'

'Where you taking us?' growled Hank.

'I'm taking you home—to the Circle 3 T.' The smile on Cole's face was blandly derisive. 'You boys are too innocent to be let out alone. We're going to herd you back to Chet. A coyote or a skunk might rise up and bite you before you get back to your little trundle-beds. I dassent risk it.'

The prisoners clumped down the cañon on foot in their high-heeled boots. Two of Cole's men herded the seventeen saddled horses in the drag.

Slim watched the pedestrians, a grin on his face. Before they reached the mouth of the cañon, some of them were beginning to limp. Cowboy boots are not made for tramping trips. The high heels fling the weight forward against the cramped toes. It was seven long miles to the Circle 3 T ranch-house. By the time they came to it, every man on foot would be in torment.

Cole rode beside Slim.

'You figure there won't be more than two or three men at the Circle 3 T,' Sanborn said, raising a point that had been discussed before.

'Can't be. There's always a dozen or more out on the range looking after the stock. Jerry picked up every last man he could when he came tearing over here to help skin yore hide.

I'd say not more than two besides Chet, and one of those will be the cook who is a tenderfoot and doesn't know how to fire a gun.'

'That's about the way I figure it, Slim. I want to get out of this without having to kill anybody. We've had nigger luck so far. Hope it will hold.'

'A fellow with luck like you ought to go hunting for lost gold mines,' Calhoun said.

Slim moved a few steps forward at a road trot, to listen to some remarks from Jerry Haskell.

'You were saying something,' he suggested.

Haskell turned on him a furious face and blistered the air with oaths.

Chapter XXV
'Seventeen of Them— Count Them'

Cole realized that his luck had stood up better than he could have reasonably expected. He had, to be sure, planned the counter-traps into which the enemy had fallen, hoping that Chet would be hoist with his own petard. But it had been sheer good fortune that events had dovetailed perfectly enough for him to achieve victory without the loss of a life. This ought to help his cause greatly, for it would prove, far better than any statement he could make, that he was trying to win Mary's rights peaceably and was not seeking a feud with Radbourne.

Moreover, his triumph held just the flavor that the frontier relished. The biter had been bit. The Circle 3 T men had been caught, not once but twice, in the trap they had set for Sanborn. The story of how he had outgeneraled them, forced a surrender, and driven them on foot like a herd of cattle back to Chet, would be told in every ranchhouse within a hundred miles. Radbourne's stock as dictator of Boone County, already declining, would go down with a crash in the market of public opinion.

The party trailed through the desert, strung out for a distance of several hundred yards. Guards on horseback flanked the prisoners. Back of these were the saddled broncos. Heat shimmered in front of the moving men. Dust rose in clouds from their dragging feet. The dry throats of those on foot were like lime-kilns.

The Circle 3 T men took their punishment according to the nature of the individual. Gray Shirt plodded on stoically, his lips closed. He knew he had no grievance. Sanborn's gang might justifiably have killed him, since that was the fate he and his associates had meant for them. Hank whined for a horse. His feet were killing him, he complained almost tearfully. Curses dripped from the lips of Haskell.

Two riders crossed the desert in front of them and stopped to find out what this strange drive could be. The men were Preston and Lutz.

They stared in astonishment at what they saw.

'I'm herding these boys home,' Cole explained. 'They got off their own range and wandered up to the Lazy B. Lucky I found them, or they would probably have starved to death. This is no country for amateurs. They're some gaunted, but after Chet has nursed them up, they won't look so whipped out, don't you reckon?'

Rusty Hunter took pains to let the two travelers know exactly what had occurred. He told the story in picturesque language, and it lost nothing in the telling. Preston and Lutz were headed for Jonesboro. In another hour or two everybody in town would know of the crushing defeat Cole had inflicted on the warriors of Radbourne.

The cavalcade moved slowly. The sun, a ball of fire, was dropping behind a peak in the sawtoothed range when the party drew close to the home ranch of the Circle 3 T.

Three men and a girl came out of the buildings to find out what this invasion meant. One of the men was Chet Radbourne. His vast bulk shook like a jelly while he watched Slim cut the ropes on the wrists of his men.

Cole swept off his hat to Mary, dismounted in front of her, said a word or two in a low voice, then turned his attention to Radbourne as the young woman vanished inside the house.

'I've brought back your boys, Chet—seventeen of 'em, count 'em,' he said. 'You oughtn't to let them stray so far. When greeners like these get off their range, they get into trouble right away.'

Radbourne's fat tallowy face was ghastly. He was so completely taken aback he did not know what to say. It was astounding. Seventeen hard-bitten fighting men, well-armed, had gone out to finish Sanborn, and they had come back disarmed, bound, scarcely able to drag one foot before the other. Did Sanborn know they had set out to murder him? Had he come here to destroy his arch-enemy before them all?

227

'I—I—don't reckon I—understand, Cole,' he gasped out. 'If my boys have been annoying you in any way—'

'It wasn't by any order of yours,' Cole interrupted. 'We all understand that. You wouldn't hurt a hair of my head.'

Gray Shirt laughed, with sardonic and bitter mirth. 'Go ahead, Chet. Explain everything nice. Talk him out of it. Tell him you aimed to have him rubbed out easy and gentle. Make him believe Mrs. Sanborn came up here of her own free will. Likely he'll swallow anything you say.'

Haskell sank down on the porch and pulled the boots from his tortured feet. 'What's the use of lying, Chet?' he spat out, with a vile curse. 'He knows we acted under yore orders. I'll say this. He'd better kill me right now. If he don't, first chance I get I'll drop him like I would a wolf.'

'No use talking thataway, Jerry,' the master of the ranch reproved. 'The idea is to fix this up with Cole. I aim to be reasonable, and I reckon he does.'

'There's nothing to fix up, Chet,' said Sanborn. 'I'm not having any dealings with you. Keep your hands off my affairs and those of my wife. You've made one bad mistake about her. Don't make another. I'm a law-abiding man, but don't presume on my reputation for wanting peace. You sent these boys out to kill me and my men. We had a chance to get every last one of them.

This time you and they are lucky. But you won't get a break like that twice. I ought to shoot you down now. You're a black-hearted scoundrel, and it would be better for this country if you were dead.'

'You don't get me right, Cole,' the fat man whined. 'Haven't I taken care of your wife like a father since I saw you last?'

'You threatened to whip her with a quirt, you villain. I ought to wipe you out for that.'

'No, Cole. That doesn't matter. He hasn't hurt me.' Mary had come out upon the porch. She was wearing a riding costume. Her voice was low and urgent. 'All I want is to get away and never see him again.'

'That's all right with me,' Radbourne said, in a whining, ingratiating plaint. 'You can go any time you like, Mrs. Sanborn. I don't wish you anything but well.'

Cole told him, his face like the Day of Judgment: 'Mrs. Sanborn will be staying with friends in Jonesboro. You'll not annoy her, you or any of your dogs. If you do, or if they do, you'd better pray to the Devil you serve for an easy death.' Before he turned away, he flung a piece of information at Radbourne, as one would a bone to a cur. 'You'll find your horses at the Longhorn Corral.'

Most of the prisoners had dropped down where they were to take the stiff boots from their swollen and inflamed feet. But Gray Shirt stood erect, his cold light blue eyes fixed on Sanborn.

'What do you mean about annoying Mrs. Sanborn?' he asked. 'Maybe you're the sort of yellow dog that pesters women. I'm not, and I don't reckon many of these boys are.'

'Not even your boss, Mr. Radbourne,' Cole said, with icy sarcasm.

'He can talk for himself, and I'll talk for myself. For a red cent I'd send you out in smoke, and I wouldn't touch her for a million dollars.'

Cole gave the man his sudden friendly smile. 'You're a man, Gray Shirt. I'll take back what I said about annoying Mrs. Sanborn. Just the same, you're fighting with this scoundrel to take her property from her. You're in the wrong camp. He's not worth the powder to blow him up. I'll tell you something else. You're backing a losing horse. Radbourne is bucked out. This country has had enough of him. He's through.'

Gray Shirt turned to his boss. 'Tell him he's a liar, Chet. Tell him you'll hang his hide on a fence to dry inside of a week.'

'You boys get on the prod too much,' Radbourne said irritably. 'I got nothing against Cole, except he's so damn rambunctious. Someone has been filling him with lies about me. I'm a man of peace. Not looking for trouble.'

Disgust in his face, Gray Shirt looked the owner of the Circle 3 T up and down. 'Sanborn is right. You're a yellow-bellied, crawling side-winder. That's what you are. And I'm through with you. I never did like you or your outfit. You can dish out orders to bump off some other guy and it doesn't hurt you any, but when it's yore own turn you can't stand up on yore hind legs and take it. Me, I'm going down the trail tonight.'

'Rats and a sinking ship. That the idea, Jim?' sneered Haskell.

Gray Shirt looked the foreman over with a cold, implacable eye. 'Say that again when we're both heeled, Jerry.'

Cole gathered his party to leave. Before going, he spoke to Gray Shirt. 'After what you've said, it isn't going to be healthy for you up here.' He waved a hand toward the saddled horses. 'Pick out your bronc and fag along down the trail. If you don't, I'd hate to bet you ever do.'

The level eyes of the hired killer looked into those of Sanborn. They were still as hard as jade.

'I'll take you up on that,' he said. 'It's lean forward and shove for me. That palomino is mine.'

He reclaimed his horse and came back to where Cole stood. 'You are one of these high-heeled smart alecks I never could go. I reckon you're all swelled up like a poisoned pup because you ran a whizzer on us today. But I'll say for you that you act like a white man. Listen. This skunk Radbourne isn't through. You want to

231

watch him every lick of the road. If you don't, you'll never be the big auger here you're figuring on being.'

Gray Shirt rode to the bunkhouse and presently emerged with a roll. He was tying it behind the saddle as the Sanborn party passed.

Cole stopped, to hand him a revolver. 'You might need this,' he said.

'So I might,' the man said with cool hardihood. 'For you or for Haskell one.'

'If it has to be one of us, make it Haskell,' Cole answered, grinning at him.

The former Circle 3 T man permitted himself a sour sardonic smile.

'It won't be you, fellow. Too many coals of fire. I'll say one thing. I'm almost glad I didn't get a chance to fill you full of lead today.'

'So am I,' Cole told him.

Gray Shirt put his horse to a gallop and vanished down the road.

Chapter XXVI
In the Dusk

Mary rode beside her husband, an odd breathless excitement filling her being. It was absurd, she told herself, that she should feel any emotion in the presence of this harsh dynamic stranger who by some strange quirk of fate happened to be the man to whom she was married. Their partnership was a business arrangement. Nothing more than that. Yet she felt not only the prickling in the throat that adventure brings, but a queer suffocation around the heart ridiculously unnecessary. She told herself it was embarrassment. This straight-backed rider with the hard-packed muscles and the granite face was a man she did not know at all; yet he was the man she had promised to love, honor, and obey, the one she had given her word to cherish until death parted them.

'Tell me about it,' she said, in her low, melodious voice. 'How did you disarm and capture all those men? It seems impossible. Yet you did it.'

He told her, simply, as if what he had done had been easy and a matter of course.

'Why didn't they think you might take the cutoff up the arroyo in the gulch?' she asked.

'Nobody had ever been up there.' He modified his statement. 'I did go up once when I was a boy. But it never struck them seven men could make it. Fact is, the slide is rather a breakneck precipice. We were lucky that none of us were hurt.'

She looked at him, with parted lips and shining eyes. A wave of emotion crashed through her. She would never love him. Frequently in the past weeks she had told herself so. That was not possible, since he had lived as he had, but she would know, would never forget as long as she lived, that she had married a man among ten thousand.

'And you were lucky when you trapped the first bunch of men, and lucky again when you got the others,' she said, with warm and friendly derision.

'Yes.'

'Just like Napoleon at—at Marengo and his other battles.'

Cole laughed. 'Don't pull that before any of the boys, or they will never quit joshing me.'

'Why?' she challenged. 'Isn't that what a good general does—takes the enemy by surprise?'

'It may be the other way round next time,' he said.

'We're going to win,' she cried vibrantly. 'I

didn't think so—at first. It was a desperate jump in the dark . . . what we did. I was selfish, thinking only of myself. But I've had plenty of time since to think of the danger into which I've dragged you. The worst of it is that I can't be sorry. I know you walk every hour in danger, with so many men ready to destroy you. Sometimes I am shaken with fear. Then I know that no harm can come to you.'

'I've rocked along all right so far,' he reminded her.

'You've saved me from that man,' she went on. 'Very likely you will save my property. It is fine for me. But all you get out of it is terrible danger. Assassins try to kill you. Men lie in wait.'

'Is that all I get?' he asked, smiling at her.

His rock-ribbed face did not betray him. She had no guess that he found her loveliness sweet and glamorous.

'Wouldn't it be best for you to guard me to the nearest railroad station, put me on a train, and send me home? I wouldn't be responsible then if—if anything happened to you.'

'You won't be responsible, anyhow. Radbourne had a black mark against my name before I ever met you. No. This fight is on. It will have to go to a finish. When I began this thing it was personal. Cole Sanborn against Chet Radbourne. There's more to it than that now. All over Boone County men are watching to see if the

235

influence of the Circle 3 T, which has corrupted public life and made honest citizens walk in fear, can be destroyed. Nesters who were scared to call their souls their own are saying what they think. Square-shooters in Jonesboro are speaking out. If Radbourne's killers get me, this fight won't stop. He is coming to the last mile of his crooked trail. I think he sees it himself, but he daren't quit. He has gone so far he has got to go on to the finish.'

As she listened, the color in her violet eyes deepened. She had married a man practically an outlaw, one generally believed to be a criminal, known as a desperate gunman, a mocker at the fine and decent things in life. But this man telling her quietly of the fight for right, seeing himself as one who carried a banner for others, was not at all the villain public opinion had pictured him. Mary knew that on the frontier the borderline between good and evil is sometimes shadowy. Circumstances may sweep men who are not bad along lawless paths. Along such trails Cole Sanborn had galloped wildly. But this she knew. Whatever wrong there might be in his past, he had now turned his back forever on dishonor. The blood beat stormily, exultantly, to her heart.

'Yes, he is afraid,' she agreed. 'I could see it in the way he treated me. But won't that fear drive him to desperation? He will see his one chance is to—to get rid of you. If he can do that—and tighten his grip again on those who have been afraid of him—'

She did not finish her sentence. To pass a clump of prickly pear she had swung away from him for a moment.

'That's on the cards,' he assented, after they were again riding knee to knee. 'We'll have to be on guard every minute.'

'Where are you going to leave me?' she asked.

'At the Peters house, if that suits you all right.'

'Would they be in any danger because of me?'

'No. You heard what that man in the gray shirt said, the one called Jim. I don't know his last name. What he says is true. He and his kind respect women. I would trust you on the desert with him just as I would with Dave Pope or Dunc McCoy. He isn't fighting women. Neither are the other Circle 3 T riders.'

'And Chet Radbourne—isn't he fighting women either?'

'Not now he isn't,' Cole answered. 'He daren't. For the first time he has come to understand the power of public opinion. He can kill me and get away with it because I have the reputation of being a bad man. But he won't bother you any more. 'Far as he is concerned, you're dynamite from now on. He knows that if he lifts a hand against you, he is likely to blow himself up.'

'So it comes to this,' she said. 'I'm safe, and you are in more danger than ever. And it started in as my fight, not yours.'

'Before I ever said a word to you or had become acquainted, you heard Haskell serve notice on me that he was going to wipe me out. I had chips in the jackpot then, and even if the pot has built up a lot since, I'm still playing a stack.'

'You say that out of kindness to me, to keep me from worrying about having got you into trouble.'

He looked at her, smiling. 'I've been in trouble ever since I landed in this country.'

'You win the battle, then I get all the rewards,' she told him reproachfully.

She felt his gaze burning into her. It seemed a long time before it shifted to the dying light on the distant hills. Night was dropping down over the valley. Soon it would envelop them.

'How do you know what rewards I get?' he asked, his voice studiedly light and casual.

'The Lazy B—and the cattle. I don't suppose you would let me divide them.'

'I reckon not.'

'Then you haven't anything to gain.'

'I'll tell you some day what I have to gain,' he said, still carelessly. 'Or else I won't.'

Mary heard him, with a fluttering heart beating against her ribs. This might mean nothing, or it might mean a great deal. She did not want him to explain his words, not yet at least. The barriers in her soul, defenses built as safeguards against the emotion he always stirred in her, were falling far too fast. She was a fool, of course, she told herself accusingly. Never for an instant had he broken the compact made the day of their marriage. He seemed to be cased in hard chill steel. Yet when he looked at her flashes burned her bosom. Always she had been high-headed and independent, but when she was with him her arrogant will melted into his. She had made him promise not to break faith. It had not been necessary, she felt then, to make herself do the same.

She had to say something, for silence was too significant.

'Is that a riddle?' she asked, after she was sure of her voice.

'I'll say this now, no more. I've fooled away my time, with nothing worthwhile to live for. You know what my reputation is. I earned it, partly at least. Now I am at work on a good job, for others as well as myself. That's something, don't you reckon?'

'Yes,' she said. 'That's a lot.'

From somewhere back of them a voice was lifted in song:

239

'Oh, old Ben Bolt was a fine old boss,
Rode to see the girls on a sore-backed hoss;
Old Ben Bolt was fond of his liquor,
Had a li'l' bottle in the pocket of his slicker.'

'I was like that boy, with a heap more of the devil in me,' Cole said. 'I was on the road to ruin, and hellbent to get there in a hurry. It's funny. I don't understand it myself. The way it seems to me is that the man you saw sitting on the porch of the Jonesboro House has quit living and another one is here in his place. Of course I'm talking foolishness, and yet I'm not.'

'I don't think you are talking foolishness at all,' she told him, almost in a murmur.

A wild and primitive joy beat a drum in her.

Chapter XXVII
Cole Advertises

The return of Sanborn to Jonesboro was almost a triumphal procession. Men had watched him go, the opinion strong in them that he was leading a forlorn hope and would probably never come back. Now, within twelve hours, he was leading his victorious band up Main Street, beside him the lovely girl whose plight had transformed this private war from a sordid feud to a thrilling romance. During that time Cole had captured more than half of Radbourne's men, had dragged them back to the den of the old fox, had reclaimed his wife, and was bringing to town with him the spoils of battle in the form of the mounts and the weapons of the gunmen he had taken.

This was the most amazing episode that had occurred in Jonesboro's turbulent life. If Sanborn had fought a bloody battle and won, he would have found a divided sentiment. Many good citizens would have felt the feud was lawless, and that one gang of ruffians had defeated another. But to have captured the enemy without firing a shot, to have had the Circle 3 T men completely in his power, to have freed them unharmed after making them ridiculous; this was a triumph approved by all the good people of the county seat.

Preston and Lutz had brought the incredible story to town. It had swept like wildfire from house to house. Now men, women, and children lined the road to see the victors. Cole rode straight-backed, imperturbable and grim, nodding now and again to someone he recognized.

But Mary was all smiles. When a good old deacon of the church called to her a fervent 'God bless you!' she waved a hand at him gaily. It did not occur to her that she supplied the element which made this dramatic entry romantic. Her eyes were bright as Arcturus because of the sweeping tide of approval the actions of Cole had met. She glowed at the cheers, at the frank comments flung out by men on the sidewalk.

'You sure combed Chet's hair for him, Cole! . . . Good old scout, you can carry weight and whop that old devil any day of the week! . . . They was certainly duck soup for you, boy, but you want to watch out some of 'em don't dry-gulch you. . . . I wouldn't make no holler if you had rubbed out that bull rattler Haskell, for he just naturally wore out his welcome with me first time I met him. . . . Hi-Yi, Cole, you're the curly wolf for my money.'

Mary loved it all. She felt the campaign was won, an illusion Cole did not share for an instant.

But he felt it wise to make the occasion as impressive as possible.

'Will someone get Jim Poston the blacksmith and tell him to open up for business?' he asked an acquaintance. 'I'll be round at his shop in ten minutes.'

He ordered the saddled but riderless horses driven to the Longhorn Corral. 'Stick together, boys, and meet me in ten minutes at the blacksmith shop. Bring all the Circle 3 T guns with you.'

'You want to look out for yoreself, Cole,' Dave warned. 'There are still two-three birds in town would like a peck at you. Don't forget that.'

'Maybeso, but they aren't likely to do their pecking tonight,' Sanborn answered. 'Still, I'll keep an eye cocked.'

Cole and Mary rode to the residence of Hal Peters. The lawyer was just returning with his wife. They had been down to Main Street.

'Quite a Roman triumph,' Peters said dryly. 'All it needed was Radbourne in chains at your chariot wheels.'

They could still hear the pop of revolvers celebrating the event.

Cole smiled, a little sheepishly. 'The boys overplayed it some.'

He lifted Mary from the saddle.

'Mr. Peters and I are so glad you are back, Mary. We are hoping you will come to our home and spend a long visit.' A hearty sincerity was in the voice of the lawyer's wife.

Mary loved her for her gracious kindness. 'If you are sure I won't be a nuisance,' she said, and added impulsively: 'I won't ever forget how good you are to me.'

'Nonsense,' the older woman said at once. 'It will be good for us, as it was before, to have a young person in the house to brighten it.' She spoke to Cole, offering her hand. 'Mr. Peters tells me he has hopes that you will save this country from the corrupt ring that has run it so long.'

'I'll try to help him do that,' Cole answered, with his swift rare smile.

'We'll all have to do our part,' the attorney said. 'I think from what I hear folks say that you have them on the run. I'll dig up some evidence of their corruption and worry them some more. No trouble to find traces of crookedness. It is all over the place.'

Cole excused himself. 'Have to get back to the boys,' he said. 'The show isn't quite over.'

'Think I'll go along with you,' Peters said.

'He's afraid I'm going to start something,' Cole told Mrs. Peters. 'Can't trust me out of his sight.'

'You'll be back before you leave town,' Mary said in a low voice to her husband.

'I'll be back,' he promised.

Sanborn led the horses back to Main Street, the

244

lank lawyer walking by his side. They moved down between the false-front buildings to the blacksmith shop. Several hundred people were gathered in front of it, most of them men. A cheer greeted Cole. He paid no attention to it.

'Poston is inside, and we've brought the guns,' Slim said. 'What you aiming to do with them?'

Within fifteen minutes each rifle and revolver had been put on the anvil and its usefulness ended by heavy blows from the blacksmith's hammer.

The spectators approved. They shouted encouragement.

'You'll do to take along, Cole. . . . Show Chet he can't cut it when he hatches up a fuss and lays it on yore lap. . . . We're with you, boy. We'll show his slit-eyed sons-of-guns they can't bully puss this country.'

Cole understood that this enthusiasm would not last. These men would go home and get to wondering if after all Radbourne would not strike back at his foe swiftly and mercilessly. Tomorrow they would be much more careful in the expression of their opinions. They would remember that Chet had spies in town who reported to him all that went on.

After the guns had been smashed, Cole paid a visit to the office of the *Boone County Beacon*. Tim Alderson was setting type on an editorial, composing it as he went along.

The little man's gimlet eyes fastened on the visitor. 'The *Beacon* comes out tomorrow. You want to read it, young fellow. I'm sure going to make the eagle scream. I'll betcha when the Circle 3 T gallows birds read it, they will want to sell themselves a dozen for thirty cents.'

'Much obliged, Tim. I've got another job for you, if you have time to set it up.'

'I'll be working half the night, anyhow,' Alderson said. 'I haven't any time to take on odd jobs. What is it you want?'

Cole explained.

The bright eyes of the small man fairly smoked. 'Say, I'll take on that job. You sit right down at my desk and write your poster.'

Sanborn was no journalist. He spent some time at his task before he got it finished. Alderson made some suggestions, then set up and ran the job.

'How many you want?' he asked before he finished the printing.

'A hundred will do. I want to plaster the town with them and stick some up at crossroads here and there in the country.'

'Then I'll strike off two hundred,' the editor said. 'There are going to be a lot of citizens in this town come to me to get a copy of this poster as a souvenir. If you whip Radbourne, they will paste this masterpiece of yours on their walls; if you don't, they will bury them deep in their trunks.'

'Looks like I'm going to be either a live hero or a dead dog,' Cole said dryly.

'One or the other,' Alderson agreed. 'And I can tell you this, that if you slip up and don't have eyes in the back of your head, you won't be around to have any medals stuck on your chest by an admiring public.'

The poster read:

FOUND

Sixteen Broomtails with the Circle 3 T Brand Straying at the Foot of Big Pine Point. Picked Up Wednesday Afternoon. May be Reclaimed at the Longhorn Corral by Paying Feed Bill.

Also Sixteen Rifles and Sixguns Come Upon at Same Time and Place After having been Abandoned by Tenderfoot Owners. These May be Called for at Poston's Blacksmith Shop and can be Gathered from the Junk Pile of Scrap Iron.

COLE SANBORN

An eruption of six bowlegged men in chaps created a diversion.

'I got the hammers and the tacks for you, Cole,' Dave shouted. 'Though what in time you want with them is more than I can guess. I found Dink Blossom at Pete Casey's and dragged him to the Emporium. The old coot said he could understand how you might want six Colt's forty-fours, but he'd be dad-gummed if he could figure what you could do with a mess of hammers and tacks. I told him you were plumb crazy anyhow, and let it go at that, seeing I didn't know myself what yore plans are.'

Cole divided the posters. He gave each of the men fifteen.

'I want them posted all over this town. Stick 'em on trees, walls, fences, in saloons, and any other conspicuous spots you notice.'

The six bowlegged bipeds read the poster and whooped.

'That'll bring the lid off'n Jerry Haskell's private can of cuss words,' Rusty said. 'Dawged if it won't peel the thick hide from two-three gents who don't feel noways loving toward you. I recollect onct when I was sitting the buck[1] in a corral on Colonel Goodnight's ranch in the Panhandle a galoot cracked down on me with his cutter and—'

'Did he kill you?' asked Dave anxiously.

The old man slewed his wrinkled eyes round at Dave and considered him. 'No, sir, he didn't kill me. After the buckjumper had got through with his meanness, I got down from the saddle and asked this bird what was eatin' him. He was sure a whipped-out lookin' specimen. Well, gents, he explained he was married and had a little pest at home was a holy terror. This kid was

[1]Riding an outlaw horse.

such a nuisance he couldn't make up his mind whether he oughtn't to drown the brat in the Cimarron. Even when he was fur from home he'd get to thinking about the little devil and it would make him so crazy he didn't know what he was doing. When he had fired at me he was having one of these spells. He said his name was Pope. Seems the kid was called Dave.'

Rusty finished his story on a note of placid indifference and turned to ask a question of Cole.

'Meet me at Hal Peters's house in about half an hour,' Cole said. 'And don't get careless, boys. We corralled most of the Circle 3 T riding stock, except what is on the range or in the big pasture. I don't expect the warriors of Chet will be down here on the peck for quite some time yet, but you never can tell. I wouldn't want any casualties among you at the end of a perfect day.'

The six men in chaps trooped out to see that Cole's advertising got a good display.

Chapter XXVIII
Lauret Makes His Choice

Cole talked with Alderson a few minutes before he followed his men into the street. He pulled the slipknot that tied the bridle rein of his horse to the hitch-rack in front of the *Beacon* office.

As he swung to the saddle, a puff of wind lifted the hat from his head. Almost at the same time there was the crack of a revolver. Swiftly Cole slid to the ground, on the same side of the horse from which he had mounted. Before his feet touched earth a forty-four had leaped from its holster to his hand. Back of the animal he waited, watching the dark alley where he had seen the flash.

He heard a rustling sound and flung a random shot into the alley.

Alderson's voice came from behind him. 'What is it?' the editor asked.

'Someone fired at me from the alley,' Cole explained. 'He's there yet. Better drift back into the office, Tim. You're in the line of fire.'

'You better come too,' Alderson advised, and vanished.

Cole did not take his advice. He had important business on hand. His senses were keyed to an acute pitch. Intently he listened. The faintest murmur of a sound might be invaluable information. His eyes bored into the patch of blackness that was the alley. Crouched against the wall there somewhere was a man with murder in his heart.

Again the stealthy rustling. Cole's gun flashed. There came to his ears the pounding of feet in rapid retreat. The ambusher was no longer trying to conceal his whereabouts. He was flying in panic for his life.

Snatching up his hat, Cole vaulted to the saddle, swung the horse, and drove straight for the alley. A shadowy figure ducked round a corner. The rider wheeled his peg pony into an alley at right angles with the first. Abruptly he pulled up. Nobody was in sight. No sound came to him, except the roar of many voices from the Arcadia. The back door of the gambling-house was open.

Cole dismounted, pushing the sixgun back into its holster. A black object on the ground caught his eye. It was a hat. Cole picked it up. He trailed the bridle reins and passed through the door into the Arcadia.

The place was filled with drinkers, gamblers, loafers milling about, and onlookers 'sweating' the games.

Cole's entrance created some attention from those nearest him, and that interest moved with him as he walked through the crowd. A dozen men greeted him. He answered perfunctorily, his eyes sweeping the place, back and forth, back and forth. He was looking for some man who might be an enemy, and he did not want notice of that person's presence to come to him in the form of a bullet.

His glance picked up Lutz. The cattleman did not even look at him. He was playing poker and his attention was concentrated on the cards. Evidently he was trying to make up his mind whether to throw away his hand or call a bet. No, not Lutz, Cole reflected. His mind was too easy, and in any case he had not had time to get set and into a jackpot. Moreover, Lutz was not the assassin type. He might kill in the open, if he could bring himself to scratch, but he would not fire from ambush.

Cole continued toward the front of the house. He saw Lauret. The man was pretending to watch a faro game, but Cole observed that he was breathing deeply. He noticed also that he could not keep his eyes on the table. They went stabbing here and there uneasily. As yet he had not seen Cole.

Sanborn stepped in close to the man, back of him, on his right side.

'I've brought the hat you dropped, Mr. Lauret,' he said evenly, in a low, distinct voice.

Lauret could not prevent a start. He swung round, hand at hip.

'What do you mean—my hat?' he demanded.

'Isn't it your hat?' Cole drawled, his words spaced. 'You dropped it at the back door, and it has your initials in it.'

The faro players looked up. A chill sensation ran down their spines. The words were simple, but the manner of them was ominous.

There were tiny beads of perspiration on the white forehead of the gambler. He swallowed a lump before he replied.

'Not my hat,' he answered huskily.

It was his opinion that the breath of death was fanning him. Should he draw now, before his enemy moved, and take a chance, he might prevent the other's bullets crashing into him.

'Never saw you without a hat before,' Cole said, watching him intently. 'Where *is* your hat?'

'That's my business.'

'And mine. You look like you have been running, Mr. Lauret.'

'That's not true.'

'Bad for the heart when a man leads the kind of life you do,' Cole told him. 'You're out of practice, both as a runner *and with a sixgun.*'

The eyes of Lauret narrowed. Now was the time, while Sanborn was still talking. In a fraction of a second, if there was no hitch, this jeering mocker might be lying dead at his feet. *If there was no hitch.* That was the joker. A picture flashed before his eyes. He saw Curt Jordan standing at the side door of the Arcadia, his six-gun blazing. He saw him sagging to the floor, muscles limp and lax. The gambler tried to flog his courage to action. But he could not bring himself to it, not with that chill bleak gaze boring into his.

'This is no country for shorthorns, Lauret,' Cole said, his voice low and steely.

One of the faro players rose abruptly. He was in a panic to get away from this spot.

'Sit down,' Cole ordered swiftly. 'You're not in this.'

The man sat down, white-faced and shaken. He was a young tenderfoot just out from Ohio.

Cole had not lifted his eyes from Lauret. His implacable voice carried on. Its message was for the gambler.

'Not safe for a man like you to carry a gun. I'll take yours now.'

He held out his *left* hand. The other was hitched by the thumb to the cartridge belt, not an inch from the butt of a revolver.

Lauret moistened his dry lips with his tongue. Something was gripping him tightly by the throat. He told himself he was going to kill the fellow now. Sanborn was making it easy. He would pre-tend he was going to hand the weapon over, and instead would fling bullets into the stomach of his enemy.

Sanborn read his thoughts aloud. 'No, it won't

be that way, Lauret. You don't get another crack at me. Draw the gun out slowly, with the butt pointing my way—*and don't make a mistake.*'

This was his chance, the professional gambler told himself again. A tilt of the wrist and a crook of a finger. The thing would be done.

Once more Cole guessed his impulse. 'Don't let a finger wander to the trigger. Remember you're an amateur.'

Lauret found he could not do it. His flaccid will was not able to drive his trembling fingers to action. He drew out the six-shooter and passed it to the iron man whose gaze held him hypnotized.

Cole examined the revolver. 'Like I thought,' he said. 'One chamber empty—fired recently. You're not thorough enough, Lauret. It will take a better man than you to kill me.' He gave an order, in a voice through which a blizzard seemed to sweep. 'Get out of this country and never come back. I'll give you an hour—no longer. If you're not gone—'

He did not finish the sentence. It was not necessary.

'I didn't shoot at you,' Lauret said, lips color-less. 'Must have been someone else.'

'An hour,' Cole repeated.

He handed the revolver back to the gambler, not even taking the precaution to remove the cartridges.

Apparently Cole dismissed him completely

from mind. The young man turned to the tender-foot who had been playing faro. His smile was friendly and apologetic.

'Sorry if I spoke roughly,' he said. 'I wanted not to start any stampede.'

The tenderfoot looked at him, awe and admiration in his face. He would have a story to tell when he went back home that would last him the rest of his life. 'It's all right, Mr. Sanborn,' he said.

Cole turned and walked out of the Arcadia. His erect flat-backed body was a mark Lauret could not have missed. But he knew the West too well to shoot now. If he killed Sanborn while the man's back was toward him, after he had been given his chance and lacked the nerve to take it, inside of an hour he would be hanging from a cottonwood.

A dozen men looked at Lauret, gravely, silently. He had been judged and found wanting. Head down, he moved toward the door. He noticed that a path opened for him as he went.

Chapter XXIX
Mary Picks up a Hat

The roan was waiting patiently in the alley for its master. Sanborn swung to the saddle and rode to the house of Peters.

He found Mary at the table eating a meal Mrs. Peters had cooked for her. An extra place had been set.

'Your wife couldn't wait for you, Mr. Sanborn,' explained Peters. 'She didn't know when you would get back. Draw right up.'

Cole hesitated.

'Only bacon and eggs,' the lawyer's wife said. 'But I have hot coffee and biscuits in the kitchen.'

Cole took the proffered chair. He was hungry. But this supper satisfied more than his physical appetite. It had been a long time since he had sat as a guest at a table set with immaculate linen, old china, and silver spoons worn thin with age. That this girl with the wild hyacinth eyes sat opposite him was even more significant. Peters had called her his wife. She was far from that, even though the law had formally declared her so. What she thought of him he could only guess, but it was impossible for her to be indifferent to him. They had been flung into a wild adventure together, were partners in it. In her behalf he had risked his life, not once but several times. He had seen the eager interest shining in her eyes. Her future was wrapped up in his success. He must be in her mind often. Did she think of him as a ruffian with redeeming traits?

'Any new adventures since I left you, young man?' Peters asked.

'None of any importance,' Cole answered. He knew they would hear tomorrow of his encounter with Lauret. Better not tell it now, since he could not even sketch it without seeming to boast. The facts would do that for him no matter how he related them. 'I had a talk with Alderson.'

'A good man, Alderson. He is with you, of course.'

'I found him writing an editorial on our side.' Cole chuckled reminiscently. 'I had him do a piece of job work for me.'

He rose, found the posters he had left with his hat, and passed one to each of the three present.

'You rub it in,' Peters said, after he had read the poster. 'It will make Chet and his beauties sore.'

'They are some annoyed already,' Cole suggested mildly.

'I shouldn't wonder,' the lawyer agreed dryly. 'Maybe it is a good plan to broadcast something of this kind. Shows you are not afraid of them.'

'Does he need to show that now after what he has done?' Mary asked demurely.

'I was going to add, young lady, that it is a good thing to set everybody laughing at these scoundrels. This town is doing that already, but it will get another chortle out of this poster.' Peters turned to Cole. 'I don't need to tell you that this is more fuel to the Circle 3 T anger. Those fellows can't hold up their heads until they wipe out the score.'

'By rubbing me out,' Cole said.

'Yes, sir,' agreed Peters bluntly. 'No sense in not recognizing facts. They will get you if they can. From now on every last one of them will be trying to hunt you down.'

'What were they trying to do at Big Pine Point?' Cole asked, helping Mary and afterward himself to another biscuit. 'I gathered they had some sort of notion like that.'

'Yes, but—Don't get the idea Radbourne will quit after he has gone this far.'

'No, he won't quit.' Cole lifted his eyes and looked straight at the lawyer. 'But I'm through going easy on him. If he asks for war, he'll get it. I've gone a long way to avoid trouble. Twice I have had him at the end of a gun and let him go. Wouldn't you say that was often enough? If he keeps crowding me?'

Peters said deliberately: 'If he lifts another hand against you, the verdict of the people will be that he is one hundred per cent wrong and that you must defend yourself.'

Mrs. Peters rose from her chair and drew the window blinds down. All of them knew why she had done it, but none of them mentioned the reason.

'We're a little tired, Mr. Peters and I,' she said. 'If you young people will excuse us, we will retire to our room. I hope you will decide to stay all night and eat breakfast with us, Mr. Sanborn. You must have a great deal to talk over with your wife.'

Cole flushed. He did not dare look at Mary. 'It is very good of you to ask me, Mrs. Peters,' he told her. 'But my men will be here in a little while. 'Soon as they come I must take the trail with them.'

As soon as Peters had followed his wife from the room, Mary flung a question at Cole.

'They don't know you are here, do they? They couldn't have followed you?'

He did not ask her whom she meant by *they*. 'No,' he answered.

'A lot of people saw you bring me here. If the Circle 3 T men have reached town, and if they asked questions—'

'They haven't reached town,' he assured her.

'You can't be too careful,' Mary urged. 'It's as Mr. Peters says, from now on every man of them will want to get you.'

'Don't worry. We've a hundred miles of hills to camp in. We'll hop around like fleas.'

'If anything happened to you, I would never forgive myself.' There was a note of passionate wistfulness in her voice. In her heart flamed the fire of primitive woman for her mate. He might think of her whatever he liked. She was afraid. She could not let him go from her with that manner of negligent indifference. It was all very well to show contempt to the enemy. But in reality he must be wary to the verge of caution. She tried to impress this on him.

He listened gravely. 'I'll be watching every minute,' he promised.

There came a clatter of horses' hoofs. Evidently the riders had drawn up in front of the house.

Someone knocked on the door. Dave Pope called to Sanborn. 'Ready when you are, Cole.'

'Be out in a minute,' Cole answered.

He looked round for his hat. Mary picked it up, perhaps because of some vague impulse to hold him a moment longer. She glanced at it, and her eyes grew fixed. Her finger pointed to two small holes, one in the side and the other in the crown.

'They weren't there this afternoon,' she said, and looked to him for an explanation.

He could not find one readily. Before he had formulated an answer, she put her thought into a charge.

'Someone shot at you.'

Cole smiled, as if it were of no consequence. 'He didn't hit me.'

'Who was it?'

'A man named Lauret. He is a professional gambler with whom I once had some trouble. He hid in an alley and shot at me. You need not worry about him. He is leaving this part of the country tonight, never to come back.'

'Did you—kill him?' she asked quickly, her heart a-flutter.

'No. I advised him to leave. He will go. You can forget him.'

She flung out her hands in despair. 'That's just it. Things like that. You are in danger all the time.'

'That troubles you?' he questioned.

'Of course it troubles me.' A glowing color poured into her cheeks. 'Didn't you ask me once if—if a husband couldn't be a friend too?'

'A husband could even be a lover,' he said, 'if it wasn't in the agreement that he was only a foreman.'

Her eyes held to his. She had a sudden sense of stilled pulses followed by a clamor of beating drums. Then she was in his arms.

Chapter XXX
At the End
of a Wagon Tongue

The two men rode through a patch of greasewood to the end of a spur which looked down upon a little oasis in the desert. Evidently there was sub-soil water here, for in the valley hemmed in by low cowbacked hills the ground was green with alfilaria. Against the bluff at the far side of the park were a sod house, a corral of thorny ocotillo, and a barn built of sahuaro poles and mud.

'Looks like some nester had settled here onct and gave it up,' the younger man said. He was almost a boy, still red-cheeked, with only a soft blond down on his face.

His companion was Rusty Hunter. They had ridden down close to the deserted homestead. The roof of the sod house had caved in and there were gaps in the corral.

'He settled here and he gave it up,' Rusty said significantly. 'There was a spring, and he put in a windmill and did some irrigating. He was a young fellow no older than you, Morse. Name of Reincke. Soon as he got things to growing, he was figuring on getting married and bringing his girl up here. Only he didn't.'

'Why didn't he?' Morse asked.

The old man's faded eyes came back from surveying the landscape to the cowpuncher by his side.

'He disappeared.'

'Disappeared?'

'He was in Chet Radbourne's way. Chet wanted the spring and the grass for his stock. He served notice to Reincke to skedaddle. But the nester was a German, and some obstinate. This was his property, taken up lawfully, and he figured on staying, he said. Chet tried to scare him out, but he had sand in his craw. Well, like I said, he disappeared.'

'Maybe he lost his nerve and lit out.'

'No, sir. The girl wrote out. He hadn't been seen back there from where he came. He never was seen again.'

'You reckon Chet had him dry-gulched?'

'Do yore own guessing, son. He started to town to file his final proofs, but he never got there. Maybe a hydrophobia skunk bit him.'

'I'll bet that skunk's name was Radbourne.'

'You couldn't get me to bet with you on that.' Rusty's gaze had rested on a small bunch of grazing cattle. 'There's a two-year-old over there would do, boy.'

They were out to get meat for the camp.

'With the Circle 3 T brand,' Morse said.

'Meat with that brand tastes sweeter to me than any other,' the oldtimer said placidly.

'But Cole told us not to kill any of Chet's stuff.'

'What Cole don't know won't hurt him none.'

Rusty rode forward and raised his rifle. At the crack of the gun the steer fell.

The men dismounted and started to skin the animal. They would carry only the hind quarters back to camp.

The old man stopped work, knife poised in hand. 'Looky here, boy. Here's something funny. This brand has been blotted. Notice how the hair hasn't hardly grown yet round the circle and the upper part of the 3 and the T. By jacks, the original brand was a Lazy B. That's what it was. Some more of Chet's dirty work. The old scalawag has been stealing our stock. He's nothing but a damned rustler.'

The indignation of Rusty was so genuine that Morse grinned. Evidently Hunter considered there was a moral distinction between rustlers. To prey on the enemy was one thing, to steal from a girl quite another.

'I'm gonna take this part of the hide back to Cole,' Rusty said. 'My idea would be for him to nail it on the courthouse wall. A kind of Exhibit A, you understand. It won't do Chet any good.'

Morse heard a sound and looked up quickly. A man on horseback was on a grassy knoll about sixty yards away. The young man glanced round. His eyes picked up two other riders. All of them carried rifles.

'Reach for the sky,' one of the men called to them.

There was no help for it. The rifles of the men skinning the steer lay on the ground half a dozen yards away. They might as well have been stacked in an armory at Santa Fe or Denver. Four hands were lifted reluctantly.

The men with the rifles rode forward. They kept their captives covered every instant. One of them swung from the saddle, bowlegged to the prisoners, and relieved them of their revolvers.

Rusty nodded to the leader, a big ugly man with a scowling face. 'Can't say I'm glad to see you under these circumstances, Jerry,' he said.

Haskell swore violently. 'Rustling. Caught in the act. A rope round yore gullets is what you need and what you'll get.' There was savage triumph in his voice.

The old man continued to chew his cud of tobacco. 'You got us wrong, Jerry,' he said equably. 'We ain't either one of us rustlers. I'm old enough to be yore daddy, I reckon, and I never blocked a brand or ran one over, nor never bought a wet horse. My eyes ain't what they onct were, and maybe I didn't read the brand right. Anyone is liable to make a mistake.'

'You've made yore last, you old rascal,' Haskell

jeered. 'Tie 'em up, boys. We'll drift back to the ranch and see what Chet has got to say.'

'Chet will be reasonable,' Rusty said. 'I been in tights a heap worse than this. Onct when I was gathering bones near Dodge after the buffalo days—'

'Slip a rope round their necks,' the foreman ordered. 'I'd drag 'em at our horses' heels if I had time, but I want to get to the Circle 3 T soon as I can. These birds will wish they had never been born before we're through with them.'

The warm color had deserted the cheeks of Morse. He knew that Rusty was making talk to ease the strain, but he had no hope the old fellow could talk Radbourne out of his vengeance. The young fellow walked to his horse firmly enough, but already a sickness was creeping over him. The pleasant sunshine no longer held any heat. A chill ran down his back.

The prisoners were lifted to their saddles. Due westward the party rode, as straight for the Circle 3 T as the contour of the country would permit.

'Don't you weaken, son,' Rusty said to his companion. 'They haven't stopped our clocks yet, not by a jugful. Cole will cut loose his dog soon as he learns what has happened.'

'Yes,' the boy agreed huskily.

It was all very well to talk, he thought, but long before Sanborn knew they were missing,

Radbourne and Haskell would blot them out. Neither of the Circle 3 T men would forget the part they had had in humiliating them.

They rode the hills across a land creased by draws. From the summits, as far as the eye could see, the long swells stretched like waves of an ocean. Once they saw a small band of antelope moving through the mesquite. The riders left the miles behind them. A horseman in the chaparral watched the party pass. He chose not to make his presence known.

At the Circle 3 T, Haskell strode into the ranchhouse and summoned his chief.

'Come here, Chet,' he roared, 'if you would like to take a look at a couple of wolves I've got roped out in front.'

Radbourne shambled to the porch. His little eyes gleamed with triumphant malice.

'Where did you jump them up?' he asked.

'Found 'em skinning a Circle 3 T steer at the old Reincke place.'

'Rustlers, eh? Well, they know what happens to cattle thieves in this country when caught,' Radbourne gloated.

A cold prickling of the skin ran over Morse. He opened his parched lips to mention that the steer had originally been a Lazy B calf, but he caught sight of Rusty frowning at him. It came to the boy that to mention this incriminating fact would be to seal his fate. Radbourne would never let them live if he thought they had evidence of brand-blotting against him.

'Now, Chet, that ain't any way to talk,' Rusty remonstrated amiably. 'We ain't rustlers. You know that dog-goned well. Like I told Jerry, I'm some nearsighted and read the brand wrong.'

'You'll hang just the same,' Radbourne retorted cruelly. 'Don't I know you both? Didn't I see you here the other day with that villain Sanborn? Would you try to tell me you don't belong to his gang?'

'We been riding with him a few days,' Rusty admitted. 'That's true. But, dad-gum it, we never done you any meanness, Chet. When we had the dead wood on you, we didn't hurt you a bit. Let's be reasonable about this.'

'I'll be reasonable,' Radbourne said, showing his bad teeth in an evil grin. 'You're outlaws and rustlers. I'll hang you reasonably to a wagon tongue. This country will be well rid of you both.'

'The quicker the sooner,' Haskell said callously. 'Prop up that wagon tongue, boys. You first, Rusty. We got to pay a proper deference to age.'

'Don't push on the reins, Jerry,' Rusty suggested, still chewing his quid evenly. 'Time is one thing we all got plenty of. I've knowed many a man's sixgun go off half-cocked who rued it later. Any fool can take life, but even God Almighty doesn't bring it back onct its gone.'

'All right. I'll give you a chance,' Radbourne

said. 'If you will lead us to the place where Sanborn is camped, I won't hang you, but will turn you over to the authorities.'

The washed-out eyes of Rusty met steadily the small black ones of the Circle 3 T owner.

'That's a subject on which I've got no information,' he said.

'You'd better have,' Radbourne snarled, and spat out a vile epithet. 'You're going to talk, or have that scrawny gullet burned with a rope. Better men than you have tried to stand up to me and yelled for mercy before I got through with them.'

'I'm brush-bred, and I don't scare, Chet,' Rusty told him quietly. 'I learned when I first turned waddy to hold up my end or turn in my string of horses.'

'We'll find out about that,' the fat man sneered. 'String him up, boys.'

The man called Hank spoke to Radbourne in a low voice. Chet looked at the younger prisoner. The face of the boy was colorless.

'Wait a minute,' Radbourne said, with a te-he of mocking laughter. 'Here's a game young cock will find his tongue and tell us where Sanborn is roosting. Say your piece, young fellow.'

From a dry throat Morse murmured that he did not know where Sanborn was just now.

'You'll tell me or you will hang,' Radbourne flung at him furiously. 'Don't play with me, you poor fool.'

'Don't be a hog, Chet,' Rusty cut in. 'One of us is enough. If it has got to be, hang me and let this boy go. Don't you see he's only a kid?'

'Are you going to talk?' Radbourne demanded of the boy angrily. 'Or hang?'

Young Morse was sick with fear. He thought of Reincke, blotted out of life when he had everything to live for. It would be that way with him. He would never again see the sun rising over the hills. He would never ride along the high trails with the cool wind blowing in his face. Not ever again would he kiss a girl. His mother would wait for his letters . . . and wait . . .

Again Rusty intervened. 'If you and Haskell do this, Chet, I wouldn't give either of you a week to live. Cole will get you both, and these warriors of yours, too, sure as two nickels make a dime.'

Radbourne slammed a fat fist down on the railing of the porch. 'Last chance, fellow!' he shouted at Morse. 'Which is it to be? I'm through fooling with you.'

Morse looked at the propped-up wagon tongue. The landscape tilted upward. His body swayed, so that the man holding the other end of the rope had to steady him. Waves of nausea swept through him.

'I . . . don't know where Cole is at,' he gasped, summoning the last remnants of his resolution.

'Suits me if it does you, Mr. Rustler,' Radbourne

said. 'We'll get that business out of the way right now, Jerry.'

Someone put an arm under the elbow of Morse and began to propel him toward the wagon. The young fellow looked at Radbourne piteously. The ranch-owner was smiling, but his smile was malignant.

Morse cried out a strangled word. 'Wait.'

The boss of the Circle 3 T lifted a fat clammy hand to stop the procession. 'Your memory better?' he asked, sneering at the young man.

'I'll . . . tell what I know,' Morse said brokenly.

'You'd better know enough. No playing horse with me. I'd as soon bump off a fool like you as take a drink, if you get in my way. Listen. Do you know where Sanborn is?'

'Y-yes.'

'And you'll lead my men there?'

'Yes.'

'If you don't, you'll be riddled with lead.' An unholy triumph lit the evil, pasty face of Radbourne. 'Tote this old coot Rusty to the bunk-house. You, Bill, tie him up there and guard him. Four more of you stay here close to your guns. Jerry, take all the rest of the men you can gather and go with this young squirt. If his actions look bad to you any time, you know what to do. Round up Sanborn and his gang. Don't take any chances. If they resist, mow them down. You don't have to bring them in alive. Dead will suit me just as well.'

Rusty was taken to the bunkhouse and fastened to a heavy staple in the wall. Through the window he could see men roping and saddling. In a cloud of dust they swept past noisily and vanished. For a minute he could hear the diminishing clatter of the hoofs. Then the last faint tinkle died away.

The heart of the oldtimer was heavy. Sanborn and his men would be surprised and shot down. Chet would be top dog again, as he had been for years before Cole challenged his supremacy. Well, that would not matter to old Rusty, he told himself bitterly. He would not live to see the evil days that would come upon Boone County. Probably the story given out by Chet would be that he had been shot with a gun in his hand trying to escape.

The guard sitting on the bunk next to the one upon which Rusty lay rolled and lit a cigarette.

'Might as well take it easy. I don't reckon you'll be paying us a long visit, but you're an old vinegarroon, and I don't reckon you got much ahead of you anyhow,' he said callously.

'Old nothing,' retorted Rusty, with energy. 'To hear some of you one-gallus brakemen talk, I must of come out to this country when the Chiricahuas were a hole in the ground.'

'You're old enough to know better than to buck Radbourne, even if you are only eighty or ninety. We got you and yore friend Sanborn where the wool is short.' He spoke with rancor. 'That geezer has been putting on lugs long enough. I don't reckon he'll ever reach this ranch alive. He druv the last nail in his coffin the other day when he pulled the funny business on us. Making us walk. Jerry ain't liable to forget that.'

The lean jaws of the prisoner moved evenly. He aimed at a knothole six feet away and scored a center shot with tobacco juice. 'I never did see such birds for counting up yore chickens before they are hatched as you Circle 3 T roosters. Betcha four bits to a plug of tobacco you don't get Cole dead or alive.'

Rusty spoke with a manner of sprightly confidence not reflected in his thoughts.

'Take you,' the guard said promptly. ' 'Course it won't make no difference to you whether we get him or not. Either way of it you're a dead 'possum.'

'By jacks, I'll live to tromp the ground down on yore grave,' Rusty flung back in his high falsetto.

The guard laughed. He had his own opinion about that.

Chapter XXXI
Cole Guesses

A voice shouted. 'Hello the camp! 'Lo, Cole—Dunc! It's Art Simmons. I'm coming up.'

'Swing to the left,' Cole answered. 'The trail is better.'

A small brown man in chaps with an unshaven face like a bristly brush wound up among the rocks.

'Bad news for you uns,' he said bluntly. 'I was in the brush when a bunch of Radbourne's men passed. Jerry Haskell was with them. They had two prisoners. One of 'em was Rusty Hunter.'

This was a jarring blow. McCoy was the first to speak.

'The other must have been young Morse.'

'Were they headed for the Circle 3 T ranch?' Cole asked.

'Straight as a crow flies.'

'Any of them see you?'

'No, sir. I took good care of that.' Simmons had not finished his story. 'I lit out soon as it was safe to bring word to you. Had to pass through the Reincke place. Well, sir, I found a dead steer there. Shot today. Partly skinned.'

'The boys were out after meat,' Dave Pope explained.

From his saddlebags Simmons drew a piece of fresh hide. 'This was jammed kinda under the steer. I'm wondering if Rusty shoved it there when he found Haskell had got him.'

Cole examined the bit of hide. Upon it was the Circle 3 T brand. But that was not all he read there. The brand had been blotted over another one. The first one was the Lazy B.

'What will Chet do with the boys?' Pope asked.

Slim laughed, without mirth. He, too, had been examining the branded bit of hide. 'Ask a harder one, Dave. Jerry will know from the earmarks it was a steer claimed by his outfit. Chet will hang the boys as rustlers. That will give him a good excuse. Or if he is scared to do that, he'll pull the old one of shooting them while they are trying to escape.'

Cole's mind swept over the probabilities. When he looked up, his harsh face was bleak.

'Will he do that right away, Slim?' he inquired. 'You know the old fox, maybe better than I do. Won't he first try to get out of them information about our hide-out?'

Slim assented. 'That's right. He'll sweat that out of the boys if he can.'

'And I reckon he can,' Cole added, thinking aloud. 'Morse is only a kid. Likely he'll break down. I wouldn't blame him if he did. Then what will Chet do?'

'He'll start his warriors out to collect our scalps.'

'Not knowing we've been warned by Art.'

'That's right,' Slim nodded. 'We're one up on the old wolf there.'

'We would be if Rusty and the kid weren't his prisoners,' Cole corrected. 'Our first job is to save them. How?'

'Bust straight for the ranch. Rescue the boys. Jerry and his crowd will be hightailin' it over the hills to get us.'

'So they will, if we've got this guessed right. But where will Rusty and Morse be? Jerry isn't going to start for us without a guide.'

'That's so,' Pete Daggett spoke up. 'D-dad-gum it, we got to mix with Jerry's bunch of w-warriors first.'

'Where? On the plains, with them two or three to one against us. That would be bad medicine. We might get three-four of them, but they would come pretty nearly wiping us out.'

'T-that's right, too,' Pete admitted. 'W-what's the matter with sticking right here in camp where we got rocks for cover?'

Cole shook his head. 'We've got to strike first—and hard. I want a prisoner, so I can come back at them and say if they hurt our boys we'll retaliate. Who would be the best one to round up?'

'If I had my ruthers I would gather in Jerry—or

the old man himself,' Slim said. 'But of course that's just talk. We'll have to take whoever we can get, if any, don't you reckon?'

'Would it stop Radbourne if we captured one or two of his men? The old scoundrel would play his hand just the same, wouldn't he?'

'Y'betcha,' Slim replied promptly. 'He'd sacrifice them quick as he would a couple of worn-out broomtails.'

'My opinion, too,' Cole said. 'I say let us try to make a good gather, boys. We'll try to get Radbourne himself. Let's pack our stuff, catch, and get going.'

While the others were catching the mounts, saddling, and putting the camp equipment on pack-animals, Cole was writing a note.

It read:

You and your boys have a nice picnic among the rocks, Jerry. Don't let any diamond-backs bite you. Remember, we'll be watching you every minute. If you do any harm to Hunter or Morse, I'll skin you alive. This goes for your whole bunch. See you later.

COLE SANBORN

He weighted the note down with a large rock on a conspicuous flat boulder.

Before they started, Cole had a word for his men. 'If I've guessed this thing wrong, boys, I'll only be leading you into a trap. Now is the time to drop out if any one of you doesn't want to take a chance.'

Dave Pope looked at him irritably. 'Fellow, what do you take us for? We'll go from hell to breakfast to help the boys. Push on, you dog-goned idjit.'

'I only mentioned it,' Cole said apologetically. 'There's liable to be ructions before we're through.'

Cole did not ride straight for the Circle 3 T. He did not want to meet the party sent from the ranch to get him. The group followed a wide circle among the hills. It swung through defiles, up steep slopes, across sunbaked mesas. Whether the men were in heavy chaparral or on shale ridges Cole knew exactly where he was going. This country was as familiar to him as a spelling-book is to a teacher.

Though they traveled fast, Cole could not outride his apprehensions. There hung heavy over him a premonition of trouble brewing. The other day at Big Pine Point he had outguessed and outgeneraled Radbourne. But the old scoundrel was a wily fox. He had got where he was by the shrewd, unscrupulous way in which he had duped others; by that, plus the ruthlessness which had never hesitated to destroy anyone interfering with his plans. It was not likely that he would be caught napping a second time.

In single file the riders emerged from a gorge to the plateau above. Dave and Slim moved forward to ride beside Cole.

'We're going to be in time, wouldn't you say?' Dave said, voicing the fear in his heart. 'The old toad wouldn't do the boys a meanness right off. He'd play his hand more careful than that, I'd figure.'

'We don't know what he would do,' Cole said gloomily. 'All we can do is guess.'

'I'd hate for anything to happen to that old donker Rusty. Or the kid either for that matter.' Dave essayed a manner entirely casual, to cover his feeling. 'It's kinda fun having the old gazabo around and listening to his windys. I run on him just to get him started on new ones.'

Cole turned abruptly to Slim. 'Am I making a mistake? I don't want to butt into a nest of guns waiting for us. Have I got this worked out right? The way it looks to me, there are two big *ifs* in this problem, assuming that Haskell took our boys to the ranch and didn't hang them when he came to the first tree. The first is this: Would Morse weaken? I'll leave Rusty out of it. I doubt if Chet could get a word from him. But Morse is another proposition. He hasn't been long in this country. Could he go through what Chet would put him up against?'

'Don't think so,' Slim answered. 'Chet is one devil spewed out of hell. When young Morse feels a redhot branding-iron against his bare feet, he will break down. I have watched that boy. Not meaning to knock him or anything, my opinion is he couldn't stand the gaff. He'll come through with the information Chet wants.'

'That is what I think,' Cole said.

'Me too,' Dave corroborated.

'All right. If Haskell took the boys to the ranch—and it looks like he did—Radbourne would make them sweat blood until he got what he wanted.'

'What he would want would be the spot where we were camping,' Dave said.

'Right. When he got it, what would he do?' Cole threw up a hand to forestall a possible comment. 'Yes, I know we've been all over that. But I don't want to overlook any sleeper. Put yourself in his place. What would you do?'

'I'd tell Haskell to burn the wind getting to our camp,' Dave replied promptly. 'And I'd made it stick out like a sore thumb that I wanted our whole outfit wiped out.'

Cole looked at Slim.

Calhoun nodded. 'Dave has about said it. That's what I would do, too, if I was as black-hearted a villain as Chet. Only there's one more thing I would do. I'd make sure enough men stayed at the ranch with me to protect me against another surprise attack.'

'How many would he keep there?' Cole asked.

'Not so many. He couldn't. Chet can't keep all his riders around the ranch eating their heads off. He has to have the cattle looked after. I've never known him to have more than a dozen or so there. Of course there's a chance he has called back the lads from the Lazy B. Say he can get hold of fifteen right off. He might send ten of them off to get us. The other five he would have sit tight where they are at, with their guns handy, to look after Mr. Chet Radbourne's hide. He made a mistake once about that. He won't do it again. Where you are concerned, he's gun-shy. You've got him buffaloed. He will play safe.'

'So we can figure we're going up against as big a crowd as we are, if we are lucky; if not, about three times as many. That's a sweet outlook. You know the lay of the ranch, Slim. How would you approach?'

'I would come through the live oaks back of the house, cut the wire fence, and take the last hundred yards on the jump.'

'We'll try it that way,' Cole decided.

The black-haired Texan grinned. 'I don't give any written guaranty with my advice, Cole. They may empty our saddles before we reach the house. If anyone has a better idea, it will be all right with me.'

Art Simmons rode forward and joined them. 'I'll be leaving you here,' he said. 'Luck, and lots of it.'

'Wait a minute.' Cole wrote in a notebook with the stub of an old pencil, tore out the sheet, and handed it to Simmons. 'Give that to my wife, Art, if anything happens to me. Otherwise, hold it till I see you.'

The nester nodded. 'I'll be pulling for you, Cole. Most everyone but the rascals in Boone County are for you now. This looks like a crazy business to me, but if anyone can make it stick it will be you.'

Simmons turned and rode off. He had a wife and three children. Once he looked back at the five men dropping over the hill. He was glad he was not one of them. His opinion was that most of Cole's men would be wiped out before sunset and the rest of them would be flying into the hills for their lives. Cole was a good man all right, but this time he had bit off more than he could chew.

Chapter XXXII

Radbourne Waves a White Flag

Radbourne sat in front of his desk, the great body of the man slumped together like that of some huge invertebrate. The beady eyes had a staring, glassy look. His mind was spinning one of the webs that meant destruction for his enemies.

The owner of the Circle 3 T realized he was in danger. The rebellion against his rule was spreading fast. Unless he quelled it, evidence could be found that might put him in the penitentiary. Peters had raked up a lot of scandal connected with various political deals he had maneuvered. For one thing there was the court-house building contract. Radbourne had made a fifteen-thousand-dollar rake-off on that. Some fool had failed to destroy a memorandum which showed it. There were road pacts and bond issues put over contrary to law. It would never do to let these go to a grand jury investigation. Judge Fairley was weakening. He was afraid of prison himself and could not be depended upon to go through against the rising tide of resentment showing itself everywhere.

Sanborn was the spear-point of the revolt. His

exploits lent courage to all those who would like to see the big boss defeated. With him out of the way, rubbed out by the man they feared and hated, the opposition would melt like snow in warm sunshine and wind.

This time Jerry Haskell would wipe out the Sanborn gang. He would probably surprise them in their camp and mow them down before they had a chance to fight back. At the worst he would defeat them, kill two or three, and scatter the rest in the brush. What Radbourne hoped for was that Sanborn, trying to rally his men, would be riddled with bullets.

If not, the thing to do would be to have the Peters house watched. Some night Sanborn would try to steal in to see his wife. He could be shot down by any man with a little nerve. Curt Jordan would have been the fellow to do it if he had not got drunk and played the fool. But there were others ready to take a chance for a thousand bucks or . . .

The crack of a rifle lifted him to his feet. He heard the blast of guns, swift as the popping of firecrackers. Through the window he caught sight of horsemen charging the house from the live oaks. One saddle was empty. A man had been shot from it. He saw a rider drag his mount to a halt, leap to the ground, pick up the body of his fallen comrade, and stagger forward with it.

Radbourne reached into a desk. As the door of

the room burst open he fired. The man in the doorway stared at him, blank surprise in his shocked eyes, then staggered forward to fall heavily upon the desk. The owner of the Circle 3 T cursed. He had shot too soon and killed one of the men set to guard him.

It seemed to him that the room filled instantly. Sanborn he saw, and Slim Calhoun. Also Dunc McCoy. His heart went down like a plummet into icy water. All of them were enemies, men marked for death by him at one time or another. Hurriedly he tossed his revolver upon the desk.

'I'm unarmed!' he cried. 'Don't kill me, boys.'

'Where are our friends, Rusty Hunter and young Morse?' Cole asked.

'Rusty is in the bunkhouse, Cole. We haven't hurt him a mite. Morse is riding with the boys.'

Cole did not ask where they were riding. 'How many of your men with Haskell?' he demanded.

'Eight. I sent 'em out to—'

'How many here at the ranch?'

'Six. Now, looky here, Cole. I ain't and never have been looking for trouble. You're such an all-fired trouble-hunter yourself you can't understand a peaceable man like me. I sent Jerry to have a conference with you because he caught two of your boys skinning a Circle 3 T beef. I figured that you would want to know so you could—'

Through the open door Slim saw Daggett carrying the body of Dave Pope.

'Dave dead?' he asked.

'N-not when I p-picked him up. He's done f-fainted now. Where is there a b-bed?'

'I'll show you,' Slim said, and led the way down the hall.

Pete followed, the feet of the lank puncher dragging on the ground.

Cole spoke to McCoy. 'I'm going to have a look at Dave's wound, Dunc. Watch this rat. If he tries to get away, shoot him down as he did his own man. I'll send one of the boys back to keep an eye on those in the bunkhouse.'

'What is the idea of you boys jumping me this way, McCoy?' Radbourne asked when they were alone. 'I'm trying to 'tend to my own business and you pester me all the time.'

McCoy looked at him with disgust and scorn. 'Man, I never saw your like as a liar. What's the sense in talking that way to me? Was I pestering you when you ran me from my homestead? Was I pestering you when you set Gildea on to murder me?'

'You're wrong about that, McCoy. I offered to buy your claim, and whatever Gildea did was on his own. I hadn't anything to do with it.'

Slim came into the room. He looked at the body of the dead man lying across the desk.

'Makes two for our side,' he said coolly. In explanation to Radbourne, he added: 'There's another lying on the porch, the man they call

Hank. He shot down Dave, so it is even steven as far as he is concerned.'

'Any chance for Dave?' asked McCoy.

'Don't know. He got it in the right lung. Cole is trying to fix him up.'

Radbourne shook his head mournfully. 'All this gunplay is bad medicine. I don't like it.'

'Except when your side does it,' Slim replied.

Calhoun walked to the window and looked cautiously at the bunkhouse. 'The boys over there seem to have got over their fogging. Quiet as a prayer-meeting now,' he continued. 'It will be too bad for you, Chet, if they pull any trouble.'

After a time Cole returned. He found Radbourne explaining what a good citizen he was and how much he wished his captors well.

'I can't understand what I've ever done for you fellows to run on me so,' he complained. 'I have enemies who go around black-naming me, and you boys believe everything you hear.'

'I'll give you a chance to show how well-meaning you are,' Cole told him grimly. He passed a white handkerchief to the prisoner. 'You are going out to be a messenger of peace. Order the boys in the bunkhouse to turn over Rusty to you. Every second you will be under three rifles. If you make a break—if you don't bring back Rusty with you, that will be good-bye for you. Understand! You will go halfway to the bunkhouse, and then you will stop.'

'Can I go on to the bunkhouse if the boys send Rusty out?'

'No. You're coming back with him. Maybe you have forgotten that you are our ace in the hole, Chet. For a while I'm going to stick closer to you than any brother.'

'You got no right to act this way, Cole,' Radbourne protested. 'You ought to know that you are getting in bad with the law when you pull high-handed stuff like this. By rights, I ought to refuse to do what you are asking me.'

'I'm not asking you,' corrected Cole. 'I'm telling you.'

'Better waddle along,' Slim suggested cheerfully. 'Take a chance. Maybe we won't plug you in the back after you have delivered the message, Chet. You can't ever tell. All you know is that you're going to turn up yore toes to the daisies if you don't do like Cole tells you.'

Radbourne moistened his lips with his tongue. He slid an oblique look from Slim to Sanborn.

'You aren't aiming to kill me while I carry a white flag, Cole,' he whined.

'Not if you come through and don't try any shenanigan. You're worth more to me alive. Get going.'

'We ought to fix up any difficulty there is between us, Cole, and not get into all this killing,' Radbourne said virtuously. 'Here you come jumping my ranch for no reason at all.

Consequence is two of my boys have been killed already and one of yours wounded. That's bad. If we don't come to an understanding there will be more bloodshed. What I say is, let's drop this helling around and show we're decent citizens in a law-abiding country. It's not right to slaughter human beings like you are doing.'

Slim spoke, drawling out his words: 'And this same mangy son-of-a-gun offered me fifteen hundred dollars to bushwhack you, Cole, and when I told him where to get off at he pumped lead at me till I was out of range.'

'You're mistaken, Slim,' the ranchman explained in an oily voice. 'I said there was a reward of fifteen hundred dollars for the fellow who led the express robbers, and my notion was it would be a good thing for you to find out who did it and arrest him, so we could have it all cleared up and Cole wouldn't be suspected. Now wasn't that what I said?'

'Can you beat that?' Slim asked, turning to Cole. 'And I reckon after I turned down yore generous offer, Chet, you was just practicing when you whanged away at me.'

'I was trying to scare you because you had been impudent to me. That was all.' Radbourne appealed to Cole. 'I want peace, boy, all the time.'

'Too much talk, Chet. Step along. Carry out with you the body of the man you killed. You can tell your boys they can come and get the two bodies. We won't hurt them while they are doing it if they don't bring rifles with them. One thing more. Have them pass the word to Haskell when he arrives that if he hurts Morse we shall certainly get him if it is the last thing we ever do. Might as well explain, too, that we shall be sticking around a while, and if they did happen to storm the house and take it, they would have to order a large-size coffin for their late lamented master.'

'I don't believe that for a minute, Cole,' Radbourne replied. 'You're too square a man to make me pay for something these crazy gunmen did against my wishes. But I'll take your messages.'

Radbourne waved the handkerchief vigorously before exposing his great bulk on the porch. He did not want a second man on his side to be killed by mistake, not if the man was Chet Radbourne. Presently he sidled out, dragging with him the inert body of the man he had shot. Almost at once he began to shout to his men not to shoot, that he wanted to have a talk with them. Two or three times he stopped, panting, to rest. He looked back nervously at the house. With three rifles in the hands of the enemy trained on him, he felt far from comfortable. One of these men he had injured might decide impulsively to even the score.

In the no man's land between the two houses, Radbourne halted and waved his flag again. At a corner of an opened window in the bunkhouse a head appeared cautiously.

'We're listening, Chet,' a voice called.

'First off, boys, Cole says you can pick up the bodies of the two men he has killed. You won't be shot at while you're doing it if you don't carry rifles with you.'

'He wouldn't fool us?'

'No, I don't think he would. Then I want you to turn over Rusty to me.'

'A swap of prisoners. That the idea?'

'No. I have to go back to the house. I hate to do it, but he has me covered.'

'What kind of a trade would that be?' Bill demanded. 'Sanborn sure has a gall. He's the one in a hole, not us. I've done sent a man after Jerry. Why, dad-gum it, soon as the boys get here we'll rush the ranch-house and finish this job pronto.'

'Don't you do it!' Radbourne screamed. 'They would kill me sure, soon as you started. Nothing like that, Bill. No matter what happens. Fix up a deal to get me away from them first. Well, I got to be going now,' he said ruefully. 'I've got to take Rusty back with me. No two ways about that.'

'If they shoot you we'll hang every last one of 'em soon as we rush the house,' Bill answered. 'He can't get away with any such thing.'

'What good would that do me if I was dead?' Radbourne demanded irritably. 'Get Rusty out to me quick. This isn't my say-so or yours. Sanborn has got hell in the neck, and we've got to do like he says.'

Bill withdrew his head for consultation with his fellows. After a time it reappeared.

'All right, Chet. You're the doctor. If I was doing this, I would give Cole a battle before I turned over our prisoner free gratis. But since you say it's to be thataway, we got no option.'

The door opened and Rusty walked out from the bunkhouse. He joined Radbourne. The oldtimer walked jauntily, chewing tobacco as he strutted forward.

'I could of told you to lay off Cole,' Rusty said jubilantly to Radbourne. 'Some folks are like a watermelon. You can't tell how good they are till you thump them. But Cole—say, after one look in his eye you'd ought to have known his come-back would have a kick like a mule. If you had had a lick of sense, you would have sent me and Morse back with yore compliments and said the war was over. Instead of which you went crazy in the head. Don't say I didn't warn you. I said Cole would round you up inside of a week, and, by jacks, he did it in two hours.'

Radbourne said nothing. He clumped back to the house, his head sullenly down between his heavy rounded shoulders. This fellow Sanborn had all the luck. It was all very well for Bill to talk about rushing the house when Haskell got back. Chet was of opinion that if they did, his riders would find their boss no longer alive.

Chapter XXXIII
Smoked Out

Rusty said nonchalantly to Cole: 'Hello, old socks! It's sure been a hundred years since I saw you this morning. This old scalawag here got notions of a necktie party for me and the kid. He made the mistake of postponing it. I just been telling the old diamondback that opportunity is like a bald-headed man with a beard; you can grab it for a hair holt coming but not going. I'll say this for you, Cole. You certainly came on the jump and all spraddled out. None of you boys hurt?'

'Dave Pope. Shot in the chest. A bad wound. Wish we had a doctor here.' Cole spoke crisply. He had just now no time to waste words.

'Lemme look at him,' Rusty suggested. 'I been doctoring busted buckaroos all my life, even if I ain't any licensed M.D. I would hate to lose that boy. I've took a smile to him, even if he does run on me something scandalous.'

'Hop to it, Rusty, and take care of him,' Cole said.

'The boys in the bunkhouse got a messenger off to Jerry Haskell to tell him to burn the wind back here,' Rusty mentioned. 'If you're aiming to hit the trail, I would say the quicker the sooner.'

'We're staying here,' Cole replied. 'Dave can't be moved, and Morse is still in their hands. I wouldn't put it beyond Haskell to fix it so that Dave would die of his wound if we left him here. No, we've got to hole up here.'

'Suits me,' Rusty said, and departed to look after his patient.

Cole ordered the prisoner tied hard and fast. He did not want him making trouble when the pinch came. Slim superintended the barring of all the doors and windows after several buckets of water had been carried in from the well just back of the house. He reported to Cole that with the meat and vegetables brought in from the root house there was food enough for two or three days.

'By that time,' Calhoun concluded, with his intrepid grin, 'we either won't be needing food or we'll be where we can get it.'

'Right you are,' McCoy agreed. 'Though I wouldn't give three cheers about it.'

'My dad was in the siege of Vicksburg,' Slim explained. 'I've stood at his knee and heard him tell about it, so I reckon it's in my blood to want to have a siege of my own to brag about to my kids.'

'If you live to have any,' McCoy added dryly.

'I've never been bumped off yet, and I'm betting my luck will stand up,' the Texan answered cheerfully. 'I aim to have six boys and four girls, the same as my parents did.' He added, to forestall what McCoy might be about to retort: 'Sure, you hope I'll have better luck than they did, if the ornery offspring you've seen is a fair sample. The answer to that is, I'm the black sheep of the bunch.'

Cole went over the house, studying it from the point of view of defense. 'We'll have tough sledding,' he told his men. 'Haskell will call in every rider on the Circle 3 T payroll. There will be five of us and over thirty of them. But we'll have two advantages. One of them is that we hold Radbourne a prisoner. The other is that we are under cover, and to get us they will have to come out into the open. They can wipe us out, if they want to pay the price. But it will come high for them. When they find out how high, they may give up and quit.'

'You figure they will attack us, anyhow, even with Chet in our hands?' McCoy asked.

'Haskell will certainly try to collect us now he has us trapped. If he didn't he would lose face in this country. He will take a chance on us injuring Radbourne. There is no love lost between him and his boss anyhow.'

'W-what's the m-matter with you fellows lighting out?' Pete Daggett wanted to know. 'Dave and I been sidekicks ever since we were kids. I'll stay with him. Haskell has got nothing particular against me. I don't reckon he would do me a meanness, anyhow not when you have Radbourne a prisoner.'

'That is just what we don't know, Pete,' replied Cole. 'I would hate to guess what goes on in that sulky mean mind of Haskell. If I took you up on that proposition, we would be leaving three of our friends in his hands. Too big a risk. Maybe he wouldn't ask any better than to have us finish off his boss. No, boys. As we stand we're a pretty strong combination. If we split up, we're only a bunch of hunted men on the dodge in the scrub.'

'And what about our horses?' McCoy asked. ' 'Soon as Haskell gets here he will send men back into the live oaks to shoot our mounts so that we can't get away on them if we make a break.'

'We shall have to unsaddle and turn the horses loose,' Cole said. 'I don't like to do it. We'll be burning our bridges. But we can't let the animals be shot down.'

Slim and Pete walked out to the back porch where the horses were tied. They unsaddled the geldings and freed them. The saddles they carried into the house.

After that the hours dragged. The men tightened the defenses. McCoy cooked dinner. Potatoes, ham, eggs, biscuits, and coffee disappeared down the throats of the diners with amazing rapidity. They lived outdoors, and their appetites were voracious.

'The c-condemned man ate a h-hearty breakfast of burned p-potatoes and s-soggy biscuits,' Pete said, scooping two more eggs to his plate.

McCoy eyed him malevolently. 'You don't like this grub, young fellow?' he asked.

Daggett knew the old camp rule. If anyone complained about the food, he did the cooking. Hastily he offered an amendment to his previous remark.

'S-sure I l-like it, Dunc. I never could stand p-potatoes that aren't burned nor b-biscuits cooked clear through.'

Someone outside gave a triumphant yell. Cole was lookout man at the moment and he conveyed information to the others.

'Arrival of Mr. Jerry Haskell and his bunch of warriors. The kid is still with them. Things will begin to happen right soon, boys. If you have that dinner tucked under your belts you had better get to your posts, don't you reckon?'

Slim walked to the window. Haskell was swinging from the saddle. They could hear his raucous curse as he dragged Morse to the ground.

'There he is, big and ugly as life,' Slim commented viciously. 'I'd like to plug him right now. I could do it, too, while that bird in the door is telling him we're here in his little rat trap. You're too dog-goned lawful, Cole. If I was to bump him off, that would throw the fear into their hearts, especially when Radbourne is in our midst. You know he'll start in to collect us. Me, I'd start the collecting.'

'We have to give him his chance, Slim. He won't take it, but we can't assume that. If there is to be a war, he will have to start it.'

'How can he start what is already started? Two of their men are dead, and Dave is a mighty sick Missourian.'

'Haskell wasn't in on that. He might be willing to talk turkey.'

'When he has us bottled here, with the cork drove in!' Slim laughed derisively. 'Not little Jerry.'

The riders dismounted and scattered. Some of them vanished into the bunkhouse. Others took cover in the stable.

After a time a man with a white towel emerged from the bunkhouse. He waved it. Cole opened the front door slightly and waved one in return.

The man was Bill. He bowlegged forward, his body looking slender above the wide chaps. In front of the house he stopped.

'We got you fellows sure,' he announced. 'No two ways about that. Fifteen of us here already, and more coming in lickety-split. Jerry says he will give you the best of it. Turn over to us Radbourne and Sanborn and he will let the rest of you go. That is more than you have got any right to expect.'

'What guaranty have we that he won't wipe us

all out soon as we get out from cover?' Slim asked.

'You have his word—and ours.'

'I don't reckon anyone could ask for more than that,' Slim jeered.

'Say, young fellow, if I was Jerry, you wouldn't be included in this peace pact after turning traitor the way you did,' Bill flung back at him angrily. 'Well, fellows, what is it to be? One way or the other. Make up yore minds.'

'Get back to Jerry and tell him to turn his wolf loose if he feels like it,' McCoy cried to the man.

'And tell him we'll get a whole passel of you before we're through, including him,' Rusty added.

Bill made one more try before leaving. 'If any one of you wants to quit a bunch of outlaws before the massacree begins, now is the last chance.'

'S-sashay back to that bunkhouse!' Daggett shouted. 'We d-done heard enough. Wouldn't one of us trust any of you farther than he could sling a bull by the tail.'

Cole himself had not spoken until now, since he had not been included in the offer of amnesty. But he had a last word.

'Tell Haskell if he injures that boy Morse I'll never rest till I have his scalp.'

The envoy had had no more than time to turn in his report when there came a blast of guns from the bunkhouse and the stable. Windows in the big house crashed. From the front door splinters flew. A spatter of bullets against the walls continued. Those inside the ranch-house did not answer the fire.

'Trying to scare us,' Rusty said. He patted the sawed-off shotgun in his hand. 'This old scatter-gun won't do any talking till she has got something to talk at.'

'My guess is that Haskell is trying to distract our attention.' Cole called to Slim, who was guarding the rear, 'Watch out they don't charge from the live oaks.'

'That is what they're aiming to do,' Slim answered. 'Four or five on horseback. Maybe more. Here they come!' He raised his rifle, took steady aim, and fired. 'Hi yi yippy yi! Got one.' His yell had risen in triumphant crescendo.

Cole sent Daggett and McCoy to support Calhoun. Rusty remained to help him defend the front of the house. Smoke began to fill the rooms. All three of those at the rear were firing.

From the bunkhouse there came a yell. Out of that building and out of the stable men poured. They scattered, running toward the house. Cole blazed away at them. Rusty waited till they were nearer before he sent a load of buckshot at them. One of the running men stumbled and went down. The others wavered. Rapidly Cole fired twice more. The attack broke. Like frightened rabbits the Circle 3 T men scuttled back for their warren.

The roar of guns outside had been heavy. Now it died away.

Daggett called excitedly to Cole: 'They're s-skedaddling for the l-live oaks.'

Cole walked into the kitchen. Through a peephole he saw the last of the horsemen disappearing in the grove. One man, on foot, limping heavily, was dragging himself toward the live oaks. He stopped every few yards to rest, looking back apprehensively at the boarded windows. Out of the woods a man rode swiftly, leaped to the ground, and helped his wounded comrade to the saddle. None of those in the kitchen fired at the rescuer as he ran for cover.

'That was Bud Calloway,' Slim said. 'Bully for Bud. The fellow he picked up was Mex.'

'Mex is luckier than the one Rusty's old scatter-gun got,' Cole told them. 'He will never ride again.'

Rusty went to the bedroom where his patient lay.

'You fellows are making a lot of Fourth of July,' Dave said feebly, with a faint grin. 'Did you stand 'em off?'

'Y'betcha! The fireworks won't be lively again for quite some time. Altogether to date we've got four.' Rusty frowned at Dave. 'You keep yore mouth shut, fellow. If you stay quiet an' behave, you'll make the grade.'

'That ain't noways news to me,' Dave managed to answer. ' 'Course I'll make it.' He ended with a fit of coughing.

'You crazy buckaroo!' Rusty reproached. 'Didn't I warn you?'

The defenders were jubilant.

'We'll learn 'em to h-hello the house before they come cavortin' around,' Daggett said.

'Don't get the idea they are through,' Cole said. 'Likely they will lay off us till dark. Then we'll hear from them again.'

His prediction was true in part at least. The firing died away, flared up intermittently in a listless fashion, became once or twice animated. But none of the attackers showed themselves in the open. They had had their lesson.

The hours wore away. The sun in the copper sky slid down behind the hills. A soft violet glow tinted the range. Dusk fell, and after dusk a night of painted moonlight.

'Soon now,' Slim said. 'Can't come too quick for me. This waiting makes me goosey.'

He had not long to wait now. In the distance the Circle 3 T men could be seen busying themselves about something which looked like a haystack.

'I'm going out to find what they are doing,' Cole announced. 'If my guess is right, they are fixing to fire the house.'

'I know the lay of the land better,' Slim protested. 'Lemme go.'

Cole shook his head. 'No. It's my job. I may come back on the jump. Be ready to let me in.'

He slipped out of a back window where the shadow of the woodshed offered convenient darkness. From here he cut across to the root house. Stretching out his head, he reconnoitered. There did not seem to be anybody in sight. A horse corral built of posts lashed with rawhide ran down one side of the yard toward the stable. Cole dodged to the fence and crept forward along it. He moved very carefully, crouched low to avoid attracting attention. Not far from him was a live oak, under which was the outdoor blacksmith shop. Keeping the trunk of the tree between him and the moving figures, he worked his way to the live oak.

From its cover he could make out more clearly what the Circle 3 T men were doing. They were slowly rolling forward a wagonload of hay. Evidently their intention was to push it to the crest of the slope and send it the last fifty or seventy-five feet of its own momentum. The hay, of course, would be fired before it started down the descent toward the porch.

Someone called for an axe. A man volunteered to get it and moved toward the live oak. The trunk of the tree split, two or three feet from the ground, into two great spreading branches. Cole squatted low, hoping not to be seen.

The man reached the live oak and glanced

round, his eyes searching for an axe. Cole saw his body stiffen suddenly. His gaze had fallen on the crouched figure.

The Circle 3 T rider let out a yell, and at the same instant Cole leaped. Too startled to draw a weapon, the fellow fell back a step or two, flinging up an arm to protect himself. Sanborn's revolver moved up and down. The force of the blow broke the defense, and the barrel of the long sixshooter came down heavily on the head of the victim. Helplessly, the man staggered against the forge and sank to the ground.

But his cry had warned those around the haywagon. Cole ran for the corral fence. Someone caught sight of him and yelled. A shot rang out. Sanborn raced along the corral. Bullets struck the posts in front of and behind him. The guns of the enemy poured a fusillade in his direction. As he scudded across the open to the root house, he felt a shock in the left shoulder. He knew he had been hit, but he was not thrown out of his stride. From the root house he dashed to the shelter of the woodshed. Through the back window he clambered into the house.

'Didn't get you?' Slim asked quickly.

'No. We've got to get out of here. By the kitchen. They're going to fire the house. We can't stop it. We'll make for the horse corral.' Cole spoke with crisp decision. He had made up his mind while he was edging back along the fence.

'We'll be trapped there,' McCoy said. 'Like rats. Why not try for that clump of live oaks? From there we might work back into the hills if we could stand them off long enough.'

'No. Haskell must have sharpshooters posted there. They would pick off two or three of us before we ever reached the woods. Dunc, you guard Radbourne. Pete and I will carry Dave on a mattress. We'll pile food on top of it. There's a windmill in the corral, so we won't have to take water. Rusty, you and Slim will have to carry food-packs and guard us if we're rushed. It's not far. If we're lucky, we'll make it.'

Pushed by willing hands back of it, the hay-wagon reached the crest before the defenders were ready to evacuate. It stood there for a few moments while those back of it got the wheels pointed in the direction of the house. The Circle 3 T men were careful not to expose themselves, but Cole stood at the window and fired several times toward the wagon. He knew that those maneuvering the wagon into position would scatter back to safety as soon as it started down the slope. At that precise moment Cole intended that his party should decamp.

The hay flamed up and the wagon gathered momentum. Those back of it scattered like a covey of young quails. Out of the kitchen door the Sanborn group moved. Rusty and Slim went first. Those bearing the wounded man followed.

Duncan McCoy and Radbourne came out last.

They had to move slowly, and they were careful not to let themselves get bunched. Slim had dropped back to guard the rear. Cole and Pete had almost reached the root house with their burden before those in the live oaks discovered what was taking place.

A bullet sank into a log of the root-house wall. The crash of guns filled the night. Someone in the escaping party gave a groan. Rusty led the way into the last open stretch, the two with the wounded man at his heels. Momentarily the moon was under a cloud, so that the fire directed at them was loosely aimed.

'Another t-twenty yards,' Daggett said, between his teeth. 'We're gonna m-make it.'

'From the fire into the frying-pan,' Dave told him. 'I wish I wasn't holding back you boys.'

They reached the corral gate and passed inside. Slim dragged it shut and made fast the heavy bolts.

Radbourne slumped down to the ground and groaned.

'Look out for a rush, boys,' Cole ordered. 'I don't reckon they will try it yet, but they might.'

From his post Slim made a comment and asked a question. 'That trip was a hundred miles to me. Anybody hurt?'

'I got plugged in the foot,' Rusty mentioned. 'Lucky for me we didn't have far to go.'

'I'm shot,' Radbourne said. 'In the leg. We've got to stop this wickedness and get me a doctor.'

'Fine,' Slim said derisively. 'Only you better tell that to Haskell. This is his battle, not ours.'

'I'll bleed to death,' the owner of the ranch wailed. 'I'll let all you boys go if you will quit now. We can't go on with this. I want a doctor.'

'So do Dave and Rusty, you yellow coyote,' McCoy retorted. 'But you don't hear them yelping. Get those pants off and let me have a look at yore wound.'

'I tell you I'll give orders to my men not to interfere with you,' Chet insisted.

'Yes, and a fat lot of attention they would give to yore orders,' Slim told him. 'We would be put out of business before we had got twenty yards. Peel down those pants if you want a doc so dog-goned bad. We'll patch you up after we've took care of Rusty and made Dave comfortable.'

Daggett brought hay from the feed-rack and scattered it on the ground close to the fence. Upon this they put the mattress where Dave Pope lay.

'We gave you a jolty trip, old hoss,' Daggett said. 'D-did we s-start your wound to bleeding again?'

Dave grinned at him, cheerfully but feebly. 'I'm all right. Look after Rusty, or he'll start a windy on us. I ain't in any condition to listen to one of the old donker's stories.'

Already Cole was pulling the boot from the

wounded foot of Hunter. Sweat beads stood out on the forehead of the oldtimer, but no sound came from his clenched lips. Cole washed and bound the wound, with the help of Daggett. This finished, they looked after Radbourne's leg.

McCoy and Caldwell kept guard at the stockade. The posts had been buried in the ground, set very close, and woven together with rawhide thongs. The fence had been modeled from the primitive ones of the early days in the Texas brush country and had been built very strongly to withstand the plunges of wild horses. Against the solid timbers bullets thudded, for the attackers kept up a sporadic bombardment. Occasionally Slim or Dunc answered the challenge through their loop-holes.

The porch of the house was crackling and long flames shooting skyward, for the hay-wagon had rolled straight to its destination. The Circle 3 T men were making no effort to put out the fire they had started, since they dared not expose them-selves in the bright light to the marksman-ship of those within the stockade.

Cole finished with Radbourne and turned to Daggett.

'Skin this coat off kinda gently, Pete,' he said.

'You been hurt?' Daggett asked.

'In the left shoulder. That's the idea. Ease her off.'

'When were you hit?'

'While I was out scouting. Nothing to make a fuss about. But since we are running a hospital, I'll ask for a little service myself.'

It was a flesh wound, not dangerous unless infection set in. Pete washed the blood away and tied up the hurt as best he could.

'They're p-pickin' us off one by one,' he said.

'We're all alive and kicking yet,' his chief replied. 'Three of them have handed in their checks, and at least one more is wounded.'

From McCoy's corner of the stockade a rifle sounded.

'Make it two wounded,' McCoy corrected. 'I been watching that bird for several minutes. He leaned out to take a crack at us and I got him in the arm.'

Rusty limped to his post. 'Dawged if I don't get into this myself,' he said.

Cole looked up at the starlit sky. The moon was shining down on a land touched to silvery magic. Peacefully the windmill clicked away. It should have been, he thought with a sardonic grin, a night for lovers and not for warfare. He recalled the lines of a hymn he used to hear when as a boy he had gone to church. How did it go?

> '. . . every prospect pleases,
> And only man is vile.'

Chapter XXXIV
Mary Urges Haste

Into Pete Casey's Haven of Rest walked a little brown man in chaps whose bristly face had not seen a razor in a week. Within three minutes Art Simmons was the center of a group which hung on every word he said. For the nester was telling a story of amazing interest. Rusty Hunter and young Morse had been captured by Jerry Haskell, and with four men at his side Cole Sanborn was marching on the bailiwick of the enemy to rescue his friends. That he could succeed in doing so seemed scarcely a possibility.

'I knew Chet would get him in the end,' Lutz exclaimed. 'Sanborn never had a chance with that wily old bird.'

A man sat at a table on the edge of the group. He was playing solitaire. Before he spoke he moved a queen.

'Has Chet got him yet?' he asked evenly, skepticism in his voice, eyes still on the cards.

The man who asked the question was Gray Shirt, by name Jim Faust.

'I'll bet he has,' Lutz replied triumphantly. 'Did you ever know anything so crazy as for Sanborn to walk right in to where Chet is waiting for him?'

'He rode in there twice before, I seem to recollect,' Gray Shirt mentioned. 'And the only luck Chet had either time was that Cole didn't bump him off like he ought to have done.'

'He missed his chance,' someone said. 'I reckon Cole was afraid to start something he couldn't finish.'

Gray Shirt found he could get the jack of spades on the heart queen by careful manipulation. 'I was there both times. If he was afraid, he certainly fooled me. He could have wiped out the whole outfit, including Haskell and Radbourne. No, sir, he wasn't scared. Not none. He was putting it up to Chet that if trouble came he wasn't going to be to blame for it. I had a little run-in with him, and I made up my mind about that young fellow. He's a white man, and he'll do to take along any time, any place.'

Faust rose from the solitaire game and drew Simmons to one side.

'Do you know where Mrs. Sanborn is staying?' he asked.

'With Mrs. Peters. I'm going round there. Got a letter to deliver to her.' Simmons had been told to deliver the note if anything happened. He considered that the condition was fulfilled. Cole was in a tight.

'I'll trail along,' Gray Shirt said.

They found Mary watering a box of geraniums on the porch.

Simmons explained who he was and gave her the note from her husband. Mary opened and read it. The color ebbed from her cheeks and lips.

'Is—is he—dead?' she gasped.

'No, ma'am. I don't reckon so.'

'But he says I won't receive the note unless— unless—'

'He told me to give it to you if anything happened to him,' Simmons said. 'I would say if a fellow walked into a nest of wasps something would happen to him.'

'Or to them,' Gray Shirt added.

'Who are you?' Mary asked Faust. 'A friend of his?' Her eyes dilated. 'You're the man my husband helped to leave the Circle 3 T.'

'Correct. And I owe him one for that. So I'm here.' Swiftly he outlined the situation. 'This is what we've got to do,' he told her, after he had made clear the danger Cole was facing. 'Get a posse up to the Circle 3 T soon as we can. Magruder won't lift a hand for me. He won't trust me. But if you go to him yoreself, he will stir his stumps. Tell him he has got to hustle together a posse and rock along fast as he can to the Circle 3 T. He may be in time. We don't know how things stand up there, but there is no use fooling ourselves. Your husband may be in desperate need of help.'

Mary did not go into the house. She put down

313

the watering-can and walked to the gate. 'Let us hurry. Please.'

'Got to see a fellow,' Simmons said, and gave his disreputable hat a slight tilt upward in lieu of a bow.

Curious eyes followed Mary and her hard-faced companion as they moved along Main Street toward the office of the sheriff. The girl had already outraged public opinion by marrying Cole Sanborn, recognized as a gambler and a 'bad man.' The frontier town had its social dividing line. Such men as Gray Shirt was and Cole had been might move with friendliness and a sense of equality among those of their own sex, but they were not expected to know the good women of the place. A bow at passing was permissible if they had met, but that was the limit of acquaintanceship. An accepted rule was that tough citizens like Faust must confine their attentions to the women who lived below the cottonwood grove and were *déclassées*.

Faust was conscious of public disapproval, but went his poker-faced way regardless of it. He was not a man to overstep the line, but just now lives were at stake. Mary did not even know she was violating the proprieties. The panic in her bosom had swept away minor considerations. Her eyes were haggard with anxiety. Fear tortured her soul. Cole was in peril. She must save him.

Two men were in the office with Magruder. Both of them were tall and rangy, strangers in town. They were deputy United States marshals.

Mary did not even take time to apologize for intruding.

'My husband!' she cried. 'He is in danger, sheriff.'

This was not news to Magruder. It had been true for many months. He had risen at her entrance and stood frowning. What was this sweet and lovely but reckless girl doing on the street with one beyond the pale like Faust?

'Two of his men have been captured and taken to the Circle 3 T,' she explained swiftly. 'He has gone there to rescue them. With only three or four men. Against more than thirty. We want you to send up a posse at once. Every moment may count. Will you hurry, please?'

'We,' repeated the sheriff, looking at Faust. 'You mean you and—'

The sentence tailed away unfinished. What he had in his mind was clear.

Gray Shirt smiled, a hard dry smile. 'I'm not in this, sheriff. It's up to you and her. I told Mrs. Sanborn to see you because I know what her husband is against. He can't cut it this time. Unless you want his men massacred you'll have to send them help—and damn soon.'

'Who brought word that Sanborn had gone to the Circle 3 T?' Magruder asked.

315

'Art Simmons. They were headed there when Art left them.'

'Where is Art? Bring him here.'

From a fold in her dress Mary pulled the note Cole had written. She passed it to Magruder.

'He would never have written this if he had not known he was—in great danger. Mr. Simmons wasn't to give it to me unless he knew my husband was—dead. But he did. Mr. Magruder, you aren't going to stand there and not try to save Cole, are you?' The voice of the girl was choked with fear. All that was worthwhile in her life hung in the balance. They might be killing Cole now—this very moment.

Magruder read the note. It was a cry of love from one who longed passionately to comfort the girl left to mourn his loss.

'All right,' the little sheriff said. 'We'll start right off.' He introduced the strangers to Mary. 'These gentlemen are United States marshals. Mr. Clement—Mr. Brand, meet Mrs. Sanborn. They are here about the robbery of the K. & J. We have found new evidence.'

At another time this would have greatly interested Mary. Now there was nothing in her mind but the immediate jeopardy in which her husband stood.

'How soon can you start?' she begged.

'Now.' Magruder turned to Faust. 'I'll look after the men and guns. Round up for me a bunch of horses. About a dozen. Have them brought here. Try the Longhorn and the Alamo corrals. You'll have to jump.'

Faust turned without a word and walked swiftly from the office.

The sheriff passed back to Mary the note from her husband. He spoke to the officers. 'This fits in with what we had in mind. Might as well start now. It gives us an excuse to take more men with us.'

He led the way to the street. The deputy marshals followed. Mary had done her part and was for the moment forgotten.

But she could not stay out of the picture. She could not fold her hands and sit quietly while all her future was at stake. This day had brought the decisive hour of her life. That certainty filled her being.

That Magruder would not let her ride with his posse to the Circle 3 T she knew. Yet she longed desperately to be near her husband. What Radbourne wanted was her property. Perhaps she could make a bargain with him to let Cole and his men go if they had fallen victims to their eagerness to rescue their friends and were his prisoners.

Every day Mary went riding on a little sorrel cowpony which she kept in a stable half a block from the Peters house. She walked back down Main Street and along the road to the stable. Some boys were playing marbles. One of them saddled the sorrel for her.

Following a little traveled hill road, she left town at a gallop.

The posse of the sheriff took the main road ten minutes later. In the posse were Preston, Gray Shirt, a doctor, and the deputy United States marshals.

Chapter XXXV
A Challenge

Cole raised above the stockade a pole from the end of which a white rag fluttered.

'Looks to me sometimes like you don't know sic' 'em, Cole,' grumbled Rusty. 'We lose on yore proposition any way you take it. If Haskell agrees to fight you, it will be because he has the deck rigged to win high, low, jack, and the game. That *hombre* isn't going to shoot it out with you on the square. Sure as hell's hot he will have it fixed to stop yore clock. We're doing fine the way things are. Let's rock along for a while.'

Sanborn did not answer. He moved the pole back and forth to attract attention.

'Rusty has the right of it,' Slim said, picking up the protest where the old man had dropped it. 'Jerry won't agree to meet you unless he has about six of his sharpshooters posted to blast you off the map soon as you show up. There isn't a straight hair in that bird's head.'

'I'll agree to what you say about Haskell,' Cole replied. 'Some of his men might be willing to dry-gulch me, but if he takes me up to fight a duel, they will make him stick it out on the level. He couldn't rue back on a bargain without losing face. No use loading ourselves, boys. We are in a trap, and we can't fight our way out of it. But if I could put Haskell out of business his men would quit and let us go. They would figure it too expensive to dig us out of our hole.'

'What you mean *us,* Cole?' Slim asked. 'You know blamed well you wouldn't be here. Maybe we're not sitting wide and handsome, but they haven't got our hides nailed to a fence yet. Betcha they are getting pretty sick of their job. Soon they will begin to figure this ain't their war anyhow.'

Cole glanced at the stained handkerchief tied around the head of the black-haired Texan. A bullet had creased Slim's forehead a few minutes since.

'They are wearing us down,' Cole answered. 'Presently one of us will be killed, then another. I don't say we can't hold out through the night, but when morning comes some of them will climb the hill back of the stable and pick us off from there. . . . Someone with a white flag. Will you meet him and have him take my offer to Haskell, Slim?'

'Don't like it a bit,' Rusty disapproved, scowling. 'They're not crowding us now, but if Haskell gets you they will sure rush the corral.'

Slim walked out to meet the envoy of the enemy. He strolled forward jauntily, a figure of debonair ease. The man who met him was Bud Calloway.

'You fellows ready to surrender?' Bud asked.

'Surrender?' Slim echoed, apparently much surprised. 'Hell's bells, no! We ain't started yet. Whatever put that into yore nut? We've got all the water and the food, and you fellows are stranded in the desert, as you might say. The trouble is that Cole is too dog-goned tender-hearted. He's plumb sorry for you misguided ducks who are getting shot up to pull Jerry's chestnuts out of the fire. You can't win, and if you did what would you get out of it but a kick in the pants, the few of you that were left? Already you have shot up old man Radbourne, after he gave you orders to lay off us. Do you reckon he is going to forget that when payday comes? Not that old wolf.'

'Was the old man hit, Slim?' Bud inquired, plainly disturbed.

'In the leg. He was bleeding like a stuck pig when we bandaged him up. Of course, if you ever should get the stockade, which isn't likely, Radbourne won't be alive. But what I'm here for is to send a message from Sanborn to Haskell. We have had orders from Cole not to kill any more of you fellows than we could help. I had a bead drawn on you when you picked up Mex. So did two more of us. We could have dropped you in yore tracks. Well, no more of that. If this fight goes on, we aim to kill from now on. Here is Cole's proposition. To save the lives of a lot of you boys who don't stand to get anything but trouble out of this, Cole will meet Haskell in a duel and settle this difficulty man to man.'

'Fair enough,' Bud said. 'If Haskell will fight him.'

'I warned Cole he was a treacherous devil, but Cole says you boys wouldn't stand for any bushwhacking if Haskell agrees to his proposition.'

'We wouldn't, either,' Bud spoke up quickly.

'Tell Haskell he can have his choice of six-shooters or rifles. Cole doesn't care what kind of a gun he kills Jerry with.'

'You talk big, Slim. Jerry is some fighter himself.'

'That so?' Slim asked, with an impudent grin. 'Cole has made him take to the tall timber two-three times that I know of. I was among those present when he bluffed Jerry off the map in Pete's place. I'll lay a little bet, Bud. Give you odds of a dollar to four bits Mr. Haskell crawls out of the fight unless he thinks he has got it fixed for him to win, and a dollar to two bits that if they ever face each other, yore bully-puss boss will go down.'

'Take you on both of the bets,' Bud retorted. 'Cole has had luck so far. He's about due for a run of bad cards. . . . All right. I'll take yore message to Jerry and be back with his answer.'

Slim returned to the stockade and made his

report. The talk with Bud Calloway had encouraged him. He had gathered an impression that there was considerable dissatisfaction in the camp of the enemy, less from what Bud had said than from his manner. There had been a complete absence of the aggressiveness one displays who feels he is a victor. Bud knew that three Circle 3 T men were dead and four others wounded, and he had no knowledge of any serious losses among the defenders. Plainly he was ready to discuss an armistice. Very likely he represented a majority opinion.

After he had told what had been said by himself and Calloway, Slim summed up his feeling.

'We're not in as bad a jam as I thought, Cole, unless I'm fooling myself. A lot of those lads would like to turn loose of the bear if they get a good excuse. It's up to Haskell now. Looks to me as if he has got to take up yore offer. You have called for a showdown. He will have to let us see his hand or throw it in the discard.'

Cole cleaned his revolver. He knew that if Haskell decided to accept the challenge, he would not choose rifles. With a six-shooter the foreman of the Circle 3 T could hit a playing-card four times out of five at twenty paces.

Chapter XXXVI

Haskell Gets the Acid Test

As soon as Bud Calloway came into the bunk-house, Haskell flung a question at him.

'Did you tell them my terms—that they would have to turn Sanborn over to me before I would even talk turkey?'

'We didn't get that far,' Bud answered. 'They haven't got any notion of surrendering.'

'Then whyfor the white flag?' Haskell demanded angrily. 'Can't fool me if they did you. They want to quit. We've got them where they can't do a thing.'

'Except kill us,' a red-headed cowpuncher grumbled.

'There won't be any more of that either,' the foreman promised irritably. 'We'll wait till morning and pick 'em off from the hill.'

'Maybe we better find out what the white flag was about if you're not too busy,' a dark, sullen-faced man suggested satirically.

'Sanborn says he doesn't want to shoot up any more of us if he can help it,' Bud explained. 'The old man has been wounded and wants to call it off. Slim says they had orders from Cole to go easy on us, but from now on it will be different.

Something in what he says, too. They sure could have finished me when I went out to get Mex and they didn't even take a crack at me.'

'Is this all you've got to say?' Haskell asked, his face dark with rage.

'Not all.' Bud looked straight at the foreman. 'Cole claims we hired hands haven't got any interest in this fight, and he is blamed near right. Thirty dollars a month doesn't cover getting shot up and bumped off the way so many of us have been. So he offers to fight a duel with you, Jerry, to settle the thing without any more of us getting hurt. He says rifles or sixguns, take yore pick.'

Haskell thumped a heavy fist down on a table. 'He's squawking. Knows we've got him and is trying to crawl out.'

There was a moment of heavy silence. The foreman was not sensitive to atmospheres, but even he felt something ominous in that lull of suspended judgment.

'Sanborn is through—bucked out,' he went on hastily. 'Making a bluff to bull through a busted flush against a full house.'

'I dunno, Jerry,' a bald-headed, heavy-set man said slowly. 'Let's talk that over. The way I look at it, plenty of us have been killed already. Sense in what Sanborn says. You've been wanting a crack at this fellow, Jerry. Rub him out, and the war is over. Nothing more to it.'

The sullen-faced man showed a set of ragged

teeth in an ironic grin. 'That's all. One crack with a gun. After that, peace along the Potomac.'

'You talk like a fool, Arkansaw,' Haskell ripped out with an oath. 'Don't you get the point, you lunkhead? I've got him. He is at the end of his trail and making a last play. Like I said, he's trying to crawl out. You aren't so dumb you can't see that, are you?'

Hard-eyed, Arkansaw met his angry gaze steadily. 'Someone is trying to crawl out. I'm not so sure it is Sanborn. You claim you have got him. He's in the wild-horse corral, waiting for you with a gun in his hands, but I don't notice you going out there and roping him. I'd say you haven't got him by a jugful.'

Bud Calloway went a step farther. 'We've all heard you make yore brags, Jerry. Now you get a chance to demonstrate. You wouldn't want better than an even break, would you?'

'Sure he wouldn't,' a wounded man put in savagely. 'Jerry has been honing to get him a man, and here's his chance for the one he wants. I say, let him hop to it.'

Tiny sweat beads broke out on Haskell's forehead. He looked round on cold, harsh faces, not one of them in sympathy with him. Whenever he had dared he had bullied these men. Now he could see a cruel jubilation at his predicament. Angry at the situation into which he had led them, they had risen against him. Victory they no longer cared for, since it must be bought at a high price. Already they had paid too much in dead and wounded. They were gloating at the chance to shift the danger to the foreman by driving him into personal combat with the man who had always outmaneuvered and outfought them. Jerry had started this battle, had promised them a cheap success. All right. Let him finish it himself.

Hardy ruffian though he was, Haskell felt a cold pressure round his heart. They had decided ruthlessly to drive him to this duel. It satisfied their anger, perhaps too a crude sense of justice. He was a gunman, and he had a reputation for nerve. Why shouldn't he face Sanborn and settle this trouble once for all? That was what they were thinking.

It came to Haskell, clear as the ringing of a bell, that if he stood up against Sanborn he was lost. The question was not as to who was the better shot. The foreman would back himself as a marksman against any man alive. But this fellow had the Indian sign on him. Cole Sanborn was his Nemesis. It would be like standing against a wall before a firing squad.

'You boys aren't looking at this right,' he said, his voice dead and heavy. 'All we have to do is wait till morning and pick them off from the corral hill. They won't have a chance.'

'That's what you told us when we started this thing.' Bill spoke up, an edge to his contradiction.

'So far I've got a busted leg out of it. That's enough. You claim we oughtn't ever to have let Sanborn's crowd out of the house. Now you show us.'

'Unless you are just a windbag, Jerry,' added Arkansaw. 'I'm beginning to wonder about that. We're buzzard heads. You've told us that plenty often. And you're there every way from the ace. By yore own say-so. Make good yore brags.'

'It has got to be one way or the other, Jerry,' Calloway said stonily. 'Either Jordan's way or Lauret's. Take yore choice.'

Looking round on the cold, expectant faces that seemed to hem him in like a ring of waiting wolves, Haskell knew Calloway had told him the truth. He could not dodge. He had to make a choice.

'I never saw the day I was afraid of this fellow or anyone else,' he said, with a bold front, and the sound of his own words heartened him. 'Tell him it will be sixguns, at twenty yards, and that I'll kill him sure as he's a foot high.'

'That's the way to talk,' Calloway said cheerfully. 'Cole is human, and can be got just like any of the rest of us.'

The others began to talk. There were smiles and laughter, the sudden relaxation prior to exciting tragedy which did not involve them. Haskell hated them all, black rage in his heart struggling with the chill of fear. Their lives were not at stake. They could jest and chatter, after having driven him to a declaration from which there was no retreat. Not one of them cared a jackstraw whether he lived or died, except the ones who were hoping Sanborn might get him.

Haskell waited while the messenger carried back to Sanborn word of the acceptance of his challenge. His eyes darted here and there, seeking help. The muscles in his face twitched. He had to fight for self-control in order not to betray his desperation.

Mechanically he joined in the talk, listened to advice. He wondered if they knew how shaken he was.

'You'll get him all right, Jerry,' someone predicted. 'Any day in the week you're as good a shot as he is.'

'Y'betcha!' Haskell heard himself answer.

'Take yore time. Don't hurry. He's liable to miss his first shot. Be nervous, maybe.'

'Yes,' the foreman agreed.

How many shots would it take? Would he have to stand up and feel bullet after bullet tearing through his vitals? A chill drenched him at the thought that within a few minutes he might be lying with the life stricken out of him.

Calloway returned, full of pleased importance. 'Everything all set, Jerry. Just the way you want it. Six-shooters at twenty yards. After the first shot you move toward each other firing as you please.'

Just the way he wanted it. Haskell could have wept with self-pity. He had come to the most terrible hour of his life, and he was alone— absolutely alone. Not a soul to wish him well except with lip cheer. There had been a woman once. She had loved him passionately and devotedly, and after he had squeezed all the joy and hope out of her young life he had flung her aside and let her go to destruction. If he had her here, to comfort him, to pray for him . . .

Better not think of her now. The thing to do was buck up and go through.

'Someone give me a drink,' he said hoarsely.

A man handed him a bottle. He saw them watching him, gravely, appraisingly. Jerry tilted the bottle and drank, the raw liquor scorching its way down his throat.

'Better go a little slow on that stuff,' the bald-headed man suggested. 'You want yore nerves steady.'

The whiskey left Haskell cold. The leaden lump inside of him did not dissolve from warmth.

'I reckon we better be moving,' he heard Calloway say.

The foreman did not answer. His legs carried him automatically to the door and into the night. The sky was now clear of clouds and the stars shone down. A silvery light flooded the land.

'Moon's out again,' a man said. 'Plenty of light to see.'

Haskell felt a sickness run through him. He almost mentioned it, but stopped himself just in time. Already they were wondering if he was game.

His gaze fell on a saddled horse tied to a hitch-rack. If he could swing to the saddle and gallop into the desert! But never again. He had been caught in a trap from which he could not escape.

How long had it been since he had fastened the chestnut there with a slip-knot? A few hours only. Then he had been riding on the top of the world. Now . . .

He had to go through. No other way to it. And suddenly, in an instant, while he was flogging his courage to face the ordeal, panic swept over him and submerged his self-respect. By God, he wouldn't be the goat. He wouldn't let them drive him to death.

Through his slack limbs warm blood poured. He had made up his mind.

'They're waiting for us,' Calloway said. 'Slim is with him, I reckon. It will be even steven, Jerry. We'll have Sanborn covered all the time. If he fires too soon, or doesn't play square in any way, he's a dead coon.'

'Yes,' Haskell said.

His gaze was on the chestnut gelding. In a moment they would pass close to it. He fell back a pace, to get on the other side of Calloway.

Now was the time. A hand went out to the bridle and pulled the slip-knot. Haskell swung the animal round and vaulted into the saddle. A spur touched the flank. The horse leaped to a gallop.

While the Circle 3 T men stood motionless in their tracks, frozen by surprise, Haskell vanished down the road.

Chapter XXXVII

'Two is Company, My Dear'

Mary struck the main road half a mile from town. Already darkness was dropping down over the hills. The moon was up, and the first stars were in the sky. In the cottonwood tops, as she crossed a dry wash, was a murmur of wind. The night was peaceful as old age.

Its peace did not bring her any assurance. Fear rode her, as she pushed the sorrel up the dusty ribbon of a road. This was a mad thing Cole had done, to ride into the stronghold of the enemy.

He was a fighting man, and he would have the advantage of surprise, perhaps, but it would not be possible for him to overpower so great a force. Radbourne was wily as a fox. One of these days he would trap Cole. The heavy weight on her heart told her that this was the time.

When she married Cole she had not bargained for this. Love had been the farthest thing from her mind. All she had wanted to do was to save herself. From the time of her arrival in Boone County, she had begun to hear about this super-bad man Sanborn. His audacity was a legend. She had listened to incredible stories of his exploits. He was a killer, an outlaw, yet one who

333

drew to him devoted friends just as he created deadly enemies. Meeting him by chance, at a time when despair was driving her hard, she had entered into her mad compact with him.

And now she loved him. All the happiness that might be in her life depended upon him. To think of him filled her with warmth. Every fiber of her being, it seemed to her, went out to meet him. She was so young. It could not be that Fate would be so cruel as to snatch away the joy she had not yet tasted.

This torture served her right. In asking him to aid her she had been moved wholly by selfishness. Her thought had been to buy his help, regardless of what it might cost him. He had known that, of course, yet he had taken up the burden for her cheerfully and gaily, as if it had been an equitable agreement between them.

Now . . .

Though she rode fast, she could not outride her dread. Her imagination saw his splendid body lying lax and inert, with Radbourne's shapeless shadow hovering over him.

She came to the fences of the Circle 3 T. They lined the road down which she galloped. Soon she would know the worst.

A horse was racing up the lane toward her. She drew up, her heart drumming, to meet the rider.

The man dragged his horse to a halt. 'Who's there?' he demanded hoarsely.

'Mary Sanborn,' she answered. 'Is—is everything all right at the ranch?'

A violent oath exploded from him.

'Is my husband there?' she asked tremulously. 'Cole Sanborn. I heard—'

He broke out in savage, furious profanity.

Mary had recognized the man by this time. He was Jerry Haskell, foreman of the Circle 3 T. There was in him a malignant rage that appalled her.

'He's there—the damned killer.'

'Is he . . . a captive?'

Through the anger and shame that possessed him reason was pushing its way. By means of this woman he could strike at Sanborn, the man he hated, the man who had made him lose face forever among the ruffians he had led. This part of the country was closed to him for the rest of his life. He had to sneak away, as quickly as he could, for the news of what he had done would travel fast. Idaho would not be too near. Or Oregon. He would have to take another name. The first thing would be to strike for the railroad.

But not alone. A sweet revenge had offered itself. He could reach Sanborn through his wife. Afterward, he would be lost in some obscure corner of the cow country a thousand miles from here.

'You're going with me,' he told the girl hoarsely.

'With you? What do you mean? Where?'

335

'Never mind where.' He caught the bridle rein of her horse and turned the animal.

In his distorted face was something so demoniac that panic swept her. She lifted her quirt and lashed it across his mouth, then gave the sorrel the spur and dashed up the road in the direction from which she had come. For an instant he sat there, his mouth a streak of fire, before he took up the pursuit.

The horses pounded through the dust. Mary was wild with fear. She did not know exactly of what she had to be afraid, but the evil passion in his face had been something dreadful to see.

Presently she knew he was gaining on her. Though she used the quirt, she could get no more speed out of the little sorrel. The big chestnut came closer at every stride. Its head overlapped the flanks of the pony. Haskell drew even with her. He reached over and caught the reins. The two horses slackened their pace, came to a jarring halt.

They were on the desert now, beyond the last fence. Haskell guided from the road.

'Two is company, my dear. Three would be a crowd,' he told the girl, with a jeering laugh.

'I'm not going with you,' Mary cried. 'Where are you taking me? Have you gone mad?'

She tried to turn her horse, and when she found she could not do that, slipped from the saddle and started to run through the brush back to the road. At once he was after her. The chestnut was a cowhorse, and it turned and twisted after her as she dodged. She was driven deeper into the brush.

From his saddle Haskell swung when at last she stood at bay.

'So, you little vixen, you can bite, eh?' he cried. 'So can I.' He snatched the quirt from her wrist and lashed the rawhide three times around her supple body.

The tortured flesh of the girl quivered. She gave an agonized cry for help, and the one to whom she called was her husband.

Unexpectedly, out of the night there came an answer, a faint far shout.

Haskell stopped, quirt in hand, mouth open, to listen. Again Mary lifted her voice in a scream, and once more, almost like an echo, there came back a reply.

With an oath, the foreman dropped the quirt. He turned, caught his horse, swung to the saddle, and galloped into the chaparral.

Chapter XXXVIII
'The War is Off'

Slim came back from his second meeting with Calloway and reported to Cole.

'You've picked you a fight,' he said. 'Bud says Haskell dodged every which way to duck it, but his men wouldn't let him crawl out. It will be on the level. You don't need to worry about that. 'Far as I can make out, the Circle 3 T riders are a heap more sore at Jerry than they are at you. They are ready to call off this battle with us. If they win, it won't buy them a thing. I hammered it into their coconuts that Radbourne isn't liable to hand out any Christmas presents to the fellows who shot him.'

'With rifles or revolvers?' Cole asked quietly.

'Revolvers, at twenty yards, to start with,' Slim answered. 'After the first shot it is to be go-as-you-please. All bars down.'

'Good. It's the way it should be. However this thing goes, things will be better afterward. Radbourne is whipped. You can see that by looking at him. We had better move on out, don't you reckon, and be ready?'

'Yes, you don't want to act backward. Be out there waiting for Haskell. Show him you mean business.'

Rusty limped forward. 'We're all pulling for you, Cole,' he said. 'Every last one of us. We hate to have it this way, though we know you've got it on Haskell every jump of the road. You're in the right, too. That counts. Boy, I feel it in my bones you're going to win.'

The others chimed in, one after another.

The harsh face of Sanborn was immobile as a piece of granite. 'Much obliged, boys,' he said. 'See you later.'

He walked out with Slim through the gate of the stockade.

In the moonlight they waited for Haskell to appear. Out of the bunkhouse a jet of men poured. Slim talked, as casually as he could, to prevent a heavy silence while Cole waited.

The Circle 3 T men were moving toward them.

'Jerry has talked big, but he never did want a showdown with you,' said Slim. 'Twice I know of he threw in his hand rather than call. It's been forced on him now. He's noways happy now, I'll bet.'

Cole did not answer, but his friend found no weakness in that grim silence. Sanborn stood at ease, giving no sign that the delay affected his nerves.

There came a sudden commotion, the sound of clattering hoofs, voices raised in excited surprise.

'By crikes, he's done lit out,' someone cried.

Slim peered into the semi-darkness of the

339

starry night. A horseman was disappearing in the gloom. The pounding of galloping feet came fainter.

From the Circle 3 T men came curses and yells of derision.

Slim slapped his chaps, letting out a whoop. 'Jerry has taken to the tall timber!' he cried. 'Couldn't stand the gaff, the big four-flusher.'

Some of the men from the bunkhouse joined Calhoun and Sanborn.

'Drinks on us, boys,' Calloway said sheepishly. 'Jerry had a date, anywheres but here. No sand in his craw. He hit the saddle on the jump. 'Far as we're concerned the war is off. We've had aplenty. You lads are free to go or stay, whichever you like. What we need more than anything else is two-three doctors.'

'We could use one ourselves,' Slim admitted. 'A couple of us are stove-up considerable, not to mention yore old man.'

'We'd better move all the seriously wounded into the bunkhouse,' Cole said. 'Send someone| to Jonesboro for doctors, Calloway. Until they come we'll make the boys that are hurt as comfortable as possible. We'll need four or five of you fellows to carry Radbourne and Dave Pope from the corral.'

The Circle 3 T men brought the door of the bunkhouse, and on it carried first Radbourne and then Pope to the temporary hospital. Daggett and Slim held each other's wrist to make a seat, and upon this transported Rusty, the old man protesting irritably that he could walk as well as not.

Magruder and his posse arrived while this was being done. The little sheriff listened to the news. He turned to the deputy United States marshals.

'Our bird has flown,' he said. 'We're about ten minutes too late.' To Sanborn he explained that witnesses had been found with strong evidence linking up Haskell with the train-robbery.

Slim had drifted back in time to hear this. 'I told you he was guilty quite some time ago,' he drawled.

There was something else on Magruder's mind. 'Down the road a way we heard a cry. Sounded like a woman's voice. Some of the boys stopped to investigate. What would a woman be doing out in the brush away up here?'

'Sure it wasn't a coyote,' Calloway suggested.

'No coyote,' the sheriff negatived. 'There hasn't been any woman around the ranch, has there?'

Calloway shook his head. 'Couldn't have been a woman.'

Within ten minutes four riders reached the ranch. Gray Shirt was one of them. From a sorrel pony a woman dismounted.

She stood beside her horse, a slender, girlish

figure, her gaze searching for someone in the huddles of shifting men.

A tall figure strode toward her.

'Cole!' she cried, with a sob.

Her hands went out, as might those of a little child who has been lost and frightened and at last has found safety. Sanborn took them in his, looked into her haggard eyes, and drew his wife close.

Mary clung to him, much as a frightened infant does to its mother, fearful that some evil fate might still tear them apart. She was trembling like an aspen leaf in the breeze.

'I've been so afraid,' she wailed. 'Ever since I knew you had come here. I had to ride up. I thought—I didn't know—'

A well of joy surged up in Cole and for a moment choked him. He was a hard man, brought up in the outdoor frontier school of stoicism where strong men learn to ride their emotions with a tight rein.

Imperturbably he had gone his own way, regardless of the approval of others. But he knew he could never be hard with her. His love for her had made some kind of chemical change in his being. It had affected profoundly his relations with his fellows. He was no longer playing a lone hand.

After the turbulent years he had been swept by strong currents into charted waters peaceful and serene. A verse he had read once sang itself in his mind.

> '. . . port after stormie seas,
> Ease after warre . . .'

Fate had been driving him to happiness. This was far better than he had deserved, better than he had dared hope.

'It's all right,' he said. 'Everything—at last.'

Under the stars they moved to the live oak which sheltered the blacksmith shop where the Circle 3 T did its horseshoeing. The weariness had fallen from her. She walked with the rhythmic grace of happy youth in a world wonderful. Cole was a lover, and her beauty and vitality stabbed him. It seemed to him that God spoke through her rapturous bloom.

'I didn't mean it to be this way,' she said, making proud confession. 'I was to take everything and give nothing. You ought to despise me.' She laughed a little, ruefully but happily, wondering at her emotion. Because a man walked by her side the world had been reborn. 'I thought some day I would marry a nice safe man, and we would do the proper things in the proper way. And instead—I get you. Would you call yourself safe and tame?'

Looking at him, so strong and forceful, an arresting and exciting personality, Mary smiled at her own question. Anything but safe, anything but tame. Life would be a risk if she tried to match her steps with his. But it came to her, with a glowing warmth that swept through her, the certainty that one could not live in any reality except cour-ageously. To decline danger was to reject life.

'Are you so set on doing the proper things in the proper way?' he asked, with fond derision. 'You, who married the bogy man of this part of the country the first hour you met him?'

She answered that with a low, full-throated laugh of happiness. He was kissing her with a keen-edged hunger that stirred within her a clamor of the blood.

It was then she made a discovery.

'You're wounded.'

'Nothing serious. A scratch. Some have been killed, others badly hurt. I have been lucky.'

'But you must have it dressed by the doctor. Perhaps . . . one never knows about wounds. Infection. You don't know it isn't serious. And you must go to bed.'

'She's bossing me already,' he said aloud.

'But—please. We must be sure.'

'The doctor will be busy for a while looking after those really hurt bad. He'll get round to me then. Don't you worry, honey. Pete Daggett washed this scratch and tied it up for me. Doc Burns couldn't have done any better. Out in this country so many buckaroos get arms and legs busted we all learn to be doctors.'

None the less, she took him back to the bunkhouse and had Doctor Burns look at the wound and dress it again. Cole submitted, a little sheepishly, with a whimsical smile. For the rest of his life he would be shepherded and mothered. He had given up his freedom and gone into captivity.

'Happier now?' Cole asked her after Doctor Burns had finished.

'Much. You don't take any care of yourself. You ought to go to bed, but I don't suppose I can get you to do that.'

'Got too much to do just now. I'll get round to that after a while. In an hour or so we can start for Jonesboro.'

He put an arm round her shoulder after they had left the hospital.

Mary winced. The pressure of her dress upon the wheals left by the quirt made the throbbing pain fiercer. In spite of herself she wriggled her body a little to shift the embrace. She dared do no more. Cole must never know what she had endured. Already she had made one mistake and had tried to rectify it. To the men who had found her sobbing in the desert she had let out the truth, but almost at once had asked them not to tell. They would talk about it among themselves, of course. It would be gossiped about at every ranch for fifty miles. But since the parties concerned are the last to hear such stories, she hoped that knowledge of the indignity would never come to her husband.

'I've got to go back now and help Doctor Burns,' she said.

'Yes,' he agreed, smiling warmly at her. 'And soon as we can we'll take the trail to—Paradise.'

She nodded, eyes gleaming. 'That's a lovely name for an ugly little town like Jonesboro. Maybe Heaven hasn't any streets of gold. Maybe it is just any place where you and I are together.'

With that she ran back into the bunkhouse and left him.

Chapter XXXIX
An Important Fool Butts In

Gray Shirt drew Slim to one side. 'Listen, fellow. There's something yore friend Sanborn doesn't know yet, and when he does know it he will see red. That cuss Haskell met up with Mrs. Sanborn down the road a ways and quirted her.'

'He—what?'

Slim stared at the man incredulously.

Faust nodded. 'Like I said. 'Seems he tried to take her with him. She cut him across the face and lit out. When he caught her, he took the quirt and lashed her. The fool must have been crazy.'

The eyes of the black-haired Texan blazed. 'Crazy or not, Cole will take after him and kill him.'

'I've got another notion,' Faust said. 'Cole is wounded. I don't know how bad. That little girl of his will be worried sick if he takes off after Haskell now. You and I both owe that yellow coyote something. What-say we get Magruder to deputize us to go after him? There seems no manner of doubt but that these United States deputy marshals have got it on him that he bossed that job of train-robbing. If we find Haskell we'll drag him back to be hanged.'

'You've got my company,' Slim said promptly.

'How about that head you've got bandaged? I don't want any invalids with me.'

'A scratch. We'd better see Magruder right off. Before Cole finds out what Haskell did to his wife.'

In every large company there is an important fool who feels it his duty to spread news that will make trouble. One of them went to Cole now to express sympathy. He took it for granted that Mrs. Sanborn had told her husband what Haskell had done to her.

'That wolf ought to be shot—treating a woman the way he did your wife,' the man said.

Cole looked at him, sized him up, and dismissed the fellow with the first casual remark that came to mind.

'Talk is cheap.'

The man was disconcerted. 'Sure. All I meant, for a skunk like that to lay hands on a good woman—'

'Lay hands on her?'

Cole's body stiffened and his eyes froze.

'Why, he tried to make her go with him, didn't he?'

'Did he?'

The busybody wished he had kept his mouth shut. Apparently Sanborn did not know the story.

'I dunno. There was some talk. Probably nothing to it.'

'What talk?'

'I kinda gathered—'

At that the gossip stuck. He did not know how much or how little to tell.

'Who from?'

'Well, Mrs. Sanborn—she said—'

'Just what did she say?'

The man tried to back out from responsibility. 'Why don't you go ask her, Cole?'

'I'm asking you.'

The cold, steely eyes of Sanborn would not release his reluctant informant. Having begun, the fellow had to go through.

'Jerry he started to take Mrs. Sanborn with him. We heard her calling for help and he lit out.'

'Anything more?'

'I thought you knew all about it. He—quirted her.' The words seemed to be dragged out of the man. He knew he had been a well-intentioned fool and interfered with the business of other people. Mary had begged him and the others who had found her not to tell what she had confided in the first shock of relief, but he had not supposed Cole was not to be in the secret.

The face of Sanborn was white and set. 'Quirted her,' he repeated. 'Did Mrs. Sanborn say so?'

'She was crying, and—she let it out, then asked us not to tell. 'Course I thought—'

What he thought was of no importance to Cole. Abruptly Sanborn turned away and strode into the bunkhouse. He stood above Mary, where she was assisting Doctor Burns with a bandage.

' 'Soon as you're through I want to see you,' Cole said, his voice rough and low.

She looked up, surprised. In his manner was something ominous. His stern eyes were like live coals. Not five minutes ago she had left him, a lover gay and cheerful, his strength irradiated and softened, his harshness melted. What had made this change in him? Did he think she had been forward—unwomanly? Perhaps. Men felt that way about women. Her sex must simper and decoy, deny and allure. She had told him the truth simply. Was that an offense against decorum?

Mary finished with the bandage, then rose and walked beside him from the room. Outside, he flung a question at her.

'Did Haskell—use a quirt to you?'

He gulped the last words out, as if he found it hard to say them.

'Oh, Cole, does that matter now?'

She caught one of his hands in hers. It was very important that she get him to see this as she did. 'That is part of our bad dream that's past,' she continued. 'It goes with all the rest of it—with your wound—with all the bloodshed. You and I have blotted all that out. We have no room for such baggage—on the trail to Paradise.'

He would not meet her pleading little smile. 'It's true, then.'

'If you have got to know about it, I lashed him first with the quirt—across the face.'

'Why did you do that?'

'I think he was a little mad,' she explained. 'He wanted me to go with him. His eyes glared and his face was distorted. You know what the Bible calls it, possessed of a devil. When he caught hold of my bridle rein and wouldn't let go, I became panicky and struck him with the quirt. After he caught me he still acted like a madman. Cole, I want you to forget it. After all, I hit him first. He is out of our lives. Forever. We'll never see him again. There is so much we must forget, and that is just a little part of it.'

'No,' he said hoarsely. 'In this country a man can't treat a woman in that way and get away with it. What kind of a husband would I be if I sat down and didn't call him to account?'

'Something beautiful has come into our lives, Cole,' she said. 'I didn't expect it. You weren't anything to me except a bad man strong enough to fight my battles. Then I found I was wrong. You weren't bad at all. You were brave and strong, and you were generous to those trying to destroy you. Even then I didn't want to love you, but I was swept from my feet. I couldn't help it. And since, when I haven't been afraid for you, I've been the happiest woman in the world. Do you

351

want to wipe all that out, by killing this man who means nothing at all to us?'

'When he did what he did he knew I would have to hunt him down,' he said doggedly.

'No, Cole. No—no—no!' The protest burst vehemently from her. 'We can't start killing all over again. Think of tonight, of all the bloodshed, of those men lying cold and still in the stable. I was thanking God we had come to the end of it. And you say you are going to begin again. If you love me—'

Her plea broke down on that sobbing note. Cole did not answer at once. He was distressed and troubled. What she had said was all true. He longed to do as she wished. But all his life training, the code of the frontier, rose up in him protestant against letting Haskell escape punishment for what he had done. With characteristic swiftness he made up his mind.

'I won't kill him,' he promised. 'I'll drag him back with a rope around his neck. Magruder can have him. There is plenty of evidence he led the K. & J. express robbers. He'll hang for that job.'

'You talk as if bullets couldn't kill you!' she cried. 'He is a desperate man, and he will shoot you down. It's the sheriff's business to get him, not yours.'

'It's my business, after what he did to you. But you don't need to be afraid. He won't hurt me.'

'How do you know he won't? Don't go, Cole. Please.'

He took her hands and looked down into her troubled face. 'I have to go, dearest,' he said gently. 'It's my job. I can't shirk it. I'm sorry. I wish I didn't have to do it.'

All the sternness had gone from his face. A few minutes ago he had been hard as iron. What alchemy was there in her presence that so softened and changed him? He could not understand or explain it.

She clung to him passionately. How could she let him go back into danger so soon?

Cole held her in his arms and kissed her. 'It won't be long, sweetheart,' he promised. 'I'll be back—for good this time.'

With that promise she had to be content.

As Cole walked to the stable, he caught sight of Slim Calhoun and Gray Shirt moving down the road. He hailed them.

'Where you headed for, boys?'

Without stopping, Slim shouted back an answer.

'We've got a hen on, oldtimer. See you at Sunday School.'

'If you'll wait I will ride with you,' Cole called to them. 'Going that way myself.'

They did not wait. Sanborn was surprised at that.

Chapter XL
Cole Bluffs

As Cole plodded through the chaparral he put himself for the twentieth time in the place of Jerry Haskell. Given the same circumstances, with the temperament of the ex-foreman of the Circle 3 T, what would he do? The pride of Haskell had been given a terrific blow. Before the men who counted most with him he had shown the white feather. To meet anybody he knew would be a humiliation almost beyond endurance. He would get out of the country as soon as he could. That meant he would make for the nearest railroad point.

There was one possible flaw in this reasoning. Haskell would not leave behind him the money gained from the express car robbery. Did he have the loot on his person in the form of bills? Or was it buried at some convenient place? If the money was cached, he would have to recover it before he crossed the desert and made for Sundown, the nearest railroad station. Knowing Haskell, Cole was of the opinion that the man carried his plunder always in a belt around his waist. For if suspicion should be directed his way, he might have to leave on the jump.

Cole had traveled very steadily all day. He wanted to get to Rabbit Ear Pass before Haskell in order to lie in wait for him. A fight in the open was barred. That would mean he had to kill or be killed, and he had promised Mary to avoid so drastic an issue. He had to trap the man and get the drop on him.

Probably Haskell would not hurry. He could not know that the officers had evidence enough to convict him of the train-robbery. For Magruder had moved with extraordinary secrecy. Nobody knew in what direction he had gone after the desert swallowed him. He could afford to take his time. So he would argue.

Once Cole saw a little dust-cloud far to his right. That would be Haskell, he guessed. Sanborn quickened his pace. He would be in time all right. The man was off a direct line and would have to bear to the left.

A rampart of hills cut across the skyline. They had been sculptured by erosion to strange and fantastic shapes, the softer rock underneath having been washed away by the floods of a million years. To the left was a fortress, with bastions and parapets and openings for disappearing cannon, the whole so lifelike that one could imagine mediaeval sentinels pacing the towers flanking the walls. Between this and the rimrock opposite ran Rabbit Ear Pass.

Cole rode into the pass, but drew up at a sandy

draw near the entrance to examine the ground for footprints. What he saw surprised him. This was a country of few travelers. The hot and dusty desert deflected traffic, which went by way of Jonesboro and skirted the hills. Only those in a hurry, or those who had reasons for not wanting to be seen, took the short cut through Rabbit Ear. Yet two horses had passed here within an hour or two. The crumbling dirt that had fallen into the tracks was still soft and loose.

Did that mean Haskell had picked up a companion and was still in front of him? In that case, who was the rider to the right whose dust he had seen?

Cole decided to wait for the solitary traveler. He would still have time, by hard going, to reach the railroad as soon as Haskell, if it turned out that the ex-foreman of the Circle 3 T was one of the two ahead of him. Sanborn led his horse up a draw and tethered it among the rocks at the head of the little gulch. Rifle in hand, he walked back and selected a spot from which he could cover the trail.

He waited, with the patience that comes to one who has spent years in the untenanted outdoors. A half an hour passed, three quarters. Cole began to think his calculations had gone wrong. It was possible the traveler had seen the footprints and was doing a little thinking on his own account. If so, and if the man was Haskell, how would he meet the situation?

Cole found out, sooner than he desired. A raucous voice called an order to him.

'Stick yore hands up!'

Cole's heart went down like a thermometer plunged into icy water. Instead of trapping his man he had been trapped.

He put his hands up and turned, a cheerful smile on his face. 'So it's you, Mr. Haskell,' he drawled. 'We've been looking for you and you've decided to save us trouble. Good enough.'

'Don't fool yoreself,' Haskell jeered, a look of ugly malice on his face. 'I'm going to bump you off—now. You came here asking for what you're going to get. I'll say this. You never saw the day I couldn't beat you from the chunk. Try to run me down, would you? I'll show you.'

Cole kept his impudent grin working. 'Haven't you forgotten one little thing, Mr. Haskell? There are three of us. If and when you shoot, my friends will close in on you. That wouldn't be so good—for you.'

'I don't believe it. You're playing a lone hand. Who are yore friends?'

Haskell spoke boldly, but he felt a chill premonition of disaster. Three sets of horses' hoofs had entered the pass. Where were the other riders? Somewhere among these rocks likely.

Sanborn's mind worked in flashes. He spoke without hesitation, without haste, choosing the names of men known to be game and with reputations for hard riding and fighting.

'Slim Calhoun and Faust,' he said, a touch of derision in his cool voice. 'It won't do, Haskell. Better put down that gun before you commit suicide. I'll make you a proposition that will give you a run for your money. You've always claimed you are the best man in Boone County with your dukes. I'm going to find that out, now.'

'What you mean?' Haskell demanded suspiciously.

'We'll settle this if you have enough sand in your craw in a fist-and-skull fight. You win, and the road is open to the railroad. Neither I nor my friends will molest you. If I win, you go back with me to Jonesboro.'

'Whyfor would I go back to Jonesboro?'

'To answer a few questions Magruder wants to ask you about the K. & J. robbery,' Cole said quietly.

'I ain't scared to answer any questions he asks me, and I ain't scared to put up my dukes with you. I could whop you the best day you ever saw with one hand tied behind me,' blustered Haskell.

'That's what I'm going to find out, as I said before. You can use a quirt on a woman, you cowardly dog. Let us see how you stack up when you face a man.'

'Ask yore friend Slim about that,' the ex-foreman boasted. 'And how do I know you'd stick to yore word and let me go after I've whopped you?'

'You know it because I'm not a liar like you,' Cole told him curtly. 'Make up your mind in a hurry. What's it to be? Do you want a chance for your life? Or don't you?'

Haskell hesitated. The urgent impulse was on him to pour lead into the body of the man he hated. If he only knew where the other two riders were who had come into the pass! Sanborn could not stand there facing him with that impudent grin unless he was sure of where his friends were. The sound of a gun would probably bring them on the run. On the other hand, he was sure he could beat Sanborn in a fist-fight. He had twenty-five pounds on the man. Moreover, much as he feared and hated this fellow, he knew Cole was a man of his word. If he said the road was open, the road would be open.

Jerry ripped out a savage oath. 'You've got a licking coming to you, fellow!' he cried, and put down his revolver.

Cole unbuckled his belt, dropped it, and stepped forward. In him was a cold, vindictive joy. Haskell had delivered himself into his hands. He had promised Mary not to kill the man, but he had said nothing about beating him as long as he could stand and take it.

Haskell shuffled forward awkwardly. He was strong as a bear, and his great power had always brought him victory in a hand-to-hand rough-

and-tumble. His big fist swept round in a wide swing. Cole beat him to the punch with a hard right to the chin. An uptilted elbow deflected the swing. Before Cole stepped back, he had landed two heavy body punches.

The bigger man grunted and rushed, head down and arms flailing. An uppercut snapped back the head and a straight left reached an eye. Once more Sanborn was out of reach, still untouched except for blows his arms and shoulders had smothered. Cole's muscles were long and rippling, like those of a panther. He moved in and out lightly, easily, and his arms lashed out with precision and perfect timing.

The foreman was already panting heavily. Both eyes were swollen and his cheeks were puffed. What worried him was that he could not land his blows effectively. He did not know he was telegraphing them in time for his foe to sidestep, duck, or drive home counter-punches a fraction of a second before his own were due to arrive. Jerry was never a fast thinker, but it was clear to him now that he was beaten unless he could close with this fellow and throw him down so that his skill would be wasted.

He rushed again and caught a ringing clout on the side of the head. His reaching arms did not close on the elusive enemy. To him it seemed that a dozen flying fists were hammering at his face and body. He stopped to gather breath, his lungs gasping. The noise of hammers and of buzzing saws were singing in his dizzy brain. Sanborn would not let him rest, but swarmed all over him.

Haskell fought back with all he had. A red bruise showed on Cole's cheekbone. His lip was cut. But Jerry did not deceive himself. He knew he was staggering, that legs and arms were heavy with weariness. Nothing could save him if he was not able to throw Sanborn down and beat his head against the ground till he was unconscious. The big man went forward drunkenly, trying to get a grip on his antagonist.

Cole knew his time had come. Out of the corner of an eye he saw a boulder behind him and avoided it. Jerry stumbled into the outcropping rock, and at the same instant Cole's right lashed to the chin.

The foreman crashed down like a log and lay as motionless.

Cole stood panting above him.

From the pass below a voice hailed him. 'Aren't you a good ways off yore range, oldtimer?'

Slim Calhoun and Gray Shirt were looking up at him.

'Come up here,' Cole called down. 'Got something to show you.'

They rode up the draw. What they saw surprised them.

'Not dead, is he?' Faust asked, with a nod toward the unconscious man.

'No. We had a shindig with our fists. I knocked him out.'

Slim took a look at his friend and another at Haskell. 'You certainly worked his face over handsome,' he said. 'It sure warms my gizzard. Not so long ago I was on the receiving end from this *hombre*. I wish you had given me an invite to the party. I'm the dog-gondest guy for getting places just too late.'

'What are you going to do with him?' Faust asked.

'Going to take him back to Magruder.'

'We aimed to save you this job, Cole,' said Slim. 'But I reckon it had to be this way. Better let me bandage up yore shoulder again. I notice it's bleeding. I would say, offhand, that getting into a hand-to-hand rookus with Jerry Haskell was no respectful way to treat a wound.'

Faust took charge of the prisoner while Slim attended to the shoulder. This done, they assembled their horses and headed down the pass for Jonesboro. Haskell kept a sullen and dejected silence. Not only had he been whipped. They were taking him back to pay for his crime. He had a well-grounded fear that the tide had turned. He would be tried for killing the express messenger the night of the train-robbery. Unless he was lucky he would be hanged. They probably had not a great deal of evidence against him, but it would not take a great deal to convict if Chet

Radbourne's power was smashed. Everybody would have a knife out for him.

Slim rode beside Haskell and lifted his voice in a ballad more or less plagiarized, more or less unmetrical. Sometimes the inspiration failed, since there were eleven stanzas, at which times he repeated himself unblushingly. The theme of the song was the recent doings of one Cole Sanborn. It narrated various adventures, in all of which one Jerry Haskell took a humiliating and ignominious part.

It began:

'Old King Cole was a merry old soul,
A merry old soul was he;
He called for his hoss, and he called for his
    roll,
And he called for his side-kicks three.'

It ended:

'Old King Cole was a merry old soul,
A merry old soul was he;
He dragged home this cat, and the cat was a
    pole,
To be hanged on a cottonwood tree.'

'If you are quite through, Slim,' suggested Cole at last.

'I was only entertaining our guest,' Slim protested, aggrieved.

Chapter XLI

'Port After Stormie Seas'

Mrs. Peters was just leaving the house, a shopping-bag on her arm. 'I'm glad to see you, Mr. Sanborn,' she said. 'Is—everything all right?'

'Couldn't be more right,' he said. 'How about here, at this end?'

She smiled. 'I'll answer in your own words. I think Mary is in her room. You might knock.'

With which Mrs. Peters continued on her way. She judged she was not needed at home just now.

Cole walked into the house, put down his hat, and looked at the closed door of his wife's bedroom. He felt extraordinarily shy. A small cough did not attract attention. He knocked on the door.

'Come in,' a low throaty contralto invited.

He turned the knob and walked into the bedroom.

Mary was doing some kind of embroidery work.

She rose, startled, the color washed out of her face.

'You're back,' she said, with a catch of the breath.

'Yes,' he said. 'My job's done.'

'You didn't—?'

The question hung suspended.

'No. We brought him back. He is in jail now.'

She gave a little sob of relief. 'He didn't hurt you?'

'No. One time he thought he would, but he changed his mind. You got back to town all right, not too tired?'

'Yes. Sheriff Magruder brought me back. They searched Haskell's cabin and found the clothes he wore at the hold-up of the train. There is any amount of evidence piled up against him. He was the one who killed the express messenger.'

'I saw Magruder when I turned him over. The sheriff says he hasn't a chance to beat the testimony against him. He'll hang.'

'Mr. Radbourne is in trouble, too,' Mary said. 'His gang is falling away from him. The politicians he ruled are afraid. They see the tide has turned, Mr. Peters says, and they are all scrambling to make themselves safe by telling what they know.'

Both of them were talking commonplaces to escape the tide of emotion sweeping them into each other's arms.

'He's through,' Cole said. 'He'll go to the penitentiary. Too many of his chickens will come home to roost.'

'Yes,' she agreed.

'And we—we're just beginning.' He moved toward her.

There was color enough in her face now. 'Yes,' she murmured.

He looked at her, soft and dewy and adorable. Love poured through his veins, irradiated him, filled him with keen-edged desire for this girl who was to be his mate. At last. 'Port after stormie seas.'

Closing the door, he strode forward. He put his arms around her. Mary lifted a rapt young face to his kiss.

Center Point Large Print
600 Brooks Road / PO Box 1
Thorndike, ME 04986-0001 USA

(207) 568-3717

US & Canada:
1 800 929-9108
www.centerpointlargeprint.com